A HISTORY
of the
AMERICAN
PEOPLE

Volume I: to 1877

CONFUSIONS:
1) ELECTORAL COLLEGE
2) MARBURY VS. MADISON
3) FUNDING—ASSUMPTION

A HISTORY
of the
AMERICAN PEOPLE

Volume I ❧ *to* 1877

BY

Harry J. Carman

Harold C. Syrett & Bernard W. Wishy

BROOKLYN COLLEGE   FORDHAM UNIVERSITY

THIRD EDITION

Alfred · A · Knopf   NEW YORK

TO

HARRY J. CARMAN

(*1884–1964*)

the man, the teacher, the scholar

THIS IS A BORZOI BOOK,
PUBLISHED BY ALFRED A. KNOPF, INC.

PUBLISHED 1952, REPRINTED SIX TIMES
SECOND EDITION, REVISED AND RESET, 1960, REPRINTED THREE TIMES
THIRD EDITION, 1967
FIFTH PRINTING

Library of Congress Catalog Card Number: 67-20622
Manufactured in the United States of America.

HERE individuals of all nations are melted into a new race of men, whose labours and posterity will one day cause great change in the world. Americans are the western pilgrims, who are carrying along with them that great mass of arts, sciences, vigour, and industry, which began long since in the east; they will finish the great circle. The Americans were once scattered all over Europe; here they are incorporated into one of the finest systems of population which has ever appeared, and which will hereafter become distinct by the power of the different climates they inhabit. The American ought therefore to love this country much better than that wherein either he or his forefathers were born. Here the rewards of his industry follow with equal steps the progress of his labour; his labour is founded on the basis of nature, *self-interest;* can it want a stronger allurement? Wives and children, who before in vain demanded of him a morsel of bread, now, fat and frolicsome, gladly help their father to clear those fields whence exuberant crops are to arise to feed and to clothe them all; without any part being claimed, either by a despotic prince, a rich abbot, or a mighty lord. Here religion demands but little of him; a small voluntary salary to the minister, and gratitude to God; can he refuse these? The American is a new man, who acts upon new principles; he must therefore entertain new ideas, and form new opinions. From involuntary idleness, servile dependence, penury, and useless labour, he has passed to toils of a very different nature, rewarded by ample subsistence.—This is an American.

MICHEL-GUILLAUME JEAN DE CRÈVECŒUR:

Letters from an American Farmer (1782)

Notes on the Revised Editions

IN THE YEARS since the first edition of this volume appeared there has been an impressive revaluation of much American history, and substantial scholarship has been published to support ideas that were largely suggestive and tentative at the end of the 1940's. This revision attempts to balance this newer scholarship against traditional interpretations but without, it is hoped, emphasizing what may turn out to be mere fashions in contemporary history. The book remains loyal to the original intention of providing a full analysis of American history that is true to the complexity of events and a fair test of the student's best possibilities as a serious scholar.

HARRY J. CARMAN

HAROLD C. SYRETT

BERNARD W. WISHY

THE SIX YEARS since the second edition have continued to bring changes in the interpretation of the various aspects of American history. Although most of the revisions for the previous edition still stand up in the light of the latest scholarship, increasing interest in contemporary history has demanded a fresh look at the events of the last fifteen years. The bulk of the revisions in this edition accordingly take account of the vast changes sweeping the world. These have brought with them not only new problems for statesmen but new perspectives for the historian.

One of Harry Carman's many remarkable gifts was his capacity to take innovation shrewdly as well as gracefully. The loss of his advice for this edition is deeply felt by his collaborators.

HAROLD C. SYRETT

BERNARD W. WISHY

Preface

J. B. Black in *The Art of History* contends that every age interprets "the record of the past in the light of its own ideas." We have preferred to take Black's words as a warning to historians rather than as a definition of written history, for we have made a conscious effort to judge the past in the light of the past and to avoid imposing the standards of our generation upon preceding generations. On the other hand, we have not renounced our right to interpret the past, for we have constantly tried to present the events of American history with a thesis in mind and to point out what we think is the significance of these events.

Our approach to history is eclectic. We do not think that the past should be studied from a single viewpoint or that it can be explained by one theory to the exclusion of all other theories. But, while rejecting any over-all thesis, we have not failed to take a stand on controversial issues. In each instance the nature of the issue has helped to determine our stand; and the fact that we have advanced a succession of different interpretations rather than used the same interpretations for a succession of events accurately reflects our conviction that every historical event is unique.

The organization of these volumes represents a compromise between the chronological and topical approaches to the material under consideration. We have divided American history into a number of comparatively large periods, and within each period we have dealt with a series of major topics. This method necessitates some repetition, but in a book that is designed for students repetition, in our view, is an asset rather than a defect. We have proceeded on the hypothesis that no part or period of American history is inherently

more important than any other, and we have therefore
sought to present in all its aspects the history of the
American people.

HARRY J. CARMAN

HAROLD C. SYRETT

BERNARD W. WISHY

Acknowledgments

FOR THE FIRST AND SECOND EDITIONS

A HISTORY OF THE AMERICAN PEOPLE is an outgrowth of Professor Carman's *Economic and Social History of the United States*. We have used the earlier work, which covers the period from the first settlements in America to 1876, as a point of departure for our first volume. At some points we have expanded Professor Carman's material, and at others we have cut those portions of it that seemed unsuitable for a general textbook, but in every instance we have subjected it to extensive revisions. In addition, we have supplemented it with a full account of American diplomatic and political history.

Throughout the preparation of the first edition of these two volumes we received considerable assistance from a number of friends and colleagues. Professors Herman Ausubel, Donald N. Bigelow, Henry F. Graff, and Chilton Williamson of Columbia University, Professors Michael Kraus and Oscar Zeichner of the College of the City of New York, Professor Oscar Handlin of Harvard University, Professors Frank Freidel and Fred A. Shannon of the University of Illinois, Professor James A. Barnes of Temple University, Professor Joe L. Norris of Wayne University, Professor R. J Ferguson of the University of Pittsburgh, Professor Burke M. Hermann of Pennsylvania State College, and Mr. Thomas R. Hay furnished us with invaluable criticisms and suggestions. Lois Green Clark of Alfred A. Knopf, Inc. read the entire manuscript and showed unusual skill and knowledge in criticizing both its form and content. Mrs. Patricia Syrett typed most of the manuscript, and both Mrs. Syrett and Miss Margaret Carscadden performed a variety of generally unpleasant tasks associated with the work on this book. Both, moreover, treated its authors with remarkable tolerance and patience. Mr. James P. Shenton and Dr. Walter P. Metzger of Columbia University helped us in the preparation of the bibliography. We are also indebted to Professor Bigelow and Mr. Charles E. McCarthy for the assistance they gave us in checking the proof.

In the preparation of the second edition we are grateful to Mrs. Syrett and to Mrs. Carman for their aid in typing and to now Professor Shenton for re-editing the final bibliographies. We are jointly responsible for whatever errors this book may contain.

HARRY J. CARMAN
HAROLD C. SYRETT
BERNARD W. WISHY

CONTENTS

Part IV · *Energies of Democracy*

Part V · *"... That that nation might live"*

Illustrations

Maps and Charts

PART I

THE
IMPERIAL
GENERATIONS

[EUROPEAN ENGRAVING OF INDIANS IN THE NEW WORLD, CA. 1505. COURTESY, NEW YORK PUBLIC LIBRARY]

>>>->>>->>>->>>->>>->>>->>>->>

An Old World Expands

COLONIAL AMERICA gave a fresh start to an old civilization. The settling of the Americas five hundred years ago started a long imperial movement over the face of the globe, of which the surrender of Western colonies in Asia and Africa in the middle of the twentieth century is the latest phase. The first timid probes for empire beyond the Atlantic fringes of Europe took place in ships often no larger than some of the lifeboats carried by a modern ocean liner. But these dangerous voyages started a new era, for the opening of America was the first chaper in the history of a momentous worldwide expansion.

Medieval Europe Discovers Asia and Africa

A thousand years ago western Europe was a small, isolated portion of the earth, practically unknown to, and largely ignorant of, the rest of the world, and suffering from the loss of its political unity. The Roman Empire of antiquity, stretching from the Atlantic Ocean almost to the Persian Gulf and entirely surrounding the Mediterranean, had long since disappeared. Charlemagne's great empire founded about the year 800 had also disintegrated. Feudal barons and weak kings now struggled for mastery in northern Europe. Most of the relatively sparse population knew only the bare necessities of life. With the decline of imperial power, European life had in many ways turned in on itself. In the ninth and tenth centuries inland cities lost touch with distant horizons, and intercity trade became insignificant. Compared with ancient and modern times, there was little travel or communication between one locality and another, and each community, whether manor or town, was forced to produce most of its own food, clothes, weapons, and tools. Both the lay and ecclesiastical lords of these communities spent their time carrying on petty warfare, administering the affairs of their private estates and their principalities, and conducting the growing business of the universal church. For support they depended upon the labor of a peasantry often tied to the soil.

With the slow growth of population and wealth, this process of decline and shrinkage began to reverse itself. By the opening of the eleventh century, foreign invasions had ceased, civil anarchy was declining, and life and wealth were a little more secure. A revivified city life began to spread inland from centers in Flanders and on the Mediterranean shores in which urban commercial culture had never died out. The trading classes regained importance and, settled under the walls of towns, merchants handled increasing amounts of both local and distant business. Daily or weekly markets in the open square, in the closed market hall, or more often in shops or stalls, provided facilities for the exchange of goods, and the growth of great international fairs brought the stimulus of a more cosmopolitan existence. Barter thus tended to give way to a money economy, and manufacturing, though still primitive in character and small in scope, increased along with trade and agricultural production and brought into being a distinct but not unified class—the *bourgeoisie*—whose social and political ambitions came to figure more prominently in the life of the times.

The barriers of isolation were further broken after 1095 by the Crusades, which drew all Europe into a common enthusiasm and opened new scenes and new ways of doing things to Europeans. When Englishmen met Venetians and Swedes traveled with Spaniards, they discovered common needs and desires, common feelings and ideals as Europeans and fellow Christians, especially when the crusaders saw that the Moslem's food and clothing, his art, customs, and view of the world were different from theirs. When the crusaders came home, they brought exotic tales of what they had seen and experienced and further stimulated curiosity about life outside Europe.

The Crusades also greatly speeded the European drift to a more active commercial life during the twelfth century. Trade between the the East and the West, extensive under the Romans, had never completely disappeared despite Arab and Norse invasions from the eighth to the tenth century. During the Crusades the Christians recaptured control of the Mediterranean. The constant demand for men and supplies led to improvements in navigation and an increase in the number and size of ships, which now returned to Europe with such commodities as muslin, damask, rice, sugar, lemons, apricots, and garlic. Trade grew in these and other Eastern articles. The European trader in turn established new markets for western European products in the Near East and North Africa, opened up new commercial routes, added to his knowledge of geography, and adopted and exploited new business techniques. With the growing attraction and scope of trade, it was no wonder that European cities increased in size and number and that men became increasingly intent on conducting business for private profit. In Italy especially, where a large number of Oriental industries were introduced, merchants and bankers grew more powerful and challenged the rule of prince and prelate.

Inspired by the sense of power and possibility that came with this growing activity in business life, Europe began by the beginning of the thirteenth century to penetrate the unexplored lands to the East, and Christian missionaries, adventurers, and traders visited many parts of Asia. Europe thus accumulated a wealth of information about Tartary, China, Japan, Persia, and India; in the cloisters of monasteries and on the quays of seaports, priests and merchants alike told of the wonders of these Far Eastern lands to people who marveled at stories of populous cities with walls of silver, of palaces roofed with gold, of rivers of pearls and other precious stones. None of the accounts written by many of these travelers is more famous than *The Book of ser Marco Polo, the Venetian, concerning the kingdoms and marvels of the east,* with its picturesque, though astonishingly accurate, description of Cathay and of the civilization of the Great Khan, its vivid, though exaggerated, account of *Cipangu* (Japan), which Marco Polo never actually visited, and its vague and extravagant statements about the "twelve thousand seven hundred islands" of the Pacific and Indian Oceans.

Europeans Probe the Atlantic

Long before Europeans had the money and inspiration to move into uncharted lands, learned men had believed that the earth was a sphere and that India could be reached by sailing around Africa. The theory that the earth was round, first entertained by the Egyptians and later by the Greeks and Romans, had come to be accepted generally by scientifically minded men, navigators, and pilots. "I have always read that the world, comprising the land and water," Columbus said, "is spherical, as is testified by the investigations of Ptolemy and others, who have proved it by the eclipses of the moon and other observations made from East to

West, as well as by the elevation of the Pole from North to South." Moslem travelers and geographers who had seen ships on the Indian and Pacific oceans also believed that the "Golden East" could be reached by sailing around Africa. Even before Marco Polo had returned from China, two Genoese seamen had attempted "to go by sea to the ports of India to trade there." Their galleys passed through the Strait of Gibraltar and headed southward; they never returned.

It is difficult to appreciate the bravery necessary for such journeys. The dangers and difficulties were great enough on established ocean routes, and long sea voyages into unknown regions were not generally practicable before a number of important advances had been made in the art of navigation. After 1300, however, marked improvement was made in cartography. Instead of basing their work on half-mythical data gathered in part from biblical and literary lore, many mapmakers began to strive for exact measurements and outlines and made especially notable advances in drafting sailing charts, which by the fifteenth century pictured with considerable accuracy the coasts of Europe, North Africa, and western Asia. The mariners of the fifteenth century also had access to world maps constructed by learned geographers and cartographers and used the compass and the astrolabe (a Moslem invention, the forerunner of the quadrant) during the latter part of the fourteenth century. With these two instruments sailors could determine both direction and latitude, and before the end of the fifteenth cenury they also had a chronometer and longitude tables. With new instruments, larger ships, and improved navigating charts, the mariner could now more freely sail the western seas.

As early as the eighth century, adventurous Vikings bent on trade and plunder had piloted their vessels out of the Baltic and North seas. In the next century they colonized Iceland, and before A.D. 1000 they had touched the coast of Labrador. In 1341, Portuguese sailors had rediscovered the forgotten Canaries, earlier identified by the Italians, and before the end of the fourteenth century, Europeans visited both the Madeira Islands and the Azores.

These achievements were dimmed by the subsequent discoveries and explorations made under the auspices of Prince Henry of Portugal. Interested in trade, anxious to spread Christianity, and curious about the unknown world, this remarkable man was an accomplished cartographer and seaman and became a great patron of exploration. While engaged in a campaign against the Moors in Africa in the early years of the fifteenth century, he learned of the caravan routes from the Mediterranean towns of North Africa southward across the Sahara. Moorish prisoners aroused him with their tales of the gold, wines, textiles, and slaves that came from the Senegal and Gambia river regions and from the gold and ivory coasts on the Gulf of Guinea. News of this rich trade "inspired him to seek those lands by way of the sea." Returning to Portugal, he established a maritime school, whose equipment, precise methods, and royal sponsorship attracted the leading navigators of Europe. Year after year increasing numbers of caravels sailed southward from Portugal, and slowly the western coast of Africa was put on the maps. By the beginning of the fifteenth century, Portuguese mariners had sailed along six hundred miles of the west African coast; in 1460, when Prince Henry died, they knew the landmarks of two thousand miles of the African shores.

National Rivalry Requires New Route to the Indies

Within Europe itself, by 1450 merchants and bankers had laid the basis of modern business systems by accumulating small amounts of capital from trade and other sources. They substituted money for barter, they loaned money at interest to government and Church, and they developed an elaborate banking technique. Bookkeeping, bills of exchange, stock companies, investment in commercial and industrial enterprises, and speculative trading were all well known by the time of Prince Henry of Portugal. Powerful Florentine houses financed Edward III of England and the Papacy. Rich German bankers invested extensively in enterprises as diverse as mining and wheat growing. These men, typical in their own way of the restless, willful quality of life in Renaissance Europe, constantly sought new markets and new investments. These bankers and merchants helped finance overseas trade and exploration.

Commerce between Europe and Asia developed rapidly from the thirteenth to the fifteenth century. From the markets of the Orient an ever increasing volume of expensive luxuries flowed to Europe's lords and kings, bishops and abbots, and wealthier merchants and their families. The East sent articles of personal adornment, spices to preserve food, and furnishings for palaces and manor houses, cathedrals and guild halls. In return, Europe sent to the East woolen fabrics, wines, coral, metals, furs, sulphur, slaves, oil, honey, amber, and grain.

These exports, however, were often insufficient to pay for the imports, and the balance of trade in favor of the East drained gold and silver from Europe. During the Crusades Europe had increased her gold supply by exploiting and plundering Syria and Asia Minor. This source was cut off by the loss of the Holy Land about the year 1300. For 150 years or more the gold and silver coin and bullion of Europe flowed from northern Europe to the commercial centers of the Adriatic and Mediterranean, and thence eastward, much as it had in centuries past. Between 1350 and 1450 a long economic decline set in, marked by falling prices, debasement of the coinage, forced loans, bankruptcies, attempts to prevent the export of gold and silver, and the retarding of many industrial enterprises.

What commerce there was over the routes between Europe and Asia was dangerous and expensive. Journeying over bleak mountains, hot deserts, and sparse plateaus, through all kinds of weather, the merchant was subject to assault and robbery by highwaymen and lawless tribes. He was often forced to pay expensive tribute to foreign rulers and officials. The merchant sending his goods by sea often fared just as poorly. Pirates might steal or storms destroy the cargo. Port dues were usually more excessive and unreasonable than were tributes in the inland towns. All such losses and taxes were passed on to the consumer. Added to his price were the cost of transshipment and the middlemen's profit, for no merchant brought goods all the way from India to Europe. A pound of pepper or a piece of fabric, for instance, might change hands a dozen times before it reached a Mediterranean port, and each seller made a profit. The commodities that were purchased for a mere trifle in the markets of the East sold often for exorbitant prices in the West.

Italian statesmen, geographers, and merchants answered the complaints of other Europeans by blaming the non-Christian middlemen for the high cost of Oriental goods. In fact, however, as soon as the products of the East reached the Levantine cities scattered along the shores of the Black Sea and the eastern Mediterranean, they were monopolized for the most part by Italian merchants, especially Venetians. For centuries the Italian traders, who frequently formed an influential part of the population of many of the Near Eastern cities, handled the bulk of the commerce between Europe and Asia. To the wharves of these cities came Venetian galleys laden with European produce for Oriental consumers, they carried homeward cargoes of coveted products from the East. The goods not consumed in the Italian cities were sold to foreigners. Through the passes of the Alps came the traders and merchants of south Germany and the "backcountry" of northern Europe. They carried back wares that they disposed of in their home cities of Augsburg, Ulm, or Nuremburg, or sent to the French fairs or to the merchants of the Hanse towns of north Germany and the Netherlands. The Venetians traded directly with England and Flanders, and, year after year, until 1560, their merchant fleets passed through the Strait of Gibraltar on the way to these northern countries.

By 1400, Venice had become the commercial-maritime center of

Europe, overshadowing her Mediterranean rivals, Pisa, Genoa, Marseilles, and Barcelona. With a population of approximately 190,000, she had an army of 40,000 men, a commercial fleet of 3,000 ships, and an enormous annual revenue. She was the distributing point for the goods of the East. To her markets and warehouses came the products of Europe for her ships. Her merchants and princes, because of their almost exclusive monopoly of the Levant trade, grew rich—some of them fabulously rich—to the envy of the rising nations on the Atlantic. Their jealousy of Venice and the growing need and will of their princes to compete for the world's power and glory lay behind their determination to seek a new cheap route to the wealth of the East.

In earlier centuries, the kings of these new national states—Portugal, Spain, France, Sweden, Denmark, and England—were only nominal rulers; effective authority rested in the hands of powerful lords, each of whom was practically sovereign over one or more of the many regions into which each country was divided. The monarch depended on these lords for funds, military forces, and the administration of the law. They resisted every effort by the king to limit their authority or to change the existing order. The monarch soon realized, however, that he had a powerful ally. Many merchants hated and sought escape from the feudal system with its rigid class distinctions, private wars, robber barons, arbitrary exactions, and varying customs duties, its hundred systems of coinage, and its multitudinous local courts from which there was often no appeal. The merchant wanted order, uniformity, and above all security. He soon realized that these objectives required stronger central government. Such government would in all probability bring better roads and bridges, wider markets, and increased protection for his interests. The merchants, therefore, often rallied to the support of the monarch in his struggle against the feudal lords. Taxes paid by the merchants enabled the king to raise a paid standing army and to hire loyal officers. In short, the success of the monarch in his efforts to unify his country and to extend and exercise his royal prerogatives depended in large measure on the prosperity of the members of the middle, or bourgeois, class. Their wealth spelled power and prestige. Together kings and merchants were to make common cause in the opening age of maritime exploration and discovery.

It was once customary to attribute the intense exploration of the late fifteenth century to a crisis in western Europe brought on by the Ottoman Turks. These "infidels," so the accounts ran, having conquered Syria and Asia Minor, cut off the old trade routes to the East and made it essential to find new commercial arteries to the Orient. This theory, however, has been disproved. In the first place, not all the trade

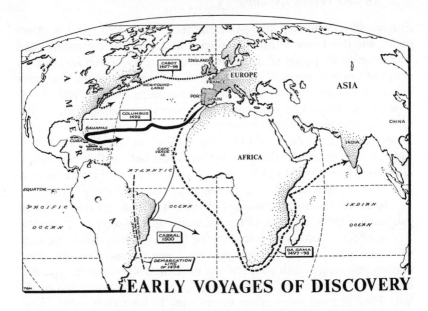

EARLY VOYAGES OF DISCOVERY

routes had been blocked by the Turks. The growing inability of the West to pay for eastern goods had put Constantinople into decline long before its capture by the Turks. The Turks did not deliberately interfere with the remaining trade. Under their regime commerce was little or no more hazardous than it had been under their predecessors. Next to the Italians, the Turks themselves were to be the heaviest losers by the opening of the New World.

The European Struggle for Empire Begins

The costs, rather than the closing, of trade with the East and the common need for kings and businessmen to expand or die in a world where wealth was scarce lay behind the drive for a direct route to the Indies. By 1471, Portuguese explorers had crossed the equator. In 1486, Bartholomew Diaz rounded the Cape of Good Hope and turned northward into the Indian Ocean, only to be forced back by threats from his mutinous crew. Nevertheless, the long-sought passageway had at last been found. Six years later an ambitious and expert Genoese sailor, successful after many years in selling his scheme of reaching the East by sailing directly westward, returned to Spain and informed his sponsors, King Ferdinand and Queen Isabella, that he had reached the outer edge of the Indies. In fact, Columbus had done something different and more important. He had introduced the New World as a permanent fact in the life of the Old.

The exploits of Columbus and Vasco da Gama, who reached India in 1498 by way of the Cape of Good Hope, were soon equaled and even excelled by others. In 1497, John Cabot, another Genoese, sailing under the English flag, anchored off the North American coast of Nova Scotia, Newfoundland, or Labrador. In 1500, attempting to follow the da Gama route to India, Cabral was driven off his course and discovered the region now known as Brazil, which he claimed for the king of Portugal. During the same year, other Portuguese sailed along the greater part of the northern coast of South America. In 1501, Americus Vespucci, a Florentine for whom America was named, followed a long stretch of the same continent. About a decade later, Balboa discovered the Pacific, and in 1522 the *Victoria*—sole survivor of Ferdinand Magellan's fleet of five ships—reached Spain after sailing around the globe.

Spain and Portugal were the first European states to obtain territory as a result of the new discoveries. The Portuguese began the colonization of Brazil and established a trading empire in India and the East Indies. They controlled most of the slave-trading stations along the coast of Africa and thus increased the enormous profits accruing from the Oriental trade. Their commercial ventures in the East helped to make the Indian Ocean and western Pacific regions better known to Europeans. Despite the fact that Portugal profited most from bringing spices to western Europe at one fifth their former cost, she was unable to support such a far-flung empire. With a relatively small population and few resources, with a government honeycombed by graft and corruption, and with no adequate means of distributing her Eastern merchandise or protecting her monopoly, it was only a question of time before she would be compelled to relinquish what she had so long worked for. Her dreams and ambitions finally died in 1580 when the Spanish monarch Philip II became ruler of Portugal and subordinated Portuguese interests to those of Spain.

The Spanish kings had been as active as the Portuguese. By the end of the sixteenth century, they laid claim to Portuguese holdings in the Eastern hemisphere and all the coastal regions and portions of the interior of South America, the West Indies, Central America, and Mexico. Adventurers like Ponce de Leon, De Soto, and Coronado—attempting the conversion of the natives or searching for treasure, slaves, or a short passage to the South Seas—explored much of the southern half of the present United States. Comparatively few permanent settlements were made in this region, however, and it was never an important part of the Spanish colonial empire. Until 1630, the little town of Santa Fe, with 250 Spaniards and twice as many half-breeds and Indian dependents, was the only Spanish settlement in New Mexico. Fifty years

*Columbus Reaches Hispaniola in
the New World*

[NEW YORK PUBLIC LIBRARY]

later, the Spanish population of New Mexico numbered approximately 2,500, nearly all of whom were living in the upper Rio Grande Valley. In Florida, St. Augustine was the only important town founded by the Spanish; it had a population of about 5,000 when the English took possession of it in 1763.

Both Spain and Portugal attempted to monopolize the commerce of their colonies. By a papal line of demarcation of 1493, supplemented the following year by the Convention of Tordesillas, the two countries agreed to divide all newly discovered lands between them, Spain obtaining all to the west of an imaginary line 370 leagues (1,110 miles) west of Cape Verde Islands, and Portugal all to the east. Within their respective spheres, each country attempted to keep trade and wealth for itself. All trade with the Spanish colonies was supposed to be carried on by Spaniards in Spanish vessels from specified Spanish ports to specified colonial ports, and Portugal followed the same system. It was reasoned that such a policy would enable the home merchants to market their goods in the colonies in return for raw materials or gold and silver. At the same time ship owners would benefit, and the government would obtain large sums in export and import taxes as well as a share of the products of the mines.

The Rivalry for Empire Spreads

Before the middle of the sixteenth century, no nation seriously challenged the title of either the Portuguese or the Spanish to their far-flung empires. But the spread of Protestantism and Spain's determination to maintain a monopoly of the world's mineral wealth made competition for empire more active. The countries that turned Protestant had often objected to the restraints imposed by the papal line and no longer felt bound to respect the claims of the Iberian states. Already the Dutch, on the verge of revolt against Spanish Catholic rule, were earning a large portion of the profits of the Portuguese trade with the East. English adventurers—Sir John Hawkins, Sir Francis Drake, and others—waged an unrelenting offensive against the Spanish monopoly, raiding and plundering the coast towns of Spanish America and capturing Spanish treasure ships on the high seas. Even the port towns of Spain did not escape molestation.

Although she was the greatest power in Europe for the century after Columbus, Spain protested in vain. Her smaller but alert rivals increasingly realized that her power rested in large measure upon the wealth that she obtained from the New World. For example, Richard Hakluyt the younger, Anglican clergyman and leading geographer of

Elizabethan England, wrote: "If you touch him [Philip] in the Indies, you touch the apple of his eye; for take away his treasure, which is *Nervus Belli*, and which he has almost out of his West Indies, his old bands of soldiers will soon be dissolved, his purposes defeated, his power and strength diminished, his pride abated and his tyranny utterly suppressed." In similar vein Francis Bacon wrote:

> Money is the principal part of the greatness of Spain; for by that they maintain their veteran army. But in this part, of all others, is most to be considered the ticklish and brittle state of the greatness of Spain. Their greatness consists in their treasure, their treasure in the Indies, and their Indies (if it be well weighed) are indeed but an accession to such as are masters of the sea.

Spanish mastery of the sea was seriously impaired by the growing power of the Protestant English. King Philip II of Spain, wishing to restore England to Roman Catholicism, first tried to marry Queen Elizabeth, who came to the English throne in 1558. Failing in this, he engineered several conspiracies against her, among them a plot to supplant her with her Catholic rival, Mary, Queen of Scots. His efforts, however, succeeded only in uniting the English people in their enmity toward Spain. Elizabeth, on her side, lost few opportunities to weaken those who would destroy her. She assisted the Huguenots, or French Protestants, secretly and then openly; she intervened in favor of the Dutch, who were rebelling against Spain; and she connived with the English "sea dogs" in their warfare on the Spanish monopoly. Philip finally resolved to subjugate England and humble its Queen by means of his "Invincible Armada." This great fleet sailed proudly into the English Channel with enormous crosses blazing on its sails and priests chanting in anticipation of the reconquest of England for Christ and Rome. The defeat of the Armada in 1588 by English skill and treacherous weather did not fully end Spanish maritime supremacy; yet within three years, 800 Spanish ships were taken, and in 1596 the Englishman Sir Thomas Howard captured and plundered Cadiz. These attacks on the Spanish fleet paved the way for the establishment of rival empires beyond the sea.

The Netherlands built the first of these empires. Beginning their maritime career as fishermen, the Dutch, long before they revolted from Spain, had built up a profitable carrying trade, bringing cloth, tar, timber, and grain from the Baltic and North seas to Spain and France in exchange for wines and liquors and other products of southwestern Europe and the East Indies. The revolt of the Netherlands gave the

Dutch a golden opportunity to secure colonial possessions. In 1595, the year following their exclusion by Philip II from the port of Lisbon, they made their first voyage to India. Direct trade with the Spice Islands increased annually, and by 1602 at least sixty-five Dutch merchantmen had made the return voyage from India. In the thirteen years from 1602 to 1615, the Dutch also captured 545 Spanish and Portuguese ships. In 1602, the Dutch East India Company was chartered, and in a few years it established new trading posts along the African and Asiatic coasts and succeeded in ousting the Portuguese from the rich islands of the Malay Archipelago and in monopolizing the bulk of their commerce. Under the auspices of the Dutch West India Company, trading posts were also established in the Americas. The most important of these included settlements along the coast of Brazil, in Guiana, in the Antilles, and at the mouth of the Hudson. But the Dutch were unable to maintain their empire; in 1654, they lost their last stronghold in Brazil, and ten years later the New Netherlands, their most important American colony, passed into the hands of the English. Throughout the seventeenth century, however, they dominated the carrying trade between Asia and Europe and increased their Baltic and Mediterranean commerce. Their power was to be challenged by the French and English.

France was more tardy in building up an overseas empire than her continental neighbors, Portugal, Spain, and Holland. During the religious wars that continued intermittently from 1562 to 1598, French commerce and industry suffered serious setbacks. French merchant vessels practically disappeared from the Atlantic. With the exception of one or two attempts by the Huguenots, the French Protestants, to make settlements in the New World, nothing was done to follow up the work of the Florentine Verrazano, sent out by Francis I in 1524, or of Cartier, who made his first voyage to America in 1534.

As soon as civil strife ceased, however, foreign and domestic trade began to revive, and the French renewed interest in overseas expansion. Henry IV and his Huguenot minister Sully subsidized a merchant marine, built up a navy, and encouraged the formation of powerful mercantile companies. In 1603, Champlain, in the employ of one of these companies, sailed up the St. Lawrence to the rapids above Montreal and explored the Acadian coast as far as the Bay of Fundy. Five years later, he laid the foundation of Quebec, destined to be the capital of New France and the center of French endeavor in America. Under Richelieu, who virtually ruled France from 1624 to 1642, and Colbert, minister of Louis XIV, the French Empire in America was expanded until it included all eastern Canada, the great central valley of North

America, French Guiana, Haiti, and over a dozen of the Antilles, including Guadeloupe and Martinique. The French also established trading posts on the African coast, laid claim to Madagascar, and gained a strong foothold in India, where they had thriving commercial centers at Surat, Chandernagor, and Pondicherry.

Sweden also made settlements in America. During the seventeenth century Sweden rose to the position of a first-class power in Northern Europe and, like her neighbors, desired to extend her commerce. In 1638, a Swedish company established a trading post on the Delaware. The venture, however, proved unsuccessful, and in 1655 New Sweden surrendered to the Dutch.

Monarchs and Merchants Establish the Greatest of Europe's Empires

In comparison with her rival empire builders, England enjoyed certain advantages. The English Channel protected her against the ravages of ambitious and warlike neighbors. Because she was not forced to maintain powerful armies to safeguard her boundaries against dangerous enemies, she supported no military caste. Her insularity did compel her to concentrate on a navy. As her navy grew in power, she was increasingly able not only to protect the homeland but also to seize and colonize distant lands and to incorporate them into her growing empire.

England's neighbors across the Channel were cramped in their efforts to establish colonial empires. The Dutch were handicapped by their small numbers, and they mistakenly concentrated upon trade instead of settlement. Although France had leaders interested in colonization and a much larger population than England, she dissipated her resources in interminable and futile dynastic wars on the continent and in domestic religious strife. Portugal, as we have seen, made a gallant start in colonial enterprise, but she had neither the resources nor the power to compete successfully with Britain. And Spain, administratively and financially mismanaged, headed for disaster after the defeat of her Armada.

By the opening of the seventeenth century, England also had a flourishing commercial class ready to embark on colonization. The backbone of the old feudal order had been broken by the Wars of the Roses. Tudor reforms had further subjugated the lay and ecclesiastical aristocracy. Changes in the English rural economy helped prepare leaders and common folk for colonization. With the increase in woolen manufactures in the sixteenth century and the consequent demand for wool, tillage gave way to sheep raising. Landlords extinguished the traditional rights of peasants and enclosed sizeable portions of the common lands. The dispossessed tenants, who were forced to become rural workers in the wool trade, as well as gentlefolk who lost out in the race for wool profits and, later, political patronage, furnished England with prospective New World emigrants.

England did practically no exploring or colonizing for half a century after the Cabot voyages of 1497–8. During this period, she was insufficiently wealthy, too small a power, and too absorbed in domestic affairs to engage in colonial experiments. As long as she was loyal to the Church of Rome, she was debarred from any part of the newly discovered world by the papal bull of demarcation. As English fishermen visited the banks of Newfoundland with greater frequency and increased the rumors about the unexplored wealth of the New World, interest in America was kept alive. With Elizabeth's accession to the throne and the ensuing contest with Spain, this interest grew rapidly.

Many leading Englishmen, even before the destruction of the Armada, expressed the opinion that by planting colonies in America England would be strengthened and Spain correspondingly weakened. In 1583, for instance, Sir George Peckham, after calling attention to the enormous wealth that Spain derived from the New World, declared that it was time for his countrymen to awaken "out of that drowsy dream wherein we have so long slumbered" and to set about colonizing America. The following year Hakluyt in his *Discourse Concerning Western Discoveries*, written for the enlightenment of Elizabeth, urged the government to establish posts between Florida and Cape Breton as bases for attacks on Philip's fleets in order to weaken his grip on America. Sir Walter Raleigh was especially outspoken "against the ambitious and bloody pretences of the Spaniards who, seeking to devour all nations, shall be themselves devoured."

As a result of the skill of Queen Elizabeth I and of her ministers, an uneasy religious peace and national security were achieved. With independence from Rome, an incipient national patriotism developed. In Shakespeare's *Henry VIII* the infant princess Elizabeth is said to promise "Upon this land a thousand, thousand blessings, which time shall bring to ripeness . . . In her days every man shall eat in safety under his own vine what he plants; and sing the merry songs of peace to all his neighbors."

Many Englishmen began to argue that colonies would strengthen England by adding to her resources, and would enhance her prestige and standing. Sir Ferdinando Gorges advocated expansion in these words: "Nothing adds more glory and greatness to any nation,

The Armada Faces the English Fleet Off England (*a contemporary print*)

[BRITISH MUSEUM]

than the enlargement of their territories, the multiplying of their subjects."

The desire to get rich quickly, the hope of every adventurer in every age, was another motive for colonization. The achievements of the great seamen, so admirably depicted by Hakluyt in his *Voyages*, stirred the English in much the same way as, generations before, the adventures of Marco Polo and the other Asiatic travelers had roused the curiosity of Europe about the East. The stories of profits ranging from 100 to 400 per cent whetted the appetite for riches. Englishmen would find mountains of precious metals, just as the Spanish had found riches in Mexico and Peru. This idea helped inspire Gilbert and Raleigh to undertake their abortive experiments in America. The same idea in 1607 enticed the first Englishmen to Virginia, where gold and silver were said to be "more plentiful than copper is with us." Even as late as 1760, Thomas Jeffreys incorporated the following item on the Far Northwest in his standard atlas of America: "Hereabouts are supposed to be the Mountains of Bright Stones mentioned in the Map of Ye Indian Ochagach." All the earlier American colonial charters were granted on the assumption that the gold and silver needed by monarch and merchant would be found. Each contained a clause reserving a fixed amount, usually one fifth, to the monarch.

English Protestants in this intensely religious age were especially alarmed by the fact that "Spanish Papists" were winning the red man in the New World to their "noxious notions" of Christianity. Most men in the seventeenth century, whether Protestant or Catholic, felt it their duty for the sake of the true faith to "instill into the purged mindes" of the heathen "the sweet and lovely liquor of the Gospel." Supporters of earlier colonizing companies asserted from time to time that the spread of Christianity was one of their chief aims. "The Kingdom of God will be enlarged," said one, "and the tidings of His truth will be proclaimed among so many millions of savage men and women who now live in darkness in those regions." Captain John Smith declared that "gaining provinces adds to the King's crown; but the reducing Heathen people to civility and true Religion, brings honour to the King of Heaven." Nearly all the colonial charters specifically mentioned the spread of Christianity as an object of settlement.

The belief that England was overpopulated also stimulated interest in expansion. An increased money supply, expanding trade, the extension of the wage system, and the multiplication of enclosures marked English economic growth. They also increased social inequality and intensified social unrest. England was wealthier in 1600 than in 1500, but her wealth was largely concentrated in the hands of the upper and

THE

THIRD AND LAST
VOLVME OF THE VOY-
AGES, NAVIGATIONS, TRAF-
fiques, and Difcoueries of the *Englifh Nation*, and in
fome few places, where they haue not been, of ftrangers, performed within and before the time of thefe hundred yeeres, to all
parts of the *Newfound* world of *America*, or the *Weft Indies*, from 73.
degrees of Northerly to 57 of Southerly latitude:

As namely to *Engronland*, *Meta Incognita*, *Eftotiland*,
Tierra de Labrador, *Newfoundland*, vp *The grand bay*, the gulfe of *S. Lau-*
rence, and the Riuer of *Canada* to *Hochelaga* and *Saguenay*, along the coaft of *Aram-*
bec, to the fhores and maines of *Virginia* and *Florida*, and on the Weft or backfide of them
both, to the rich and pleafant countries of *Nuena Bifcaya*, *Cibola*, *Tiguex*, *Cicuit*,
Quinira, to the 15. prouinces of the kingdome of *New-Mexico*, to the
bottome of the gulfe of *California*, and vp the
Riuer of *Buena Guia:*

And likewife to all the yles both fmall and great lying before the
cape of *Florida*, *The bay* of *Mexico*, and *Tierra firma*, to the coafts and Inlands
or *Newe Spaine*, *Tierra firma*, and *Guiana*, vp the mighty Riuers of *Orenoque*,
Diffekebe, and *Maranom*, to euery part of the coaft of *Brafil*, to the Riuer of *Plate*,
through the Streights of *Magellan* forward and backward, and to the
South of the faid Streights as farre as 57 degrees:

And from thence on the backfide of *America*, along the coaftes, harbours,
and capes of *Chili*, *Peru*; *Nicaragua*, *Nuena Efpanna*, *Nuena Galicia*, *Culiacan*,
California, *Noua Albion*, and more Northerly as farre as 43 degrees:

Together with the two renowmed, and profperous voyages of Sir *Francis Drake*
and M. *Thomas Candifh* round about the circumference of the whole earth, and
diuers other voyages intended and fet forth for that courfe.

Collected by RICHARD HAKLVYT *Preacher, and fometimes*
ftudent of Chrift-Church in Oxford.

¶ Imprinted at London by *George Bifhop Ralfe*
Newberie and ROBERT BARKER
ANNO DOM. 1600

Title Page of Hakluyt's "Voyages"

middle classes. With the influx into Europe of approximately one and a
half billion dollars in gold and silver from America between 1500 and
1600, prices shot upward and the cost of living increased at least 300
per cent. Production did not keep pace with the ability to buy, and
population increased the pressure on prices. English beef, for instance,
rose from one cent a pound in 1548 to four in 1588; pork and mutton
more than doubled in price during the same period; and the cost of
other food products and of clothing rose accordingly.

With most income and wages already pitifully low by our standards, people moved close to starvation and violence. Thousands were
reduced to beggary and vagabondage; jails were filled, and crime increased. Contemporary authorities attributed this economic distress to
overpopulation and suggested colonization as a remedy. In 1576, Sir
Humphrey Gilbert pointed out: "We might inhabit some part of these
countries, and settle there such needy people of our country, which
now trouble the commonwealth, and through want here at home are
enforced to commit outrageous offences whereby they are daily consumed with the gallows." Hakluyt had the same view. "These petty
thieves," he said, "might be condemned for certain years in the western
parts." In a pamphlet entitled *Nova Britannia*, published a generation
later, in 1609, after stating that money and people were necessary for
successful colonization, the author declared that England had "swarms
of idle persons, which having no meanes of labour to relieve their
misery, do likewise swarm in lewd and naughty practices." It would
be most profitable for England, he went on to say, "to rid our multitudes of such as lie at home, pestering the land with pestilence and
penury, and infecting one another with vice and villainy worse than
the plague itself." Still another pamphlet declared that there was nothing "more dangerous for the estate of commonwealths than when the
people do increase to a greater multitude and number than may justly
parallel with the largeness of the place and country; for hereupon comes
oppression, and diverse kinds of wrongs, mutinies, sedition, commotion
and rebellion, scarcities, dearth, poverty, and sundry sorts of calamities, which either breed the conversion, or eversion, of cities and
commonwealths."

Improvising a National Economic Policy

Of all these influences upon English expansion, none perhaps was
more important than the desire of Elizabeth I to make England
economically self-sufficient and politically independent. The diverse
economic policies that Elizabeth and other European monarchs devised

to reach these goals are collectively called *mercantilism*. More the counsel of necessity than deduction from theory, mercantilism was a series of practical proposals for survival in a world in which warfare was accepted as the normal or expected condition among states. With the further assumption that the wealth of the world was inherently limited, national safety seemed to depend on competition for a large and permanent stock of gold and silver. It was common belief that these commodities, always in demand and always acceptable payment for services or goods, represented the chief wealth of a country. The nation's strength and prosperity depended absolutely upon the amount of specie at its command. Spain seemed powerful and prosperous as long as gold and silver flowed into her coffers from the New World. Since England did not own rich deposits of precious metals, she had to seek mines outside of Europe or to build up her stock of gold and silver by means of privateering and favorable trade balances. She used both means, but as the image of America as a treasure house of gold, silver, and precious stones gradually vanished, statesmen came more and more to depend upon commerce as a source of specie supply.

The cardinal feature of the later merchantilist outlook was admirably expressed by Thomas Mun. In a pamphlet entitled *England's Treasure by Foreign Trade* (1664), Mun declared: "The ordinary means . . . to increase our wealth and treasure is by foreign trade, wherein we must ever observe this rule, to sell more to strangers yearly than we consume of theirs in value." In other words, the value of a country's exports should always exceed that of her imports, and the difference, or balance of trade, would be earned in money or additional goods. The mercantilists made many suggestions for fostering a favorable balance of trade. In general, however, they advocated a population just large enough to supply adequate labor and consumers; the promotion of trade and circulation of money within the state for the purpose of ensuring prosperity; the encouragement of home manufactures and the export of home-manufactured articles; the prohibition of foreign manufactures through high customs duties; the granting of government subsidies or bonuses to infant industries; the negotiation of treaties favorable to the commercial class; the establishment of colonies as markets and sources of raw materials; and the fostering of the fishing and shipping industries as valuable auxiliaries of trade and naval strength. Proposals such as these were to form the basis of England's treatment of the American colonies down to the eve of the American Revolution.

At the time of Elizabeth and the first Stuarts it was not easy for England to apply mercantilist ideas. Lacking many natural resources, she had long been compelled to import certain essential commodities from foreign countries. Two thirds of the fish consumed by the English, for example, was purchased from foreigners, principally the Dutch, who were entrenched in the fishing industry.

England was also overdependent on her rivals for staple necessities. She faced the problem of finding adequate markets abroad for her own commodities, now increasing in both variety and volume. Trade with Catholic Spain was precarious, and the Spanish habitually confiscated English vessels that dared to trade with the Barbary States of North Africa on the ground that the English brought "armor, munition, and forbidden merchandise to strengthen the infidells against these parts of Christendom." Venice opposed English commercial activities in the eastern Mediterranean; Denmark imposed onerous charges on English merchantmen passing through the Danish straits; and France excluded English goods by tariffs and arbitrary taxes. Prolonged civil strife had undermined the Flanders market for English wool, and English traders in Russia no longer enjoyed exemption from customs duties. Even the privileges that English merchants had long been granted in the German towns were being withdrawn.

To statesmen and businessmen, commercial and colonial expansion seemed the remedy for these pressing problems. Direct trade with India would procure the products of the Orient independently of the Dutch and at less cost. New markets might be opened up for English goods. Similarly, colonies in America might provide both a source of supply and a market for English products. England would not need to depend on the Dutch for fish, or on the Baltic States for naval supplies, or on European markets for the sale of manufactured goods. If her trade could be diverted from foreign channels into a closed network of empire, she would become economically self-sufficient, prosperous, and strong. "Our moneys and wares," an advocate of colonization wrote in 1606, "that now run into the hands of our adversaries or cold friends shall pass unto our friends and natural kinsmen and from them likewise we shall receive such things as shall be most available to our necessities, which intercourse of trade may rather be called a homebred traffic than a foreign exchange."

In the last quarter of the sixteenth century, gentlemen adventurers like Gilbert and Raleigh, dreaming of glory and wealth beyond the seas and of a greater England, composed of extensive feudal or proprietary estates, made their first efforts to plant colonies in the New World. Though they failed, they inspired others. Less than a century later the foundation of the greatest of the European empires had been securely laid. Although among the last of the Old World nations to move overseas, England had founded colonies in Virginia, Maryland, New England, the Bermudas, the Bahamas, Guiana, and the lesser Antilles. The English flag also flew over remote but thriving trading posts along the verdant shores of Africa and the teeming coasts of India.

FOR SUPPLEMENTARY READING

NOTE: In this and subsequent chapter bibliographies, (Pb) following the date means that the work cited exists in a paperback edition. Due, however, to the rapid changes in paperback availability, readers should consult the latest *Paperbacks in Print* to determine if any book cited hereafter continues to appear or has become available as a paperback since this volume went to press.

A fine general survey of the history of the West since the Middle Ages is R. R. Palmer and Joel Colton, *A History of the Modern World* (3rd ed., 1965). The most important name in the interpretation of the revival of European life in the eleventh century is still Henri Pirenne, whose mature ideas are to be found in *Mohammed and Charlemagne* (1939) (Pb). A leading critic of Pirenne is Alfons Dopsch. See his *The Economic and Social Foundations of European Civilization* (1923, 1937). The Americas before Columbus are studied in J. Jennings and E. Norbeck (eds.), *Prehistoric Men in the New World* (1964). On the general background of the era of discovery after 1450, see E. P. Cheyney, *The European Background of American History, 1300–1600* (1904). The most recent survey of English society at the start of the seventeenth century is Wallace Notestein, *The English People on the Eve of Colonization 1603–1630* (1954). This volume can be supplemented by the colorful works of A. L. Rowse, *The Expansion of Elizabethan England* (1955) and *The Elizabethans and America* (1959). For the explorers themselves, students should start with J. B. Brebner's outstanding work, *The Explorers of North America 1492–1806* (1933) (Pb), and S. E. Morison's famous study of Columbus, *Admiral of the Ocean Sea* (1942) (Pb). The classic work on mercantilism is Eli Heckscher, *Mercantilism* (2 vols., 1935).

The influence of much of this scholarship can be found in the general studies of C. P. Nettels, *The Roots of American Civilization* (1938), and L. B. Wright, *The Atlantic Frontier* (rev. ed., 1960).

2

Settling Colonial America

ALL AMERICANS were originally immigrants. All had traditions that conflicted with what life in America demanded. All knew the pain of breaking off an old established life and starting a new one. Many of the first English settlers in North America were unable to pay their way to New England or Virginia and arrived in debt to men in the home country who had financed their voyages. The financial sponsors of the first generation of Americans made immigration into a business. The colonizers, as they are sometimes called, were either proprietors or members of trading companies that backed the establishment of colonies in the New World. The colonists—or actual settlers in America—came from a wide range of classes, nationalities, and intellectual backgrounds. Most were Englishmen, but many came from the European continent, and still others from Africa. Some hoped to escape persecution; some viewed the New World as a land of unbounded economic opportunities; and some emigrated because they were forcibly seized and shipped across the Atlantic. But all—however reluctantly—were to become Americans, and all were to contribute some portion of their past to the new civilization they were shaping.

First of Millions

The first English attempts to colonize North America were controlled by individuals rather than companies. Sir Humphrey Gilbert was the first Englishman to send colonists to the New World. His initial expedition, which sailed in 1578 with a patent granted by Queen Elizabeth, was defeated by the Spanish. A second attempt ended in disaster in 1583, when Gilbert and his ship were lost in a storm. In the following year, Gilbert's half-brother, Sir Walter Raleigh, having obtained a renewal of the patent, sponsored an expedition that explored the coast of the region that he named "Virginia." Under Raleigh's direction, efforts were then made to establish a colony on Roanoke Island in 1585 and 1587. The survivors of the first settlement on Roanoke returned to England in 1586, but the second group of colonists disappeared without leaving a trace. The failure of the Gilbert and Raleigh ventures made it clear that the tasks they had undertaken were too big for any one colonizer. Within a short time the trading company had supplanted the individual promoter of colonization.

Trading companies were chartered by the state, and rich merchants, as well as noblemen of high rank, gentlemen, and government officials, became members by contributing money and influence to the enterprise. The Virginia Company of London, for example, which planted the first successful English colony in America, was composed at one time of 659 persons, including 21 peers, 96 knights, 58 gentlemen, 110 merchants, and 282 citizens. Each member of a trading company shared in the profits according to his subscription. Such a company might be given quasi-governmental powers. It usually enjoyed complete authority in the region specified in its charter, electing its own officers, making its own by-laws, raising and coining money, regulating trade, disposing of corporate property, and providing for defense. It was not, however, completely independent of the crown. Often it could do nothing contrary to the laws of the mother country, upon whom it constantly relied for protection. The company was expected to strengthen the nation by opening up new commerce, by maintaining a favorable balance of trade, by supplying timber and supplies for the navy, and by weakening commercial and political rivals.

More than fifty of these companies were chartered by England, France, Holland, Sweden, and Denmark before 1700. By 1588, England alone had chartered the Muscovy, Cathay, Baltic, Levant, Moroccan, and African companies, and in 1600 the famous English East India Company was founded. Later trading companies also furnished the money and leadership necessary to bring emigrants from the Old World to the New, and founded four of the colonies that were to become part of the United States. Virginia was founded in 1607 by the Virginia Company of London. New Netherlands was planted by the Dutch near Albany, New York, in 1614. Massachusetts was established by the Massachusetts

*"James VI, King of Scotland and After of Great Britain
Under the Name of James I"*

Bay Company in 1630. A Swedish commercial company founded Delaware in 1638 and the Pilgrims who settled Plymouth in 1620 were financed by an English merchant, Thomas Weston, and his associates.

In 1606 James I gave the Plymouth Company and the Virginia Company of London charters that granted each of them a tract of land on the American coast a hundred miles in width and a hundred miles in depth. The land of the Plymouth Company was to lie between the thirty-eighth and forty-fifth parallels, roughly the area today between the mouth of the Potomac River and the northern borders of New York and Vermont. The Virginia Company was entitled to settle between the thirty-fourth and forty-first parallels, a region bounded today by Cape Fear, North Carolina, on the south and New York City on the north. It was further stipulated that the settlements of each of the companies had to be separated by at least one hundred miles. The Virginia Company immediately began preparations for colonization, and on May 24, 1607, its first group of settlers founded Jamestown.

The men who came to Jamestown hoped to find gold. Although

tough and aggressive, they suffered countless hardships. By the autumn of 1607, 76 of the 104 original settlers were dead; in 1616, only 350 of the 1,600 that had been sent by the company were still alive; and in 1624, despite the fact that there had been more than 4,000 arrivals since the colony's founding, only 1,200 had managed to survive Indian attacks, lawlessness, and disease. There was no gold in Virginia, but about 1616 an improved method for curing Virginia's tobacco was discovered, and the ultimate success of the colony was assured.

Although the stockholders of the Virginia Company viewed Jamestown as a business venture, they obtained no returns on their investment. The expense of maintaining the colony always exceeded the value of the relatively small amount of products that the settlers shipped to the mother country. The company's charter was liberalized in 1609 and in 1612. In 1619, communal ownership of the land in Virginia gave way to private holdings, and in the same year the colonists were permitted a representative assembly, the House of Burgesses. In 1624, the company's charter was annulled. Virginia became a royal colony, and the control of its government passed to the Crown. The first royal governor in America appeared in Virginia. He was a hint of things to come elsewhere, for by the eve of the American Revolution eight other colonies had come under direct royal supervision.

Thirteen years after the founding of Jamestown, a small band of Englishmen settled at Plymouth in the present state of Massachusetts. The so-called Pilgrims, some of whom had previously migrated from Scrooby, England, to Holland, sailed for the New World in the *Mayflower* and reached Plymouth Bay in December, 1620. Before landing, forty-one of the one hundred settlers signed the "Mayflower Compact," which provided for the establishment of a form of popular rule in the new colony. This famous agreement was also designed to preserve order in America, for each signer pledged himself to obey the laws to be passed after arrival. Despite a severe first winter during which more than half the inhabitants died, the colony survived, and most of its members were soon making an adequate living from the fur trade, farming, fishing, and lumbering. Although the Pilgrims had been given permission to settle on the land granted to the Virginia Company, their ship had been blown off its course, and their colony was situated on territory that had been assigned originally to the Plymouth Company. The Council of New England had taken over the Plymouth Company's grant, but it made no move to remove the Pilgrims. In 1630, William Bradford, the Governor of Plymouth, secured title to the land occupied by the colonists. By 1641, the leaders of the colony succeeded in paying off the last of the debts to the group of London merchants who had financed the *Mayflower* voyage. For the next fifty years the settlements in and around Plymouth comprised a self-governing community. The Pilgrims were a pious, hard-working, sober people drawn mainly from what we would call the lower middle classes. In comparison with their Puritan neighbors, they achieved little eminence or distinction. In 1691, William III transferred the political control of the Plymouth colony to the Massachusetts Bay colony.

The Puritan settlers at Massachusetts Bay surpassed the Pilgrims at Plymouth both in numbers and in their influence on later American life. In 1628, some English businessmen, most of whom were Puritans, secured from the Council of New England the land between the Merrimack and Charles rivers. In the following year this grant was confirmed in a charter that Charles I issued to the Massachusetts Bay Company. By chance or connivance this charter omitted the usual provision that the control of the company was to remain in England. Within a short time the company had dispatched ships with settlers to the New World. When John Winthrop, the company Governor, reached Massachusetts in 1630 with the charter, the colony and company became one. By the end of 1630, there were well over a thousand settlers in the towns of the Massachusetts Bay colony. During the "Great Migration" of the 1630's, 25,000 more arrived. In 1684 Massachusetts' charter was annulled, and in 1691 it became a royal colony.

Emigrants from Massachusetts helped establish the colonies of Rhode Island and Connecticut. In 1635, Roger Williams, a Puritan minister, was forced out of Massachusetts because of his religious and political views. The following year he settled at the present site of Providence, Rhode Island. He was soon joined by others, and by 1643, Portsmouth, Newport, and Warwick had been founded. In 1644, Parliament conferred on the Narragansett Bay settlers the right of self-government, and in 1663, Charles II granted Rhode Island a charter. Massachusetts Puritans also migrated to the Connecticut Valley. In 1635 and 1636, they founded the towns of Hartford, Wethersfield, and Windsor. Other settlers in the valley included former inhabitants of Plymouth who had a trading post in the vicinity of Windsor. Saybrook, a fort at the mouth of the Connecticut River, and the Puritan colony of New Haven were also established in the 1630's. In 1662 the various valley towns and the colony of New Haven were placed under a single administration in a charter granted by Charles II. The new self-governing colony was named Connecticut.

In 1623, Sir Ferdinando Gorges and Captain John Mason, both Englishmen, were granted the region between the Merrimack and Kennebec rivers. Six years later they divided the area; Mason took the western portion and named it New Hampshire, while Gorges assumed control over the eastern part and called it Maine. Neither however, was successful in attracting settlers from England, although the lands under their jurisdiction did entice settlers from Massachusetts. Within a short time the Bay colony was claiming jurisdiction over the inhabitants in both New Hampshire and Maine. New Hampshire was separated from Massachusetts and made a royal colony in 1679. Maine continued as a part of Massachusetts until 1820.

The Proprietors Promote Colonies

Several colonies were founded by individuals rather than by trading companies. In these so-called proprietorships a tract of land was granted by the king to an individual family or group of men.

Sir George Calvert, a talented Roman Catholic gentleman from Yorkshire, was raised to the peerage as Viscount Baltimore by Charles I, and he received a charter for Maryland in 1632. Primarily interested in colonization as a business venture, Calvert and his successors were largely indifferent to the political and religious creeds of their settlers. William Penn was born of moderately wealthy parents and trained at Oxford, where he cast his lot with the despised Protestant sect, the Society of Friends—or Ranters, or Quakers, as they were more frequently called. Penn looked to America for haven for his persecuted brethren and for wealth, and he obtained the right to establish a colony in 1681. Lord Berkeley and Sir George Carteret launched the project that led to the founding of New Jersey because they thought it promised a fortune in land speculation. Shortly before the Duke of York's conquest of New Netherlands in 1664, he gave New Jersey to Berkeley and Carteret. Other favorites of Charles II who received the vast ocean-to-ocean tract known as Carolina in 1663 dreamed of immense profits from a reconstituted feudal order in America. James Oglethorpe, on the other hand, viewed his colony primarily as a refuge for imprisoned debtors but made the colony attractive to the crown by emphasizing its role as a buffer state against Spanish and French expansion. In 1732, he and his associates won a charter for Georgia.

Like the trading companies, proprietors were free to establish whatever institutions they pleased, provided that these institutions did not conflict with the laws and government of England. The proprietor had to supply the capital for establishing his overseas domains: although this represented a considerable investment, he could expect profits from the leasing or sale of land, feudal dues, and a share in whatever mines might be discovered. The Penns and the Calverts, as well as less well-

The Landing of Penn

[NEW YORK PUBLIC LIBRARY]

known proprietors, induced as many people as they could to settle in their "plantations," much as modern boards of trade or chambers of commerce boost their towns or cities. The proprietors were ingenious advertisers for settlers. Penn's handbills that circulated in Europe did not differ materially in their appeal from the advertisement of a modern real estate man: "The Richness of the Air, the navigable Rivers, and thus the prodigious Increase of Corn, the flourishing conditions of the City of Philadelphia make it [the colony] the most glorious Place. . . . Poor People both men and women, can here get three times the wages for their Labor they can in *England* or *Wales*."

Maryland and Pennsylvania followed the path of Virginia and were eventually placed under royal control. Pennsylvania was mortgaged by Penn in 1708 but was returned to the Penn family in the middle of the eighteenth century. New Jersey was divided into East New Jersey and West New Jersey in 1664, but in 1702 the parts were reunited to form a royal colony. The settlers in the northern part of Carolina, most of whom were drawn from Virginia, had little in common with those in the settlement at Charleston. In 1719, South Carolina rebelled against the authority of the proprietors and began its separate existence as a royal colony. Nine years later North Carolina was also made a royal colony. Despite the high hopes of its founders, Georgia grew more slowly than the other colonies. When it, too, became a royal colony in 1752, it had less than 9,000 inhabitants.

Two of the English colonies in North America—New York and Delaware—were acquired by conquest. In 1664, an English expedition demanded and obtained the surrender of New Netherlands from its Dutch Governor, Peter Stuyvesant. The Duke of York, who was the brother of King Charles II, became the proprietor of the province. With his acquisition of New York, the Duke of York also claimed authority over the Dutch settlers and the Swedes the Dutch had conquered in what is now the state of Delaware. In 1682, however, he transferred jurisdiction over the Three Lower Counties—as Delaware was then called—to Pennsylvania. Delaware became a separate colony with its own assembly in 1703, but it remained under the ultimate authority of the proprietor of Pennsylvania until the Revolution.

Fortune Calls Settlers to Colonial America

No single reason or general word like *merchantilism* can explain why thousands of Europeans migrated to America in the seventeenth and eighteenth centuries. The rapid influx of gold and silver following the discovery of the New World brought economic hardship in many places. In England, particularly in the eastern and southeastern counties where the great English wool trade was centered, this distress was aggravated by the economic upheaval that came with the enclosures of the common lands for private use, by the depreciation in the value of money, and by European wars, which deprived England of her cloth markets. The towns and countryside swarmed with those unable to secure a livelihood, and the jails and almshouses were filled with beggars and those who had resorted to petty thievery to stay alive. "Our country," Sir William Pelham wrote, "was never in that want that now it is . . . for there are many thousands in these parts who have sold all they have even to their bed straw, and can not get work to earn any money. Dog's flesh is a dainty dish."

Unemployed wool workers, dispossessed farmers, and bankrupt wool traders were open to the inducements offered to settle in America. Often the government authorities compelled the more timid to emigrate by authorizing colonial agents and patentees of land to seize for their uses men and women of the lower classes, especially paupers and prisoners. An English commission in 1633, for example, was appointed "to reprieve able-bodied persons convicted of certain felonies, and to bestow them to be used in discoveries and other employments." Even the gentry felt the pinch of hard times. Many of them were reduced to straitened circumstances in their effort to "keep up" with the standards of enterprising traders or the *nouveaux riches*. Under Charles I many also lost social prestige or political privileges because they were opposed to royal policies. John Winthrop, a country squire of Suffolk, a man of modest estate, and one of the leaders of the emigration to Massachusetts Bay, complained that his "means here are so shortened as he shall not be able to continue in that place and employment where he now is"; the standard and cost of living had so increased that "no man's estate will suffice to keep sail with his equals." Winthrop shared the current opinion that England was overpopulated:

> This land grows weary of her inhabitants, so as man is here of less price amongst us than a horse or ship. . . . We stand here striving for places of habitation . . . and in the meantime suffer a whole continent as fruitful and convenient for the use of man to lie waste without any improvement.

The Struggle for God's Word in England

Although minor revolts against the authority of the Church of Rome had broken out for centuries, the formal unity of European Christianity was not shattered until after Luther began his attack on the Papacy in 1517. For Luther and Calvin, the foremost leaders of the Reformation, the chief issues of the age were theological. They wanted a militant, disciplined Christianity, purged of the tendencies to laxness and ecclesiastical corruption that seemed offensive in Renaissance Rome. Their attack in the name of "truth" tied in, however, with other resentments of Rome's political and economic power. The alliances made in the sixteenth century between religious reformers and powerful princes, merchants, and aroused common folk were too diverse to permit generalization. But questions of faith and practical power were inextricably linked with each other as the fires of faith flamed across Europe. Religion was taken too seriously to permit it to remain nonpolitical.

It is almost impossible for modern students to capture the excitement of men in the sixteenth and seventeenth century over religious issues. The growing number of Christian sects at the time only suggests the diverse ways and the minute particulars (to the modern mind) with which men sought God's truth. It took over 150 years for the fires kindled by the Reformation to die down. If something like modern religious diversity began to emerge at the end of the seventeenth century, this was furthest from the intentions of most Christians, Protestant as well as Catholic, in the earlier generations of the struggle. With truth conceived exclusively as the voice of groups believing themselves to be called by God to lead all Europe to salvation, it was not surprising that ideas of separation of church and state or toleration were either unknown or offensive to conscience. Men were prepared to take great personal risks over such issues as the use of the sign of the cross, the age at which baptism should take place, and the decoration of churches and the arrangement of altars. Those who could read devoured books with titles like *Episcopacy Asserted* or *The Liberty of Prophesying.* The "sweetest day I have seen in England" was described by one worthy as lasting continuously from nine to five with prayer, confession, bible-reading, preaching, and ending with a warning against various heretics.

In England in 1529 Henry VIII broke with Rome largely over personal and political matters. Henry wanted no significant changes in Christian belief or practice. At the same time, however, the long tradition of English criticism of the religion of Rome was reactivated and strengthened by the exciting news from the continental Protestants about a purified faith. The subsequent history of the Reformation in England was a complex struggle between those who, following Henry, conceived of the Reformation largely as a practical political matter and those, like many later emigrants to America, who thought of it primarily as the opportunity to establish God's holy word throughout the realm.

Under Henry VIII and his immediate successors, Edward VI and Queen Mary Tudor (Henry's Catholic daughter by his first marriage), the tides of theological controversy rolled back and forth with accompanying bloodshed and killing. Slowly, however, a distinctively English form of Christianity took shape, with the monarch as the executive of the church acting through his bishops. This religion came to be called Anglicanism. The cornerstones of the Anglican faith were the Thirty-nine Articles (1563) and the Book of Common Prayer (1552). The essentials of English religion were based on conflicting Lutheran, Calvinist, and Roman Catholic doctrines and worship and were consequently full of compromises and ambiguities. Sensing this, the more radical Protestants, eager, as zealous reformers usually are, for the clearest truths about faith, decided that the reformation had not yet gone far enough, particularly in the reorganization of the Church and in the conduct of religious services. Their discontent was increased by Queen Elizabeth's skill at avoiding quarrels over doctrine and parrying the demands of the discontented extreme Protestants. By shrewd maneuver and by requiring, in the main, mere conformity in religious practice, Elizabeth was able to keep an uneasy religious peace. In contrast to the policy of her predecessors, those who refused to conform were put to death only for actual acts of treason. There was a marked decline in the more terrible forms of persecution, although imprisonment and other restrictions of those out of sympathy with Anglicanism continued.

The Rise of Puritanism

Down to about 1580, the only significant Protestant opponents of the Elizabethan religious settlement were the Presbyterians. Because they wanted to purify the creed and practices of the Church of England, they came to be known as Puritans, a term of abuse at the time. Puritanism, however, should not be associated only with the Presbyterians, for as time passed and English Protestantism split into an increasing number of sects, Puritanism was used to describe many groups and many ideas. Puritanism encompassed a view of man and history, an attitude toward the Bible, and ideas about the organization of the Church.

The major influence shaping the Puritan view of man was John Calvin, one of the great leaders of the Reformation on the continent. The English had come into direct touch with the ideas of his followers when some Englishmen fled to Europe in anticipation of persecution under the Catholic Queen Mary Tudor (1553–8). When they returned to England under Elizabeth, they spread what they had learned through the pulpit and ministry. Cambridge University especially became a famous center of Puritanism. Significantly, a large number of the leaders of early New England were trained at Cambridge or influenced by preachers who had been educated there. It happened that Cambridge was also in the center of the wool region and many of the unemployed or dispossessed common folk and gentry who left the area near Cambridge for America around 1630 had become deeply committed to Puritan ideals.

According to Calvin, when Adam ate the apple from the tree of knowledge, he rebelled against God and changed the course of history. From that time forward all mankind was to pay for this "original sin." Man's life was to be marked by unhappiness and strife. Death in most cases would bring damnation, for Adam had so cut man off from God, had so corrupted human nature, that there was nothing man could do to earn God's forgiveness. God "by a just and irreprehensible but incomprehensible judgment" knew whom he had chosen to save and those whom he had damned. He exercised "His gratuitous mercy, totally irrespective of human merit." The world and human history were to be the scenes of momentous struggles in the life of every man and woman. If a man would at least try to struggle against sin and follow the word brought by Jesus Christ, his ability to resist sin might show that God had in fact chosen him for salvation.

Understandably in a world that took religious questions so seriously, this message had a stunning impact. Awesome and restricting as Calvin's message may appear today, to many people living in the sixteenth century, it came as a liberation. Here was a discipline of holiness that suggested a chance for deliverance from misery and wickedness. This was the powerful word spread by the Puritan preachers in the last quarter of the sixteenth century. The flexible religious policy of Queen Elizabeth made it possible for this potentially revolutionary view of life to take powerful hold on the English imagination. When translated, as it was to be, into political and religious policy it was an immense force that inspired not only the Puritan leaders in America but those who stayed in England.

Even most Anglicans accepted this Puritan view of life until the early seventeenth century, when they began to take a less severe view of man's fate. Indeed, the growing emphasis of Anglican thinkers on man's power to *earn* God's favor helped convince Puritans that, unless they hurried their reformation, a monstrous pride in man would soon replace their emphasis on man's fallen nature. Although the Puritan psychology, as we might call it, was a powerful inducement to faith and inspired an intense personal discipline, it had however, to be connected with practical advice about how the reformed Christian life was to be led.

The second major feature of Puritanism was, consequently, an attitude toward the Bible. Puritans believed that God in both Old and New Testaments had given His only authoritative word about personal conduct and religious worship. The Bible was to be read as literally and as strictly as possible. It was ultimately superior to the writings of the Christian fathers, to the traditions of the Church, and to the word of priests, bishops, or Popes. Each man stood alone before God in judgment. No other human authority, no matter how trained or disciplined, could affect the results of man's search for evidences of God's grace within himself. No church could gain or increase man's chance for salvation. Puritans read the Bible as forbidding anything except the simplest worship. Most of the practices of English religion they claimed were "anti-Christian, and devilish and contrary to the Scriptures." They hotly debated such issues as the proper clothing for ministers who officiated at services, the use of the sign of the cross, and whether altars should be enclosed by a railing. Since the Anglican faith had retained priests and bishops, richness of liturgy, ceremony, and the authority of tradition as well as the Bible, conflict between Puritans and Anglicans was inevitable.

The struggle between Puritanism and Anglicanism was intensified by a bitter dispute over the nature of the church. It was unthinkable at the time that a citizen not attend church. Since it was nearly universally believed that religious duty was all inclusive and man's primary concern and that there was only one true church or religion, the question of the nature of the church was inseparable from ideas of what English life and government should be. Even if the monarch had been an atheist, the influence of Christian faith, with its then comprehensive views of man and morality, and the immense power of the church would have created unavoidable issues for the Crown. With many Puritans insisting that the Bible be used as a basis for civil law, the actual issue was made even more complex.

Down to about 1580, most reformers sought a Presbyterian church. Objecting to the special spiritual authority implied in a priesthood and in a system of bishops, and angered by the royal role in choosing religious leaders, the Presbyterian group wanted to substitute councils of elders to be elected by the individual churches. These councils, or Synods, as they were called, would have the right to define religious doctrine and practice and to instruct the crown in its religious and civil duties.

As time passed, however, even this system came into question. Puritans began to ask whether Presbyterianism itself was sanctioned by the Bible. Would it not be a truer faith if individual congregations banded together only loosely to define doctrine or ceremony? Cooperation and consultation among churches might be needed, but the idea that a council outside an individual church could dictate the forms of worship seemed to challenge the notion that communion with God depended on the individuals within their own churches. A very loose system of churches was suggested to replace both Presbyterianism and Anglicanism. This came to be known as Congregationalism, and it was the form of church organization favored by most of the leaders of the Massachusetts Bay Colony.

Given the desire of Puritan ministers to find the truest possible realization of God's word, it is not surprising that the challenge to centralized or hierarchic religious authority was soon carried even further. Many people became convinced that the earliest church, that closest to Christ and His apostles, had been independent of all external authority. Did not the reformation ideal logically imply that a church could only be composed of men moved by the Holy Spirit in a unique way? Could any church beyond that be more than a spiritual fellowship without any visible structure? Was not the true church, then, the single gathering, pursuing independent of or separate from other churches, the word of God? This suggested a third form of Puritan church, which came to be known as Independency or Separatism.

Modern students find it difficult to understand that for most of the past, Western societies have esteemed order and stability rather than progress and change. What Englishmen on the eve of the settlement of America respected as stability, we might construe as social stagnation. Given a general desire for order and clear lines of authority, it was understandable that men believed that every person should have his station in life and all groups in society an assigned place. Society could never actually be a neat package, but the ideal of the individual's station and duties was a powerful one. Separatism was a challenge to this traditional attitude. In effect, it proposed the removal of external control from religion. It further asserted that mere birth in a place did not assign a man membership in the local church, as nearly all Christians other than Separatists agreed. Faith and church were not matters of geography but of conscious individual choice. It is therefore understandable, once the Crown decided to tighten the lines of religious control, why the Separatist churches were in the most exposed or anomalous position. Some of the Separatists who fled England rather than surrender their beliefs are more familiar to us as the Pilgrim fathers.

The Calvinist view of man, the high place of the Bible, and conflicting views of the church provided the major issues in an increasingly bitter debate initiated by the Puritans, in the fifty years between 1580 and 1630. Because religious issues were inseparable at the time from other questions, foreign policy toward Catholic France and Spain was bound to become a source of religious quarrels. Similarly, economic interests could not be separated from religious beliefs. Massachusetts leaders like John Winthrop may have suffered a loss of wealth and prestige in England, but they were also devout Puritans, as were many of the unemployed weavers or ousted yeoman who followed Winthrop to America. Their economic and political grievances against the Court were accented by Puritanical scorn and disgust at its lushness and sexual corruption. The violence and open immorality in "low places" seemed to demand a strict and swift justice by "God's elect" as the Puritans thought of themselves. Inspired by the call to holiness, seeking, in full confidence that they alone had the truth, to reform England for Christ, the Puritans clearly were ready for a clash if policy was changed from a politics of compromise to a politics seeking to establish Anglican doctrine more clearly than Elizabeth had.

The Fight for True Faith Becomes Political

Elizabeth did attempt to make Puritans conform, but only to the Anglican *forms* of worship. Her successor in 1603, James I, had been James VI of Scotland, where the Presbyterians had triumphed. With James now King of England, that wing of the Puritan group, successful in Scotland, hoped that England's moment for redemption had also arrived. King James, a florid, arrogant, but accomplished man, welcomed the throne of England not as a chance to deliver England to the Puritans, but as a deliverance from the Scottish Presbyterians. Seeking to clarify doctrine and to settle religious affairs, he invited the Puritans to debate the issues with him at the Hampton Court Conference in 1604. James's arrogance was more than matched by the doctrinaire bias of the Puritan leaders. When Presbyterianism was mentioned, the King flew into a rage and promised the assembly that only when he was old and "his windpipe was stuffed" would he "hearken unto them." The Puritans, adamant, would not compromise or conform. James I finally asserted that he would make them conform or harry them out of the land, "or else do worse."

Although the conference authorized the great King James version of the Bible, little else came of the intransigence on both sides. A few years later, when the King tightened the rule of doctrinal conformity, several hundred ministers resigned. Among these were the future leaders of Plymouth Colony who in 1608 fled to Holland, then the most tolerant nation in Europe. After this, however, religious trouble in England subsided for nearly a generation. Under Charles I, conditions again deteriorated. The suspension of the laws against Catholics filled the reformers with alarm. Matters came to a head when in 1629 Charles dissolved Parliament and set himself, with the assistance of Archbishop Laud, to destroying Puritanism in all its forms. Although the Anglican faith had become philosophically more humane and enlightened (in modern terms) than the faith of the Puritans, it was now to be imposed by force. Its very liberality of doctrine struck the Puritans with horror. Charles and Laud were determined to get rid of the many-sided Puritan challenge to the Crown. Harsh laws were enacted and harsher decrees promulgated. As persecution increased, thousands of Puritans, having lost hope of securing control of the established church, turned toward America as the only avenue of escape. A few were noblemen possessing landed estates; some were merchants of considerable wealth; others were professional men and university graduates; but by far the greatest number were landed gentry and yeomen farmers.

With the overthrow of Charles I and the establishment of the Commonwealth, in 1651, the tide turned. The Puritans, now in the saddle, resolved to impose their own orthodoxy on the English people. As early as 1641, orders were issued for the demolition of all images, altars, and crucifixes. Two years later, the "Solemn League and Covenant" pledged Parliament and the Puritan leaders to do away with "church government by archbishops, bishops, their chancellors and commissaries, deans and chapters, archdeacons, and all other ecclesiastical officers depending on that hierarchy," and to "reform religion in England" in doctrine, worship, discipline, and government according to the Word of God and "the example of the best reformed churches." The Commonwealth guaranteed toleration for various Christian beliefs, "provided this liberty be not extended to popery or prelacy." Both the Anglicans and Roman Catholics were threatened. From 1640 to 1660, those who had persecuted the Puritans found themselves on the defensive. This persecution of Anglicans and Roman Catholics added to the turmoil and ill-fortune of civil war and sent hundreds of them to the New World.

The recall of Charles II to the throne in 1660 marked the end of Puritan domination in England. The Anglican Church, which twenty years before had seemingly received a death blow, rose again, apparently more vigorous and powerful than ever. Puritans, Quakers, other Protestant groups, and Catholics now became targets of oppression; rather than risk or undergo persecution, another wave of Englishmen elected to join their brethren beyond the seas.

Because of its intensely personal appeal and bracing moral outlook, Puritanism attracted converts from all classes. The Puritan thought he was required to throw himself into his daily job as part of his Christian discipline. This demand helped stimulate his "drive" to business success and capital accumulation. Believing as he did that the distinctions of the world separating men were nothing in the eyes of God, that kings as well as common laborers were sinners, the English Puritan gradually moved to the belief that no man or government was good enough to be trusted with arbitrary power. The idea of the sinfulness of all men came to be used as a basis for attack on the doctrine of the Divine Right of kings.

The combination of their growing wealth with the conviction that they walked with God made many Puritans increasingly self-confident, even though they lacked the titles and trappings of nobility. When King Charles I seemed to unite personal arrogance, unholiness, and unwarranted absolutism in restricting such "rights" as freedom from arbi-

trary arrest and imprisonment, lawful taxation, and the power to petition over grievances, he precipitated a genuine controversy in England
over political and religious principles that cut across class lines. Rather
than suffer the costs and trials of long conflict with the Crown, many
Englishmen chose the uncertainties of distant colonization. Others
stayed at home to fight the King. Puritans who followed the conflict
with the King from the distant shores of New England awaited confidently the day when they would be recalled to an England purged of
corruption and eager for the word of the Lord that the colonists had
kept pure by their decision to settle in the wilderness of America. But
the effect of the wilderness on the practice of God's word was to bring
unforeseen results.

What was to happen in America might suggest, in Puritan terms,
the real inscrutability of God's providence. The Massachusetts colonists
of the 1620's and '30's were confident that they had read God's word
correctly. Faced with a loss of political privilege, of social status, and
of economic opportunity, and threatened by the victory of a "horrid"
religion, they sought in the New World that reformed faith and world's
work seemingly only temporarily denied to them in their ancestral villages and manors.

Peopling a Continent

When the first ships with settlers dropped anchor in the waters off
the mysterious coasts of North America, from Atlantic to Pacific the
land before them supported a few hundred thousand Indians scattered
over three million square miles of territory. The best Indian trails were
swallowed by forest, tall grasses, or deserts after a few pitiful miles of
successful struggle against an incredibly raw nature. Nearly every
American today has had ancestors who approached America's shores
with mixed feelings of apprehension and hope similar to those of the
first colonists.

Exact figures are lacking, but as early as 1640 there were more
than 65,000 Englishmen in America. Of this number, approximately
14,000 had settled in Massachusetts, 1,500 in Maine and New Hampshire, 300 in Rhode Island, and 2,000 in Connecticut. Between 1620 and
1642, 1,500 English colonists settled in Maryland and 8,000 in Virginia.
During the same period, more than twice the number of Englishmen
that went to New England settled in the English West Indies. New
England in 1689 had about 80,000 people; Maryland, Virginia, and the
Carolinas together boasted a slightly larger number; and the Middle
colonies from New York to Pennsylvania had 40,000—in all, about

South Carolina in the 1670's

(*a contemporary print*)

200,000 settlers. The population of the English West Indian islands increased even more rapidly.

Second only to the English in numbers and influence after 1700 were the English-speaking Presbyterians from Northern Ireland, the so-called Scotch-Irish. These were the descendants of the Presbyterians from the Scottish lowlands who had moved to Northern Ireland following the expulsion of the indigenous Irish in 1611 and had settled as tenants in the six northern counties of Ulster. The land there had been confiscated from the Irish and regranted to English speculators (composed for the most part of London merchants) as part of James I's program for subduing Ireland by settling it with Scottish and English colonists. Despite the hostility of their Catholic neighbors, frequent friction with the English government, and the vicissitudes of war, the Scotch-Irish had prospered. By the close of the seventeenth century, Ulster alone had a Presbyterian population of more than a million farmers and businessmen. The economic and religious grievances of the Ulsterites weighed very heavily on them. British landlords and businessmen, with an eye to greater profits, induced the government to enact legislation to check Irish competition. The Navigation Acts (1660–63) cut off direct trade with the colonies; heavy duties practically prohibited the importation into England of Irish exports, including stock and dairy products; the Woolens Act of 1699 forbade exportation of Irish raw wool and woolen cloth; and discouraging regulations of other sorts and inadequate markets ruined the linen industry. Even the cultivation of tobacco was forbidden. These restrictive measures applied to all Ireland, but their effect on Ulster was especially disastrous. Moreover, the Test Act of 1704 further oppressed these Presbyterians of the Irish north. It questioned their marriages, closed their chapels, and discontinued their schools. They were compelled to pay tithes for the support of the Church of Ireland, an Anglican organization cordially hated by the great majority. Finally, when their original leases began to expire between 1714 and 1718, absentee landlords doubled and in some instances trebled the rents. At the same time, prolonged droughts ruined the crops, and smallpox and other diseases took a heavy toll of life.

Angered and discouraged, thousands of Scotch-Irish turned toward America. By the eve of the Revolution, it is estimated that more than 300,000 had made new homes on the other side of the Atlantic. Fifty-four shiploads reached the port of Boston between 1714 and 1720, and an even larger number landed in Philadelphia during the same years. Although the Scotch-Irish came to all the colonies, by far the greater number settled in the frontier regions of New Jersey, Pennsylvania, Maryland, Virginia, and the Carolinas. In New York and New England, their settlements were small and scattered.

The Germans ranked next to the Scotch-Irish in numbers. Many of them were victims of the Thirty Years' War (1618–48) and the seventeenth-century wars of Louis XIV. They sought escape from the poverty and destruction that surrounded them on all sides. By the opening of the eighteenth century, a steady stream of German farmers and artisans from south Germany, the valley of the Rhine, and the German cantons of Switzerland was pouring into the colonies of the Atlantic seaboard. The advertising of Penn and other proprietors helped to attract the Germans. During the reign of Queen Anne (1702–14) books and other literature were distributed through the Palatinate and other German provinces encouraging Germans to come to England so that they might be sent to English colonies. It is estimated that fully a third of Pennsylvania's pre-Revolutionary population was German. Other thousands settled in New York, in the frontier regions of Maryland, Virginia, the Carolinas, and in other colonies. By the end of the colonial period there were 200,000 Germans in America.

Besides the Scotch-Irish and Germans, hundreds of Huguenot or French Protestant exiles established homes in South Carolina and in the colonies of the North, where families like the Delanos, the Devereuxs, and the Faneuils became leaders in business and in society. Scot-

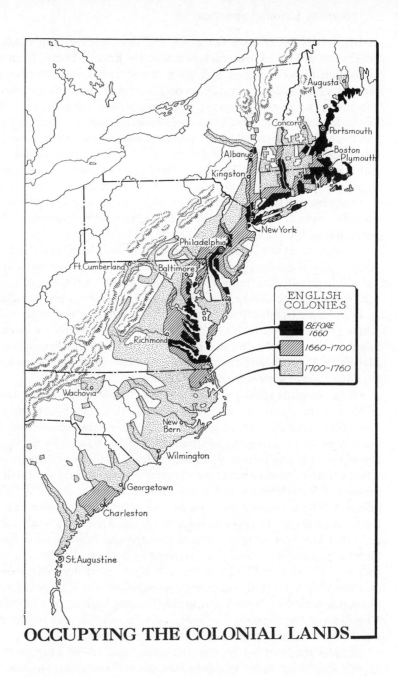

ENGLISH
COLONIES

BEFORE 1660

1660-1700

1700-1760

Augusta
Concord
Portsmouth
Albany
Boston
Plymouth
Kingston
New York
Philadelphia
Ft. Cumberland
Baltimore
Richmond
Wachovia
New Bern
Wilmington
Georgetown
Charleston
St. Augustine

OCCUPYING THE COLONIAL LANDS

tish Presbyterians settled in New Jersey and New England. Welsh-men—many of them Quakers—made their homes in Pennsylvania, the Carolinas, and New England, where men like Thomas Bardin played an active and useful role in their respective communities. From Switzer-land a band of 600 Swiss under De Graffenried founded New Bern, North Carolina. Other Swiss pioneers found homes in Pennsylvania and South Carolina. From southern and eastern Ireland came thousands of Catholic Irish. Approximately 400 Swedes settled in New Sweden on the lower Delaware, and the Dutch in New Netherland numbered about 8,000 when their colony was taken over by the English in 1664. By 1776, practically every colonial port town had a small Jewish group. Long before the Declaration of Independence it was obvious that America was not a homogeneous society.

Free and Forced Immigrants

Throughout the colonial period, an insignificant number of upper-class Europeans emigrated to the English possessions in North America. The early settlers in the Massachusetts Bay colony and in Virginia were drawn largely from the rural areas of England. Few actual paupers and few of the really rich were among them. Nevertheless, the colonies were not peopled exclusively by members of what today would be de-scribed as the rural middle class. Many settlers were so poor that they paid for passage across the Atlantic by selling their freedom for a given number of years; poverty forced others to leave their native lands for the New World against their will.

The average landless workingman's lot in England was harsh and insecure. By law, he was, in effect, confined to his native parish, where he had little or no opportunity to improve his status. He lived in an environment dominated by economic scarcity. His wage, sure to be low in any case, was fixed by land-owning justices of the peace, who were interested in keeping it as low as possible. An adequate living for himself and his family was almost impossible. His children at an early age were forced to contribute to the support of the household. He was always close to starvation and penury, and however much he might struggle and economize, he could save nothing for sickness or old age. What public relief there was was pitifully inadequate. The English economists of the time regarded him as a useless weight upon the com-munity rather than the potential consumer of the goods he produced. He existed only to contribute his labor to production. The New World, with its opportunities for earning at least a decent living, seemed to af-ford the English laborer the only escape from his miserable condition

To the poorer classes on the Continent as well—particularly to the Germans—America was the land of promise.

If their poverty turned them toward America, poverty also stood between these people and America. To overcome this barrier, tens of thousands sold themselves into servitude to ship captains, agents of planters, professional speculators, and others, in return for the payment of the cost of their transportation, varying from six to eight pounds sterling per person. These people who came to America already in debt were generally known as indentured servants or redemptioners. Redemptioners, or free-willers as they were sometimes called, made an agreement with a merchant or ship captain that enabled them to find a master in the colonies who would pay their passage. Indentured servants, on the other hand, were auctioned off to the highest bidder when the vessel reached America. There were many more indentured servants than redemptioners.

Overcrowding and indescribably bad sanitary arrangements, starvation and barbarous punishments made the poor men's journey to America a nightmare—and the number who died of disease and exposure was very large. Those who reached America were at once transferred to masters to work out their terms of bondage, which generally ran from two to seven years. Individuals bound to sea captains were usually advertised and auctioned off to the highest bidder, who frequently happened to be a "soul driver," that is, a person who trafficked in indentured labor. Sometimes drivers bought "the whole and sometimes a parcel of them as they can agree, and then drive them through the country like a parcel of sheep, until they can sell them to advantage." Many who came were redeemed upon arrival by friends and relatives, but among those with this expectation large numbers were also disappointed. Frequently, the children of very old or sick immigrants, who were unable to pay their passage or to work, served time for their parents as well as for themselves.

Although every colony had these bondsmen, as they have been called, the number was exceptionally large in the proprietary colonies, where the demand for cheap labor was insistent. The Baltimores, Penns, and Carterets made every effort to secure as many indentured servants as possible. They were so successful that in all probability over half of the thousands of immigrants who came to the Middle colonies during the seventeenth and eighteenth centuries were in temporary bondage. During the seventeenth century, the number in the Southern colonies was also large, but it declined rapidly in some areas after slavery secured a foothold.

A considerable class of involuntary servants composed of kid-

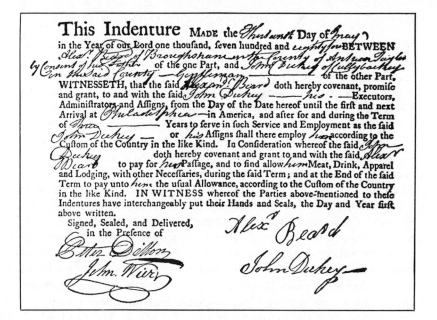

A Typical Indenture

napped individuals, political and religious offenders, paupers, and vagrants increased the white labor supply. Thousands of children and adults in English cities, particularly Bristol and London, were victims of professional kidnappers and agents of companies and proprietors who had colonies in America. Children were lured from their homes by promises of trinkets or sweetmeats and then forcibly seized and sold for long terms of servitude. As early as 1627, approximately 1,500 children had been sent across the Atlantic. Fifty years later it was estimated that at least 10,000 persons were either forcibly or fraudulently "spirited away" to America every year. In 1671, a kidnapper stated that for twelve years he had sent 500 individuals annually to the colonies. Parents in straitened circumstances often indentured their children, and English parish authorities welcomed the opportunity of sending orphans and paupers to the New World. Many of these, separated from friends and relatives and subjected to great hardships, soon died. Those of stronger constitution, after serving their term of bondage, either became independent farmers or farm laborers or joined the growing group of artisans.

Other involuntary white emigrants were the "criminals" or "transported prisoners." Almost all were either political and religious offenders or convicts from English jails. They represented some of the most outspoken and some of the worst elements of the population.

Many had dared to criticize or oppose the government—for example, the Irish transported by Cromwell during his occupation of Ireland, the Cavaliers who bitterly denounced the Puritans and championed the cause of the Stuarts, the Roundheads after the Restoration, and the Scots and English who, from time to time, rebelled or plotted insurrection against the English monarchs. Sometimes these offenders were actually men of superior training who were employed by their masters in positions of responsibility. Many of those forced to come to America were not criminals in a modern sense, but victims of a penal code which listed no less than 300 crimes punishable by death. The starving poor who committed trifling offenses were put in the same class as highwaymen and murderers. During the seventeenth century, the English courts would frequently pardon a criminal if he would leave the country. In 1717, Parliament enacted a statute that permitted certain classes of criminals to be transported at the discretion of the court for a term of not less than seven years. Between 1717 and the outbreak of the Revolution, some 40,000 convicted persons were sent to America, some for seven years, some for fourteen, and some for life. In Maryland, which received more than any other colony, they formed the backbone of the servant class. Not all of these transported convicts were petty criminals. Some were counterfeiters, robbers and even murderers; some carried disease and were a menace to master and community alike. Several colonies vigorously protested against receiving these undesirables and attempted to exclude them by law. The British government opposed these efforts, and in most instances they came to nothing.

African Labor Comes to America

For countless white men and women, life in America began in bondage and ended in freedom. Most Negroes, however, began and ended their life in America as another man's property. In 1619, "a Dutch man-of-war with 20 Negars" anchored off Jamestown, where it disposed of its human freight as indentured servants. For a century or more before this time, Portuguese, Spanish, and, especially, Dutch traders had developed a profitable slave traffic with southwestern Europe. The West Indies soon became their chief market. Throughout the seventeenth century, however, the supply of slave labor in the mainland colonies increased very slowly. The majority of the English colonists had few moral scruples against human slavery. But the Dutch monopolized the trading stations along the African coast, and the West Indies competed for slave labor. In their first fifty years in America, many Negroes were not slaves at all but indentured servants. These

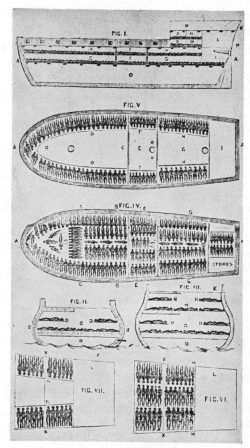

A Slave Ship

were bound, however, for far longer periods and under more precarious conditions than whites. In Virginia until 1645, free Negroes could even vote. In 1671, there were only 2,000 Negroes in Virginia, and in the colonies to the north there were even fewer. Thirty years later Virginia had only 4,000 Negroes, about 8 per cent of her total population. Except, perhaps, in South Carolina, the South throughout the seventeenth century depended, not upon Negro slaves, but upon free and indentured white and colored labor.

Toward the end of the century, however, Negro slavery began to increase. With the spread of tobacco culture, a larger and cheaper labor force became imperative. The English government after the Restoration began to restrict the supply of laborers sent to the colonies. English slavers broke the Dutch monopoly of the trade and were able to secure slave cargoes along the West African coast from native chiefs or slavedrivers in exchange for cheap clothing, hardware, ammunition, and rum of an inferior quality. In 1672, Parliament chartered the Royal African Company, an English commercial corporation, and gave it an exclusive monopoly of the slave trade with the British colonies. In 1698, English merchants who were not members of the company and traders and shipowners of Boston, Newport, New York, and Charleston were also allowed to participate in the business. The volume of the traffic increased so rapidly that approximately 250,000 Negroes were brought to the West Indies or to the American mainland within the next ten years. After 1713, when England and Spain signed the *Asiento*, which granted England the exclusive right for thirty years to bring African slaves into Spanish possessions, the traffic grew still more. Shippers of New England rivaled those of Old England in the number of Negroes they transported and in the profits they obtained.

DISTRIBUTION OF NEGRO POPULATION, 1760 [*]

Negro population north of Maryland	87,000
Negro population in Southern colonies	299,000
Total (approximately)	386,000

DISTRIBUTION OF POPULATION IN SOUTHERN COLONIES

	Total	Whites	Blacks
Maryland	164,000	108,000	56,000
Virginia	315,000	165,000	150,000
North Carolina	130,000	110,000	20,000
South Carolina	100,000	30,000	70,000
Georgia	9,000	6,000	3,000
Total	718,000	419,000	299,000

The distribution of slavery throughout the colonies was very uneven. In the North small farms and short crop seasons made slavery unfeasible. Some Negroes were employed on farms, but the majority were household servants, coachmen, boatmen, sailors, and porters. In some instances Northern slaveholders frankly confessed that slavery was too expensive for them to afford. On the eve of the Revolution only one out of every fifty of the inhabitants of New England was a Negro; in New York, one in six; in Delaware and Pennsylvania, where there was considerable Quaker opposition to slavery, about one in five.

* See Edward Channing: *History of the United States*, Vol. II: *A Centu, y of Colonial History, 1660–1760* (New York: The Macmillan Company, 1908), pp. 491–2; Marcus W. Jernegan: "Slavery and Conversion in the American Colonies," *American Historical Review*, Vol. XXI, p. 253, n. 123.

Three fourths of the 400,000 Negroes in the colonies were in the South—in Maryland, Virginia, the Carolinas, and Georgia, where in some communities they equaled or exceeded the whites in number.

Parceling Out a Virgin Land

For two thirds of our history, most Americans have made their living on the land. Their hopes for success and the extent of their failures have depended on what they could take from the soil. The vast majority of those who emigrated to colonial America hoped to become landowners. Land was the main means of subsistence, but it was also the way to wealth in a new country. In Europe wealth in land was closely related to a man's social rank. The vast untenanted areas of America offered an unexampled economic opportunity and a temptation to wealth and power. It helped nurse a prodigious appetite for success and a vast impatience with the limitations of the life into which the individual had been born. The manner in which the land in the colonies was distributed and apportioned had a profound effect on both the settlement and development of America.

In the old world life on the land was usually tightly knit and hedged in with many restrictions imposed by law, custom, and the pressure of population. For centuries, men lived in villages and went out into the fields during the day. A communal and conservative pattern of life was the rule. What sociologists call a peasant culture was dominant for ages. Even the larger landowners who lived on their property in the "great house" (a relative term), and who received the deference of the village or smaller neighboring yeomen, had a passive attitude toward the land. Despite a growing tendency to commercialize land, and to trade actively in real estate, most individuals or families had inherited their land rather than bought it. The effect of America on this comparatively changeless pattern was revolutionary. In America the peasant disappeared, and the stable estate or subsistence farm was soon subject to commercial exploitation and market values.

At first both commercial companies and individual proprietors, on receiving grants from the English Crown, planned to make America a land of great estates and tenant farmers. Those who tilled the soil were not to own the land. Under the law of primogeniture, every estate, upon the death of its owner, was to be transferred intact to the eldest son. This had been the dream of those "gentlemen adventurers," Gilbert and Raleigh, and of their successors. In the early days of Virginia, the land belonged, not to the settlers, but to the Virginia Company, which used the settlers to exploit it for the benefit of the stockholders.

Plans were made to carve the extensive territory of Carolina into feudal estates; and in Maryland sixty manors tilled by tenants were established before 1676, each containing on an average about 3,000 acres. In New York the great semifeudal properties established under the Dutch regime were confirmed and, in some instances, even enlarged under English rule.

These various attempts to introduce a closed or aristocratic land system into the New World failed, for land was too cheap and too abundant. Unlike Europe, where little land was available, settlers did not have to work merely for subsistence or for another's profit or convenience. America, with its broad expanse of undeveloped territory uncluttered by traditional rules of tenure, offered the free laborer or runaway a rare opportunity to obtain land, not by virtue of birth, title, and official influence, but by hard work and personal initiative. The constant scramble for what was, almost literally, a lease on life produced recurrent bitter fights against all forms of feudal tenure. By the time of the American Revolution, there had developed on this side of the Atlantic a system of landholding strikingly different from that of eighteenth-century Europe. In general, two types of ownership came to prevail: the freehold and the leasehold.

The New England Farm

In the three New England colonies of Massachusetts, Connecticut, and Rhode Island, most farmers were freeholders and held the land they tilled in "fee simple." "Where there is one farm in the hands of a tenant," Thomas Hutchinson wrote, "there are fifty occupied by him who has the fee of it." The charters of these colonies gave the title to the land to the colonial legislatures,* which in turn made township grants to groups of settlers who were called town proprietors. These proprietors, in turn, set apart sites for the village green and meeting-house, laid out streets, and designated house lots for the settlers. The home lot assigned each settler, on which were located his dwelling, out-buildings, and garden, ranged in size from a small plot to sometimes as much as thirty acres. The settler received in addition a share of the arable land, which, following in part the custom of the English manor, was divided into strips. The amount of land allotted to each individual usually depended upon his investment in the original town enterprise, his ability to use the land, and the size of his family. Other things being

---

* In theory the title to land in Massachusetts belonged to the Massachusetts Bay Company, but the company's General Court was also the Massachusetts legislature.

equal, the industrious man with a large family received more than his neighbor who was less ambitious or who had a smaller family. The outlying meadows and pasture land, including woods and waste, were held in common and regulated by town ordinances. As dangers passed and the countryside became more familiar, people moved from houses in the village directly onto their property. The original common lands were sold to private individuals, and New England thus became a land of compact farms. Taxes were assessed by the local authorities. In Massachusetts, suggesting the future pattern of America, there were no feudal charges such as were common in other parts of colonial America. Subject to the remote authority of Old World officials who seldom bothered him, to the dictates of some exacting creditor if he were unfortunate enough to be a debtor, and to the laws of his town and colony, nearly every New England farmer was by 1750 the master of his land. He could sell it, will it to his relatives, add to it by purchase, or do with it what he pleased.

Estates and Farms in the Middle Colonies

Outside of New England, most of the soil was disposed of according to some form of feudal tenure. A variety of land systems prevailed. In the royal province of New York, Long Island and part of Westchester County were divided into freeholds; but along either side of the Hudson were great semifeudal estates, such as the Van Rensselaer, Van Cortlandt, and Livingston manors, tilled, not by freeholders, but by tenants who paid rent to a "lord of the manor." North and west of the Hudson, extensive tracts were granted by royal Governors to favored individuals. For example, Governor Fletcher's favorite and right-hand man, Captain John Evans, received a tract amounting to about 6,000 acres. One of Fletcher's successors asserted that nearly three quarters of the available land of the province had been granted to about thirty persons during Fletcher's regime (1692–98). Not until 1768, when land in the Mohawk Valley was purchased from the Iroquois Indians, could a settler in that section of the colony obtain a farm in fee simple. Yet, despite the existence of large estates in New York, by numbers small farms predominated. Land distribution in the proprietary colonies of New Jersey and Pennsylvania was not markedly different from that of New York. Here and there were extensive manorial estates, such as those of Lewis Morris in East New Jersey and of the Penns on the Delaware. In both colonies, however, there was a notable tendency to divide large estates into small, manageable farms not unlike those of New England.

City Hall of New York, 1679

A South of Few Plantations

The seventeenth-century South was not a land of great plantations. Before 1640, Lord Baltimore made grants in perpetuity for estates as large as 30,000 acres, but he soon discovered that it was much more profitable to issue grants for smaller plots. In both Maryland and Virginia, the land was parceled out to thousands of freeholders, each of whom owned a farm varying from 50 to 500 acres. Until the eighteenth century, there were few large plantations, and even on the eve of the Civil War, most southern land was neither plantation nor slave-worked property. In Virginia, the land was distributed according to the arrangement established by the Virginia Company after its unsuccessful attempt to make cultivation of the soil a communal enterprise. To resident shareholders it allotted 100 acres for each share of stock held, and it provided that these individual holdings might be increased by "headright," a system that entitled any person to an additional 50 acres if he would pay the passage of a new settler from Europe to Virginia. Since the spread of tobacco created a chronic labor shortage, the headright neatly combined a way to increase one's land with a means to obtain men to work it. The system of headrights was made law when Virginia became a royal province in 1624. Even a freeman paying his own passage to America was entitled to 50 acres, and an additional 50 acres for his wife and for each of his children or other members of his household. The land system that eventually developed in the Carolinas and Georgia did not differ materially from that of Virginia; the mass of the population were small farmers. In all the southern colonies, clergymen, physicians, and government officials were rewarded with numerous grants, and personal favorites received large tracts gratuitously.

Except in Massachusetts, Connecticut, and Rhode Island, the colonial land system was at first closed in character. All of the land was sold or leased by an overlord, who had in turn obtained his holdings from the Crown. By the end of the seventeenth century, the personal service of tenant to lord had been superseded by the payment of what was generally known as a "quitrent." This obligation, which varied from colony to colony, ranged from the fraction of a penny to two shillings sixpence per hundred acres. Unlike ordinary rent, the amount bore no relation to the value of the land, and as long as the tenant fulfilled his obligation to his overlord, the quitrent did not in any way limit his freedom to dispose of his acres as he saw fit. As a form of revenue, the quitrent was uniformly unsatisfactory, although some landlords, notably the Penns, Baltimores, and Fairfaxes of Virginia, collected considerable sums annually. As a rule, the colonial farmer not only opposed quitrents but whenever possible evaded payment. In New York and New Jersey, attempts to collect them sometimes led to violent resistance. Efforts to enforce the feudal practices of escheat and alienation also roused animosity. By escheat, the lands of those who died without heirs or who were convicted of treason reverted to the Crown or to the proprietor; by alienation, a fee sometimes as high as one year's rent was demanded on every transfer of the property.

The Beckoning Frontier

The great plains, cowboys, and covered wagons have become so much a part of our image of the frontier that it is difficult to remember that travelers inland to Cambridge, Massachusetts, Yonkers, New York, and Richmond, Virginia, were once lucky to arrive alive after a journey over poorly marked trails through a wilderness. The college student at Cambridge today travels into Boston for an evening's entertainment in fifteen minutes. In the 1630's the journey took a half day, and safe arrival evoked a thankful prayer. From the beginning, the frontier has been a consistent pervasive influence in American life. Yet generations after Frederick Jackson Turner declared in 1893 that the frontier was the dominant influence in American history, historians are still divided over the question of what precise influence it exercised on the development of political institutions, social equality, or American liberty.

As population increased in the colonies, cheap land in the first settlements became less available. By the opening of the eighteenth century, farmers' sons and newcomers, as well as the less prosperous but ambitious and adventurous classes of the towns, had long been thinking of the sparsely settled frontier. Here the young man who did not possess sufficient capital to buy a farm in the neighborhood in which he was reared could take or acquire a tract in the unbroken wilderness. Here, too, those discontented souls who chafed under the restraints of the older communities could find freedom. Throughout the colonial period, the "Old West," as Frederick Jackson Turner called the untenanted lands between the Atlantic settlements and Alleghenies, attracted many of those who found life unacceptable in the older communities. The frontier, in other words, intensified the hope for success that was implicit in being a freeman in America.

Among the first to settle these newer lands were the Germans and the Scotch-Irish. By 1770, several hundred thousand Germans and Scotch-Irish had found their way to the New World. Although considerable numbers settled along the hilly New England frontier and in the fertile Hudson, Mohawk, and Schoharie valleys of New York, most had first settled in Pennsylvania. The Germans were located in the area around Lancaster, a region still renowned as the home of the "Pennsylvania Dutch." The first quarter of the eighteenth century had hardly passed before many of them, attracted by land, began to move slowly southward through the "great valley" that lay on the eastern slopes of the Appalachians. By 1750, they were not only occupying the Virginia piedmont in increasing numbers but were streaming into the valley of the Shenandoah and out through the water gaps to the uplands of the Carolinas. At the opening of the Revolution, they had a line of settlements extending from the Mohawk to the Savannah.

Paralleling this line were the settlements of the Scotch-Irish. Like the Germans, the majority of these aggressive, individualistic emigrants, established settlements in Pennsylvania. Taking up farms at first along the old Indian route from Lancaster to Bedford, they soon made their way into the valley of the Juniata and the Redstone country and by 1775 had established a powerful community around Pittsburgh. Like the Germans, they also filtered southward into the upcountry of Virginia and along the western bank of the Shenandoah and finally into the southern uplands. Frequently their zone of settlement overlapped that of the Germans, but in general the bulk of the Scotch-Irish lived farther to the west. From Maryland southward, both German and Scotch-Irish were in large measure separated from the tidewater planters by the Blue Ridge Mountains and the pine barrens of the Carolinas and Georgia.

While the Germans and Scotch-Irish were moving southward, other pioneers, having made their way across Virginia by way of the James River, were advancing through the Blue Ridge Gap to the Shenandoah Valley. Frederick County, Virginia, with Winchester as its seat, was organized in 1743, nearly a century and a half after Jamestown. Two years later, Staunton, the seat of Augusta County, held its first court, and by the middle of the century Virginia and North Carolina had found it desirable to extend their common boundary to the Laurel Fork of the Holston River. No love was lost between these men of the backcountry and those who resided in the coastal plain region. The easterners, who controlled the fluid capital and dominated the legislature and the courts of the colonies, were accused of forcing the frontiersmen to pay excessive taxes and exorbitant fees. During 1765–67, the backcountrymen of North Carolina organized what were known as the Regulators for the purpose of administering their own affairs. Open rebellion soon broke out and did not subside until 1771, when the Regulators were defeated by Governor Tryon's troops in the battle of the Alamance.

The entire colonial land system was affected by the mania for speculation. Individuals, companies, religious organizations, and even whole towns obtained large tracts of territory for the purpose of re-selling at a profit. Everywhere men with small or large surplus capital saw in unappropriated lands opportunity for speculative investment. In 1720, Roger Wolcott of Windsor, Connecticut, together with others, secured an unoccupied tract seven by ten miles, for speculative purposes. In the same manner, men like Colonel Samuel Partridge, Jacob Wendell, Colonel Israel Williams, and Ezra Stiles acquired immense holdings which they resold at profits that would make a twentieth-century real-estate dealer envious. In 1678, the people of Deerfield, in western Massachusetts, complained that nearly half the best land of the town belonged to eight or nine speculators. In the same colony, the land of the town of Leicester was granted to twenty-two individuals, including Paul Dudley, the Attorney General; John Clark, a political leader; and Samuel Sewall, son of the Chief Justice. Not one of the twenty-two became inhabitants of the community. Speculators, too, secured control of the greater part of the New Hampshire grants, consisting of 130 townships in the present state of Vermont.

Land agents and speculators were also active in the middle and southern colonies. In New York an extraordinary proportion of the landed wealth was in the hands of Sir William Johnson or representatives of those aristocratic families who throughout the colonial period had extensive political and economic power in the colony. Chief Justice Allen of Pennsylvania, a close friend of the Penns, was reputed to be the greatest land speculator of his time. When the American revolution broke out, speculators in Pennsylvania licked their chops over the nearly 22 million acres of the Penn family that they hoped to see confiscated. For years before the Revolution, Benjamin Franklin was engaged in land speculation. In 1763, he and several wealthy and influential Philadelphia merchants had under consideration a number of speculative undertakings, including the exploitation of western lands. In Virginia and the Carolinas, millions of acres of the rich fertile lands of the backcountry fell into the hands of speculators like Robert Beverly, Richard Henderson, the Washingtons, the Carters, and Lord Fairfax, who in turn disposed of them to German and Scotch-Irish immigrants. Prominent Charleston merchants like Benjamin Whitaker dealt in houses, tenements, and plantations as a side line, and by the time of the Revolution the sale of land in South Carolina had become a business in itself.

REFUTING THE TURNER THESIS

It is often claimed that the frontier bred a spirit of individualism. Certainly it tested a man's self-reliance as well as his physical and moral mettle. Very often, however, the moral test was not met. Since colonial days, a fever for profit in cash, the cheapest and quickest proof of success or "opportunity," has touched most Americans, whatever their station in life. Just as this fever was to weaken the moral dignity of the American's search for a place on the land, so was it to enter into every use of the abundant resources that he found or created in America.

FOR SUPPLEMENTARY READING

The best general work on the seventeenth century is G. N. Clark, *The Seventeenth Century* (1929, 1947), a master's account. On the various forms of colonial exploitation the first work to be consulted is Charles M. Andrews, *The Colonial Period in American History* (4 vols., 1934–37). On the Reformation, the study of Preserved Smith, *The Age of the Reformation* (1920), and, for balance, the Roman Catholic view of the Rev. Philip Hughes, *The Revolt Against the Church* (1947), should be consulted. There is a fine short essay on the Reformation by

Roland Bainton in *The Age of the Reformation* (1956) (Pb), but Bainton concentrates heavily on Luther For the English Reformation one book, F. M. Powicke, *The Reformation in England* (1941), leads all others. For further study of Puritanism in England read William Haller, *The Rise of Puritanism* (1938) (Pb). On the relation between Puritanism and business enterprise the famous work of R. H. Tawney, *Religion and The Rise of Capitalism* (1926) (Pb), is the easiest starting point. There is an excellent cross section of opinion on the same question in the pamphlet *Protestantism and Capitalism* (1959).

English political life in the late seventeenth century has a classical analysis in G. M. Trevelyan, *England Under the Stuarts* (1904, 1947). The economic history of the period is covered by John U. Nef, *Industry and Government in France and England, 1540–1640* (1940) (Pb). The emergence of colonial American institutions is most fully dealt with in H. L. Osgood's classic, *The American Colonies in the Seventeenth Century* (3 vols., 1904–07). Recent views on some principal problems of this period can be found in J. M. Smith (ed.), *Seventeenth Century America* (1959).

The complex question of indentured servitude is the subject of A. E. Smith's *Colonists in Bondage: White Servitude and Convict Labor in America, 1607–1776* (1947). But this volume should be read along with R. B. Morris' fine work, *Government and Labor in Early America* (1946) (Pb). On Negro slavery, students can begin with J. H. Franklin's *From Slavery to Freedom* (1947). A very full study of emigration is H. I. Cowan, *British Emigration to British North America* (1961).

There are individual studies of all the colonies, but students would do well to start with more general works. Among these are T. J. Wertenbaker's *The Puritan Oligarchy* (1947) and *The Middle Colonies* (1938). On the South, W. F. Craven's *The Southern Colonies in the Seventeenth Century* (1949) is most recommended. The opening of the colonial frontier has several chapters devoted to it in R. A. Billington, *Westward Expansion* (1949). Students should also consult T. D. Clark, *Frontier America* (1959), and T. P. Abernethy, *Three Virginia Frontiers* (1940). On colonial population there is one outstanding work: E. B. Greene and V. D. Harrington, *American Population before the Federal Census of 1790* (1932). For a study of the diversity of national and religious backgrounds in the colonies begin with L. B. Wright, *The Cultural Life of the American Colonies* (1957). Excellent "case studies" are S. C. Powell, *Puritan Village: The Foundation of a New England Town* (1963) (Pb) and B. Rutman, *Winthrop's Boston . . . 1630–1649* (1965). A revised view of the Indian problem is A. Vaughan, *New England Frontier: Puritans and Indians* (1965).

3

Creating an American Economy

ALTHOUGH for most of its history a land of farmers, America has always been a business civilization. The rich possibilities of a new continent made irresistible the temptation to acquire riches and to enter the market place. By itself the beckoning abundance of nature in America would have lured men away from a passive or stable life. Joined, however, with the desire of the new colonists to wring from nature all possible profit, the growth of an activist, calculating, competitive business psychology was inevitable. Although the psychology led to great exploitation, it also inspired a practical idealism. Money in America came to signify the individual's moral as well as practical victory over nature and circumstance.

America was started as a group of struggling frontier villages, close to poverty and destruction and very far from realizing dreams of wealth and progress. The need to band together in the face of danger initially strengthened old world traditions of a close communal existence. Limits on economic freedom were imposed by many English and local regulations in order to prevent unchristian trade practices and to preserve economic strength and political stability. It was not, therefore, until the American revolution that the desire for an unfettered economy was able to sweep away the accumulated mass of laws that attempted to control prices, wages, conditions of labor, what one could plant or manufacture, and where one might sell. For many generations after the Pilgrims first gave thanks to God for America's abundance, a growing desire to take the risks of a free market was to clash with persistent attempts to regulate the colonial economy both at home and from abroad.

Sowing the Soil

Colonial America was a land of farmers. As late as 1760, nine tenths of an unevenly distributed population of approximately 1,500,000 derived their livelihoods from the soil of the Atlantic seaboard. Cities in the modern sense of the word did not exist. There were some small towns, and the largest of these—Boston, New York, Philadelphia, and Charleston—contained only a few thousand inhabitants each. A small number of colonists made a living in trapping, fishing, lumbering, ship-building, manufacturing, and commerce, and most farmers north of Maryland spent some of their time in enterprises other than farming. For a relatively new colonial area, English North America, although overwhelmingly agrarian, had a remarkably diversified economy.

The first farmers of America did not know what to expect from their new soil. The cycle of seasons was different from England's, and they did not know what crops could be grown in the New World. All the information about the soil that had been passed on in Europe from father to son for generations might prove to be useless in the young colonies. Obviously, farming had to begin anew and without, one must recall, any of the aids from science and government that are available to the modern farmer.

Topography, climate, rainfall, and fertility of soil determined the character of American agriculture. New England, for example, cut off from the St. Lawrence and Hudson valley by mountains, was essentially an isolated coastal region. Except for the Connecticut, the rivers of New England were not navigable for any considerable distance; and, although they proved later to be of great value when harnessed for water power, they were at best of minor importance in the settlement of the section. "In the frequent harbors and bays, in the 700 miles of coast line, in the great sound stretching across Connecticut, and in the sounds about lower Massachusetts," to quote the historian Weeden, "were the physical features, the initiatory characteristics that controlled the destiny of New England." The New England colonies possessed little level territory, and what flat areas there were seemed too sandy for easy cultivation. A broken, undulating, semimountainous area lent itself neither to the formation of plantation estates nor to the profitable employment of slave labor. What good farm land there was, was scattered across the center of New England. Elsewhere the boulder-

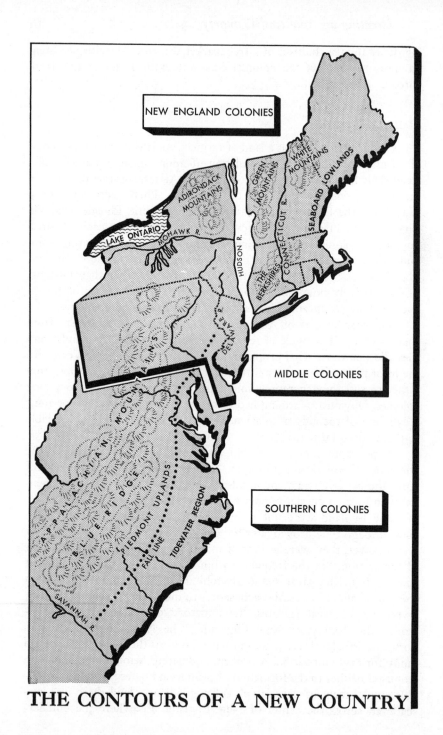

THE CONTOURS OF A NEW COUNTRY

strewn, stubborn soil made cultivation exceedingly difficult. Such topography, together with long, severe winters and short summers, tended to make agriculture in New England more difficult, less productive, and less profitable than in the middle and southern colonies.

Starting at the southern side of New York harbor, however, there swept southwards an ever widening plain for larger scale farming. Between the bay-indented coast and the "fall line," or head of navigation, of the numerous rivers that drained the area, lay the narrow, forest-covered lowlands. Once cleared and placed under cultivation, the rich, but in some places thin, soil of this tidewater region afforded the settler more than a mere living. Here and there along the coast of the Carolinas and Georgia, and especially near the river mouths, were marshlands well suited for the production of rice. This tidewater area was separated from the interior by a belt of pine barrens. On the other side of these, to the west, lay a rolling upland, the Piedmont, possessing soil of almost unsurpassed fertility. In comparison with New England, there were regions in the South that went through a long season of almost semitropical climate. The South consequently produced not only wheat, oats, barley, corn, fruit, and livestock, but also the staples tobacco, rice, indigo, and cotton. The staple region also enjoyed abundant rainfall, and, generally speaking, topography and climate made the colonial South an agrarian section.

Characteristics of both New England and the South were to be found in the physical features and climate of the middle colonies. In New York, the valleys of the Hudson and the Mohawk were, from the first, famous for their agricultural output; and the broad, sloping river valleys of Pennsylvania and New Jersey seemed to have been especially prepared by nature for tilling the soil. On the other hand, very considerable areas, such as northeastern Pennsylvania, were, like western New England, rocky and mountainous and therefore unfit for significant farming. The extensive marshes and unfertile sandy tracts of eastern New Jersey similarly limited the farmer. In New York and in the northern part of New Jersey and Pennsylvania, the climate was close to New England's. In the southern half of this region, however, climatic variation was less and the growing season longer.

Yankee, Yorker, and Pennsylvania Farmers

Despite the mediocre character of the soil and the harshness of climate, the farmers of New England managed to raise many products. Indian corn, or maize, was the most important of these. Easy cultivation, rapid growth, large yield, and general use as a food by both man and beast made it the section's staple crop throughout the colonial period. The Indians whom the early settlers met on arrival had been decimated by a plague and were not strong enough to offer significant opposition to the white men. From friendly Indians, moreover, the early settlers learned how to plant, fertilize, cultivate, grind, and cook corn. Later New England farmers grew European grains, particularly barley, oats, rye, and buckwheat, but they never raised wheat on any wide scale. A variety of fruits, vegetables, fodder, livestock, and dairy foods were other New England products sent to markets at home and abroad.

No section of colonial America was so favored by soil and climate for general farming as the region from the Hudson to the Potomac. In comparison with New England, the variety of crops was greater, and the yield was usually larger. Wheat instead of corn was the important staple crop. With only superficial tillage, the fields of New York and Pennsylvania yielded twenty to forty bushels per acre. Other cereals, hay, fruits, and vegetables were also produced in these "bread colonies." In contrast to New England, potatoes were an important food and were extensively grown. Large crops of hay and grain and rich pasture lands made the production of cattle, sheep, and swine profitable, particularly in the backcountry, where the cost of transporting grain to market was almost prohibitive. There livestock could be fattened at little expense and driven to the coast towns for sale. Philadelphia early became the colonial center for the livestock business. Splendid horses, especially the famous Conestoga type that pulled the earliest "covered wagons," were developed by Pennsylvania's German farmers. The forests, like those of New England, furnished a great variety of timber products and plenty of game and fur-bearing animals. The rivers, lakes, and adjacent coast waters provided clams, oysters, lobsters, and fish.

The Cash and Curse of the South

The South has always raised many of the crops cultivated in the North. Corn, for instance, grew better in Maryland and Virginia than in New England, and both colonies during the eighteenth century exported wheat. For variety and quality of product the southern gardens were rated among the finest in the world. Nevertheless, except for the upcountry regions, the general farmer or the grain producers, fruit growers, or vegetable gardeners did not dominate the life of the South. In volume of trade and as a source of social influence, the great staple crops were of first importance.

The old colonial South of the tidewater and piedmont—particularly Virginia, Maryland, and parts of North Carolina—with its rich soil and favorable climate, was especially adapted for the production of tobacco. Like corn, tobacco was a native American plant already grown by the Indians at the time of the discovery of the New World. The practice of smoking tobacco was introduced early into Europe, but it soon met the decided opposition of both king and priest, who denounced it as loathsome and dangerous both to the individual and to society. Nevertheless, the habit spread rapidly and created a market for the plant. In 1612, Captain John Rolfe produced a successful tobacco crop in Virginia, and within six years tobacco was the staple of the colony. The members of the struggling Virginia Company of London were anxious to have the settlers produce flax, cotton, indigo, and other commodities that they thought would be more profitable and more useful to the mother country. The profits from the initially despised tobacco leaf soon changed their minds. Less than a quarter of a century later, tobacco was raised to the exclusion of almost everything else. In 1622, Virginia exported 60,000 pounds, or three times as much as in 1619, and in 1664, Virginia and Maryland, with a total population of about 40,000, produced nearly 25,000,000 pounds; by 1750, this production had doubled to 50,000,000 pounds.

Tobacco was the greatest southern lure to the market place and to making farming a business. But the South had to pay a price for its profits. Because tobacco was often his only crop, the tobacco farmer became dependent upon other farms and other colonies for part or all of his food supply. A few early planters did understand the advantages of planting partly exhausted tobacco land with corn, wheat, and other cereals, or of turning it into pasture for sheep and cattle, and, as the center of population moved westward during the eighteenth century, areas of the South became dotted with grain and livestock farms scattered between larger, less diversified tobacco farms. Most farmers, however, found it more profitable to raise tobacco than to raise food.

Dependence on outside food supplies was perhaps less damaging than the abuse of the tobacco lands. Tobacco rapidly exhausted the soil. The planter was obliged either to fertilize his old land or to clear new land. In the short run, the second policy was cheaper, and the planter, with little concern for future generations, first used up one tract and then cleared another. This method put a premium upon waste and extravagance and encouraged greediness and the formation of larger estates which tended to crowd out the small farmer.

Most of all, tobacco helped create the South's greatest social prob-

Preparing Tobacco for the Market

lem. Tobacco production brought a demand for cheap labor. As indentured servants became more scarce and proved difficult to control, Negro slaves, supplied after the 1660's by the Royal African Company, became increasingly important on the tobacco farms. The large crops turned out by the slaves laid the basis for an oligarchic landholding class, which, although small in numbers, came to dominate the social and political life of the entire section.

Production of the other two southern staples—rice and indigo—led to similar results. Virginians were interested in both these crops, but Carolina planters made them commercially profitable. During the last quarter of the seventeenth century, experiments were attempted with an inferior grade of rice, but not until after the Madagascar variety had been introduced was the production of the crop a financial success. At first rice was grown on the uplands, but planters soon discovered that the unhealthy swamps along the seacoast, if drained and cleared of trees, were admirably suited for its culture, and here the great rice plantations developed. All things considered, rice production was less profitable than that of tobacco; yet in 1754, South Carolina alone exported approximately 100,000 barrels.

The cultivation of indigo for dyes was not introduced until 1741, but it spread so rapidly that in 1747 the shipments to England totaled more than 200,000 pounds. This yield gradually increased, and before the Revolution, South Carolina was exporting 500,000 pounds a year. As in the production of rice, Negroes did the work. On an average, one slave could handle two acres, which would produce approximately sixteen pounds of dye. Slaves also extracted the dye from the plants and prepared it for market. Indigo, like the other southern staples, was so profitable that some of the best coast lands of Carolina were devoted to its cultivation. The owners of these lands formed an important part of the landed aristocracy, which set the social standards and controlled the political affairs of the South.

Because of the time and expense in removing the seeds, cotton was not an important crop in the colonial period except in South Carolina. By the eve of the revolution the great rice colony was also producing nearly 1,000,000 pounds of cotton annually.

In both North and South farm methods and management were primitive and unimaginative. Here and there a few wealthy and enterprising farmers who were abreast of the latest developments in European agriculture attempted to apply scientific principles to the breeding of livestock and the production of crops. With these exceptions, however, there were practically no advances in agricultural technique until after 1750. As in Europe, farmers left their land fallow so that it might

THE GREAT STAPLES
OF THE COLONIAL SOUTH

regain its fertility, and they paid little or no attention to better methods of cropping or cattle breeding. The abundance of cheap, fertile land discouraged the use of artificial fertilizer and careful crop rotation. Cleared fields were not infrequently filled with roots, stumps, and stones and were cultivated only with primitive tools. The scarcity and high cost of labor made intensive farming relatively unprofitable. Inadequate markets also helped postpone the improvement of farm methods.

The colonial farmer was, generally speaking, isolated; he had neither time nor money for travel, and no modern means of communication linked him to the outside world. All his time and energy were used in securing a livelihood for himself and his family; life was so hard that he had little leisure to devise or study improvements in agricultural methods. He learned instead to develop a zealous attention to his business. To make farming pay, he devoted an increasing portion of his lands to the demands of his markets and bought more land with his profits in the hope of selling at a higher price in the future. From the outset, he was a rural businessman.

Pelts and Pines

In his quest for money, the American colonist at once recognized the potential wealth in America's forests and waters. Soon fur trading, fishing, lumbering, and shipbuilding provided employment for a sizeable ·part of the population and supplied the nonfarm products essential to an otherwise agrarian economy.

The forests abounded in beaver, otter, fox, mink, and other valuable fur-bearing animals whose pelts and skins found a ready market in the Old World. Eighteen years before the Pilgrims landed at Plymouth, Bartholomew Gosnold obtained furs from the savages along the coast of New England. The Pilgrims themselves engaged in the fur business. Their first cargo back to England in 1621 was composed of pelts and clapboards. The fur trade, in fact, bought the Pilgrims freedom from their merchant backers. Every early Massachusetts town had its fur-trading monopoly, which it customarily "farmed out" to various persons, and not always to the highest bidder. The trade in New England and elsewhere was carried on almost entirely through the Indians, who supplied the white trader, or middleman, with large quantities of furs in exchange for trinkets, blankets, liquor, and ammunition.

The fur industry developed rapidly in the Hudson Valley, where for the first two decades of Dutch occupation it was almost the only business. In 1656, Fort Orange (Albany), the Dutch trading post, exported 35,000 beaver and otter skins. Even after New Netherlands passed into the hands of the English in 1664, the fur traffic continued to be an important industry; 40,000 skins were exported annually to England. Toward the end of the century, however, the trade declined; only 15,000 skins were exported from the colony in 1699.

Pennsylvania and Virginia trappers exploited practically every valley in the eastern Alleghenies, and year after year the Potomac, the James, and the many tributaries of the Chesapeake were dotted with their fur-laden canoes. Carolina and Georgia traders did a thriving business with the Creek and Choctaw Indians. Augusta, Georgia, laid out in 1736, became, from the first, one of the foremost fur-trade centers in America. Pack trains employing 600 horses brought in 100,000 pounds of skins annually. It was estimated that at the same time the fur exports from Charleston, South Carolina, totaled between £25,000 and £30,000 a year.

"The Trapper's Return"

As the population of the English colonies increased and fur-bearing animals became scarcer in the older settled regions, trader and trapper turned westward toward unexploited territories. But as soon as they had advanced beyond the valley of the Mohawk or had pushed across the Alleghenies into the Ohio country, they came into conflict with the French, who laid claim to a vast territory stretching from the Gulf of St. Lawrence to the mouth of the Mississippi and embracing the heart of the North American continent. A system of lakes and rivers afforded easy access to the entire region, which was particularly rich in valuable furs. From 1600, when the French King Henry IV awarded a monopoly of the fur trade to a group of French traders and merchants, the fur business constituted France's chief source of wealth in the New World, and she stubbornly resisted any foreign intrusion. Much as she desired to keep her vast empire intact and maintain a monopoly of the fur trade within her boundaries, she was powerless to do so. Her empire was in many respects merely an empire on paper. As late as 1750, its white population totaled no more than sixty or seventy thousand, a number wholly inadequate to develop its resources or to defend it. Pitted against this sparse population and eager to annex the French domains were more than a million inhabitants in the thirteen English mainland colonies. While the French colonists were exploring forests and rivers, their English rivals were transforming the Atlantic seaboard wilderness into farms and plantations and were pushing westward to conquer new lands, plant new settlements, and reap new profits.

In the closing years of the seventeenth century, as the English Hudson's Bay Company became a more powerful rival of the French, English traders and speculators increasingly menaced the trade and prestige of their ancient adversary. In 1724, the colony of New York, for example, angered the French by establishing a fortified trading post at Oswego on Lake Ontario for the purpose of intercepting the Indian trade with Montreal. A few years later the French commandant at Detroit complained about the intrusion of the English and their growing influence over the Indians. Hostility was further intensified when, toward the middle of the century, English traders established posts only to have them destroyed by the French and Indians.

In 1763, after the French and Indian War, the French lost North America, but this victory had little immediate effect on the declining fur trade of the colonies. Only on the frontier did the fur trade retain a semblance of its early character. Although in 1764 England ruled that all hides and skins could be exported only to the mother country, less than $700,000 worth of furs and peltry were exported from all the North American colonies in 1770.

Fur-bearing animals could flee the Indian and white man, but trees could not. Originally, the "forest primeval" grew over much of the virgin land. Almost all of New England was covered with magnificent forests of cedar, spruce, and white pine, the last so useful for masts and spars that the British authorities regarded it as the most valuable timber in America. Hardwoods were also plentiful. Red and white oak with knotless trunks fifty to seventy feet high were greatly prized by every colonial shipbuilder. The sugar maple, the sap of which made sugar to supply many colonial households, was also abundant in New England. Extensive forests covered many sections of New York, and hardwoods abounded in all the middle colonies and even in Virginia and the colonies to the south. Vast tracts of the Carolinas and Georgia were covered with forests of long-leaf yellow pine, valuable not only as lumber but especially for the tar, pitch, and turpentine needed by sailor and settler alike.

Most colonial lumbermen, especially in the northern colonies, were farmers who turned to the forest during the winter months to supplement a slender income derived from the summer's toil. During the eighteenth century an increasing number of land speculators, merchants, and even professional men invested in lumbering. Elisha Cooke and Mark Hunking Wentworth, the latter the "lumber king" of colonial America, were typical of this group.

Britain, Spain, and Portugal, and the West Indies eagerly bought America's forest products. The masts of many British men-of-war came from some New England hillside on which choice trees had been marked by royal officials for the King's use. England, its forests being rapidly exhausted to provide charcoal for the iron industry, purchased shiploads of American spars, sawed timber, naval stores, and potash to bleach her woolens. Irish peasants packed their butter and salted food in buckets and tubs made from the woods of Pennsylvania., Spanish and Portuguese shipbuilders planked their vessels with timber from Maine and New Hampshire; and West Indian planters shipped their sugar and molasses in barrels and hogsheads manufactured from the trees of the American forests.

Naval stores were of primary importance both to the colonists and to England. Among the products England was forced to import were tar, pitch, turpentine, flax, hemp, and cordage, essential alike to merchant marine and navy. For years she had depended on the Baltic countries for these indispensable naval stores—a costly source at best and liable at any time to be cut off by war, embargo, or blockade. Accordingly, she made strenuous efforts for economic independence by securing these products from her colonies. At first she expected New England to supply her; but New England shipbuilders consumed nearly all the tar, pitch, and turpentine produced by the section. From the South, however, and especially from the Carolinas, England obtained great quantities of these stores. Between 1701 and 1718, shipments of tar from America to England increased from 177 to 82,000 barrels. Indeed, in 1718, colonial tar constituted nearly 90 per cent of all the British imports from America. In 1724, South Carolina was exporting 52,000 barrels of pitch, tar, and turpentine a year, but this remarkable rate of increase did not continue. In 1768, the total imports into Great Britain from all the colonies amounted to a little more than 135,000 barrels. Two years later, it had fallen to about 102,000 barrels. England tried to stimulate the production of naval stores by incentive payments called bounties, which provided a lucrative source of income for the eager colonial entrepreneurs.

The Fisheries

Long before the Pilgrims set foot upon the New World, English, Dutch, Portuguese, and French navigators were exploiting the rich fishing grounds that extended from Long Island to the Grand Banks of Newfoundland. In the sixteenth century, fish, rather than meat, was the chief flesh food of most Europeans. As early as 1540, the American fisheries were mentioned in an act of the English Parliament, and fifty years later Sir Walter Raleigh declared that they were the "stay and support of the west counties of England." By the close of the sixteenth century, the Newfoundland fisheries alone were employing 200 vessels and 10,000 men and boys. Four years after the Pilgrims landed at Plymouth, Captain John Smith reported that "there hath been a'fishing, this year upon the coast [of New England], about fifty English ships." And in the same connection he wrote: "Let not the meanness of the word Fish distaste you, for it will afford as good gold as the mines of Guiana and Potassie with less hazard and charge, and more certainty and facility."

In New England fishing developed into a major industry. Boston began to export fish in 1633, and in a few years the entire region began to realize the commercial importance of the seemingly inexhaustible fishing shoals. Soon every port had its fishing fleet, which brought in cod, mackerel, bass, herring, halibut, hake, sturgeon, and other deep-sea fish. To encourage the industry, the General Court of Massachusetts in 1639 exempted vessels and other property employed in the business from all duties and public taxes for seven years. Fishermen and ship-builders were also excused from military duty. The result of this legislation was soon apparent. Governor Winthrop reported that in 1641 300,000 dried fish had been sent to market, and before the end of the century New England merchants were shipping cargoes of fish to the West Indies as cheap food for slaves.

As the industry expanded, the fishermen pushed northeastward to the coast of Nova Scotia, the Gulf of St. Lawrence, and the Grand Banks of Newfoundland, where like the fur traders in the West, they at once came into conflict with the French. As quarrels became more frequent, the New Englanders began to demand the expulsion of their rivals. By 1680, the French claimed all the territory east of the Kennebec and levied tribute on foreign vessels engaged in fishing on the Acadian coast. They also incited the Indians to attack outlying English settlements and to murder crews of New England fishing boats that frequented the coast of Maine. When war broke out between England and France in 1689, New England's fishermen, shipbuilders, and merchants welcomed the chance to send a successful expedition against Port Royal, Nova Scotia, the base of the French privateers. But the Peace of Ryswick, which concluded King William's War in 1697, left the French in possession of all the coast islands and fishing grounds north of the Penobscot River, with the exception of the eastern half of Newfoundland, which was retained by England.

King William's War was the opening phase in America of the momentous struggle between France and England that was to continue for generations. When the contest was renewed in 1702, the New Englanders again welcomed the opportunity to expel the French from the fishing grounds of America. "It grieves me to the heart," wrote the French Governor of Acadia, "to see Messieurs les Bastonnais enrich themselves in our domain; for the base of their commerce is the fish which they catch off our coasts, and send to all parts of the world." Despite his plea for support, Nova Scotia was again captured in 1710 by a combined colonial and English force. By the terms of the Peace of Utrecht, which terminated Queen Anne's War in 1713, France surrendered to England all of Newfoundland and the Hudson Bay country; and she not only confirmed England's conquest of Nova Scotia but agreed not to fish within thirty leagues of the Nova Scotia coast from Sable Island to the southwest. She retained, however, Cape Breton Island, as well as the Gulf of St. Lawrence and the islands lying within its mouth, and her fishermen were to enjoy the privilege of catching and drying fish on certain parts of the coast of Newfoundland. New Englanders rejoiced, for, although their rivals had not been excluded entirely from the fisheries, their sphere of operation had been greatly curtailed. England now had exclusive possession of many of the richest grounds and an equal chance, it was thought, to compete with the French in the others. The rejoicing, however, did not last long, for the French immediately colonized and fortified Cape Breton, and, under the protection of the fortress of Louisburg, their fisheries became more flourishing and prosperous than ever before.

More than thirty years elapsed before the New Englanders had another chance to rid themselves of French competition. But, despite their capture of Louisburg during King George's War (1744-48), the Treaty of Aix-la-Chapelle in 1748 provided for the return of Cape Breton Island to France, and the quarrel over the fisheries remained unsettled. Not until the French colonial empire crumbled in 1763 did the business interests of New England have the satisfaction of seeing France lose all her territory in the northern fishing grounds except for two small islands, Miquelon and St. Pierre.

Despite French competition and three quarters of a century of intermittent warfare, the New England fisheries had a remarkable growth. In 1731, almost a hundred years after its establishment, the industry employed between 5,000 and 6,000 men. Gloucester alone had a fleet of 70 vessels, and fishing developed so rapidly in Marblehead that a fisherman's reproof to an exhorting preacher seemed literally true: "Our ancestors came not here for religion. Their main end was to catch fish." Salem, Ipswich, Yarmouth, Plymouth, and Chatham all had their cod fleets, and it is estimated that 665 vessels carrying approximately 4,400 men were annually employed in cod fishing during the ten years before the Revolution. In 1765, the industry furnished employment to 10,000 men, yielded approximately $2,000,000 per year, and kept 350 vessels busy carrying fish to the markets of Europe and the West Indies.

The whaling industry grew just as impressively. As early as 1614, Captain John Smith had visited the New England coast "to take whales and make trials at a mine of gold and copper." Richard Mather, who came to Massachusetts in 1635, related that he had seen off the New England coast "mighty whales spewing up water in the air like the smoke of a chimney . . . of such incredible bigness that I will never wonder that the body of Jonah could be in the belly of a whale." At first those engaged in the industry depended entirely upon the occasional drift whales cast ashore by the sea; but they soon learned the art of harpooning the whales from small boats. By the close of the seventeenth century, Plymouth, Salem, Nantucket, and the fishing towns on the eastern end of Long Island were doing a profitable whaling business, and New England merchants were exporting considerable quantities of whale products. But the peak of colonial whaling came after 1715. In that year Christopher Hussey of Nantucket fitted out a vessel to pursue sperm whales and tow them ashore. Less than a dozen years later, arrangements were developed for extracting the oil on shipboard; thus the Nantucket whalers were able to extend their cruising radius to the coast of Brazil and to the Arctic Ocean. Whalers of other New England towns soon followed their example, and 360 vessels were engaged in the industry by 1774. Of these, at least 120 belonged to Nantucket, 180 to other Massachusetts ports, and the remainder to Connecticut, Rhode Island, and New York.

Hearth and Home Industries

Despite the fact that the colonists were expected to secure their clothing and other manufactures from England, they early produced textiles in their homes. In 1643, the author of *New England's First Fruits* wrote: "They are making linens, fustians, dimities, and look immediately to woolens from their own sheep." Two years later the General Court of Massachusetts appealed to the towns to increase and preserve the number of sheep. This appeal, together with certain stringent measures taken by the Massachusetts authorities, bore results, and by 1662, sheep fell in price to one fourth of their cost in 1645.

Between 1650 and 1700, all the New England colonies tried to raise the production and to lower the price of sheep. Before 1700, New England was producing enough wool for her domestic manufactures. South of New England, flocks of sheep could be found everywhere, but seldom enough to meet local needs as successfully as the New Englanders had.

Once supplied with wool or the other chief colonial raw materials, flax and hemp, the majority of the colonists made their own cloth and rope. At first all the processes of textile manufacture were carried on in the home. All the tools used came from the family workbench or the village cabinet shop. Dyes were made from plants found in the forest. There was little specialization until the middle of the eighteenth century, when mills began to be erected for the more difficult processes of dying, carding and fulling.

Before these mills appeared, colonial workmen and their wives needed simple tools for making cloth and utensils, and the call for iron-wares grew. The colonies had plentiful deposits of bog-iron ore from which iron of good quality was readily produced. Thanks to the business sagacity of the younger John Winthrop, who secured capital and skilled laborers from England, Massachusetts Bay was able to establish a forge and a furnace at Lynn in 1643. Within a short time the capacity of this plant reached eight tons per week, a figure that compared favorably with the production of some of the larger establishments of the Old World. For a quarter of a century, Lynn supplied the farm tools, pots, kettles, and other domestic utensils for the growing communities of eastern Massachusetts. Furnaces and foundries were subsequently built in other parts of the colony, the rest of New England, and the other colonies. By 1750, the center of the industry had shifted from New England to Pennsylvania, and wealthy ironmasters of the valleys of the Delaware and Susquehanna eventually joined hands with the merchant princes of Philadelphia to dominate the colony.

Ships and Spirits

Of all the specialized colonial industries, shipbuilding was in many respects the most important. Without a fleet, the colonists would have had to distribute the products of forest, farm, and sea through outsiders. Ships were built in every colony, but chiefly in New England and the middle colonies. The southern colonies did try from time to time to develop the industry through bounties, but without success.

New England's first seafaring vessel, the *Blessing of the Bay*, a little thirty-ton seagoing sloop, was launched in 1631. Cheap building materials and a ready market for the sale of the ships caused the industry to grow rapidly, and in less than thirty years the coast was dotted with shipyards. At nearly every major port from Newburyport, Massachusetts, to New Haven, wrights and master builders plied their trade. Villages far up navigable streams and even inland towns engaged in the business. The English Navigation Acts of the mid-seventeenth century, which attempted to confine colonial commerce to English and colonial vessels, further stimulated building. In 1676, an accurate English observer declared that Massachusetts had up to that time built 730 vessels. The golden age of New England shipbuilding, however, dates from 1700 to 1735, a period in which New England sold vessels to every part of the Atlantic world. In no other country were ships built so skillfully and inexpensively; timber was plentiful and easily available, and its cheapness more than offset the cost of labor, which was somewhat higher than in Europe.

Although New Amsterdam passed into the hands of the English, her shipyard did not decline, and during the eighteenth century, yards at Albany and Poughkeepsie were also active. Pennsylvania most closely rivaled New England. Both Philadelphia and Wilmington had large shipyards, and their ships formed an important part of the colonial merchant marine. Many vessels were also built on the eastern shore of Maryland.

New England's ships were put to busy use transporting her products. Her dried fish and lumber were often shipped in her own bottoms. Of special importance for New England's shippers was her most important industry, the distillation of rum from cheap West Indian molasses. Beginning in New England before the middle of the seventeenth century, the business from the first proved profitable, the product sometimes selling for as high as a dollar a gallon. In 1774, the sixty-three distilleries of Massachusetts alone produced 2,700,000 gallons. In the North, rum replaced beer and cider as the favorite drink for the rank and file of the population, and many considered it almost as much of a necessity as flour. Large quantities of it were consumed at home, and it soon came to be regarded as indispensable for the fishing fleets, Indian trade, and slaving business. By 1775, the foundations of many New England fortunes had been laid from profits derived in part from this flourishing industry.

Trade with the West Indies for molasses did much for the commercial and industrial prosperity of the northern colonists. This commerce, including the trade with the French, Dutch, and Spanish islands, also enabled the northerners to utilize their fisheries, forests, and fertile soil, to expand their manufactures, to supply cargoes for their merchant marine, to build up their towns, and, above all, to secure the necessary gold and silver for the goods and bills of exchange with which to pay their adverse English trade balances. The sugar islands, as the West Indies were often called, afforded an excellent market. Their slave labor produced by far the major portion of the world's sugar, but they were forced to import every necessity of life. From New England they obtained horses, dairy products, oil, lumber for their houses, the "refuse fish" for their slaves, and goods of both domestic and British manufacture. In return, the New Englanders received many cargoes of sugar and cheap molasses for the distilleries of Massachusetts and Rhode Island. New York, Pennsylvania, Maryland, and Virginia supplied practically all the grain, flour, bread, vegetables, and potatoes for these islands. Like the New Englanders, the merchants of the middle colonies received in return sugar, molasses, and other tropical products, such as coffee, and often Spanish coin or bills of exchange. Even the Carolinas shipped staves of red oak for sugar hogsheads, white oak for rum casks, yellow pine for siding, and cypress for shingles. Northern vessels trading in the islands also brought quantities of mahogany and logwood from Central America for reshipment to Europe.

Obviously, in one way or another almost all the mainland colonies had a stake in a flourishing West Indian trade in exports and imports. Of the salable commodities Great Britain herself at first would take only furs, forest products, and ships. Cereals, meats, and fish were not wanted, for they were supplied to the English by domestic producers who were protected by tariff legislation. The Corn Law of 1689 practically prohibited the importation of grain; similar duties were levied on fish, and the importation of salted beef and pork was forbidden altogether. With their many burgeoning industries, the American colonies had to find markets. The British and foreign West Indies seemed obvious targets for trade. They supplied a variety of tropical products wanted on the mainland. Yet, of the £950,000 worth of West Indian products imported to the thirteen mainland colonies in 1770, more than half was accounted for by rum; molasses ranked next, and sugar third, and the three together made up four fifths of the total.

At first the colonists traded mostly with the British islands in the Caribbean, but soon, despite mercantilist regulations, smugglers began to sail to the French and other foreign West Indies. Because of the greater fertility of the soil, premiums on the importation of slaves, and better methods of cultivation resulting in larger production, a French

West Indian sugar planter was able to undersell his British rivals by 25 to 50 per cent. The French also needed the food products, horses, and lumber that New England and the middle colonies wished to market. This trade, though carried on illegally, enabled New England and the middle colonies to secure an adequate supply of desperately needed specie with which to make good their adverse balances with the mother country.

The West Indian trade was also inextricably bound up with the traffic in African slaves. Rum-laden vessels from New England, and other colonies as well, sailed for the Guinea Coast, where they exchanged their cargo for slaves that they in turn disposed of in the slave markets of the West Indies. The vessels were then loaded with sugar, molasses, rum, indigo, and other West Indian products which were sold in the mainland colonies or in Europe. There were many variations of this triangular trade, but the West Indies, with their slave markets and their tropical products and hard cash so necessary to the northern colonies, were essential to them all. Without this trade with the islands, the rum industry would have been seriously crippled, and without rum the slave traffic, in all probability, would have been much hampered.

Trading and Selling at Home and Abroad

The importance of seafaring and trade in colonial life can scarcely be overestimated. Many colonists derived the greater part of their wealth and profits from shipping and devoted considerable time to commerce. In the colonies north of Maryland, the men of the prosperous trading centers dominated every phase of colonial life. The colonial merchant did not confine his activities to his local community or even to the narrow fringe of coast from Maine to Georgia; his interests radiated beyond the West Indies to every part of the known world.

Local trade was carried on in crossroad stores, town shops, weekly markets and quarterly fairs, and by the itinerant peddlers who were to become such familiar figures in American folklore. Intercolonial trade originated when the older settlements began to furnish provisions to their newer neighbors. Such commerce had to be carried on almost entirely by water. Roads were few and at times almost impassable; often they were little more than widened Indian trails. During the eighteenth century, as population increased and settlers pushed farther west, more attention was paid to the development of internal improvements, which soon became a key issue in American politics. Inland farmers with grain and other foodstuffs for the market were naturally anxious to have bridges built and roads improved, and by the eve of the Revolution, the Indian trails in the upland country from New York to Georgia were gradually taking shape as passable highways. People in settled areas, however, objected to paying taxes for roads that did not benefit them directly. At best, overland transportation throughout the entire colonial period was slow, difficult, and costly; merchants and shippers were forced to make use of the sea with its many harbors and tributary waterways. The ocean, rather than the highway, linked Boston, New York, Philadelphia, and the southern colonies.

By far the greater portion of all colonial shipping was in the hands of enterprising northerners, who with hundreds of small craft penetrated every harbor, bay, estuary, and navigable river. Because the northern colonists produced few commodities that could be sold in England, they had to market their surplus lumber, beef, and fish whereever they could. The need for ships grew rapidly. Fishing also stimulated shipbuilding, and both industries, together with local manufacturing and small-farm agriculture, contributed to the growth of commercial towns. With its comparative lack of harbors and with a ready foreign market for its staples, the South failed to develop its navigation and shipping, an important town life or, except in Charleston, a significant merchant or trading class. To the southern planter large-scale agriculture was vastly more profitable than commerce.

The southern colonies furnished the growing trans-Atlantic commerce with tobacco, rice, wheat, indigo, and naval stores and received in return cargoes of manufactured goods. Since they had no overseas shipping of their own, the southerners depended upon English merchants and northern carriers for the transportation of goods and produce. Each year about Christmas time, scores of English merchantmen set sail for the Chesapeake, where they delivered their manufactured goods and took in return thousands of hogsheads of tobacco. The tobacco fleet alone in 1706 numbered 300 sails.

Because the imports and exports of the southern colonies were more than double those of all the other colonies, it was the southern rather than the northern colonies that did the major share of the business with or through Great Britain. In 1769, about seven ninths of the exports from Virginia and Maryland, five sevenths of those from the Carolinas, and more than five sixths of those from Georgia went first to the mother country. At the same time, Great Britain received only one fourth of New England's total exports, and less than half of New York's and Pennsylvania's. Virginia and Maryland obtained nearly seven eighths of their imports from Great Britain, the Carolinas three fifths, and Georgia over five sixths. New England, on the other hand, secured only two fifths of her imports from the mother country, New York less than half, and Pennsylvania only a very small fraction.

Financing Economic Growth

Against many natural and legal restrictions, the extraordinarily diverse colonial economy made steady headway. This continuous long-term growth should not obscure, however, the many short-run hardships, individual failures, and frustrations. At every turn the businessmen on the farm, the plantation, and in the town had to maneuver carefully to avoid large losses or even bankruptcy. Diversification of the colonial economy came about partly in response to the risks of pursuing only one line of work or trade; a side-business gave some additional security in case of loss of the wheat crop or shipment of lumber.

Since all Americans were active or prospective businessmen, all were vitally concerned with the supply of money. Then as now, in a market economy organized for private profit, control over the money supply was of vital importance. Throughout the colonial period, all Americans were adversely affected by lack of capital and by the absence of a uniform system of money and adequate credit facilities. The colonies were without gold or silver mines. The northern colonies' unfavorable balance of trade with Great Britain drained them of what specie they were able to acquire from the West Indies. Although the southern colonies obtained specie from England, it was usually spent for additional manufactured goods or for more slaves or indentured servants. Because credit institutions were largely wanting, merchants and others were obliged to make their payments for the most part in cash or kind or bills of credit. Under mercantilist policies, the export of coin from Great Britain was forbidden by law, and the colonies had no common currency of their own.

Without adequate coin, the colonists were at first compelled to resort to barter, or payment in kind. Bead money, or wampum, redeemable in beaver skins, passed as currency in New England and the middle colonies until about the beginning of the eighteenth century. Staple commodities like corn, cattle, furs, and wheat were declared by law to be legal tender in payment for merchandise, labor, and taxes. For years many Harvard students paid their tuition in produce, livestock, and meat, and "occasionally with various articles raked up from the family closets of student debtors." In the southern colonies, tobacco and rice as well as other commodities were used as currency. In 1730, the Virginia assembly provided for the establishment of warehouses for the storage of tobacco and the issue to owners of transferable notes that might be used to satisfy debts in the county or district in which they were issued. Because tobacco had no staple value, the notes fluctuated in worth. Value in tobacco, furthermore, could not easily be translated into value in another commodity. Other products used in place of money, like tobacco, deteriorated or rotted. All things considered, barter and "commodity money" failed to meet the needs of the colonists.

Although some hard money of foreign denomination reached the colonies as a result of trade, the ratio of value between the English and non-English coin varied from colony to colony, despite all attempts of the home government to establish a common rating. The Spanish "piece of eight"—a silver coin worth eight of the basic Spanish "reals" was generally rated as worth four shillings and six pence of English money, but in New York and North Carolina it was equivalent to eight shillings; in New Jersey, Pennsylvania, Maryland, and Delaware to seven shillings and six pence; in New England and Virginia to six shillings; and in South Carolina and Georgia to four shillings and eight pence. Subsidiary coins had equally diverse value. Sometimes the value of the coins was impaired by clipping or reduced in weight by "sweating," the process of removing small particles of silver or gold by shaking a number of coins together in a bag. Massachusetts was the only colony to establish a mint, which issued small pieces of silver known as pine tree shillings, but in 1684 this mint was closed by order of the Crown.

Facing a chronic shortage of cash and finding no relief from the mother country, the colonies were almost forced to turn to paper money. First adopted by Massachusetts in 1690 to meet the expenses of a disastrous expedition against French Quebec, paper money was soon issued by the other New England colonies and by South Carolina, New York, and New Jersey. Ultimately all the colonies, with the exception of North Carolina, resorted to this means of supplying an adequate currency. Of the numerous issues, all were more or less alike in purpose and in result. Some bore interest, while others did not; some were made legal tender for payments of all sorts, while others could be used for future obligations but not for past debts; some could be used for all public payments but not for business transactions between private individuals; some were made payable on demand, and others were not. Some papers were retired promptly, according to the terms of their issue, but others were not; some were irredeemable. All eventually depreciated and therefore tended to drive "good" money out of circulation. Silver in Massachusetts, for instance, rose to a premium of 1100 per cent between 1700 and 1750.

At first paper money had the enthusiastic support of the great majority of colonists. But as soon as it began to depreciate and commodity prices began to climb, many businessmen, especially moneylenders and merchants, became lukewarm in their approval and finally bitterly denounced it. The manufacturer often aligned himself with merchant and moneylender, but fights among the colonists about this currency were not always over paper money as such but over what group would profit from government contracts to print and issue the certificates. Initially, paper inflation stimulated industry, but when depreciation set in, the cost of production generally increased rapidly or would go up in one area while in a more stable locale it remained low. The situation in New England was typical. In 1736, a vessel could be built more cheaply on the Thames in Connecticut than in Massachusetts; consequently, the quantity of imported molasses distilled annually in Boston between 1735 and 1742 fell off one third. Wage earners as well as those with fixed incomes had not prospered in proportion to the cost of living. A Massachusetts pamphleteer declared that "Salary Men, Ministers, School-Masters, Judges of the Circuit, President and Tutors at College, Widows and Orphans, etc. are pincht and hurt more than any." After stabilizing her currency in 1749, Massachusetts again enjoyed commercial and industrial prosperity, while Rhode Island, with depreciated paper, lost a large part of her West Indian trade, and her distilling and manufacturing industries languished. Nevertheless, the farmers with goods to buy, as well as those who were obliged to borrow money, were generally supporters of cheap currency, even though they too sometimes found fault with the prices they received for their produce.

The persistent blindness of the mother country to the needs of colonial business expansion more than matched the irresponsibility of those in the colonies who thought paper money a cheap release from debt. The continuous struggle for an adequate money supply lasted for more than a century. In itself an indication of the growing size and diversity of the American economy, it also dramatizes more than any issue the entrepreneurial character of the English colonists. Their constant fevers over specie were a result of their drive for material success, and their increasingly active business life on land and in the towns created problems that the English currency policies eventually could not answer.

FOR SUPPLEMENTARY READING

There are numerous studies of specific aspects of the colonial economy. For general investigation, however, a start may be made in C. P. Nettels, *The Roots of American Civilization* (1938), and L. B. Hacker, *The Triumph of American Capitalism* (1940). L. C. Gray, *History of Agriculture in the Southern United States to 1860* (2 vols., 1933), and P. W. Bidwell and J. I. Falconer, *History of American Agriculture in the Northern United States, 1620–1860* (1925), are two starting points for scholars interested in land and farm problems. Other classic studies are V. S. Clark, *History of Manufactures in the United States, 1607–1860* (1916–28), and E. R. Johnson and others, *History of Domestic and Foreign Commerce of the United States* (2 vols., 1915).

On the complex question of the commercial relations between the colonies and England the primary work is G. L. Beer, *The Commercial Policy of England toward the American Colonies* (1893). Beer's subsequent volumes are more detailed analyses. These should be followed by two studies: L. H. Harper, *The English Navigation Laws* (1939), and C. P. Nettels, *Money Supply of the American Colonies before 1720* (1924). The last volume of C. M. Andrews, *The Colonial Period of American History* (1938), is lucid on the subject of imperial regulation. Bernard Bailyn, *The New England Merchants in the Seventeenth Century* (1955), should be read as the leading case study on the question of the profitability of trade in the early empire. R. Pares, *Merchants and Planters* (1960), is a splendidly lucid account with wider scope than Bailyn's work.

4

‒⟩⟩‒⟩⟩‒⟩⟩‒⟩⟩‒⟩⟩‒⟩⟩‒⟩⟩‒⟩⟩

Colonial Culture

EVEN the most loyal English colonists were profoundly affected by living on the edge of an alien wilderness, months away from ancestral homes, with only the most sporadic news from the old hearths. Those who tried to cling to old customs in their American homes could not completely copy the home country and were forced to make many compromises with the new raw world in which they had settled. For nearly three centuries, American life was to be dominated by provincial codes of conduct appropriate to a society of small Christian businessmen, living in comparative ignorance of the world and much of their own society.

Although European in origin, colonial institutions and beliefs had to be reshaped to fit the needs of an isolated, essentially agrarian people. The small farmer had to cope with frontier conditions, and, as time passed, his sense of having created afresh a new civilization exerted great power over his imagination. Relentlessly battling for a place in the sun against a harsh resisting nature, with little opportunity for recreation, he tended to be frugal, shrewd, and tenacious. His intellectual and religious attitudes were adjusted to his simple, individualistic way of life; by and large, he had no counterpart in Europe. He was, in short, an American.

God's Word in America

Few, if any, atheists or skeptics were among the first American settlers. Even the colonist most hungry for wealth was profoundly influenced by Christianity. In the early history of Jamestown, the Word of God always came with plans for finding gold. In the first generations of colonial life most men believed that religious diversity or religious freedom were offenses to conscience. In the preceding century all Englishmen had persecuted, Protestants no less (and at times even more) than Catholics, and the English in America were not at first exceptions.

Most Americans in the early seventeenth century had no interest in the separation of church and state. In Virginia the Anglican church was established, and in Massachusetts Congregationalism, founded by men from the most militant wing of English Protestantism, was the state church. In the first colony the Anglicans persecuted the Quakers, and in the second a Puritan oligarchy silenced nonconformists by social pressure, exile, and even death. Religious intolerance generally characterized American life until well past the colonial period. It declined only as an increase in religious sects made peace essential and as the lure of material success and poor church organization blunted the power of the ministers to arouse men to follow God's word. The Englishman who first settled along the Atlantic coast believed in God, obeyed his church, and accepted the consequences of disbelief just as had the medieval serf of the twelfth century. The hand of nature in flashes of lightning or comets, in untimely frosts or floods, in earthquakes or destructive windstorms reinforced religious faith and substantiated the belief that both God and the devil took an active interest in man's affairs. In moments of sorrow and misfortune the colonist invariably turned to God for solace and comfort. The death of a son or daughter, for example, was "God's will," and there was everywhere unquestioned faith in a divine system of reward and punishment. "An age of faith" was as much a description of the religious climate of seventeenth century America as of England.

When the first Englishman settled in the New World, the fervor of the Reformation was still strong. Indeed, many emigrants to America came to fulfill the Reformation in their own way in the New World. In England the Puritans fought the hated Roman church and other Protestants, particularly the increasingly "Romish" Anglicans. Puritanism, as an attitude toward man, the Bible, and the church together, was an immensely potent force on both sides of the Atlantic. In England it helped to precipitate a civil war; in America it strongly affected the thoughts and acts of the vast majority of English colonists.

Although New England and Virginia had different churches, the colonists in each area lived under similar religious controls. The Virginian, like the New England farmer, was expected to be a church-attending and God-fearing man. To fish, travel, or transport or sell goods on the Sabbath was illegal and subject to punishment in most of the colonies. As late as 1699, the Virginia legislature enacted a law compelling every citizen of the colony to attend some place of worship. Inventories of seventeenth century estates in Virginia often contained the entry of "one old Bible and the practice of piety." In every colony the minister was an important person, who believed himself divinely ordained to guard the members of his flock. In both domestic and civil matters he was their adviser, and his opinions probably carried more weight than those of any other individual. He comforted his parishioners in time of misfortune and sorrow and was quick to reprove them when they fell into sin or violated the codes of the community. He read his long, expository sermons in tones that were convincing and unmistakable, and he never tired of exhorting his flock to avoid swearing, drunkenness, fornication, sleeping in church, and other "temptations of the Devil."

Although the Calvinist views of man and of the Bible affected all the English colonies in the seventeenth century, it was in Massachusetts—and later in Connecticut—that they became entrenched. The leaders of Massachusetts, like other Calvinists, believed that all men were born in sin and that only those individuals who were "elected" by God obtained salvation. All others were damned. At most, a man might search himself for "signs" that God had chosen him. Conveniently, the power to act morally was taken as proof that one was meant to be moral, or, in other words, that one had been saved. Good conduct, outer piety, worldly success were tribute, not to man, but to the infinite power, mercy, and wisdom of God.

Because the leaders of Massachusetts Bay proposed that "the elect" establish God's word in America, free of the corruptions that had infected England, only those who showed evidence that God had chosen them were to be trusted with a voice in the management of the church and society. The elect called themselves Saints and believed that they alone constituted "the church." Everyone in the settlement, however, was compelled to live in accordance with the rules laid down by the Saints. These rules were taken from both the Old and the New Testament. The Saints thought that mankind was still subject to the ancient Hebrew code, the code of the "chosen people" of the Old Testament. Like the Hebrews, they claimed to have been brought together and entrusted by God with a mission to exemplify righteous living for all the world. The early legal code of Massachusetts Bay—the Body of Liberties—reflected these beliefs.

All settlers were not Saints or members of the church. The outsiders, nevertheless, were forced to contribute to the support of the established religion and to attend services together with the Saints.

Non-Saints, however, could not receive Communion, nor could they have a voice in choosing the leaders or rules for living or worship.

A hierarchical scheme for governing church and state was developed. At the bottom were all inhabitants of the village and neighborhood, elect and nonelect. Collectively, these constituted the Congregation from which the Saints who made up "the church" were chosen. The Saints in turn selected, with what was assumed to be the inspiration of God, their leaders, or Elders. In the early years, only about 20 per cent of the population were Saints. The whole system tended to concentrate great power and prestige in the hands of the Elders, who were likely to be the secular rulers as well.

The inspiration of this religious society was the idea of the Covenant. The Covenant was in part an answer to the dilemma of those who believed in predestination. If God was all powerful and man could do nothing to earn his way back from sin to grace, then how could he believe that anything he did, whether righteous or wicked, made any difference? Did a man who strove to follow God have any guarantee that God had truly chosen him? The Covenant theology told men to search for signs of Grace. If they found the power to live in a Godly way, if they could buttress their feeling that God had made this possible by quoting some texts from Scripture that would satisfy the Saints and Elders, only then might they "own the Covenant." God would then be presumed to have entered into an unbreakable agreement (or Covenant) to help them on life's way and to save them after death.

These ideas, which provided the blood and marrow of New England life for nearly a century, were to have an incalculable effect on American history. Carried to the rest of the continent by New England school teachers and future pioneers sprung from New England stock, the Puritan sense of life was to color American life deeply. That great harvest of literary genius that America was to reap in the nineteenth century—exemplified by writers like Hawthorne, Melville, Henry James—cannot be understood without appreciation of its relation to the Puritan ethos. The idea of America as a special holy experiment, the concept of the "world" mission of America, the preoccupation of American moralists and educators with conduct and character, even the idea of government originating in a compact, have all been influenced by the ideas of the Puritans. The persisting American wish to make life perfect and pure, which has so often conflicted with the will to be powerful and rich, also goes back to Puritan sources. Even when Puritan theology eventually died, the moral fervor and zeal it nourished shifted to the support of such ideals as republican government, human equality, or a world made "safe for democracy."

Making a Holy Society

The Saints and Elders of the church were the leaders of what was conceived as a moral revolution in the world's affairs. It is no wonder that the church played such an important role in the government of the Massachusetts Bay colony. The company charter itself vested authority over the colony in the General Court of the company, which consisted of stockholders, or freemen. At first Governor Winthrop ruled the colony with the help of a deputy governor and a General Court of eight assistants, all of whom were freemen and Saints who had emigrated from England to Massachusetts. In 1630, however, 108 settlers asked to be made freemen, and Winthrop—who feared that if he refused, the petitioners would move elsewhere—agreed. But the Puritan leaders soon took care to prevent those who did not share their religious views from gaining political power. By an act of 1631, only covenanted members of the colony's churches could become freemen, and another act, adopted three years later, provided that no church could be established without the approval of the General Court. Not all church members, however, had political power, for only the General Court could make a man a freeman. From 1630 to 1634, the freemen were permitted to vote for the governor and council of assistants, who continued to compose the General Court. In 1634, the voters of each town obtained the right to elect two representatives to the General Court, which in 1644 became a bicameral body. Since all freemen were church members, and since the church members were a minority of the population, Massachusetts was largely controlled in these years by a Puritan oligarchy.

Although Puritanism has been depicted as a drab and gloomy faith, it did not seem so to the Puritans. Convinced that they alone were true Christians, they were exalted by their efforts to create a New Zion in the midst of a wilderness. They looked on their moral discipline as a delivery from a fetid world of sin. In the demanding conditions of the New World, where militancy was needed to cope with many new problems, the Puritan discipline and a frontier code complemented each other in many respects. Hard work, an eye for the main chance, and disdain for frivolity were dictated by both the inner logic of Puritanism and the demands of the wilderness. Still, it would be wrong to think that these first pioneers were "puritanical" in the modern sense of the word. Hard work and strict church-attendance represented one side only—they dressed in gay as well as somber clothes, drank wine, and enjoyed the company of their neighbors. Unlike latter-day puritans, they were not particularly squeamish about sex, and John Cotton, a Puritan divine, wrote: "Women are creatures without which there is no comfortable Living for man: it is true of them what is wont to be said of Governments, *That bad ones are better than none.*"

The authoritarianism used by the Massachusetts leaders to enforce religious conformity invited nonconformity; for when an official creed is defined very narrowly, the range of forbidden opinions is enormously increased. It was difficult, moreover, for the Puritan rulers to hold their fellow colonists in line, for there was no way to prevent dissidents from migrating to the wilderness that lay beyond the jurisdiction of the oligarchy. As early as 1636, Thomas Hooker, pastor of the church in Newton, moved with most of his small congregation to the present site of Hartford, Connecticut. Hooker believed that the "foundation of all authority is laid . . . in the free consent of the people," and, with the adoption of the "Fundamental Orders of Connecticut" in 1639 by the towns of Hartford, Wethersfield, and Windsor, his ideas were translated into law. This document, which served the colony as a constitution—Connecticut had no charter until 1662—provided that the religious and civil governments were to be in the hands of representative officials elected by freemen. The Fundamental Orders, which have been viewed by many as the first attempt at political democracy in America, were more democratic in theory than in practice. To become a freeman in Connecticut—that is, to secure the right to vote in elections to send representatives to the assembly—required certification from a magistrate; and the magistrates were careful to certify only church members as freemen. Connecticut, like Massachusetts, was a Bible Commonwealth.

Roger Williams was another Massachusetts clergyman who objected to the oligarchy's administration of religious and civil affairs. An inveterate individualist and a man of undoubted courage, Williams openly attacked the fusion of church and state within the colony and the expropriation of Indian lands by the English settlers. In many respects, however, Williams was more somber in his view of man's sinfulness than his opponents. What in fact separated him from them was his belief that with the coming of Christ all men had to stand individually before God and that no tribe, community, or nation had the right to constitute itself as *the* church as the Puritan divines had done. Williams believed that only the ancient Hebrews were entitled to establish religious qualifications for membership in civil society; the Puritan attempt to do the same thing was, therefore, a violation of Christ's message. He thought that the relation of the individual to God was so important and so personal that no man could dare interfere in another man's search for Christ. This idea obviously struck at the heart of the Puritan belief in a Bible Commonwealth.

Given the genuine conflict of beliefs between Williams and the oligarchy, the consequences seem inevitable. In October, 1635, the General Court of Massachusetts convicted Williams of spreading "new and dangerous opinions against the authorities of magistrates," and a short time later he fled the colony to avoid arrest. In 1636, he settled at Providence and was soon joined by a few loyal followers. Under Williams's direction, the Rhode Island colony established religious freedom up to the point that religious opinions did not lead to shirking civil duties like military service. Williams also separated church and state and set up a civil government in which each head of a family had one vote. The new colony grew rapidly and attracted many settlers whose religious views had brought them into conflict with the authorities in the other colonies.

Among the settlers in Rhode Island was Anne Hutchinson. Her ideas had previously attracted some of the leading citizens of Boston. Essentially, she preached that mere learning in the scriptures or following the forms of piety did not guarantee that one was a true Christian. What mattered more than doctrine or Biblical knowledge was the feeling that one was with Christ. Being an extremely gifted woman, she was able to defend her ideas with a wealth of learning. One implication of her ideas was that the tests established by the Saints for admission to the Covenant or to the ministry might be insufficient and might, in fact, be passed by a shrewd sinner. Her opinions were too dangerous to be permitted circulation by the oligarchy, and in 1638 she was forced to leave Massachusetts because of her heretical views. Claiming that she was directly inspired by God, she had set herself against the clergy as an interpreter of the Scriptures. After a short stay in exile in Rhode Island, this remarkable woman moved on toward New Amsterdam. In 1643, she was killed by the Indians before she could reach a new home. Williams, for his part, continued to move from creed to creed. Following a short period as a Baptist, in 1639 he became a Seeker, or "one who accepted no creed, although clinging to the fundamental belief of Christianity."

Although Puritanism was in many ways the most forceful and dynamic creed in the colonies, it was not—as Williams had demonstrated—the only one; and by the first decades of the eighteenth century, colonial America had a remarkable religious diversity. In the

South the Anglicans predominated. The Baptists were established in Rhode Island, in other parts of New England, and in South Carolina. Pennsylvania became the home of Quakers, Lutherans, Moravians, and other denominations. The Dutch Reformists, who practiced a form of Calvinism that had developed in Holland, centered in New York. There was a scattering of Jews in Newport, New York, Philadelphia, and Charleston; and the majority of the Catholics in English America lived in Maryland. The Scotch-Irish, who settled along the frontier, were almost exclusively Presbyterians—that is, Calvinists—who thought that church matters should be decided by elected groups (presbyteries) of elders rather than by individual congregations. Methodism did not secure a foothold until the decade preceding the Revolution.

The multiplicity of sects in the colonies was one cause of the growth, however slow, of religious toleration in English America. Roger Williams had shown the way in Rhode Island, but there were other colonies that provided at least a measure of religious freedom. Most often toleration arose out of the need to attract colonists; it seldom came out of a conviction that toleration was a positive moral good. The Maryland Toleration Act of 1649 granted religious freedom to all those who professed to believe in Christ; New Jersey in 1665 provided a very wide liberty of conscience; and four years later the charter of South Carolina included a similar provision. Pennsylvania in 1682 assured equal liberty to all "who confess and acknowledge the one Almighty and Eternal God to be the creator, upholder, and ruler of the world." The report in 1683 of Thomas Dongan, Roman Catholic Governor of New York, provides some indication of the increasing ability of people of different religious views to live side by side in colonial America. "Here be not many of the Church of England," he wrote, "few Roman Catholics; abundance of Quaker preachers, Men and Women especially; Singing Quakers; Ranting Quakers; Sabbatarians; Antisabbatarians; some Jews; in short of all sorts of opinion there are some. . . . The most prevailing opinion is that of the Dutch Calvinists." Despite this growth of diversity and the adoption of toleration laws, many colonists, given the chance, continued to discriminate against those of other faiths.

The Long Crisis of Orthodoxy

The growth of diverse sects created a profound problem of conscience for the established churches. Quite apart from their pleasure in power and the harsh pride that came from their monopoly over religious life, a great number of church leaders were sincerely troubled about the purity of their faith in what seemed a world rife with error and corruption of God's word. The decay of "Christian living" and the loss of religious ardor among the young was bad enough. Positive heresy was even worse. Certainly, the hunger for "religious experience" remained powerful for generations after religious uniformity had passed. What restrictions and what discipline one would accept from a church, rather than infidelity as such, was the principal cause of trouble for the ministers. Rhode Island had at once provided for separation of church and state, and in the middle provinces no colony, with the exception of New York, had a state church. In the other colonies established churches waged what proved to be a losing battle with the frontier; in the long run, the clergy could not continue to control people who were free to leave the immediate neighborhood. Hooker and Williams had freed themselves from the domination of the Boston ministers by migrating, and many others who never left the colony were still able to get far enough away from Boston to escape its influence. In Virginia the Anglican church, with an even more centralized organization than the Massachusetts Congregationalists, was unable to keep pace with the westward movement of its communicants. An increasing number of Virginians took the church with decreasing seriousness, and many who went to church did so only as a matter of form or for social reasons. The colony's clergy repeatedly complained—but apparently in vain—of those who desecrated the Sabbath by drinking, fighting, gambling, swearing, and dancing.

In no colony were the problems of church discipline and church membership more dramatically fought out than in Massachusetts. Having driven out theological opponents like Hutchinson and Williams, the Puritans seemed free to make their Bible state. Their deepest dreams, however, were undone within a generation after they had hammered out their holy code in the 1640's.

By 1660, it was apparent that the Puritan settlers were in America for good. Charles II brought Anglicanism back to England as the state religion, and the incentive to return to England with the true Puritan faith unimpaired was at best indefinitely postponed, at worst given up. The initially strange and hostile environment of the New World, furthermore, was now better understood and controlled. The first need to survive on the edge of the wilderness and in the face of the Devil's minions declined. People drifted away from Boston and other centers of authority. For the first generation Puritanism had been a fighting faith against English or colonial opponents. As it triumphed, it tended to become habit, routine, and commonplace. Given the wealth of the New World, many still outside the church could not take seriously the

The Reverend Cotton Mather

notion that only the elect would prosper in this life. Among the Saints the "drive" to work, thrift, and accumulation that was construed as a search for a sign of God's favor became detached from its theological purpose. Worldly success was becoming an end in itself and brought with it a more relaxed sense of life. The prestige and power of the learned ministry could be maintained only so long as deep theological interests dominated the public mind. Indifference to the church reversed the tide. Now the minister became increasingly dependent on the willingness of the Christian to come to hear him, let alone heed him. Originally, the Puritan theologians, who were not emotionalists, had depended on every resource of human reason to discern what a stern God demanded of man and to justify His word. After 1660, the use of reason took more secular and more humane directions. Cotton Mather, for example, one of the greatest of the latter day oligarchs, was an active member of the Royal Society in London (which helped to popularize the science of Newton and the ideas of Locke), a proponent of toleration, and an advocate of inoculation against smallpox.

The ultimate test of the Puritan always had been in his conduct, but in Massachusetts concern with conduct was slowly dissociated from the question of loyalty to a single authoritarian church. Deep interest in the conditions of man's moral life in the eighteenth century and after was associated with a variety of views of man, ranging from a traditional Calvinism to optimistic views of his nature and of the powers of human reason. At the same time, however, the deep feelings that had found fulfillment in the powerful and dramatic role of the Calvinist "moral athlete" who constantly tested his God-given powers were set free. This "enthusiasm" was to provide a source of inspiration and support for the most serious and bizarre of reform programs and crusades for many generations after the twilight of the Puritan oligarchy.

By 1660, these several currents away from orthodoxy were already in motion. The Puritan leaders first came to grips with the failure of those who had been baptized to go on to "own the Covenant" and to replenish the church. When these mere "half-saints" asked to have their children baptized, what was to be done? If one failed to baptize the children, both parents and children might turn further from the church. If one admitted these children to baptism, what happened to the Covenant? In an effort to increase church membership, in 1662 Massachusetts adopted the Half-way Covenant, which, although permitting children of the merely baptized to receive baptism themselves, still denied them the rights of communion and the power to vote until they had fully owned the Covenant. But this compromise, although it reversed the downward trend in church membership for a time, did not measurably increase the influence of the church over the people.

As the years passed, the Saints and the ministers had to make one compromise after another to maintain the church. Slowly the whole nature of the church, of the position of the minister, and of the tone of religion were altered. Starting with an authoritarian ministry and an elite church that could challege a petitioner to prove his worth, by the middle of the eighteenth century the minister was often on his knees begging vast throngs of simple folk assembled in a holiday atmosphere to come to Christ and to testify to their conversion, not in the form of Biblical knowledge or logic, but by openly showing the fervor of their feelings. The church became democratized in membership and in leadership, although, paradoxically, the emphasis on human sin and wickedness was deepened in the attempt to stir people to seek conversion.

Before these changes were realized, the orthodox made a last desperate attempt to save the older Covenant ideal. In the final years of the seventeenth century, many people in Europe and America still believed in the active power of the devil and of witches over human

Delivery from Witchcraft

life. In 1684, Massachusetts Bay Colony lost her original charter. There followed a decade of continuous political turmoil and social unrest, at the end of which a new charter was negotiated. The new Charter of 1691 forbade religious tests for voting and converted Massachusetts into a royal colony in which a governor named by the king replaced the choice of the freemen. In the midst of political agitation and social upset, the persistent belief in witches was reactivated by the tales of some hysterical young girls of Salem. Soon the combination of the general belief in witches, the unrest of the times, and the thought of some leaders that such incidents could be used to bring many drifters back to owning the Covenant helped spread general hysteria. Cotton Mather interpreted the Salem events as an "Assault of the *evil Angels* upon the Country" and resolved to "sett the *Covenant of Grace* yett more evangelically and explicitly before the Children of God." If the devil was active, did this not suggest that God had abandoned Massachusetts for turning away from the Lord's Word? Unfortunately, too many men and women felt guilty for their worldliness, their disregard of the church, and their failure to esteem the Covenant, and before sanity reasserted itself 200 people were accused of being in league with the Devil. Of these, 150 were imprisoned for a time, and more than 20 were put to death. Intervention by the governor just as charges of witchcraft began to be made against people in high places and revulsion against the use in the trials of "spectral evidence" helped bring this dreadful affair to a close. This awesome last effort (however sincere) to save souls in Massachusetts brought many to doubt the wisdom of a religious and political system that could produce such a tragedy. As New England entered the eighteenth century, it lived within a Puritan heritage, but it tried to forget the rule of the old Puritan oligarchy.

Elsewhere in the colonies in the seventeenth century moral and intellectual life was thoroughly imbedded in Protestant theology. As in Massachusetts, each of the growing number of sects had its own particular problems of organization and of maintaining the Word of God against the growing claims of the world. In the Anglican South, the weakness of the church was particularly increased by the absence of a bishop in America, for under Anglicanism only a bishop could ordain new clergymen and confirm new communicants. The problem of religion on the frontier was especially acute. There, people raised with a strong religious sense were cut off from churches for many years. Although their freedom bred strong resistance to ministers who did not meet their needs, it also nourished a profound spiritual hunger.

Deism and Revivalism

Men in every age can be said to be falling away from God, and there are always keepers of the flame to remind them of their errors. The history of every religious group in colonial America turns on the growing conflict between the world and the Word of God, the difficulty of reconciling tightly knit or orthodox churches with the diversity, the size, and the tempting wealth of America. Although impatience with churches was far more important than disbelief in Christianity itself, even within Christian belief notable changes took place. In the more settled areas of the country, a more benign view of human possibilities and an image of a more approachable and loving God began to attract people. This change was helped along by the new intellectual currents embodied in the work of Isaac Newton and John Locke. Newtonian physics, set in a religious framework, prepared the way for an interpretation of the universe as a rational, knowable, and controllable cosmos created by a benign God and operating under the universal laws of mechanics. John Locke interpreted the nature of the human mind in such a way as to suggest that there were no inherent limitations on the power of men to perfect human nature and to reform civil society. It is impossible to determine the precise effect of the ideas of such men as Newton and Locke on colonial religion, but that it had an effect cannot be doubted. On both sides of the Atlantic many men and women, particularly the better educated, accepted a Christianity increasingly influenced by the rationalist theories of the European Enlightenment. This faith did not disturb their pursuit of comfort, the world's rewards, and their notion that good conduct was the essence of religion.

If some men in Europe and America sought to reconcile reason and religion, others protested that too much reason had already robbed religion of much of its vitality. In the German states the Pietists turned to the inner voice of the heart and emphasized a degree of individual judgment in spiritual matters that stood in sharp contrast to the original teachings of both Luther and Calvin about the authority of the Bible or the learned ministry. In England, in the early eighteenth century, John and Charles Wesley and their friend George Whitefield launched a frontal attack against rationalism, formalism, and skepticism. Both these movements were to have a direct effect on religious developments in America. A group of Germans, known as Moravians, settled in Pennsylvania, where they preached and practiced pietism. Whitefield toured the English colonies in 1739–41. Renowned as a man of personal magnetism, undoubted oratorical ability, and obvious sincerity, he preached to enormous audiences in every colony, converting countless thousands, and playing the most spectacular role in the religious revival that was known as the Great Awakening.

The Great Awakening, which has been aptly described as a "tidal wave of religious fervor," swept over the colonies about 1740 and left its mark on every one of them. Offering faith to common folk in terms that they both understood and appreciated, it gave a new vitality to religion in the colonies.

The Awakening was the greatest of a long series of attempts to satisfy the religious hunger that was not fulfilled by the older churches or that had been unsatisfied on the churchless frontier. It was also the culmination of the changes in religious organization that were so important in the history of New England. A religion of the heart, open to all and often brought by a traveling minister, was a real challenge to older churches with a fixed ministry. These churches had lately accepted a more rational theology and had helped to spread a liberal faith in man and reason to a church membership open largely to "the best people."

The preachers of the Great Awakening used a revivalist technique, a way of eliciting feelings of man's despondency without God. George Whitefield spoke for the other preachers in the movement as well as for himself when he said: "I love those that thunder out THE WORD. The Christian World is in a dead sleep. Nothing but a loud voice can awaken . . . it." In sermons that appealed to the heart rather than to logic the preachers of the Great Awakening sought to arouse people to a personal and public repentance. They did not describe a rational world but emphasized the torments of Hell in minute detail, while, at the same time, they offered the delights of Heaven to those who were ready for redemption and were prepared to accept God. Free from denominational control and directed to all Protestants regardless of sect, the Great Awakening achieved its most enthusiastic response in those regions of colonial America where the hold of the established churches was weakest. The Awakening was the forerunner of evangelism, one of the most notable traditions in the history of American religion.

Long before Whitefield reached America, however, opposition to the formalism of the older denominations and the conflict between the dissenting sects and the established churches had prepared the ground for a less inhibited approach to religion. The harvest that Whitefield reaped in 1739–41 had been sown some years earlier by others. As early as 1720, Theodore J. Frelinghuysen, a German pietistic pastor of four Dutch Reformed churches in New Jersey, was advocating an "inner religion" based on a mystical relationship of man to God. By 1726, Frelinghuysen's influence had spread beyond his own congregations to other Dutch Reformed churches and to several newly organized Presbyterian churches in the colony. Among the Presbyterians, Gilbert and William Tennent soon became leading revivalists, and in 1736 William founded the "Log College"—the forerunner of Princeton—to train young men for the ministry. The graduates of this institution were among the most influential preachers in the Great Awakening.

Although the Great Awakening represents a democratization of the church, the view of man presented by the preachers at the meetings was illiberal in the extreme. All the old Calvinist themes were played with a vengeance amid shrieks and groans from the crowds. The consequent difficulty in determining whether the Awakening was a "forward movement" is made clearer when we recall that liberal views of man were at the time largely heard in elite churches whose members were horrified by the "enthusiasm," disorder, and "open-to-all-comers"

Jonathan Edwards

atmosphere of the revivals. Later, however, a more polite form of evangelism was also to take hold among "the better churches."

The complexity of the intellectual changes in the colonies in the eighteenth century is dramatically demonstrated in the career of Jonathan Edwards. Edwards was descended from a great line of Massachusetts ministers. His grandfather, Solomon Stoddard, had helped draft the Half-way Covenant of 1662. Edwards was convinced that the impiety and wickedness of the age of the Great Awakening were due to a failure to recognize the utter depravity of man. Even the earlier Covenant theology had gone too far in assuring the elect that God would respect their efforts to live the moral life; man did not deserve so much credit. Edwards, in other words, introduced the starkest Calvinism yet heard in America in an age when "sophisticated people" were increasingly arguing for man's God-given potentialities for a rational and moral life. Edwards had little connection with the main movements of the Great Awakening, but he did use revivalist techniques and Calvinist images with terrifying effect in "nice" churches. But the paradox of Edwards is that he attempted to buttress his appeal for converts by using Locke's belief that men build their ideas on the basis of accumulated sensations of pleasure and pain. Edwards hoped to arouse his audience to feel the agony of a life without God and then to make them implore the Lord's deliverance in anticipation of the joy of His love. At a time when Locke seemed to many to suggest the growth of man's power to control his environment, Edwards was using him to drive home the need to recognize man's complete depravity and the wickedness of his worldly pride.

There were few features of American life that were not in some measure affected by the great religious revival of Edwards's time. Stimulating a widespread interest in religion, the Great Awakening also weakened the control of the formalists—or "Old Lights"—over church affairs and contributed to the growth of Christian humanitarian efforts to save men from such "morally corrupting habits" as drinking and gambling. The colleges of Princeton, Hampden-Sydney, Pennsylvania, Rutgers, and Dartmouth also had their roots in the Awakening. By emphasizing that God offered grace to the commonest men, and by permitting lay preachers—in contrast to ordained clergymen—to conduct religious services, the Awakening gave wide currency to the idea that all men were equally sinners before God. And from the idea that all men were equally sinners before God it was only a step to the belief that no sinful king had the right to rule men just because it was his wish or power to do so. If the Great Awakening was not a liberal movement, its democratic implications were unmistakable.

Educating the Early Americans

For the century before the Great Awakening and after, the most important American book was the Bible. The Bible was not then read as literature or as folk myths but as the directly inspired word of God. Since most Protestants placed the Bible at the center of religious life, it was imperative that men learn to read. Of course, men like the leaders of the Massachusetts Bay Colony also valued reading as a gentleman's accomplishment, but reading served best when put to Godly purposes.

Throughout the colonial period, however, formal teaching was limited and inadequate. The widely scattered farms and plantations in the southern colonies made it impossible to establish an effective general school system. Virginia, Maryland, and the Carolinas, however, had a number of private schools of which the "Old Field Schools" of Virginia were typical. These schools, which received their name because of their location in abandoned fields, were formed by the families of a neighborhood and were taught by the wife of one of the planters, the local clergyman or—if the families were sufficiently well off—a professional teacher. There were also a few grammar schools and endowed free elementary schools. Some plantations had their private tutors, and the records show that there also were endowed parish schools. In the northern colonies, opportunities for schooling were a little better. In Pennsylvania, where a halfhearted attempt was made to make education a function of the state, all parents were required under penalty of a heavy fine to see that their children could read. New Jersey in 1693 authorized towns to levy taxes for the support of public schools, and a number of them appear to have been subsequently established. As late as 1756, however, the schools of the neighboring province of New York were described as being of "the lowest order."

Even in New England, which has often been pictured as the cradle of the American educational system, opportunity for schooling was limited. The Puritans of Massachusetts, it is true, decreed in 1642 that, owing to "the neglect of many parents to train up their children in learning and labor, which might be profitable to the Commonwealth," education should be compulsory. This act did not establish schools but simply provided that children should be taught to "read and understand the principles of religion and the capital lawes of the country." Five years later this act was followed by another requiring every town of fifty families to provide for primary education by maintaining a teacher of reading and writing; each town of one hundred families was to establish a grammar school "with a teacher able to instruct youth so as they may be fitted for the university." Many towns failed to comply, and in 1701 the legislature complained that the law was "shamefully neglected in divers towns." The part of Massachusetts that is now the state of Maine did not have a single school until after the opening of the eighteenth century. Rhode Island and New Hampshire were almost entirely without schools in 1700. Connecticut, however, was slightly better off than her northern neighbors. School attendance was not compulsory in any of the colonies, and even in those communities where school was maintained throughout the year, attendance of farmers' children was very poor.

More notable advances were made in higher education than in secondary schooling. Harvard, the first college in the colonies, was authorized by the General Court of Massachusetts in 1636 and endowed two years later by John Harvard, a Charlestown minister. Established principally for the purpose of training men for the ministry, for more than fifty years this institution was the only college in North America. After more than thirty years of attempts, William and Mary was finally founded in Virginia in 1693. Even after its principal sponsor, a Scottish churchman, had secured a royal charter and funds for its en-

Harvard College, about 1740

dowment, the attorney general declared that there was not the slightest need for such an institution. When he was reminded that the principal purpose of the college was to educate young men for the ministry in order that the souls of the colony might be saved, he replied: "Souls! Damn your souls, make tobacco." Despite opposition and many misfortunes, the college survived. In 1729 its faculty consisted of President Blair and six professors, but its work was that of an academy rather than a college. Though not as influential as Harvard, it nevertheless trained many men who played important roles in Virginia politics and in the struggle for independence. A few years after William and Mary had been founded, the third college, Yale, was chartered (1701), partly as a protest against the growing religious liberalism of Harvard, and also to meet the demand of the wealthy citizens of New Haven for a college of their own. Endowed by Elihu Yale, a son of Massachusetts who had made a fortune in East Indian trade, it soon became the stronghold of orthodox Calvinists. Six other colleges were established before 1775, four of them primarily sectarian. The College of New Jersey (Princeton), founded in 1746, was Presbyterian in inspiration; King's College (Columbia) chartered in 1754, required its President to be an Anglican; Brown, established in 1764, was Baptist; and Rutgers, founded in 1766, was Dutch Reformed. Of the other two, Dartmouth, chartered in 1769, was an outgrowth of Eleazar Wheelock's Indian school, and the Philadelphia Academy, forerunner of the University of Pennsylvania, was established by Benjamin Franklin in 1751 for the purpose of training young men for social and political leadership.

All these colleges, except the Philadelphia Academy, were largely under church control, and most of the professorships were filled by clergymen. One's position in student life was determined by the wealth and social eminence of his family. As in the Old World, entrance was based almost entirely upon a knowledge of Latin and Greek. Harvard as early as 1643 stated that "when any scholar is able to understand Tully [Cicero] or such like classical Latin authors extempore, and make and speak true Latin in verse and prose . . . and decline perfectly the paradigms of nouns and verbs in the Greek tongue, let him then, and not before, be capable of admission into the college." The course of instruction did not differ basically from that of the medieval university. Although arithmetic, geometry, physics, astronomy, ethics, politics, and divinity were included in the curriculum, the chief emphasis was placed upon the classics and sometimes on Hebrew. At Harvard a student could not receive his degree until he was "found able to read the originals of the Old and New Testament into the Latin tongue, and to resolve them logically." Only the Philadelphia Academy paid any marked attention to English and the sciences; history, literature, geography, and political economy had no place elsewhere in American schools, and even Franklin was forced to compromise with those at the Academy who favored the traditional curriculum. The classics and the other scholastic subjects were provided for those who wished to train for law, medicine, or the church, but Franklin insisted that for the man who wanted to follow some other calling, or who desired a liberal education, there should be a variety of courses in the sciences, modern languages, and what we call social studies.

Books were included in the endowments of the colonial colleges, for the earliest settlers, especially those trained in the universities, brought their libraries with them and subsequently added to them. At the time of his death in 1643, William Brewster owned nearly 400 volumes, Miles Standish about 50, and John Winthrop, Jr., had a library of more than 1,000 volumes. Inventories of the possessions of seventeenth-century Virginians show that many persons possessed sizable libraries. By 1750, there is also evidence of an increased number of colonial booksellers. There were more frequent book advertisements in the press, and a public library movement was making slow headway. Charleston, South Carolina, claims the distinction of having the first library supported by public funds. Through the initiative of Franklin, a public subscription library was founded in Philadelphia in 1731; similar institutions were soon opened in Boston, Newport, New York, and Charleston. Between 1745 and 1763, seventeen subscription libraries were founded. The Philadelphia library, according to Franklin, "soon manifested its utility, was imitated by other towns and in other provinces . . . reading became fashionable; and our people . . . in a few years were observed by strangers to be better instructed and more intelligent than people of the same rank generally are in other countries."

The Colonial Intellectuals

Despite the pre-eminence of theology and philosophy in colonial colleges, there was also considerable interest in scientific work. Curiosity about the new plants and animals found in America, the great need of the colonists for practical knowledge, and the traditions of humane learning brought from Europe to American colleges and freshened by lively exchanges with European university and learned circles—all these helped broaden the scope of the colonial mind. But most of the advances in knowledge in the colonies ran along lines parallel to those being followed in Europe.

Famous men in colonial politics, such as John Winthrop, Cotton Mather, and Cadwallader Colden of New York, were also well known for their work in mathematics, physics, and botany. European scientists, such as Linnaeus, Buffon, and the members of the British Royal Society and the *Académie Française*, kept in touch with American associates.

Most gentlemen in the colonial period looked upon "book learning" not as the barren abstractions of the effete, but as a necessary manly accomplishment of persons of wealth and prestige. Any claim by a "man of the people" that intellect was not a strong recommendation for a political career would have seemed to them confirmation of their suspicions about the tendencies of democracy to ignorant mob rule. Most of the colonial intellectual elite were not systematic or thorough thinkers but possessed the minds of gifted amateurs. Like Thomas Jefferson, they enjoyed learning for its own sake as well as for the expertness it gave in such practical matters as farming and government. From one point of view their minds were often stocked only with bits and pieces of "interesting information." But this fund of facts often strengthened a native shrewdness and feeling for the immediate and concrete that was already such an important characteristic of the American intellectual tradition they were helping to form.

The most famous figure in colonial intellectual life was Benjamin

Franklin. There were few issues in his lifetime in which Franklin did not have an interest. He was also one of the foremost figures in what has been called the "Atlantic Civilization" of the middle eighteenth century, an international society of lettered men carrying on extensive correspondence with each other about electricity, plants, optics, theories of education, and schemes for moral and political improvement. Although Franklin did not have a deeply disciplined mind capable of reordering man's sense of the world through fresh and profound insights, he did exemplify the virtues of disinterestedness, flexibility, genuine curiosity, and deference to ideas that constitute the traditions of intelligence. His variety of interests, humanitarian concerns, and efforts at public betterment helped make him the model of an ambitious practical busy-ness. His intelligence, moreover, was admirably suited for organizing public purposes. As he said in proposing the formation of the American Philosophical Society for the enlargement of human knowledge: "The first drudgery of settling new colonies is now pretty well over, and there are many in every province in circumstances that set them at ease, and afford leisure to cultivate the finer arts and improve the common stock of knowledge." The outgrowth of a Philadelphia literary-scientific club called the Junto, the American Philosophical Society had as its purpose the promotion of the applied sciences and practical arts and the encouragement of "all philosophical experiments that let light into the nature of things, tend to increase the power of man over matter, and multiply the conveniences and pleasures of life." Included in its membership were virtually all the principal representatives of secular learning in the colonies, as well as such eminent Old World scientists as Buffon, Linnaeus, Condorcet, Raynal, and Lavoisier. Franklin's achievements soon won him membership in the Royal Society in England and an international reputation. "We are waiting with the greatest eagerness to hear from you," wrote Buffon and his fellow physicists from France in 1754.

Creating an American Public

Franklin started life as a printer. In many ways his other later interests continued to exemplify some of the best journalistic qualities: liveliness, attention to immediate fact, and a lucid prose style. The members of the American Philosophical Society also had to acquire those gifts if they were to influence the public mind. Even at its best, however, this organization could not hope to equal the power of the colonial newspapers.

Of all the agencies that deeply influenced the responses of the colonists to their various problems, probably none was more important than the press. Although the first printing press in English America was set up in Massachusetts in 1639, not a single newspaper had been published in the colonies as late as the close of the seventeenth century. A three-page pamphlet entitled *Public Occurrences, both Foreign and Domestic*, published in Boston in 1690, was promptly suppressed by the authorities for uttering "reflections of a very high nature" on a current political problem. In 1704, the *Boston News-Letter*, the first regular newspaper in the colonies, appeared. By judiciously refraining from criticizing the authorities and by printing only belated news from Europe and reports of customs house clearings and entries, this tiny, four-page, two-column sheet managed to survive; but fifteen years elapsed before it had an American rival elsewhere. In 1719 the *Boston Gazette* and *The American Weekly Mercury* (of Philadelphia) were started. Shortly afterward James Franklin, Benjamin's brother, began the *New England Courant* in spite of the advice of his friends, who assured him that America did not need another newspaper. Yet by 1765, forty-three American newspapers had been established, three of which were in German.

Some of these papers were short-lived. All were small-sized weeklies with crude, rough type and narrow, crowded columns. Considerable space was allotted to local news, gossip, and advertisements. All ran letters from home and abroad, sermons, poetry, essays, and reprints of English articles. Cartoons were few, but some, like Franklin's sketch of a snake cut into eight pieces and entitled "Join or Die," were very effective. With improvement in communication and the growth of greater interest in what the other colonies were doing, items such as legislative acts, speeches of governors, and brief notes about crimes and accidents were copied from other papers. A few were bold enough to print editorials of an independent and unbiased character; most, however, were guarded and circumspect.

A number of magazines also began to be published toward the middle of the century. In Philadelphia in 1741, Benjamin Franklin founded *The General Magazine and Historical Chronicle for all the British Plantations in America*; it contained some general news, lengthy extracts from new books, and reprints of original poems and prose essays from various colonial newspapers. The intention behind this magazine was to produce something culturally American and intercolonial. Its content was entirely American; the poems and essays, instead of being copies from English journals, were domestic productions. The "Accounts of or Extracts from New Books, Pamphlets, etc., Published in the Plantations" was, as the title implied, a department devoted exclusively to the review of publications from the colonial press. The reprints were selected from the press of all the Anglo-American provinces, including the West Indies. The content of Franklin's magazine is a guide to the direction of the intellectual changes that the colonies were undergoing: a growing diversity of interests united with a sense of the importance of purely American events.

The widening popular press was to play a large role in late colonial politics and in the coming of the Revolution, but it had to contend constantly with censorship and restraint. Following English precedent, Massachusetts established a system of official licensing for presses that lasted until 1755. In all the colonies any publisher who dared to criticize the government or even inadvertently printed anything displeasing to the officials was liable to arrest, but censors did not always have their way. In 1735, John Peter Zenger, a German immigrant and editor of the *New York Weekly Journal,* was brought to trial on the charge of criminal libel preferred against him by Governor Cosby of New York. Shortly before, Cosby had removed the chief justice of the province for rendering an adverse decision in a matter in which Cosby was personally interested. Articles that appeared in Zenger's paper sharply criticizing the governor's action led to the editor's arrest. The new chief justice, a tool of the governor, ruled that the jury had to decide only whether Zenger had published the articles or not, thus leaving to the court the decision as to their libelous character. But Andrew Hamilton of Philadelphia, probably the most brilliant and distinguished lawyer in America, argued that the jury had the right to decide whether the statements in question were false and libelous. This argument and his eloquent appeal for free public discussion as a safeguard for free government won the jury, and Zenger was acquitted.

The Young American Towns

Towns were the homes of the colonial newspapers, and the growth in the size and influence of the colonial press is one index of the expansion and importance of "cities" in the century preceding the Revolution. With the rise of the towns, an antagonism sprang up between townsfolk and the more isolated rural backcountry people that was to be a continuous and important rivalry in American life. Because both town and country, as we have seen in examining the colonial economy, were committed to a businessman's ethos, bitter fights between them over proper shares of the profits of farming and commerce were to be expected. The location of markets in the towns, the dependence on town merchants as the distributors and exporters of produce, and the

Boston, 1722

role of the merchant as salesman to the farmer were sources of continuous conflict. The more liquid and more easily massed wealth of the town often gave the leading citizens political power out of proportion to their numbers. As centers of communication for the colony, the towns could provide a general knowledge of affairs and a degree of sophistication that the isolated farmers of the interior could not easily match.

Both town and country soon formed flattering images of themselves which, if taken literally, would distort our understanding of the nature of the conflict between them. The farmers used the image of an innocent yeoman defending himself against the moneybags. And the townsman, although less openly, proclaimed himself the only possible source of imagination and spiritedness, given the hopeless simplicity of the farmer.

Colonial America was overwhelmingly rural, yet by the beginning of the eighteenth century the role of the towns in a business civilization gave them an importance far greater than can be suggested by their small population. By the eve of the revolution, moreover, American commercial centers rivaled many of the leading ports of Great Britain even in population and wealth. Ranking first at the end of the colonial period was Philadelphia, with about 25,000 people. New York ran a close second, and Boston stood third, with a population of slightly more than 20,000. Fourth was Charleston, with about 10,000 inhabitants; and Newport, a prosperous manufacturing and commercial center and outranked only by Boston among the New England ports, stood fifth, with a population of approximately 7,000. Baltimore, Norfolk, Portsmouth, Salem, Providence, New London, and New Haven were promising a large future growth, and, with the increase of population during the eighteenth century, a number of inland towns also became important. Among these were Albany, at the junction of the Hudson and Mohawk valleys; Lynn, Massachusetts, the center of colonial shoe manufacture; Hartford, Connecticut; and the substantial Pennsylvania towns of Lancaster, York, and Germantown. However, a number of towns, like Richmond, Virginia, Reading, Pennsylvania, and Springfield, Massachusetts, destined to become important inland urban centers, were only struggling villages of a few score houses at the outbreak of the War of Independence.

Although these towns housed only one tenth of the population, they exercised a tremendous influence in colonial affairs, largely because they were the homes of the wealthiest and most cosmopolitan colonists. Here lived the prosperous merchant princes—the Whartons, Pembertons, Willings, and Morrises of Philadelphia; the Amorys,

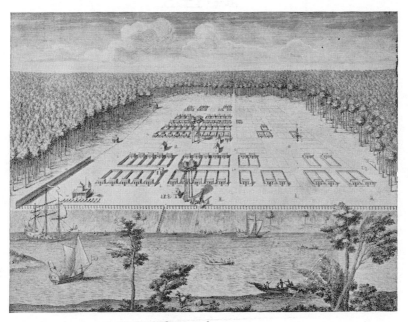

Savannah, 1734

Faneuils, Hancocks, and Boylstons of Boston; the Lows, Livingstons, Crugers, and Waltons of New York; the Redwoods, Lopezes, and Wantons of Newport; the Browns, "Nicky, Josey, John and Mosey," of Providence; and the merchant planters—Manigaults, Mazycks, Laurenses, and Rutledges—of Charleston. These men were owners of stores, merchant ships, wharves, warehouses, fishing craft, and whalers; they were speculators in town real estate and frontier lands. Many were private bankers and underwriters of marine insurance. Together with the proprietors of the estates along the Hudson and the southern planters, the town elite formed the backbone of an aristocracy which virtually ruled colonial society and politics. In the commercial colonies petty shopkeepers, vendue-masters, ropemakers, sailmakers, sailors, coopers, caulkers, smiths, carpenters, and fishermen were dependent upon the merchants for a livelihood, but most of them also looked forward to becoming businessmen in their own right. Even the northern farmers "felt the ebb and flow of seaborne commerce," for they looked to the merchant to market their surplus goods. "If the merchant trade be not kept on foot," wrote a contemporary historian, "they fear greatly their corn and cattle will lie in their hands."

Like the men of the great estates, the merchant aristocracy of the

RULES
OF THIS TAVERN

Four pence a night for Bed

Six pence with Supper

No more than five to sleep
in one bed

No Boots to be worn in bed

Organ Grinders to sleep in
the Wash house

No dogs allowed upstairs

No Beer allowed in the
Kitchen

No Razor Grinders or Tinkers
taken in

A Colonial Tavern Sign

[BETTMANN ARCHIVE]

colonies lived well. Many of its members owned country houses as well as spacious town mansions of wood or brick, both furnished with imported articles. Their wives and daughters wore gowns of broadcloths, silks, and linens, modeled after the latest London fashions. Feasts and pageants, and dinners and dances at some country inn were common occurrences. Speaking of the merchants of Boston in 1740, an English traveler declared that both "ladies and gentlemen dress and appear as gay, in common, as courtiers in England on a coronation or birthday." This statement was equally true of the rich merchants' families of the other seacoast towns. Individually and as a class, the merchants jealously guarded their interests against both overzealous officials and "radical" voters. More intent on business than politics, they nevertheless were quick to enter politics (but not always on the same side) when their interests were jeopardized or when they wished to secure some particular end through legislation.

As centers of communication the commercial towns were scarcely less important than as centers of wealth. During the early colonial years, settlements were cut off for long periods from the Old World and from each other. Practically the only means of travel was by foot, horseback, or water. Every community had its inns or taverns, but many of them were cheerless, ill-kept places. There were few newspapers, and only with the arrival of some vessel from overseas or some coastal trader was news of the outside world received. It was not until 1691, when postal service between Massachusetts, New York, and Pennsylvania was established, that the semblance of a postal system came into being. Under such conditions, it was difficult to break down the barriers of provincialism or to develop a common intellectual life. By 1750, however, there was marked improvement. Although roads over which a wheeled vehicle might pass with safety were as yet comparatively few, there were many highways and postroads connecting the several colonies with each other. Regular "lines" of stagecoaches and stageboats were beginning to operate between Boston and New York, and New York and Philadelphia. Larger ships and better inns also made travel and postal communication easier. In 1753, Benjamin Franklin and William Hunter of Virginia were appointed deputy postmasters general by the King. They helped reorganize and expand the primitive mail service.

Life on the Land

Despite this steady over-all growth of prosperity and ease of communication, most colonists lived under crude and isolated conditions. The great majority of farmers had started their careers in dwellings as humble as caves, lean-tos, wigwams, and huts of wattle and clay. "For our houses and churches in these times," stated the Virginia General Assembly of the early years, ". . . were so mean and poor . . . that they could not stand above one or two years."

As time went on, the more prosperous colonists in the settled regions erected clapboarded frame houses, most of which at first were small one-story buildings. Only the more prosperous settlers were able to have solidly built homes that rose two stories high in front and sloped down to one story in the rear. Enormous chimneys of brick and stone extended through the house, providing flues for the open fireplaces. Writing about these frame dwellings in 1656, a contemporary observed that "although for the most part they are but one story besides the loft, and built of wood, yet contrived so delightfully that your ordinary houses in England are not so handsome, for usually the rooms are large, daubed with whitelime, glazed and flowered, and if not glazed windows, shutters which are made very pretty and convenient." But even the frame structures were often unpainted on the outside, and the same was true of the barns and other outbuildings. The permanent home of the ordinary farmer was seldom constructed of any material other than wood. Much of the more romantic picture of rural colonial America is taken from surviving big houses and mansions, but at the time there were extraordinarily few of these, and they were often separated from each other by several days' journey.

The day-to-day demands of rural life placed severe limitations on refinements in the colonies. In as much as the first settlers were practically compelled by circumstances to devote all their time and energy to making a living, they enjoyed little or no leisure. Whatever desire they had for beauty had to be expressed in the homes they built, the tools and furnishings they made, and the many tasks they performed. They showed little originality, either borrowing freely from or imitating Old World patterns. Nowhere is this fact better demonstrated than in seventeenth-century colonial architecture. The Dutch, for example, closely followed the models familiar to them. "New Amsterdam," as Lewis Mumford points out, "was a replica of the Old World port, with its gabled brick houses and its well-banked canals and fine gardens." The simple, square, frame house of the New Englander, with its large fireplace and single chimney, as well as the gabled structures of the South, were based on medieval designs, and the Puritan meetinghouse and the Anglican church were copies of English models.

The patroon estates of New York had luxurious, well-built houses of brick or stone. Although the early home of the southern planter was built of undressed logs, by the opening of the eighteenth century a few imposing, well-constructed mansions were being erected, such as Tuckahoe, the seat of the Randolphs on the James River; Westover, the beautiful residence of William Byrd; and Mount Vernon, the home of Washington. Surrounded by gardens and neatly trimmed hedges, homes like these, with their broad lawns sloping down to the banks of the stream on which they were located, equaled the residences of the wealthy English country gentleman for room, comfort, and beauty. Clustered about these mansions with their great halls, high rooms, and graceful staircases, were small villages of barns, Negro cabins, stables, offices, and other buildings.

The country homes and personal wardrobes of the wealthy patroons and the southern planters were lavishly furnished with articles from abroad. From the cabinetmakers of London came chairs, tables, and settees of carved mahogany, upholstered in rich fabrics or the finest of Russian leather; walls were hung with expensive tapestries or decorated with paintings and engravings. Sleeping chambers were furnished with highboys, chests, and bedsteads of finished oak and walnut.

An Early "Great House" in North Carolina, circa 1712

The Cape Cod Cottage

The New England "Salt Box"

Like the wealthiest townspeople, planters and patroons dressed on occasion in fashionable and expensive clothes that were often imported from Europe.

The few great planters or patroons might have fine clothes and handsome mansions, but these were luxuries that the ordinary farmer could not afford. Economy was the watchword in the farm family, and furniture and utensils were used until worn or broken beyond repair. Rural people dressed in plain homespun and leather, both of which were produced on the farm. During the summer months they wore garments of coarse linen and towcloth; the children and many of the men went barefoot except on the Sabbath, but even then it was not uncommon for country folk to carry their shoes and stockings until near the church in order to save leather and shine. In winter the men and boys and women and girls wore heavy flannels, woolens, or buckskins and heavy, double-soled, calfskin or cowhide shoes or boots. Deerskin was frequently used for coats. Each member of the household had a "best suit" or a "best dress," which was worn only on Sundays and on special occasions. Whether for "every day" or "dress up," the clothes were unstylish in both cut and color; but they wore well. The same clothes served one member of the family after another until even the patches were worn out. By the middle of the eighteenth century, many people could afford to dress better, and a few, anxious to imitate their wealthier neighbors, did.

These obvious contrasts in home and dress symbolized differences in social status, wealth, and intellectual opportunity. Burdened with the responsibility of securing a livelihood for himself and those dependent on him, the farmer was wrapped up in material interests, and his best energies were expended in grappling with nature for an existence. He and his children were busy conquering the forest, building a home, tilling the soil, harvesting crops, and fighting Indians. The planter, on the other hand, could send his children overseas or north to be educated, or he obtained tutors for them from England, Scotland, or the northern colonies. If sufficiently wealthy and interested, he had his own library. The average day of the planter was, however, largely taken up with practical matters of supervising his estate accounts, haggling with shippers or merchants on his own wharfs, acting as justice of the peace or as member of the colonial legislature, arranging for his latest speculation in western lands, and, above all, running local politics. Although he was often not far removed in time from a log cabin or simple farm, his wealth and offices brought him social prestige and the deference of his "inferiors." Colonial America was not an egalitarian society.

The Emergence of the American

By the middle of the eighteenth century, Benjamin Franklin considered himself not merely a Pennsylvanian, but an American; King's College in New York enrolled students from other colonies; and Boston papers circulated in New York and Charleston. The towns had emerged from the hardships of the pioneering period. Among the established clergy a broader spirit was noticeable; sectarian prejudices, although still strong, were less likely to go unchallenged. Hearing from western Europe was easier and news more constant; schools and colleges were improving; the number of professional men was larger; and a wealthy class with leisure and a taste for intellectual pursuits had come into existence.

Many of these changes in colonial religious beliefs and standards of living and much of the growth of American knowledge and science were similar to changes in the western European life of the late seventeenth and eighteenth centuries. What most set off the colonists from Europe were differences in psychology. The "feel" of the new world was different. America was nourishing, within its Christian heritage and a business ethos, a vast impatience with the traditional European restraints of church and crown, corporation and class. It was already raising an image of human fulfillment that probably no people had ever known before. Human will in the New World, whether for wealth or freedom or God's word, could be and often was amply rewarded. By 1776, Americans had thus begun to think of the New World as the home of a new man accepting the chance to prove his worth against a harsh and stubborn environment.

FOR SUPPLEMENTARY READING

L. B. Wright, *The Cultural Life of the American Colonies* (1957), is a respectable survey of colonial social and intellectual life. Regional studies, however, have more merit. Of the many works on New England none can compare with Perry Miller's three volumes: *Orthodoxy in Massachusetts* (1933); *The New England Mind: The Seventeenth Century* (1939); and *The New England Mind: From Colony to Province* (1953). A smaller work that shows the influence of Miller's scholarship is Alan Simpson, *Puritanism in Old and New England* (1955). Miller's *Jonathan Edwards* (1949) and *Roger Williams* (1953) and E. Bates, *Anne Hutchinson and the Antinomian Controversy in the Massachusetts Bay Colony* (1962), are also indispensable for understanding three of the most controversial colonial figures.

Next to Miller's the works of Carl Bridenbaugh have done much to change the interpretation of colonial life. His *Cities in the Wilderness: The First Century of Urban Life in America 1625–1742* (1938), *Cities in Revolt 1742–1776* (1955), and *Myths and Realities: Societies of the Colonial South* (1952) are good places to begin study of two important subjects. F. B. Tolles, *Meeting House and Counting House: The Quaker Merchants of Colonial Philadelphia* (1948), and T. J. Wertenbaker, *The Middle Colonies* (1938), do well by the large area between Connecticut and Maryland. For New England, two works by E. S. Morgan are recommended: *Visible Saints, The History of a Puritan Idea* (1965) and *The Gentle Puritan: A Life of Ezra Stiles 1767–1795* (1962).

The complexity of the change from Calvinism to Deism is suggested in Miller's *Jonathan Edwards* and is treated less dramatically but more formally in H. W. Schneider, *History of American Philosophy* (1946). There are three studies of the Great Awakening that should be consulted: E. C. Gaustad, *The Great Awakening in New England* (1957); W. M. Gewehr, *The Great Awakening in Virginia* (1930); and A. Heimert, *Religion and the American Mind* (1965). Paul Monroe has a survey of colonial education in *The Founding of the American Public School System* (1949), but its limited scope is broadened by Bernard Bailyn, *Education in the Forming of American Society* (1960); R. Middlekauf, *Ancients and Axioms* (1963); and R. Gummere, *The American Colonial Mind and the Classical Tradition* (1963). Michael Kraus in *The Atlantic Civilization* (1949) has much useful material on the colonial intellectuals. Recent good starting points for the study of Benjamin Franklin are V. W. Crane, *Benjamin Franklin and a Rising People* (1954), and P. W. Conner, *Poor Richard's Politicks* (1965). Before doing any extensive work in American intellectual history, however, students should read V. W. Brooks, *America's Coming of Age* (1958) (Pb); D. H. Lawrence, *Studies in Classic American Literature* (1953) (Pb); Richard Chase, *The American Novel and Its Tradition* (1958) (Pb); and Lionel Trilling, "Reality in America" in *The Liberal Imagination* (1950) (Pb).

An important and distorted issue is made clearer in L. W. Levy, *Freedom of Speech and Press in Early American History: Legacy of Suppression* (1960).

PART II

THE BIRTH
OF A NATION

5

⇉⇉⇉⇉⇉⇉⇉⇉⇉⇉

Administering Colonial Affairs

THE BRITISH EMPIRE grew in an unsystematized way, largely in response to a variety of motives and needs. The American settlements became parts of a large group of more than thirty colonies, and only the final struggles with the home country welded the Englishmen together as *the* thirteen colonies.

Throughout the colonial period, British authorities attempted to regulate both the governmental and economic affairs of their overseas possessions. Colonial government was largely a product of trial and error. In comparison with empires ruled by an alien people, English government did not press heavily on the inhabitants of the American colonies. In economic matters many colonists enjoyed a considerable degree of practical freedom. Despite numerous mercantilist regulations that applied to the commerce and manufacturing of all the colonies, restrictive laws passed in America and England were not always rigorously enforced. Although Edmund Burke exaggerated when he referred to England's colonial policy before 1760 as one of "salutary neglect," there was considerable truth in his statement.

The Politics of Empire

The British government never put the American colonies under an effective systematic plan of administration. Long separated from each other by almost impassable forests or by long stretches of water, each colony, within certain limits, developed its own institutions and traditions to which the home government in so far as possible adapted itself. Instead of regarding the colonies as parts of an English community, England treated them as disconnected, semi-autonomous political entities. As virtually self-governing units, each colony developed its own land policy, its own method of dealing with the Indians, and its own system of administration.

Although colonial political views and institutions differed in some respects from those of England, the colonists were nevertheless Englishmen and were governed ultimately by the laws and regulations made by the officials of the home government. The colonist was compelled to obey the laws of Parliament that specifically applied to the colonies; but, at the same time, he had to obey the laws that were passed by the legislature within his own colony. In time many colonists came to assume that Parliament's legislative rights were limited to a colony's external affairs, while strictly intracolonial matters fell within the province of the local assemblies. The English authorities, for their part, never accepted this distinction. In their minds there could be no doubt concerning the supremacy of Parliament.

Instead of establishing a single bureau or office to formulate and coordinate colonial policy, the English government parceled out the control of the colonies among a number of agencies. Originally the most important of these from the colonial viewpoint was the Privy Council, which was made up of the King's chief advisers. The Privy Council's principal function in colonial affairs was to serve as a clearinghouse for policies that had been proposed by other officials of the home government. The Privy Council approved or disapproved of the instructions and commissions for the royal governors, settled bureaucratic disputes among the colonial administrators, ruled on complaints from the colonies, and heard appeals from the colonial courts. Its most important power was the right to disallow those acts of the colonial legislatures of which it disapproved. Although the Privy Council theoretically had considerable authority over colonial life, the steady growth of Parliamentary power in the eighteenth century resulted in a corresponding decline in the power of the King and his advisers. By 1750, many of the duties of the Privy Council had become perfunctory, despite the fact that it still could disallow colonial legislation.

Virtually every important agency in the English government exercised either direct or indirect control over some aspect of colonial administration. A secretary of state, whose primary concern was with foreign affairs, selected the royal governors for the colonies. The commissioners of customs appointed the customs collectors and sought to

THE

EXPANSION

OF BRITISH

NORTH

AMERICA

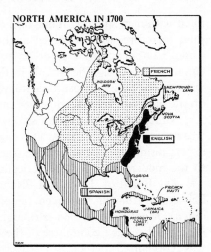

NORTH AMERICA IN 1700

NORTH AMERICA AFTER 1713

NORTH AMERICA AFTER 1763

prevent illegal commerce. The Treasury controlled royal revenues and expenditures in the colonies. The Admiralty and War Office were responsible for colonial defense and also cooperated with the customs officials in suppressing illegal trade. Finally, the Bishop of London exercised control over the Anglican church in the provinces.

English politics in the eighteenth century turned increasingly on questions of favors and patronage. Most of the colonial posts were often filled with men allied with one of many competing "factions." Colonial jobs, therefore, were involved in the vagaries of the English political game. Considerations extraneous to the good administration of the empire played a significant role in the choice of imperial personnel. It was not until the nineteenth century, in fact, that English politics took on the now familiar tone of sober caution and responsibility.

Although England had a strong central government by 1700, she was not yet a modern state. The relatively clear lines of authority, the expert disinterested civil service, the research offices that are essential to the modern state were practically unknown.

The Board of Trade and Plantations was the only agency in the British government that even remotely resembled a genuine colonial office. Originating in 1660—although there were precedents for it before that date—as a committee of the Privy Council, the Board of Trade was reorganized in 1696 as a powerful instrument of colonial supervision. Its principal interest was in commerce, but it was concerned with every detail of colonial affairs. All colonial legislation was subject to its review. It recommended that the Crown disallow any act of a colonial assembly that was contrary to the laws of England, that threatened the maintenance of the royal prerogative, or that jeopardized the property rights of any citizen of the Empire; and its recommendations were almost without exception accepted. The Board also heard complaints. Any colony could present any grievance through an agent who represented it in England, and any British merchant or manufacturer was equally free to lodge objections against any colonial authority and to make suggestions that he thought would prove to his advantage. Although the percentage of laws disallowed was not great, the colonists increasingly mistrusted and disliked the Board and thought of it as an agency created to limit their freedom of action for the benefit of grasping English businessmen and politicians.

Unfortunately, with English politics and administrative procedure in so crude a state, the worthwhile work the Board might have accomplished depended excessively on the personality and politics of its officers, particularly the president. Times of intense activity would be followed by years of sloth. Inaction pleased many colonists and accustomed them to freedom; effective administrators like Lord Halifax (1748–61), on the other hand, might seem intolerable to Americans. The Board's powers, like the quality of its leadership, also varied in line with the changes in English politics.

The American Governments

Within a colony, authority was divided between the representatives of the colonial voters and the royal officials. Each colony had its distinctive political institutions and traditions, but all had a governor, a representative assembly, a judicial system, and the Common Law of England, which guaranteed trial by jury, and freedom from arbitrary imprisonment. Eight out of the thirteen—Georgia, the two Carolinas, Virginia, New Jersey, New York, New Hampshire, and Massachusetts—had lost their original forms of government and had become royal colonies by 1752, each with a governor appointed by the king. In the proprietary colonies of Maryland, Pennsylvania, and Delaware, executive authority was vested in the proprietor or in a governor or lieutenant governor appointed by him. Only in Connecticut and Rhode Island, the so-called "corporate" or self-governing colonies, was the governor chosen by representatives of the enfranchised voters, and in both he was little more than a figurehead in functions and power.

Selected for the most part from the English political factions, the royal governors differed greatly in culture, training, and ability. Some were efficient administrators, and men of undoubted integrity and ability. Others used their office to enrich themselves and friends by sinecures, patronage, land grants, and the acceptance of bribes. Nearly all gained the reputation—which in some cases was undeserved—of being overbearing. Franklin, in a statement that perhaps reveals more about its author than its subject, wrote:

> Their office makes them insolent; their insolence makes them odious; and being conscious that they are hated, they become malicious; their malice urges them to continual abuse of the inhabitants in their letters to Administration, representing them as disaffected and rebellious, and (to encourage the use of severity) as weak, divided, timid, and cowardly. Government believes all; thinking it necessary to support and countenance its officers. Their quarreling with the people is deemed a mark and consequence of their fidelity. They are, therefore, more highly rewarded, and this makes their conduct still more insolent and provoking.

American officials and American colonial politics were also tainted by corruption; the governors were not all devils in a land of angels. In the colonies honesty received little or no financial reward. Factional fights and patronage squabbles, remote from genuine public issues, had as much interest for American officials as they did for the English at home. The colonial governor was in a delicate position. He had to walk a line between the genuine needs and "party politics" of his charges in America and the demands of law, administration, and politics in England. As a group, the governors were as good a cross section of talent and knavery as can probably be found at any level of public life in the eighteenth century.

With the exception of Pennsylvania, each colony had developed a bicameral legislature. The members of the upper house of councilors, or assistants, as they were called, were, in all the colonies except Connecticut and Rhode Island, chosen by the king on the recommendation of the governor, who usually named those who he had reason to believe would support his claims. The colonial assembly or lower house, however, was in every instance chosen by the qualified voters. It did not take the colonists long to discover that the colonial governor represented royal prerogatives. With his sweeping power to enforce laws, to grant reprieves and pardons, to remove councilors, to summon, adjourn, and dissolve the popular assembly, to veto measures he deemed objectionable, to propose laws desired by the Crown, to levy troops for defense, and to enforce martial law in time of invasion, war, and rebellion, he was not favorable toward the degree of self-government the colonists wanted. The favoritism shown by the governor in filling offices at his disposal and in making land grants irritated some colonists, particularly those passed by in the awards. They were even less pleased when he granted special privileges to a select few or countenanced the wrongdoings of corrupt or overbearing officials. Gradually a struggle developed between a "royal party," comprised of English officials with their colonial favorites, and colonial leaders anxious for the favors, prestige, and the governing rights of those in power. The lines separating the groups were by no means fixed or determined only by considerations of principle, but these lines did become clearer as the break with England neared.

Among genuine grievances, the landowner as a taxpayer resented what he believed to be exorbitant taxation. At all times he was a caustic critic of those officials who, in his judgment, lavished spoils on favorites or were guilty of wasteful or unnecessary expenditures.

Disputes over taxation, political favors, centralized government, Indian policy, and land policy were continuous throughout the colonial period. These were constantly interlaced with questions of political opportunism, although all sides took care to appear in the best possible light as men of principle. Colonial politics were very bitter, and the slowly growing ideal of an American world free from the intrigue and "statecraft" that had so defaced European life must be contrasted with the usual experience of colonial leaders. Sometimes the struggle for power and prestige in the colonies broke out into bloody civil wars that were only indirectly connected with imperial questions. Such struggles as Bacon's Rebellion in Virginia (1675–76), Leisler's Rebellion in New York (1689–91), and the Regulator Wars in North Carolina (1768–71) were bitter factional fights which do not lend themselves to generalizations about democracy opposing aristocracy or the virtuous frontiersman challenging the corrupt tidewater oligarchs.

The Rise of the Assemblies

One of the most significant themes in colonial political history is the rise of the assemblies and their effective challenge to the governors' power. The struggle between the governors and assemblies is continuous in the eighteenth century and runs parallel to the growing challenge of the legislature to the crown in England. By the eve of the American Revolution, there had already been a century of political conflict between the lower houses of the colonial legislatures and the royal governors.

The colonial assembly, although not representative of all the people, championed self-government. Like the House of Commons, its greatest power was in laying taxes and making appropriations. It was determined to control the colonial purse strings and to use that control for advancing the welfare of those whom it represented. Among other things, it succeeded in stripping the upper house of all power over money bills. It stipulated that money grants be made annual, not permanent, and that they be paid out by a treasurer appointed by the assembly. By withholding, or threatening to withhold, the governor's salary, it often succeeded in making him amenable to its wishes. The assembly led the important fight against appointing colonial judges for life, subject only to the king's pleasure, instead of for a limited term, with his return depending on good behavior. During the eighteenth century, the governors complained about "republican principles" practiced by the colonists and elaborated plans to reduce all the colonies to the status of royal provinces, free the royal governors from financial dependence upon the colonial assemblies by parliamentary imposition of taxes, maintain a British standing army in the colonies, and increase the use of the royal veto on colonial laws. As a result, the colonists became more bitter and vindictive toward royal authority and more determined in their insistence that their growing powers of self-government be respected.

In the continuous struggles between governor and assembly, both sides had effective weapons. Through its control of the purse, the assembly could block any program put forward by the governor and could even withhold the funds needed for the salaries of the royal officials within a colony. The governor, for his part, could prorogue the assembly and veto its acts. These, however, were negative powers, for they did not enable the governor to compel the assembly to do what it did not wish to do. But behind the governor was British authority; and if the assembly became openly defiant, there was always the possibility of abolishing the colony's representative government.

In 1684, when Massachusetts refused to obey the orders of the crown and the laws of Parliament, its charter was revoked, and in the course of the next four years, the New England colonies were combined with New York and the two Jerseys to form the Dominion of New England. Sir Edmund Andros served as royal governor of the united colonies, none of which was permitted to have an assembly. In 1689, however, the colonists, following the lead of Parliament in the Glorious Revolution, successfully rebelled against the king's representatives in the Dominion; and with the accession of William and Mary to the throne, the colonies constituting the Dominion of New England were again separated, although they had to accept changes in their new charters.

The events of 1684–89 revealed, but did not resolve, the problems inherent in the British system of colonial government. To the colonists, representative government would increasingly become a tradition and a right to which they were entitled as Englishmen. To the royal officials, the powers of the colonial assemblies constituted privileges granted by the crown which could also be revoked. The differences between the two points of view were so pronounced that a determined policy on either side would leave little room for compromise. Eventually force rather than constitutional argument was to settle the long struggle for power.

Democracy in Colonial Politics

One of the persistent issues in colonial politics was the adequacy of representation for newer settlements. In most cases the backcountry, more sparsely populated than the regions along the coast, would, on the fairest reckoning, have been outweighed and outvoted by the older areas. But the leaders of the more settled regions, in an effort to guarantee their predominance, often restricted the power of the frontier by malapportionment, juggling of votes, and failure to provide adequate polling places.

The issues of adequate representation or fair elections should not, however, be confused with the question of the degree of democratic suffrage in the colonies before the Revolution. The evidence suggests that there was a far greater popular participation in voting than was formerly believed to be the case, but this feature of colonial politics should not be considered a sufficient test of democracy. In too many nations in the modern world, universal suffrage exists without a democratic way of life.

Although the laws regulating suffrage changed from time to time, in general the individual's actual influence and participation in political affairs varied with his economic status or his religious affiliation or both, depending upon the voting requirements of the colony in which he lived. In Massachusetts, until 1684, suffrage was restricted to members of the Congregational Church; after that date, freeholders of an estate worth at least 40s. a year or the owner of other property to the value of £40 sterling could vote. In Pennsylvania, the right to vote was limited to freeholders of 50 acres or more of land well seated, 12 acres of it cleared and under cultivation, and to other persons worth at least £50 in lawful money; the prospective voter also had to believe in Christ as the Savior of the world. To vote in Virginia, the colonist had to be a freeholder who owned at least 50 acres of land if there was no house on it, or 25 acres of land with a house 12 feet square. In South Carolina, the franchise was limited to communicants of the Church of England who possessed 50 acres freehold or a personal estate of £10. There were similar requirements in the other colonies; in law, suffrage was strictly limited to male property holders and taxpayers, and in some cases, to communicants of some particular church.

Judging by tax lists, in some places considerable numbers of people could not meet the property qualification. In Pennsylvania, one examination of tax lists suggests that only 8 per cent of the country population were legally eligible to vote. Studies of Massachusetts, New York, New Jersey, and Virginia indicate, however, that a numerous electorate was legally available to competing candidates. In general, there could be few truly propertyless people in an overwhelmingly family-farm, small business, and plantation economy. In Virginia and South Carolina, for example, the qualification for voting was equal to only a single head right. Slaves, indentured servants, and hired hands in town and farm could not vote by law, but whites who were without any property throughout their lives were unusual.

Whatever the property or religious qualifications in law and whatever the economic worth of the citizens, the real test of the issue of suffrage must be how many people actually voted. Here we can say with some confidence that by 1776 in many places American suffrage was substantially democratic. Whatever the actual extent of voting, colonial politics were generally controlled by shifting alliances within an elite of the influential, wellborn, and rich. By and large, although there was a broad suffrage at the base, the mass of voters were under the unsteady control of an oligarchy. This pattern of American political life of the late colonial period persisted, despite the dramatic break with England, down to the early nineteenth century. The key offices in the colonies and states had very high property qualifications, and these were probably maintained in fact as well as in law. This mixed pattern of "democratic" voting and oligarchic rule was helped by a diminishing yet powerful habit of deference by "inferiors" to "superiors" and, even more, by the practices of the colonial "machines."

Any discrepancies between the formal qualifications for voting and actual participation in elections can be explained in several ways. Since there was a constant struggle for office, favors, and patronage among the colonists, the temptation was great to look the other way when the unqualified but reliable voter appeared at the polls. In many areas, if voting qualifications could not be met, they were ignored. In smaller communities it might be difficult not to let one's neighbors vote even if formally disqualified. Low votes in specific elections cannot be taken as conclusive proof of the lack of a democratic suffrage, for an exciting election before or afterwards might have brought out a much larger vote. Unjust apportionment, insufficient polling places, tampering with ballots, and numerous protests and challenges in the Assembly when the voting news arrived at the colonial capital were all means for controlling or blunting unfavorable results. With the growth of population and its expansion westward after the Revolution, the possibilities of a genuine restriction in law and fact of a potentially larger electorate cannot be ignored.

Even before American independence, however, election districts were large, and means of communication inadequate. The older settled regions, particularly the towns, often refused to apportion representation in elective bodies on the basis of population. In Virginia throughout the colonial period, control rested with the tidewater aristocracy rather than the small farmer class. Similarly, in Pennsylvania the three eastern counties elected twenty-four of the thirty-six representatives to the colonial assembly, with the result that a Quaker merchant oligarchy usually dominated the German and Scotch-Irish farmers of the other counties.

These elite leaders of the colonies were the men who were called upon in 1776 to decide finally whether to stay under English rule or

gamble ousting the royal party from their governments without opening the door to the direct rule of "the people" and their leaders. A
struggle among Americans for the control of American political
life was to be one of the momentous results of the decision taken
on July 4, 1776.

Paying for Empire and Making Empire Pay

The men who controlled colonial politics were called upon to
make clear their own grievances and the complaints of their people
against English imperial controls. England's administration of the colonial economy was intended to fill the needs of a mercantilist empire.
A state, to be wealthy, independent, and powerful, had to possess a
large and permanent stock of gold and silver. As England lacked rich
deposits of precious metals, it had either to seek mines in other parts
of the world or to build up its stock of gold and silver by favorable
trade balances. To help assure an excess of exports over imports, the
state had to protect and aid home agriculture, encourage the production of raw materials for home manufacture, protect and stimulate
home industry, encourage native shipping in every possible way, and
provide an efficient navy. The English colonies were for all these purposes a special blessing. They supplied the mother country with the
necessary raw materials it did not produce, furnished a market for
home manufactures, afforded home merchants and shipowners a means
of additional profits, and directly or indirectly added to the wealth of
the nation by increasing its specie supply.

England first endeavored to regulate colonial trade by a series of
laws and ordinances. Among the most important of these regulatory
measures were the so-called Navigation Acts, which began to be applied to the colonies soon after the importation of tobacco began. In
the days of Cromwell, when England and Holland were engaged in a
struggle for the commercial supremacy of the seas, more drastic and
sweeping legislation was enacted. In 1650, the bulk of the British colonial trade was in the hands of the Dutch. Parliament, therefore, forbade foreign vessels "to come to, or Trade in, or Traffique with" any
of the English colonies in America unless licensed by Parliament or by
the Council of State. At the same time, the colonies were forbidden to
have "any manner of Commerce or Traffique with any people whatsoever." In short, the colonies were to carry on their commerce solely
with England. It did not matter if the Virginia planter could derive
a greater profit by doing business with the Dutch; the interests of the
Empire demanded the elimination of foreign competition and an Eng-

lish monopoly of the Empire's shipping. This measure was followed the next year by the Navigation Act of 1651, which provided that all goods grown or manufactured in Asia, Africa, or America and imported into England or its possessions must be brought in English-owned and English-manned ships. European goods could be imported into England or its possessions only in English ships or in vessels belonging to the country where the goods were produced or to which they were usually shipped for re-export. With few exceptions, no foreign goods could be brought into England except from the place of production or from the usual port of shipment. Salted fish, fish oil, or whale fins could not be imported into England unless the fish had been caught by English vessels; no fish could be exported from England or its possessions except in English ships; and the English coastal trade was closed to foreign vessels.

The acts of 1650 and 1651, although only partially enforced (because there were too few English ships to carry goods), did cause some complaint in the colonies. Virginia planters asserted that the measures worked great hardship and that they had been passed because of "the Avarice of a few interested persons, who endeavor to rob us of all we sweat and labour for." Even Governor Berkeley declared that those who sponsored the legislation "would faine bring us to the same poverty wherein the Dutch found and relieved us; would take away the liberty of our consciences and tongues, and our right of giving and selling our goods to whom we please." In 1655, the legislature of the colony resolved that "all freedom of trade shall be maintained, and all merchants and traders shall be cherished." Massachusetts condemned the seizure of a Dutch vessel in its waters, and the legislature of Rhode Island went so far as to declare that in times of peace commerce with the Dutch was lawful.

In 1660, the Restoration government passed an "Act for the Encouraging and Increasing of Shipping and Navigation," which stipulated that goods imported into or exported from any British colony must be carried in ships owned and manned by Englishmen. Englishmen were defined as "only his Majesty's subjects of England, Ireland, and the plantations [colonies]." This policy was intended to give English shippers a monopoly of the carrying trade of the Empire and to encourage shipbuilding both in Great Britain and in the colonies. The act also ruled that certain "enumerated" articles—sugar, tobacco, cotton, wool, ginger, indigo, fustic, and other dye woods—grown or manufactured in the colonies could not be sold directly to foreigners, but had first to be sent to England or to some other part of the British domain. This list was subsequently extended: rice, molasses, and the naval stores—tar, pitch, turpentine, hemp, masts, and yards—were added in 1706; copper, ore, beaver, and other skins in 1722; whale fins, raw silks, hides, pot and pearl ashes, pig and bar iron, lumber, coffee, pimento, and coconuts in 1764. Up to 1766, nonenumerated articles, including a number of the more important colonial commodities, such as fish, grain, and rum, could be disposed of directly to any part of the world, unless, of course, their sale in this way was prevented by foreign restrictions. In 1766, although 96 per cent of the volume of colonial trade already went to England first, England forbade the shipment of any colonial goods to any foreign country north of Cape Finisterre. By requiring the colonists to sell enumerated commodities only within the Empire, England sought to supply her manufacturers with needed raw materials, to enable the home merchants to obtain a profit as middlemen or distributors, to increase her revenue (since all goods imported from the colonies were, as a rule, like goods from foreign countries, subject to heavy duties), and to provide more business for the English merchant marine.

The act of 1660 did not prevent the colonists from evading the English tariff by importing directly from foreign countries. Articles manufactured in Holland or in France, for instance, might be brought directly to Virginia or Massachusetts in English ships and sold at a lower price than like goods of English manufacture. English merchants, unless they owned the ship, derived no profit from such transactions. To remedy this situation and to keep the colonies "in a firmer dependence upon it [England] and rendering them yet more beneficial and advantageous unto it," Parliament in 1663 provided that all European goods bound for the colonies must first be sent to England and from there reshipped in English ships to colonial ports. The only exceptions to this rule were salt from Spain for the New England fisheries, wines from Madeira and the Azores, and a few commodities from Ireland and Scotland. This act enabled the English merchants to collect profitable commissions on all European goods consumed in the colonies. At the same time, by bringing the colonies within the English tariff system, it provided a means for increasing the revenue of the home government.

Like their predecessors, the acts of 1660 and 1663 roused opposition in the colonies. Before 1673, colonial merchants managed to send enumerated articles direct to Europe without landing them in England, under the pretense that they were destined for some other part of the Empire. In that year, however, Parliament endeavored to put an end to this practice by providing that every vessel leaving the colonies and carrying enumerated articles must give a bond that it would land the articles in England or else pay the equivalent of the import tax levied on such articles by the home country. It also authorized the appointment of colonial customs collectors to supervise and enforce the act. But these officials made little headway, for evasions continued at an increasing rate, and some of the colonists even went so far as to dispatch their commodities directly to Europe through privateers and pirates. Both corruption and inefficiency thus worked on behalf of colonial freedom.

Businessmen in England, who understandably objected to these infractions, repeatedly demanded that the Navigation Acts be more strictly enforced. In 1695, merchants of Bristol, Liverpool, and London petitioned the House of Commons for action. These complaints, the growing realization that England had gained an empire which now had to be put in order, the inefficiency of the old supervising agencies, and the energy of King William III and his ministers brought a turning point in imperial administration. In 1696, the Board of Trade was established with a new fullness of powers. With it came an act "for preventing Frauds and regulating Abuses in the Plantation Trade." This act affirmed and clarified the earlier Navigation Laws. It provided that all English vessels, whether owned in England or in the colonies, must be registered; that all colonial laws at variance with the Acts of Trade were null and void; and that all colonial governors must take an oath to enforce the Navigation Acts or suffer penalty of fine and loss of office. It also authorized collectors and inspectors to visit and search ships, wharves, and warehouses, and to seize unlawful merchandise. Furthermore, cases involving penalties could now be brought before colonial admiralty courts. Up to this time, it had been almost impossible to secure convictions in revenue cases from colonial juries. For a few years after its passage, the act of 1696 was fairly effective, and by 1701 the balance of trade, long in favor of the mainland colonies, stood in favor of England.

After 1696, two important trends mark the laws regulating trade. A slow shift from royal to parliamentary supervision took place as George I and George II increasingly let policy fall into the hands of parliamentary leaders. Between 1696 and 1763, when a comprehensive policy for the empire was again attempted, the history of regulation is primarily the story of many new specific prohibitions and adjustments. For example, Georgia and South Carolina were permitted to ship rice directly to Mediterranean countries in 1730, and the bounties paid for naval stores were raised and lowered several times.

Of these various trade regulations few, if any, proved more objectionable to the colonists than the Molasses Act of 1733. The northern colonies, unable for the most part to sell their surplus products in

England, turned to other markets—particularly to the French possessions in the West Indies, where they readily exchanged their provisions,
horses, cattle, timber products, and cargoes of African slaves for rum,
sugar, molasses, and money or bills of exchange. By far the greater part
of this West Indian trade was carried on with the French, who were
able to undersell the British from 25 to 50 per cent. In addition to this
competition, the English West Indian planters were injured by the
"enumeration" of sugar. The home country was unable to consume
the entire sugar crop or to market the surplus profitably; still, by law,
the sugar had to go first to England. The planters sought relief, and in
1730 and 1731 they petitioned the Privy Council to prohibit trade with
the French islands. Failing to gain assistance, they carried their petition
to Parliament, where it was debated at length. Spokesmen for the
northern colonies pointed out that any interference with the West Indian trade would paralyze the commercial provinces. This trade, as we
have seen, enabled them to profit from their fisheries, forests, and farm
crops, and, above all, to secure the necessary hard money with which to
satisfy their English creditors. On the other hand, absentee planters,
who were members of Parliament and were backed by a powerful
lobby, relentlessly pressed their case. Many persons both in and out of
Parliament asserted that, although the dispute grew out of a clash of
interests within the Empire, it was in reality part of the greater contest
between France and England for commercial supremacy. They argued
also that the northern colonists, though promoting their own interests,
were violating the idea of imperial self-sufficiency by enriching foreign
sugar colonies and impoverishing those of their own empire. It was
on this broader political ground that the matter was in large measure
decided. In its final form the act passed was restrictive rather than prohibitory. It imposed a duty of 9*d.* a gallon on rum, 6*d.* a gallon on
molasses, and 5*s.* a hundredweight on sugar imported from non-English
West Indies.

The argument that the act was aimed primarily at France failed to
impress the commercial provinces. In both New England and the middle colonies, merchants and distillers regarded the act as a piece of class
legislation that would enable "a few pamper'd Creolians" to "roll in
their gilded equipages through the streets" of London at the expense
of two million American subjects. But England was without adequate
customs service to enforce the law, and, as many had anticipated, it
was frequently ignored. Even though it was evaded, however, the law
was not without effect. Because it failed to take account of what the
colonists regarded as their right to develop the natural resources of
their country and to utilize them as they saw fit, it constituted a per-

Anno sexto

Georgii II. Regis.

An Act for the better securing and encouraging the Trade of His Majesty's Sugar Colonies in *America*.

WHEREAS the Welfare and Prosperity of Your Majesty's Sugar Colonies in America are of the greatest Consequence and Importance to the Trade, Navigation, and Strength of this Kingdom : And whereas the Planters of the said Sugar Colonies have of late Years fallen under such great Discouragements, that they are unable to improve or carry on the Sugar Trade upon an equal Footing with the foreign Sugar Colonies, without some Advantage and Relief be given to them from Great Britain : For Remedy whereof, and for the Good and Welfare of Your Majesty's Subjects, we Your Majesty's most dutiful and loyal Subjects, the Commons of Great Britain assembled in Parliament, have given and granted unto Your Majesty the several and respective Rates and Duties herein after mentioned, and in such Manner and Form, as is herein after expressed; and do most humbly beseech Your Majesty that it may be enacted,

Bbbb2

First Page of the Molasses Act, 1733

petual grievance against England; it irritated the colonists to have their interests subordinated to those of a small coterie of West Indian sugar planters.

The extent of colonial smuggling to evade the Molasses Act should not be exaggerated. The colonists who evaded the law comprised only a small percentage of the population. Merchants who carried on a legitimate trade within the Empire could often accumulate large fortunes, and recent studies indicate that the legitimate traders outnumbered the smugglers.

Controlling Colonial Industries

The growing diversity of business in America created rivalries between English and colonial industries. During the seventeenth century and the earlier part of the eighteenth, conditions in the colonies discouraged industrial enterprises. The person who wanted to engage in manufacturing on any considerable scale was handicapped by lack of capital, an unstable currency, and an inadequate labor supply. In spite of these obstacles, many lines of manufacture appeared in New England and the middle colonies. Because the development of these rival industries in the colonies lessened the market for English manufactures, the English merchant and the manufacturer turned to Parliament for protection. Many of the specific prohibitions passed by Parliament after 1696 were, in part, answers to the complaints of English producers.

The passage of the Woolens Act in 1699 marked the first important step in restraint on colonial manufactures. At the time it was passed, all the northern colonies were producing considerable quantities of woolen goods on a small scale. Massachusetts supplied a large part of its own needs and even exported woolen goods to other colonies. The English woolen manufacturer naturally opposed this colonial enterprise because every skein of woolen yarn and every yard of woolen cloth produced in America limited his market. The landed groups in England that produced the raw wool, the persons who fabricated it, and the merchants who handled the finished product, all supported the manufacturers in their contention that an industry affecting more than a million Englishmen and accounting for nearly half of all exports should not be endangered by rivals in some other part of the Empire. The act of 1699 provided, under heavy penalty, that no woolen goods of any description could be sent from one colony to another or from any colony to a foreign country. This act, however, had more effect on Ireland than on the colonies. The law was not prohibitory, for any colony could still manufacture for consumption within its borders.

A second law restricting colonial manufactures was enacted in 1732. Favored by an abundance of beaver and unhampered by government regulations, New Yorkers and New Englanders had for several years been manufacturing beaver hats in increasing quantities. Because of their peculiar advantages, they were often able to undersell the British manufacturer not only in the colonies but in foreign lands, particularly Spain and the West Indies. The home interests complained about this competition and in 1731 asked the Board of Trade to suppress the manufacture of hats in the colonies. A parliamentary inquiry, disclosing the fact that New York and New England were turning out 10,000 hats annually, resulted in legislation. The Hat Act of 1732 provided that no American-made hat could be exported from one colony to another, or from the colonies to England and Europe. No master could have more than two apprentices, and each had to serve for not less than seven years. No one could engage in the manufacture of felt hats unless he had served a seven-year apprenticeship. The act also forbade the employment of Negroes in this industry. These labor restrictions were intended to cut down the work force available to colonial producers.

A series of laws were applied to the iron industry. England was anxious to obtain from the colonists additional bar and pig iron, but she wished to monopolize the manufacture of finished iron products. As early as 1719, a bill was introduced in Parliament prohibiting the manufacture in America of hollow ware and castings and the erection of forges for refining iron. Twenty years later, pressure on Parliament was renewed, but the desired legislation was not enacted until 1750, when a law was passed providing that bar and pig iron should be admitted to Great Britain duty free, but absolutely prohibiting, under penalty of £200, the erection in the colonies of slitting or rolling mills, plating forges, or steel furnaces. Such establishments already in operation were allowed to continue. British iron interests, which were chiefly responsible for the passage of this law, intended that the colonial ironmasters should furnish them with raw material, but should not compete with them by manufacturing bar and pig iron into tools and hardware.

Just as the English depended on the colonists for raw iron, so did they want a large lumber supply for their needs as a seafaring nation. England had always depended upon the forests of New England for masts for the royal navy, and at an early date it had taken steps to reserve the larger trees for that purpose. The last clause of the new charter granted Massachusetts in 1691 reserved for the Crown all trees not growing on private lands that were more than twenty-four inches in diameter at the base. About a decade later, a parliamentary statute provided a penalty of £15 for the felling of such trees anywhere in the colonies of New York, New Jersey, and New England. In 1711, the penalty was raised to £100, and surveyors of the "King's Woods" were appointed to mark suitable trees with a broad arrow signifying that they were reserved for the use of the navy. Still later, Parliament ruled that no white pine trees outside the bounds of a township should be cut without a royal license. Evasion of this statute led Parliament in 1729 to enact that no white pine trees might be felled unless they were on the property of private persons.

Because lumbering was one of the most important part-time and full-time colonial industries, these restrictive measures and the unpopular officials who endeavored to enforce them created perennial friction. Colonial lumber interests constantly broke the laws by cutting forest giants reserved for masts and sawing them into planks or splitting them into shingles. Arrests were made, but convictions were impossible, for judge and jury alike were on the side of the lawbreakers. In 1720, the Massachusetts assembly advanced the claim that the timber described as belonging to the Crown was royal property only while standing and that as soon as it was cut it belonged to the colony. The Lords of Trade labeled this fantastic doctrine a "scandalous evasion" of the law. Colonial land speculators joined lumbermen in defying the restraints, and some even declared that Parliament had no right to infringe the economic liberties of the colonies.

Regulating the Land and Money Markets

As soon as land became a marketable commodity in America, the very size of the domain and the inadequacy of governmental power effectively to regulate its sale spelled trouble. Frequent controversy over land titles and quitrents was a constant source of friction among the colonists and between the colonies and England. Opportunity to acquire land had attracted many settlers to America, and they and their descendants vigorously resisted every move that threatened their ownership. In New England during the administration of Governor Andros (1684–89), popular feeling was aroused when the home authorities questioned the validity of all land titles on the ground that the original colonizing companies had had no power to make grants to the towns and that the towns in turn had been powerless to grant land to individuals. Andros was instructed to grant all lands "yet undisposed of" in return for a minimal quitrent for every hundred acres. Although the quitrent was small and Andros was cautioned not to molest any man's "Freehold or Goods," this move was bitterly resented by the colonists as unjust meddling. Outside of New England, attempts to alter land titles in favor of home interests or to levy and collect quitrents also met with opposition. The intense competition for land among English and colonial land agents, the squatters, new legal settlers, and the original Indian owners slowly built up an impenetrable maze of conflicting interests that not even the most gifted statesmanship (had it existed) could have put right. When England tried to bring reason to bear on the western land question in 1763, inevitably she had to offend many colonists deeply.

A similar difficulty developed over the colonial currency policy. During the first quarter of the eighteenth century, British merchants repeatedly informed Parliament that many colonies had enacted laws that favored colonial creditors but seriously impeded British creditors in collecting debts lawfully due them. In asking for redress, they characterized the discriminatory legislation as "bare-faced fraud." As a result, Parliament in 1732 provided that the affidavit of a resident in Great Britain should have the same weight as evidence given in open court in the colonies. Lands, tenements, and slaves owned by the colonists were made liable for debts in much the same way as was real estate in England. Spokesmen for the unthrifty and less fortunate colonists upon whom this regulation weighed most heavily condemned it on the ground that Parliament was interfering with the internal affairs of the colonies. They presumed that home rule on the debt question would mean less pressure to pay their debts.

Hard pressed constantly for a circulating medium, all the colonies, with the exception of North Carolina, turned to paper money. During the decade 1730–40, several colonial governments, particularly those of New England, added large quantities of paper currency to the amount already in circulation. They also formed "banks." As early as 1722, Pennsylvania had established a loan office that issued and loaned small bills secured by land of double the value. "The poor middling people who had any land or houses to pledge," observed Sir William Keith, "borrowed from the loan-office and paid off their usurious creditors. The few rich men who had before this given over all trade, except that of usury, were obliged to build ships and launch out again into trade." In 1732, the New London Society United for Trade and Commerce was started in Connecticut. It had a short and stormy career but in many respects served as the model for the more famous Land Bank of Massachusetts, founded in 1740.

The Massachusetts assembly requested proposals for supplying the colony with "more money" and "an additional medium of trade." The resulting "bank," which had no capital stock, planned to issue £150,000 in paper money notes to be secured by land. Those not owning land were to be allowed to secure loans of not more than £100 on personal security, provided that they had proper sureties. The notes, which were not to be redeemed for twenty years, might be paid off in commodities.

This credit scheme and the demand for paper money had the almost solid backing of the debtors among all groups who believed that land banks and cheap money would remedy their economic ills. The creditors—for the most part moneylenders, merchants, manufacturers, and their lawyer-allies—opposed the issue of paper money when such issues made it possible to scale down the value of debts. These groups, although creditors within the colony, were often in debt to the English. Having to receive hard money to pay overseas obligations in the specie that was demanded in England, they had to fight the debtor banks at every turn, for rival banks and increasing issues of paper currency meant competition, inflation, and possible ruin. In Massachusetts creditors endeavored to counter the Land Bank by setting up a bank of their own, known as the Silver Bank, which issued notes based on silver; similar action took place in Rhode Island and New Hampshire. Some creditors, however, wanted only to profit from the banking business itself. They tried to induce the Massachusetts assembly to veto the Land Bank plan, but that body, dominated by a majority of small and large debtors, refused. The Governor, loyal to the King, then issued a proclamation cautioning all persons not to use the Land Bank notes, on the ground that they tended "to defraud men, to disturb the peace, and to injure trade." Shortly afterward an address signed by 130 prominent merchants of the colony warned the public to have nothing to do with the scheme.

Entreaties and warnings had no effect, and the Privy Council was forced to intervene. All persons were forbidden to pass Land Bank bills. Certain classes of officials found guilty of doing so were threatened with removal; military officers were forced to ascertain whether their subordinates had passed the bills; and registrars of deeds were ordered to return all Land Bank mortgages. Despite these edicts, the Land Bank bills continued to circulate. Finally, in 1741, Parliament suppressed the institution. Following the destruction of the Bank, and responding to complaints of the English merchants "that many fair creditors and other persons not in debt lost half or three-fourths of what was due to them, and of their personal estate" because of the issues of paper money by New England, Parliament passed an act in 1751 forbidding the New England governments to issue any additional legal-tender bills of credit. In 1764, Parliament forbade the use of legal-tender paper money in all the colonies on the theory that it was "false in its principles, unjust in its foundations, and manifestly fraudulent in its operations."

Many colonial business interests approved the action of the home government, but the more numerous debtors condemned it. The Land Bank had had the support of nearly two thirds of the Massachusetts assembly, and John Adams, writing in 1774, thought that its suppression was more important than the Stamp Act in "creating ferment" and rousing opposition in Massachusetts to British authority. Benjamin Franklin in 1766 informed British leaders that one of the principal reasons for American ill-feeling toward England was the prohibition of paper money.

Regulation and Revolution

What was the total effect of English restrictions on the Colonial economy? At every point, inefficiency, corruption, the ease of lawbreaking, and friendly officials helped the colonists. Over all, the colonial economy grew. By the eve of the American Revolution, the requirement to ship via English ports and to pay the vexatious numerous extra costs did prevent a favorable general balance of trade for the colonists. Even so, in analyzing the colonial response, it is most important to know exactly what groups suffered from English regulations or profited by the "salutary neglect" of enforcement of the laws on the books. The colonists objected to all restrictive enactments and repeatedly asserted that it was their right to engage in any sort of industry and to trade with whom they wished. But they usually forgot that the mother country also did much to promote the well-being of the colonies. She gave them preferential customs rates, so that the rates on colonial tobacco, for example, were much less than those on Spanish tobacco. Similarly, the rates on colonial indigo, iron, whale oil, hemp, lumber, silk, ginger, pot and pearl ashes, and molasses were less than those on similar nonimperial commodities. England, it may be argued, adopted this preferential system because she needed these products; nevertheless, these particular commodities enjoyed a special advantage in the British market.

The duty on many commodities exported to the colonies by way of England was refunded in part or entirely, so the colonists could buy some goods—Dutch linens, for instance—more cheaply than such goods

"The Colonies Reduced"

could be purchased in England. These refunds, or drawbacks, were
not, however, granted to everyone. Bounties and other financial inducements encouraged colonial production of certain commodities.
Parliament in 1705 passed a measure granting bounties on naval stores
imported from the colonies— £4 a ton on pitch and tar, £6 a ton on
hemp, £3 a ton on rosin and turpentine, and £1 a ton on masts, yards,
and bowsprits. Increased production and a rapid decline in the price of
these commodities, however, led to a considerable reduction of the
bounties during the reign of George II. To free England from
dependence on French indigo, a bounty of 6*d*. a pound on indigo imported directly into England from her overseas possessions was provided in 1748. Parliament also helped colonial tobacco growers by
prohibiting tobacco growing in England and Ireland. As part of the
British Empire, the colonies also enjoyed military and naval protection,
free or privileged trade with other parts of the Empire, and the benefit
of Great Britain's commercial treaties.

There can be no doubt that psychologically English regulation was
generally detrimental to good feelings between colonies and mother
country. But bad feelings do not always lead to effective political action or vigorous protest, and even less often do they result in revolutionary war. The question of the great break with England turns not
so much on the balance of discontents over feelings of amity but on
how the discontents led to the famous solemn declaration of "the Rep-

resentatives of the United States of America, in General Congress Assembled."

FOR SUPPLEMENTARY READING

J. H. Plumb, *The First Four Georges* (1956), is an ideal introductory summary of recent scholarship on eighteenth-century English politics. Despite its age, O. M. Dickerson, *American Colonial Government 1696–1765* (1912), is still reliable and first-rate, as are L. W. Larabee, *Royal Government in America* (1930), and C. M. Andrews, *Colonial Self Government* (1904). H. L. Osgood, *The American Colonies in the Seventeenth Century* (3 vols., 1904–07), and Edward Channing, *A History of the United States* (6 vols., 1905–25), are still good places for details on political life in the colonies before 1763. They should be supplemented, however, by the following newer studies: C. S. Grant, *Democracy in the Connecticut Frontier Town of Kent* (1961); C. S. Sydnor, *Gentlemen Freeholders: Political Practices in Washington's Virginia* (1952); R. E. Brown, *Middle Class Democracy and the Revolution in Massachusetts 1691–1780* (1955); R. E. and K. Brown, *Virginia, 1705–1786: Aristocracy or Democracy?* (1964); Theodore Thayer, *Pennsylvania Politics and the Growth of Democracy 1740–1766* (1953); W. E. Washburn, *The Governor and the Rebel* (1957); C. P. Nettels, *The Roots of American Civilization;* C. M. Andrews, *Colonial Period of American History* (1938); O. M. Dickerson, *The Navigation Acts and the American Revolution* (1951); L. H. Gipson, *The British Empire before the American Revolution* (12 vols. to date); and G. L. Beer, *The Old Colonial System 1660–1754* (1912). All are pertinent to the subject of imperial regulation. The inescapable world setting of colonial affairs is underscored by H. Peckham, *The Colonial Wars 1689–1762* (1964).

6

The Conflict
of Interests

D ESPITE maladministration, inefficiency, and neglect, for more than a century the British Empire in America both survived and expanded; but in 1776, with the outbreak of the Revolution, the inadequacies of the British colonial system were fully revealed. It is often easier to state what did not cause the American Revolution than to ascertain what did. It was not caused by a "wicked, stubborn, German King," George III; by "taxation without representation"; or by the righteousness of the colonists and the wickedness of their rulers. Its origins were both more prosaic and more deep-seated than any of these. Ignorance and misunderstanding, opposing ideals and conflicting interests, stubborn pride and hasty willfulness all played their part.

Two Ways of Life

By 1750, the British colonists in North America had developed a way of life that they sensed set them apart from Great Britain in many ways. Separated from England by three thousand miles and conditioned by an environment unknown to Englishmen at home, they had been forced by circumstances to modify the institutions of the Old World. The colonists were Englishmen, but they were Englishmen whose attitudes and behavior often little resembled those of their countrymen on the other side of the Atlantic Ocean. In the words of St.

Jean de Crèvecoeur, a Frenchman who had settled in the colonies, the American was a "new man." Writing during the American Revolution, Crèvecoeur asked: "What, then, is the American, this new man?" And his answer was:

> He is an American, who leaving behind him all his ancient prejudices and manners, receives new ones from the new mode of life he has embraced. . . . Americans are the western pilgrims. . . . The American is a new man, who acts upon new principles; he must therefore entertain new ideas, and form new opinions. From involuntary idleness, servile dependence, penury, and useless labor, he has passed to toils of a very different nature, rewarded by ample subsistence.—This is an American.

Many Englishmen regarded the colonists as socially inferior, frequently snubbing them and often referring to them harshly. A London pamphleteer wrote that the English ministry might well dub the Americans "a race of dastardly cowards, sprung from our bastards, our swindlers, and our convicts." Bostonians were characterized as "people of coarse, insolent manners" and New Englanders in general as little short of slaves, the only difference being "that they were not bought and sold." General Wolfe, the hero of Quebec, declared that the Americans "are in general the dirtiest, most contemptible, cowardly dogs that you can conceive." Some Englishmen seemed to take pleasure in constantly stressing the poverty of the colonists and ridiculing their dress, manners, speech, and customs.

The British by no means monopolized such invective. Many colonists thought and spoke of England as a den of iniquity given over to every debasing luxury and dissipation. Henry Laurens and other Americans who had visited eighteenth-century England were astonished at the frivolity and immorality of the ruling class. "Chastity," wrote Laurens in 1772, "is certainly out of fashion in England." Such characterizations did not breed a sense of common destiny. Loose talk and flippant generalizations about their separate heritage and their mode of life, whether true or not, embittered the colonists and aroused a rebellious spirit. Those familiar with conditions in London wondered whether the colonists ought to obey a government controlled by "licentious and unprincipled men."

Intellectually, eighteenth-century America was still a pioneer community, largely provincial in outlook, and out of close touch with the Old World. America supported only a few men of leisure and produced little architecture or painting that could compare with that of the English. No great cathedrals, ancient universities, or palaces graced its landscape. It had no rivals for Gainsborough, Romney, or Reynolds. It lacked all the elements of a splendid civilization. Only in acquaintance with political literature were some colonists on a par with the English. Their general failings in intellectual attainment, like the social differences, were constantly emphasized.

The numerous differences between the colonists and England were aggravated by repeated misunderstandings and conflicts that arose over the government and administration of the colonies. By the middle of the eighteenth century, each colonial assembly was a miniature House of Commons, claiming and exercising the right to levy and collect taxes, borrow money, raise troops, regulate trade with the Indians, issue currency, fix the salaries of government officials, and appoint agents to represent the colony in its dealings with England. These assemblies were not interested in promoting the interests of England or of her appointed colonial officials. The assemblies' efforts centered on their own ends and ambitions, and on the interests of those who elected them. The royal governor, on the other hand, was not chiefly concerned with the liberties of the colonists. Sent to protect imperial interests, anxious to enlarge his own private fortune or to secure a lucrative post for some dependent relative or friend, he regarded the colonial assembly as a troublesome barrier.

In their attempts to check or limit royal authority, the colonists buttressed their position with constitutional theories borrowed from England and reshaped to meet their particular needs. The example of the House of Commons was always before them, and on frequent occasions royal governors had to listen to the same arguments used by parliamentary leaders in their conflicts with the king. The colonists argued that their charters, tradition, and God had given them rights that the English were violating. Andrew C. McLaughlin, the eminent constitutional historian, has stated that there is considerable evidence to support the conclusion that with the colonial protests "the England of the seventeenth century arose to combat the England of the eighteenth; . . . and that America separated from Britain in the seventeenth century rather than in the second half" of the eighteenth century.* The Englishmen in the mother country, having imposed strong constitutional limits on the monarchy, were in a position to forget—or, at least, to ignore—the principles that they had championed at an earlier period; but to Americans these same principles seemed altogether relevant to their own situation. The colonists believed that they were

---

* Andrew C. McLaughlin: *A Constitutional History of the United States* (New York: D. Appleton-Century Company, Inc., 1935), p. 91.

asking officials in England to be nothing more than consistent—to grant to Americans those same limits on royal rule that they had once gained for themselves.

John Locke, in his *Two Treatises concerning Government* (1690), had written a very famous English defense of popular rights, and they seemed to have been vindicated in the English Revolution of 1688-9. But his work, like that of many other English political philosophers of his day, also provided the colonists with a theory of government that they thought both to describe and solve their problems. Maintaining that every human being possessed the natural rights of life, liberty, and property, Locke declared that a people created government to safeguard these rights. But if a government failed to preserve such rights—if the rulers failed to abide by the contract made between them and the people when the government was created—then the people had the right to supplant the government with one that would protect these rights and observe the contract. So long as a majority of the people supported a government, whether by king or parliament, it was entitled to obedience. Locke had thus advanced ideas with which educated Englishmen had become acquainted during the seventeenth century; to the later colonists, he was writing, not about theories, but about facts. When Americans quoted Locke before the Revolution, they accepted him primarily as an authority who had codified certain obvious and eternal political truths and not as a writer of a program for a glorious republican future.

The concept of natural rights and the theory of government by compact were very familiar in colonial America in the eighteenth century. They had been spread by newspapers, pulpit, and books. Locke's writings could be found in the personal libraries of many educated Americans, and his ideas were discussed not only in legislative chambers, but also in churches, drawing rooms, and taverns. When James Otis in 1761 defended the Boston merchants against general search warrants, he did not maintain that his clients were innocent, but that the law in question violated certain fundamental rights that all Englishmen enjoyed. Patrick Henry used the same reasoning in a case concerning the disallowance of a Virginia statute by the Privy Council. Arguing that with the disallowance the Privy Council had broken the compact that bound colony and mother country, he concluded that act of tyranny had deprived Virginians of their basic rights as Englishmen. To Henry, government was "a conditional compact between king and people," and "a violation of the covenant by either party discharges the other from obligation." It would be a mistake to assume that Otis, Henry, or many others used Locke's ideas only as a device for concealing and dignifying their ulterior motives. Genuine constitutional issues were involved, and if Locke had never existed, the colonists would have been compelled to invent him.

Religious differences also widened the gulf that separated the colonies from Great Britain in the eighteenth century. John Adams asserted that the religious question served "as much as any other cause to arouse the attention, not only of the inquiring mind, but of the common people, and urge them to close thinking on the constitutional authority of parliament over the colonies." Apprehension was aroused by the repeated attempt to spread the Anglican faith in the colonies at the expense of the Presbyterians, Quakers, and other groups, and by the scheme to establish an Anglican episcopate in America.

In the South and in three New York counties, Anglicanism was legally established. Naturally, some Anglican leaders hoped for a time when it would be the dominant faith in all the colonies. Not all American Anglicans, however, were happy with the thought that their religious life would be controlled by a bishop appointed by the king, for whose support they would have to be taxed. The Anglican churches in America without their own bishops were relatively free to go their own way. The dissenting Protestant groups were well aware of the hope of some Anglicans for the triumph of their church in America. In 1763, the famous Massachusetts preacher Jonathan Mayhew launched a bitter attack against the Anglican Society for the Propagation of the Gospel in Foreign Parts on the ground that it was trying to "root out Presbyterianism." This opinion, widespread among the Dissenters in the North, was strengthened by recurrent rumors that an episcopate was to be founded in the colonies. After 1750, opposition to the plan was universal outside the Anglican Church. New England Congregationalists declared that with its establishment the colonies would be deluged in a flood of episcopacy and victimized by "right reverend and holy tyrants." An American bishopric, they warned, would mean additional taxes, priest-controlled courts, and the assumption of secular functions by episcopal authorities. Discord and apprehension were bound to develop when Dissenters labeled all officials appointed by the British government as "ruffle-shirted Episcopalians" and tools and allies of "tyrannical monarchialism," and when Anglicans replied in turn that all Dissenters were steeped in "republican principles." Nearly a century and a half after the great religious fight in England between Anglicans and Puritans the religious issue still smouldered.

The dissenting clergy exerted a tremendous influence upon the political ideals of the people. Year after year, especially at election time, Presbyterian and Congregational preachers directly or indirectly advocated the ideas of Locke. In their sermons they analyzed the origin and nature of government and asserted that people had a right to rebel against a government that took their money or property without their consent. A Presbyterian minister taught the young Patrick Henry that the British Constitution was "but the voluntary compact of sovereign and subject." Preachers like him and ideas like his were typical of every Calvinistic community and many anti-bishop Anglican areas. The sermons, usually printed in pamphlet form, were virtually political textbooks. At the meetings called to protest against various British measures, the preacher, mingling freely with lawyer and mechanic, had real influence in building resistance to the British authorities.

Reorganization and Reform

For more than a century, the English had allowed the colonies to drift. They had not enforced laws affecting the colonies, and overlapping agencies had worked at cross purposes. By 1750, a number of English statesmen who were critical of this inefficient system were proposing a series of administrative reforms for British North America. The plans they advanced eventually became the official policy of the British government. They called for centralized control of the trans-Allegheny region, a closer association of the colonies for administrative purposes, the imposition of a greater share of the expenses of colonial defense and administration upon the colonists, and the enforcement of the mercantilist system.

The home authorities were particularly alarmed at growing Indian hostility in the West. Unscrupulous traders and eager landgrabbers repeatedly cheated the natives. The lands of the Indians had been stolen, their children kidnapped, and their hunting grounds destroyed. Time after time their spokesmen had pleaded in vain with the individual colonies for just treatment. Failing to secure redress, the Indians, hostile enough at all times, were increasingly embittered against the English. Because of the possibility of Indian warfare and of the probable renewal of the long struggle with France, the friendship and support of the Indians, especially of the Iroquois tribes, were vitally important to Britain. She could no longer afford to trust relations with the natives to the colonists. A centralized system of administration that would effectively defend the rights of the Indians and retain their allegiance was therefore planned to replace thirteen separate, selfish, and often conflicting Indian policies.

A second major reason for centralized control of the West was intimately bound up with the first. Both the home authorities and many of the colonists wanted to substitute for chaotic colonial controls over the frontier domain a uniform policy that would eliminate, or at least minimize, the numerous squabbles and hard feelings over the disposition of western lands. To frame such a policy, however, was not easy. In the colonies and in England there were at least two groups whose interests in the problem were diametrically opposed to each other. The opponents of opening the West to settlement included Americans and Englishmen who had invested heavily in lands east of the Alleghenies and who therefore wished to prevent transmontane competition. The Indians and their supporters, who wished to preserve the native hunting grounds from further encroachments, desired to keep the trans-Allegheny country an untenanted wilderness in which the fur-bearing animals and the Indian hunter might continue to thrive and from which England might continue to receive furs. Another group, however, viewed expanding colonies as markets for British manufactured goods. They also envisioned opportunities for speculation in land beyond the Alleghenies and regarded the colonies as a dumping ground for surplus population. This second group wanted the land in the trans-Allegheny region settled as rapidly as possible. The manufacturers would then have more consumers for their products and the speculators more buyers for their land.

The task of devising a land policy that would satisfy these two conflicting groups was probably impossible. The problem was aggravated by the fact that several of the colonies, including Massachusetts, Connecticut, Virginia, the Carolinas, and Georgia, claimed extensive tracts of land beyond the mountains. Many colonists, particularly the Virginians who used profits from land sales to meet their English debts, were aware of the great wealth to be gained from these western lands and were reluctant to accept any plan that would stop or slow the exploitation of the West. On the other hand, the less fortunate colonies pointed out that if the colonies having western territory were allowed to retain it, they would soon overshadow the others in wealth and power. Many English leaders thought that the home government should ignore the original charter grants, carve the western tracts into new colonies, and control the sale of the land so as to provide additional revenue for the imperial treasury.

Many motives prompted British statesmen to advocate a more unified administration of the colonies. All, however, sprang from the conviction that the colonies were no longer isolated units, each with its own peculiar problems, but one continuous settlement confronted with common problems and dangers. The early wilderness barriers that separated one settlement from another had in large measure disappeared. Although the colonists still thought of themselves as Virginians or New Yorkers, many of their problems were strikingly similar. Virginia had an Indian problem, a military problem, a financial problem; but so had each of the other colonies, and often the action of one colony affected all. Many spokesmen on both sides of the Atlantic believed that divided control should be abandoned for concerted action on certain problems. In the 1750's, with the renewal of the struggle with France impending, the argument for this policy gained ground. "The French," wrote Governor Dinwiddie of Virginia, "too justly observe the want of connection in the colonies and from them conclude (as they declare without Reserve) that although we are vastly superior to them in Numbers, yet they can take & secure the Country before we can agree to hinder them."

The agitation for closer association of the colonies culminated in the Albany Congress of 1754, which was attended by twenty-five delegates representing the New England colonies, New York, Pennsylvania, and Maryland. An alliance with the Indians was the primary subject before the Congress, but this problem was inextricably bound up with the deeper question of permanent colonial union. After lengthy discussion, the delegates reached the unanimous conclusion that some form of union was "absolutely necessary for their preservation" and that it could be established only by parliamentary action. There were numerous difficulties, however, and only after extended debate was a plan adopted. Advanced by Benjamin Franklin, it provided for a chief executive (president-general) to be appointed and supported by the Crown and a legislature (grand council) of forty-eight members to be chosen by the several colonial assemblies largely on the basis of population and wealth. The legislature was to exercise general control over Indian affairs, raise and equip a colonial army and navy, erect forts, and make laws and levy taxes necessary for the execution of its policies. All acts of the legislature, however, were to be subject to the veto, first of the president-general and then of the Crown.

Because none of the delegates, with the exception of those from Massachusetts, was empowered to enter into any form of union, the plan was submitted to the respective assemblies. If approved by them, it was to be transmitted to Parliament. But the plan met with a cool reception; the colonial assemblies either rejected it outright or failed to ratify it. Although disappointed, Franklin was not surprised. He wrote:

ALBANY CONGRESS

All the Assemblies in the Colonies have, I suppose, had the Union Plan laid before them, but it is not likely, in my Opinion, that any of them will act upon it so far as to agree to it, or to propose any Amendments to it. Every Body cries, a union is absolutely necessary, but when they come to the Manner and Form of the Union, their weak Noddles are perfectly distracted.

The rejection of the Albany plan revealed that the colonists were politically still particularistic and provincial. Despite the fact that they formed continuous settlements along the Atlantic seaboard and were faced with many common problems, they were narrow in outlook and jealous of their prerogatives. Local pride and local patriotism were strong, and no colony was willing to surrender any part of its power or authority to any other colony or to any central government. All the colonists knew that England was anxious to have them bear a greater portion of the cost of colonial defense, and they feared that the Albany plan would mean not only additional taxation but taxation by an authority other than local legislatures. If they took no steps to assume a greater share of the expense, England would have to continue defending them. In rejecting the Albany plan the colonial assemblies were also undoubtedly influenced by speculators in western land. The records, for example, clearly indicate that the official action of Connecticut was influenced by the stockholders of one of the great land organizations, the Susquehanna Company, which did all within its power to block the plan for union.

Closely bound up with the question of colonial union was the problem of imperial defense. From the outset, the burden of protecting the Empire had been borne primarily by the mother country. The navy was financed entirely by the British taxpayer. During the four years 1708 through 1711, for example, nearly £2,000,000 was added to England's debt for naval protection for the colonies. Theoretically, each colony was supposed to provide for its own military defense except when war disturbed Europe or when the Empire as a whole was endangered. In reality, the mother country was frequently called upon to erect forts and to send arms, ammunition, and troops. The refusal of the colonies to cooperate for defense against the Indians compelled the home authorities to station garrisons in the two most exposed colonies, New York and North Carolina. England was also obliged to spend large sums annually for presents for the Indians in an effort to retain their friendship. By 1750 the national debt stood at approximately

JOIN or DIE

Device Invented by Franklin (1754) Commonly Used as a Newspaper Heading in 1776

£72,500,000, and the English landowner was paying taxes of 6½s. per pound, or about 30 per cent of his income, not including tithes and poor rates; something had to be done to lighten what the British taxpayer considered, not unreasonably, an excessively high tax burden. The logical answer was to require that the colonists contribute more to the cost of imperial defense. There had already been various proposals for a direct parliamentary tax upon the colonists, apart from the impositions under the trade regulations. Sir William Keith, for example, had suggested a stamp tax as early as 1728, but the proposal had been rejected on the ground that the colonies would oppose it. By the middle of the century, however, relief for the English taxpayer by a tax upon the colonies was being widely discussed in both press and pamphlet.

The Crisis in Colonial Administration

The English movements for colonial reform came to a head at the end of the long struggle between France and England for commercial and colonial supremacy. King William's War (1689–97), Queen Anne's War (1701–13), King George's War (1744–8), and the French and Indian War (1756–63) were the colonial parts of a world-wide conflict between the two powers, but they were also struggles for the American fur trade and fisheries, and for the Ohio-Mississippi rivers region. At the conclusion of the French and Indian War (Seven Years' War) the French were finally driven from North America. After the Treaty of Paris in 1763 the English flag floated triumphantly over Canada and the territory east of the Mississippi with the exception of New Orleans. This city, together with Louisiana, France transferred to her ally Spain. Of her former extensive territories in North America, France retained only two small, rocky islands off the coast of Newfoundland. The French colonial empire on the American continent was gone, and Spain was forced to cede Florida to England in exchange for Cuba, which the British had seized during the war.

Although the French and Indian War delayed the inauguration of sweeping changes in colonial policy and worked against those changes made in the 1750's, it also emphasized the need for reform. Because the colonies had refused to accept the Albany plan of union and had failed to take any concerted action for their common defense, England was forced to rely during the war on the old decentralized requisition system. During the first two years of the conflict, the total military expense of the colonies was estimated at £170,000, an amount that Parliament voted to refund "as an Encouragement to exert themselves for the future in their mutual and common Defense." In 1757, England required the colonies to raise, clothe, and pay provincial soldiers, but the home government was to furnish provisions and equipment. The British authorities also suggested that the colonists might be reimbursed for their expenses if they showed the proper vigor in raising troops.

Despite these inducements, the results were far from satisfactory. Only three colonies, Massachusetts, Connecticut, and New York, made anything like the expected contribution. Although these contained only about one third of the colonial white population, they furnished seven tenths of all the colonial troops. Georgia, New Hampshire, and North Carolina were too poor to do much; but Maryland and Pennsylvania, both wealthy and populous, contributed almost nothing. Loudoun, the commander in chief during 1756–57, declared that Rhode Island was unwilling to do its share and that Virginia had failed to furnish its quota. The Maryland assembly refused to let what few troops it did raise serve under Loudoun, who declared that it was "the constant study of every Province here to throw every expence on the Crown, and bear no part of the expence of this War themselves." Often the colonial levies were so late in arriving at the place of assembly that they seriously delayed military operations. General Amherst complained in 1760 that "the Sloth of the Colonies in raising their troops and sending them to their Rendezvous made it impracticable for me to move the Troops on as soon as I could have wished." All in all, the war strengthened the growing conviction of the home authorities that the colonies could not be relied upon to defend themselves, that the system of requisition was inefficient, and that some system of centralized colonial control for purposes of defense was imperative.

The need for reform was further demonstrated by colonial wartime trade with the French. All trade between any part of the Empire and the enemy was prohibited in wartime. But this principle, which had been violated by the colonies during the earlier struggles between England and France, was again ignored during the French and Indian War. The French forces in Canada were supplied with beef, pork, and other provisions from Pennsylvania, New York, and New England. The colonies also traded either directly or indirectly with the French West Indies. Northern shippers, especially Rhode Islanders and Pennsylvanians, operating openly or under thinly veiled disguises, did a flourishing business. As a general rule, their vessels were protected from seizure by licenses granted by French officials, who welcomed the illicit intercourse, or by flag-of-truce passes issued by colonial governors, theoretically for facilitating the exchange of prisoners of war. The flag-of-truce passes were at once in great demand. Governor Denny of Pennsylvania sold them at first in small numbers at high prices. Later, as the number issued increased and their value declined, he resorted to selling blank ones for £20 each. Speculation in flag-of-truce passes became common in port towns. Exactly what portion of the trade with the French was carried on by way of neutral Spanish and Dutch ports is unknown. The records, however, indicate that it was large.

As the war progressed, it became increasingly evident that this illegal trade seriously thwarted the efforts of the British military and naval authorities. By furnishing the French islands with an ample supply of provisions and a market for their produce, the colonial merchants enabled these islands to hold out longer than they otherwise could have; and by draining the colonies of provisions, they forced the British government to send supplies from England to the English armies operating in America. General Crump in his communications with Pitt bitterly denounced this trade, Admiral Cotes called it "iniquitous," and Commodore Moore called those engaged in it "traitors to their country." Pitt himself, in ordering the colonial governors to suppress it, declared that through it the enemy was "principally, if not alone, enabled to sustain and protract this long and expensive war."

The end of the war brought to a head all the important questions of colonial administration. In the Treaty of Paris in 1763, Britain retained Canada and the West, and East and West Florida, in preference to the French sugar-planting island of Guadaloupe and the Spanish island of Puerto Rico. This decision was in part the result of opposition from the British West Indian planters, who feared that additional sugar-producing territory would destroy their monopoly of the home market; but it was also the result of changes taking place in the English economy. England was increasing her manufactures, and the tem-perate zone colonies, with their rapidly expanding population, afforded a better market for manufactured goods than the tropical islands, with their limited population. Finally, the British decision was affected by the desire to end the French menace to the English colonies in North America.

The decision to retain Canada and the West brought with it a number of perplexing administrative problems. What, for instance, should be done with the immense territory beyond the Alleghenies? Should the half dozen seaboard colonies that claimed the region be allowed to administer it as they pleased, or should it be administered by the mother country? Should it be left as a hunting ground for the Indians, as advocated by the influential Hudson's Bay Company and others interested in the development of the fur trade, or should it be opened up to settlement? If it were opened for settlement, should the colonists be left free to derive all the profits from land sales, or should the disposition of the territory be regulated to give land speculators in every part of the Empire an opportunity? How should Canada, with its 80,000 French inhabitants, and Florida, with its Spanish population, be governed? Now that the French had been driven out of Canada, what steps would be necessary to keep the colonies loyal and prevent them from seeking complete independence? William Burke, kinsman of the famous statesman, in opposing the retention of Canada, declared that while it remained in French hands it bound the North American colonies to Great Britain. "A neighbor," said he, "that keeps us in some awe," is not always the worst of neighbors. Great Britain had no adequate colonial machinery to grapple with these problems. To solve them she needed new methods and new policies.

The enormous expense occasioned by the Seven Years' War also emphasized the need for overhauling the British colonial system. The conflict cost England more than £82,000,000, of which £60,000,000 were added to the already existing national debt of about £70,000,000. England was now convinced that a standing army of 10,000 men was needed in America to protect both the old and the recently acquired parts of the Empire. It was estimated that such a force would cost about £300,000 annually, an increase of approximately £220,000 over the prewar period. In addition, about £1,500,000 had to be raised annually for the navy. For England to bear the whole burden of this expense was out of the question. The British landowner was already weighted down with taxes, and the government considered it unwise to shift the added expense to the shoulders of the laboring classes. It therefore turned to the colonies for revenue. The war, it reasoned, had been fought partly for the colonies; the standing army was to protect them against possible French and Indian attacks; and the navy was to be used in part to safeguard their commerce. Many British leaders believed that under the existing system of colonial administration the colonies had demonstrated both their inability and their unwillingness to bear their share of the military burden. Reform was the only alternative.

Lord Grenville's Program for the Empire

The great need for imperial reform was thrust upon a parliament ill suited for serious and principled work. In Parliament, instead of two major parties, Whig and Tory, were some half dozen factions, nearly all of Whig origin (that is, supporters of the principles of constitutional monarchy) and composed of individuals motivated almost entirely by personal ambitions and interests. Of these, the followers of William Pitt and the Old Whigs, made up for the most part of the representatives of some of the former great Whig families, opposed the royal prerogative and stood for mild reform. Lord Hardwicke, the Duke of Newcastle, and the Marquis of Rockingham were prominent figures in the Old Whig group, but its outstanding leader was Edmund Burke.

The Pittites and the Old Whigs were on the whole the factions most sympathetic toward America. Their sharpest opponents were in the Court faction, composed of four allied groups, whose chief spokesmen were the Earl of Bute and Lord North.

George III, who came to the throne in 1760, was primarily concerned with gaining back the powers his predecessors had let slip into the hands of the leaders of Parliament. In fact, George III was a defender of the principles of 1688-89, but after generations of erosion of the king's constitutional privileges his attempt to regain them seemed like illegal usurpation. He had no use for either parties or factions, which he believed were interested in purely selfish ends at variance with his own plans and the welfare of the people. On this point the Pittites and a faction led by Grenville more or less agreed with him, but the feud between the two made it difficult for the King to unite both of them with the Court faction and thus command a safe majority in Parliament. In order to put an end to faction, the king had to work within the existing system, that is, to use factions himself, and this necessity clouded his claim to be above politics. Consequently, throughout the period after 1760 weak coalition ministries, made up of representatives from at least three of the warring factions, were necessary. From the point of view of devising a sane and stable imperial policy, nothing

George III

could have been more disastrous than the combination of headstrong king and strife-ridden Parliament. From the close of the Seven Years' War to the end of the American Revolution, England had four ministries: the Grenville ministry, 1763–65; the Rockingham ministry, 1765–66; the Grafton-Pitt ministry, 1766–70; and the North ministry, 1770–82. All four had to work with a Parliament that represented interests that thought of the colonies as sources of profit, raw materials, markets, and national strength. "For what purpose," asked an English official, "were they suffered to go to that country unless the profits of their labor should return to their masters here. I think the policy of colonization is highly culpable if the advantage of it should not redound to the interests of Great Britain."

When the Grenville ministry came to office in 1763, it set to work to establish unified and efficient control over Britain's newly conquered territory, to readjust and tighten the British trade laws, and to lighten the financial strain on the English taxpayer by raising revenue in the colonies. Even before Grenville became Prime Minister, the problem of the West had become acute. Canada and the Floridas, with their alien populations, had to be provided for. Pioneers from the older, settled colonial regions were staking out claims in the valleys of the Ohio country; and speculative land companies and colony promoters, who before the war had turned their attention to the trans-Allegheny country, were renewing their attempts to obtain grants. In 1763, George Washington and other Virginian soldiers, to whom Governor Dinwiddie promised 200,000 acres "of His Majesty the King of Great Britain's lands on the east side of the River Ohio" in partial compensation for their services, pressed their claims in a petition to the King. In the same year, the Ohio Company, which as early as 1747 had petitioned for 500,000 acres on the upper Ohio, sent a special agent to London to protect its interests; and a new concern, the Mississippi Company—composed of fifty prominent Virginians and Marylanders, including George Washington, the Lees, and the Fitzhughs—memorialized the King for a grant of 2,500,000 acres on the east bank of the Mississippi. In New York, Pennsylvania, and other colonies, there were also speculators who hoped to obtain grants in the great valley territory.

Coupled with the problem of Western settlement was that of Indian policy. The colonies' administration of Indian affairs had been a dismal failure. By 1761, the situation had become so chaotic that the home government took complete charge and appointed two English commissioners to control and supervise all Indian matters; but their task was so great that they had made little headway when the Grenville ministry came into power. English settlers and land speculators continued to steal the Indian's land and to defraud him of his furs. To make matters worse, the British military authorities had abandoned the practice of giving the natives presents of guns and clothing. General Amherst attempted to prevent the Indians from receiving ammunition and rum, but at the same time he approved a plan to supply them with blankets that had been used by smallpox patients. Furthermore, the French fur traders led the Indians to believe that France was about to regain control of the Mississippi Valley. Aroused by these tales, tribes of the Old Northwest, under the leadership of Pontiac and other chiefs, organized a confederacy. By May, 1763, they were on the warpath, and within a few weeks they had captured or destroyed almost every British post west of Niagara. Months of warfare followed, and peace did not begin to be restored until the spring of 1764.

Fortunately for the Grenville ministry, Lord Shelburne, President of the Board of Trade, had already formulated a policy for the West.

This policy with certain modifications constituted the Proclamation of 1763. Boundaries were established for three new mainland Crown colonies—Quebec, East Florida, and West Florida. All other lands "lying to the westward of the sources of the rivers which fall into the sea from the west or the northwest" and not yet acquired from the natives by the British government either by cession or purchase, were "for the present" reserved for Indians. All territory between the crest of the Alleghenies and the Mississippi, from Florida to 50° north latitude, was closed to settlers and land speculators. The sale of Indian lands, except to the Crown, was also prohibited, and all those who had inadvertently settled within the reserved region were ordered to withdraw. No person could carry on trade with the Indians unless he was licensed by the governor or commander in chief of some colony. To obtain this license, the trader had to give bond to observe such regulations as "we shall at any time think fit to . . . direct for the benefit of the said trade." Fugitives from justice taking refuge in the reserved territory were to be apprehended and returned.

As soon as the Proclamation of 1763 was announced, it created conflict. The colonists, not understanding or not choosing to understand that its framers regarded it as a temporary expedient to allay the fears of the Indians, looked upon it as an arbitrary and uncalled for obstacle to their westward expansion. Ambitious pioneers, colony promoters, and speculators were especially vexed. Six of the older colonies questioned the legality of the measure on the ground that it conflicted with their claims to western territory.

The proposals to tighten the British mercantile regulations and to raise revenue in America were closely intertwined. As Chancellor of the Exchequer, Grenville calculated that the colonists ought to be responsible for at least one half of the £300,000 annual estimate for the defense of Britain's American possessions. In part to raise about one third of the £150,000 and in part to make the colonies more useful to England commercially, he suggested that immediate steps be taken for the strict enforcement of the old trade regulations. The Navigation Acts, particularly the Molasses Act of 1733, had been notoriously evaded. Many customs officials in the colonies either turned smugglers themselves or were bribed by smuggling merchants and carriers. The few who conscientiously attempted to perform their duties were either hampered or completely blocked. "If conniving at foreign sugar and molasses, and Portugal wines and fruit," wrote Governor Bernard of Massachusetts in 1764, "is to be reckoned corruption, there was never, I believe, an incorrupt Custom House official in America till within twelve months." The various acts were so laxly enforced that, according to the Board of Trade, the collection of £1,900 a year was costing £7,600. In most colonies smuggling had become respectable.

Parliament received Grenville's proposals favorably and took immediate action. It authorized sending additional revenue cutters to American waters, permitted naval commanders to act as customs officials, enlarged the jurisdiction of courts of admiralty in revenue cases, made colonial governors responsible for the strict enforcement of all trade laws, and allowed the use of "writs of assistance," or general search warrants. It also passed a modified version of the Molasses Act, which was about to expire, and in 1764 it supplemented this with a new measure, the Sugar Act. Imposed for the express purpose of "defraying the necessary expenses of defending, protecting, and securing the British colonies and plantations in America," this new legislation lowered from six to three cents a gallon the duty on foreign molasses brought into the colonies, raised the duty on refined sugars, forbade the importation of foreign rum, and placed a heavy tax on Oriental and French textiles, Portuguese and Spanish wines, coffee, and pimentos, unless these were shipped by way of England. It also provided that, with few exceptions, no drawbacks should be allowed.

Because the prosperity of the northern colonies depended on the foreign molasses trade, the Grenville measures drew bitter protests from colonial businessmen. Massachusetts merchants asserted that enforcement of the Molasses Act would ruin the rum distilleries, fisheries, and slave trade. John Hancock wrote that "the times are very bad," and "will be worse here, in short such is the situation of things here that we do not know who is and who is not safe." Rhode Island and Connecticut merchants were equally discouraged and apprehensive. Leading citizens of New York complained about the restrictions and the dwindling trade. Clement Biddle of Philadelphia declared that "the restrictions we are lay'd under by the Parliament puts us at a stand how to employ our vessels to any advantage, as we have no prospects of markets at our own islands and cannot send elsewhere to have anything that will answer in return." Merchant organizations in nearly all the commercial provinces drafted formal protests. The Rhode Island assembly, in a remonstrance to the Board of Trade, stated that the colony could not exist without the foreign West Indian trade. As attempts were made to enforce the legislation, the complaints became more insistent and more frequent. Even some English merchants, whose trade with the colonies began to decline as a result of the new legislation, joined the opposition.

But Grenville, paying little attention to the protests, proceeded to carry out the remainder of his program. All duties and forfeitures under the Sugar Act, he declared, had to be paid in gold or silver. The colonists were in a quandary; they had no mines of precious metals, and their principal source of specie supply, the foreign West Indies, was at least partially cut off by enforcement of the Trade Acts. To make matters worse, Grenville, at the solicitation of British creditors, induced Parliament in 1764 to pass the Colonial Currency Act, which forbade further issue of paper money as legal tender in the colonies and prevented colonial debtors from settling their accounts in depreciated currency.

Grenville's third measure was the Stamp Act. To raise the remaining two thirds of the £150,000 that he hoped to obtain from the colonies, he suggested a direct tax in the form of "certain stamp duties." Far from acting in a tyrannical manner, he informed the colonists a year in advance that if they did not like this method, already in use in England, for raising the necessary funds, he would be glad to have them "signify" a more satisfactory means. Since the only replies proposed the old requisition system or denied the right of Parliament to tax the colonies at all, Grenville pushed the stamp bill through Parliament in March, 1765. By its terms, revenue stamps, ranging from a $\frac{1}{2}d$. to £10, were required for commercial and legal documents, liquor licenses, pamphlets, newspapers, almanacs, advertisements, playing cards, and dice. Infractions of the law were to be punished by heavy fines and forfeitures that, at the option of the informer or prosecutor, might be collected through the vice-admiralty courts. Forgery and counterfeiting were punishable by death. Unfortunately for Anglo-American amity, this act affected directly the most influential and articulate colonial groups, the lawyers and the press.

Less than a month later Grenville, still intent on cutting down expenses, induced Parliament to pass the Quartering Act. It provided that where the colonial barracks were insufficient to house the proposed army of 10,000 men, public hostelries were to be used. If more room was needed, vacant houses, barns, and other buildings were to be rented. The act also directed the colonists to furnish the troops with fuel, candles, vinegar, salt, bedding, cooking utensils, and small quantities of beer, cider, and rum. Persons furnishing quarters and supplies were to be reimbursed by the province in which the troops were stationed. Rates for transporting troops or supplies from one colonial point to another were fixed in the act. Any excess over these rates had to be borne by the colonies.

Organizing Colonial Protest

The opposition to the Sugar and Currency Acts was mild in comparison with the storms that followed the passage of the Stamp Act and the Quartering Act. Newspaper publishers, pamphleteers, lawyers, bankers, and merchants, on whom the Stamp Act fell most heavily, were especially outspoken. Northerners, like James Otis of Massachusetts and Stephen Hopkins of Rhode Island, declaring such legislation tyrannical, asserted that the mother country had no right to tax the colonies without their consent. The Virginia House of Burgesses, led by Patrick Henry, passed a series of resolutions stating that the inhabitants of the colony could not be bound by any law or ordinance imposing any tax upon them unless the law had been passed by the Virginia legislature. A Stamp Act Congress, composed of delegates representing nine colonies, met in New York in October, 1765, and issued a declaration of rights and grievances drafted by John Dickinson of Pennsylvania. The document approved by this illegal meeting stated that the colonists were entitled to the inherent rights and liberties of native-born Englishmen—petition, trial by jury, and self-taxation. The Congress drafted petitions to the King and to each of the two houses of Parliament, requesting repeal of the Stamp Act and of other obnoxious legislation, and pointing out that the colonies could not be represented in the House of Commons.

Had the colonists been content with congresses, constitutional discussions, protests, remonstrances, and memorials, the Grenville legislation might have remained unchanged. But opposition of a more formidable character began to appear even before the Stamp Act went into effect—an opposition which marked the beginning of a ten-year struggle that was to culminate in the Revolution. Boycotts against England and violent resistance began to be used. The first use of the boycott was almost accidental. The depression following the French and Indian War as well as the Grenville legislation forced the colonies to economize. They stopped eating certain articles of food, replaced imported tea with domestic sage, sassafras, and other herbs, and substituted homespun for British textiles. British imports began to decline, and the colonists soon perceived that nonimportation and nonconsumption were weapons that could be used to force the repeal of the measures. Accordingly, one day before the Stamp Act went into effect, 200 New York merchants voted not to purchase British goods until the Sugar Act had been modified and the Stamp Act repealed. A week later, more than 400 Philadelphia merchants agreed to make all their orders for British merchandise contingent upon the repeal of the Stamp Act.

Less than a month later, Boston merchants made a similar agreement, and smaller New England towns and southern towns followed suit.

The effect of these agreements was soon felt in the mother country. English exports to the commercial colonies declined by more than 20 per cent in one year. Exports to the tobacco colonies fell even more during the same period. With the mainland colonists owing British businessmen between £4,000,000 and £6,000,000, British merchants, manufacturers, and workingmen flooded Parliament with petitions demanding the immediate repeal of the Stamp Act. Benjamin Franklin, who was in England at the time, was summoned to appear before the House of Commons to be questioned about the attitude of the Americans. He declared that the colonists were angered by "the restraints lately laid on their trade, by which the bringing of foreign gold and silver into the colonies was prevented; the prohibition of making paper money among themselves; and then demanding a new and heavy tax by stamps, taking away at the same time trials by jury, and refusing to receive and hear their humble petitions." The colonists, he asserted, would never submit to the Stamp Act unless compelled to do so, and compulsion might mean revolution.

Meanwhile, the more militant colonists, generally among the smaller businessmen and lawyers, organized societies known as "Sons of Liberty." These people expressed opposition to the Grenville legislation by a series of popular demonstrations. They held parades; they intimidated stamp collectors, burned them in effigy, and forced them to resign; and they destroyed stamps and the property of the stamp collectors and of others who favored the Grenville measures. In Boston, a mob led by a shoemaker named Mackintosh and incited by those who were most seriously affected by the Sugar and Stamp Acts burned the stamp collector Oliver in effigy, tore down a new building of Oliver's that they thought he intended to use as a stamp office, partially destroyed the Oliver home and the library and residence of the chief justice, attacked the houses of the registrar of the admiralty and the comptroller of the customs, and destroyed the records of the admiralty courts. Oliver resigned, and merchants forced the sheriff who had arrested Mackintosh to release him.

While such disturbances were occurring in both the mainland and West Indian colonies, the King, vexed by the troubled state of American affairs and hostile to Grenville, forced his ministry out of office. The new ministry, led by the young and inexperienced Marquis of Rockingham, did not know which way to turn. On the one hand, it was bombarded with petitions and remonstrances asking for the immediate repeal of the Stamp Act and modification of the other Grenville measures. On the other, the majority of those who wanted to avoid high taxes at home, who supported a narrow colonial policy, and who were angered by the action of the American militants, was just as firmly opposed to repeal or modification. The merchant interests, however, finally triumphed, and Parliament repealed the Stamp Act. Although next year it also reduced the tariff on molasses to 1*d*. per gallon and lowered other customs duties, the income was still used as revenue. As late as 1772, the Sugar Act still provided England with more than 90 per cent of its colonial revenue. To appease the opposition and to safeguard itself, Parliament issued a Declaratory Act that asserted its right to tax the colonies at any time.

The passage of the remedial legislation brought great rejoicing in America. The nonimportation movement quickly collapsed, local manufacturing declined, British goods again began to flow into the colonies, and toasts were drunk to King George. New York voted a statue of the King. Few of the colonists noticed that with the passage of the Declaratory Act, the basic cause of grievance still remained.

Charles Townshend Opens the Wounds

The unstable Rockingham ministry was ousted in July, 1766, and was succeeded by the Pitt-Grafton coalition. The Chancellor of the Exchequer in the new cabinet was Charles Townshend. Like Grenville, he maintained that the colonies were, and ought to be, subordinate to the mother country and that they should contribute to the support of the Empire. With Lord Shelburne, the officer chiefly concerned with America, preoccupied with the American West, Townshend had little difficulty in inducing Parliament in 1767 to pass the series of acts that bear his name. The most important of these was a new revenue bill that imposed duties on glass, lead, painters' colors, tea, and paper and provided for the collection of these duties by British commissioners stationed in American ports. It authorized the use of writs of assistance and the trial of smugglers in courts without juries. The revenue derived from the act was to be used for the upkeep of the military establishment and for "defraying the charge of the administration of justice, and the support of civil government in such provinces where it shall be found necessary." Another act suspended the New York Assembly for refusing to comply fully with the provisions of the Quartering Act. Since the Townshend duties would in fact bring in only a small revenue, the political purposes of the acts seemed all the more glaring.

The passage of the Townshend Acts was the signal for renewed colonial opposition. Still suffering from the postwar business depression and from the effects of the Currency Act of 1764, the colonists complained of "high taxes," the "unfavorable balance of trade," the "deluge of bankruptcies," the "alarming scarcity of money," the "stagnation of trade," and the "load of restrictions." Many regarded the Townshend legislation as a plan to embarrass them further. Few understood Britain's financial dilemma. The vast majority thought that the mother country was determined not only to ruin their economy, but to curtail what they had long regarded as their right of self-government. The plans in the Townshend Acts to undercut the colonial assemblies, judges, and juries could lead to no other conclusion.

The opposition took many forms. Lawyers and pamphleteers who had opposed the Grenville legislation on constitutional grounds were again outspoken. James Otis declared that the colonies "must instantly, vigorously and unanimously unite themselves . . . to maintain the Liberty with which Heaven itself hath made us free." John Dickinson of Pennsylvania in his *Letters from a Farmer in Pennsylvania to the Inhabitants of the British Colonies*, although urging the colonists to refrain from the use of force, asserted that the Townshend measures were unjust, un-English, and dangerous for the future well-being of the colonies. "Let us," he said, "consider ourselves as . . . freemen . . . *firmly bound together* by the *same rights, interests*, and *dangers*. . . . What have these colonies to *ask*, while they continue free; Or what have they to *dread*, but insidious attempts to subvert their freedom? . . . They form one political body, of which *each colony* is a *member*." Dickinson denied Parliament's right to tax for revenue and attacked the suspension of the New York Assembly. His moderate tone and reasoned argument won the American cause many friends. Samuel Adams induced the Massachusetts assembly to send a circular letter to the other colonial assemblies urging them to cooperate in defending their natural and constitutional rights. Several colonies passed sympathetic resolutions in reply, and Virginia issued a circular letter calling upon the other colonies to support Massachusetts. In Massachusetts and Virginia the governors dissolved the protesting legislatures.

But colonial pamphlets and resolutions were not so effective in securing the repeal of the Townshend Acts as were the renewal and extension of the commercial boycott. In 1767, leading Bostonians agreed not to purchase certain imported articles; interest in home manufacture revived; and the newspapers carried reports describing the increase and perfection of local manufacturing. Harvard graduates, for example, wore homespun and printed their theses on paper manufactured in a nearby town. In 1770, the *Boston Gazette* declared that the "very impoverishing custom of wearing deep mourning at Funerals is now

almost entirely laid aside in the Province." By 1769, New York, Philadelphia, and the lesser commercial centers were following a similar custom. Even the Virginia planters, headed by George Washington,
formed a nonimportation association. Although some of the colonists,
including many of the merchants, failed to live up to these agreements,
English merchants and manufacturers felt the effects of nonimportation, and in a single year imports from Great Britain fell off by 40
per cent.

Violent expressions of opposition not only disturbed the British
leaders, but alarmed the more conservative colonists as well. In Boston
the radical element became so menacing that the new customs commissioners asked for a warship and a regiment of soldiers to protect them.
After repeated requests the British authorities in 1768 sent the man-of-
war *Romney*. Soon after its arrival, the sloop *Liberty*, one of John Hancock's vessels, sailed into Boston harbor with a cargo consisting in part
of Madeira wine on which there was a heavy tax of £7 sterling per ton.
When the customs official went on board he was "hoved down" into
the cabin, the wine was taken ashore, and a false entry made. A few
days later the *Liberty* was seized by the customs officers and moored
under the guns of the *Romney*. Infuriated by this action, a mob soon
terrorized the town; it assaulted a customs official, burned a small boat
belonging to the service, and damaged the homes of the comptroller
and collector. The commissioners, fearing for their lives, took refuge
on the *Romney* and later in Castle William. A short time afterward,
when the Inspector-General, who had been away from Boston, returned, he was roughly handled by a small mob. In the other commercial colonies there were similar disturbances. In Providence a customs
official was tarred and feathered, and at Newport a revenue cutter was
destroyed. In Philadelphia, a mob stole smuggled wine that the customs
officers had seized, and assaulted a protesting official.

Even America's friends in England maintained that such colonial
violence should be suppressed and that the colonies should be compelled, by force if necessary, to accept any law or policy that the
mother country might see fit to devise. Accordingly, the ministry decided to station a military force in Boston. Despite the fact that regular
garrisons were already maintained in more than a score of places in
America, rumors that troops were to be sent caused great excitement.
The various acts of the British officials were denounced in the *Boston
Gazette*, and a Boston town meeting summoned a convention of delegates from all the towns of the colony to take steps to safeguard the
colony's interests. Governor Bernard, however, refused to call the
Assembly, which he had prorogued, or to receive petitions prepared

On the Death of Five young Men who was Murthered, *March* 5th 1770. By the 29th Regiment.

Patriots Make the Most of the "Massacre"

by the convention reciting the colony's grievances. The substitute "Assembly" recommended that the people obtain arms.

When the first contingent of soldiers arrived from Halifax on September 28, 1768, the Boston selectmen, in defiance of the Quartering Act, refused to provide food and shelter for them within the limits of the town. During the next few months, the more militant colonists—urged on by Samuel Adams, a graduate of Harvard, a member of the Massachusetts legislature, and a consistently outspoken critic of British rule—did all they could to stir up trouble between the citizenry and the soldiers. Both officers and privates were dubbed "Red Coats," "Lobsters," and "Bloody Backs" and on several occasions were pelted with oyster shells, snowballs, and the like. Unfortunately, these soldiers were allowed to earn off-duty pay by hiring themselves out for labor. This only increased the tension between town workers and the military. Many conservative Bostonians—property owners and businessmen—hated and feared the mobs more than they did the soldiery, but they were powerless to prevent trouble. Late in February, 1770, an informer among the customs officials, while being dragged from his home by a mob, fired into the crowd and killed an eleven-year-old boy named Seider. It is difficult to imagine how any event could have better served the purposes of Sam Adams and his associates. The unfortunate official was arrested and, in spite of the order of the court, found guilty of murder by a local jury, but Seider was pictured as a martyr to the cause of liberty. Feeling ran high, and soon there were stories that the soldiers were insulting civilians. Finally, on March 5, a sentry on guard at the customshouse, having been repeatedly bullied and snowballed by a crowd, called for assistance. When a sergeant and six men were sent to his relief, the crowd began to assault them with sticks and stones, daring them to fire. The soldiers, however, refrained from action until one of them was knocked down with a club; the guard then opened fire, killing three outright and wounding several others. This was the celebrated "Boston Massacre." Captain Preston, the commander of the guard, immediately surrendered to the civilian authorities, and the other members of the squad were arrested. Although a Boston town meeting led by Sam Adams promptly labeled them "murderers," all but two of the accused, after a trial in which they were defended by John Adams and Josiah Quincy, Jr., were found not guilty. But men like Sam Adams and Paul Revere, and a great public funeral for the "martyrs," made the incident seem something quite other than what it was.

The South Moves to Resistance

As resentment against the English increased in the North, the southern planters—particularly those in Virginia—also had growing reason for complaint. Wasteful methods of cultivation and the rapid increase in population resulted in a fairly sharp advance in the price of meadowlands in the tidewater and piedmont sections between 1750 and 1775. As early as 1759, Governor Dinwiddie had informed the Board of Trade that the best lands of the colony had already been pre-empted, and by 1774 the available supply east of the Proclamation Line of 1763 had practically all been taken. To colonial planters and speculators, who coveted the fertile expanses beyond the Alleghenies, the Proclamation of 1763 seemed a selfish policy designed to promote the interests of British Court favorites, politicians, and alien speculators. The proposal of the home government to hand over the Kentucky and Ohio country to the Walpole Company—an English organization sponsored by George Grenville—instead of granting it to Virginian land companies, alarmed the Virginians. They were also angered by England's refusal to

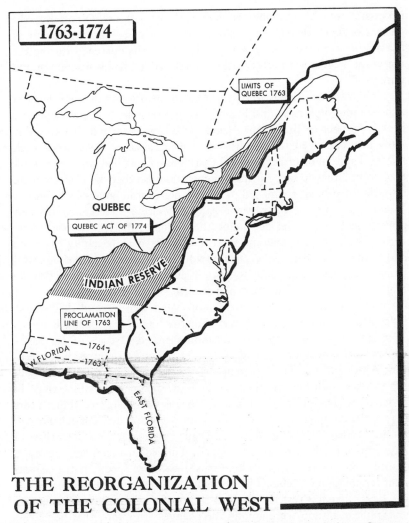

1763-1774

LIMITS OF
QUEBEC 1763

QUEBEC

QUEBEC ACT OF 1774

INDIAN RESERVE

PROCLAMATION
LINE OF 1763

W. FLORIDA — 1764
— 1763

EAST FLORIDA

THE REORGANIZATION
OF THE COLONIAL WEST

permit the survey of certain trans-Allegheny bounty lands that George
Washington and other Virginians had purchased.

Less important perhaps than the land question in alienating the
planters was the system of public finances. Virginia secured its revenue
from three principal sources: quitrents, customs duties, and poll taxes.
The total public income from these sources varied from year to year,
but there was usually a substantial balance after expenses, including the
salaries of royal officials, had been paid. But these balances, instead of
being at the disposal of the colonial assembly, went into the royal treasury. Since the cost of local government was mounting annually, it was

necessary for the assembly to increase the poll tax. Naturally, the planter believed that he was again being victimized for the benefit of the mother country. The rapid curtailment of the currency during the ten years preceding the Revolution greatly added to his discontent and unrest.

The vast majority of the great landed proprietors of the tidewater also resented high taxes and loss of colonial revenue because they were heavily in debt to British merchants. Jefferson estimated that the Virginia planters owed the English at least £2,000,000 because of their wasteful system of marketing and that "these debts had become hereditary from father to son, for many generations, so that the planters were a species of property annexed to certain mercantile houses in London." In 1791, a group of British merchants submitted a statement to their government listing the debts due them from American customers in 1775. The total principal and interest amounted to nearly £5,000,000 and of this more than £4,000,000 was due from states south of Pennsylvania; Virginians, including Randolph, Jefferson, and Lee, owed more than £2,300,000. With their plantations, slaves, and sometimes their furniture and still ungrown crops, mortgaged well beyond their value, it seemed that nothing less than repudiation could save them. Between 1750 and 1775, the provincial assemblies passed a series of lax bankruptcy acts as well as other measures detrimental to nonresident creditors. Although these laws were nearly always killed by royal veto, they nevertheless indicated the ends to which the planter was willing to go in order to extricate himself from a precarious financial state. Some years before the complete break with England, Jefferson and Patrick Henry, in an extralegal meeting of the Virginia Assembly, proposed that all payments on British debts be stopped. The leading planters, however, wanted only more time in which to secure more specie, not a permanent repudiation of debts. The stopping of speculation in western lands, the new currency restrictions, and the threat of new taxes to support an Anglican bishop were among the changes after 1763 that helped to convince many debt-ridden planters that the English government was determined to crush the colonies completely.

Militants and Reluctants

The new issues created by the imperial policy after 1763 inevitably became involved with the complexities of colonial politics. The royal governors, who had been in conflict with the assemblies for generations, were asked by London to enforce more rigorous policies at a time when their power had been effectively limited by the legislatures.

To secure support for the royal program, the governors had to increase their influence among colonial leaders. This led to renewed charges of meddling and corruption similar to those made against George III in his fight against factions in Parliament. Among the colonists themselves new choices had to be made and new stands taken for or against London. The vast majority of the colonial leaders would have gratefully accepted honorable peace and compromise with George III even after the battles of Lexington and Concord. The King either ignored or spurned their offers.

Whether the imposition of new British regulations after 1763 produced a struggle between two fairly distinct social and economic classes within colonial America must be carefully analyzed. The rich and the well-born—merchants, large landholders, and moneylenders—dominated colonial life. They owned or controlled the economic resources of the colonies—the bulk of the land, forests, fishing grounds, the agencies of commerce, and the fluid capital. By property qualifications for office holding, and by shrewd political maneuvers, they were able to limit greatly the political power of the rank and file of voters Socially, these men considered themselves superior to common people, and, on the surface, they would appear to have been reluctant to risk a rebellion; yet the most humane, gifted, and patriotic American leaders came from this group.

The poorer people—small farmers, mechanics, shopkeepers, and frontiersmen—were conscious of the barrier that separated them from the advantages of wealth, education, and social position. Quitrents, tax systems favoring the rich, unequal representation, restricted or manipulated suffrage, and economic monopoly were constant complaints. Neither the privileged classes in the colonies nor royal officials and British "profiteers" were spared the invective of the small man with his Calvinist morality; yet on the southern frontier many of these men were to be defenders of the King.

Struggles among the Americans opposed to the King at no time divided clearly along class lines. Both wings of the colonial cause cut across professions, religion, geographical location, and income. Even the royal party had within itself large and small merchants and farmers, big shippers and petty smugglers, and many other equally contrasting groups, all of whom had a stake in the maintenance of royal government in America.

For understandable reasons, those who held power did not sympathize with the desire for change. They staunchly defended the existing order, belittled protests, and repeatedly attempted to blunt harsh demands. On occasion colonial antagonists cooperated against Great

Britain, but at no time did the colonial ruling interests have any intention of releasing their grip on colonial affairs or of removing the barrier separating classes. Although many of these men believed that they were entitled to the ultimate voice in American affairs, they were wary that the open door of independence would also let in "levellers."

Should the royal government fall, those who stood closest to winning power in America had to be cautious. In the eighteenth century gentlemen did not take easily to revolutions, especially when one could not be sure that the revolution could be contained. "Direct action" was generally led by men less close to the top of the colonial élite. These militants had more to gain by a rush to revolution, for only a fundamental alteration in colonial politics would bring them to the power, privilege, and prestige that they coveted. Even if the militants, the Henrys, Sears, Reveres, Warrens, and Adamses, were drawn from below the top drawer of colonial leadership what principles or social program they had in common would be difficult to say. Jefferson and Madison, for example, remained convinced that Patrick Henry was primarily an opportunist.

The militants in various colonies came into closer touch with each other as the crisis deepened. By skill and energy and helped by English blunders they pulled the reluctants to their side. It would be a mistake, however, to think of the militants as a coherent conspiratorial group inspired by sheer expediency. Genuine issues of the gravest nature were at stake. But issues do not create events, and men do. In the coming of the Revolution the struggle between militants and reluctants was most important, for, in the words of Carl Becker, to the issue of "home rule" within the Empire had been added the question "Who shall rule at home?" Reluctants had to be careful in talking about "natural rights," for the militants might take them too seriously for comfort.

As the militant spirit in the colonies increased, the more moderate opposition to British policy declined. Merchants who had once sought and gained the support of what they termed the "mob" began to realize that in winning their battles with England they might conceivably lose all that they had in America. If the price of the repeal of British trade regulations was majority rule in the colonies, many merchants preferred the British regulations. But they soon discovered that they were not free to choose, for the despised "mob" was getting out of hand. In the demonstrations against the Townshend Acts, the militants directed their antagonism against the reluctant merchants as well as against the local representatives of the Crown. What had once seemed to be a clearcut conflict between two vested interests within the Empire was converted into a movement that seemed to strike at the very foundations of oligarchic rule in the colonies.

Despite the split between militants and reluctants, there was a temporary lull in the struggle from 1770 to 1772. The Townshend Duties, with the exception of the duty on tea, were repealed—partly because of the colonial boycott on British goods, partly because the acts, while yielding little revenue, had increased the military establishment in America and had brought the colonies to the brink of rebellion, and partly because Lord North, who became Prime Minister in 1770, maintained that the taxation of British goods was contrary to the principles of mercantilism. The tax on tea was retained in order to keep the colonies aware of British authority and because, of all the Townshend duties, the tea tax had brought in the most revenue. "The properest time to exert our right of taxation," said North, "is when the right is refused." At the same time, fears that the "mob" might become too powerful if the agitation against England continued tended to check the discontent. "All men of property," said Cadwallader Colden, Lieutenant Governor of New York, "are so sensible of their danger from riots and tumults that they will not rashly be induced to enter into combinations which may promote disorder for the future, but will endeavor to promote due subordination to legal authority."

For two years comparative calm prevailed, and the reluctants seemed to have things well in hand. The militant spokesmen, however, were unwilling to let sleeping dogs lie. Spurred on by restless leaders like Samuel Adams, they did their best to keep opposition alive by repeating the old cries about British oppression and colonial rights. Adams, hoping for complete independence, declared that the rank and file of the people were not dependent upon "merchants or any particular class of men"; and William Lee advised his brother in Virginia not to "trust anything to the merchants for, in general, gain is their God; but force them to cooperate with the wishes of the people." The alliance between the merchants and masses was for the time being clearly at an end.

Although the militants did not make as much headway as they wished during these years, one event—the so-called *Gaspée* affair—played directly into their hands. For some time before 1770, the English East India Company had been running behind financially, and to make up for its losses, it had advanced the price of tea on the London market. This policy led to widespread smuggling by American merchants, who could buy tea in Holland much more cheaply than in England and at the same time avoid paying duty. England resolved to enforce the law, and her revenue cutters and customs officials became extremely active. Riotous scenes occurred in Falmouth and in Philadelphia in 1771; but it was in Rhode Island, with its numerous inlets and islands, that the chief trouble occurred. Among the revenue boats sent to apprehend the illicit traders was the *Gaspée*, commanded by Lieutenant Dudingston. In the eyes of the colonists, Dudingston was overzealous. He stopped and searched ships under the flimsiest pretext, seized goods illegally, and fired on market boats as they entered Newport harbor; he antagonized the farmers living on the islands by cutting down their trees for fuel and seizing their sheep for meat. The chance for revenge came when on June 9, 1772, the *Gaspée* ran aground seven miles below Providence. At midnight, men and boys headed by John Brown, the richest merchant of Providence, attacked the boat. Dudingston was wounded, he and his crew were put ashore, and the vessel was burned. English officialdom condemned the act as treasonable and directed that those responsible for it should be apprehended and sent to England for trial.

The *Gaspée* affair, together with the report in 1772 that judges' and governors' salaries would be paid by England out of revenue derived from colonial customs, furnished Sam Adams and his fellow militants with new fuel. The power of the assemblies to limit the royal power by withholding salaries or other funds could now be bypassed by the crown. The militants urged the people to consider whether they wanted to be "freemen or slaves," whether they wanted to submit everything "dear and sacred" to the decisions of "pensioned hirelings." Adams, fully realizing the reluctance of the merchants and wishing to keep the people roused, was especially active. Whether in town meeting, on the street corner, or in tavern or grogshop, he constantly advocated the need for union and common action. Finally he moved in a Boston town meeting of November, 1772, that a committee of twenty-one be appointed "to state the Rights of the Colonists and of this province in particular, as men, as Christians, and as Subjects; with the Infringements and Violations thereof that have been or from time to time may be made"; and to communicate and publish the same to the several towns of Massachusetts and to the world as the sense of Boston, requesting of each town "a free communication of their Sentiment on this Subject." This resolution, passed without a dissenting vote, in reality provided for the establishment of an agency that was to be used to stir up popular sentiment in favor of revolution and to resist the will and authority of the British government. By January, 1773, more than eighty Massachusetts towns had similar committees. Two months later the Virginia assembly appointed a standing committee of correspondence, and the majority of the other colonies followed suit. The militants now had at least the beginning of a permanent organization divorced from control of the reluctant colonists.

The Boldest Strike Yet Made in America

At the beginning of the year 1773, the reluctants in America still dominated the situation. With few exceptions, they flatly opposed independence, and they supported a policy of expediency and passive resistance. At this stage, just as the outlook for more peaceful relations between England and the colonies seemed encouraging, Lord North and his colleagues decided to intervene. The advance in the price of tea in England had not materially aided the East India Company, and at the beginning of 1773 the company found itself on the verge of bankruptcy with seventeen million pounds of tea in its warehouses in England and its dividends cut in half. In an effort to aid the company and at the same time increase the revenue of the government, North induced Parliament in May, 1773, to enact a measure that gave the company a virtual monopoly of the tea trade in America. By this act, the company was permitted to ship its tea, not through colonial dealers, but directly to the colonies in its own vessels and to dispose of it to retailers through its own agents. The British and colonial importers—both of them middle-men—were thus eliminated. Although the company had to pay the three-penny customs tax in the colonies, it did not have to pay English export duties. The company could undersell both the honest merchant and the dealer who dealt in smuggled tea by 25 per cent.

Angered by the grant of a monopoly to what seemed to them a powerful, grasping corporation, aroused by the prospect of the loss of profits from a lucrative trade, and fearful lest other articles should be similarly monopolized by the East India Company or other companies, the merchants again joined the militants. They had no intention of supporting demands for more drastic measures; they wished only to avoid the ruin of their trade. If American commerce were to be controlled by great monopolies, one of their number said, the colonies might find themselves in the power of a monster that could "destroy every branch of our commerce, drain us of all our property, and wantonly leave us to perish by thousands." To protect their trade the merchants were willing to enter into almost any sort of an alliance. Besides, they apparently expected to control the militants as they had on previous occasions.

Long before the East India Company's ships arrived at the colonial ports, the question of how to "safeguard" colonial interests was discussed. The more conservative merchants and the moderates were inclined to resort to the old method of economic boycott and to bring pressure to force the company's consignees to resign. The militants, on the other hand, determined to make the most of the opportunity, advocated sterner measures. In Boston they soon gained the upper hand, and tarring and feathering and other forms of violence were frequent occurrences. The company's consignees, among whom were the two sons and the nephew of Governor Thomas Hutchinson of Massachusetts, were labeled "Traitors to their Country, Butchers," who were "doing everything to Murder and destroy all that shall stand in the way of their private Interests." Hutchinson's refusal to allow the tea ships to leave the harbor and the consignees' refusal to resign at the repeated requests of the merchant-controlled town meeting opened the way for Sam Adams to summon a great mass meeting. This body, in which the rank and file greatly outnumbered the merchants, refused to obey the governor's order to disperse and unanimously adopted a resolution stating that the tea should not be landed and that the duty on it should not be paid. The governor, however, was equally determined that the tea should not leave the harbor until it had first been landed and the duty on it paid. As a result, on the night of December 16, 1773, a band of men disguised as Indians boarded the company's vessels and dumped 342 chests of tea into the harbor while a great crowd on shore looked on. The deed was performed quietly, and there was no other damage. Among the "Indians" at this "tea party" were merchants who toiled "side by side with carpenters, masons, farmers, blacksmiths, and barbers."

In the other colonies the East India Company also met opposition. In Philadelphia, 8,000 citizens adopted resolutions directing Captain Ayers, commander of the company's tea ship, not to enter his cargo at the customshouse and to resail at once for England. Ayers wisely obeyed. In New York, as in Philadelphia, people from all classes were opposed to the company's tea shipments, and a document entitled "The Association of the Sons of Liberty" denounced as enemies—and declared a boycott against—all persons who in any way should aid in bringing dutied tea into port. Furthermore, the militants of the city held a meeting and appointed a committee of correspondence to communicate with the other colonies. Many merchants, thoroughly alarmed, attempted to hold the militants in check, but soon found themselves powerless. Fortunately for the company, its consignees, realizing the strength of public opposition and having no desire for another Boston Tea Party, resigned and advised the captain of the company's tea ship to return to sea "for the safety of your cargo, your vessels, and your person. . . ." In Charleston, where the militants, composed mostly of planters and mechanics, found it more difficult to secure the cooperation of the merchants in opposing entry of the tea, resistance was less marked than in the northern ports. Here the tea was unloaded and placed in the government warehouses, where it remained until it was auctioned off three years later for the benefit of the new Revolutionary government.

Reluctants denounced the Boston Tea Party as a "diabolical" act that was contrary to the best interests of the country. Even liberal-minded men like Franklin and Dickinson disapproved of it, the former labeling it "an act of violent Injustice" for which the East India Company ought to be fully compensated. Only the extremists approved of it, and throughout the colonies, for the moment at least, it injured their cause. In the eyes of the British ministry and British leaders including Pitt and Burke, the refusal of the colonists to accept the East India Company's tea and the lawless assaults on the company's property, coupled with refusal to obey Crown officials, was nothing short of open defiance.

The Royal Fist is Clenched

Unfortunately, the news of the Tea Party reached England at the height of a scandal involving Benjamin Franklin, the Massachusetts House of Representatives, and several English friends of America. Angered at reports in letters forwarded to them by Franklin, the Massachusetts House petitioned the Privy Council to remove two important royal officials in Boston. Fury at Franklin in London increased with the arrival of the reports of the Tea Party. Franklin was dismissed from his postmastership and was dreadfully humiliated in a riotous scene in the House of Commons.

Following this alienation of the best Anglo-American statesman, Parliament passed the "Intolerable Acts." The first of these, the Boston Port Bill, closed the port of Boston until such time as the British authorities were satisfied "that the trade of Great Britain may safely be carried on there, and His Majesty's customs duly collected." It also stipulated that the port should not be opened until the inhabitants of Boston had made restitution to the East India Company for the destruction of its property. The Massachusetts Government Act practically reduced that province to the status of a Crown colony, and the Administration of Justice Act ordered that all persons indicted for murder or other capital crimes be sent to England or to some other colony for trial if the governor or his lieutenant thought that such persons could not obtain an unbiased trial in Massachusetts. Royal officials were also protected against certain suits in provincial courts. A fourth measure, a new Quar-

"The Mitred Minuet": The Colonists Feared Freedom for Catholics in the Quebec Act, 1774

tering Act, provided that if ample barracks were not ready for troops within twenty-four hours after they had been ordered, the local authorities must find suitable quarters for them. This act was to apply to all the colonies.

The Quebec Act, though not a punitive measure, was extremely irritating to the colonists. Actually the culmination of eleven years work after the Proclamation of 1763, it added to the Province of Quebec the great stretch of territory west of the Alleghenies and north of the Ohio to which several of the colonies and a new proprietary company laid claim, and provided that the whole province should be governed by Crown officials. In accordance with the previous practice among the French, there was to be no elected assembly, no privilege of self-taxation, and trials were to be without jury. Moreover, all Catholics were to enjoy complete religious toleration. Some Englishmen and many colonists looked on the Quebec Act as a means to keep the settlers near the seacoast and thus under better control. Among these men was General Gage, commander in chief of the armed forces in America. With the passage of the Intolerable Acts, he was appointed Governor of Massachusetts, and four additional regiments were dispatched to the disaffected New England area. It was generally believed in England that the colonists would not and could not resist. Hutchinson and some of the loyal colonists entertained this opinion, and Gage himself informed George III that the Americans "will be Lyons whilst we are lambs but if we take the resolute part they will undoubtedly prove very meek."

The passage of the Intolerable Acts and the administrative measures taken for their enforcement widened and deepened the chasm of misunderstanding and hard feeling between the colonies and England. The North ministry, instead of adopting a conciliatory policy and sending a commission of inquiry to America to ascertain the exact state of affairs, chose to treat the colonies as dependencies whose citizens should be punished for disobeying the edicts of the mother country and for resorting to violence. The colonists, who had enjoyed a large degree of home rule for 150 years, bitterly resented the North measures. The King's arrogant attempt to restore the colonial dependence that had long vanished and the determination of the more militant Americans to create a new political situation in the colonies were from this time forward to complement each other handsomely.

The American Policy: Naked Fists or Velvet Gloves

Although the majority of the colonists condemned the passage of the Intolerable Acts, there was sharp division of opinion among them as to what course of action they should pursue. The extreme militants, bent on obtaining colonial self-government or even independence, advocated a strong retaliatory policy. They opposed any restitution to the East India Company, and they wanted the colonies to suspend all commercial intercourse with Great Britain and with the British and foreign West Indies. The less radical leaders, on the other hand, anxious to reach a peaceful understanding with the mother country and to avoid any move that would strengthen the militants, hesitated to endorse a rash program.

In the midst of the heated discussion between the two factions, a movement spontaneously developed for an intercolonial congress to discuss the situation. On May 17, 1774, a Providence town meeting proposed such a congress, and a few days later a similar suggestion came from the New York and Philadelphia committees of correspondence and from the Virginia House of Burgesses. Finally, on June 17, the Massachusetts assembly, at the instigation of Sam Adams, invited the other colonies to send delegates to a Continental Congress to be held at Philadelphia the next September. The delegates, the invitation ran, were

to consult upon the present state of the colonies, and the miseries to which they are and must be reduced by the operation of certain acts of Parliament respecting America, and to deliberate and determine upon wise and proper measures to be by them recommended to all the colonies, for the recovery and establishment of their just rights and liberties, civil and religious, and the restoration of union and harmony between Great Britain and the colonies, most ardently desired by all good men.

It was suggested that the delegates, might be chosen by the colonial assemblies, by popularly elected conventions, or by committees of correspondence.

When the illegal Congress assembled on September 5, all the colonies were represented except Georgia, where the royal governor had prevented the selection of delegates. Of the fifty-six delegates who eventually appeared, only eleven were merchants. More than two thirds were lawyers, but many of these derived a large part of their income from agriculture. Many, especially those from the southern colonies, were among the ablest men in America. Although every shade of opinion in the colonies was represented, and most of the men wanted to avoid an irrevocable break with England, the militants gained a narrow control.

The first test of strength between the antagonistic groups came on the opening day; the Congress declined the invitation of Joseph Galloway, a wealthy Pennsylvanian and leader of the conservatives, to meet in the state house and voted to hold its sessions in Carpenter's Hall, to the great satisfaction of "the mechanics and citizens in general." The militants scored a second victory by securing the election of Charles Thomson as secretary despite the fact that Galloway deemed him "one of the most violent Sons of Liberty (so-called) in America."

These victories were of minor consequence in comparison with the endorsement of the Suffolk Resolves, obtained by the militants, on September 17. Adopted a few days before in Suffolk County, Massachusetts, the Resolves declared in bold language that the Intolerable Acts were unconstitutional and void and that the government of Massachusetts, as then established, was illegal. The people of the province were advised to organize their own civil government to which they should pay all taxes, to raise troops for defense, and to suspend all commercial intercourse with Great Britain, Ireland, and the West Indies. Alarmed at this action, which they asserted was nothing short of a "complete declaration of war," the more conservative men submitted a plan prepared by Galloway for a union between the colonies and the mother country. This plan became the platform of the Galloway group. It had behind it Franklin's Albany Plan of 1754. Others like it at the time and later were to become the middle way between independence and coercion. Galloway's federal scheme provided for a Crown-appointed president-general and a council of deputies chosen every three years by the colonial legislatures. Parliament might veto acts of the council, and acts of Parliament relating to the colonies might, in turn, be vetoed by the council. Although the plan was supported by John Jay and James Duane of New York and by other moderates, the militants just managed to defeat it. "Measures of independence and sedition," Galloway said long afterward, "were . . . preferred to those of harmony and liberty."

The rejection by the militants of the conciliatory plan did not prevent the two factions from agreeing to the Declaration of American Rights. Adopted on October 14, this manifesto declared that Parliament had imposed unjust taxes on the colonies, had burdened them with standing armies in times of peace, had dissolved their assemblies, and had treated their petitions for redress with contempt. The Intolerable Acts were characterized as "impolitic, unjust, and cruel, as well as unconstitutional." The colonists, the Congress asserted, were "entitled to life, liberty, and property and . . . had never ceded to any foreign power whatever, a right to dispose of either without their consent." Inasmuch as they were not and could not be represented in the British Parliament, they were "entitled to a free and exclusive power of legislation in their several provincial legislatures where their right of representation can alone be preserved, in all cases of taxation and internal policy. . . ." These ideas were embodied in addresses to the King, the British people, and the inhabitants of the Province of Quebec. The Americans had now claimed *all* taxing powers for themselves. By allowing only a royal veto to interfere with their rights, they implied the end of Parliamentary supervision. For the English to accept this, however, would involve giving the monarch the very prerogative that Parliament had fought against for generations. Here again American and English politics were at cross purposes.

The militants also wanted something more than declarations and petitions. They succeeded after a hard struggle in pushing through a scheme known as the Association—a nonimport, nonconsumption, nonexport agreement. Beginning December 1, 1774, no goods of any description were to be imported from the British Isles, directly or indirectly; if this failed to bring redress, then all export of colonial goods to Great Britain, Ireland, and the West Indies was to cease September 10, 1775. "Utmost endeavors" were to be made to meet the economic difficulties that were bound to follow. Agriculture, particularly the breeding of sheep, was to be stimulated. Local arts and manufactures were to be encouraged and profiteering forbidden. Extravagance and dissipation, "especially all horseracing, and all kinds of gaming, cock-fighting, exhibitions of shows, plays, and other expensive diversions and entertainments," were to be discouraged. Even the luxury of mourning was to be curtailed, as in the days of 1765–66.

Because the Congress had been chosen in a highly irregular manner, it was an extralegal body that could not give legal sanction to its acts. Nevertheless, the militants decreed that the Association covenant applied, not just to its signers, but to all the colonists, and it provided for committees of "safety and inspection" in every county, city, and town, to be chosen by those qualified to vote for representatives in the colonial legislatures. The committees were to enforce the Association covenant by boycotting and by branding as an enemy of American liberties anyone who dared violate its provisions. They were to seize, and either store or sell, all imported goods. If necessary, an entire province might be boycotted.

The less rash patriots fully realized the revolutionary character of the Association. Merchants asked why they should be compelled to sacrifice their trade for the benefit of farmers and mechanics and "designing" men of the stamp of Sam Adams. Many declared that the more conservative members of the Congress had been outwitted and outmaneuvered by radicals. "You had all the honors," wrote one, "you had all the leading cards in every suit in your own hands, and yet, astonishing as it may appear to by-standers, you suffered sharpers to get the odd trick." In New York and Connecticut, conservatives held protest meetings and adopted resolutions derogatory to both Congress and the Association. Men like Galloway defended themselves by saying that if they had not accepted the Association, the militants would have gone even further than they did.

Protest was useless, for the militant movement was too strong to check. Between November, 1774, and the following June, one after another of the colonies approved the work of the Congress; some ratified the Association unanimously. Enforcement machinery was quickly set up in every colony but Georgia, and most of the committees were composed of militants. According to conservative observers in New York, Philadelphia, and Boston, the committees were made up of "nobodies" and "unimportant persons." Governor Wright of Georgia declared that the Savannah committee was merely "a Parcel of the Lowest People, Chiefly Carpenters, Shoemakers, Blacksmiths, &c." But the committees, even though composed of the rank and file, functioned well, and the Association was vigorously enforced. In all the colonies, import trade from England in 1775 declined almost 97 per cent in comparison with the preceding year. English businessmen with financial interests in America bombarded Parliament and the British ministry

William Pitt as the Earl of Chatham

with petitions demanding the repeal of the legislation of 1774. But many merchants also became anti-American.

Lord North and his followers were in no mood to listen to petitions and declarations. The colonists, they asserted, by refusing to obey the laws of Parliament and by creating revolutionary agencies such as the Association, had openly rebelled. And open rebellion must be suppressed, even though it worked hardship for the time being on the British merchant and manufacturer. "An enemy in the bowels of a Kingdom," said Solicitor General Wedderburn to the House of Commons, "is surely to be resisted, opposed, and conquered; notwithstanding the trade that may suffer, and the fabrics that may be ruined." Even the eloquence and arguments of Pitt and Burke, both of whom urged the repeal of the Intolerable Acts and the adoption of a conciliatory policy, were largely in vain. Pitt warned the House of Lords:

Every motive of justice and of policy, of dignity and of prudence urges you to allay the ferment in America; by the removal of your troops from Boston, by a repeal of your Acts
of Parliament, and by a display of amicable disposition towards
your colonies. On the other hand, every danger and every
hazard impend to deter you from perseverance in your present
ruinous course. Foreign war hanging over your head—by a
slight and brittle thread; France and Spain watching your conduct and waiting for the maturity of your errors, with a vigi-
lant eye to America and the temper of your colonies.

But the ministry, newly returned to power in a general election,
refused to heed this advice. Lord North did sponsor a set of "conciliatory resolutions" (February 27, 1775) that offered to relieve from Parliamentary taxation any colony that would assume its share of imperial
defense and make provision for the support of local officers of the
Crown. This plan, however, was, in effect, nullified by an address to
the King assuring him of support in suppressing the rebellion and by
the Restraining Act of March 30, 1775, which was designed to destroy
the commerce of New England. By this act, the people of New England were cut off from the northern fisheries, and their trade was confined to Great Britain, Ireland, and the British West Indies until "the
trade and commerce of His Majesty's subjects may be carried on without interruption." Less than a month later, the act was extended to
New Jersey, Pennsylvania, Delaware, Maryland, Virginia, and South
Carolina. Wittingly or unwittingly, British conservatives again cooperated with colonial militants in closing the door against conciliation.

While Parliament was listening to the entreaties of Pitt and Burke
and adding to its coercive measures, the militants were busy strengthening their organization, enforcing the Association, stirring up a spirit of
resistance among the people, drilling troops, gathering military supplies,
and gaining a firmer foothold in the existing provincial governments or
setting up governments of their own. The reluctants appeared to be
either defeated or bewildered, and without organization or program.
With extremists in control on both sides of the Atlantic, each determined to coerce the other, armed warfare seemed inevitable. In the
words of George III, blows would "decide whether they are to be
subject to this country or independent."

From Lexington to Liberty

The first blow was struck on April 19, 1775, when General Gage, military Governor of Massachusetts, attempted to arrest two of the militant leaders, Sam Adams and John Hancock, and to destroy military supplies that had been collected at Concord. Paul Revere and William Dawes warned the countryside of Gage's intended action, and the colonial "minutemen" battled with the British regulars at Lexington and Concord. The English now became more resolute, and the militants welcomed the additional fuel for propaganda. In every hamlet and town from Maine to Georgia, Gage and his British redcoats were represented as "massacrers of innocent people," "butcherers," and the agents of "tyrannous despoilers of liberty."

While these reports were being circulated, thousands of New England troops, collected for the most part by the militant committees appointed to enforce the Association, began to gather in Cambridge, just outside Boston. It was now evident that the extremists, especially those in New England, were determined to supplement peaceful coercion with military force and that they would make every effort to gain support from the Second Continental Congress, which was to assemble at Philadelphia on May 10, 1775.

Similar to its predecessor in the irregularity of its election and in the fact that it included all shades of opinion, the new Congress was nevertheless much more radical in membership. Nearly all the delegates had had some political experience, either in their local communities or in their colonial legislatures. Among them were a large majority of those destined to be the outstanding leaders of the Revolution. With the election of John Hancock as president, it was evident that the militant delegates were in control. But the conservatives, though outnumbered, strenuously resisted any move away from conciliation and toward independence. "Every important step," wrote John Adams, "was opposed and carried by bare majorities." Largely because the more conservative representatives were convinced that pressure of public opinion together with commercial coercion would force the English authorities to yield, the Congress shortly after convening again petitioned the King for a redress of grievances. But the move was in vain, and the Congress moved steadily in the direction of putting the colonies on a war footing. Lord North's offer of peace was rejected on the grounds that the Intolerable Acts had not been repealed and that Parliament had not renounced its right to tax the colonies. Steps were taken to raise and equip an army; Washington was appointed commander in chief; and plans were made to encourage privateering, to es-

N. W. View of the State House in Philadelphia (Independence Hall)

tablish a fleet, to protect the frontiers, to secure alliances with the Indians, to enforce more strictly the Association, to secure foreign assistance, particularly from England's European rivals, and to establish a system of currency and credit and a national postal system.

Outside the Congress, the idea of absolute independence spread. Strengthened by the course of events in both Great Britain and America and impatient with halfway measures, the militants employed every means at their disposal to advance the scheme of complete separation. Other apologists, who never tired of emphasizing the necessity for loyalty to the mother country, were smothered by the more fiery pamphleteers.

Most effective of these pamphleteers—more influential, even, than Sam Adams—was Thomas Paine. Born in England of Quaker parentage, Paine was in his thirty-seventh year when he first set foot on American soil in December, 1774. Already branded a social misfit and an enemy of all things aristocratic and monarchical, he threw himself wholeheartedly into the colonial dispute. In January, 1776—thirteen months after his arrival—he published his famous pamphlet *Common Sense*, in which he set forth the economic and political arguments for complete independence. Sweeping aside legal questions, he based some of his principal arguments on economic considerations. Government, he asserted, was merely a means to an end, and governmental policies always rested squarely on economic foundations. Whether the colonies ought to remain a part of the British Empire or not should be determined, not on the basis of legal or constitutional precedents, but on the ground of economic advantage or disadvantage. He maintained, with disregard for fact, that the colonies had from the first suffered economically and that whatever prosperity they enjoyed had been won in spite of English hostility and English exploitation. England had never shown generosity in its dealings with the colonies and instead of helping them had hampered their development by restrictions. "As Europe is our market for trade, we ought to form no partial connection with any part of it," he said. "It is the true interest of America to steer clear of European connections, which she never can do while by her dependence on Britain she is made the makeweight in the scale of British politics." It was nonsense to assume that England was the mother of the colonies: "Europe and not England is the parent country of America. This new world hath been the Asylum for the persecuted lovers of civil and religious liberty from every part of Europe. Hither they have fled, not from the tender embraces of the mother but from the cruelty of the monster." It was absurd that an island 3,000 miles away should control a continent. The Crown, with all that it symbolized, was the great enemy; the King could only make war and give away places. "A pretty business, indeed, for a man to be allowed eight hundred thousand sterling a year for, and worshipped into the bargain! Of more worth is one honest man to society, and in the sight of God, than all the crowned ruffians that ever lived." The colonies, he concluded, should abandon their petitions and their expressions of loyalty and should formally declare their independence.

The work of Paine and other pamphleteers, the news of the Restraining Act, and the numerous military encounters between the British and the colonists aided the militant cause. There was a pronounced drift of public opinion in favor of independence during the early months of 1776. The hiring of German troops against his own people by George III speeded the Americans toward freedom. The King had indeed closed every door. Nowhere, perhaps, was recognition of this more apparent than in the action of the provincial assemblies. As early as 1774, all the colonies except New York and Georgia, where conservatives were strongly entrenched, had laid the foundations for new governments in the form of provincial congresses, conventions, or conferences. By the autumn of 1775, the old colonial governments had in large measure disappeared, and patriot governments had come to power.

Though usually controlled by militants, these governments did not immediately decide for complete independence. The five middle colonies specifically instructed their delegates to the Second Continental Congress to oppose any move in the direction of independence, and as late as January, 1776, not more than a third of the members of the Congress were willing to vote for a definite break with England. By the spring of 1776, however, the tide was flowing strongly in the opposite direction. The news of the coming of the Hessians to America was confirmed. In the South, the royal governor in Virginia frightened the planters when he called for the Negro slaves to revolt. Massachusetts informed her delegates at Philadelphia that she was in favor of independence. In April, North Carolina explicitly approved such a step, and a month later Virginia instructed her representatives in the Congress to propose it. One after another, the several colonies fell into line, until by the end of June even the more reluctant had given their consent.

Only a semblance of the old colonial regimes remained, and sentiment in favor of separation was strong and daily growing stronger. Militants both in and out of Congress declared that the hour had come to break completely with Britain, and on June 7, Richard Henry Lee moved on behalf of the Virginia delegation that "these united colonies are, and of right ought to be free and independent states," that a plan of confederation be prepared, and that effectual measures be taken to secure foreign alliances. John Adams, in seconding the motion, argued for an immediate declaration. But some of the delegates still held back. The people, they asserted, had not yet demanded such a measure, and the middle colonies "were not yet ripe for bidding adieu to British connection." After considerable debate, final decision on the question was postponed for three weeks, and a committee consisting of four militants (Thomas Jefferson, Benjamin Franklin, John Adams, and Roger Sherman) and one moderate (Robert R. Livingston) was appointed to prepare a formal declaration. When the motion was again brought before the Congress on July 1, nine colonies voted for it; Pennsylvania and South Carolina opposed it, the Delaware delegation was tied, and New York was excused from voting. On the following day, when the final vote was taken, all except New York cast their ballots in the affirmative. On July 4, the final draft of the declaration was formally adopted, although it was not signed until some weeks later.

Written under high emotional pressure and designed to win support on both sides of the Atlantic, the Declaration of Independence consisted of two principal parts: a preamble and a list of grievances. The preamble, an eloquent statement of the Lockian philosophy of natural rights, held as "self-evident" the following "truths":

(335)

The PENNSYLVANIA EVENING POST.

Price only Two Coppers.   Published every *Tuesday, Thursday,* and *Saturday* Evenings.

Vol. II.]   SATURDAY, JULY 6, 1776.   [Num. 228.

In CONGRESS, July 4, 1776.

A Declaration by the Representatives of the United States of America, in General Congress assembled.

WHEN, in the course of human events, it becomes necessary for one people to dissolve the political bands which have connected them with another, and to assume, among the powers of the earth, the separate and equal station to which the laws of nature and of nature's God entitle them, a decent respect to the opinions of mankind requires that they should declare the causes which impel them to the separation.

We hold these truths to be self-evident, That all men are created equal; that they are endowed, by their Creator, with certain unalienable rights; that among these are life, liberty, and the pursuit of happiness. That to secure these rights, governments are instituted among men, deriving their just powers from the consent of the governed; that whenever any form of government becomes destructive of these ends, it is the right of the people to alter or to abolish it, and to institute new government, laying its foundation on such principles, and organizing its powers in such form, as to them shall seem most likely to effect their safety and happiness. Prudence, indeed, will dictate that governments long established should not be changed for light and transient causes; and accordingly all experience hath shewn, that mankind are more disposed to suffer, while evils are sufferable, than to right themselves by abolishing the forms to which they are accustomed. But when a long train of abuses and usurpations, pursuing invariably the same object, evinces a design to reduce them under absolute despotism, it is their right, it is their duty, to throw off such government, and to provide new guards for their future security. Such has been the patient sufferance of these colonies; and such is now the necessity which constrains them to alter their former systems of government. The history of the present King of Great Britain is a history of repeated injuries and usurpations, all having in direct object the establishment of an absolute tyranny over these states. To prove this, let facts be submitted to a candid world.

He has refused his assent to laws, the most wholesome and necessary for the public good.

He has forbidden his Governors to pass laws of immediate and pressing importance, unless suspended in their operation till his assent should be obtained; and, when so suspended, he has utterly neglected to attend to them.

He has refused to pass other laws for the accommodation of large districts of people, unless those people would relinquish the right of representation in the legislature, a right inestimable to them, and formidable to tyrants only.

He has called together legislative bodies at places unusual, uncomfortable, and distant from the depository of their public records, for the sole purpose of fatiguing them into compliance with his measures.

He has dissolved Representative Houses repeatedly, for opposing with manly firmness his invasions on the rights of the people.

He has refused for a long time, after such dissolutions, to cause others to be elected; whereby the legislative powers, incapable of annihilation, have returned to the people at large for their exercise; the state remaining in the mean time exposed to all the dangers of invasion from without, and convulsions within.

He has endeavoured to prevent the population of these states; for that purpose obstructing the laws for naturalization of foreigners; refusing to pass others to encourage their migrations hither, and raising the conditions of new appropriations of lands.

He has obstructed the administration of justice, by refusing his assent to laws for establishing judiciary powers.

He has made judges dependant on his will alone, for the tenure of their offices, and the amount and payment of their salaries.

He has erected a multitude of new offices, and sent hither swarms of officers to harrass our people, and eat out their substance.

He has kept among us, in times of peace, standing armies, without the consent of our legislatures.

He has affected to render the military independant of and superior to the civil power.

He has combined with others to subject us to a jurisdiction foreign to our constitution, and unacknowledged by our laws; giving his assent to their acts of pretended legislation:

For quartering large bodies of armed troops among us:

For protecting them, by a mock trial, from punishment for any murders which they should commit on the inhabitants of these states:

For cutting off our trade with all parts of the world:

For imposing taxes on us without our consent:

For depriving us, in many cases, of the benefits of trial by jury:

For transporting us beyond seas to be tried for pretended offences:

For abolishing the free system of English laws in a neighbouring province, establishing therein an arbitrary government, and enlarging its boundaries, so as to render it at once an example and fit instrument for introducing the same absolute rule into these colonies:

For taking away our charters, abolishing our most valuable laws, and altering fundamentally the forms of our governments:

For suspending our own legislatures, and declaring themselves invested with power to legislate for us in all cases whatsoever.

He has abdicated government here, by declaring us out of his protection and waging war against us.

He has plundered our seas, ravaged our coasts, burnt our towns, and destroyed the lives of our people.

He is, at this time, transporting large armies of foreign mercenaries to complete the works of death, desolation, and tyranny, already begun with circumstances of cruelty and

The First Newspaper Printing of the Declaration of Independence

That all men are created equal, that they are endowed by their Creator with certain inalienable rights, that among these are life, liberty, and the pursuit of happiness. That to secure these rights, governments are instituted among men, deriving their just powers from the consent of the governed, that whenever any form of government becomes destructive of these ends, it is the right of the people to alter or to abolish it, and to institute new government, laying its foundation on such principles, and organizing its powers in such form, as to them shall seem most likely to effect their Safety and Happiness.

Of the list of grievances, the majority of which concerned George III, some were overstated, and others were difficult to prove. "The history of the present King of Great Britain," so ran the indictment, "is a history of repeated injuries and usurpations, all having in direct object the establishment of an absolute tyranny over these states." By refusing to give his assent to laws passed by the colonial legislatures, by repeatedly dissolving representative bodies, and by obstructing the administration of justice, he had done all in his power to destroy local self-government. The King was charged with having "erected a multitude" of new offices in the colonies and of filling them with his henchmen, of quartering troops on the colonists, of cutting off their commerce, of arbitrarily imposing taxes on them, of plundering and burning their towns, and of murdering their people. Against such acts, warnings, petitions, and remonstrances had been in vain and had been "answered only by repeated injury." "A prince, whose character is thus marked by every act which may define a tyrant, is unfit to be the ruler of a free people."

Three or four days after its formal adoption, the Declaration was publicly read in Philadelphia, and copies of it soon appeared in every community. Its publication marked the triumph of the strategy of the intransigent colonists, and it put an end to any immediate prospect of adjustment and conciliation. In England, those who favored the American cause were powerless to effect any change in the policy of the administration; and in America the militants wanted no conciliation. To the moderates, who had desired some sort of a compromise, the adoption and publication of the Declaration was tragic, for it forced them to choose between those who would establish a new order and those who would remain within the fold of the British Empire. Outwardly at least, one had to be either a Patriot or a Loyalist—and each was a traitor in the eyes of the other. Having made at last what they then understood only as a break with England, the Americans were free to test their ardor for popular sovereignty in the fires of war.

FOR SUPPLEMENTARY READING

The best volume on the outbreak of the Revolution is L. H. Gipson, *The Coming of the Revolution 1763–1775* (1954), whose bias needs correction by C. M. Andrews, *The Colonial Background of the American Revolution* (1924). There is an effective short synthesis of views on the imperial crisis in E. S. Morgan, *The Birth of the Republic: 1763–1789* (1956) (Pb). The same author and his wife, H. M. Morgan, have done the best book available on the Stamp Act, *The Stamp Act Crisis: Prologue to Revolution* (1953). B. W. Labaree, *The Boston Tea Party* (1964), does equally well by a famous event. The English politics of the time are expertly analyzed by Sir Lewis Namier and J. Brooke, *Charles Townshend* (1964), and C. R. Ritcheson, *British Politics and the American Revolution* (1954). The temper of American politics in the late colonial period is vividly portrayed by George Dangerfield, *Chancellor Robert R. Livingston of New York* (1960).

The complexity of the western lands issue is amply demonstrated by C. W. Alvord, *The Mississippi Valley in British Politics* (2 vols., 1917), and T. P. Abernethy, *Western Lands and the American Revolution* (1937). The greatest historian on the clash of England and France in the West is still Francis Parkman, *France and England in America* (8 vols., 1851–1892). More than mere pieces of this work can be found in S. E. Morison's finely edited volume, *The Parkman Reader* (1955).

A. M. Schlesinger, *The Colonial Merchants and the American Revolution 1763–1776* (1917), is a famous study of an important subject. Carl Becker, *The Eve of Revolution* (1918), has the classic statement that class differences separated the two wings of the patriot cause. On John Locke the best study is Willmoore Kendall, *John Locke and the Doctrine of Majority Rule* (1941). The political and legal theory in the years of protest before the Revolution is well analyzed in R. L. Schuyler, *Parliament and the British Empire* (1929). Religious disputes affecting the Empire are the subject for Carl Bridenbaugh, *Mitre and Sceptre . . . 1689–1775* (1962). The complexity of issues dividing the colonists is a theme of R. M. Brown, *The South Carolina Regulators* (1963), and P. H. Smith, *Loyalists and Redcoats* (1964).

Two special subjects are attractively treated in H. T. Colbourn, *The Lamp of Experience: Whig History and the Intellectual Origins of the American Revolution* (1965), and J. Shy, *Toward Lexington: The Role of the British Army in the Coming of the American Revolution* (1965).

7

>>>->>>->>>->>>->>>->>>->>>->>>

Revolution

THE AMERICAN REVOLUTION was a double struggle. It was a rebellion against imperial authority, affecting the international balance of power. It was also a conflict between two parties or groups—Patriots and Loyalists—and, as such, Europeans construed it as a momentous social revolution. Although the issues were never altogether clear to the Americans, their importance in the perspective of history cannot be exaggerated. The Revolution ended British sovereignty over the thirteen colonies, and also brought about fundamental and far-reaching changes in American and European life.

The Divided Americans

On the eve of the Revolution, America was composed of the commercially dominated North, extending from the port towns of Maine to the Chesapeake; the tidewater region from Maryland to Georgia; and the indefinite frontier stretching from Canada southward, bounded on the east by the older settled districts and on the west by the Alleghenies. By far the greater part of the northern population was composed of small farmers, tradesmen, and mechanics. Most of these small property holders were individualistic, ignorant, and provincial. Dominated by the ruling oligarchy, they had little influence in governmental affairs, and Cadwallader Colden of New York was not far wrong when in 1765 he declared that the lower classes were "the most useful and the most moral, but allwise . . . the dupes" of the wealthier classes.

Whether the small holder supported the Revolution depended on the balance of his grievances against the Crown and against the patriot oligarchy. Those who had received harsh treatment from landlords or merchants in their colony were understandably reluctant to fight a war whose victory would guarantee their enemies power over the social life and politics of the new state.

For the wealthy land owners and merchants of the North, the question of supporting the Revolution was perplexing. They feared that independence might lead to radical regimes that would undermine their position. Complete separation from the Empire might also seriously interfere with their customary trade operations. On the other hand, the distance from England and a large measure of economic freedom had developed in them a spirit of home rule that had been severely strained by British policy after 1763. Many of them undoubtedly realized that opposition to the Revolution might mean business failure, ostracism, imprisonment, confiscation of their wealth, and even banishment. The militant propaganda that independence would materially benefit the men of means was not without its effect. One writer declared that independence would probably mean "a free and unlimited trade; a great accession of wealth; and a proportionate rise in the value of land; the establishment, gradual improvement, and perfection of manufactures and science; a vast influx of foreigners . . . ; an astonishing increase of our people from the present stock." Another wrote: "Some think they say everything against a state of independence by crying out that in a state of dependence we enjoyed the protection of Great Britain. . . . But do we not pay dearly for this protection? The restriction of our trade alone is worth ten times the protection, besides the sums we pay in customs and other duties to the amount of more than a million annually. . . ."

Like the farmers and mechanics in their colonies, the northern élite split over the Revolution. Ties of interest and family and fears or hopes for the future pushed some to join the patriot cause and left others in support of the Crown.

In the tidewater region, long controlled by the larger planters, the question of complete independence also led to sharp divisions. In Georgia a majority opposed the movement, for the colony was little affected by the new imperial policy of the mother country and was still dependent on the home government for subsidies and protection against the Indians. In South Carolina more than half the people were opposed to the Revolution. Some feared radicalism and the loss of the European rice market; some small farmers in the north did not want to put the colony permanently into the hands of the tidewater oligarchy. Virginia, on the other hand, socially and religiously more akin to England than any of the other colonies, was a Patriot stronghold. The Lees and

Washingtons and other Virginians like them, who imitated the manners and tastes of the English gentry, who educated their sons in English universities and supported the Anglican Church, nevertheless joined the revolt against England. In debt to the merchants of England, prevented from taking up new land beyond the Proclamation Line of 1763, and opposed to English financial and religious policies in the colonies, most tidewater planters saw little advantage in remaining within the Empire. They looked back on a long and acrimonious political struggle with the royal representatives in their own colony. Although the planters had little use for democracy, they had already proved their awareness of their interests as colonists and their willingness to defend these interests. They were confident that independence would leave them in control of Virginia and free from the financial grip of the British merchants and factors.

The merchants in the tidewater region, fewer in number than in the commercial provinces and composed for the most part of factors and agents for British trading houses, opposed the Revolution. Yet even here there were exceptions, like Henry Laurens of South Carolina, one of the foremost merchants in America. The southern merchants had little in common with the northern groups who supported the Revolution. The Continental Association was injurious to their business, and England's commercial policy, which the northern provinces had attempted to break down, was either beneficial to them or less onerous to bear.

The frontiersmen seemingly should not only have favored the American cause, but should have given it impetus. By training and environment, they were democratic. Nearly all were Dissenters, and few social or economic ties bound them to England. Like the mechanics and artisans of the older settled regions, they resented the domination of the seaboard aristocracy. In the South, however, the very resentment against tidewater Patriots and the fear, in places, of inadequate protection against the Indians kept the bulk of the frontier people loyal to the King. Even in the north, there were frontier areas in which local grievances worked against revolutionary enthusiasm.

With so many interests involved in the momentous events after 1776, it is not surprising that there was no completely coherent and predictable pattern of response to independence and the Revolutionary war.

1.) GUESSWORK AS TO WHICH SIDE AN AMERICAN WOULD TAKE IN CONSIDERING REVOLUTION.

The Energetic Minority

Despite widespread opposition to English policies, the majority of the colonists did not consistently support the Revolution. In John Adams' opinion, one third of the people opposed it at any given time. On the other hand, Joseph Galloway, Tory exile from Pennsylvania, testifying before a parliamentary committee in 1779, declared that at the beginning of the struggle less than one fifth of the entire colonial population favored independence and that even after three years more than four fifths of the colonists favored union with Great Britain "upon constitutional principles," rather than independence. Both Adams and Galloway probably exaggerated, for both were biased. Moreover, they failed to take into account the fluctuation of opinion with the fortunes of war. Lecky, the English historian, was probably much nearer the truth when he stated that "the American Revolution, like most others, was the work of an energetic minority who succeeded in committing an undecided and fluctuating majority to courses for which they had little love, and leading them step by step to a position from which it was impossible to recede."

If the actual number of active supporters of the movement at any particular time was not large, it was not the fault of the more militant Patriots, who worked incessantly for the American cause. From pen and printing press came hundreds of pamphlets, letters, newspaper articles, and cartoons, all calculated to inform, encourage, and inspire. Patriot preachers denounced "British oppression" and sought to advance the cause of independence. The Tory diarist, Nicholas Cresswell, complained:

> The few that pretend to preach are mere retailers of politics, sowers of sedition and rebellion, who serve to blow the coals of discord and excite the people to arms. The Presbyterian clergy are particularly active in supporting the measures of Congress from the rostrum, gaining proselytes, persecuting the unbelievers, preaching up the righteousness of their cause, and persuading the unthinking populace of the infallibility of success!

But in every class there were many colonists who could not be persuaded, by either propaganda or threats, to forsake their loyalty to Great Britain. Included in the Tory or Loyalist ranks were great landowners, such as the Van Cortlandts, Crugers, De Lanceys, De Peysters, Jessups, and Philipses of New York; rich merchants like the Whartons, Penningtons, and Pembertons of Philadelphia, and the Higginsons,

"The Tory's Day of Judgment"

Chandlers, and Hutchinsons of Boston; large numbers of professional men—lawyers, physicians, and college authorities; many prosperous farmers; the majority of Crown officials; almost all of the Anglican clergymen; those who aped the English aristocracy and who for one reason or another hated radicalism. From the lower ranks of society, those who depended on Loyalist merchants or landowners for a livelihood, or on royal bounties, purchases, and military protection, remained loyal to George III. In all probability the Loyalists comprised at least one third of the entire population of the thirteen colonies; in three—New York, Pennsylvania, and South Carolina—they approached or exceeded a majority. Many Loyalists had suffered from the arbitrary acts of King and Parliament and were as anxious for reform as the most ardent Patriot, but they insisted that whatever the wrongs, they should be righted by petition and compromise, not by war, violence, and mob rule. In the opinion of the Loyalists, the Revolution was a conspiracy and the conspirators, in the words of one of the Loyalist leaders, "an infernal, dark-designing group of men . . . obscure, pettifogging attorneys, bankrupt shopkeepers, outlawed smugglers . . . wretched banditti . . . the refuse and dregs of mankind."

Against the Loyalists, who lacked both the organization and aggressiveness of the Revolutionists, the Patriots waged warfare that was even more bitter and relentless than that carried on against Great Britain. During the conflict, great numbers of Loyalists enlisted in the royal forces or organized militia companies of their own under commissions from the Crown. New York alone furnished the King 15,000 men. Much to the disappointment of the British authorities, however, their actual service was not commensurate with their numerical strength; their only outstanding exploits were an expedition against the coast towns of Connecticut that burned Fairfield and Norwalk and their cooperation with the Indians in the Wyoming Valley and Cherry Valley massacres. In addition, many Loyalist privateers attacked Patriot shipping.

Those Loyalists not under the immediate protection of the British armies suffered considerable hardship. Even before the Declaration of Independence was signed, Revolutionary committees in every colony were warning the Loyalists to be quiet, depriving them of their arms, and compelling them to adhere to the Association. As the struggle progressed and it became evident that some of the Loyalists could not be intimidated or coerced into supporting the Patriot cause, the Revolutionists resorted to more drastic measures. All who refused to take an oath of allegiance were denied the rights of citizenship; they could not vote, hold office, or enjoy court protection. In many cases they were forbidden to pursue their professions or to acquire or dispose of property. They were denied free speech, and they were forbidden to travel or to trade with the British armies. When many of these laws failed to accomplish their purpose, the more ardent Loyalists were banished. It is to the credit of the Patriot leaders that, despite the enthusiasm for the revolutionary cause, tarring and feathering and killing Tories were sporadic and never developed into a systematic policy. The American ardor for liberty did not bring with it a national reign of terror.

Paying for the Patriot Cause

Faced with the opposition of both the Loyalists and the imperial government and without an army or navy, a national treasury, or a well-organized central government, the Patriots were confronted with overwhelming obstacles. Each of the states regarded itself as absolutely independent and was jealous both of its sister states and of the Continental Congress. Each was more concerned with its own civil and military problems than with those of the common cause, and within each state there was often lack of unanimity about policy among the Patriots.

The inexperienced Continental Congress had no problem more perplexing than that of raising money. Created in an emergency and regarded merely as the instrument of thirteen sovereign states, the Congress did not have the power to tax. Consequently, it was compelled to resort to other sources to secure the revenue necessary for carrying on the war. Paper money was its most obvious expedient. Less than a week after the battle of Bunker Hill, Congress authorized an issue of $2,000,000 in paper money. Before the end of 1779, when Congress voted to limit the amount of bills in circulation, forty issues totaling nearly $250,000,000 had been authorized. To these Continental issues the individual states, especially Virginia and the Carolinas, added more than $200,000,000 of their own, making the total in paper currency more than $450,000,000.

As Congress did not have the power to tax, it did not have sufficient funds to redeem the Continental notes; nor could it declare them legal tender. It could only recommend that they be redeemed by the states and that the states make them legal tender for all debts. Congress itself did resolve that if any person should "be so lost to all virtue and regard for his country" as to refuse to accept the notes, he should be "deemed an enemy of his country." The states for their part did make the notes legal tender but paid little attention to the proposals for redemption. When in 1780 Congress recommended that the extant Continental currency be exchanged for new, interest-bearing notes redeemable in specie, 80 per cent of the original value of the paper money was lost, and both the new paper and old continued to decline in actual worth throughout the 1780's. By January, 1781, it took $100 in paper to acquire $1 in silver; less than six months later the paper was practically worthless and had all but ceased to pass as currency. Prices rose, and many persons were unable to pay their debts. In 1781, a pair of shoes cost $100 in paper money, a bushel of corn $40, a pound of tea $90, and a barrel of flour $1,575. From the beginning of the war, speculators had added to the inflation by attempts to control markets by purchasing available goods or by buying them up before they reached the market. "One great reason," resolved a Boston town meeting in 1778, "of the present Excessive Price of Provisions in this Town arises from the Avarice, Injustice and Inhumanity of certain Persons within Twenty Miles of it, who purchase great Part of the same as Farmers living at a greater Distance and put an exhorbitant Advance upon it." In some states monopolizers and engrossers were denounced, fined, and imprisoned. At the suggestion of Congress, attempts were made to fix the price of both labor and commodities, but generally they were ineffectual.

In its desperate effort to secure funds, Congress also resorted to requisitions. This method, however, was little more successful than when employed by Great Britain within the colonies in earlier times. The four requisitions between November, 1777, and October, 1779, were dreadful failures, as were the three specie requisitions of 1780–81. The net revenue obtained from all the requests to the states for money up to January 1, 1784, was only about $5,800,000 in specie. Each state, ignorant of or indifferent to the facts, insisted that it had paid more than its share, or was afraid that it might do so. Although many more supplies than money were obtained by Congressional requisition, the system was both wasteful and inefficient. Grain and flour, for example, spoiled for lack of money to transport them. Often when horses and wagons were requisitioned, the owners would hide their horses and make their wagons useless by removing a wheel or some other indispensable part. The method of requisitioning supplies, Washington informed Congress, was the "most uncertain, expensive and injurious that could be devised."

Domestic and foreign loans were also floated by Congress to secure funds. Between $60,000,000 and $70,000,000 in paper was subscribed for domestic bonds, which in specie were worth approximately $7,500,000. Millions of dollars worth of certificates were also issued for army supplies, and small short-term loans were also obtained during the closing years of the war from the new Bank of North America.

The foreign loans, though their face value was less than that of the domestic bonds, were more than equal in specie value to all the interest-bearing certificates sold at home. Beginning in 1777, small subsidies from France and Spain were supplemented by state loans, and during the last years of the struggle, when victory for the Patriot cause was assured, private Dutch bankers loaned the new nation more than $1,000,000. Most of the money obtained from the foreign loans was used to purchase European supplies. One installment from France, however, was used to pay interest on the domestic loans in America, and another to furnish the specie necessary for founding the Bank of North America.

The fiscal machinery set up by Congress during the Revolution invited chaos. Persistent jealousies in the Congress and among the states and fear of centralized authority prevented the establishment of an independent treasury until the Revolution was almost over. Congress tried several experiments with committees and boards but finally, early in 1781, provided for a single superintendent of finance. For this position it chose Robert Morris, an experienced Philadelphia merchant and financier.

Morris was given wide powers on paper, but state pride, jealousy, and bickering made his job exceedingly difficult. For three years he tried to increase the requisitions from the states, to put new life into the domestic and foreign loan policy, to create a national revenue, and to place the currency of the country on a specie basis. Discouraged with the results of his labors and by many charges that he was using his office to further his private interest, Morris resigned in 1783. Whether he was guilty of irregularities in his accounts and of speculating with public funds—two of the most serious charges made against him—is still a matter of dispute. Morris himself denied the accusations, which he answered in detail. His friends also asserted his innocence. Others, including those who have investigated the matter, believe that he knowingly allowed his private interests to become entangled with public affairs and that he was not impartially devoted to the welfare of the public. Nevertheless, Morris did vastly more than had previously been done to bring order out of chaos. Despite his efforts, American finances remained in a chaotic state throughout the Revolution and, in many areas, for years following the Patriot victory.

The Battlefields of Freedom

The Second Continental Congress handled the finances of the Revolution as poorly as it dealt with every other phase of the struggle. Lack of experience, authority, and ability to get things done was manifest everywhere. During the first years of the conflict, the Congress underrated British strength and assumed that Great Britain would yield rather than fight to a finish. But Britain had no intention of yielding. At the outset her military leaders reasoned that New England was the center of rebellion, and that they would isolate it by sending expeditions up from New York along the Hudson and down from Canada by way of Lake Champlain and then crush it with an army operating from Boston. But this plan was given up as impossible and was succeeded by another; British naval forces were to occupy and bottle up all the principal colonial ports and use them as centers from which to destroy colonial shipping. But this plan was in turn abandoned in favor of a scheme for occupying colonies like New York, Pennsylvania, and South Carolina, where the Loyalists were numerically strong.

The colonists were almost completely unprepared to meet these plans. Without an experienced army or the means of supporting one, and fearful that a powerful armed force might mean military dictatorship, they had to transform the motley array that had rushed to besiege the British in Boston into the Continental army with Washington as commander in chief. A few months later the Continental Congress advised the states to enroll all able-bodied men between sixteen and fifty in the militia. The size of Washington's task is difficult to imagine. The supply of arms and ammunition was scarce, and the men undisciplined and inclined to desert. "Such a dearth of public spirit, and want of virtue, such stock-jobbing, and fertility in all the low arts to obtain advantages of one kind and another, . . . I never saw before, and pray God I may never be witness to again," wrote Washington. "Such a dirty, mercenary spirit pervades the whole I should not be at all surprised at any disaster that may happen." In February, 1776, when he found how few troops he had under his command, he urged Congress to abandon the militia and to create a national army, a step which that body took eight months later when it voted to raise eighty-eight battalions totaling 63,000 men. Even then it was unable to secure recruits—despite the fact that it offered a bounty of £20 and 100 acres of land—and was obliged to "advise" the states to fill their quotas by draft. At no time did the army have ready for service more than a small part of its paper enrollment, and what was true of soldiers was equally true of equipment and supplies. Furthermore, by listening to Horatio Gates, Thomas Conway, Thomas Mifflin, and Charles Lee—all of whom wished to curb Washington's authority and if possible, oust him from command—and by establishing a military board of control, the Congress undoubtedly handicapped and embarrassed Washington.

The weakness of the Patriot army and the dilatoriness of Congress were reflected in the operations of 1776–77. General William Howe, after abandoning Boston, withdrew to Nova Scotia, where he organized and strengthened his forces for an attack on New York. But Washington, who anticipated Howe's strategy, moved his troops in April, 1776, to Brooklyn Heights on the western tip of Long Island. Three months

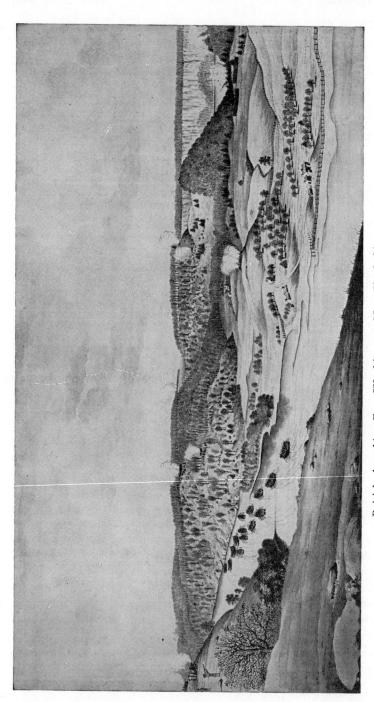

British Attacking Fort Washington, New York City, 1776

later, Howe with approximately 33,000 soldiers—8,000 of whom were Hessians—occupied Staten Island. The British then crossed over to Long Island and defeated the Americans at the battle of Brooklyn Heights (August 27, 1776), and the Continentals were forced to withdraw to Harlem Heights in northern Manhattan.

Washington's success in averting a complete disaster after the defeat at Brooklyn Heights can be attributed in part to the British desire to achieve peace through negotiation rather than by military victory. Lord Richard Howe, General Howe's brother and in command of the British fleet in New York, had been sent to America with authority to conclude a generous settlement with the Patriots if they would abandon the fight. But when he offered his terms to John Adams, Benjamin Franklin, and John Rutledge, who had been selected by Congress to confer with him, they rejected the proposal on the ground that they could accept nothing less than complete independence. As the American demand went beyond Lord Howe's instructions, he refused it, and the negotiations were concluded.

When Howe occupied New York City in September, 1776, Washington was compelled to withdraw across the Hudson River to New Jersey. The British soon followed and undoubtedly could have captured the Americans before they reached the Delaware if Howe had been willing to abandon his leisurely tactics for a more aggressive campaign. During the retreat across New Jersey, Washington repeatedly asked General Charles Lee for reinforcements; but Lee, who had been given an independent command by Congress, and hoped to supplant Washington, refused to cooperate. On December 13, Lee was captured by the British. A week earlier, Washington had ferried his troops safely across the Delaware, and within a month he was able to inflict two severe defeats on the British. On December 25, 1776, the Americans captured 1,000 Hessians at Trenton, and on January 3, 1777, they achieved an even more brilliant victory at Princeton. Following the Trenton-Princeton campaign, the British returned to New York, and Washington's troops went into winter quarters at Morristown, New Jersey.

The operations in New York City and New Jersey were paralleled by equally significant campaigns in Canada. As early as May, 1775, an expedition of Connecticut and Massachusetts troops under Ethan Allen had opened up the invasion route to Canada with the conquest of Forts Ticonderoga and Crown Point. In November of the same year, a force of Continentals under Richard Montgomery occupied Montreal, and Benedict Arnold led still another expedition across Maine to Quebec. But Arnold could not take Quebec, and even after he had been joined by Montgomery's troops, the combined forces were unable to capture it. In June, 1776, after repeated failures and the death of Montgomery, the Americans withdrew, and the British began to formulate a plan for a counteroffensive that would crush resistance in the northern states. This plan, which was drawn up in London by Lord George Germain, called for the junction of three British forces in the vicinity of Albany. General John Burgoyne was to lead one army southward from Canada, Lieutenant-Colonel Barry St. Leger was to attack with another through the Mohawk Valley, and Howe was to send part of his troops up the Hudson from New York while using the remainder to conquer Philadelphia.

From the outset the British plan was mismanaged. Instead of co-operating with Burgoyne, Howe set sail for Philadelphia. His decision to go by sea rather than land gave Washington ample opportunity to place himself between Philadelphia and the British, who disembarked at Elkton, Maryland. On September 11, 1777, the Americans, who were hopelessly outnumbered, were able to check, but not halt, the British advance at the battle of Brandywine. Two weeks later, Howe occupied Philadelphia. Following an American defeat at Germantown, the war entered a stalemate as Washington took up winter quarters at Valley Forge, and Howe remained in Philadelphia. While the Continentals suffered hardships at Valley Forge because of poor supplies, the British lived in luxury on the provisions sold to them by Americans in and near the city.

The British campaigns in New York state, which were disrupted by Howe's removal to Philadelphia, were completely upset by the successful resistance of the American Patriots. St. Leger, after a severe defeat at Oriskany (August 3, 1777) by a band of German-Americans under General Nicholas Herkimer, withdrew to Canada when he heard that Benedict Arnold was advancing with re-enforcements. Only Burgoyne's force of 7,000 remained to threaten the American position in the North. After capturing Ticonderoga on July 6, 1777, Burgoyne reached Fort Edward on the Hudson at the end of the month. But a shortage of supplies delayed his advance, and it was not until early September that he was able to resume his march to the south. Meanwhile, the decisive defeat of a British foraging expedition by a band of Scotch-Irish militiamen under Colonel John Stark at Bennington, Vermont, had raised American hopes and enlistments; and when Burgoyne reached Saratoga, he was confronted by a formidable force of Patriots under General Horatio Gates. After two bloody battles (September 19 and October 7, 1777) at Freeman's farm, Burgoyne's army surrendered on October 17, 1777. The battle of Saratoga was an important turning

Burgoyne's Surrender

[THE NEW YORK HISTORICAL SOCIETY]

point in the war, for it not only was a major setback for the British, but it was also decisive in enabling the Americans to secure military and financial assistance from Britain's enemies in Europe.

Victory and Peace

Long before the beginning of the war, men like Benjamin Franklin, John Adams, John Jay, and Thomas Jefferson, steeped in the history of contemporary Europe, were fully aware of the old rivalry between Great Britain and the continental powers, particularly France, for the commercial and imperial supremacy of the world. They knew, for example, that France, remembering her defeat in the Seven Years' War and the loss of her American empire, was watching every opportunity for revenge. They also knew that Holland, France, and Spain had long carried on a lucrative trade with the colonists and that they would undoubtedly welcome any chance of increasing that trade at the expense of Britain. A few of the more far-sighted British leaders, such as Chatham, also had foreseen these possibilities and repeatedly warned their countrymen to take the Bourbon powers into consideration in their plans for coercing the colonies.

At the outset of the revolt, Congress created a secret committee to correspond and negotiate with foreign powers. Early in 1776, it despatched Silas Deane of Connecticut to Paris and a few months later sent Franklin and Arthur Lee to be his collaborators at the French Court. Subsequently, it sent John Jay to Spain, John Adams to Holland, and other agents to the other leading European capitals. No aid was secured from Vienna, Berlin, or St. Petersburg, but the Bourbon states from the first cooperated with the American envoys. American ships were sheltered in their ports, where their cargoes were sold and the vessels reloaded with manufactured goods. In a single year the Spanish firm of Gardoqui and Sons shipped to the Americans at the expense of its government 11,000 pairs of shoes, 18,000 blankets, 41,000 pairs of stockings, and great quantities of shirting, tent cloth, and medicines. In France, Beaumarchais—author, publisher, courtier, musician, shipowner, manufacturer and financier—acted as go-between for the struggling rebels and his government; under his direction, an almost steady stream of supplies destined for America poured out of French ports in spite of British protests.

The American representatives desired something more than funds and supplies, however; they wanted an alliance that would bring armed assistance. France was their one likely prospect, and on France Americans centered their efforts. For a time the French government, despite the efforts of Franklin and the pressure of Frenchmen like Beaumarchais, was unwilling to support the revolutionists openly. France was not in sympathy with the idea of popular sovereignity back of the American revolt; her finances were badly disordered; and she knew that open recognition of America would mean war with England. Besides, the progress of Americans arms was far from promising. The surrender of Burgoyne, however, radically altered French opinion, and on February 6, 1778, treaties of alliance and commerce were signed; France recognized the independence of the United States and openly declared war on Great Britain. Spain, fearing that the revolution of the English provinces would set a bad example for her own colonies, refused to ally with the Americans. But her desire to strike a blow at England in retaliation for despoiling her treasure ships, violating her commercial codes, and taking Gibraltar caused her to enter the struggle on the side of France in 1779. In 1780, the Dutch also entered the conflict. Wishing to increase their trade at England's expense, they had from the outset been friendly to the Americans, furnishing them ammunition and other supplies on credit or in exchange for tobacco. Great Britain accordingly declared war on Holland in 1780.

The French marked their entry into the American war by dispatching several regiments and a fleet under the Comte D'Estaing. The

American Rifleman (left) and American General in Full Uniform

British, realizing that the conflict was rapidly developing into a general European war, quickly readjusted their policies. Commissioners were sent to America with still another peace proposal; but when the Americans, who recognized the significance of the French alliance as fully as the English did, rejected the offer, the British attempted decisive military steps. Howe was replaced by Sir Henry Clinton, who was instructed to evacuate Philadelphia, to attack the French in the West Indies, to devastate the coast of New England, and to center his operations at New York. When Clinton withdrew from Philadelphia, Washington pursued him across New Jersey. Americans under Charles Lee (who had been exchanged by the British) fought an indecisive engagement with the British at Monmouth (June 28, 1778), and Lee was not able to prevent them from returning to New York. The French fleet refused to attack Clinton, and after an abortive attempt to capture Newport, Rhode Island, it sailed for the West Indies. Although Washington was able to limit British activity to a series of largely ineffectual raids, the task of confining Clinton to New York deprived the American forces of any freedom of action. Neither side could obtain a decided advantage.

Despite the British failure to gain military control, Benedict Arnold's treason came perilously close to wrecking the American cause. After playing a major role in the American victory at Saratoga, Arnold had gone first to Valley Forge and then to Philadelphia following the British evacuation of that city. When it was rumored that he was fraternizing with the British, he demanded a court martial so that he could exonerate himself. Although the court found him guilty of some of the charges brought against him, Washington nevertheless granted Arnold's request that he be placed in command of West Point, the key fort in the American defenses of the Hudson. Even before Arnold received this position, he was passing military information to the British, and he was now planning to turn his new command over to them. The plot, however, was discovered in 1780, when Major John André, the go-between in Arnold's negotiations with the British, was captured while carrying incriminating papers. André was executed as a spy, and Arnold escaped to the British lines.

Although neither side could achieve a decisive victory in the East, in the West the British were no match for the American frontiersmen. During the first two years of the war, the British, who had their principal base at Detroit and could rely on the support of the Indians, had dominated the region beyond the Alleghenies. But they lost their position to the Americans after George Rogers Clark, a frontier farmer and surveyor from Virginia, took over the command of the American forces in 1778. Commissioned a major by Governor Patrick Henry of Virginia, Clark with only 175 volunteers captured Kaskaskia on July 4, 1778, and then seized Cahokia and Vincennes. When the British retook Vincennes, Clark marched a band of frontiersmen through the wilderness in the middle of winter to capture it a second time (February 25, 1779). For the remainder of the war he continued to attack along the entire frontier, and almost entirely because of his efforts the Americans were able to control all of the Northwest except Detroit.

The Americans had successes in the West, but the war was finally decided in the South. By the end of 1778, the British were shifting their attention from the northern states to the South, in which, except for the British attack on Charleston in 1776, there had been no major fighting since the outbreak of the war. In December, 1778, the British occupied Savannah. A combined American and French blockade and siege to recapture the town during September and October, 1779, failed. By the summer of 1780 the British controlled all of Georgia and South Caro-

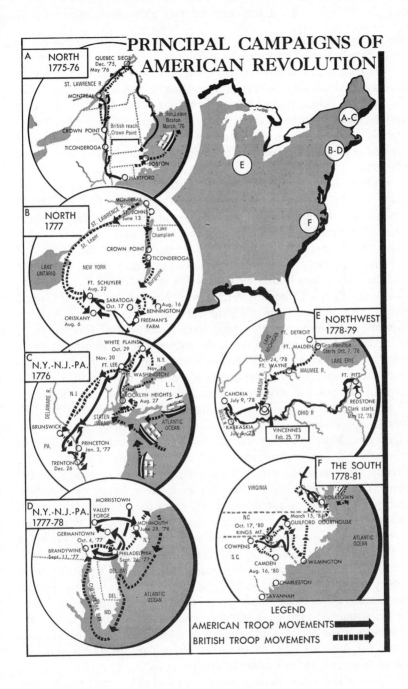

PRINCIPAL CAMPAIGNS OF AMERICAN REVOLUTION

A NORTH 1775-76

QUEBEC SIEGE Dec. '75, May '76
ST. LAWRENCE R.
MONTREAL
CROWN POINT
British reach Crown Point
TICONDEROGA
British Leave Boston March, '76
BOSTON
HARTFORD

B NORTH 1777

MONTREAL
ST. JOHNS June 13
ST. LAWRENCE R.
Lake Champlain
St. Leger
CROWN POINT
TICONDEROGA
LAKE ONTARIO
NEW YORK
Burgoyne
FT. SCHUYLER Aug. 22
SARATOGA Oct. 17
Aug. 16 BENNINGTON
ORISKANY Aug. 6
FREEMAN'S FARM

C N.Y.-N.J.-PA. 1776

WHITE PLAINS Oct. 29
Nov. 20
FT. LEE
N.Y.
Nov. 16
FT. WASHINGTON
L.I.
DELAWARE R.
N.J.
BROOKLYN HEIGHTS Aug. 27
STATEN ISLAND
ATLANTIC OCEAN
BRUNSWICK
PA.
PRINCETON Jan. 3, '77
TRENTON Dec. 26

D N.Y.-N.J.-PA. 1777-78

MORRISTOWN
VALLEY FORGE
MONMOUTH June 28, '78
GERMANTOWN Oct. 4, '77
N.J.
BRANDYWINE Sept. 11, '77
PHILADELPHIA Sept. 26, '77
DEL. BAY
DEL
CHESAPEAKE BAY
MD.
ATLANTIC OCEAN

E NORTHWEST 1778-79

LAKE MICHIGAN
FT. DETROIT
FT. MALDEN
Gen. Hamilton Starts Oct. 7, '78
LAKE ERIE
Oct. 24, '78
FT. WAYNE
MAUMEE R.
FT. PITT
WABASH R.
CAHOKIA July 9, '78
MISS. R.
OHIO R.
REDSTONE Clark starts May 12, '78
KASKASKIA July 5, '78
VINCENNES Feb. 25, '79

F THE SOUTH 1778-81

VIRGINIA
YORKTOWN
March 15, '81
N.C.
GUILFORD COURTHOUSE
Oct. 17, '80
KINGS MT.
COWPENS
CAMDEN Aug. 16, '80
S.C.
WILMINGTON
CHARLESTON
ATLANTIC OCEAN
SAVANNAH

A-C
B-D
E
F

LEGEND

AMERICAN TROOP MOVEMENTS ▬▬➤
BRITISH TROOP MOVEMENTS ▪▪▪▪➤

lina. Although Clinton, who had been commanding the British forces in the South, had to return to New York to prevent the city's capture by Washington, his departure had no appreciable effect on the war in the South. At Camden, South Carolina (August, 1780) Lord Cornwallis, Clinton's successor, inflicted an ignominious defeat on the Americans under General Horatio Gates, the hero of Saratoga who was subsequently relieved of his command. American spirits were somewhat revived in October of that year by a victory at King's Mountain, South Carolina.

After Gates' dismissal, General Nathaniel Greene assumed command of the Patriot troops in the South. Placing General Daniel Morgan in control of the American forces in the backcountry, Greene assumed command over the troops on the east of Cornwallis' northward line of march. In January, 1781, Morgan defeated the British and Loyalists at Cowpens, South Carolina, but in March of the same year Greene's army was beaten by Cornwallis at Guildford Court House. Cornwallis then withdrew to Wilmington, North Carolina, and Greene with the aid of backcountry Patriots, led by Francis Marion, Andrew Pickens, and Thomas Sumter, forced the British out of Charleston.

Although the French alliance, the entrance of the Bourbon powers into the conflict, and the shifting of British plans undoubtedly brightened the prospects of the Revolutionary cause, the situation at the beginning of 1781 was still precarious. Patriot finances were desperate, Washington's army showed no improvement, and many who had formerly supported the American leaders were becoming apathetic and indifferent. More assistance was necessary if the Revolutionists were to triumph. No one in America sensed this fact more than the young French nobleman, Marquis de Lafayette, who at an early age offered his services to the Patriots. With Baron de Kalb, Baron von Steuben, and a few others, Lafayette stood out from the dozens of European officers who joined the American forces and who, as Washington wrote, were "men who in the first instance, tell you they wish for nothing more than the honor of serving so glorious a cause as volunteers, the next day solicit rank without pay, the day following want money advanced to them, and in the course of a week want further promotion, and are not satisfied with anything you can do for them." In the winter of 1779–80, Lafayette returned to France to induce the French government to send an army to continental America. He procured for America 5,500 of the finest French troops, commanded by the experienced soldier Comte de Rochambeau.

The military and naval assistance provided by the French made possible the final defeat of the British. In April, 1781, Cornwallis moved from North Carolina to Virginia and was followed at a respectful distance by a smaller force of Americans commanded by Lafayette. In August, Cornwallis' troops, along with those sent south from New York by Clinton, established their camp at Yorktown on the York River. The French Fleet, commanded by the Comte de Grasse, arrived in Chesapeake Bay during the summer and defeated the British in a naval engagement on September 5. When the British fleet withdrew to New York, Cornwallis lost his last chance to obtain relief from the sea. Meanwhile, reinforcements were rushed to Lafayette by land. Rochambeau, who had been at Newport for a year following the town's evacuation by the British, marched his troops south. Washington, after hoodwinking Clinton into believing that the Americans were about to attack New York, also turned south and met Rochambeau at Elkton, Maryland. Both armies then joined Lafayette before the British army at Yorktown. Cornwallis, who was surrounded by the French fleet and by an army that was three times as large as his own, was in a hopeless position, and on October 19, 1781, he surrendered. The capitulation of Cornwallis' army at Yorktown marked the end of the military phase of the Revolution.

Winning the Peace

The American victory in the Revolution can be attributed as much to the British as to the Patriots. Fighting 3,000 miles from home over virtually unknown terrain, the British entrusted their troops to inferior commanders, repeatedly altered their over-all strategy, and failed to coordinate the efforts of armies that were operating at great distances from one another. The continuing fights among the factions in the English Parliament and the awarding of war contracts and commands to favorites of the ministry also helped to vitiate the British war effort. English political leaders who were out of power hoped that an American victory would discredit the King's party in Parliament and in the country. Although the American cause was also hindered by "party politics," and although several American officers were inept—and one was an open traitor—in George Washington the Patriots possessed an inestimable asset. Although not a brilliant commander, he was a man of undoubted integrity who commanded unlimited respect. Above all, he had an extraordinary tenacity that made him ideally suited for the type of war he was forced to conduct.

Britain's greatest military disadvantage lay in the fact that she gained relatively little from her naval supremacy. British naval operations were continually hampered by the fleets of France, Spain, and

Holland and by American war vessels under the command of such able leaders as John Paul Jones and James Nicholson. The Americans were also able to inflict considerable damage on British shipping. "The success of the American cruisers has given a prodigious wound to the British Trade," ran one account. "It is computed in England that £1,500,000 sterling has been taken in the West Indian trade alone. The consequence has been several capital houses in England have failed for large sums, and more are expected to share the same fate." Great Britain was finally defeated because of the extensive aid that the Americans received from their European allies. The results of this assistance were dramatically illustrated at Yorktown; but throughout the war, and especially after 1778, it was the single most important factor contributing to the American victory.

For some time before the surrender of Cornwallis at Yorktown, it was evident that Britain was losing the struggle with her former colonies. Her merchants and manufacturers, finding it difficult to market their goods, began to increase their protests. In spite of mounting taxes, the government's income decreased, and expenditures during the war exceeded those of peaceful days by more than £120,000,000. Government loans could be floated only at ruinous rates. At the same time, the Ministry had to meet the growing opposition, headed by Edmund Burke, which advocated the termination of the conflict with the Americans. Those who had preached coercion of the colonies still hoped that by some means the allies might be defeated and the Empire saved, and they were therefore reluctant to yield; but in the spring of 1782 the British emissaries began to put out peace feelers. A year was to elapse, however, before Great Britain signed the Treaty of Paris, by which she acknowledged the triumph of the Patriots and the political independence of her former colonies.

The American commissioners Benjamin Franklin, John Jay, and John Adams, fully aware that neither France nor Spain had entered the contest for the sake of establishing a powerful republic in the New World, conveniently ignored their instructions to include America's allies in any treaty negotiation and agreed upon a preliminary treaty of peace with the British agent, Richard Oswald, without consulting either of the Bourbon powers. The French, deeply concerned about the unsatisfied desires of Spain for territory west of the Appalachians, took Franklin to task; but he proved more than equal to the occasion. The American envoys, he said, had been guilty of bad manners, but they hoped that all that had been accomplished as a result of the struggle with Great Britain would not be undone by "a single indiscretion." Franklin not only appeased the French, but within a few weeks he in-

Edmund Burke

[NATIONAL PORTRAIT GALLERY, LONDON]

duced them to grant another loan of 6,000,000 livres to the United States.

By the terms of the final draft of the Treaty of Paris, Great Britain acknowledged the independence of the United States and her claim to the territory west to the Mississippi, north to Canada, and south to the Floridas. She also agreed that the people of the new republic should continue to enjoy unmolested the right to fish on the banks of Newfoundland and in the inshore waters of all the British dominions in America as well as "to try and cure fish in any of the unsettled bays, harbors, and creeks of Nova Scotia, Magdalen Islands, and Labrador so long as the same shall remain unsettled." Furthermore, she agreed to evacuate the territory of the United States without carrying off American property. The United States, for its part, promised that no lawful impediment should be thrown in the way of British creditors in recovering their debts from American debtors, that there should be no further persecution of the Loyalists, and that Congress should recommend to the legislatures of the states that they take steps to restore the rights of the Loyalists. The navigation of the Mississippi from its source to its mouth was to remain forever "free and open to the subjects of Great Britain and the citizens of the United States." Efforts of the American negotiators to secure Canada and Nova Scotia and to induce Great Britain to agree to a commercial treaty failed. If the terms of the treaty were liberal to the Americans, as many Englishmen at the time asserted, it was undoubtedly because Great Britain desired to weaken as much as possible the existing relationship between her Bourbon rivals and the young American republic.

Life Behind the Battlefronts

Throughout the Revolution the civilian population suffered much less from privation and want than did the men in the army. Because most Americans were farmers, they were to a large extent self-sustaining. With the exception of certain manufactured articles, some luxuries, and a few foods such as sugar and tea, the rural population managed to produce the needed essentials.

By drawing upon the farm population for soldiers, the war may have reduced food production somewhat, but the principal difficulty was inadequate means for getting the food from the producer to the consumer, and in many towns there were shortages. "Food is getting scarce and money scarcer," wrote a New Englander early in 1777; two years later the same writer declared that the seaboard towns of Massachusetts "will soon have nothing to eat." Rhode Island and Connecticut towns also suffered. "Nearly one-quarter of the best plow-land is now in possession of the enemy," Governor Greene of Rhode Island wrote in 1779, "and other considerable tracts are so exposed that the occupiers have not dared, nor been able, to plant them for two years past." The situation was similar in the middle states. In the South, however, where there were few towns, the war was only slightly felt until 1780.

More important than the scarcity of food was the increase in prices. Salt, for example, which sold for $.18 a bushel in 1774, cost $6.00 a bushel in specie in 1781, and a similar change took place in the cost of practically every other commodity. This advance in prices, although partly the result of decreased production and increased demand, was in large measure due to speculation, the increased cost of doing business, and the depreciation of paper money. In a letter to her husband Mrs. John Adams wrote:

> I blush whilst I give you a price current. All butcher's meat from a dollar to eight shillings per pound; corn twenty-five dollars, rye thirty per bushel, flour fifty pounds per hundred, potatoes ten dollars a bushel . . . labor six and eight dollars a day; . . . a common cow from sixty to seventy pounds; and all English goods in proportion . . . I have studied, and do study, every method of economy in my power; otherwise a mint of money would not support a family.

Throughout the Revolution, luxury and extravagance existed side by side with hardship. Private letters, ship records, and merchants' advertisements in newspapers abound in evidences of luxurious and extravagant living. ". . . this dreadful war," Dr. Orne, Salem physician, wrote to Colonel Pickering, ". . . is attended with such irregular distribution of property, such evasion of order, such decay of morals, so much public distress and private extravagance." "You can scarcely form an Idea of the increase and growth of extravagance of the People in their demands for labour and every article for sale," a friend wrote to John Adams in 1778. "Dissipation has no bounds at present; when or where it will stop, or if a reform will take place, I dare not predict." Sam Adams complained about the "Superfluity of Dress and Ornament" of the people at a time when the army was half-starved and semi-naked. Newspapers, diaries, and travelers' accounts were filled with stories of dancing, horse racing, and gay living.

War, however, usually accentuates opposing tendencies to dissipation and puritanism. How much actual increase in extravagance there was over peacetime, and to what degree wartime conscientiousness exposed dissipation that would otherwise have gone unnoticed, we shall never know. Men of the time, however, thought in ways like John Adams.

Contemporaries noted another classic effect of war: a marked increase in class fluidity during the Revolution. Many old families, whose fortunes had been derived from the fisheries or trade, suddenly found themselves reduced nearly to bankruptcy. Others whose large incomes came from fixed investments were not much better off. Many from the lower ranks of society, on the other hand, improved their social and economic position. Former laborers, shopkeepers, peddlers, and small farmers were among the *nouveaux riches* who rose in rank, to the dismay of established families.

The energy released and accented by wartime profiteering was very great. How many persons accumulated fortunes as army contractors is unknown, but there were enough to cause Congress to complain in 1777 that in every state there were profiteers, "instigated by the lust of avarice," who were endeavoring to enrich themselves at the expense of the public. One observer wrote:

The war has thrown property into channels where before it never was and has increased little streams to overflowing rivers; and what is worse, in some respects by a method that has drained the sources of some as much as it has replenished others. Rich and numerous prizes, and the putting six or seven hundred per cent on goods bought in peace times, are the grand engines.

Profiteering was not confined to newcomers. Old mercantile establishments—Otis and Andrews of Boston, for example—were obtaining profits of 50 to 200 per cent on army clothing at the very time when Washington's ragged troops were stationed at Valley Forge.

The effect of the war upon manufacturing was much more apparent than that upon agriculture. The sudden absence of English goods and the urgent demand for war supplies stimulated manufacturing. Patriot homes produced not only enough homespun for the family but a surplus for sale. Southern planters and wealthy merchants in New England and middle states, who had once dressed in imported fabrics, now wore garments that came from the home spinning wheel and loom. Many states offered prizes and encouraged the formation of societies to encourage manufacturing and the mechanical arts. After privateers began to place their cargoes on the market and foreign goods began to come in through new channels, there was a decline in household output. Even before the Revolution, however, small manufacturing establishments had developed outside the home in many Northern towns—as early as 1767, Haverhill, Massachusetts, had forty-four workshops and nineteen mills—and during the war, paper mills, potteries, and other establishments were set up with capital contributed mainly by the mercantile class. Here, as elsewhere, the Revolution accelerated certain tendencies that were already active in colonial life.

Great interest centered in the manufacture of munitions and other war supplies. Gun, munitions, and powder factories were founded in New England to supplement the small factories already in existence in such places as Lancaster, Pennsylvania. Lead was obtained from abroad or by melting down roofs and window weights. Several of the states offered bounties for the manufacture of guns, textiles, and other materials needed for war.

The war seriously handicapped internal trade. There was no adequate means of transportation, no uniform and stable monetary system, and no central authority with power to regulate interstate commerce. Attempts to replace the maze of pre-war economic regulations failed against the tides of particularism and new business energies. Trading with the enemy was forbidden, but the records indicate that many Patriot farmers and shopkeepers carried on business with the British armies.

Shipping along the coasts was practically ruined by British privateers. Foreign trade, however, fared better. No longer restricted by mercantilist regulations, the rebellious provinces at the outset threw open their ports to all traders except the British, and even this exception was subsequently waived. American warehouses were almost bare of foreign goods, and the merchants of France, Holland, and Spain welcomed the chance to secure profits and markets at the expense of their hated rival. Soon many ships laden with continental goods destined for America were on their way across the Atlantic; but not all reached their destination, for the British admiralty reported the capture of 570 vessels between 1776 and 1779. Despite the vigilance of the British naval authorities and the activities of enemy privateers, an increasing number of foreign cargoes made their way to American ports, and by 1778 there was an adequate supply of foreign merchandise available. In return for their goods, foreign merchants received tobacco, rice, flour, and other commodities. Indirect trade with Britain, although forbidden until 1780, was also carried on secretly. Commerce with the British West Indies, on the other hand, was all but eliminated by the war, for a new British navigation law effectively excluded the Americans from trade with these islands. Without doubt, one of the most momentous effects of the war was the stimulation of American business enterprise and, with it, the rising prestige of the ideal of *laissez-faire*.

The Democratic Spirit and the War

The Revolution was far more than a successful fight for political independence, for it touched virtually all phases of American life. If it did not introduce many novel political ideas or practices, it accelerated trends that had been developing for many years before the outbreak of hostilities.

For more than a century and a half the colonists had lived under royal government, which, despite changes and turbulence, had created some sense of social continuity and political predictability. Suddenly, almost at once, the old systems of politics and administration were shaken or undone. From 1774 to 1777, the British ruling class was eliminated, the old colonial governments were changed or destroyed, and new state and "national" governments emerged. Many colonial leaders were convinced that the foundations of society were being threatened. The "leveling spirit" of the Revolution alarmed many conservative planters, merchants, and large landholders in the Patriot ranks. "Every one who has the least pretensions to be a gentleman," Samuel Johnston of North Carolina complained, "is borne down *per ignoble vulgus*—a set of men without reading, experience, or principles to govern them." The suffrage, another conservative said of his state, was being extended "to every biped of the forest." For a time the breaking of old ties helped loosen the grip of the former colonial, now Patriot, élite. In Pennsylvania, a radical upthrust made for temporary retirement of "the best people" from political power. Elsewhere, the Revolution, by causing British withdrawal from American domestic politics, narrowed the struggle for political control and left Americans free to institute such changes and reforms as they saw fit.

The way in which the new state governments were organized revealed the deep-seated faith of the Americans in contract theories of government. Even before July, 1776, four colonies—New Hampshire, New Jersey, South Carolina, and Virginia—had drafted constitutions. During the war seven others followed suit. The two remaining states—Rhode Island and Connecticut—retained most of their colonial charters, merely deleting from them all references to royal authority. In the overwhelming majority of the states, the provincial congresses drafted these new constitutions. Because these bodies also served as legislatures, no distinction was made between the sources of constitutional and statute law. Massachusetts voters were the first to select special delegates to write a constitution in 1779–80, and Massachusetts was also the first state to submit its constitution to the voters for ratification.

Although all the new constitutions provided for representative government, little that could be called direct popular rule prevailed in the various states. The governments of Delaware, Georgia, North Carolina, and Pennsylvania had more democratic features than those of the other states. In Pennsylvania, for example, a unicameral legislature, elected annually by the taxpayers, was supreme. The legislature controlled the state's judiciary, and the governor and an executive council of thirteen were little more than figureheads. In most other states, high property qualifications for the chief offices and seaboard domination of politics were recurrent features of government. In a majority of states, because of reaction against royal rule, the first wish was to reduce executive authority and to enhance legislative powers, but slowly the governors gained greater powers. The "radical" constitution of Pennsylvania, moreover, was detested by most of the leading citizens of the state, one of whom was reported to have died of a broken heart over the extremism of the new state charter. In Pennsylvania also the "democratic" constitution at first contained a provision for a loyalty oath for voters, aimed in part at Tories, conservatives, and the pacifist Quakers. Gradually, in Pennsylvania as elsewhere, the sober and well-set citizens moved into the offices left vacant by the departure of the members of the royal party.

Despite differences in both the letter and spirit of the new constitutions, most of the state governments had certain common liberal features. The preambles of all the constitutions contained a summary of the Lockian philosophy of government. Eight states, moreover, adopted bills of rights; and the Virginia Bill of Rights, which antedated the Declaration of Independence, rested on the same philosophical foundation as its more illustrious successor.

Significant changes were also made in the nation's land system. All the vacant lands within the boundaries of the United States were now free from British control. Royal edicts such as the Proclamation of 1763 could no longer keep fur-trader, settler, or land speculator out of the region beyond the Alleghenies. Although many colonists had successfully evaded royal regulations on the use of the forests and had avoided paying their quitrents, the regulations still on the books seemed potential threats to economic independence. Similarly, although primogeniture and entail had long ceased to exert any force in maintaining family estates intact, they remained symbols of an older aristocratic order that Americans had been liquidating for a century and a half. Like other limits on land tenure, they suggested needless or artificial barricades against the intensely acquisitive and speculative temper of American landowners and merchants, and within a generation after the war nearly every state had abolished them.

With the collapse of imperial and colonial controls, land and forest regulations were swept away in many places. Surveyors or other royal agents would no longer try to set aside trees for the British navy. The quitrent system was also abolished for most farmers. Crown and proprietary lands were put into the hands of the state legislatures; but whether these and other changes in law helped the spread of equality is difficult to assess. Lands of the Crown or of the Loyalists were often confiscated, not to advance democracy, but as a war measure to strike back at the enemy and for sales in order to raise revenue. Most of the land eventually fell into the hands of speculators who in turn sold some of it to small farmers but also a large part to already wealthy Patriot landholders. In Pennsylvania the improved lands of the Penn family, the old proprietors under the Crown, amounted to about a half million acres. These were not even confiscated but were guaranteed with their quitrents to the Penns forever, and this was done under the supposedly most democratic of the new state governments. In southern New York many of the vast holdings of the Loyalist De Lanceys and Bayards were bought up or taken by the wealthiest patriots, like the Livingstons and Roosevelts. On the other hand, a Loyalist estate of 5,000 acres in Putnam County, New York, went to 250 persons.

If the Revolution brought these changes in land ownership and inheritance, it no less profoundly affected industry and commerce. As parts of the British Empire, the colonies had been forbidden to issue bills of credit, to make paper money, to engage in certain manufacturing pursuits, or to carry on trade with whom they pleased. Like the restrictions on land, many of these had been evaded or had fallen into disuse. Still their disappearance, like the land laws, added to the Americans' exuberance. The Revolution swept away all sorts of business restrictions, and the former colonists were at liberty to organize and develop their industry and commerce as they saw fit, subject only to limitations, such as the lack of capital, and to external circumstances over which they had little or no control.

Church as well as state felt the effects of the Revolution. When the Revolution broke out, nine colonies had established churches. In New England, outside of Rhode Island, the Congregational Church was established by law and supported by general taxation, and the same was true of the Anglican Church in Virginia, Maryland, New York, the Carolinas, and Georgia. Only religiously diverse Pennsylvania and Rhode Island approached complete religious freedom in law. Taking all the colonies together, there probably existed nearly 3,000 active religious organizations in 1776. The Revolution did not greatly reduce the number, and not at all the variety, of religious organizations. But it did adversely affect the Anglican Church in those areas in which its ministers had remained loyal to the head of that church, George III. In all the states except Virginia the Anglicans were soon deprived of their privileges and immunities and placed on an equal legal basis with the Baptists, Quakers, and other nonestablished groups. In Virginia the Anglicans were most firmly entrenched, and it was not until 1786 that the legislature passed Jefferson's long cherished and much debated "Statute of Virginia for Religious Freedom," which divorced church and state. In New England, the Congregationalists enjoyed supremacy; there, the fight for disestablishment was even more bitter and long-drawn-out, and this last stronghold of church privilege did not yield until the nineteenth century. Disestablishment took place in New Hampshire in 1817, in Connecticut in 1818, and in Massachusetts in 1833.

Separation of church and state did not, however, produce complete religious freedom. Religious disputes and intolerance still continued, for many people believed that their religion, and theirs alone, afforded the means to eternal salvation. It was still common opinion that society was not safe without the aid of an established religion. At the close of the war, no man could take any office in Massachusetts or Maryland without subscribing to a declaration that he believed in Christianity. In Pennsylvania he had to declare in addition that he believed the Scriptures to be divinely inspired; and in Delaware he had to believe in the Trinity. In New Jersey and the Carolinas he had to be a Protestant. The constitution of North Carolina stated:

> No person who shall deny the being of God, or the truth of the Protestant religion, or the divine authority either of the Old or New Testaments, or who shall hold religious principles incompatible with the freedom or safety of the State, shall be capable of holding any office or place of trust or profit in the civil department within this State.

The various religious organizations suffered many hardships during the Revolution. Decrease in income, depreciation of paper money, and destruction of property created serious difficulties for many clergymen and their congregations. In some instances congregations broke up or were abandoned by their ministers. In Hampshire and Berkshire counties in western Massachusetts thirty-three towns had ministers, but thirty-nine had none. Lack of large public buildings forced the military authorities to convert churches into hospitals, barracks, prisons, and storehouses. More than fifty churches were destroyed by the enemy during the conflict, and several Anglican churches suffered a similar fate at the hands of the Patriots, who regarded them as strongholds of Toryism.

Immediately following the Revolution, practically all religious groups attempted to improve their spiritual and material fortunes. Several reorganized their forms of government. The Anglicans, thinking that they could no longer continue to be a part of the diocese of the bishop of London, established an American episcopate with Bishop Seabury at its head, and renamed their church The Protestant Episcopal Church. The Catholic clergy, who had been under the control of the vicar apostolic of London, in 1784 erected the separate and distinct Catholic Church in the United States with Father John Carroll at its head. The Methodists also found it increasingly difficult to remain under

Old World control, and in 1784 Francis Asbury, on the authority of John Wesley, was ordained as "superintendent" of the American Methodists, a title that was shortly changed to "bishop." Other religious groups, with the exception of the Congregationalists, also developed more independent and comprehensive organizations. In 1789, the first general assembly of the Presbyterian Church in the United States convened at Philadelphia. The Dutch Reformed Church held its first general synod in 1792, and the Universalists their first general convention in 1786.

One of the unanticipated and paradoxical events of the war was a reaction against the benign philosophy of the Enlightenment. The social dislocations brought on by the hard years of battle and all-out efforts by the ministry, particularly the Methodists, brought a great wave of revivalism throughout the colonies in the 1780's. Once again the themes of man's sinfulness and of dangers of pride in reason brought many to "open profession of faith in Christ." These revivals represented in part a freshening of the spirit of the Great Awakening of the 1740's. But this time the evangelical ministers managed to force men with more liberal views on the defensive. Yet the Methodist leaders of this "Protestant Counter Reformation" were different from earlier preachers. Unlike the strict Calvinists, they announced that sinners did have the ability to choose the paths that could lead to redemption or hell. This emphasis on the power of human will, although coming from premises radically different from those of Benjamin Franklin or Thomas Jefferson, strengthened in its own way the belief of many Americans that the Revolution had given men a new lease on life and greater chances to make the future depend on their own choices.

Both fundamentalists and rationalists, however, increasingly agreed that the Revolution required that Americans do something about slavery, and opposition to slavery increased markedly during the war years. Of all American institutions, slavery was most obviously contrary to the doctrines of liberty and equality. In his original draft of the Declaration of Independence Jefferson had condemned George III for supporting the slave trade and for violating the "most sacred rights of life and liberty of a distant people, who never offended him, captivating them into slavery in another hemisphere or to incur miserable death in their transportation thither." Although the paragraph containing this clause was struck out in deference to the wishes of the planters of the Carolinas and Georgia and of the slave traders of the North, it represented the attitude of many famous men in every part of the new nation. Memorials advocating antislavery legislation increased in number after 1776. Patrick Henry stigmatized slavery as an "abominable practice," and a "species of violence and tyranny repugnant to humanity, inconsistent with religion, and destructive of liberty." Even south of Virginia, where condemnation of slavery was rare, a few protested. Henry Laurens, the wealthy and influential South Carolinian, writing in 1776, said: "You know, my dear son, I abhor slavery. . . . The day, I hope, is approaching when from principles of gratitude as well as justice every man will strive to be foremost in showing his readiness to comply with the golden rule. . . ." In Pennsylvania the Quakers, Mennonites, and other sects carried on an energetic campaign against slavery. The Methodists in conference resolved that "slave-keeping was hurtful to society and contrary to the laws of God and nature." Abolition and manumission societies, headed by such prominent men as Benjamin Franklin and Tench Coxe of Pennsylvania and Melancthon Smith of New York, also condemned slavery as morally iniquitous.

Those opposed to slavery in the South were, however, a distinct minority of the white population. Every state in the region except South Carolina did abolish the slave trade, not for equality's sake, but rather as a blow against the English shippers of slaves. In the North, Vermont, though not a member of the Continental Congress, abolished slavery by constitutional provision in 1777. Three years later Pennsylvania made provision for gradual emancipation. New Hampshire, Connecticut, and Rhode Island, with very few slaves, soon followed these pioneers. But not until 1799 did New York provide that all children born of slaves should be freed when they had reached a certain age; and emancipation for all slaves was not completed until 1827. New Jersey was even more dilatory; it was 1804 before the legislature took the first step to put an end to slavery, and 1846 before the last slaves in the state were converted into apprentices. By 1800 slavery in Massachusetts had been eliminated by statute as well as by custom.

When the Declaration of Independence was issued, the colonial penal codes, although more humane than those in Europe, were by modern standards both barbarous and illiberal. In New York sixteen crimes were punishable by death on the first offense, and for many second offense felonies there was also capital punishment. Delaware listed twenty crimes for which death was the penalty. Connecticut had fifteen, and Rhode Island only a few less. At the instigation of men like Jefferson, who were familiar with the efforts of Beccaria to improve the criminal laws of Europe, Virginia led the movement for reform, but, as with slavery, actual reform came slowly. Although movements against imprisonment for debt and for reform of the dreadful prison conditions of the time started during the revolutionary generation, they made little headway.

The Revolution also had limited effects on education. On the one hand, it tended to drain teachers and money from schools. Common schools, both public and private, as well as some colleges, were forced to close or to curtail their activities. Despite the concern of Jefferson, John Adams, and others, only four of the state constitutions—those of Georgia, North Carolina, Pennsylvania, and Massachusetts—mentioned either schools or education. The first constitution of Vermont, which did not join the Union until 1790, made provision for an educational system from town school to university. Before 1789, little legislation affecting the common school was enacted by any state. On the other hand, during this period several academies were established, of which Phillips Andover (1778) in Massachusetts and Phillips Exeter (1781) in New Hampshire were perhaps the most outstanding. Before 1790, eight new colleges were founded, and in the last decade of the century more than a half dozen others. Meanwhile, a medical department had been added to Harvard in 1783, and general improvements in medical and dental education came elsewhere. The first law school in America was opened at Litchfield, Connecticut, in 1784 by Judge Tappan Reeve. General reform of the legal profession made the American bar more responsible, but also more conservative. With the first printing of two future classic text books, Noah Webster's speller (1783) and Jedidiah Morse's geography (1784), and with the revival of the American Philosophical Society and the founding of the American Academy of Arts and Sciences, American cultural life started on new paths.

Of all the social consequences of the Revolution, the gains for equality were much smaller than the growing strength of spirit of individualism and nationalism that had been slowly developing from the day the English planted their first permanent settlements on American soil. In the future, the former colonists, though copying some Old World customs and manners, were to think of themselves more strongly than ever before as Americans. Many social changes in the years after 1776 cannot be traced directly to the effects of the Revolution or of the principles of the Declaration of Independence. But the America of 1783 was psychologically different from the America of 1775. America was to be neither a playground for English officials nor a market to be exploited by British businessmen. The destinies of America had passed into the hands of people whose sense of life was markedly different from that of the English and of other Europeans. Although most citizens of the new republic were still extremely provincial, a spirit of national identity was undermining the old strongholds of particularism and foretelling the day when the dozen or more independent commonwealths would be knit together in a federal union.

FOR SUPPLEMENTARY READING

The best one-volume general works on the Revolution are J. C. Miller, *Triumph of Freedom* (1948), and P. Mackesy, *The War for America* (1965). For military history, Willard Wallace, *Appeal to Arms* (1951), has more grace and style than J. R. Alden's more comprehensive *The American Revolution 1755–1783* (1954). H. S. Commager and R. B. Morris have made a most impressive collection of contemporary accounts in *The Spirit of Seventy-Six* (2 vols., 1958). Lynn Montross, *The Reluctant Rebels* (1950), is a recent good study of the patriot leadership. Elisha P. Douglass, *Rebels and Democrats* (1955), restates the classic view of the war on the home front as a struggle for equality. For a more recent view, use J. T. Main, *The Social Structure of Revolutionary America* (1965).

Three books can be used to start study of the political theory of the time: Clinton Rossiter, *Seedtime of the Republic* (1953) (Pb); C. L. Becker, *The Declaration of Independence* (1922); and R. G. Adams, *The Political Ideas of the American Revolution* (1922) (Pb). Allan Nevins, *The American States During and After the Revolution* (1927), has the fullest examination of wartime politics within the states. This work—together with J. F. Jameson, *The American Revolution Considered as a Social Movement* (1926) (Pb) and Merrill Jensen, *The Articles of Confederation* (1940)—ought to be read in the light of the article by F. B. Tolles, "The American Revolution Considered as a Social Movement: A Revaluation," *American Historical Review*, Vol. LX (Oct. 1954).

There are two books to begin study of the diplomacy of the Revolution: S. F. Bemis, *The Diplomacy of the American Revolution* (1935) (Pb), and E. S. Corwin, *French Policy and the American Alliance* (1916). They take places behind the recent work of R. B. Morris, *The Peacemakers: The Great Powers and American Independence* (1965). The international setting is also the theme of R. W. Van Alstyne, *Empire and Independence, The International History of the American Revolution* (1965).

Historians' debates about the Revolution are found in E. S. Morgan (ed.), *The American Revolution: Two Centuries of Interpretation* (1965), and E. Wright (ed.), *Causes and Consequences of the American Revolution* (1966). A famous older English study has been compressed by R. B. Morris: G. M. Trevelyan, *The American Revolution* (1964).

8

-≫≫-≫≫-≫≫-≫≫-≫≫-≫≫-≫≫-≫≫

Confederation
and Constitution

FTER 1776, the American people moved by trial and error toward new forms of government. In less than a generation, they abandoned their time-honored status as thirteen separate units in a far-flung British Empire and became the citizens of a new nation.

No man in 1776 had in mind the form of political life adopted in the Constitution of the United States of America. In the movement toward the Constitution, Americans debated many complex questions about the nature of political power and discussed the roles that prominent American leaders and their states could expect to play in a new government.

Because the American Revolution had cut across class lines, the enthusiasm for independence had bound together such different people as Thomas Jefferson and Sam Adams, but the nearer America came to securing her freedom, the more the differences among the Patriots were accentuated. As soon as the Patriots severed the ties that had bound them to England, they had to find a substitute for the centralized authority they were seeking to overthrow. The task was not easy. Any attempt to create an effective union among the new states had to reckon with many disputes that divided the population. Despite these difficulties, the Americans in little more than a decade seemed to have solved the problem of authority that had so long plagued the British Empire, and the Constitution still stands as a monument to the political genius of the founding fathers of the United States.

Unity and Diversity

The problem of union in 1776 was not a new one. At times—particularly when the Empire was threatened by France—officials in England had done all in their power to promote a spirit of unity and cooperation among the colonists. To the colonists, union seemed merely a device that would enable Great Britain to increase its authority over the provincial economies and governments. Even without formal union, they argued, they had frequently been able to protest against British acts they considered oppressive. Conflicting and shifting views of union on both sides of the Atlantic explain in large part both the origins of the Albany plan of union and the failure of either the British or the Americans to accept such proposals.

Demands for union both before and during the Revolution raised psychological as well as administrative problems. The average American tended to be loyal to a locality rather than to a distant government. Living in small communities or on isolated farms, eighteenth-century Americans were inclined to view anyone outside their immediate neighborhoods as a foreigner. The marked physical contrasts between the various sections produced decidedly different customs, traditions, and economies. New Englanders had little in common with Virginians; a wide gulf separated farmers from city dwellers; and the frontiersmen and the inhabitants of the coastal regions had developed two distinct—and often diametrically opposed—ways of living.

The outbreak of the Revolution played down, but did not eliminate, the powerful spirit of localism in every section of America. In many instances, the rivalries that had divided the colonies were carried over to the states. Each state was convinced that it was contributing more to the cause than the others, and each believed that the others were not altogether trustworthy. Boundary disputes also continued to provoke conflicts. New York and New Hampshire both sought to annex Vermont; Maryland viewed Virginia's expansionist moves with understandable alarm; and those states without western lands resented the claims of the others to territory beyond the Alleghenies. Any union that was capable of solving such problems would require an effective central government; yet, in many respects, the Revolution itself was a protest against centralized political authority.

Despite the strength of the particularist tradition in revolutionary America, the struggle for independence made some form of union imperative. A common enemy gave the states common problems and a common objective. Above all, the exigencies of war made clear to the Patriot leaders the need for a unified policy. The alternative to union was defeat. The difficulties faced by the Continental Congress—with its lack of authority and divided responsibility—indicated both the need for cooperation in a period of crisis and the reluctance of the American people to relinquish cherished local rights. In addition to the demands imposed by the war, other forces impelled many Americans to realize that they had some common ties with citizens in other sections of the country. Members of the same religious denominations had some sense of oneness regardless of where they lived. Class lines, which cut across political borders, sometimes helped to produce a spirit of solidarity. Growing intercolonial trade also tended to bind together Americans who lived in widely scattered regions of the new nation.

The Declaration of Independence proved to be the turning point in the movement for establishing an American union. Before 1776, all plans for union had of necessity to make some provision for British control. But, with the removal of British authority, the character of the problem changed. The desirability of union had become an academic question; for, like their former rulers, the Americans now had to decide how much authority should be granted to the states and how much should be granted to the central government. Regardless of how the issue was resolved, large numbers of Americans were bound to be dissatisfied with the answers to these pressing questions.

In the struggle over forming the new government, no clear lines of class division emerged. Just as the colonial farmers, merchants, frontiersmen, and plantation owners had split on loyalty to England or revolution, so did the Patriot forces disagree on the questions of the division of power in the new nation. Small southern frontier farmers wanted stronger national government for protection against the Indians. Some of their counterparts in New England feared that a stronger government would interfere with their local interests. Merchants in Newport or Norfolk might resist closer union, while men of the same calling in New York or Philadelphia might desire it. Local problems and interests largely determined where a particular group stood on the question of an effective national government.

At the beginning of the war, most of the Patriot leaders viewed the Revolution as essentially a war against unjust central authority. They were determined that the disruption of the British Empire would not be followed by the reimposition of a type of government that they had fought to destroy. To the more radical Patriots, the Revolution was more than a war for independence. They were convinced that the more remote a government was from those that it governed, the more likely it was to become tyrannical. As a consequence, they wished to exchange British centralization for a series of nearly autonomous state units that would provide popular leaders with the greatest possible opportunity to govern themselves. In this sense the radicals were democrats who believed that the states should be given authority over taxation, coinage, trade, property rights, military forces, and foreign affairs. In advancing this program, men like Sam Adams and Patrick Henry were not, of course, disinterested, for they were fairly confident that they would be able to control the government of the states of the proposed federation.

The fear that revolution might provide a political opportunity for radicals had held back many other Patriot leaders from a final break with England. The majority of the signers of the Declaration of Independence had not taken that fateful step in order to deliver themselves into the hands of the back country "levellers" or town "mobs" manipulated by men like Sam Adams. Opposed to certain features of British rule on principle, they had also objected to the relatively subordinate position they had occupied in the hierarchy of imperial authority. Their principal aim was to take over the power that had been exercised by British officials, without changing the existing class and political structure in other ways. If they could carry out this policy, they would then be in a position to check any radical movements in the states and thus prevent the movement for independence from becoming a social revolution.

Opposition to radicals within the states did not make substantial men supporters of a strong central government. A wealthy man like John Hancock of Massachusetts enjoyed much power and prestige in his state, and only large enticements finally induced him to risk losing prestige to the leaders of a national government. Others, however, who were his equals in local power, moved to demand more effective national government as the years after 1783 seemed to show America drifting to helplessness and anarchy.

The first round in the struggle over the form of the new government ended with the adoption of the Articles of Confederation. As early as July 21, 1775, Benjamin Franklin had submitted a revised version of his Albany plan of union to the Congress for its consideration. When almost a year later (July 2, 1776) the Congress adopted Richard Henry Lee's resolution for independence, it also approved a motion to appoint a committee to draw up a plan of confederation for the states. John Dickinson, who served as the committee's chairman, dominated the proceedings, and the document that was submitted to the Congress on July 12, 1776, was largely his work. Because Dickinson's plan contained a number of centralizing features that were unacceptable, the entire subject of union was thrashed out in the committee of the whole. When the Articles of Confederation were approved by the Congress on

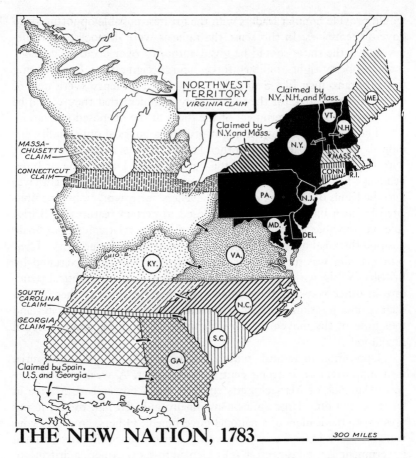

THE NEW NATION, 1783 ———— 300 MILES

November 15, 1777, they reflected a general fear of strong government.
The Articles were not put into operation immediately, for an acrimonious controversy over western land claims delayed their acceptance by
all the states. It was not until 1781, when Maryland finally granted its
approval, that the Articles of Confederation went into effect.

Under the Articles of Confederation, the United States was a league
of sovereign commonwealths. The Federal government consisted of a
Congress in which each state enjoyed equal power. The Congress, composed of delegates chosen annually by the states, was empowered to
declare war, make peace, send and receive diplomatic representatives,
make treaties, regulate the value of coin both of the United States and
of the several states, borrow money and issue bills of credit, raise armies,
build a navy, control Indian affairs, fix weights and measures, and establish post offices. It had, however, no power to levy taxes or to regu-

late commerce. No amendment could be added to the Articles unless it was ratified by every state. To secure adoption, practically every important measure had to have the assent of nine states.

The Articles of Confederation were the product of neither ignorance nor experience, but of the conscious desire of Patriot leaders to devise a system of government that would promote their own state interests and conform to their principles. Consequently, the Articles of Confederation differed in every important essential from the British administration they supplanted. The central government under the Articles could not control commerce, trade, banking, and currency; it could not tax the people directly; it had neither executive nor judicial branches; and it did not have an agency like the Privy Council that could disallow the laws passed by the state legislatures.

The two most objectionable features of English government had been King and Parliament. When Americans set up their own government, they made no attempt to create a position equivalent to that held by the King, and the closest approach to an executive office in the Confederation was a committee of thirteen (one representative from each state) selected by Congress to act as that body's *alter ego* when it was not in session. In place of Parliament, the Americans established a Congress that had practically none of Parliament's powers. The Confederation Congress could make commercial treaties, but it could not make the states live up to the treaty terms. It could pass laws, but it could not make the states obey them. It was the most important branch of the new government, but it had no way of coercing states that were recalcitrant. Under the Articles of Confederation, the states were free to work out their own destinies without the threat of outside interference or domination.

The Confederation Congress did possess numerous rights on paper. But the one power it lacked was the power to coerce. The extent of its authority was therefore always dependent on the willingness of the states to accept its measures. In the years after the Articles went into effect, the states displayed limitless capacity for either ignoring or defying the government of the Confederation. The Congress, therefore, lacked the *sine qua non* of every effective government—the power to govern; it could suggest, but it could not command.

In the Declaration of Independence the American colonial leaders announced their philosophy of government, but the Declaration was a statement of views and intentions rather than a framework of government. The Articles of Confederation was the first American attempt to apply the Declaration's philosophy of the sovereignty of the people. Although subsequent events were to demonstrate that the Articles failed to provide the kind of government needed by a new and divided nation, they nevertheless accurately reflected the spirit of the leaders of the American Revolution in the first flush of their enthusiasm over freedom from the interference of a distant, centralized government.

The West and the Confederation

Throughout its brief but turbulent history, the government of the Confederation was much involved with developments on the frontier regions beyond the Alleghenies. On the one hand, problems in the West were primarily responsible for the four-year delay in the ratification of the Articles. On the other, one of the outstanding achievements of the new government was the system it eventually developed for the disposal of the public domain and its effective and statesmanlike method for the political organization of the territories of the United States.

The interval between Congress' approval of the Articles of Confederation in 1777 and the completion of ratification in 1781 was due to Maryland's refusal to ratify any plan of government that sanctioned existing land titles west of the Alleghenies. At the outbreak of the Revolution, Connecticut, Georgia, Massachusetts, the two Carolinas, and Virginia claimed extensive tracts of the western domain that they had obtained from the British government during the colonial period. New York also had claims based on a treaty that the colony had concluded with the Indians. The remaining states had no title to any western lands. Although twelve states had approved the Articles of Confederation by 1779, Maryland refused on the ground that lands that "had been secured by the blood and treasure of all, ought, in reason, justice, and policy, to be considered a common stock, to be parcelled out by Congress into free, convenient, and independent Governments." Since neither side showed any willingness to give way, there seemed a strong likelihood that the Articles of Confederation would never go into effect. Finally, in January 1781, Virginia, which had the largest claim, offered to relinquish its territory north of the Ohio River. Maryland immediately ratified the Articles, and on March 1, 1781, they officially became the law of the new nation.

Virginia's agreement to cede its western lands contained certain stipulations that were not acceptable to Congress, and it was not until 1784 that the Old Dominion turned over most of its territory north of the Ohio to the government of the Confederation. Meanwhile New York had surrendered its title to its western lands in 1782, and the other northern states soon followed suit. In 1785–86, Massachusetts transferred its western lands to the Confederation, and in the same year

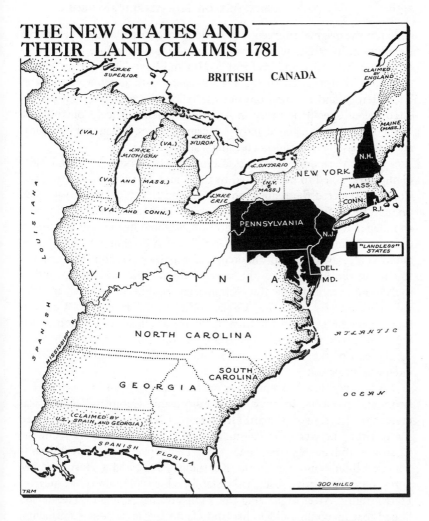

THE NEW STATES AND
THEIR LAND CLAIMS 1781

BRITISH CANADA

LAKE SUPERIOR

CLAIMED BY ENGLAND

(VA.)

(VA.)

LAKE HURON

LAKE MICHIGAN

MAINE (MASS.)

N.H.

L. ONTARIO

NEW YORK

(VA. AND MASS.)

(N.Y. & MASS.)

LAKE ERIE

MASS.

CONN.

(VA. AND CONN.)

R.I.

PENNSYLVANIA

N.J.

"LANDLESS" STATES

DEL.

MD.

V I R G I N I A

OHIO R.

NORTH CAROLINA

ATLANTIC

SOUTH CAROLINA

G E O R G I A

OCEAN

(CLAIMED BY U.S., SPAIN, AND GEORGIA)

L O U I S I A N A

S P A N I S H

MISSISSIPPI R.

SPANISH FLORIDA

300 MILES

TRM

Connecticut gave up all its western territory except the Western Reserve (now northern Ohio), which was not ceded to the United States until 1800. The southern states were much more reluctant than those of the North to abandon their claims. But South Carolina ceded its western lands in 1787, North Carolina (which had made and retracted an earlier cession) did the same in 1790, and Georgia followed suit in 1802. Virginia's claim to the region south of the Ohio was erased in 1792 with the admission of Kentucky to the Union.

While Congress was negotiating with the states over the western land claims, settlers in the interior were attempting to establish new commonwealths in the wilderness. Vermont, the first state later to be added to the original thirteen, was settled more than a decade before the Revolution. Its affairs were largely controlled, even before the Revolution, by Ethan Allen and his brothers, Ira and Levi. "The Green Mountain Boys" contributed to the Patriot cause with notable victories at Ticonderoga and Bennington; but the Allens were always more interested in land speculation than in American independence. Controlling a land company that claimed 300,000 Vermont acres, Ethan and his brothers were masters of business chicanery and intrigue.

When Vermont, which was claimed by both New York and New Hampshire, asked to be admitted to the Union in 1776, the Continental Congress rejected the request on the ground that New York had been granted the region by the Crown. Refused as a state, Vermont became an independent republic. Its constitution, adopted in 1777, was the most democratic in America. In the republic of Vermont all adult males could vote, slavery was prohibited, and religious freedom was granted to all. But the Allens were still worried about their land claims, and in the closing years of the Revolution they sought to have their titles validated, first by promising English officials in Canada that Vermont would become a neutral and then by assuring officials in London that it would side with the British. These negotiations, however, were cut short by the end of the war. Throughout the 1780's Vermont remained an independent nation.

Kentucky, like Vermont, was opened to settlement by both speculators and pioneers. In 1775, the Transylvania Company, which was under the direction of Richard Henderson of North Carolina, purchased the territory between the Kentucky and Cumberland rivers from the Cherokee Indians. In the same year, Henderson and Daniel Boone founded Boonesborough on the Kentucky River, and a short time before some Pennsylvanians had established a community at nearby Harrodsburg. After organizing the Transylvania Company, Henderson hoped that he could validate his land claims by having the Continental Congress recognize his settlements. But Congress refused to grant his request, and Virginia in 1776 organized the lands in Kentucky into a county. Henderson's efforts, however, were not altogether fruitless, for the Transylvania Company was given 200,000 acres in the new county.

As early as 1769, a band of Virginia frontiersmen had settled near the Wautauga River in Tennessee, where they were soon joined by backcountry farmers from North Carolina. In 1772, the inhabitants of the region organized a government and negotiated a treaty with the Cherokee Indians. The new government, which operated under a constitution known as the Wautauga Association, lasted until North Carolina reasserted its claim to the region in 1776 and converted it into a

county. Eight years later, when North Carolina ceded its western territory to the Confederation and stopped its annual payments to the
Cherokees, the Wautaugans again had to fend for themselves. At two
conventions, they drew up a constitution, elected a governor, and named
their territory the state of Franklin. The new state had a short, perilous,
and chaotic history. Torn by internal dissension and menaced by hostile
Indians, it also had to contend with North Carolina, which had cancelled its 1784 cession and attempted to regain control over its former
western lands.

While pioneers were creating in the wilderness south of the Ohio
a series of new commonwealths, only a comparatively small number of
settlers were moving into the Northwest. In 1784, there were less than
4,000 white inhabitants in the entire region, and most of these were in
communities that had been established by the French. Between 30,000
and 40,000 Indians lived north of the Ohio, and the land could not be
settled until the Indian titles had been extinguished. Treaties were negotiated in 1784 with the Iroquois and in 1785 with the Chippewa, Delaware, Ottawa, and Wyandot tribes. These agreements cancelled the
Indian claims to virtually all of Ohio.

Although the states did not finally relinquish their claims to the
Northwest until 1786, Congress began to take steps to organize this immense colonial domain soon after the Articles of Confederation had
gone into effect. After considering two other proposals, Congress in
1784 adopted an ordinance drafted by Jefferson that provided that the
territory should forever remain a part of the United States; that it
should be subject to the Congress and the Articles of Confederation;
that it should be divided into ten states with constitutions modeled after
those of the original states; that a permanent government should be
formed and a delegate elected to Congress when the population numbered 20,000; that each state should be admitted to the union when the
number of inhabitants equaled "the least numerous of the thirteen original states"; and that each state formed from it should pay its share of
the Revolutionary debts. An article forbidding slavery in any of the national territories after 1800 was rejected by a single vote, and Congress
refused to approve Jefferson's proposal that the new states be given such
names as Assenisippia, Pelisippia, Cherronesus, Metropotamia, and
Polypotamia.

Because the Confederation Congress was always hard pressed for
funds, it was more interested in the revenue that could be produced
from land sales in the Northwest than in the territory's political organization. Accordingly, in 1785 Congress passed a Land Ordinance that
stated that as soon as the Indian title to the lands north of the Ohio had

Selling American Lands in France in the 1780's

[THE NEW YORK HISTORICAL SOCIETY]

been acquired by the government, the territory should be surveyed into townships six miles square. Each of the townships, in turn, was to be divided into thirty-six lots or "sections" of 640 acres each.

After reserving to the national government one seventh of every township, to be used to satisfy the claims of the soldiers of the Continental Army, and one third of any mineral ore that might be found, the measure directed that the land be distributed among the states and auctioned off alternately by townships or by lots at a minimum cash price of $1 per acre plus $36 per township to cover the cost of survey. The Ordinance further provided that the sixteenth section of each township be set aside for the support of education, and that each purchaser receive with his deed a definite description of his holding.

In the months immediately after the adoption of the Land Ordinance of 1785, the Northwest was more attractive to speculators than to settlers. Because Congress made no move to carry out the provisions of the Ordinance of 1784, individuals were reluctant to take up land at a relatively high price in a region where Indians were a constant menace and where no government existed to protect property rights. But none of these considerations stopped the land speculators, and within a short time a plan for pre-empting large tracts in the Northwest had been drawn up by the Ohio Company of Associates. Organized at the Bunch of Grapes Tavern in Boston on March 1, 1786, by a group of Revolutionary officers, the Ohio Associates hoped that Congress would give them an enormous land grant in exchange for the almost worthless Continental certificates that they had been paid for their military service. They also wanted Congress to organize the territory so that the settler-purchasers would be assured adequate protection.

To achieve their objectives, the Ohio Associates were compelled to undertake delicate—if not illegal—negotiations with Congress. After General Samuel Parsons had tried his hand at this work and failed, the task was entrusted to Manasseh Cutler. A Massachusetts clergyman, botanist, philosopher, and businessman, Cutler also proved to be an adept lobbyist. When Congress refused to listen to his original proposals, he included the Scioto Company of New York in the arrangements, and the deal was consummated. According to Cutler, the transaction involved "a private speculation in which many of the principal characters of America" were concerned. In any event, both companies were given charters by Congress. The Ohio Associates bought 1,500,000 acres of land at approximately nine cents an acre, and the Scioto Company obtained an option—which it never took up—on 3,500,000 acres.

Two weeks before Cutler had concluded his negotiations, Congress adopted the Northwest Ordinance (July 12, 1787) for the organization of the territory. Under the terms of the Ordinance, the territory was to be divided into not less than three or more than five states. Until the area had a population of 5,000 free males, it would be administered by a governor, three judges, and a secretary, all of whom were to be appointed by Congress. In the second stage of its administration, the territory was to have a representative assembly with power to make laws subject to the governor's veto, a council selected from a list of names submitted by the territorial legislature, and a nonvoting delegate in Congress. When any of the proposed states within the territory had a population of 60,000 free inhabitants, it could be admitted to the Union "on an equal footing with the original states." Finally, six "articles of compact" in the Ordinance provided for personal liberty, religious freedom, the introduction of a system of free public education, and the exclusion of slavery. General Arthur St. Clair was appointed first governor of the territory.

The Northwest Ordinance settled a vexing American problem but was somewhat less democratic than Jefferson's proposals of 1784. It was, nevertheless, a radical departure from the colonial policies of the

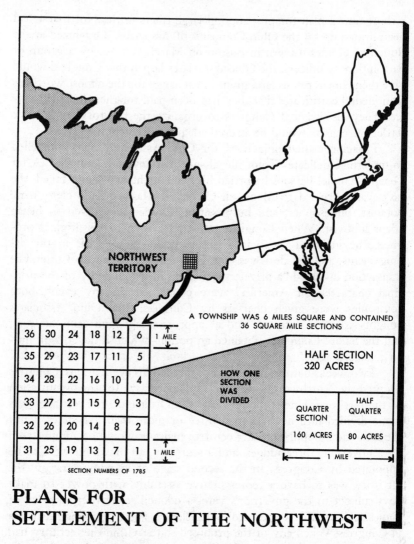

NORTHWEST
TERRITORY

A TOWNSHIP WAS 6 MILES SQUARE AND CONTAINED
36 SQUARE MILE SECTIONS

36	30	24	18	12	6
35	29	23	17	11	5
34	28	22	16	10	4
33	27	21	15	9	3
32	26	20	14	8	2
31	25	19	13	7	1

1 MILE

SECTION NUMBERS OF 1785

HOW ONE
SECTION
WAS
DIVIDED

HALF SECTION
320 ACRES

QUARTER
SECTION
160 ACRES

HALF
QUARTER
80 ACRES

1 MILE

PLANS FOR
SETTLEMENT OF THE NORTHWEST

major powers of the Old World. In the past, colonists had been viewed as fit subjects for exploitation, but the Northwest Ordinance granted certain fundamental rights to all the inhabitants of the territory, and assured them that their political status would soon be the same as that enjoyed by the residents of the established states. In this fashion the traditional rivalry between colony and mother country was largely eliminated before it had an opportunity to develop, and a plan was devised for the orderly incorporation of new areas into the United States. The Northwest Ordinance demonstrated both the determination of the new nation to avoid the British mistakes of the colonial period and the ability of its people to translate the theories of popular sovereignty into the reality of self-government.

Outstanding Accounts with Europe

American pioneers in the Northwest were constantly menaced by the British and their Indian allies. In the Treaty of Paris the British had agreed to abandon their military and fur-trading posts in the Northwest as rapidly as possible. But at a secret meeting in the British Colonial Office on April 8, 1784—the day before the treaty went into effect—the British decided to retain these posts in order to enlist the aid of friendly Indians in checking the advance of American settlement and to protect the lucrative Scottish Canadian fur trade in the Northwest. Many officials in London were predicting that the collapse of the new United States was only a matter of time—these posts would then enable the British to obtain the Northwest by default. The British therefore not only ignored Congress's repeated requests to evacuate the posts, but also forbade the use of the Great Lakes to Americans and opened a customs office at Oswego.

Great Britain's refusal to withdraw from the Northwest was matched by the United States' violation of the Treaty of Paris' provision for the payment of the debts that individual Americans owed the British. Under the terms of the peace treaty, it was "agreed that creditors on either side shall meet with no lawful impediment to the recovery of the full value in sterling money, of all *bona fide* debts heretofore contracted." But Congress was unable to prevent the states from passing bills that did place "lawful impediments" in the way of British creditors seeking to collect the money owed them. If the dispute over the Northwest posts made manifest Congress's inability to achieve its aims in international affairs, the debts controversy just as fully demonstrated that Congress was powerless to coerce the American states.

The disagreements with Great Britain over treatment of the Loyalists and compensation for stolen slaves also revealed Congress's impotence. The Treaty of Paris provided that persecution of the Loyalists "be discontinued" and "that Congress . . . also recommend to the several states, that the estates, rights and properties [of the Loyalists] . . . be restored to them." There was practically no persecution of the Loyalists after the war; but all the states refused to abide by the compensation clause. Congress lived up to the letter of the treaty by making repeated recommendations to the states, but there the matter ended. To many Americans, failure to compensate the Loyalists seemed balanced by Great Britain's refusal to abide by the treaty provision that required her to pay for the 3,000 slaves stolen by her soldiers during the war. In a short time, however, these questions were pushed into the background by more important matters.

The relations of the United States with Spain were no more satisfactory than those with Britain. The Spanish in the Southwest were pursuing a policy in many respects similar to that of the British in the Northwest. Although the Treaty of Paris granted the United States all the territory north of Florida and gave the Americans the right to navigate the Mississippi, the Spanish ignored both provisions. Maintaining that the southern border of the United States was farther north than that claimed by the Americans, the Spanish made every effort to occupy the disputed territory. Like the English in the Northwest, they refused to relinquish their posts in the region and enlisted the aid of powerful Indian tribes—in this instance, the Creek, Choctaw, and Chickasaw—to check the westward advance of American settlers. The Spanish also purchased the temporary allegiance of a number of American frontier leaders. Many westerners—among them, James Robertson, George Rogers Clark, and John Sevier—negotiated with the Spanish, but no other American went as far as James Wilkinson. In 1787, Wilkinson, who had fought in the Revolution, moved from Kentucky to New Orleans, where he swore allegiance to the Spanish Crown and accepted an annual payment in return for his efforts to create a secessionist movement in the Southwest.

Far more important than either Spanish gold or hostile Indians in the conflict between the United States and Spain in the Southwest was the control of the Mississippi River. Because the cost of sending produce overland to the East was prohibitive, pioneers in the West were forced to use the Mississippi as a highway for shipping their surplus produce to New Orleans, where it could be transferred to ocean-going vessels. Consequently, when the Spanish in 1784 closed the river to Americans, the economic life of the Southwest was jeopardized. The westerners immediately appealed to Congress for assistance, and in 1785, John Jay, the Secretary of Foreign Affairs, sought to work out a compromise with Diego de Gardoqui, the Spanish minister to the United States. Although the two diplomats also discussed the boundary dispute, Indian problems, and a possible commercial treaty, the Mississippi remained the most important item on the agenda throughout the negotiations. At one point, Jay, who was closely affiliated with Northeastern business interests, declared that the United States would renounce its right to navigate the Mississippi for twenty-five to thirty years in return for a favorable trade agreement. But this proposal was not acceptable to either the South or West, and in 1787 the negotiations ended with nothing accomplished except an increased suspicion by westerners that the Confederation government could not be trusted to protect their interests.

Great Britain also refused to conclude a commercial treaty with the United States. At the end of the war the Americans were anxious to resume their trade with England, but the British quickly revealed that they were determined to make their former colonies pay dearly for independence. In 1783, Parliament adopted a Navigation Act that restricted all trade with the British West Indies to British-built and British-owned ships and imposed heavy tonnage duties on American vessels in English ports. Another Navigation Act, adopted in 1787, prohibited the indirect import of American goods into England by way of foreign lands. Furthermore, the British refused to send a diplomatic representative to the United States before 1791; and John Adams, the first American minister to the Court of St. James, was treated with "dry decency and cold civility" until he returned home in 1788.

The weakness of the Confederation government prevented it from retaliating against Great Britain or Spain. Throughout these years, moreover, the Barbary pirates from Algiers, Morocco, Tripoli, and Tunis seized American sailors and ships in the Mediterranean; and Congress did not possess either the power to prevent such seizures or the money to ransom the American sailors who had been captured.

Postwar Prosperity and Depression

In the last years of the Confederation period, the Americans also had to contend with a severe depression. In the immediate postwar years, however, the new nation was undeniably prosperous except for those people who had depended on army contracts and privateering. Direct trade with Europe and new commerce with China, Hawaii, and other Pacific areas helped make up for losses in the areas of the British Empire now formally closed to American citizens. Manufacturing increased in volume and diversity. Commercial banks, which had been forbidden by the English were now organized. Corporate enterprises were also set up in manufacturing, insurance, and for the construction of turnpikes. Great profits accrued to the various land companies organized after 1776.

The general economic expansion lasted until 1785, when excessive optimism and overly rapid growth led to too large commitments in inventories and private credit. Accordingly, the new republic found itself in the midst of a depression that lasted until after 1787. Between 1785 and 1787, many businessmen found themselves in financial straits, and farmers, unable to market their surplus products, had difficulty in meeting their taxes and interest charges on mortgages. Soldiers returning from the army were obliged to sell their wage certificates at one eighth of their face value. Thousands of artisans and laborers were jobless. Between 1785 and 1789, commodity prices dropped 30 per cent. By 1787, farm wages fell to a low of forty cents a day and foreclosures and judgments for debt climbed to all-time highs in many areas.

Congress' inability to carry out either its domestic or foreign policies aggravated the impact of the depression. Since the Confederation could not establish import duties and since Great Britain was determined to regain its pre-Revolutionary markets at all costs, the American manufacturer could not withstand British competition. During the months immediately following the signing of the Treaty of Paris, Great Britain glutted the former colonies with cheap manufactured goods, and, although Congress was unable to help, the home producers' efforts to put pressure upon the state governments met with some success. Between 1783 and 1788, all the states except Connecticut, New Jersey, and Delaware levied tonnage dues upon British vessels or discriminatory tariffs upon British goods. But the effect of this action was minimized or completely neutralized by the fact that the duties were not uniform, and the British vessels therefore used the free or cheapest ports.

Great Britain had persistently refused to negotiate a commercial treaty with the United States. While continuing to encourage the former colonists to send her needed commodities, England closed her doors to American whale products. She also forbade the United States to participate in the carrying trade of her West Indian possessions, or to send salt meats or fish to them even in British vessels. The interruption of the West Indian trade seriously interfered with the coastal trade and the slave traffic, made it impossible for the Americans to secure much-needed specie and bills of exchange with which to pay for foreign goods, and severely handicapped the rum and ship-building industries.

During the lean years after 1785 American merchants were also hard hit. Like the manufacturers, they had to compete with the British —who, not content with flooding the country with their goods, also distributed them directly. Every town of any importance had its British agents or factors. In April, 1785, Boston merchants held a meeting in Faneuil Hall and voted to petition Congress "for laws putting our commerce on an equality." Following precedents established in the years preceding the Revolution, they made arrangements to communicate with committees in other colonies and pledged themselves not only to boycott the British factors, but to prevent others from doing business with them. They agreed not to lease warehouses to the British and not to employ any person who helped the British. The British refusal to vacate the trading posts in the Northwest deprived these Americans of a large share of the profits of the fur trade and added to the feeling against Great Britain.

Lack of a uniform national currency and of governmental machinery for facilitating interstate trade also worked hardships on the domestic merchant. The heavy imports of foreign goods in 1783–4 drained the country of much specie, and what was left was debased in value by clippers and counterfeiters. Paper currency, with its constant fluctuations, was hated by most businessmen, for they could never be certain of its value. New Jersey paper money, for instance, was practically worthless in New York. Although there were also numerous conflicting state tariffs on goods that originated "abroad," such tariffs seldom applied to commodities originating in other states, and interstate trade was therefore not excessively hampered by these regulations.

The public debt was an especially vexing question under the Confederation. At the beginning of 1784, the indebtedness of the states was approximately $21,000,000, and that of the national government totaled almost $40,000,000. Although the national debt was slightly reduced during the next few years by receipts from the sale of public lands, the interest on it remained unpaid. Of the approximately $4,500,000 spent by the national treasury from 1784 to 1789, about half came from foreign loans and the remainder from requisitions on the states. In 1786, the national financial system broke down completely. Loans, domestic or foreign, could be obtained only with the greatest difficulty; requisitions were ineffectual; and efforts to secure funds by means of a national tax failed. Holders of government bonds, whether original subscribers or speculators who had acquired them at greatly reduced figures, were alarmed. The creditors were even further injured by the widespread use of paper money and by the enactment of stay laws closing the courts to people seeking payment of debts.

Because sovereignty was vested in the states, the central government, even if so disposed, was powerless to aid the nation's economy. It could not, for example, raise funds with which to pay the interest or principal on public securities, for, under the Articles, Congress was forced to rely on a requisition system similar to that employed by England in colonial days. As early as 1781, Congress, acting on the suggestion of "divers inhabitants of the state of Pennsylvania," proposed that the Articles be amended so as to authorize a national 5 per cent duty on imports. But this and similar proposals were blocked by the dissenting voices of Rhode Island and New York. And what was true of the attempts to secure revenue was also true of Congress' efforts to prevent the several states from enacting conflicting tariffs against non-American articles.

Despite these great difficulties the Confederation government did manage to reduce the principal of its debt. The individual states were even more successful. None of the states entered the federal union in 1789 with a very high debt. Some states had quickly brought their debts to a low level without outside help. But this very rapid amortization of the debt in a state like Massachusetts helped bring on and aggravate the depression. It induced a large deflation which, combined with high taxes and strict laws about the collection of debts, drove the small holders to desperate measures. Thus, while it is possible to praise the state governments for their contributions to economic stability up to 1785, paradoxically, the reduction of the debt also helped precipitate the crisis that brought an end to the Articles of Confederation.

The Critical Years: 1785–87

With the onset of the depression, the Articles of Confederation seemed to confirm their detractors' worst predictions. Congress had failed in its dealings with foreign nations, and it had demonstrated that it was totally incapable of preventing the various state legislatures from going their own ways. During the dark years of 1785–86, farmers, small retailers, laboring men, and debtors in general often found themselves unable to meet their obligations; their possessions passed into the hands of tax gatherers and creditors through foreclosures and seizures, and they themselves were thrown into prison. They resorted to drastic measures. Stay laws, impairment of contracts, legal tender acts, increased issues of paper money, and the closing of the courts to suits for debt were among the more important legislative steps taken to ward off harassing sheriffs. These attempts sometimes produced violence; mobs in Windsor and Rutland counties, Vermont, tried to prevent the courts from holding sessions, and the courthouse at Plymouth, New Hampshire, was burned.

In Rhode Island the struggle over paper money produced a memorable judicial decision. In an effort to enforce the state's paper money regulations, the legislature adopted a law providing for the trial before a juryless court of three judges of anyone who would not accept paper money. This legal tender currency was so debased that many creditors temporarily fled the state to avoid having to accept it.

Throughout the Confederation period in Massachusetts as elsewhere the former Patriot elite and the forces of law and order never lost control of their states. Every effort of the rank and file to attain some political influence beyond the right to vote was fruitless. Fear of the demands of the small propertied men for increased participation in the political life of Massachusetts had caused conservatives to draft a state constitution in 1780 that doubled the property qualification for voting, but this did not prove to be an effective deterrent to a wide suffrage when there were grave issues at stake. The situation in Massachusetts was already tense when in 1786 the legislature, acting on the suggestion of the new Governor, James Bowdoin, voted a tax of £311,000, an average of about $20 for every household of five. The proceeds of this tax, which fell more heavily on the farmer than on the merchant and creditor, were to be used in part to pay off more of the state's Revolutionary debt, now mostly in the hands of speculators. But this tax, together with the charges on the indebtedness incurred during the boom period, was more than the poorer families of the state could pay, especially during the deflation that came after 1785. Local retailers and moneylenders, however, pressed by Boston merchants, who in turn were being crowded by British creditors, had to have money. Thousands of debtors lost everything, and the jails overflowed with prisoners confined for debt.

The debtors, particularly in the central and western portions of the state, hurriedly called town and county conventions, which demanded that the legislature redress their grievances. Their petitions criticized the continued existence of the state senate and some of the higher courts (notably the Court of Common Pleas), the system of representation, exorbitant fees, the method of paying the state debt, unequal taxation, and the lack of currency. They wanted the state debt scaled down, the special privileges enjoyed by property eliminated from the Constitution, additional paper currency issued, and the lot of the debtor, whether farmer or townsman, made easier. "They are determined," wrote General Henry Knox to Washington "to annihilate all debts, public and private, and have agrarian laws, which are easily effected by the means of unfunded paper money, which shall be a tender in all cases whatsoever. . . . We shall have a formidable rebellion against reason, the principle of all government, and against the very name of liberty." One creditor wrote: "Instead of cheerfully paying as far as they are able their own private debts, retrenching their idle,

The Shaysites in Retreat

unnecessary expenses, and contributing their portion to support a government of their own making, we see them assembling conventions to do acts treasonable to the State." Their leaders, he continued, were "destitute of property, without reputation, hardy and factious in their tempers, and eminent only for their vices and depravity." Still another conservative labeled them "bankrupts and sots who have gambled or slept away their estates" and a "multitude of tavern-haunting politicians."

There was some truth to these assertions. In the Massachusetts countryside were a number of former revolutionary soldiers who had been village idlers and local toughs. Drifting together into small gangs, these rootless men had been especially irritated by the fall in value of their service certificates. They helped organize the debtors and inflame their grievances, but they had not created those grievances out of thin air.

Condemned by leading citizens and unable to secure redress from the legislature, the debtors rebelled. In August, 1786, insurgents seized the courthouse in Northampton and forcibly prevented the court from sitting and granting foreclosure notices to creditors. Less than a week later another insurgent band took possession of the courthouse in Worcester and compelled the court to adjourn. A little later a mob

prevented the court from sitting at Great Barrington and released all
the imprisoned debtors. Similar disturbances occurred in other disaffected areas. Alarmed at the turn of events, Governor Bowdoin summoned a special session of the legislature; but since several of its members were more or less in sympathy with the insurgents, the legislature
failed to get at the heart of the difficulties. It promised to redress grievances and took steps to protect the courts. Meanwhile an insurgent
force led by Daniel Shays, who had fought at Lexington, Bunker Hill,
Saratoga, and Stony Point, forced an adjournment of the court at
Springfield. Early in 1787, General Benjamin Lincoln was dispatched
with a force of 4,000 troops to suppress Shays's insurrection and during
the winter of 1787 he succeeded in quashing it. Despite demands that
the rebels be severely punished, the legislature, sensing majority opinion, granted amnesty to all—even to Shays. Law and order had triumphed, but so deep-seated was the feeling on the part of the poorer
classes that Governor Bowdoin was decisively defeated when he stood
for re-election.

Moving Toward a New Constitution

When news of Shays's Rebellion, as it came to be called, reached
the leaders of 1776, dismay was added to their apprehension about the
Confederation. George Washington, who wrote many anxious letters
trying to find out the causes of "all these commotions," worried that
America was rendering itself "ridiculous and contemptible in the eyes
of all Europe." The president of the Confederation Congress had already written to Prince Henry of Prussia about the possibilities of his
accepting a constitutional kingship in America. Increasingly, talk of
dictators was heard. James Madison, John Jay, Alexander Hamilton,
Edmund Randolph, and Thomas Jefferson all recorded their deep fears
concerning the country's future or expressed belief that political reform
was necessary. Even some of those who later opposed the new Constitution believed that stronger powers had to be given to the central
government. By 1786, it was evident to all but the most prejudiced
contemporaries that the government of the United States was a government in name only. To most of the leaders who had set America free
the ills of the country were primarily due to the lack of coercing power
in the Confederation government. In place of a weak government at
the beck and call of sovereign states, these men wished to establish a
centralized government that would itself exercise sovereign powers.
Such a government would pay the nation's debts, establish a sound
currency, regulate commerce, protect manufactures, properly distrib-

ute the western lands, carry out treaty agreements, and protest against aggressions of foreign nations.

Suggestions for a stronger central government had their beginnings even before the close of the war. As early as 1780, Alexander Hamilton, then only twenty-five years of age, had written: "The idea of an uncontrollable sovereignty in each state . . . will defeat the other powers given to Congress, and make our union feeble and precarious. . . . Congress should have complete sovereignty in all that relates to war, peace, trade, finance." During the next two years, in a series of papers, Hamilton enlarged upon what seemed to him to be the shortcomings of the Articles and urged that the Federal government be given the powers of taxation, regulation of commerce, and disposal of ungranted land. Others asked for similar reforms.

In 1785, Governor Bowdoin of Massachusetts, aware of the discontent in his own state, suggested the need for a stronger union, and the legislature of the Commonwealth adopted a resolution declaring the Articles of Confederation inadequate and recommending that a convention be called to revise them.

As early as 1784, the Virginia legislature had adopted a resolution framed by James Madison appointing commissioners to meet with agents of Maryland to discuss proposals for improving the navigation of the Potomac. Washington, who had large holdings in western lands, was understandably interested in this project, and at his suggestion the delegates met at Mount Vernon in 1785. After the spokesmen for the two states had agreed on plans for the Potomac, the Maryland legislature proposed that representatives from Delaware, Maryland, Pennsylvania, and Virginia meet to examine their common commercial problems. The Virginia legislature, after seconding this proposal, issued a call to all the states for a convention to meet at Annapolis on the first Monday in September, 1786. In its invitation, the Virginia legislature stated that the states would "consider how a uniform system in their commercial regulations may be necessary to their common interests and their permanent harmony."

Although nine states appointed delegates to the Annapolis Convention, only five—Delaware, New Jersey, New York, Pennsylvania, and Virginia—were actually represented. Instead of carrying out the express purpose for which it had been called, the convention adopted a report by Hamilton that pointed to the critical situation in the states and advised them to send delegates to another convention to meet in Philadelphia in May, 1787. Hamilton recommended that the delegates to this convention "devise such further provisions as shall appear . . . necessary as to render the constitution of the federal government adequate to the exigencies of the union." To allay the suspicions of local interests, he added that any amendment that the Philadelphia Convention might propose, must, in accordance with the Articles, be submitted to the states for their approval.

Hamilton's proposal was at once forwarded to the state legislatures and to Congress, and on February 21, 1787, Congress issued a call for the convention. It was even more explicit than Hamilton in stating that the sole purpose of the convention was to revise the Articles. Neither the Annapolis gathering nor the Congress specified the manner in which the delegates were to be chosen. In no instance were they chosen by popular vote. By May, 1787, all the states except New Hampshire and Rhode Island, acting through their legislatures, had chosen delegates. New Hampshire subsequently sent two delegates, after John Langdon, a wealthy Portsmouth merchant, offered to defray the expenses of a delegation. Rhode Island, where creditors had lost control of the legislature and the government had repudiated its financial obligations to the Confederation, refused to participate in the convention.

A Summer at Philadelphia

The Philadelphia Convention of 1787 was strikingly different from the First or even the Second Continental Congress. Of the sixty-two delegates appointed, fifty-five attended the sessions with more or less regularity, and thirty-nine put their names to the final draft of the new Constitution. Though not an "assembly of demi-gods," as Jefferson described it, the convention contained a good number of the outstanding men in America. On the other hand, there were no radicals like Patrick Henry, Sam Adams, or Thomas Paine; but, nevertheless the convention represented a cross section of American groups, sections, and interests. The majority were lawyers with experience in politics: seven, for example, had been state governors; nearly thirty had served in Congress; and eight had signed the Declaration of Independence. Washington, certainly one of the most respected men in America, was unanimously chosen president of the convention. Those who sat under him—including Robert Morris, Luther Martin, John Dickinson, Charles C. Pinckney, James Wilson, Charles Pinckney, Benjamin Franklin, Alexander Hamilton, James Madison, Roger Sherman, Elbridge Gerry, Edmund Randolph, Nathaniel Gorham, John Langdon, John Rutledge, and George Wythe—were men of affairs who believed that they could save the country from ruin and possible civil war by establishing a more effective system of government.

In the course of the debates in the convention, the delegates repeatedly demonstrated that they were not interested in political theory but in the practical problems with which they had to contend. Madison, Hamilton, Martin, and others were students of history and political theory, but such excursions as were made into these fields were, as Professor Robert L. Schuyler has said, "purple patches"—embellishments as it were—rather than integral parts of the proceedings. Uppermost was the delegates' desire to provide the kind of government that would function best for the ends they had in view. This desire was responsible for the numerous utterances in the convention about the dangers of direct democracy. Gerry of Massachusetts, for instance, opposed the election of the House of Representatives by popular vote. "The evils we experience," he said, "flow from the excess of democracy," and he decried "the danger of the levelling spirit." William Livingston of New Jersey declared that "the people ever have been and ever will be unfit to retain the exercise of power in their own hands." Charles Pinckney of South Carolina so distrusted popular rule that he proposed high property qualifications for Federal officeholders. Edmund Randolph of Virginia, who was even more skeptical of the political wisdom of the untutored and propertyless, attributed all the distress suffered during the post-Revolutionary years to "the turbulence and follies of democracy." Roger Sherman of Connecticut advocated keeping popular influence in the new government to a minimum. Alexander Hamilton of New York elaborated upon the "imprudence of democracy." "All communities," he said, "divide themselves into the few and the many. The first are the rich and well-born, the other the mass of the people," who "seldom judge or determine right." Clearly what such men wanted was a government powerful enough to provide stability without itself becoming a threat to the commonwealth. This was in fact what they achieved in the Constitution of the United States.

The Rising Sun at Philadelphia

Although the convention was scheduled to open on May 15, 1787, the first meeting, which was attended by twenty-nine delegates, was not held until May 25. In the ensuing months, the delegates deliberated behind closed doors, maintained the strictest secrecy, kept no official account of their debates, and recorded only propositions before the convention and some of the votes for and against them. Soon after the opening session, the delegates decided to draw up a new constitution rather than to attempt to revise the Articles of Confederation. By a vote of six states to one, with one state divided, the convention resolved that "a national government ought to be established consisting of a supreme legislative, executive, and judiciary"; the word "national" was subsequently eliminated from the resolution. The separation of powers with an accompanying system of checks and balances were the principal ideas on which the new charter was to be based.

The central question confronting the delegates was how much authority to grant to the states and how much to give central authority—a problem that neither the British rulers of the colonies nor the authors of the Articles of Confederation had been able to solve. The first suggestions came from the delegates of Virginia, who had arrived at Philadelphia before those from the other states and who had used the time at their disposal to draw up a plan for a new central government. What came to be known as the Virginia Plan provided for a two-house legislature composed of members apportioned among the states on the basis of free white population; the members of the lower house were to be elected by the people of the several states and those of the upper house were to be chosen by the lower house from persons nominated by the state legislatures. An executive—either an individual or a group of men—was to be selected by the legislature and to be ineligible for a second term. The judiciary was to consist of a supreme court and inferior courts. The acts of the legislature, which itself was to be authorized to pass on the constitutionality of state laws, were to be subject to review by a council of revision consisting of the executive and part of the judiciary. The Virginia Plan reflected the interests of the larger states and clearly revealed that its framers believed in a far greater degree of centralization than prevailed under the Articles of Confederation.

Four days after the opening of the convention, Edmund Randolph presented the Virginia Plan to the delegates. In the ensuing debate, which lasted for two weeks, it became apparent that the smaller states— in this instance, Connecticut, Delaware, Maryland, and New Jersey— and New York were opposed to many features of the Virginia Plan.

On June 15, William Paterson of New Jersey laid before the delegates the small states' program. Known as the New Jersey Plan, it called for the revision instead of the abandonment of the Articles of Confederation. Federal rather than national in spirit, the New Jersey Plan provided for a single-chambered congress in which each state was to have one vote, a plural executive chosen by Congress, and a federal judicial system. Congress was to have the authority to admit new states, to obtain funds through requisitions on the states, to impose tariffs on imports, and to regulate trade.

After a week of debate, the convention failed to take any action on the New Jersey Plan. But the small states were still unwilling to accept the Virginia Plan, and a committee was appointed to devise a formula that would be acceptable to both factions. On July 16, the committee's report was approved, and the way was cleared for the resolution of this most vexing problem. Under the plan that was finally adopted, provision was made for a two-house legislature; members in the House of Representatives, or lower house, were to be apportioned among the states largely on the basis of population, elected biennially by popular vote, and paid from the national treasury. In the Senate, or upper house, each state was allotted two members to be elected for a six-year term by its legislature. Unlike the members of the Congress of the Confederation, each senator could vote individually, and he also was to receive his compensation from the national treasury.

Slavery was another troublesome question that split the convention into two clearly defined groups. Although the delegates made a conscious effort to avoid the subject and although the word "slave" does not appear in the Constitution, the problem could not be ignored. The northern delegates, while accepting the southern view that the slaves were property, wanted them taxed as such. The South, on the other hand, wished to consider slaves as men in apportioning representatives in Congress. After much jockeying, this issue was settled by the so-called "federal ratio" compromise, which counted five slaves as three whites for both taxation and representation.

The slave trade, however, presented another problem that was closely related to the general controversy about the regulation of commerce. Northern commercial interests, anxious to promote their special advantages, thought that Congress should have full power to enact navigation acts, levy duties on imports and exports, and regulate the foreign slave trade. The South was opposed to export taxes and to any step that would sacrifice its interests as a staple-exporting section. Although the slave trade was denounced in the convention such prominent southerners as George Mason of Virginia and Luther Martin of Maryland, the delegation from South Carolina and Georgia threatened to oppose the Constitution if Congress was given power to interfere with the slave traffic. But the North fully realized that unlimited importation of slaves, coupled with the "federal ratio" compromise, might give the South a preponderance of political power that it might use to the detriment of the North. Another bargain adjusted this difficulty: Congress was authorized to regulate commerce but was forbidden to prohibit the foreign slave trade before 1808; Congress was given the power, however, to levy an import duty upon slaves of not more than $10 each.

When the convention turned to the problem of creating an executive for the new government, the delegates had to choose from a number of possibilities. Those who feared the dangers of popular rule thought that the President should serve for life; those who feared autocracy favored a relatively short term. Some delegates believed that the executive should be granted extensive powers; others thought he should be a figurehead. Finally, there was a sharp cleavage between those who advocated that the president be selected by Congress and those who proposed that he be elected by the people. The problem was solved by putting the selection of the president in the hands of electors who in turn were designated by each state in any manner that its legislature might direct. Each state was entitled to as many electors as it had senators and representatives in Congress. In case the electors failed to give a majority to any one person, the choice of a president then devolved upon the House of Representatives, where each state would have one vote. The President could be removed from office after the House had instituted impeachment proceedings and if the Senate, sitting as a court, had by a two-thirds majority voted for his conviction. His term was four years, and he was eligible for re-election.

The President was given extensive authority by the convention. He was directed to "take care that the laws be faithfully executed"; he had the right to call Congress into extraordinary sessions; and he could veto acts of Congress (although a two-thirds vote in both houses could override his veto). In addition, Section 2 of Article II of the Constitution provided:

> The President shall be Commander in Chief of the Army and Navy of the United States, and of the militia of the several states, when called into the actual service of the United States. . . .
>
> He shall have power, by and with the advice and consent of the Senate, to make treaties, provided two thirds of the senators present concur; and he shall nominate, and by and with the advice and consent of the Senate, shall appoint ambassadors, other public ministers and consuls, judges of the Supreme Court, and all other officers of the United States, whose appointments are not herein otherwise provided for, and which shall be established by law; but the Congress may by law vest the appointment of such inferior officers, as they think proper,

in the President alone, in the courts of law, or in the heads of departments.

The President shall have power to fill up all vacancies that may happen during the recess of the Senate, by granting commissions which shall expire at the end of their next session.

The judicial system of the new government was one of the few major subjects that produced practically no disagreement in the convention. Both the New Jersey and Virginia Plans called for a federal judicial system, for the delegates were fully aware of the unsatisfactory results under the Confederation of delegating all judicial authority to the state courts. Consequently, the convention created an independent federal judiciary headed by a Supreme Court, the members of which were appointed by the president, with the advice and consent of the Senate, for life or during good behavior. Provision was also made for such inferior courts as might from time to time be deemed necessary. The federal courts were given jurisdiction over:

all cases in law and equity, arising under this constitution, the laws of the United States, and treaties made, or which shall be made, under their authority;—to all cases affecting ambassadors, other public ministers and consuls;—to all cases of admiralty and maritime jurisdiction;—to controversies to which the United States shall be a party;—to controversies between two or more states; between a state and citizens of another state;— between citizens of different states;—between citizens of the same state claiming lands under grants of different states, and between a state, or the citizens thereof, and foreign states, citizens or subjects.

In cases "affecting ambassadors, other public ministers and consuls, and those in which a state shall be a party," the Supreme Court was granted original jurisdiction. In all other cases, it had appellate jurisdiction. Most of the delegates at the time thought that review of the constitutionality of state and national laws was an inherent power of the judiciary, and they did not think it necessary to specify it.

The delegates' fear of concentrated political power, whether in a popular majority or in a small "faction," accounted in large part for their system of checks and balances. After prolonged debate, it became obvious that proposals for restricting the suffrage entailed serious administrative problems; they then decided that direct popular rule could be just as effectively thwarted by an ingenious division of powers and responsibility among the three branches of the government. The legislature was checked by its division into two houses, by the president's veto, and by the power of the judiciary to declare its acts null and void. Even if a popular majority should control the lower house, as Madison feared it would,* there seemed little likelihood the Senate and President would permit it to put on the statute books legislation detrimental to the minority. The executive was checked by the Senate in the matter of treaties and appointments. The Supreme Court, the members of which were appointed for life by the President with the approval of the Senate, was far removed from the people. Finally, the several states were forbidden to enact legislation detrimental to the propertied business interests, and the President was empowered, upon call from the state authorities, to send troops to suppress domestic insurrection.

The system of checks and balances was not the only way in which the delegates sought to prevent the growth of concentrated political power. Although the Constitution provided for popular participation in the government, the people were permitted to vote directly only for members of the House of Representatives. The President was to be chosen by electors, and Senators were to be selected in whatever way the state legislatures might decide. Equally significant was the complicated method devised for amending the Constitution. Although the Constitution was far easier to alter than the Articles of Confederation, it nevertheless could not be changed by a simple majority. Before a proposed amendment could go into effect, it had to be approved by a two-thirds vote in both houses of Congress and to be ratified by the legislatures or conventions of three fourths of the states.

It is frequently asserted that the Constitution is a "bundle of compromises," but it should also be noted that there were certain major issues on which the delegates were in substantial agreement. They did not disagree on the dangers of direct democracy, and they did not disagree on the desirability of having the federal government assume

---

* Madison expressed his view on this point as follows: "The landed interest, at present, is prevalent, but in process of time . . . when the number of landholders shall be comparatively small . . . will not the landed interests be overbalanced in future elections? and, unless wisely provided against, what will become of our government? In England, at this day, if elections were open to all classes of people, the property of landed proprietors would be insecure. An Agrarian law would take place. If these observations be just, our government ought to secure the permanent interests of the country against innovation. Landholders ought to have a share in the government, to support these invaluable interests, and to balance and check the other. They ought to be so constituted as to protect the minority of the opulent against the majority." Jonathan Elliot: *Debates in the Several State Conventions on the Adoption of the Federal Constitution*, Vol. 1 (Washington, D.C.: printed by the editor, 1836), pp. 449–50. It must be remembered, however, that the great majority of Americans at the time were landholders and devoted, as the Shaysites had been, to the protection of their property rights.

many of the powers that had been left to the states under the Articles of Confederation. There was therefore general unanimity in the convention on practically all the economic and protective provisions in the final draft of the Constitution. With extreme particularists not represented in the convention, the delegates granted Congress the power to lay and collect taxes, duties, imposts, and excises; coin and borrow money; regulate interstate and foreign commerce; fix the standard of weights and measures; provide for patents and copyrights; establish post offices; raise and support armies; maintain a navy; and pay all debts contracted by the United States before the adoption of the Constitution. To safeguard against the passage of radical economic legislation, the states were forbidden to coin money, issue bills of credit, make anything but gold and silver coin legal tender in payment of debts, make any law impairing the obligation of contracts, or lay imposts or duties on imports or exports or on tonnage.

Despite the large number of specific powers granted to the new Congress, including what would become known as the "elastic clause"—to make all laws "necessary and proper" to fulfill the listed specific powers—the delegates at Philadelphia wished to emphasize that most authority was still to be lodged in the states. Federal power was not intended to proceed beyond the specifically delegated authority in the Constitution. More comprehensive grants of power, as envisioned in the original Virginia Plan or in Hamilton's early suggestions to the convention, had been rejected.

In effect, the Constitution had established a series of filters through which proposals about public policy would have to pass before becoming law. The federal system and checks and balances went together in this respect. Yet, after all was done, on the central issue of the location of final political authority the Constitution was ambiguous. Presumably, there was no voice beyond that of three fourths of the state legislatures or of state conventions called to consider amendments; these were supposedly the final source of the will of the people mentioned in the Preamble to the Constitution. Nothing in the Constitution is exempt from amendment except the provision for two senators from each state. The amending process, however, is slow and clumsy, and it has been seldom used. No man at Philadelphia seems to have fully understood that even so superb a plan as the Constitution was, at bottom, only a piece of fine machinery. When issues would arise over which compromise seemed impossible, not even machinery made by demi-gods could prevent the inflexible partisan from refusing to abide by the constitutional process. It took a Civil War to establish clearly that, whatever its results, the peaceful constitutional process could not itself be rejected. But even today the possibilities remain of using the Constitution for conflicting ends, and a skillful minority can find ample chance within the law of preventing a decision hostile to its interests.

Although it is difficult to ascertain the precise nature of any individual's motives, it seems reasonable to conclude that many of the delegates at the Philadelphia convention were motivated at least in part by their belief that law, order, the "proprieties," and stability were necessary to permit men to pursue their legitimate interests. Certainly the men of 1787 wanted to protect property rights, and most Americans at the time joined the fathers of the Constitution in respect for private property. Their experiences under the Confederation, their remarks both before and during the convention, and the fashion in which they assigned the major economic powers to the federal government rather than to the states, all tend to support the conclusion that the fathers unashamedly had drafted a Constitution to protect their own and their countrymen's "stake in society." On the other hand, various delegates also repeatedly and sincerely referred to the sheer inefficiency of the Confederation government and its weakness in foreign affairs. Saving property and other rights and strengthening the central government were not mutually exclusive objectives. It seems reasonable to assume that most delegates were swayed by both, rather than by only one, of these considerations; yet any final estimate of the motives of the founding fathers becomes relatively insignificant when compared with their accomplishments.

The lasting and unique achievement of the framers of the Constitution was the discovery of a way to strengthen the central government without destroying the individual states. They discovered a plan that permitted both the federal and state governments to act effectively. At the same time, they were able to overcome the principal deficiency of the Confederation by circumventing the question of how to make a state obey the Federal government. Under the Constitution, the national government operates directly in regard to the individual rather than indirectly through the states. In this fashion the inability of the Confederation Congress to command a state was supplanted by the national government's power to coerce individuals in the states. Federal power beyond that of the states was further assured by requiring state officials to take an oath to uphold the federal Constitution. Finally, by making the Constitution the "supreme law of the land," the founding fathers made it impossible for the states to adopt an act contrary to the Constitution.

The framers of the Constitution succeeded where all others before them had failed. By devising new methods to reconcile the diverse political units of the nation, they established an effective federal government and made a notable and far-reaching contribution to the development of constitutional theory and practice.

The Fight for the New Charter

As soon as the final draft of the Constitution had been completed, its framers set to work to secure its ratification. The fathers feared that the state legislatures might be unwilling to accept the new instrument of government with its numerous new restraints on state activity. The authors sent it to the existing Confederation Congress with the advice that that body transmit it to the state legislatures which in turn would call special ratifying conventions. As a further aid to the success of their undertaking, they cast aside the old provision in the Articles of Confederation that the fundamental law of the land could not be altered or amended without the unanimous consent of the states and inserted in the new Constitution a provision that it should go into effect as soon as it received the approval of nine states.

The submission of the Constitution to the several states for ratification led at once to an intensive campaign between those who favored its adoption and those who opposed it. The former, styling themselves Federalists, were, with few exceptions, the same individuals who had labored so indefatigably for a central government. At the time, David Humphreys of New Haven wrote to Washington that "all the different classes in the liberal professions will be in favor of the proposed Constitution. The Clergy, Lawyers, Physicians & Merchants will have considerable influence on Society. Nor will the Officers of the late Army be backward in expressing their approbation." General Knox, another correspondent of Washington's, declared in October, 1787, that the new Constitution was "received with great joy by all the commercial part of the community." Shortly afterward, Madison wrote Jefferson that in New England "the men of letters, the principal Officers of Government, the judges and lawyers and clergy and men of property furnished only here and there an adversary." And Hamilton, surveying the situation at the close of the Philadelphia Convention, felt certain that the new Constitution had "the good will of the commercial interests" and "the hopes of the creditors of the United States."

The Anti-Federalists, as the opponents of the Constitution were called, were, like the Federalists, generally recruited from all classes of society. Some of the Anti-Federalists distrusted men of superior education and large property. "An apprehension that liberties of the peo-

Campaigning for the Constitution in New York

ple are in danger, and a distrust of men of property or Education," Rufus King wrote to Madison in January, 1788, "have a more powerful Effect upon the minds of our Opponents than any Specific Objections against the Constitution." Shortly afterward, he asserted that the opposition arose chiefly "from an opinion that is immovable that some injury is plotted against them—that the system is the production of the rich and ambitious, that they discover its operations and that the consequences will be the establishment of two orders in the Society, one comprehending the opulent and the great, the other the poor and illiterate." The opposition in New Hampshire, a citizen of that state informed Washington, "was composed of men who were involved in debt, and in consequence would be averse to any government which was likely to abolish their tender Laws and cut off every hope of accomplishing their favorite plan of introducing a paper currency." Hamilton pointed out, however, the variety of motives among the opponents to the Constitution. There were "inconsiderable men in possession of considerable offices under the state governments who will fear a diminution of their consequence, power, and emolument by the establishment of the general government and who can hope for nothing there." He added that "some considerable men in office possessed of talents and popularity who partly from the same motives and partly from a desire of *playing a part* in a convulsion for their own aggrandisement will oppose the quiet adoption of the new government." To these causes there should be added he said:

> the disinclination of the people to taxes and of course to a strong government—the opposition of all men much in debt who will not wish to see a government established one object of which is to restrain the means of cheating Creditors—the democratical jealousy of the people which may be alarmed at the appearance of institutions that may seem calculated to place the power of the community in few hands and to raise a few individuals to stations of great prominence.

Between the Federalists and Anti-Federalists were many middle-grounders who did not know which party to support. It was this diverse group that Richard Henry Lee had in mind when he wrote:

> One party is composed of little insurgents, men in debt, who want no law, and who want a share of the property of others; these are called levellers, Shaysites, etc. The other party is composed of a few, but more dangerous men, with their servile dependents; these avariciously grasp at all power and property; you may discover in all the actions of these men, an evident dislike to free and equal government, and they go systematically to work to change, essentially, the forms of government in this country; these are called aristocrats, moneyites, etc. Between these two parties is the weight of the community; the men of middling property, men not in debt, on the one hand, and men, on the other, content with republican governments, and not aiming at immense fortunes, offices and power. In 1786 the little insurgents, the levellers, came forth, invaded the rights of others, and attempted to establish governments according to their wills. Their movements evidently gave encouragement to the other party, which in 1787 has taken the political field and with its fashionable dependents, and the tongue and the pen, is endeavoring to establish in a great haste, a politic kind of government. These two parties are really insignificant, compared with the solid, free and independent part of the community.

Though inferior in numbers in competing for support, the Federalists enjoyed advantages over their opponents. The majority of the signers of the Declaration of Independence were among them, as well as the leading men in winning the Revolution. Allies among the professional classes and among the majority of the more influential newspaper proprietors enabled them to exercise greater influence than would otherwise have been possible. Although many wealthy, educated and equally antidemocratic men led the Anti-Federalists, on balance the Federalists probably possessed better resources for waging a strenuous campaign, and they were better organized. They had, moreover, the powerful backing of Washington and the Order of Cincinnati, which had been established by Revolutionary officers.

During the campaign, the country was flooded with oratory and pamphlet literature. There were acrimonious attacks and counter-attacks. For sagacity and insight into the nature of government and politics, two documents among the many produced during the struggle for ratification are unequalled: the *Federalist*, a collection of eighty-five essays, most of which were written by Hamilton and Madison, with a few by Jay, and *Letters from the Federal Farmer to the Republicans* by Richard Henry Lee. The former considered by the Federalists as an unanswerable defense of the Constitution, is remarkable for its comprehensiveness, cogency, and simplicity of statement. Of the *Federalist* essays, number ten, written by Madison, admirably sets forth the sense of society that had inspired the framers of the new organic law. Asserting that there were various sources of political interests, Madison went on to say that "the most common and durable source of factions" had always been the unequal distribution of property.

> Those who hold and those who are without property have ever formed distinct interests of society. Those who are creditors and those who are debtors fall under a like discrimination. A landed interest, a manufacturing interest, a mercantile interest, a moneyed interest, with many lesser interests, grow up of necessity in civilized nations, and divide them into different classes actuated by different sentiments and views. The regulation of these various and interfering interests forms the principal task of modern legislation and involves the spirit of party and faction in the necessary and ordinary operations of the government.

It was Madison's hope that the new Constitution, with its federal system and checks and balances, would fulfill the legitimate interests of competing factions while not permitting any one group to dominate the nation. While far more restrained than many of his Anti-Federalist compatriots, Lee in his *Letters from the Federal Farmer* stated the principal objections of the opponents to the Constitution. He argued that it was undemocratic, that it was planned to serve the interests of a propertied minority, and that it did not represent the judgment and wishes of the rank and file of the country's population. "Every man of reflection," Lee said, "must see that the change now proposed is a transfer of power from the many to the few." Lee also took exception to what he thought was unseemly haste on the part of Hamilton and others in urging the adoption of the Constitution. The people, he maintained, should have time to examine and debate the Constitution fully before being called upon for their final decision. In his attack on the Constitution, Lee did not emphasize that it lacked a Bill of Rights, but many others criticized it for this omission. It soon became clear, however, that the absence of a Bill of Rights would be remedied and that no authoritarian intention was to be inferred from the lack of guarantees of basic rights in the draft of the charter that came from Philadelphia.

Both *The Federalist* and Lee's *Letters* should be considered showpieces in an intense political campaign in which the greatest variety of motives were active on all sides. Naturally, the supporters and opponents of the Constitution wished to put the best possible construction on their positions. With feelings running high, the ratification fight led to questionable practices by Federalists and Anti-Federalists alike. In Pennsylvania the opponents of the Constitution in the legislature stayed away from the meetings in order to prevent a quorum. By absenting themselves, they sought to prevent the calling of a ratifying convention. This refusal to allow the process of deliberation to go forward was countered by the Federalists, who dragged two of the absentees back into the assembly room in order to form the quorum, and the legislature at once made provision for the election of delegates to the convention. The convention, in which the Federalists outnumbered the Anti-Federalists two to one, approved the new government on December 12, 1787, less than a week after Delaware, the first state to ratify, had registered its approval. In Massachusetts, where the opponents of a stronger federal government were powerfully represented in the convention, the Federalists delayed an early vote; as it was, the margin of victory for the Federalists was uncomfortably close, the final vote being 187 to 168. In Maryland and South Carolina, those in favor of ratification won sweeping victories. In Virginia, on the other hand, they were successful by the narrow margin of ten votes, eighty-nine delegates voting "yes" and seventy-nine "no."

Two states, New Hampshire and New York, elected conventions that seemed opposed to the new federal charter. When the New Hampshire convention met on February 13, 1788, it was apparent to the overconfident Federalists that a large proportion of the delegates had been instructed to vote against the adoption of the new Constitution. One of the Federalist spokesmen wrote:

> So confident were we of the prevailing voice in favor of the Constitution that no pains were taken to counteract the intrigues of a few notoriously vile characters, who were too successful in the dark and dirty business of seducing a great number of the interior towns by false representation to fetter their delegates with positive instructions to vote in all events against the Constitution.

Alarmed, the friends of the Constitution managed to secure an adjournment of the convention to the following June, when they were finally successful by a vote of fifty-seven to forty-seven. In New York's ratifying convention, which met in June, 1788, the opponents of the new system had a two-thirds majority. They were headed by the governor, George Clinton, an ally of the large landed families, who had helped track down the Shaysites who had fled into New York. It was only after a month of negotiation and bickering that the Federalists won by a vote of thirty to twenty-seven. So strong was the opposition in North Carolina and Rhode Island that neither state accepted the Constitution until after Washington's inauguration.

Despite the great issues at stake, the vast amount of propaganda circulated, and the sharpness of the debate, many citizens failed to express an opinion at the polls. The scanty data available seem to indicate that not more than a third of those entitled to vote participated in the selection of the ratifying conventions.

More instructive than the speeches and writing during the campaign is an analysis of the distribution of the vote on the Constitution. Studies of the election map indicate that there was no clear over-all division along economic lines on the Constitution and that such other issues as frontier defense, local political squabbles, the fear of loss of political office or prestige, and religious conflict strongly affected opinion. In New Jersey, all classes welcomed the Constitution. In Georgia, with citizens anxious for adequate national defense forces against the Spanish and Indians, the Federalists swept the state. The economic interests of both sides of Virginia and North Carolina were essentially the same, although in North Carolina some of the very rich seem to have been opposed to and the very poor in favor of the Constitution. The small farmers in the Great Valley of Virginia were Federalist, while the mercantile city of Norfolk was Anti-Federalist. Large enclaves of favorable votes could be found in the western areas of Massachusetts and New Hampshire, where the small farmer debtor or

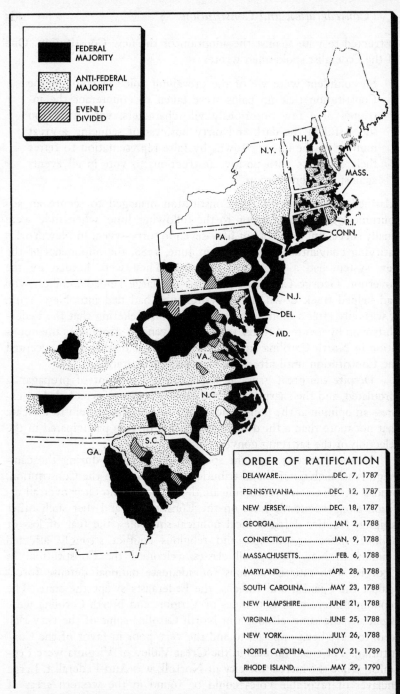

| FEDERAL MAJORITY |
| ANTI-FEDERAL MAJORITY |
| EVENLY DIVIDED |

N.H.

N.Y.

MASS.

R.I.

CONN.

PA.

N.J.

DEL.

MD.

VA.

N.C.

S.C.

GA.

ORDER OF RATIFICATION

DELAWARE	DEC. 7, 1787
PENNSYLVANIA	DEC. 12, 1787
NEW JERSEY	DEC. 18, 1787
GEORGIA	JAN. 2, 1788
CONNECTICUT	JAN. 9, 1788
MASSACHUSETTS	FEB. 6, 1788
MARYLAND	APR. 28, 1788
SOUTH CAROLINA	MAY 23, 1788
NEW HAMPSHIRE	JUNE 21, 1788
VIRGINIA	JUNE 25, 1788
NEW YORK	JULY 26, 1788
NORTH CAROLINA	NOV. 21, 1789
RHODE ISLAND	MAY 29, 1790

RATIFYING THE NEW CONSTITUTION

the "democratic frontiersman" might be expected to have been opposed to the Constitution.

During the ratification of the Constitution the country had been promised a bill of rights, and it was assumed that George Washington would be the first president. Those who had opposed ratification were somewhat placated after the campaign. Economic revival in 1788 also encouraged Americans to look forward more hopefully to the new government. They now anticipated less troubled national growth and the ultimate vindication of the principles of the Declaration of Independence that seemed embodied in the new Constitution.

FOR SUPPLEMENTARY READING

All students should begin by reading Marcus Cunliffe, *The Nation Takes Shape* (1959); Merrill Jensen, *The New Nation* (1950); and Charles A. Beard, *An Economic Interpretation of the Constitution of the United States* (1913). Allan Nevins, *The American States During and After the Revolution* (1924), has details about state politics that cannot be found collected elsewhere. All these books should be read in the light of R. B. Morris's find analysis of recent evidence, "The Confederation Period and the American Historian," *The William and Mary Quarterly*, Vol. XIII (April 1956). Many of Morris's own conclusions are strengthened by Forrest McDonald's thorough restudy of the Philadelphia convention, *We the People* (1958), and by R. E. Brown, *Charles Beard and the Constitution* (1956). A counterview is in Lee Benson, *Turner and Beard* (1960).

R. A. East, *Business Enterprise in the American Revolutionary Era* (1938), is of first importance in interpreting the postwar economy. Lynn Montross, *The Reluctant Rebels* (1950), is an attractive history of the Continental Congress.

On western land questions consult R. M. Robbins, *Our Landed Heritage* (1942), or R. A. Billington, *Westward Expansion* (1949). On Shays' Rebellion the classic background study of the period is John Fiske, *The Critical Period of American History, 1783–1789* (1888). The uprising itself is analyzed in M. L. Starkey, *A Little Rebellion* (1955), and with deeper perspective by R. B. Morris, "Insurrection in Massachusetts," in D. Aaron (ed.), *America in Crisis* (1952).

The political and legal theory of the Constitution can best be studied in the meticulous edition of *The Federalist* edited by J. E. Cooke (1961) (Pb). James Madison's *Journal of the Federal Convention* is presented in Max Farrand (ed.), *Records of the Federal Convention* (4 vols., 1911–37), and in an easier rearrangement in A. T. Prescott (ed.), *Drafting the Federal Constitution* (1941). A useful guide to the debates is Max Farrand, *The Framing of the Constitution of the United States* (1913), and the best study of the drafting is R. L. Schuyler, *The Constitution of the United States* (1923). On ratification, the indispensable work to begin with is Jonathan Elliot (ed.), *The Debates in the Several State Conventions on the Adoption of the Federal Constitution* (5 vols., 1836–45). There are many studies of ratification in individual states, but of first importance is O. G. Libby, *The Geographical Distribution of the Vote of the Thirteen States on the Federal Constitution 1787–1788* (1894). The opposition to the Constitution has had several recent students: J. T. Main, *The Antifederalists: Critics of the Constitution* (1961); C. M. Kenyon (ed.), *The Antifederalists* (1961); M. Borden (ed.), *The Antifederalist Papers* (1965); and R. A. Rutland, *The Ordeal of the Constitution* (1966).

There are biographies of nearly all the major statesmen and politicians of the period 1763–89. Among the books on leading figures are: Dumas Malone, *Jefferson the Virginian* (1948), *Jefferson and the Rights of Man* (1951), and *Jefferson and the Ordeal of Liberty* (1962); Carl Van Doren, *Benjamin Franklin* (1938); Irving Brant, *James Madison* (6 vols., 1941–61); Broadus Mitchell, *Alexander Hamilton* (2 vols., 1957, 1962); A. J. Beveridge, *The Life of John Marshall* (4 vols., 1916–19); John C. Miller, *Sam Adams: Pioneer in Propaganda* (1936); Marcus Cunliffe, *George Washington: Man and Monument* (1958); Gilbert Chinard, *Honest John Adams* (1933).

PART III

THE
SUCCESSFUL
EXPERIMENT

9

The Federalists in Power

THE MEN who led America to independence and later gave her the Constitution also determined national policies in the decade following the election of George Washington. Drawn from many parts of the country and representing various powerful interests, as a group they came to be known as the Federalists.

The Federalist party occupies a unique position in American history. Composed of many of the ablest men in the United States, it had an outstanding record and a relatively short life. During the twelve years that the Federalists were in power, they organized the new government, set precedents that have never been broken, established a sound financial system, obtained the withdrawal of the British from the Northwest, eliminated the Spanish threat to the Southwest, and prevented the United States from becoming involved in a general European war. Despite these achievements, the Federalists were defeated in the election of 1800, and they never regained full control of the national government. Possessing every requisite for political success except the ability to gauge or control the popular will, they lost the support of an electorate that preferred limited government to strong central supervision of national development.

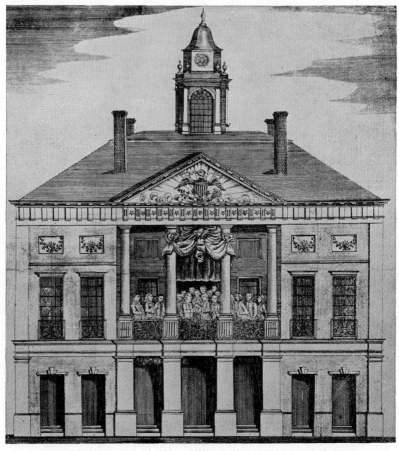

Washington's Inauguration at Federal Hall, New York, 1789

Organizing the New Government

With the adoption of the Constitution, its friends won a battle rather than a war. The Constitution was only a parchment plan of government. Economic stability and a national government strong enough to protect men in their interests and to compel foreign respect were goals still to be attained. The friends of the Constitution were unwilling to entrust these tasks to their opponents. In the interval between the ratification of the Constitution and the first presidential election, Washington wrote: "There will . . . be no room for the advocates of the Constitution to relax in their exertions; for if they should be lulled into security, appointments. of Anti-Federal men may probably take place; and the consequences which you so justly dread be realized." Many others shared Washington's apprehensions that the forces of particularism, of "direct action," and of "levelling," although dormant, were still powerful.

The opponents of the Constitution were also aware of the importance of securing control of the new government. A rural delegate to the Massachusetts ratifying convention said:

> These lawyers, and men of learning, and moneyed men that talk so finely, and gloss over matters so smoothly, to make us poor illiterate people swallow down the pill expect to get into Congress themselves; they expect to be the managers of this Constitution, and get all the power and all the money into their own hands, and then they will swallow up all of us little folks, like the great leviathan, Mr. President; yea, just as the whale swallowed up Jonah. This is what I am afraid of.

Wealthy anti-Constitutionalists feared that effective government under the new Constitution would interfere with their local economic and political privileges.

With each side distrustful of the other and with each hoping to secure control of the new government, there was an intense campaign to fill the offices under the new system. "The agitation [over ratification]," John Marshall wrote, "had been too great to be suddenly calmed; and for the active opponents of the system to become suddenly its friends, or even indifferent to its fate, would have been a victory of reason over passion, or a surrender of individual judgment to the decision of the majority, examples of which are rarely given in the progress of human affairs." In some states, he went on, some people were inclined to acquiesce in the decision that had been made and to wait for a fair trial of the Constitution; in others, the chagrin of defeat seemed to increase the original hostility to the instrument: and in "all those states where the opposition was sufficiently formidable to inspire a hope of success, the effort was made to fill the legislature with the declared enemies of the government, and thus commit it in its infancy to the custody of its foes." In every state except Georgia, those fearful of the Constitution put up congressional candidates, and in many communities the fight was as spirited as that over ratification.

The election was an overwhelming victory for the supporters of the Constitution. Washington's elevation to the presidency—he received the vote of every elector—assured them of control of the executive branch of the government. While Washington was not the demi-god subsequently pictured by Parson Weems in his eulogistic *Life of Washington*, he was nevertheless a man of enormous presence and unparalleled prestige. Fifty-seven years old when he became President on April 30, 1789, Washington had been a surveyor, plantation owner, western land speculator, member of Virginia House of Burgesses, and commander of the American forces in the Revolution. He had been critical of the Articles of Confederation and had served as head of the Philadelphia Convention.

Although his reputation in 1789 rested on his military exploits, he proved to be equally skillful in the new government. Firm, patient, and far more disinterested than most of his contemporaries, he was able both to take advice and to make up his own mind. Whatever knowledge he lacked about government, particularly in economic affairs, he made up for by surrounding himself with able subordinates to whom he did not hesitate to delegate authority. It was extraordinary good fortune for the United States to have a Washington; the Federalists were equally fortunate in that they could claim him for their side.

In the Constitution mention is made of the "principal officer in each of the executive departments." Soon after its organization, Congress established the Department of Foreign Affairs (which was soon changed to the Department of State), the Department of War, and the Department of the Treasury. Provision was also made for the appointment of an attorney general and a postmaster general. In filling these administrative posts at his disposal, Washington was careful to select those who had supported the Constitution. For the important post of secretary of the treasury he turned first to Robert Morris, the financial genius of the Revolutionary period, and a member of the Philadelphia Convention. When Morris declined, Washington turned to his former aide, Alexander Hamilton, who was to become the "giant of Federalism." General Henry Knox of Massachusetts, another ardent Federalist, was made Secretary of War; and Edmund Randolph of Virginia, a Federalist convert, Attorney General. Thomas Jefferson, the Secretary of State, had been the American minister to France during the Confederation period. He was not a delegate to the Philadelphia Convention, and he did not participate in the contest over the ratification. He had worried about the absence of a bill of rights in the original text of the Constitution and about the President's right to succeed himself, but from the first he had favored the adoption of the new charter. Supporters of the Constitution occupied the minor as well as the major offices of the new government, and the diplomatic, consular, and customs service were also manned exclusively by friends of the Constitution. Understandably, the new government could not enlist its personnel from those who had not accepted ratification or who hoped to work against the new Constitution within the government.

The judiciary was also staffed by those who had helped draft the Constitution or had worked for its ratification. Under the terms of the Judiciary Act of September 24, 1789, provision was made for the organization of the Supreme Court and the establishment of thirteen district and three circuit courts, all of which were distinct from the state courts. The first Chief Justice was John Jay, who, with Alexander Hamilton, had done most to secure the ratification of the Constitution in New York. Of the remaining five members of the Court, all had worked for ratification in the conventions of their respective states, and three had been members of the Philadelphia Convention. All the posts in the lower courts were also awarded to Federalists.

Although opposition groups were represented in Congress, the friends of the Constitution were prominent in both the Senate and the House of Representatives. Eleven out of twenty-six senators and nine out of sixty-five members of the first House of Representatives had been members of the Philadelphia Convention. Forty-four members of the first Congress had been members of this convention or of the state ratifying conventions; all but seven had supported the new system. When the first Congress met in the Spring of 1789, to be a Federalist meant that one had fully accepted the new organic law. But, as James Madison, himself a leading Federalist at this time, had feared, interests were at work in the country and in Congress that were to narrow the definition of Federalist into a description of a political "faction," identified more with an economic and political program than with loyalty to the form of government outlined in the Constitution.

The Cloak of the Constitution

The interests and factions that were to be perennial sources of political conflict had not coalesced into coherent political parties in 1789. Interest groups of many sorts obviously existed and were waiting anxiously to see in what directions the new government might move. One of the real fears in 1789 was that the United States might fall under one man rule, or monarchy, as the word was then understood. The Revolution had intensified republican sentiment in the country, and hostility to aristocratic and monarchial forms spread rapidly as Americans convinced themselves that in 1776 they had cut free from the intrigue and corruption of European politics and courts. Those Americans whose manner or sentiments seemed to suggest anything less than "republican simplicity" were often called monarchists. Washington was suspected of desiring to emulate European royalty; senators were criticized for insisting that the upper house adopt the forms and rules of Parliament; and Vice-President John Adams was ridiculed for his lengthy and pompous discourses to the Senate on the desirability of suitable titles for public officials. To William Maclay, a crusty democratic senator from rural Pennsylvania, the real or suspected desire to make the Old World courts a model for the New was intolerable, and in 1790 he wrote in his journal: "Strange indeed, that in the very country [America] where the flame of freedom had been kindled, an attempt should be made to introduce these humiliating distinctions." On another occasion, Maclay, who was disgusted with Adams's behavior as the Senate's presiding officer, wrote:

> The Senate met. The Vice President rose in the most solemn manner. This son of Adam seemed impressed with deeper gravity, yet what shall I think of him? He often, in the midst of his most important airs—I believe when he is at loss for expressions (and this he often is, wrapped up, I suppose, in the contemplation of his own importance)—suffers an unmeaning kind of vacant laugh to escape him. This was the case to-day, and really to me bore the air of ridiculing the farce he was acting. "Gentlemen, I wish for the direction of the Senate. The President will, I suppose address the Congress. How shall I behave? How shall we receive it? Shall it be standing or sitting?"

Besides questions about protocol, there were many others of graver importance to which the Constitution provided no specific answers. Under the circumstances, the officers of the new government had no alternative but to establish their own precedents. For example, when Washington, interpreting literally the provision in the Constitution stating that the president should make treaties "by and with the advice and consent of the Senate," appeared in person before that body to discuss a proposed Indian treaty, the senators were visibly offended. Washington never again asked the Senate's "advice" on a treaty, and most of his successors have followed this precedent. In similar fashion, the cabinet was a product both of Washington's personal views and of the necessity for working out a set of rules for the day-to-day conduct of the government. Although the Constitution makes no mention of a cabinet, from the outset Washington repeatedly used his constitutional power to "require the opinion, in writing" of his department heads. At first he approached his assistants individually. Before the end of his first administration, he was meeting more or less regularly with all of them at his home. Although the word "cabinet" did not appear in a federal statute until 1907, both the word and the institution were accepted parts of the American governmental system in the 1790's.

One of the most fortunate features of the new government was the almost universal acclaim accorded the new Constitution as soon as it was put into effect. Men who had criticized almost every feature of the Constitution during the struggle over ratification, and during the elections of 1788 now vied with the Federalists in extolling its virtues.

The transformation of the Constitution from a major political issue into a universally venerated symbol was caused in part by the effectiveness of the Federalists' campaign for ratification. By calling themselves Federalists, a name that more accurately described the opposition which believed in a loose union of states, they implied that the government they were sponsoring would further the interests of the states. By identifying the Constitution with progress, they implied that its opponents were reactionaries. Finally, by emphasizing—although with little or no justification—that the Constitution was an expression of the popular will, they were able to appeal to the nascent democratic spirit in America. In this vein, James Wilson, a Pennsylvania Federalist, in a speech to his state's ratifying convention, said: "Government . . . has hitherto been the result of force, fraud or accident. . . . America now presents the first instance of a free people assembled to weigh . . . calmly, and to decide leisurely and peaceably, upon the form of government by which they will bind themselves and their posterity."

The prestige of the Constitution was helped in the long run by separation of church and state. The numerous sects in America made it impolitic, if not impossible, to create a state religion; and with no official church, there was no basis for a charge that the Constitution discriminated against certain religious denominations. Instead, the Federalists could maintain that the new plan of government was a political expression of moral tenets held by all Christians. Thus, a New Haven minister wondered

> . . . whether men can be serious in regard to the Christian religion, who can object to a government . . . calculated to promote the glory of God by establishing peace, order and justice in our country—and whether it would not be better for such men to renounce the Christian name, to enter into society with the Shawnee or Mohawk Indians than to attempt to retain the blessings of religion and civilization with their licentious ideas of government.

Even Benjamin Franklin, who had little use for formal religion, wrote:

> I must avow that I have so much faith in the general govern-
> ment of the world by Providence, that I can hardly conceive
> [that] a transaction of such momentous importance [as the
> Constitution] to the welfare of millions now existing . . .
> should be suffered to pass without being in some degree in-
> fluenced, guided and governed by that omnipotent, omnipresent
> and beneficial Rule, in whom all inferior spirits live, and move
> and have their being.

The chances for success of the Constitution, of the Federalists, and
of the Washington Administration, were enormously enhanced when
economic uncertainty gave way after 1787 to more prosperous conditions in the 1790's. Although the adoption of the Constitution did not
create this prosperity except in so far as it tended to increase the confidence of business groups, Federalists were quick to attribute the upswing in the business cycle to the new form of government. William
Maclay might complain that the Federalists "paint the state of the country under the old . . . congress, as if neither wood grew nor water ran
in America before the happy adoption of the new Constitution"; but
many Americans accepted the Federalist interpretation of the change
in their fortunes.

Perhaps the most important contribution to the popularity of the
Constitution was the adoption of the first ten Amendments, or Bill of
Rights. Several states had ratified the Constitution with the understanding that it would be amended to include specific guarantees of personal
liberty, and North Carolina withheld its approval until such action was
taken. Such guarantees, which were not opposed by the Federalists, had
been omitted from the Constitution only because it was believed that
they were adequately provided by the states and in common law. But
as soon as it became obvious that the new government could both enhance its prestige and remove an important source of opposition by
making the desired constitutional amendments, the Federalists did not
hesitate to sponsor them. Accordingly, in June, 1789, Madison submitted to Congress several amendments that had been proposed by the
states. Of these, the House approved seventeen, the Senate voted for
twelve, and ten were ratified by the states. On December 15, 1791, the
first ten amendments, guaranteeing all Americans such rights from the
federal government as trial by jury and freedom of speech, religion,
and press became part of the Constitution. Men who had previously
distrusted the new form of government were now prepared to give it
their support.

Alexander Hamilton

Putting the Constitution to Work

To what use was the Constitution to be put? The new Secretary of the Treasury was ready to use the powers of the national government to the full, and he conceived himself as America's Prime Minister. Alexander Hamilton was one of the men most responsible for the success of the new government. Born in the West Indies, trained at King's College (Columbia), with a scintillating mind and a charming personality, he was a great lawyer, a skillful orator, a master organizer, a brilliant pamphleteer, and a statesman of the first rank. Temperamentally, he admired and respected aristocracy and throughout his life despised democracy. His ideal of government was rule by talented men whose wealth and leisure had given them the largest stake in society and a comprehensive view of human affairs. He thought it unlikely that talent and the real immediate sources of political power would be found among those obliged to earn their living by hard labor. He distrusted theorists and idealists and based his political philosophy on the realities of power. "That power," he said, "which holds the purse-strings absolutely must rule."

Before assuming office, Hamilton had in mind economic measures that he believed were absolutely necessary for the success of the new government. They included the funding of the entire national debt—principal and interest—at face value, regardless of whether the old bond and stock certificates were held by the original subscribers or had been acquired by speculators and others at a discount; the assumption at face value of the debts of the several states by the national government; the establishment of a national bank and a mint; the levying of customs duties to protect and encourage American manufactures and commerce; the sale of the public lands to pay for the liquidation of the national debt; and the establishment of a sinking fund for purchasing public securities in the open market from time to time. This program was in keeping with Hamilton's belief that no government could last without the confidence and support of property owners and businessmen.

Hamilton's *Report on the Public Credit*, the first of the documents in which he elaborated his program, was submitted to Congress in January, 1790. A detailed plan for funding the debt and increasing the fluid capital of the country, it proposed calling in the old national bonds and certificates, the principal and interest on which at face value totaled approximately $50,000,000, and replacing them with new securities. Hamilton also recommended that the national government assume at face value the debts of the states, incurred for the most part during the Revolution and amounting to about $20,000,000. He believed that their assumption would make for orderliness and stability and bind the Union more closely together, that it would compensate the states in part for their surrender to the federal government of the right to levy import duties, and that it would force all public creditors to look to the federal government rather than to the states for the sums due them.

Hamilton also advocated a sinking fund that the secretary of the treasury could use to buy securities in the market when in his judgment it was to the best interests of the government and of the holders of public securities to do so. He planned that the money for this sinking fund, as well as for interest on the new securities and for their ultimate retirement, should be obtained from import duties and the proceeds of the sale of public lands in the West.

Closely associated with the funding and assumption plans was the scheme for a central bank, which Hamilton outlined in his *Report on the National Bank.* A national bank, he argued, would increase the productive capital of the country by increasing the number of notes in circulation, by putting them to greater use, and by collecting what otherwise might well be idle funds. It would enable the government to obtain loans more easily, and, by increasing the circulation of money and expanding the facilities for borrowing, it would make the collection of taxes easier. Of the capital stock of $10,000,000, one fifth was to be subscribed by the government and the remainder by the public.

In still another report, Hamilton dealt with the vexatious and much debated subject of the coinage. Although he expressed a preference for gold, he nevertheless recommended that both gold and silver should be minted in the ratio of one to fifteen—a proportion corresponding to the bullion values of the time. He also advocated the use of the decimal system of coinage, and proposed gold and silver equivalents for the dollar, the monetary unit. He further recommended the coinage of $10 gold pieces, silver dimes, and copper pennies and half-pennies.

Hamilton demanded a protective tariff in 1791 in his *Report on Manufactures.* He maintained that a high tariff would help to make the United States economically independent, would lower prices, and would protect infant industries against foreign competition. His principal argument was the desirability of promoting manufacturing in the United States, and the bulk of the report is devoted to an extended and brilliant discussion of the advantages of a factory system. Manufactures, Hamilton contended, would promote a greater division of labor than agriculture; would increase production by adding the "artificial force" of machinery to the "natural force of man"; would give employment to "classes of the community not originally engaged in the particular business"; would help enrich the country by encouraging the immigration of foreign workers; would furnish "greater scope for the diversity of talents and dispositions which discriminate men from each other"; would "cherish and stimulate the activity of the human mind by multiplying the objects of enterprise"; and would furnish a home market for surplus farm products.

Hamilton argued that his many-sided program would benefit all classes in the United States. Maintaining that business expansion was the only effective means for adding to the nation's wealth and promoting general prosperity, he tried to convince the farmers that they would also profit. But Hamilton's program was essentially mercantile and industrial. An agricultural economy alone could never make America the national power Hamilton hoped it would become.

Wherever there were businessmen or farmers whose interests would not be served by the Hamiltonian program of nationally supervised, broad economic development, there was the seedbed of opposition to the Federalist supporters of Hamilton. Actually, despite Hamilton's vision and political acumen, his proposals ran against the tide of *laissez faire*, against the forces of localism and particularism, and counter to the slowly rising belief in equal rights that the American Revolution had stimulated. Hamilton had great respect for English institutions, although he did not believe that monarchy could work in America, and he was convinced that the centralized and concentrated power that the English state seemed to possess could be duplicated within a republican form of government. Within six months after taking office, he had made himself into the American prime minister. While his prestige was less than Washington's, his daily power was probably greater. His Treasury agents were everywhere in the country, collecting customs, selling lands, taking in excises. These men were also soon to become the grass roots reporters for a national political party fighting for Hamilton's policies. Hamilton never held back from the rough and tumble of politics. Convinced that America could guarantee its republican institutions and basic liberties only if it was strong and self-sufficient, he plunged into the negotiations, the "deals," even the intrigue on which political success often depends. Accustomed to thinking in the most pragmatic ways, he seemed insensitive to calls for justice that were too abstract or remote to be taken seriously. Realistically, Hamilton merely interpreted these claims as fine cloaks for interests that were being hurt by his program. His zest in power and statecraft, his intrigue, his desire to create a great American state, and his seeming lack of feeling for the needs of the small man were what first aroused Thomas Jefferson against him. In less than a year, a partisan opposition against Hamilton began to take shape. It found its roots among those interests throughout the country that felt slighted by Hamilton's proposals.

The Struggle Over Hamilton's Program

The opposition first leveled its guns at Hamilton's funding proposals. A large part of the old state and Continental bonds had been acquired by speculators at low prices. Soldiers, farmers, and crossroads merchants—ignorant of what the Federal Constitution would bring in its wake and, later, unaware of the Hamiltonian funding scheme—had been easy prey for agents who scoured the country in quest of depreciated paper. When the funding measure came before Congress, some of the opposition leaders, contending that the high debt was for goods bought at greatly inflated prices, for services rendered at exorbitant rates, or for loans of depreciated paper, proposed that it be scaled down to market value rather than, as Hamilton proposed, redeemed at face value. Another congressional group headed by Madison was especially anxious to do justice to both the original investor and the present holder. Accordingly, Madison advanced a plan that was a compromise between those who wanted the debt refunded at face value and those who would refund it at market value. It provided that the speculator be paid the highest price that had prevailed on the market and the original holder the difference between the face value and the market price. Although aware that this plan had certain defects, Madison felt certain that it was far superior to the other two. "The original sufferers," he said, "will not be fully indemnified; but they will receive from their country a tribute due to their merits, which if it does not entirely heal their wounds, will assuage the pain of them." But, on February 22, 1790, Congress rejected Madison's proposal by a vote of almost three to one. A few months later, Hamilton's plan was adopted. Of the sixty-four members of the House of Representatives, twenty-nine held these securities. The speculation to buy up the suddenly valuable paper and the involvement of Hamilton's own aide in the jobbing increased enmity toward Hamilton. He, however, simply considered these results of the funding scheme a necessary price for a good public end.

Opposition to the assumption of the debts of the states by the national government was bitter and uncompromising. Representatives of debtor, inflationary, and smaller economic interests thought the proposal merely another move in Hamilton's plan to enrich the large businessmen at the expense of the rest of the country. The opposition of the South was intense because the proportion of its debts to the population was much less than that in the North. Some southern states had also already taken care of their debts, and their citizens, through representatives like James Madison, could see no reason why they should be taxed to help pay the debts of the North. The Hamiltonians worked assiduously to overcome this opposition, but when the vote on the measure was taken in the House of Representatives on April 12, 1790, they were defeated by two votes. Following a favorable motion to reconsider, Hamilton and his supporters redoubled their efforts. Finally, after weeks of negotiations, Hamilton seized upon the idea of a bargain with the South over the site of the permanent capital. Fortunately for Hamilton, Jefferson, who had just returned from France to take up his new duties as Secretary of State and who was soon to became Hamilton's chief antagonist, listened to his plea for assistance. At a dinner party arranged by Jefferson, it was agreed that two members who had previously voted against assumption should change their minds and that the friends of assumption in return should see to it that the national capital was located

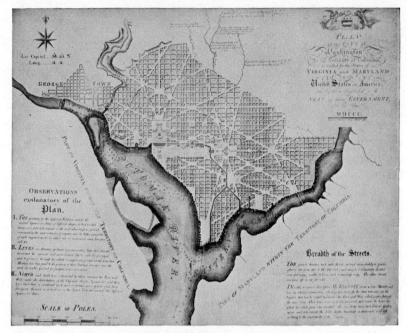

Plan of Washington, D. C.

on the banks of the Potomac in territory set off from Virginia and Maryland. To pacify Pennsylvania, which also wanted the capital, Philadelphia was to be the seat of the national government for ten years. "And so," Jefferson wrote long afterwards, "the Assumption was passed, and twenty millions of stock divided among favored states and thrown in as a pabulum to the stock-jobbing herd."

Hamilton's recommendations for a mint and a national bank were also made law by Congress. The Mint Act, which closely followed the Secretary of the Treasury's suggestions, was passed with little difficulty in 1792, but the bank measure was vigorously opposed. "This plan of a national bank," said James Jackson of Georgia, "is calculated to benefit a small part of the United States, the mercantile interests only; the farmers, the yeomanry, will derive no advantage from it." The measure, he went on to say, sought to create a monopoly and was contrary to the spirit and intent of the Constitution. Actually justifying inflationist and wild cat banking forces, his arguments foreshadowed those of Andrew Jackson forty years later. Even Madison, who had worked so indefatigably for the establishment of a strong federal government, opposed the bank as unconstitutional. The opposition, however, was not strong enough to prevent the passage of this measure. Of the twenty votes cast against the bill in the House, nineteen were by southern members. The bank was chartered for twenty years and capitalized at $10,000,000, four fifths of which were to be subscribed by individuals and the remaining fifth by the government. Authorized to serve as a depository of government funds, it could also issue notes that were receivable for government dues. In December, 1791, the bank began its notably successful career in Philadelphia; branch offices were subsequently established in Boston, New York, Baltimore, Washington, Norfolk, Charleston, Savannah, and New Orleans.

The bank bill, as Madison said, raised constitutional as well as financial issues, and before signing the measure, Washington sought the advice of the members of his cabinet. Jefferson and Randolph maintained that the bank law was unconstitutional; Hamilton and Knox took the opposite view. Jefferson, whose constitutional theories were undoubtedly colored in this instance by his economic and political opinions, took a narrow view of the Constitution and argued that the document contained no provision granting Congress authority to establish a bank. The bank was not absolutely "necessary and proper" to fulfill the grants of power given to Congress over the national economy. Hamilton, fully as prejudiced as Jefferson, rested his case on a broad interpretation of the Constitution. Reasoning that the Constitution gave the government general powers without necessarily specifying the means by which they might be used, he concluded: "This criterion is the *end* to which the measure relates as a *mean*. If the *end* is clearly comprehended within any of the specified powers, and if the measure have an obvious relation to that *end*, and is not forbidden by any particular provision of the Constitution, it may safely be deemed to come within the compass of the national authority." Washington accepted Hamilton's concept of "implied powers" and signed the bill. From the standpoint of constitutional history, the broad and strict interpretations advanced by Hamilton and Jefferson respectively set a pattern for future constitutional argument.

Because Hamilton did not wish to alienate potential support for the government among the larger businessmen by taxing them directly, he proposed that the government rely on a tariff and excise taxes as sources of revenue. John Taylor of Caroline, a Virginian enthusiast for an agricultural America, wrote that under a protective tariff, "the wealth of the majority will be as certainly diminished to enrich capital, as it should be obliged to export a million of guineas to bring back a million of dollars or to bestow a portion of its guineas upon this special interest."

There was, however, no significant argument in 1789 against the government's claim of a need for revenue. Even before Hamilton's *Report on Manufactures*, Congress adopted a modest tariff bill (July 4, 1789). No attempt was made to exact the remainder of Hamilton's elaborate program for stimulating American manufactures, largely because American industry was not yet strong enough or national enough to need or demand the privileges Hamilton had in mind.

Hamilton's proposal for an excise tax on liquor aroused far more hostility than the tariff. Despite this fact, in 1791 Congress enacted an excise law that followed most of Hamilton's suggestions. Although eastern distillers were affected by this measure, they easily shifted the burden of the tax to the consumer. Frontier farmers, who because of bad roads and high transportation costs were transforming their grain into whisky, were less fortunately situated. Much of their liquor was for their own use, and the excise duty fell on them as a direct tax. Unlike the eastern distillers, even those who sent part of their manufactured product to market were unable to shift the tax. News of the passage of the excise measure aroused widespread dissatisfaction on the frontier. Alarmed by the extent of the opposition, Congress in 1792 put through supplementary legislation abolishing the tax on the smaller stills; but even this modification of the law failed to placate the frontier farmers of Pennsylvania. Meetings, resolutions, and protests soon gave way to more drastic action: men refused to pay the tax, intimidated government collectors, and dealt summary justice to persons who gave information or other aid to revenue officers. Finally, in 1794, when a United States marshal attempted to serve warrants on those who had been indicted for refusal to pay the tax, an open insurrection known as the Whisky Rebellion broke out. Hamilton, anxious to strengthen the hand of government and to compel respect for law and order, advised Washington to treat the rebels severely. Milder counsel, however, prevailed, and with the approach of a considerable military force led by Governor Lee of Virginia, the revolt melted away. Several of the ringleaders were arrested and marched to Philadelphia where they were jailed; only two were subsequently convicted, and they were pardoned by the President. Federalists rejoiced over the triumph of the government. Yet few of them apparently realized that both the excise law and the revolt that had followed had weakened their cause and strengthened the opposition. In only a few years political power was to pass into the hands of the very men whom the Hamiltonians labeled pernicious, malignant, contemptible, and vile.

The Rise of an Opposition

Although Hamilton's financial policies were designed to unite the entire nation behind the government, they tended to produce just the opposite effect. Small farmers, small or local business interests, recent immigrants, and a large variety of other interest groups injured in some way by the Federalist laws could see little to commend in the new system. Their spokesmen pointed out the reasons for their refusal to support the Federalists. John Taylor in his pamphlet *An Enquiry into the Principles and Tendency of Certain Public Measures*, which appeared in 1794, attacked the Hamiltonian program as a device to enrich the wealthy and impoverish the poor. A year earlier, George Logan, in an anonymous tract entitled *Five Letters Addressed to the Yeomanry of the United States*, declared that the lawbooks of the Union were stained with mercantile regulations highly injurious to the agricultural interest of the country; funding systems by which the property and rights of poor but meritorious citizens were sacrificed to wealthy gamesters and speculators; the establishment of banks "authorizing a few men to create fictitious money, by which they may acquire rapid fortunes without industry"; and excise laws that disturbed domestic tranquility and prevented the farmer from enjoying the fruits of his industry. Somewhat later, J. T. Callender, another farmer pamphleteer, expressed much the same opinion in his *Sedgwick & Co., or a Key to the Six Per Cent Cabinet*. Pamphlets of lesser importance and newspaper articles also reflected the opposition to the existing order.

The controversial nature of Hamilton's financial policies did not prevent a Federalist victory in the election of 1792. The opposition— who now called themselves either Democratic-Republicans or Republicans—realized the futility of opposing a man they had no chance of defeating, and for the second time Washington received every electoral vote. But no aura of sanctity surrounded John Adams, the vice-president, and the Republicans selected George Clinton of New York to run against him. Although Adams received seventy-seven electoral votes to fifty for Clinton, the Republicans carried Georgia, New York, North Carolina, and Virginia and won a single electoral vote in Pennsylvania. Party lines were beginning to take definite shape, and before the end of Washington's second term, the two contending groups were conducting bitter partisan warfare.

The acrimonious debates over the Federalist financial policies should not obscure Hamilton's very real contribution to the success of the new government. More than anyone else, he was responsible for placing Federal finances on a sound basis. enhancing the prestige of the

United States government both at home and abroad, and making the states realize that they could never regain the powers they had enjoyed under the Confederation. An aristocrat who despised democracy, he did as much as any individual in Washington's administration to insure the survival of the world's most democratic nation.

The Long Shadow of European War

The first generation under the Constitution was passed in a world at war. The French Revolution of 1789 brought on a general European conflict that never really halted until the final allied victory over Napoleon at Waterloo in 1815. Even under the best circumstances, Americans would have been hard put to avoid involvement in so momentous a struggle and to avoid comparisons between the Revolutions of 1776 and 1789. By 1790, leading Americans like Jefferson had, in retrospect, given a new interpretation to the events of 1776. His years in France as our minister convinced Jefferson that in 1776 the Americans had not only broken with England but had taken the first steps toward a new age for mankind, an era of progress, of equality before the law, and of limited or republican government. By 1790, it seemed to many men that the American and French Revolutions were predominantly the same struggle against tyranny. Just as it seemed to Europeans that the principles proclaimed in France in 1789 were on trial before the world, so did it seem increasingly to Jefferson and his friends that the principles of 1776 were being tested in America in the 1790's. A defeat for the rights of man in America or in Europe might profoundly alter the course of history. American domestic politics thus became involved in a battle over theories of human rights, and American foreign policy was affected by the intense partisanship stirred up by the French Revolution. Federalists were accused of wishing for the victory of England over France because they were friends of monarchy and foes of the rights of man; Hamilton's policies were interpreted as an attempt to frustrate the intentions of the Declaration of Independence. The Democratic-Republicans, the opposition, were said to be Jacobins anxious to destroy Christianity, constitutional government, and property rights. Washington's troubles were great enough as it was, but the growing ideological fights of his two terms in office complicated his problems enormously. Under the circumstances, Washington's conduct of American foreign policy in many respects constitutes as notable an achievement as Hamilton's administration of the new nation's finances. As the head of a new government, Washington had neither guides nor precedents to lessen the burden of his responsibility. As President of a weak nation in the midst of a world at war, he was continually faced by the seemingly impossible task of maintaining American neutrality. Realizing that war could wreck the American experiment before it had had an opportunity to demonstrate its worth, he made peace his sole objective; and, despite the criticisms of his political opponents, he successfully steered the United States through some of the most trying years in its history.

The outbreak of the French Revolution was greeted by many Americans with unrestrained enthusiasm. From Maine to Georgia, the news that in France the old order had been overturned and that the aristocracy of Europe under the leadership of the Duke of Brunswick had been turned back at the French frontier was applauded by those Americans who believed that the Old World upheaval was inspired by their own revolutionary struggle. French ideas, French modes of speaking, and French fashions became the order of the day. Liberty poles were erected and liberty caps worn. Titles such as "Sir," "The Honorable," and "His Excellency" were discarded as too aristocratic, and "Citizen" and "Citizeness" replaced "Mr.," "Mrs.," and "Miss." Even the theaters caught the spirit, and Shakespeare and Sheridan gave way to *Tyranny Suppressed*, and the *Demolition of the Bastille*. Streets whose names were associated with aristocracy were renamed: Royal Exchange Alley in Boston became Equality Lane, and Kings Street in New York was renamed Liberty Street. Thomas Paine strengthened this enthusiasm in his *Rights of Man*, a reply to Burke's *Reflections on the French Revolution*. In answer to Burke's attack on the French leaders for their disregard for tradition in the name of purely abstract rights Paine wrote:

> Every age and generation must be free to act for itself in all cases as the ages and generations which preceded it. The vanity and presumption of governing beyond the grave is the most ridiculous and insolent of all tyrannies. . . . Every generation is, and must be, competent to all the purposes which its occasions require. It is the living, and not the dead, that are to be accommodated.

Paine's eloquent defense of the French Revolution stimulated the formation in the United States of secret democratic societies which were said to be modeled after the Jacobin clubs of Paris. These societies passed resolutions embodying democratic and equalitarian sentiments, endorsing the work of the French radicals, and condemning the efforts of the European monarchs to stamp out the Revolution. The activities of these organizations were not confined to agitation over events in

Europe; an increasing number were interested in local politics, and many explicitly stated that their avowed purpose was to discuss and disseminate information about domestic affairs.

To the Federalists, the French Revolution—with its defiance of tradition and constituted authority, its challenge to privilege, and its emphasis, in its radical phase, on democracy—was a shocking example of the dangers of mob rule. As the movement in France gathered headway and control passed from the moderates into the hands of the radicals, the Federalist leaders became almost hysterical lest the "rabble" and "Jacobins" in America should also overturn the government. Every sympathizer of the French Revolution, a New England clergyman said, was guilty of spreading "atheistical, anarchical and, in other respects, immoral principles. . . . The editors, patrons, and abettors of these vehicles of slander ought to be considered and treated as enemies to their country. . . . Of all traitors they are the most aggravatedly criminal; of all villains they are the most infamous and detestable." And William Cobbett, a Federalist editor, wrote: "I say, beware, ye understrapping cut-throats, who walk in rags and sleep amidst filth and vermin, for if once the halter gets around your flea bitten necks, howling and confessing will come too late." The answers of Anti-Federalist editors like Philip Freneau were equally spirited.

In the midst of the campaigns of abuse waged by Federalist and Republicans, "Citizen" Edmund Charles Genêt arrived in the city of Charleston as the representative of revolutionary France to the United States. Young, handsome, elegant in manner, eloquent and entertaining in conversation, and friendly in bearing, he was received with great acclaim by Republicans, and his month's journey northward to Philadelphia produced a continuous ovation. He was greeted as a conquering hero by the multitudes who paid tribute to France and the principles of the revolutionists of 1789, but when he presented his credentials to Washington and Jefferson, he was received with stern formality. Believing that the Administration did not represent the people and that the American people would support him in a conflict with the government, Genêt soon adopted a policy that led to his downfall and strengthened the hand of the Federalists.

Before Genêt's arrival, Washington, fully aware that the new minister was determined to drag the United States into the European war on the side of France, asked his cabinet for advice and suggestions. Hamilton unhesitatingly argued that the treaties of 1778 between France and the United States were obsolete because they had been negotiated with the Bourbon monarchy, which the Revolutionists had overthrown. Even if the treaties were in force, he contended, there would be no obligation on the part of the American republic to come to the assistance of France, for they stipulated American aid only if France were fighting a defensive war. Jefferson, on the other hand, maintained that since treaties are negotiated between nations rather than between governments, the pacts of 1778 were still binding. He thought that, without denouncing the treaties, America should do nothing to prejudice the French cause, to permit her to demand our entry, or, worse, to declare war on us for aid to England or for renouncing the treaty. Washington inclined to agree with Hamilton on neutrality and with Jefferson on not abjuring the treaties. In 1793, he issued a proclamation of neutrality announcing that the United States was not a party to the conflict and that all American citizens were to refrain from any act that might be considered hostile by the warring nations.

The proclamation of neutrality meant nothing, however, to Genêt. Even before he had presented his credentials, he had planned to organize expeditions in the United States against Louisiana and Florida. He attempted to use American ports as bases of operation for French privateers and commissioned American vessels to prey on British commerce. When Jefferson, as Secretary of State, endeavored to check him, he denounced the Administration as cowardly and unrepresentative. Finally the government, unable to tolerate longer his abuse and interference, asked for his recall. Genêt, knowing that his return to France might mean his execution, decided to remain in America. He went to New York, married a daughter of George Clinton, and lived quietly in the United States until his death in 1835.

Genêt's presence in America and his highhanded methods served to weaken the Republicans and correspondingly strengthen the Federalists. Jefferson, well aware of this fact, was much relieved when the obnoxious minister was removed from office. Even the democratic clubs agreed with Madison, who characterized Genêt's conduct as that of a madman. Genêt's actions did not help the cause of the French Revolution. Many Americans who had been inclined to be sympathetic now became either indifferent or openly hostile to a cause that could send so outrageous a representative to the American people.

With the removal of Genêt, Great Britain rather than France again became the immediate antagonist of the United States. The British retained their posts in the Northwest, and they continued to use their Indian allies to menace American settlers in the region. The Indians, who refused to abide by the treaties that they had signed in the 1780's, repeatedly sent scalping parties to menace the settlements in the Northwest. Britain made possible the Indian attacks on the American "Long Knives" by supplying tribes with liquor and ammunition and by permitting them to use the disputed posts as bases for their operations. Britain still seemed to hope to create an Indian buffer state that would stand as a permanent barrier to American expansion in the North-west.

Any sustained offensive against the Indians in the Northwest neces-sarily created a risk of war with Great Britain. Washington decided that it was a risk that he would have to take. In 1790 he sent General Josiah Harmar to attack the Indians on the Maumee. Harmar was able to destroy some undefended Indian settlements; but when his troops were ambushed, they were forced to retreat. A year later, a much larger expedition under Governor St. Clair was overwhelmingly de-feated by the Indians. Washington now turned to "Mad Anthony" Wayne, who had distinguished himself at the battle of Stony Point in 1779. After drilling his recruits intensively for more than a year, Wayne advanced into the wilderness and took up winter quarters at Fort Greenville during 1793–94. The British meanwhile were making every effort to rouse their Indian allies. In February, 1794, Lord Dor-chester, the governor of Canada, as much as told the Indians that they could count on British assistance in their efforts to repulse the Ameri-cans. Wayne replied by offering peace to the Indians; but after they had repeatedly refused his proposals, he resumed his advance and com-pletely routed them at the battle of Fallen Timbers (August 20, 1794). Despite this defeat, the Indians refused to agree to peace, and it was not until August, 1795, that they accepted the Treaty of Greenville. This treaty in which the Indians agreed to accept the authority of the United States rather than that of Great Britain and to abandon the warpath, led to fifteen years of comparative tranquility in the North-west.

In these same years, the United States was also compelled to deal with an equally serious British threat to its commercial rights. In 1793, Great Britain declared war on France and quickly destroyed most of her merchant marine. France, cut off from her West Indian islands, with whom she had carried on approximately two thirds of her over-seas trade, was compelled to lift her mercantilistic barriers and open her commerce to the neutrals of the world. Americans rejoiced, for here was an opportunity to enjoy legally the lucrative West Indian trade. But their rejoicing did not last long. The British were determined to starve France into submission and to prevent the development of a rival merchant marine. They ruled that all ships of neutrals were liable to capture if engaged in carrying enemy-owned goods. Even more dam-aging to the Americans was British revival of the "rule of 1756," which stated that a trade closed in time of peace could not be opened in time of war. In June, 1793, they also authorized the seizure of all vessels carrying grain and flour.

The British commanders carried out these orders even before the United States had learned of their existence. Within a short time, they had seized approximately 300 American ships. The British, however, did not stop with ships; they also impressed American sailors. When British commanders discovered on an American merchant ship British seamen who had escaped from the Royal Navy to the more attractive American merchant marine, they forcibly removed them. But often the men impressed in this fashion claimed to be citizens of the United States. Some American sailors were thus forced to serve in the British navy against their will.

The effect of these British policies on the United States was far-reaching. Shipbuilding decreased, and farmers, frustrated in their hopes for the West Indies as a market for their surplus grain and meat, complained that they were unable to get rid of their produce. Sympathizers of France, overlooking the fact that French men-of-war and privateers were also harassing American vessels, were outspoken in their hatred for Britain. Federalist leaders, through detesting France, were placed in an embarrassing position. Some Federalist planters welcomed trouble with England in the hope that debts still due British creditors would be extinguished. Others remembered that the British had failed to compensate them for the thousands of slaves that they asserted the British had carried off at the conclusion of the Revolution. Hoping to gain advantage from this split within the Federalists, the Republicans demanded that drastic measures be taken against Great Britain and made proposals ranging from sequestration of British debts to a declaration of war.

John Jay Pays for Peace

Aside from a few fanatics, no American wanted war with Great Britain. The Federal government was still in the experimental stage and in no position to embark upon a costly and hazardous war. Most of the national income came from the tariff, and goods from Great Britain accounted for almost 90 per cent of American imports. War would have impaired the public credit and would probably have destroyed the fiscal system that Hamilton had so arduously constructed. War would have meant irreparable loss to the American producer and merchant and would have closed the door to the English investor, who not only advanced credit for trade and money for land speculation and industrial

John Jay

enterprise, but who was also a heavy purchaser of government bonds and bank stock. The Federalists especially had no desire to declare war against any country engaged in curbing "Jacobinical" France.

In an effort to exact concessions from the British and to give the Administration time to devise a satisfactory settlement, Congress on March 26, 1794, adopted a thirty-day embargo that was subsequently extended a month. Steps were also taken to prepare for the unwelcome possibility of war. Congress approved a measure for the construction of harbor fortifications, authorized additional military stores, passed a bill for increasing the strength of the artillery, and made provision for calling out 80,000 militiamen. At the same time, an effort was made to settle the controversy by negotiation. In May, 1794, John Jay, Chief Justice of the Supreme Court, was sent to England to conclude a treaty with the British. At the time, Washington wrote: "If he succeeds, well;

if he does not, why, knowing the worst, we must take measures accordingly."

Jay's instructions directed him to reject any treaty that did not secure the British evacuation of the Northwest posts, indemnification for American shipping losses, and the removal of conditions impeding the peaceful commercial relations of the two countries. But the military weakness of the United States and Hamilton's desire to maintain peace at any cost made Jay's position extremely difficult. Determined to prevent a breakdown of the negotiations, Hamilton informed George Hammond, the British minister in Philadelphia, that Washington's cabinet in a secret meeting had agreed not to join the League of Armed Neutrality, which was being organized by some of the European powers to resist British maritime restrictions. When Hammond relayed this information to his superiors in London, Jay was deprived of his principal bargaining point, and the British were able to reject a number of the American demands.

Under the Jay Treaty, the New England boundary line and indemnities for shipping seized by the British were to be adjusted by joint commissions; the Northwest posts were to be evacuated by June 1, 1796; and, in return, the Mississippi was to be opened to British trade. No mention was made of pacifying the Indians or of compensation for the slaves carried off by the British army, yet the federal government was to assume the old pre-Revolutionary British debts and pay principal and interest in specie. America had to abandon the principle that "free goods made free ships," and the British contraband list was extended. Nothing was said about the impressment of American seamen. The all-important West Indian trade, which Jay was specifically instructed to secure, was opened to American ships of seventy-tons burden only, and on the express condition that American vessels should not carry molasses, sugar, coffee, cocoa, or cotton, no matter where produced, to any other ports in the world except their own. The East Indian trade was opened to Americans subject to certain conditions. Finally, British trade with the United States was placed on a most-favored-nation basis by which America had to extend to England any tariff favors given to other nations; this precluded such retaliatory and discriminatory measures as the Anti-Federalists had been proposing.

At first, the Senate tried to keep the terms of the treaty secret, but when they were made public, an uproar followed. Jay was burned in effigy, the British minister was openly insulted, and Hamilton, trying to defend the treaty, was hissed and stoned. Opponents of the Washington Administration denounced the treaty as a Federalist surrender to British power. For the first time open attacks were made on President

Washington. "His Excellency, John Jay. May he and his treason be forever politically damned" was a typical toast. "Damn John Jay! Damn every one who won't damn John Jay! Damn every one who won't put out lights in his windows and sit up all night damning John Jay" was one curse that expressed common feelings. Even Federalists like John Rutledge and John Langdon denounced the treaty.

Alarmed at the public protest, Hamilton, writing under the pen name of "Camillus," came to the rescue of the treaty. In a series of thirty-eight essays, he emphasized its more favorable provisions. But he showed that the controversy was also another phase of the conflict between Federalists and their opponents. The opposition, he said, had merely seized upon the treaty in order to discredit the Federalists and their work. Hamilton alienated the large landed interests of the South by asserting that the southern claim of compensation for slaves taken by the British was "a very doubtful one," and that the debts owing to British creditors ought to be paid. Other Federalist leaders, among them Fisher Ames of Massachusetts, also vigorously supported the treaty. Ames, in denouncing those merchants who sided with the Republicans on this issue, said that he could not disguise his "contempt for the blindness and gullibility of the rich men who so readily lend their strength to the party which is thirsting for the contents of their iron chests." To the great relief of the Federalists, the Senate in June, 1795, ratified the treaty minus the article dealing with the West Indian trade. Ten months later, the House of Representatives, despite the opposition of the Republicans, authorized the funds that were needed to give effect to the treaty.

The importance of the Jay Treaty cannot be overemphasized. Far more important than the Republican criticisms of Jay were the very real benefits that he secured for the United States. The Jay Treaty made for stronger American sovereignty in the Northwest, assured the United States of commercial prosperity, and, by forestalling war, prevented the destruction of Hamilton's financial system. In return, the Americans were compelled to defer to the English rules about trade in time of war. The Republicans complained that the price exacted by the British for a settlement was exorbitant, but it was a price that the Federalists were willing to pay to insure the survival of the American nation. In perspective, the Jay Treaty seems—just as the Federalists at the time maintained it was—the only alternative to the destruction of the United States.

The Jay Treaty also paved the way for settlement of the disputes between the United States and Spain in the Southwest. Spain, having entered the war against France in 1793, withdrew from the conflict two years later to side with France against Great Britain. Under the circumstances, the Jay Treaty, which to the Spanish looked like the first step toward the creation of a formal alliance between the two nations, convinced Spain that she could no longer retain her position in the American Southwest in the face of the combined opposition of the United States and Great Britain. Accordingly, Count Manuel Godoy, who until this time had rejected all American overtures for a settlement, indicated to Thomas Pinckney, the United States diplomatic representative in Madrid, that Spain was now prepared to negotiate a treaty. The Pinckney Treaty—or Treaty of San Lorenzo—which was concluded on October 27, 1795, and unanimously ratified by the Senate on March 3, 1796, met all the American demands of the preceding twelve years. The United States was granted free navigation of the Mississippi and the right of deposit at New Orleans; the boundary between Florida and the United States was placed at the thirty-first parallel; and Spain promised to restrain the Indians along the frontier. The Pinckney Treaty, which was enthusiastically received by all groups in the United States, was a fine triumph of American diplomacy. In contrast to the Jay Treaty, it required that the United States make no concessions. At the same time, it satisfied the demands of the westerners, guaranteed the territorial integrity of the United States in the Southwest, and opened the way for American expansion into Louisiana.

Some months before the conclusion of his second term as President, Washington, in his "Farewell Address" (September 17, 1796), offered his general reflections about the nation's foreign policy. He warned the American people against what he believed were the principal dangers to the new republic and cautioned them to avoid sectional jealousies and partisan strife. He also said: "It is our true policy to steer clear of permanent alliances with any portion of the foreign world. . . . We may safely trust to temporary alliances for extraordinary emergencies." Ignoring the circumstances in which these words were uttered and not reading Washington's full statement, later generations have used Washington's valedictory to justify a more isolationist version of American foreign policy. But placed in the context of the period, Washington's statement stands as the plea of a man who had in fact faced and withstood both the menace of foreign intrigue at home and the threat of war abroad.

The Stewardship of John Adams

The strength of the Federalist party was seriously impaired by Washington's decision to retire at the end of his second presidential term. For a dozen years or more, he had been an invaluable prop to the Federalists. He had, for example, thrown all his weight and influence into the movement for the Constitution. During his presidency he had done everything in his power to endow Federalist measures with dignity. His great name and the respect in which he was held by the overwhelming majority of his countrymen undoubtedly made it easier for Hamilton and the other Federalist leaders to accomplish all that they did. On more than one occasion, unpopular Federalist measures had been saved by recourse to the appeal "Stand by Washington." His retirement, therefore, opened the door wide to the opposition; men who up to this time had hesitated to say what they thought now spoke their thoughts. "If ever there was a period for rejoicing," wrote a grandson of Benjamin Franklin in referring to Washington's retirement, "this is the moment—every heart, in unison with the freedom and happiness of the people, ought to beat high with exultation that the name of Washington from this day ceases to give a currency to political iniquity and to legalize corruption."

After his withdrawal from the cabinet in 1794, Jefferson had helped to organize the Republicans among the nation's dissatisfied interest groups. In 1796, he was the party's obvious choice for the presidency. In an effort to form an alliance between the southern planters and northern voters, the Republicans selected Aaron Burr, the head of New York's Sons of Tammany for the vice-presidency. The Federalists had more difficulty in drawing up a ticket. After rejecting Hamilton (who had resigned as Secretary of the Treasury in 1795) on the ground that his reputation, like John Jay's, would lose more votes than it would win, the party settled on John Adams and Thomas Pinckney as their two candidates.

Hamilton, bitter over his rejection by the party to which he had contributed so much, urged the North to cast its votes for Adams and Pinckney, thinking that the northern votes for the latter, when combined with many ballots expected for him from the South would make Pinckney President. Under the Constitution at the time, before the Twelfth Amendment was added, the electors voted for two men; the man with the highest number of votes became President, with the second highest, Vice-President.

The effect on the voters of this split in the Federalist high command was probably more than offset by France's attempt to determine the outcome of the election. Pierre A. Adet, the French minister to the United States, who had been withdrawn from his post by his government in protest against the Jay Treaty, remained in the United States to campaign for a Republican victory. Although Jefferson did not solicit this assistance, it alienated many voters who resented foreign intervention in American affairs. After a vituperative campaign, conducted mainly in the press, the electors were chosen by the state legislatures. In the electoral count, Adams received seventy-one votes to sixty-eight for Jefferson. Because of the rivalry between the Adams and Hamilton groups, many Federalist electors gave their second votes to Jefferson rather than to Pinckney, the choice of the other faction. As a result, they came close to making Jefferson President, and without their votes he could not have become Vice-President.

John Adams, the nation's second President, was a realist of high intellectual ability. As a young man, he had staunchly defended human rights, but with maturing years, he became skeptical of theories about the essential goodness of man and of claims about the inevitable triumph of reason and progress. He understood history as a ceaseless struggle for power and prestige. Like Madison, he believed that motives other than the desire for wealth were at work in society. Knowing perhaps his own character, he gave, for example, great weight to the effect of the desire for esteem. Nevertheless, although the cost of progress might be high, disciplined disinterested leadership, such as an Adams might supply, could advance the claims of civilization. Men, if weak, were tractable. The problem of government was to get enough power legally into the proper hands in order to control otherwise destructively selfish factions. But government itself had to be prevented from degenerating into a mere faction. Particularly vehement against unicameral supreme legislatures directly elected by the people, Adams constantly emphasized checks and balances. He believed that social warfare could be prevented only by a government that both safeguarded the poor against exploitation by the rich and protected the rich against the leveling attacks of the poor. Although he advocated rule by the well-born and the educated, he did not believe that government should be controlled completely by any class. His refusal to defer to popular frenzy, his vanity, and his tactlessness did not make him a popular figure. Few American Presidents have possessed more integrity than John Adams, and events were to demonstrate how fortunate it was that the American people had elected a man who never hesitated to subordinate political expediency to principle.

On assuming office, Adams at once found himself face to face with many of the problems that had vexed Washington. The absence of solid party support behind him and his retention intact of Washington's last, and second rate, cabinet did not help Adams. In fact, his cabinet took orders more from Hamilton than from the President.

During the last years of Washington's administration, James

John Adams

[THE NEW YORK HISTORICAL SOCIETY]

Monroe, who sympathized with the French radicals, had been recalled as minister to France, and Charles Cotesworth Pinckney, a thorough-going Federalist, had been named to replace him. This action, together with the Jay Treaty and memories of Washington's earlier treatment of Genêt angered the Directory at Paris. The Washington government was labeled pro-British; and Pinckney, instead of being received, was first placed under surveillance as a suspicious character and then ordered out of the country; the American alliance of 1778 was declared at an end; French vessels were authorized to seize and confiscate all American vessels bound to or from British ports or engaged in carrying British goods; and Adet, the French minister to the United States, was recalled. Most Federalists demanded war; but Adams announced to a special session of Congress that he would attempt to settle the difficulty by negotiation. A committee of three—C. C. Pinckney, John Marshall, and Elbridge Gerry—was sent to France to restore friendly relations.

When the three commissioners arrived in Paris, Talleyrand, in charge of foreign affairs for the French government, refused to receive them officially. Negotiations were carried on informally through agents designated by Talleyrand. As a price for peace, these agents demanded, first, that the United States apologize for its past conduct—in other words, for what the French called its pro-British policy; secondly, that it extend to the French government a large loan; and, finally, that Talleyrand and his fellow plunderers receive a *douceur* of $240,000.

Bribery was an accepted method of conducting diplomacy in Europe at the time, but the American commissioners had no guarantee that Talleyrand would draw up a treaty after they had paid him. After months of haggling, Pinckney and Marshall returned to the United States; Gerry remained in Paris until he was recalled. When at one point in the negotiations a French agent told the commissioners that they were expected to "offer money," Pinckney had replied, "No, no; not a sixpence." In America, Pinckney's words were transformed into "Millions for defense, but not one cent for tribute." The fact that at the time the United States was paying tribute to the Barbary pirates had no apparent effect on this slogan's popularity among the American people.

The report of the negotiations (referring to the French agents as Mr. X, Mr. Y, and Mr. Z) that Adams made to Congress in April, 1798, aroused the country to such an extent that many Americans urged a declaration of war. The friends of France suffered a great defeat. The Federalists, anxious to discredit the French Revolution and to embarrass their political opponents, sought to make the most of the opportunity presented to them by Talleyrand. Homes and offices of Republican editors were attacked: Benjamin Franklin, dead only a half-dozen years, was denounced as a democrat; and Republicans were condemned as infidels by Federalist preachers, who urged their congregations to hate the word "revolution." Hamilton and William Cobbett filled the Federalists press with propaganda: French troops, the public was informed, had already landed at Charleston and were destroying farmhouses; Negro slaves were being armed and incited to insurrection by French revolutionary agents.

The Federalists did not stop with propaganda; they were soon preparing for war. The army was to be increased, and Washington, Hamilton, and Knox were summoned to take command. A Navy Department was also organized, and fighting began on the high seas, although no formal declaration of war had been made either by France or the United States. In the naval war that followed, the United States *Constellation* defeated *L'Insurgente* on one occasion and the *Vengeance* on another, and the *Boston* forced *Le Berceau* to surrender. In all, the French lost more than eighty vessels during the two years of fighting. American enthusiasm for the victories at sea was not diminished by either the comparatively large number of American ships captured by the French or by the realization that France had to fight the British as well as the United States Navy.

Throughout the undeclared naval war, preparations were also made to create an American army. Although Washington agreed to serve as commander in chief, his age would have prevented him from taking an active part in military operations, and the question of who was to be second in command soon threatened to split the Federalist party. Despite Adams's opposition, his disloyal cabinet induced Washington to indicate his preference for Hamilton as second officer. The President was compelled to give this post to his most formidable opponent within the party. Hamilton immediately began to draw up plans for an attack against Spanish America, which he hoped to capture with the aid of the British Navy and the cooperation of Latin American rebels led by Don Francisco de Miranda. But the size of the army did not keep pace with Hamilton's grandiose schemes. It was not until 1799 that an active campaign for recruits was undertaken. Adams soon had to demonstrate that he, not Hamilton, was President of the United States.

Adams never succumbed to the war fever created by his fellow Federalists. In February, 1799, he nominated William Vans Murray as minister to France. When members of the Hamilton wing of the party in the Senate objected to this apparent reversal of policy, the President relented to the extent of appointing a three-man commission instead of an envoy. He selected Oliver Ellsworth, W. R. Davie, and Murray as commissioners, who left for France only after the President had received assurances from Talleyrand that they would be received. When they reached Paris, they found Napoleon Bonaparte rather than the corrupt Directory in control. The French, for their own reasons, now proved unusually cooperative. On September 30, 1800, the treaty negotiations were concluded. The so-called Convention of 1800 abrogated the treaties of 1778—thus ending the United States' only "entangling alliance"—and affirmed the principle that free ships make free goods. On the other hand, no provision was made for indemnifying the owners of ships or of property illegally seized.

Adams's Success and Failure

To the dismay of the extremists in his own party, John Adams had almost singlehandedly prevented the United States from being dragged into war. But he had also ruined his own political career. By placing his country before his party, he made one of the most courageous decisions in the history of the American presidency. Fifteen years later, Adams wrote:

> I will defend my missions to France, as long as I have an eye to direct my hand, or a finger to hold my pen. They were the most disinterested and meritorious actions of my life. I reflect upon them with so much satisfaction, that I desire no other inscription over my gravestone than: "Here lies John Adams, who took upon himself the responsibility of the peace with France in the year 1800."

In the course of the excitement aroused by the dispute with France, a few outstanding Republicans insisted that the break with France was in large measure due to Federalist dislike of the French Revolution and of democracy in general. Prominent among these was Philip Freneau, who at the instigation of Madison and other Virginians had established the *National Gazette* in Philadelphia in the early 1790's. No Federalist escaped Freneau's vitriolic pen, and his editorials and articles were widely copied in the Republican press. Freneau's attacks, along with those of other Republicans, convinced the more extreme Federalists that the time had come to silence the critics of the existing order.

Unfortunately, the previous failure of the government to define by statute a precise meaning of the Bill of Rights about freedom of the press played into the hands of authoritarians in the Federalist party as well as irresponsible editors and demagogues in both political camps. The latter were free to use the vilest tactics, and the Federalists had a golden chance to use fear of Jacobinism to frighten their opposition. In 1798, four drastic measures known as the Alien and Sedition Acts were passed by Congress. The first of these, a new naturalization law, raised the minimum residence requirement from five to fourteen years. It was probably aimed in part at the many new immigrants who voted Republican. The second, the Alien Deportation Act authorized the President to banish at any time aliens that he judged "dangerous to the peace and safety of the United States" or that he had "reasonable grounds to suspect are concerned in any treasonable or secret machinations against the government." This measure was supplemented by the Alien Enemies Act, which empowered the President, in the event of war, to restrain,

Hot Tempers in Congress, 1798

imprison, or remove all alien enemies whose continued presence might endanger the public safety. The fourth law, the Sedition Act, was aimed at the Republican press. Skillfully, the act was made to combine powers necessary for any government to control sedition with purely partisan items. It prescribed a fine not exceeding $5,000 and imprisonment of not less than six months or more than five years for any persons who might unlawfully combine or conspire to oppose any measures "of the government of the United States . . . or to impede the operation of any law of the United States, or to intimidate or prevent any person holding a place or office . . . from undertaking, performing, or executing his trust or duty." Persons who counseled, advised, or attempted "to procure any insurrection, riot, unlawful assembly, or combination" were to be deemed guilty of a high misdemeanor and, if convicted, were liable to the same severe punishment. The most objectionable feature was the provision that any person who should "write, print, utter, or publish . . . any false, scandalous, and malicious writing or writings against the government of the United States" or against any of its officers was liable to a fine not exceeding $2,000 and to a maximum imprisonment of two years.

The Alien Acts, though not enforced, caused bitter resentment, and many persons fearing Federalist persecutions left the country. Under the vigorous enforcement of the Sedition Act, twenty-four Republican editors were arrested soon after the bill's adoption. Among these were three of the ablest journalists in America. Some of those arrested, however unjustly, were far from being heroic principled men. J. T. Callendar of the *Richmond Examiner* had printed a famous slander against Hamilton, and Matthew Lyon of Vermont was equally irresponsible. Of the fifteen men finally indicted under the law, ten were convicted. Of these, Lyon, congressman from Vermont, was perhaps the most prominent. He was sentenced to four months in jail and fined $1,000 for asserting that President Adams had turned men out of office for party reasons and for referring to the President's "continual grasp for power" and his "unbounded thirst for ridiculous pomp, foolish adulation, and selfish avarice." Jedidiah Peck, an eccentric surveyor-preacher, was dragged from his bed in Otsego, New York, placed in manacles and marched 200 miles to New York, where he was tried for sedition for having circulated a powerful and vituperative petition for the repeal of the Sedition Act. Similar was the case of David Brown, an illiterate and irresponsible Revolutionary soldier of Dedham, Massachusetts. Brown was very much involved in the erection of a liberty pole bearing the inscription: "No Stamp Act, no Sedition, no Alien Bills, no Land Tax; downfall to the Tyrants of America, peace and retirement to the President; long live the Vice-President, and the minority; may moral virtue be the basis of civil government." Fisher Ames, Federalist guardian of the existing order, at once took steps to apprehend this trumpeter of sedition. After a farcical trial, Brown was sentenced to eighteen months' imprisonment and a fine of $400. Unable to secure the money, he remained in prison for two years, until pardoned by Jefferson.

The Alien and Sedition laws were a boomerang to the Federalists. Americans in all walks of life, including prominent Federalists, vigorously protested against what they maintained were outrageous departures from the fundamental law of the land and from the tradition of liberty. President Adams had signed the acts without enthusiasm and was not active in using them. Hamilton at first objected to and then accepted the Sedition Act. John Marshall remained a constant opponent. Many men believed that these laws violated the spirit of the Federal Constitution. They openly transgressed the First Amendment, which forbade Congress to make any law restricting freedom of speech and press.

Of the many protests, the Kentucky and Virginia Resolutions were the most famous. The Kentucky Resolutions, drafted by Jefferson and slightly modified by Madison, were presented to the Kentucky legislature in November, 1798. They declared that government exists

"The Providential Detection": Jefferson Depicted as a Jacobin (circa 1800)

by compact and that certain definite powers are reserved to each state. Any acts contrary to the Constitution, such as the Alien and Sedition laws, were therefore null and void and of no force. For redress, however, a formal protest was merely to be circulated among the other states, and Congress was to be asked to repeal the laws. Similar resolutions drawn up by Madison for Virginia condemned the laws in briefer and milder form but stated the authority of a state to "interpose, for arresting the progress of the evil." The passage of these resolutions served to center public attention on the acts. The Republicans made the resolutions the occasion for denouncing the laws. The Federalists made them a pretext not only for justifying the acts, but for defending the Constitution and their administration of the national government. The Federalists were right to point out that as an answer to the acts the opposition seemed to be suggesting a way to break up the Union.

The individual most responsible for the formulation of the Kentucky and Virginia Resolutions and the subsequent defeat of the Federalists in the election of 1800 was Thomas Jefferson. A perceptive political analyst with a deep-seated belief in man's natural rights, Jefferson was also a practical politician who realized that elections could only be won by well-organized parties. Starting with the dissatisfied planters and farmers in his native state of Virginia, Jefferson eventually made agreements with important Republicans in every state in the Union. Jefferson's Republican party drew its support from various quarters—southern farmers, small businessmen, Anti-Federalist merchants, and many, but not all, frontier groups. Although these groups had little in common with each other, they all had reasons to dislike the Federalists. They were bound together, not by similar ideals, but by the belief that their grievances could be attributed to Federalist control of the central government. Jefferson did not create this opposition, but more than anyone else he was responsible for giving it national organization.

Jefferson could make no overt move to rally his supporters as long as Washington remained President, for nothing could be gained—and much could be lost—by opposing the nation's leading hero and citizen. But when John Adams succeeded Washington in 1797, the opposition forces were able to carry on their political activities in the open and to become a national party in name as well as in fact. Despite this advantage, the Jeffersonians were soon on the defensive, for, as men branded, unjustly, as Francophiles, they could not avoid being discredited by the XYZ affair and the undeclared naval war with France. During this period, they were probably saved from extinction only by the conflict between Adams and Hamilton within the Federalist party. When the Federalists sought to press their advantage with the Alien and Sedition Acts, however, Jefferson was able once again to rouse his followers against Federalist rule. Adams's decision to make peace with France also deprived the Federalists of one of their most effective issues.

In the campaign of 1800, the Federalists nominated John Adams and C. C. Pinckney; the Republicans again selected Jefferson and Burr. The outcome of the election indicates both the effectiveness of the Republican organization and the extent of the popular dissatisfaction with the Federalists. The Republicans carried New York, and most of

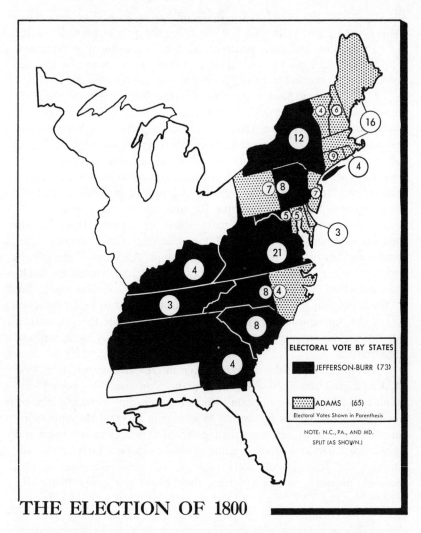

ELECTORAL VOTE BY STATES

▇ JEFFERSON-BURR (73)

▨ ADAMS (65)

Electoral Votes Shown in Parenthesis

NOTE: N.C., PA., AND MD.
SPLIT (AS SHOWN.)

THE ELECTION OF 1800

the South; Federalist strength centered in New England. Jefferson received seventy-three electoral votes and Adams sixty-five. In what for
the time was a remarkable display of party regularity, all the Republican
electors cast their second votes for Burr, who was therefore tied with
Jefferson for the presidency. Under the Constitution, it was now up
to the House of Representatives, where the Federalists had a clear
majority, to decide between Jefferson and Burr. Although a number
of Federalists preferred Burr, Hamilton, who opposed Jefferson's
policies but knew that Burr was altogether untrustworthy, eventually

prevailed on them to change their votes; and on the thirty-sixth ballot Jefferson was chosen the third President of the United States.

The election of 1800 marked the end of Federalist rule in the national capital. In a little more than a decade, the Federalists had transformed a collection of autonomous states into a firm and enduring union. Their opponents had criticized their methods and even their objectives, but nothing could rob them of their accomplishments. They had created a nation.

FOR SUPPLEMENTARY READING

The volumes to start with are L. D. White, *The Federalists* (1948), and J. C. Miller, *The Federalist Era* (1960). Dumas Malone's *Jefferson and the Rights of Man* and *Jefferson and the Ordeal of Liberty* have a good account of the Hamilton-Jefferson feud. J. T. Adams (ed.), *Jeffersonian Principles and Hamiltonian Principles* (1932), has brief, reliable, but prosaic summaries of the views of the two greatest cabinet members.

On Washington's role as President, a short guiding survey is H. J. Ford, *Washington and His Colleagues* (1921). The best study of the fiscal problems of the era is Bray Hammond, *Banks and Politics in America* (1957). An invaluable primary source is E. S. Maclay (ed.), *The Journal of William Maclay* (1928), which gives the tart and shrewd comments of one of the first U.S. Senators. On the Whisky Rebellion see L. D. Baldwin, *Whisky Rebels* (1939).

Charles A. Beard, *Economic Origins of Jeffersonian Democracy* (1915, 1949), has the influential classic statement of Hamilton versus Jefferson as *the* theme of American history. This work should be taken in the light of newer works: Joseph Charles, *The Origins of the American Party System* (1956); Nobel E. Cunningham, *The Jeffersonian Republicans* (1958); and W. N. Chambers, *Political Parties in a New Nation* (1963). Hamilton receives a glowing re-evaluation in L. M. Hacker, *Alexander Hamilton in the American Tradition* (1957), and narrower praise in J. C. Miller, *Alexander Hamilton, Portrait in Paradox* (1959). There is an excellent selection of Hamilton's writings in R. B. Morris (ed.), *The Basic Ideas of Alexander Hamilton* (1957) (Pb). A judicious introduction to these papers attempts to clear Hamilton of charges made by Jefferson's admirers. A similar pro-Hamilton view accompanies J. E. Cooke (ed.), *The Reports of Alexander Hamilton* (1964) (Pb).

John Adams has received new and deserved respect from recent scholars. The starting general study is still Gilbert Chinard's thin *Honest John Adams* (1933), but this should be subordinated to S. G. Kurtz, *The Presidency of John Adams: The Collapse of Federalism, 1795–1800* (1958), and M. J. Dauer, *The Adams Federalists* (1953). There is a good collection of Adams's rambling but insightful writings in Adrienne Koch and W. Peden (eds.), *The Selected Writings of John and John Quincy Adams* (1946). A fully balanced treatment of the Alien and Sedition Acts is still to be written, but J. C. Miller, *Crisis in Freedom* (1951), has many virtues. The best work on Adams's political theory is Z. Haraszti, *John Adams and the Prophets of Progress* (1952). A seldom read but great work is S. E. Morison, *The Life and Letters of Harrison Gray Otis* (2 vols., 1913), a study of New England Federalism.

For foreign policy between 1789 and 1801, consult S. F. Bemis, *Jay's Treaty* (rev. ed., 1962) (Pb), a landmark in diplomatic history; P. A. Varg, *Foreign Policies of the Founding Fathers* (1963); and R. R. Palmer, *The Age of the Democratic Revolution: The Struggle* (1964). For western problems A. P. Whitaker's two volumes—*The Spanish American Frontier, 1783–1795* (1927) and *The Mississippi Question, 1795–1803* (1934)—are starting points for deeper study.

Jefferson's Era: The Years of Peace

M ANY Europeans were astonished early in 1801 when the Federalist party peacefully surrendered power to Thomas Jefferson. Skeptical of all republican governments and convinced that the bitter invective of American politics of the 1790's would lead to the dissolution of the new United States, they could not believe that the Federalists would accept the decision of the electorate. They had underestimated the dedication of all Americans to the great experiment in free republican institutions. They had taken Jeffersonians and Hamiltonians at their word and had failed to discount a good part of the declared hostility of the time as mere party politics. Europeans could not have known what Hamilton had assumed in choosing Jefferson over Burr: while helping to arrange the deal by which Jefferson was finally elected, Hamilton had written an associate that however strong Jefferson's ideas, when faced with the facts, the Virginian would compromise. Hamilton's shrewd evaluation of the third President of the United States was one indication that Thomas Jefferson was not a fanatic or dogmatist and that his election in 1800 did not presage a revolution.

The Ideal World of Thomas Jefferson

Although Thomas Jefferson successfully evaded the traps of logic and abstract ideas, he has become the author of a theory of politics called Jeffersonian Democracy. Actually, Jefferson had the mind of a gifted amateur and never put into systematic or rigorous form his recurring beliefs or insights about the nature of society. His one persistent theme was hostility to concentrated political or social power. Although he believed in the long-term wisdom of the people, he was always sceptical about the reliability of immediate majorities. Ultimately, he was himself a majoritarian, but he hoped to find a way to combine the final power of the people with the daily rule of enlightened energetic leaders. These were to be men who had proved their talent for government and who constituted what he called a "natural aristocracy."

PARADOX

Jefferson was born in 1743 in Albemarle County in the Virginia backcountry. His father was a well-to-do large farmer, but Thomas was related on his mother's side to the planter-aristocracy of Virginia. He attended William and Mary College and became a lawyer. After serving in the Continental Congress, where he drafted the Declaration of Independence, he resigned, first to become a member of the Virginia legislature and then governor of "his country," Virginia. During the Confederation period he helped organize the Northwest Territory and was the United States' minister to France. Although he had little sympathy with Federalist principles, he remained an increasingly reluctant member of Washington's cabinet until 1794, when he resigned to take over the leadership of the new anti-Federalist groups. In 1796, he became Vice-President under another Federalist, John Adams. His opposition to royal rule, to entail and primogeniture, to slavery as a moral wrong, and to the alliance between church and state had made him America's leading humane statesman. He was also probably the most versatile man in the United States. In addition to being a politician, Jefferson was a botanist, linguist, political philosopher, amateur architect, practical inventor, and a student of almost every subject known to man.

When Jefferson became President of the United States on March 4, 1801, he had made public his ideas on virtually all the important issues of the day. More than any other notable American of his time, he had an abiding faith in popular government. Man, he held, "was a rational animal, endowed by nature with rights and with an innate sense of justice; and . . . he could be restrained from wrong and protected in right, by moderate powers, confided to persons of his own choice and held to their duties by dependence on his own will." At the very time when Hamilton and his fellow Federalists were expressing deep distrust of popular government, Jefferson was contending that men "habituated to think for themselves and to follow their reason as their

Thomas Jefferson

guide would be more easily and safely governed than with minds nourished in error and vitiated and debased . . . by ignorance, indigence, and oppression."

Jefferson wanted America to be a land of small land-owning farmers. He was an outspoken opponent of an urban mercantile economy and the financial edifice designed and erected by Hamilton. Instead of large urban communities with their captains of industry and their propertyless voters, he wished to keep America agrarian. In his *Notes on Virginia*, he wrote:

> Those who labor in the earth are the chosen people of God, if ever He had a chosen people, whose breasts He has made His peculiar deposit for substantial and genuine virtue. It is the focus in which he keeps alive that sacred fire, which otherwise

might escape from the face of the earth. Corruption of morals in the mass of cultivators is a phenomenon of which no age nor nation has furnished an example. . . .

His admiration for farm life was even more explicitly set forth in a letter to John Jay written in the summer of 1785:

> We have now lands enough to employ an infinite number of people in their cultivation. Cultivators of the earth are the most valuable citizens. They are the most vigorous, the most independent, the most virtuous, and they are tied to their country and wedded to its liberty and interests by the most lasting bonds. As long, therefore, as they can find employment in this line, I would not convert them into mariners, artisans or anything else.

Despite the generosity in these views, even in Jefferson's time farm life and farm people were probably, on the whole, no more virtuous or less money-minded than the city people whom Jefferson called "panders of vice and the instruments by which the liberties of a country are generally overturned."

Jefferson distrusted the large commercial cities of his time because of their possibilities for rapid accumulation of power, their social instability, their wretched poor, their Babel-like atmosphere. "The mobs of great cities," he said, "add just so much to the support of pure government as sores do to the strength of the human body." He seemed to forget the market-mindedness, the speculative temperament, and rough rural politicking of the countryside of his own day. However idealized his conception of American farm life, it was inspired by his desire for man's happiness.

Jefferson had a deep-seated dislike of everything that smacked of oppression and tended to deprave humanity. "I have sworn upon the altar of God," he wrote in 1800, "eternal hostility against every form of tyranny over the mind of man." He advocated a system of universal secular education, rejected orthodox Christianity in favor of Deism, championed freedom of press and speech, and urged all to criticize the existing order with a view to its improvement. Although he later compromised his ideal, he declared that the University of Virginia, founded under his leadership, would be based "on the illimitable freedom of the human mind. For here we are not afraid to follow the truth wheresoever it may lead or to tolerate any error so long as reason is left free to combat it."

Almost all of Jefferson's views on government stemmed from his dedication to freedom as a political first principle. He favored a nation of small landowners, for example, because he thought an agricultural nation would not invite the fevers for success and the concentration of economic and political power found in an industrial society. He believed that social stability and decentralization were essential to the preservation of freedom. Give all men land and the right to choose enlightened leaders and to voice their discontents, give them as much education as possible, maintain a vigorous political system of checks and balances, and—Jefferson believed—peace and prosperity would follow. Let each man, furthermore, be free to pursue his own economic interests under law, and the general well-being of society would be assured. Let America stay permanently free of involvements with Europe, that old world of degrading mass poverty and crafty Machiavellians, and she would fulfill the ideals of the Declaration of Independence and stand as an example for oppressed men everywhere.

Jefferson opposed war except in self-defense. He had a personal horror of debt and thought public debt an unjust burden on future generations and a favor to a minority of bond-holding commercial men. He believed that the Constitution and laws should be strictly interpreted and that the ideal constitutional government was that which governed least. Because he also believed that local governments could be more readily controlled by the voters, he did not think that the authority of the federal government should ever be permitted to overshadow that of the states. Against the relatively high degree of centralization advocated by the Federalists, Jefferson set a philosophy of states' rights and local loyalties. All these ideas suggest that we can generally characterize Jefferson as a rationalist and a cautious majoritarian who believed in a *laissez-faire* economy and in a decentralized, politically isolated America of family farms. These ideals were in conflict with the lives Americans actually led even before Jefferson's time. They were, moreover, challenged by events during his two terms in office.

Squaring Theory with Practice

Despite Jefferson's "philosophy" and opposition to the views of his predecessors, he made remarkably few changes in the policies of the government during his two terms as President of the United States. Although he later referred to his election as the "revolution of 1800," there was little in his inaugural address to substantiate such a view. Stating that "we are all Republicans, we are all Federalists," he pledged his administration to the "honest payment of our debts and the sacred preservation of the public faith; encouragement of agriculture and of commerce its handmaid." The inaugural was so conciliatory in tone that Hamilton thought it "virtually a candid retraction of past misapprehensions, and a pledge to the community that the new President will not lend himself to dangerous innovations, but in essential points tread in the steps" of the Federalists. Hamilton had the measure of the man.

Jefferson's appointment policy was as conciliatory as his inaugural. Despite the fears of his opponents and the pressure of his followers, Jefferson refused to drive the Federalists from their posts in the civil service. Although he removed a few Federalists for political reasons and filled all vacancies that occurred with Republicans, he made no attempt to emulate the partisan system of appointments that had been used by his predecessors. Jefferson did not enjoy keeping Republicans from jobs that they thought they deserved, and on one occasion he complained that few officeholders died and none resigned.

Jefferson's cabinet also revealed his desire to win the support of the opposition. He had received no New England electoral votes, but he appointed Gideon Granger of Connecticut Postmaster General. His Secretary of War and Attorney General were both from Massachusetts. The other cabinet appointments accurately reflected the growing national character of the Republican party. The Secretary of the Navy came from Maryland, and Secretary of State James Madison had for years played a prominent role in Virginia as well as in national politics. To head the Treasury Department, Jefferson selected Albert Gallatin, a Swiss aristocrat who had migrated to America during the Revolution and had become an outspoken champion of popular rights, and, at the same time, a friend of prominent financial leaders. A resident of western Pennsylvania and a former member of the House of Representatives, Gallatin owed his appointment to his ability and to Jefferson's desire to have his Administration include a man who was both close to frontier groups in the Republican party and in touch with many of the nation's financiers.

Many of the innovations introduced by Jefferson altered the surface aspects of administration without fundamentally changing the government that had been erected by the Federalists. In contrast to the pomp that attended many public ceremonies under the Federalists, Jefferson's inauguration was notable for its simplicity. At the same time, he abandoned Washington's and Adams's practice of delivering messages to Congress in person on the ground that such speeches were similar to pronouncement from the throne in a monarchy. Jefferson also sought to emphasize the republican tone of the new government by ignoring diplomatic rank at White House dinners, refusing to hold formal *levées*, and establishing a series of rules for republican behavior at governmental receptions. When Anthony Merry, the British minister to the United States, made his first call on the President, he was insulted when he was received by Jefferson in slippers "down at the heels." At a presidential dinner in honor of the Merrys, Jefferson compounded the insult by escorting Dolly Madison rather than Mrs. Merry to the table. Merry refused to attend any other functions at the White House, and Jefferson had the satisfaction of feeling that even the manners of the new Administration were republican.

Jefferson and his fellow Republicans did seek to rid the country of what they considered the most glaring abuses of Federalist rule. Congress repealed the Judiciary Act of 1801, which had been passed three weeks before Jefferson took office and which provided for an expansion of the Federal court system. Jefferson pardoned those still in prison under the Alien and Sedition Acts—which had expired—and Congress rescinded the Naturalization Law. Jefferson also made an attempt to live up to his earlier pledges to reduce both taxes and the national debt. Federal expenses were cut, and Congress repealed the whisky tax and, at Gallatin's instigation, passed itemized rather than general appropriation bills. Gallatin's efforts to scale down the government's debt were immeasurably aided by a marked increase in tariff revenues. Throughout Jefferson's administration, imports steadily mounted, and the income from duties rose proportionately. At the same time, a British admiralty court ruled in 1800 that despite the European war, American shippers could carry goods from the French West Indies to France if such cargoes were shipped through the United States. This decision legalized what had been a profitable trade to Americans and assured the government of still larger tariff receipts. Largely because of these developments, the Republicans reduced the national debt from approximately $83,000,000 in 1801 to about $57,000,000 in 1809.

One of the principal victims of Jefferson's and Gallatin's economy drive was the navy. Although the bitter war in Europe constantly threatened American involvement, Jefferson was convinced that a fleet of war vessels could serve no other purpose than to drag the United States into a war for the benefit of the nation's commercial classes. The President, accordingly, proposed that the "navy" of seven frigates be kept in the Potomac where they "would require but one set of plunderers to look after them." To guard the country at minimum cost against the dangers of invasion, he advocated the construction of several small gunboats which could be hauled up on shore when not in use. Congress appropriated $50,000 for Jefferson's program; the gunboats were built; and Jefferson's "mosquito fleet," as his opponents called it, soon proved its impracticability. One gunboat was washed some eight miles inland by a storm, and the lives of the "naval militia" were in jeopardy whenever they put to sea. Jefferson's gunboats provided Federalist wits with an opportunity to ridicule the Administration, but they did not improve the defenses of the United States at a time of international crisis.

Although Jefferson could argue that his naval program accorded with the republican principle of economy, he was soon compelled by the pressure of events in the Mediterranean to revise his theories to fit the exigencies of a practical problem. Both Washington and Adams had agreed to continue to pay tribute to Algiers, Tripoli, Tunis, and Morocco to prevent pirates from these countries from interfering with American commerce. But soon after Jefferson took office, the Pasha of Tripoli, enraged because he believed that he was not receiving his share of the money from the United States, had the flag on the American consulate cut down. Jefferson responded by dispatching warships to the Mediterranean. After considerable fighting, the United States obtained a satisfactory treaty from Tripoli in 1805, but the war against the other Barbary states, interrupted by the War of 1812, was not concluded until 1816. In taking action against the Barbary pirates, Jefferson was compelled to overlook his formal aversion to commercial wars, to a navy, and to government spending.

The President, the Constitution, and the Courts

Jefferson's efforts to put his republican theories into effect were hampered by the Federal judiciary as well as by developments abroad. When the Republicans gained control of the executive and legislative branches of the government in 1801, the nation's judicial system was staffed entirely by Federalists. In the midnight hours of his final day in office, Adams had filled the posts created by the Judiciary Act of 1801 with members of his own party. The Republicans had retaliated by repealing the Judiciary Act and postponing the next session of the Supreme Court until 1803; but neither move had had any appreciable effect on Federalist domination of the courts. In Chief Justice John Marshall the Federalists had a champion who repeatedly proved himself capable of upholding the ideals of Washington and Hamilton, and from 1801 to 1835 he handed down a long list of notable decisions that emphasized his Federalist view of the Constitution. Marshall fought economic instability and local interests hostile to national economic growth. At every turn, he did all in his power to magnify and strengthen the sovereignty of the national state and to safeguard the general American respect for the interests of private property. In the eyes of the Jeffersonians, Marshall was a thorough-going reactionary. As they were to learn to their distress, he also was one of the most powerful men in the Federal government.

Marshall first demonstrated both his ability as a jurist and the power of the judiciary under the Constitution in the case of *Marbury vs. Madison*. In 1803, William Marbury, a "midnight appointment" as a justice of the peace in the District of Columbia, asked the Supreme Court to compel the Secretary of State to grant him his commission. In support of his petition, Marbury cited Section 13 of the Judiciary Act of 1789, which stated that the Court could issue writs of mandamus in such cases. Marbury's action placed Marshall in what appeared to be a highly embarrassing predicament. If the Court granted Marbury's request, Marshall knew that Secretary of State James Madison would ignore the mandamus. On the other hand, if the Court refused the petition, Marshall knew that the decision would be interpreted as a major victory for the Republicans.

To resolve this dilemma, Marshall took a third course. The principal issue confronting him, he decided, was one of jurisdiction. The Supreme Court, according to the Constitution, has original jurisdiction "in all cases affecting ambassadors, other public ministers and consuls, and those in which a state shall be a party." In all other cases the Court was granted appellate jurisdiction. Since, however, *Marbury vs. Madison* had originated before the Supreme Court, that Court had no constitutional jurisdiction over it. Under the circumstances, Marshall might well have referred Marbury to a lower court. Instead, he declared that Marbury deserved the writ, but that the Constitution did not permit the Court to grant it. He thus neatly sidestepped his political problem; but he did not stop here. Because the Constitution and Section 13 of the 1789 law were in conflict, he declared the latter unconstitutional and therefore void. Constitutional historians have argued for years over whether or not the Constitution provided for judicial review of congressional acts; but, regardless of how this question is answered, the fact remains that John Marshall in *Marbury vs. Madison* was the first Supreme Court Justice to disallow a law passed by Congress. And in doing so he enraged Jefferson and his followers, not so much by the issue at hand—Marbury's seat—but by the implications of the decision.

Jefferson complained that Marshall's decision made the Constitution "a mere thing of wax," which the judges "may twist and shape into any form they please." But there was little that he or his followers could do about it. Actually, despite these fears, Marshall remained only a distant threat to the President after this case. The administration, on its side, did not change the Federalist complexion of the courts. They did, however, institute impeachment proceedings against John Pickering, a Federal judge in New Hampshire, and against Supreme Court Justice Samuel Chase. Pickering, a drunkard and an incompetent, was notoriously anti-Republican in his views. In a trial involving a violation of the revenue laws, he refused to grant the government an appeal and said to the Federal prosecutor: "You may bring forty thousand government witnesses, they will not alter the decree." Pickering did not appear for his own trial before the Senate, and he was removed from office after his counsel had pleaded insanity.

This minor success was insignificant, however, when placed against the failure to convict Supreme Court Justice Chase. Chase had played a prominent—and, to the Republicans, an indefensible—part in the sedition trials of the 1790's. On more than one occasion he had used his position on the bench as a pretense for delivering political harangues against the Jeffersonians. In a charge to a jury in Baltimore, he stated that any extension of the suffrage would mean that "our republican Constitution will sink into a mobocracy" and that "the modern doctrines by our late reformers, that all men in a state of society are entitled to enjoy equal liberty and . . . rights, have brought this . . . mischief upon us." Despite such remarks, the Republicans were unable to make an effective case against Chase, and he remained on the Supreme Court. With the failure of these proceedings, the Republicans made no further move to change the judiciary. John Marshall had shown some of the possibilities of the founding fathers' plan for a government of checks and balances. Although Jefferson could predict that the Federalists would use the judiciary to "batter down all the bulwarks of republicanism," Marshall did little after *Marbury vs. Madison* to block Republican legislation.

Near the end of his first term in office, Jefferson could look back on four years of unfulfilled major promises. He had changed some of the superficial aspects of the government, but the administrative system that he had inherited from the Federalists remained largely intact. He had not altered any of Hamilton's basic financial policies. He had retained the bank and the tariff system. He had violated his own theories on the role of the navy in the nation's foreign policy, and he had been unable to break the Federalists' hold on the judiciary. If it had not been for his notable—and, to a certain extent, fortuitous—accomplishments in the West, he might well have considered his first administration a failure.

Expansion Westward

When Jefferson became President in 1801, the United States had a population of approximately 5,300,000, of which nearly 1,000,000 lived beyond the Appalachian line of settlement established by the British in 1763. The frontier line ran from Maine across northern Vermont and New Hampshire to Lake Champlain, and then in winding fashion southward to just below the mouth of the Savannah River. There were three marked bulges or protuberances westward: one in New York along the Mohawk; another around Pittsburgh; and the third in the upland country of Kentucky, in the valleys of east Tennessee, and in the Cumberland district of central Tennessee. Trans-Allegheny towns were active but small and few in number; Lexington had 1,797 inhabitants; Nashville, 355; Cincinnati, 500; and Pittsburgh, 1,565.

Despite the growth of population in the West, few settlers were satisfied with the provisions of the land laws. Many thought that the law retarded rather than accelerated the occupation of frontier regions. Starting in 1796, Congress responded to pressures and progressively reduced the minimum acreage for sale and the minimum price per acre while extending the time for payment. By 1820, the government had deeded 18,117,860 acres to purchasers under the more generous terms. Often, however, the better lands sold for more than the minimum price, and much of it went to speculators.

Soon after settlers began to take up lands in the trans-Allegheny region, Jefferson was able to more than double the western domain of the United States by purchasing Louisiana. Although Louisiana had originally been claimed by France through exploration, it had been transferred to Spain in 1763 in compensation for Spanish losses to Great Britain in the Seven Years' War. Spain was able to hold Louisiana for almost forty years; but in 1800, Napoleon, hoping to re-establish in America the vast colonial empire that France had lost a generation before, forced Spain to restore Louisiana to France. Louisiana was to be the granary for a new French empire in the West. The nation that controlled Louisiana, moreover, could threaten the economy as well as the territorial security of the United States. Spain had demonstrated this fact repeatedly in the decade before the adoption of the Pinckney Treaty in 1795. In July, 1802, she demonstrated it again when the Spanish Intendant at New Orleans arbitrarily withdrew the right of Americans to deposit their goods while waiting for ships to Europe. This action was interpreted by the westerners as a forerunner of what they might expect from France, for it was now known that the rumors of cession to France were true. Expeditions were organized for the

[handwritten margin note: WANTED N. ORLEANS TO BE A FREE PORT.]

immediate seizure of the coveted territory. Protests and memorials demanding aid were sent to Jefferson. Even the New England Federalists, anxious for any move that would embarrass or discredit Jefferson and his party, did all they could to drive the country into war with France.

The President, though greatly worried, refused to be stampeded. Instead of yielding to the call for war, he set himself to settling the whole question by peaceful negotiation. He induced Congress to vote an appropriation of two million dollars "for any expenses . . . in relation to the intercourse between the United States and foreign nations," and he sent James Monroe to France to aid the regular minister, Robert Livingston, in "enlarging and more effectually securing our rights and interests in the river Mississippi and in the territories eastward thereof." Livingston had already been instructed to sound out Napoleon on the possibility of selling these regions to the United States.

Fortunately for the American negotiators, a number of events played into their hands. Unexpected opposition in Spain had delayed the transfer of Louisiana; French soldiers, who were sent to conquer Santo Domingo and who were then to be shipped to Louisiana, had been decimated by warfare against the Negroes and by yellow fever; European hostilities, temporarily stopped by the Peace of Amiens in 1802, had been resumed, and Napoleon was therefore in no position either to conquer or defend overseas possessions. Napoleon, moreover, needed money, and the sale of Louisiana would help replenish his treasury.

On April 11, 1803, Napoleon instructed his Minister of Foreign Affairs to open negotiations for the disposal not merely of New Orleans and West Florida, which Livingston for weeks had sought to buy, but of all the vast Louisiana tract. Bewildered momentarily by Napoleon's decision and by his lack of authority to acquire an empire, Livingston nevertheless accepted the proposal. Monroe quickly assented, and for two weeks the negotiators haggled over the terms. Finally, on May 2, 1803, the treaty transferring the entire province to the United States was signed; Livingston and Monroe committed the United States to pay $11,250,000 in 6 per cent bonds, and to assume claims held by American citizens against France, estimated at $3,750,000.

The purchase of Louisiana for $15,000,000 delighted the people of the West and Republicans of the middle and southern states; but the Federalists bitterly condemned it as unconstitutional and prejudicial to the best interests of the Union. New England shippers and middle-states manufacturers saw no reason for supporting a policy of westward expansion. They had no desire to see the East depopulated and business paralyzed for the sake of strengthening the party of Thomas

Jefferson, a party that had vigorously opposed Hamilton's program of assumption, the Bank of the United States, and the tariff. Their interests centered on the Atlantic seaboard; trade and association tied them to Europe rather than to the West. As men of property and social standing, they would never submit to the rule of a "hotch-potch of wild men from the Far West."

As Jefferson had been an advocate of strict construction of the Constitution, he was principally concerned with the charge that the purchase was unconstitutional. The Administration, he frankly admitted, had exceeded its powers, and he therefore considered an amendment to the Constitution that would confirm the purchase and provide for its government. The President's friends, however, less concerned with the constitutional question than with the popularity of the acquisition of the territory, unblushingly adopted the Federalist interpretation of "implied powers." The right to acquire foreign territory, they argued, existed as a result of the right to make treaties and the power to make war and peace. Besides, argument in Congress over a constitutional amendment, they pointed out, would create a political issue and lose time. In the midst of the debate about how to annex the new lands came a rumor that Napoleon might change his mind. Jefferson pressed the Senate for ratification. The Constitution, he still maintained, did not authorize the purchase, but if "our friends shall think differently, certainly I shall acquiesce with satisfaction, confident that the good sense of our country will correct the evil of construction when it shall produce ill effects." Circumstances and expediency had again forced Jefferson to abandon theory and to modify his interpretation of the fundamental law of the land. On October 17, 1803, the treaty was ratified by a vote of twenty-four to seven.

Jefferson had to overcome more than constitutional scruples to sanction the acquisition of Louisiana. The addition of this vast territory also ran counter to his notions of governmental economy and his belief that no move should be made to strengthen the power of the central government at the expense of the states. But Jefferson was inspired by other—and to his mind, much more important—considerations. He believed that the purchase of Louisiana would not only eliminate the possibility of war, but would also ensure the supremacy of the American farmer in the nation's political and economic life for centuries to come. If Louisiana were part of the United States, Jefferson had no doubt that America would always be an agrarian country.

The acquisition of Louisiana, which was undoubtedly the outstanding achievement of Jefferson's first administration, explains in large part his overwhelming victory in the election of 1804. The Federalists, moreover, were hard pressed to find a suitable issue, for Jefferson had done little to upset the program that they had inaugurated in the 1790's. For a time the Federalists considered nominating Burr, who had alienated Jefferson by his desire to forego the vice-presidency and to try for the presidency after the tie vote in the electoral college in 1800; but Burr's backers were discredited when Hamilton revealed that they were attempting to organize a secession movement in New England and New York, and the nomination went to Charles C. Pinckney. Jefferson's majority was unexpectedly large. With 162 electoral votes to 14 for Pinckney, he won every New England state except Connecticut, carried New York with the help of his running mate George Clinton, and made a stronger showing than he had in 1800 in Pennsylvania and the South. The election also reduced Federalist strength in the Senate to seven and in the House to twenty-five.

Opening the New Lands

Jefferson continued to maintain his interest in the West throughout his second administration, and it was at his instigation that the territory acquired from France was first explored. As early as 1783, he had written George Rogers Clark about leading an exploring party into the Far West, and the acquisition of the territory now enabled Jefferson to fulfill his long-cherished wish. In a confidential message to Congress in January, 1803, he asked for an appropriation of $2500 to equip an expedition that would explore the western country and lay out an overland route to the Pacific. Congress complied with his request, and Captain Meriwether Lewis, Jefferson's private secretary and a man of exceptional courage, vigor, and intelligence, was chosen to head the undertaking. Associated with him was another army officer, William Clark, younger brother of George Rogers Clark. The explorers and their party of less than fifty men left St. Louis in May, 1804. Going up the Missouri, they spent the winter near the site of the present town of Bismarck, North Dakota, and early in April, 1805, proceeded westward. Many members of the party were almost exhausted in making their way over the Rockies, but finally, late in September, the expedition came to the headwaters of the Columbia and two months later reached the Pacific. Wintering on the Oregon coast, the men turned eastward in the spring of 1806, and by September 23 they were safely back in St. Louis. In accordance with instructions, Lewis and Clark carefully recorded their observations, and their journals contained valuable information concerning the geography and resources of the western country and the opportunities for trade. Many easterners for the first time

Captain Clark Shooting Bears

grasped the possibilities of this vast region, and fur merchants immediately prepared to tap the rich resources of the upper Missouri. Officially, the door to the Far West had been opened, and the United States' claims to the Oregon country were strengthened.

Jefferson's continuing interest in the West was further revealed by his willingness to spend Federal funds to improve its communications with the seaboard. When western farmers complained of the difficulty of shipping their products to market, Republican legislators in Washington appropriated funds for the construction of a national highway to the West. Gallatin, as Jefferson's Secretary of the Treasury, urged internal improvements that would benefit the East as well as the West. In addition to recommending a line of canals paralleling the coast and a turnpike from Maine to Georgia, Gallatin proposed that the government construct in the West an extensive and integrated network of roads and canals. Gallatin estimated that these improvements would cost $20,000,000, a sum that might be obtained from the sale of public lands or from the treasury at the rate of $2,000,000 a year for ten years. Jefferson, who had declared in 1805 that the surplus revenue in the treasury could well "be applied in time of peace to rivers, canals, roads, arts, manufactures, education, and other great objects within each state," enthusiastically supported the Gallatin proposals. The Republican President was always willing to forget his objections to government spending whenever the interests of the West could be furthered by Federal assistance.

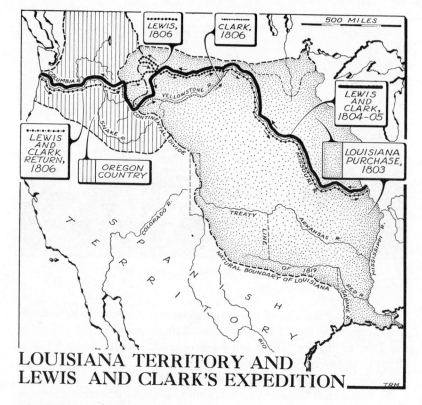

LOUISIANA TERRITORY AND
LEWIS AND CLARK'S EXPEDITION

Speculators and Conspirators

Although Jefferson derived undoubted and understandable satisfaction from his accomplishments in the West, this region was also
the source of some of the most difficult and controversial problems of
his entire administration. In the Southwest, Jefferson inherited a dispute that went back to the Confederation period and that had plagued
the Federalists throughout the 1790's. Georgia did not abandon its
western land claims until after Jefferson had taken office. In 1789, that
state granted an extensive tract in the present states of Mississippi and
Alabama to four land companies. The purchasers, however, did not
live up to their part of the agreement, and in 1795 the Georgia legislature approved the sale of an even larger area at approximately $.015
per acre to the four Yazoo Land companies. In the following year, after
it had been discovered that all but one of the legislators voting for the
measure had an interest in the companies in question, the state revoked
the grant. The stockholders, many of whom were prominent northerners, appealed to the federal government; and when Georgia relinquished

its western lands in 1802, they increased their pressure on Jefferson to confirm their grants.

Despite the speculative and fraudulent character of the Yazoo grants, the Republican administration supported the claims of the Yazoo interests. Jefferson presumably wished to gain the confidence of the northern business groups that had invested in the companies. In 1803, a committee, appointed by the President and consisting of the Secretary of State, the Secretary of the Treasury, and the Attorney General, recommended to Congress that the stockholders be paid out of the receipts from the land sales in the Yazoo tract. This proposal, however, was defeated by a group of congressmen led by John Randolph of Roanoke, a rigorously principled Virginia planter who was disgusted both with Jefferson's overtures to the North and with the corrupt acts of the Yazoo companies. In 1805, when the Yazoo claims were again presented to Congress—Postmaster General Gideon Granger served as the stockholders' representative—Randolph was once more able to prevent approval. Randolph, an extreme advocate of states' rights, accused Jefferson of going over to the opposition and broke with the Administration. As the head of a small group of congressmen known as the Quids, Randolph indiscriminately attacked both Republican and Federalist policies.

The West offered opportunities for international intrigue as well as speculative profit: Jefferson was employing threats and cajolery to obtain West Florida from Spain, a problem that was part of continuing quarrels over the exact boundaries of the Louisiana Purchase; hostile Indians and brigands in the Floridas were raiding settlements in the United States; and James Wilkinson, always willing to sell his services to the highest bidder, was in command of American troops in Louisiana. Even before the completion of his term as Vice-President (1801–5), Aaron Burr had decided to fish in the troubled waters of the West. Within a short time he was corresponding with Wilkinson, asking Anthony Merry, the British minister, for British financial and naval assistance in setting up an independent republic in Louisiana, urging the Spanish minister to help him establish a buffer state between Mexico and Louisiana, and telling still others that he planned to lead an expedition against the Spanish possessions in America. Burr's ability to alter his stories as the occasion demanded has confused historians to the present day, and it is still not known just what he hoped to accomplish. All agree that he was a scoundrel, but no one can be certain that he was also a traitor.

Soon after the expiration of his term as Vice-President, Burr began a leisurely trip down the Ohio. Following a short visit with Herman Blennerhasset, an Irishman who lived like a feudal lord on an island in

Aaron Burr

the Ohio near Parkersburg, Burr resumed his journey. He visited Andrew Jackson at Nashville, met Wilkinson at the mouth of the Ohio, and proceeded to New Orleans. Burr, who had been enthusiastically received by westerners in all walks of life, then returned to the East. A man of undoubted charm, he had an unusual faculty for making his vulgar dreams of riches and glory seem both real and noble to his listeners.

Although rumors that Burr was plotting treason were common throughout the winter of 1805–6, Jefferson appeared to ignore them, and he made no move to prevent Burr's return to the West the following summer. After gathering supplies at Blennerhasset's Island, Burr started down the Ohio with a flotilla of thirteen flatboats and sixty men. Meanwhile, Wilkinson, who could not even be honest with a fellow conspirator, wrote a lurid account of Burr's activities and plans to the President. On November 29, 1806, Jefferson ordered Burr's arrest. Burr, who did not learn of Jefferson's decision until the following January, deserted his followers and headed for the Spanish border. Captured, he was sent to Richmond, Virginia, to stand trial for treason.

Jefferson was now convinced of Burr's guilt and made no attempt to conceal his belief that he should be convicted of treason. Against all rules of fair play and propriety, Jefferson tried to assure Burr's conviction. But once again Marshall, who presided over the circuit court that heard the case, thwarted the President. On questions of civil liberties, Marshall always took extreme care to protect the rights of the individual. He gave the jury no other alternative than to declare Burr innocent. Although Jefferson thought differently, the Constitution gave Marshall little choice in the matter, for it defines treason as the actual waging of war against the United States or the aiding of its enemies. At the most, the government, whose principal witness was Wilkinson, could prove that Burr had contemplated but had not performed such acts. The Constitution had provided that no individual can be accused of treason "unless on the testimony of two witnesses to the same overt act, or on confession in open court"; the required two witnesses did not appear, and Burr did not confess. Although Marshall had refused to prove a man guilty of treason on the basis of unsubstantiated reports, Jefferson was nevertheless upset by the Chief Justice's failure to curb the activities of a man he distrusted and disliked. In the words of Andrew C. McLaughlin: "Jefferson, the foe of tyranny, and the apostle of freedom and individual rights, was angry because the Chief Justice, an advocate of strong and effective government, had so interpreted the Constitution as to protect a prisoner alleged to be guilty of treason against the nation. Marshall's decision partook of the character of Jeffersonian liberalism and modernism; and Jefferson lamented."

The Jeffersonian Legacy

Jefferson's active intervention in Burr's trial was one of the few unwholesome events in the career of a man of high principles and meticulous morality. But it was also one of many inconsistencies with which the student of Jefferson and his age must deal. In large measure, difficulty in understanding Jefferson comes less from study of the man as he was than from our belief in what later admirers have made of him. Jefferson was one of the foremost spokesmen in American history for humane ideals that have become part of our democratic heritage. In seeking to give this so called "Jeffersonian tradition" coherence and consistency, we have culled from Jefferson's very long life his recurring beliefs and ideals and have endowed them with the spirit of a system that they never possessed for Jefferson himself. We have created an image of Jefferson that in many ways obscures the tentativeness and *ad hoc* quality of his thought. It is difficult to match that modern creation—the *theory* of Jeffersonian democracy—that leads us to expect consistency, with the contradictions and nuances in the life and thought of a very practical man who never gave precision or finality to his beliefs.

We can also be confused in interpreting Jefferson by our failure to appreciate his great talents as a politician. Jefferson had distaste for personal involvement in the common intrigue of "party politics." It is very difficult to know what role he played in the daily political round of patronage, favors, and party discipline in which we know his contemporaries engaged. We can guess that Jefferson's great political success was due to more than the ideal attractions of his program or personality. Jefferson, however, seems appealing because of this seeming remoteness from partisanship and "party politics." Hamilton, a more open manipulator of men and interests, does not evoke the affection that a Jefferson, apparently "above politics," manages to create. In combining this image of a great "nonpolitical" leader with the ideals called "Jeffersonian democracy," little room is left for a Jefferson who made statements for reasons of political expediency or who constantly adjusted his never fully formulated "philosophy" to the demands of public and party life. The burden of reconciling Jeffersonian theory with practice is more ours than it was Jefferson's.

The history of his administration shows that every one of Jefferson's major ideas about America was, at some time, contradicted by his practices. Paradoxically, Jefferson, who had in mind a small farmers' America, one that would be radically different from the land we now know, has come down to us as foremost spokesman for the ideals of a twentieth-century society that probably would have appalled him. Professor Charles M. Wiltse has suggested that we can separate Jefferson's *beliefs* in human rights and in happiness as the test of government from the *institutions* of the agricultural society that Jefferson favored in his own time. In accepting this suggestion, however, we ought to remember Jefferson's own skepticism that his ideals could be fulfilled without his institutions and that other men were just as loyal to the ideals we assign only to him. Madison and John Adams, for example, were probably superior to Jefferson in their understanding of the nature of human rights, and could easily share the intellectual admiration usually reserved for Jefferson alone. If, moreover, the Jeffersonian ideal of natural rights superior to the commands of the state is "alive" and "meaningful," if it is not to be a mere piety or vague abstraction, we must analyze its consequences and not be content with uncritical enthusiasm for a creed of a great and good man.

FOR SUPPLEMENTARY READING

There is no complete, reliable study of Jefferson. Dumas Malone's fine work is still in progress. A. J. Nock, *Jefferson* (1926), is the best one-volume work, although the standard account is H. S. Randall, *The Life of Thomas Jefferson* (3 vols., 1865). Many excellent selections from Jefferson can be found in the mistitled volume edited by Saul Padover, *The Complete Jefferson* (1951). Jefferson's papers will be completely available from Julian P. Boyd, *The Papers of Thomas Jefferson* (17 vols. to date).

For the period, use E. Channing, *The Jeffersonian System* (1906). Nothing, however, can match Henry Adams, *History of the United States During the Administrations of Jefferson and Madison* (9 vols., 1889–91), available as an abridged one-volume paperback. Also see L. D. White, *The Jeffersonians* (1951). Study of Jefferson's "philosophy" can start with C. M. Wiltse, *The Jeffersonian Tradition in American Life* (1935); D. J. Boorstin, *The Lost World of Thomas Jefferson* (1948); and A. Koch, *The Philosophy of Thomas Jefferson* (1943)—all, however, less good than M. E. Petersen, *The Jefferson Image in the American Mind* (1960) (Pb).

On Jefferson and the Supreme Court, start with A. J. Beveridge, *The Life of John Marshall* (4 vols., 1916–19), and C. Warren, *The Supreme Court in United States History* (2 vols., 1937). On the Louisiana Purchase, see E. W. Lyon, *Louisiana in French Diplomacy, 1789–1804* (1934). On Jefferson and Burr, consult T. P. Abernethy, *The Burr Conspiracy* (1954). For a reassessment of Jefferson's relations with Madison, see A. Koch's *Jefferson and Madison: The Great Collaboration* (1950). B. De Voto (ed.), *The Journals of Lewis and Clark* (1953), is an obvious source. On foreign relations, use S. J. Bemis's *Diplomatic History*.

For politics, see D. Malone, *Jefferson as Political Leader* (1963); N. E. Cunningham, Jr., *The Jefferson Republicans in Power . . . 1801–1809* (1963); N. K. Risjord, *The Old Republicans: Southern Conservatism in the Age of Jefferson* (1965); and D. H. Fischer, *The Revolution of American Conservatism* (1965). An excellent summary on Jefferson is in R. Hofstadter, *The American Political Tradition* (1948) (Pb), but should be balanced by L. W. Levy, *Jefferson and Civil Liberties: The Darker Side* (1963).

11

⋙⋙⋙⋙⋙⋙⋙⋙

Jefferson's Era:
The Years of War

GEORGE WASHINGTON's inauguration in the spring of 1789 coincided with the outbreak of the French Revolution. For the next twenty years, the fate of the republican experiment in America was constantly involved with events transforming European life. From 1793 to 1815, four American Presidents had to decide how to guide the new nation to peace and prosperity in a world engaged in a bitter revolutionary war. The problems of American rights that confronted Washington and grew more intense under John Adams also continued under Jefferson and his successor James Madison. Great efforts were made to keep America at peace and to profit from trade with the belligerents. Yet, like every other world war during America's history, the Napoleonic wars eventually drew the United States into active hostilities.

Whether or not the price of peace was clearly understood, all the Presidents from Washington to Madison based their policies on the assumption that peace was essential for America. There were few men at the time who questioned whether America did not have a duty to take sides in the great struggles that were destroying the traditional basis of European life. None of the Presidents seemed to discern that the desire to trade with everyone, everywhere, must appear to both sides at some time as aid and comfort to an enemy. Jefferson hoped that the importance of American trade would force England and France to respect the United States' claims for neutral rights. He failed to realize that even if these rights were temporarily recognized, at any time the larger, vital interests of France or England were threatened by American shipments, the French or English would be required to interfere with American commerce.

Possessing no navy worth mentioning, and even less of an army, the only weapons America could use to defend her claims were her raw materials. The rationale of Jefferson's and Madison's foreign policy was to attempt to use this one bargaining point to best advantage. Had the United States of 1812 been the nation she was in 1914, the thought of losing or gaining American aid might have compelled an earlier, more thorough, more sincere respect for American claims.

Trials of a Neutral

Jefferson, like Washington and Adams before him, found it impossible to keep developments in Europe from affecting American policies. Despite an undeclared war with France during his administration, John Adams had demonstrated remarkable skill in keeping the republic out of Europe's wars. But the Jeffersonian Republicans, although fully determined to avoid being drawn into the European conflict, faced an increasingly difficult problem. When war between Great Britain and France began in 1793, the two countries entered upon an all-out struggle for world supremacy. The contest was intensified in 1803 after a short lull of a year. Since both nations were converting farmers into soldiers, both would be compelled to rely upon the United States for large exports of food. For the time being, both nations might have to abandon their cherished mercantilistic notions, throw open their colonies to trade, and depend in great measure on the merchant marine of the United States to bring them needed supplies. When it suited them, however, both would ignore the rights of neutrals and subject the United States, like every other noncombatant nation, to all sorts of indignity and inconvenience.

The very nature of the Old World struggle made interference with American commerce inevitable. Napoleon resolved to break Britain by destroying her commercial leadership and despoiling her of part of her colonial empire. Great Britain was frightened by Napoleon's success in bringing the greater part of the continent of Europe to his feet and in spreading the ideals of the French Revolution. Since she had failed to crush him on land, she determined to starve him into submission. In May, 1806, less than a year after Nelson had annihilated the French fleet at Trafalgar, Great Britain declared a blockade of the Continent from the River Elbe to Brest. Napoleon's answer to this policy came in November of the same year. His famous Berlin Decree proclaimed a blockade of the British Isles, even though he had no navy to enforce it, and announced that any vessel stopping at an English port would not be admitted to a French port. The British government retaliated with a series of Orders in Council that extended the continental blockade, closed the whole French coasting trade to neutrals, and required all neutral vessels bound for the barred zone to clear from a British port, secure a license, and pay certain "transit duties." Not to be outdone, Napoleon in December, 1807, issued the Milan Decree, which declared that the French would seize and confiscate any ship submitting to search by British officers, paying any tax or duty to the British government, or coming from or bound for a British port.

These orders and decrees were not inspired by special hostility to the United States. Ever since war began in 1793, there had been restrictions on all neutral trade. With the United States the chief neutral, however, the new decrees caused great hardship for American commerce. If a ship sailed directly for the Continent, it was liable to seizure by the British; if, on the other hand, it put in at a British port, it might be captured and confiscated by the French. Every American shipper was faced with conflicting rules not of his making. His risks were enormous, but so were the rewards for those who escaped the maze of retaliatory measures. Between 1803 and 1812, approximately 1,500 American ships were seized by the European belligerents, and most of these were confiscated for ignoring the rules imposed upon them. Nevertheless, for the first four years of this period American profits were greater than American losses.

To their numerous other restraints on American commerce the British added one more when they virtually excluded American ships from the trade between the French West Indies and France. In 1800, in the *Polly* case the British had permitted this trade if the goods from the West Indies were first landed at a port in the United States. Many American shippers had taken advantage of this British policy by merely calling at an American port without bothering to unload their cargoes. The United States government repaid these shippers for the American duties on commodities that had been imported from the French islands and were then exported to France. The Americans had thus transformed the broken voyage into a continuous voyage. In 1805, the British moved to stop this practice. In a case involving the *Essex*, a ship that had been paid a drawback, a British admiralty court ruled that French West Indian cargoes could not be sent to France by way of an American port unless their owner could demonstrate that he originally intended to send them to the United States rather than to France. As it was almost impossible to demonstrate such an intention, the British were able to shut off still another source of profit to the American shipper.

If England's interference with their trade angered Americans, the traditional British practice of impressing seamen caused even more resentment. England realized that her hope of conquering France depended on her navy. Yet its efficiency was always threatened by desertion. Long hours, low wages, filthy and often insufficient food, wretched sleeping quarters, severe punishment for trivial offenses, and the opportunity to escape the European war caused thousands of British seamen to flee to American merchantmen. Unable to spare these men, the British government applied the rule "once an Englishman, always an Englishman"; it refused them the right of expatriation and directed its naval officers to stop American vessels on the high seas, search them, and remove, by force if necessary, any man whose service might be lawfully claimed. America agreed to such searches in English ports or even at times on the high seas if a ship had visited the British Isles. But the English were not content with this. In carrying out their instructions, the searching parties more often than not did their work in highhanded fashion, and they were not always careful to distinguish between Britishers and Yankees. Many sailors born under the American flag were pressed into English service.

All efforts by the United States to induce the belligerents to respect the rights of neutrals came to nothing. American notes of protest to England were either ignored or answered in sarcastic and insolent vein. Napoleon's attitude was similar and in some respects more overbearing. He accused Jefferson of being a tool of Great Britain, issued false statements to lure American merchantmen to French waters where he knew they would be seized and confiscated, and made promises that he had no intention of fulfilling.

Desiring to trade but refusing to pay the price for aiding the enemies of other powers, the Republicans decided to try the same policies that Washington had employed with marked success in the 1790's. In 1806, Congress passed a Nonimportation Act closing American ports to certain British goods. Jefferson also sent William Pinkney to England to help James Monroe, the United States Minister at the Court of St. James, draw up a satisfactory commercial treaty with Great Britain. In the ensuing negotiations, the British agreed to exercise greater care in their impressment policy and to relax their restrictions on the French West Indian trade. A treaty containing both these provisions was signed by Monroe and Pinkney. But Jefferson, who had expressly forbidden the American representatives to conclude any agreement that did not contain a British renunciation of the right of impressment, refused to submit the treaty to the Senate for ratification. Jefferson proved himself less of a realist than Washington. The British had to continue to impress to survive. As long as the United States refused to recognize this necessity, the two countries would be unable to settle their other disputes. The Jay Treaty had been made possible by Federalist recognition of Britain's supremacy on the seas; Jefferson's refusal to do the same left him just where he was before Pinkney and Monroe began their negotiations with the British.

British naval supremacy was brought home to every American in the summer of 1807. The British warship *Leopard* halted the American frigate *Chesapeake* off the Virginia capes to search her for deserters. The British had never maintained that they had the right to impress men from American war vessels, and the commander of the American ship refused to permit the search. The *Leopard* immediately opened fire, killing three and wounding eighteen others. Unprepared for action, the *Chesapeake* was forced to yield. Four men—three of whom were Americans who had escaped from the British navy after having been impressed—were taken as alleged deserters.

The *Chesapeake* affair did more to arouse public opinion in the United States than any other single incident in the years preceding the outbreak of the War of 1812. War in the summer of 1807 would have been far more popular than it was to be in 1812. Americans of every political persuasion and from every section believed that their nation's disgrace could only be removed by a declaration of hostilities against Great Britain. Jefferson did not want war, but he knew that some action was necessary to allay popular feeling. In an effort to prevent a repetition of the *Chesapeake* affair, he issued a proclamation excluding British warships from American waters. To avoid an open rupture, he put off convening Congress until the war fever had subsided. The British, who no more wanted war than Jefferson, disavowed the action of the *Leopard*. They recalled the ship's commander, agreed to indemnify the wounded and the families of the dead, announced their willingness to return the impressed seamen, and admitted that the Royal Navy had no right to search ships of war. But these concessions were not enough to satisfy Jefferson, and he instructed the American representatives to demand that the British abandon impressments on merchant ships as well as warships. To the British this issue seemed irrelevant. Pointing out that the impressment of merchant seamen had nothing to do with the *Chesapeake* affair, they flatly rejected the American proposal and charged that Jefferson's failure to exclude French as well

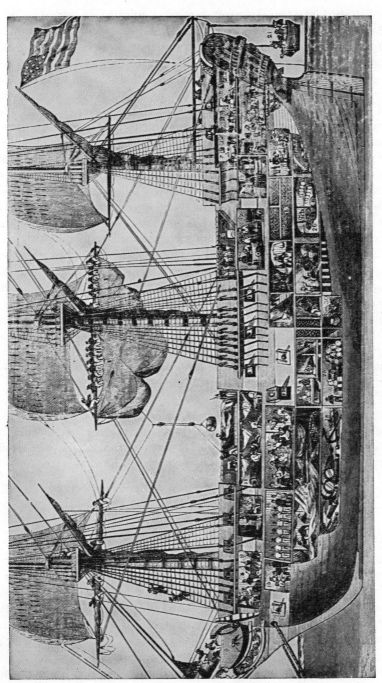

An American Warship

as British ships from American waters constituted an unneutral act. Once again, Jefferson's insistence that the British give up impressments prevented a settlement, and the larger question of respect for American trading rights remained unsettled.

The Nonimportation Act had proved wholly inadequate, but the Republicans were still committed to a policy of economic coercion. In December, 1807, Congress adopted the Embargo Act. This measure forbade all American vessels to sail from an American port to European ports and required every coasting vessel to give bond double the value of the vessel and cargo that it would land its cargo only in an American port. Instead of protecting American overseas commerce, the embargo tended to destroy it. The value of exports fell from $108,000,000 in 1807 to $22,000,000 the following year, an enormous decline for a country so dependent on foreign markets. Soon every port was crowded with idle ships; warehouses bulged with decaying goods; the shipbuilding industry languished; merchants went bankrupt; farmers lost their markets; prices of manufactured goods doubled; and the national revenue decreased approximately 50 per cent. Even those shippers who dared to evade the law by slipping out of port or by smuggling goods across the Canadian and Florida borders were always in danger of being apprehended by Federal agents. Massachusetts, the principal shipowning state in America, was especially hard hit. The embargo not only suspended at least half her commerce but greatly curtailed her fishing and whaling industries.

Before the end of 1808, the temper of the country, particularly of the commercial Northeast, was worse than before the passage of the embargo measure. Federalist politicians accused Jefferson of ruining the country. A newspaper poet in Newburyport, Massachusetts, spoke for the coastal residents of New England when he wrote:

> Our ships all in motion once whitened the ocean
> They sailed and returned with a cargo;
> Now doomed to decay, they have fallen a prey
> To Jefferson—worms—and Embargo.

Another New England critic of the embargo wrote to Jefferson: "You infernal villain, how much longer are you going to keep this damned Embargo on to starve us poor people[?] One of my children has already starved to death, of which [I am] so ashamed . . . [that I] declared it died of apoplexy." The extent of Jefferson's failure was revealed in part by the ability of the Federalists—who at times were little better than political bankrupts—to make a respectable showing in the election of 1808. James Madison, selected by Jefferson as his successor,

OGRABME: *The Snapping Turtle of the* EMBARGO

[NEW YORK PUBLIC LIBRARY]

received 122 electoral votes; but 46 electors cast their ballots for Charles C. Pinckney, the Federalist candidate, and six others voted for George Clinton, Jefferson's Vice-President. In addition, the Federalists made sizable gains in Congress, and every New England state except Vermont gave majorities to Pinckney.

Mr. Madison Has His Try with Neutral Rights

As Jefferson's second term drew to a close, the Republicans had nothing to show for their efforts to safeguard American rights on the high seas. Jefferson had believed that economic pressure would force the belligerents to accede to American demands; instead, it had split the United States and driven the New Englanders to the point of secession. At the same time, he had done nothing to prepare the country for war, the only alternative to either continued humiliation or an effective program of economic coercion.

James Madison, like Jefferson, was a Virginia planter. Before becoming Jefferson's Secretary of State, he had been a member of Virginia's first constitutional convention, the Continental Congress, the Virginia legislature, the Philadelphia Convention, and the House of Representatives. Although he played a notable role in the drafting and ratification of the Constitution, he was one of the few founding fathers to break with the Federalists after the Constitution had gone into effect. Madison was one of the most gifted students of politics in American history. As dedicated as were his predecessors to humane purposes for government, he nevertheless, had a healthy skepticism about larger pretensions of reformers and a thorough knowledge of the temptations that power offers all men, whether rich or poor, simple or gifted. The most famous statement of his views of the general problems of politics can be found in *Federalist*, number X, but his letters and private papers reveal even more than that famous propaganda piece his sharpness and insight. But, paradoxically, like his contemporary John Adams, Madison was unable to use his theoretical knowledge to enhance his prestige as a national leader. The famous Federalist from Massachusetts, Fisher Ames, has left a shrewd impression of the man:

> He is probably deficient in that fervor and vigor of character which you will expect in a great man. He is not likely to risk bold measures . . . nor even to persevere in any measures against a firm opposition . . . he excels in the quality of judgment . . . he is a studious man, devoted to public business and a thorough master of almost every public question that can arise . . . Upon the whole, he is a useful, respectable, worthy man, in a degree so eminent that his character will not sink. He will continue to be a very influential man in our country.

Scholarly though he was, Madison had repeatedly demonstrated that he was at home in the world of affairs. But, when he became President, he had lived in Jefferson's shadow for eight years. His critics—with some justification—complained that he was incapable of charting his own course.

In the interval between the election of 1808 and Madison's inaugural, Jefferson turned over most of the tasks of the presidency to his successor. With Madison's approval, Jefferson signed the repeal of the Embargo Act on March 1, 1809. Forced by popular pressure to abandon the embargo, the Republicans were immediately faced with the problem of finding a substitute. War was out of the question, for the country was unprepared; yet the thought of submission to France and Great Britain was intolerable. All that remained was a variation of the old policy. The embargo was supplanted by a Nonintercourse Act that permitted American shippers to trade with any part of the world except England and France. In what proved to be a vain effort to play one belligerent off against the other, the Republicans added to the bill

James Madison

the provision that trade would be resumed with whichever nation would first remove its restrictions on American commerce.

Soon after the adoption of the Nonintercourse Act, George Canning, the British foreign minister, instructed David Erskine, the British minister in Washington, to open negotiations with the Madison administration for a commercial treaty. Throughout the conferences, Erskine proved remarkably cooperative. Soon both parties were able to agree to a treaty that provided for a satisfactory settlement of the *Chesapeake* affair and the repeal of each country's restrictions on the other's commerce. Madison announced that the British would now withdraw the Orders in Council and that the United States would resume its commercial relations with Great Britain. His announcement was premature; Erskine had exceeded his instructions, and Canning rejected the treaty. As if to remove any doubt concerning his attitude, Canning replaced Erskine with Francis James Jackson, who made no attempt to conceal his hostility toward the United States and who felt that it was "charity" to call Erskine a "fool."

While the British refused the demands of the United States, Napoleon made a mockery of American policy. Soon after the embargo went into effect, he issued the Bayonne Decree (April 17, 1808) ordering the seizure of all American ships in French ports. In justification of this extraordinary move, he argued that, since no ships could then legally leave the United States, those in French ports must have been British vessels that were seeking to conceal their identity with the American colors. Armed with the Bayonne Decree, the French confiscated approximately $10,000,000 worth of American ships and cargoes in a single year. When the embargo was supplanted by the Nonintercourse Act, Napoleon countered with the Rambouillet Decree (March 23, 1810) authorizing the seizure and sale of all American ships that had entered French ports after the date on which the United States had severed commercial relations with France. The United States could protest against Napoleon's policies, but it could not compel him to alter them without war.

By 1810, the United States had ample justification for a declaration of war against either Great Britain or France. But a nation needs more than justification to declare war. The United States still lacked both the will to fight and adequate military power. All that remained was the opportunity to try still another version of economic coercion. Nathaniel Macon, chairman of the House Committee on Foreign Affairs, accordingly drew up a bill requiring that all imports from France and England be carried on American ships. Although this measure was passed by the House, it was defeated in the Senate. Congress then adopted an "inside-out" Nonintercourse Act that was known as Macon's Bill No. 2 (May 1, 1810). While permitting American trade with every nation of the world, Macon's Bill No. 2 provided that if either Great Britain or France revoked or modified its commercial decrees while the other did not, the President would revive the Nonintercourse Act against the offending country. Once more the United States was offering itself to the highest bidder. Once more both Britain and France spurned the offer. Like its predecessors, Macon's Bill No. 2 failed to remove a single restriction from American commerce.

Although Napoleon had no intention of complying with the conditions laid down in Macon's Bill No. 2, by pretending to do so he could add one more complication to the already strained relations between

Great Britain and the United States. On August 5, 1810, the French foreign minister, the Duc de Cadore, wrote the American minister to France that the Berlin and Milan Decrees would be revoked on November 1. But the Cadore letter did not say all that it seemed to say. The French foreign minister added that the revocation would go into effect only if England repealed its Orders in Council "or . . . the United States . . . shall cause their [the United States'] rights to be respected by the English." Madison, falling into the trap set by Napoleon, announced on November 2, 1810, that the Nonintercourse Act would be applied to the British unless Great Britain repealed its Orders in Council within three months. Napoleon, having achieved his objective, again authorized the seizure of American ships. The British ignored Madison's threat; and on March 2, 1811, Congress adopted a bill reinstituting nonintercourse against Great Britain. The Cadore letter had fulfilled Napoleon's happiest expectations.

In the dark days of 1811, the prestige of the United States had reached one of the all-time lows in the nation's history, but American spirits were temporarily revived by an unexpected naval victory. On May 11, 1811, the American frigate *President*, while patrolling the waters off Sandy Hook, New Jersey, encountered the British war vessel *Little Belt*. When the British ship was hailed and refused to come about, a battle followed in which thirty-two Englishmen were either killed or wounded. American losses were slight, and the *President* was the undisputed victor. To the American people the defeat of the *Little Belt* served as a tonic, for many believed that the British at last had been forced to pay for the *Chesapeake* affair. Once again there were demands for war, and a Philadelphia newspaper wrote that the *President*'s victory recalled the good old days of '76 when with "our hay forks, pitch forks and grubbing hoes . . . we knocked down his teeth and scowered his blackhell throat."

The War Hawks

Despite the enthusiasm for the *President*'s victory in the coastal regions, the demand for war did not come from northeastern shippers, but from nationally-minded frontier expansionists and southern planters. Despite affronts and inconveniences, the shipping interests were making money and did not want war. But the frontier West, with a eye on Canada, and the planting South, with its heart set on Florida, were now demanding war. Ever since pre-Revolutionary days, frontiersmen from New Hampshire to Kentucky had demanded that the Indian tribes of the Northwest be ousted and that Canada be acquired by the United States. The westerners' land hunger, a desire to obtain control of the British fur trade, and, above all, the wish to destroy forever the alliance between the British and the Indians were principally responsible for this double demand over the years.

Throughout Jefferson's administration there had been sporadic fighting and repeated misunderstandings between the Indians and the American settlers in the Northwest. Frontiersmen, ignoring the guarantees granted the Indians by treaties, overran Indian lands and advanced through northwestern Ohio and the Indiana territory into the Wabash country. William Henry Harrison, who had been named Governor of Indiana Territory by President Jefferson, was wholly in sympathy with the pioneer policy of excluding the Indians by any means. By treating with certain irresponsible local chiefs, he succeeded in 1804 and 1805 in despoiling whole tribes of some of their most valuable hunting grounds. This action was bitterly resented by more intelligent and foresighted Indian leaders like Tecumseh and his brother, the Prophet, sons of a Shawnee warrior. To prevent another betrayal, they proposed that all the frontier tribes from the Great Lakes to the Gulf should form a confederacy that would confer upon a congress of warriors sole authority to dispose of Indian lands. Scarcely had Prophetstown, the capital of this Indian confederacy, been founded (1808) before Governor Harrison, again meeting with the same irresponsible sachems, secured titled to the rich valley of the Wabash. Three years later the plans of Tecumseh and the Prophet were shattered. Harrison, invading unceded Indian lands, defeated the Indians in the battle of Tippecanoe (1811), and destroyed the seat of their confederacy.

In his report of the battle, Harrison stated that the Indians had fought with guns and powder supplied by the British. To the frontiersmen, the problem was long familiar; it could be solved only by destroying the British bases in Canada.

The westerners' desire for Canada was matched by the southerners' demand for Florida. As long as East and West Florida remained in alien hands, their swamps and marshlands afforded a refuge for runaway slaves, and their Indian population could be incited against the United States. Many farmers of eastern Tennessee and of the neighboring territory of Alabama could reach the sea only by rivers that passed through the Floridas. There was always the danger also that the Floridas might be used as a base by England.

Both Livingston and Monroe, who had negotiated the treaty of 1803, asserted that the Louisiana Purchase included West Florida— that is, the strip of Gulf coast between the Iberville or eastern branch of the Mississippi and the Apalachicola—but Spain claimed this territory as part of the Floridas. During the years immediately following the acquisition of Louisiana, while the United States was unsuccessfully endeavoring to induce Spain to recognize its claim, West Florida gradually filled up with Americans. In 1810, they revolted against the Spanish authorities. With the connivance of the American government they declared their independence of Spain and asked to be annexed to the United States. In October, 1810, President Madison, heeding the wishes of the frontier expansionists, issued a proclamation declaring that by the Louisiana Purchase the United States extended as far east as the Perdido and that West Florida was therefore American soil. The fact that Spain was heavily indebted to American citizens for damages to their trade afforded sufficient excuse to claim East Florida also. Early in 1811, Congress tentatively authorized the seizure of the region, and southern expansionists now urged that the United States resort to war if necessary to acquire East Florida from Spain.

The westerners and southerners were nationalists as well as expansionists, and they deeply resented the injustices heaped on the United States by both belligerents. They were disgusted with the New Englanders' refusal to put patriotism above profits and reluctance to turn against their nation's oppressors. They reserved their most intense hatred for Great Britain. In their opinion, England had been even more insulting than France, and Great Britain and her ally, Spain, controlled the regions that the American expansionists desired. To get their produce to the seas, before acquiring West Florida and Louisiana, western farmers had to float down rivers passing through foreign-owned and hostile territory. Even after America acquired these regions, British interference with American ships on the high seas cut the farmers off from European markets. This gave the westerners a solid stake in defense of American neutral rights.

However strong the demand to annex Canada or Florida or to destroy the Indians, there were arguments against these proposals. If Florida was conquered, its long coastline would be impossible to defend, given the insignificance of the American navy. Since parts of Florida had already been acquired without war and negotiations for the rest also had been started, why should the administration go to war for Florida? After Harrison's defeat of the Indians in the Northwest in 1811, there was little significant conflict between them and American settlers. As for Canada, despite the incessant boastful talk in Congress—such as "The conquest of Canada is in your power . . . the militia of Kentucky are alone competent to place Montreal and Upper Canada at your feet"—it would be difficult to induce Congress to vote for war for Canada alone.

Whatever public opinion was about Indians, expansion, or the claim that our free ships made free goods, the decision for war had to come from Congress. In the Eleventh and Twelfth Congresses young leaders from frontier areas identified themselves with the defense of American rights and honor and with expansion. Without the militancy and skill of young men like Henry Clay and John C. Calhoun in making political issues of these long-standing discontents, war might not have come by June of 1812. The news of the English repeal of the Orders in Council would have arrived in time to cancel or reduce substantially the threat of war, and to vindicate, at least temporarily, the Jefferson-Madison policy of economic coercion. As it was, Henry Clay, the young Kentuckian, and his associates called the "War Hawks," kept the agitation for war at a height. "No man," said Clay, "wants peace more than I; but I prefer the troubled ocean of war, demanded by the honor and independence of this country, with all its calamities and desolation, to the tranquil and putrescent pool of ignominious peace."

During the early months of 1812, the demand for war became more insistent than ever. Madison, whose sole objective had been the preservation of peace, on June 1, 1812, asked Congress to declare war on Great Britain. Clay and Calhoun fell to work at once to bring the war sentiment to fulfillment. On June 4, the House of Representatives by a vote of seventy-nine to forty-nine approved a war resolution, and the Senate in a nineteen to thirteen vote followed suit on June 17. On the next day, the declaration went into effect. The strongest vote for war came along a great western arc running from Maine to Georgia. The greatest opposition came from the coastal areas, especially Federalist New England. The attitude of the Federalist Northeast is admirably summed up by Julius Pratt:

In home affairs, it was convinced, not without cause . . . that the Republican administration had deliberately resolved to ruin its commerce and dissipate its prosperity. Holding these views, it could see no worse national crime than a war against England which would render indirect aid to Napoleon, and no worse disaster to its own interests than a form of expansion which would mean new states to increase the Republican strength in Congress.

The British, like the Federalists, wished to avoid war. France was still the principal enemy, and Britain had no desire to be diverted from the war in Europe by armed conflict in North America. A series of political shifts had also produced a new English ministry that favored a more conciliatory policy toward the United States. On June 16—two days before the American declaration of war went into effect—the British government announced the repeal of all the Orders in Council affecting American commerce. The British decision, by providing an opportunity for peace, converted that fall's American election into a referendum on the popularity of war. Madison, who was running for a second term, was definitely committed to the war. He was opposed by De Witt Clinton of New York, who had been nominated by dissident Republicans, and who as a peace candidate was also supported by the Federalists. Madison received 128 electoral votes to 89 for Clinton. The election followed closely the sectional pattern that had been set in the vote on the war resolution in Congress. Madison carried all the South and every western state; Clinton won every northern state except Pennsylvania and Vermont. The election reaffirmed the decision of the majority to fight, but it also revealed that a powerful minority was opposed to war.

A Sorry Little War

There was no guarantee that if the news of the repeal of the British Orders in Council had reached Washington a few weeks earlier, America would never have become involved in the Napoleonic wars. The struggle between England and France was just entering its most bitter and important stage. Had American products gone to the continent in sufficient supply to affect England's chances adversely, the blockade might well have been reimposed. English governments at the time were dependably unstable, and the next change of ministry could well have reversed the decisions of June, 1812. It is difficult to understand also how freedom to trade would have lessened the demands for Canada and Florida—granting, that is, that land hunger alone did or could cause an Anglo-American war. There was always the possibility also that the United States might eventually have gone to war against France.

Although such speculations may seem academic, they do seriously challenge the judgment that the American policy of peace through economic coercion would have finally triumphed if there had been an Atlantic cable to bring the news of the end of the Orders in Council instantaneously. As it was, war did come to a nation that could ill afford it and that was wretchedly prepared for fighting the world's greatest sea power. Jefferson and Madison never seemed to realize that if economic coercion failed, war would follow. It had been essential to strengthen American defenses while using diplomacy and economic pressure to safeguard American rights. But such was not the case and because defenses were neglected, in 1812 the military odds against the United States were staggering. Only the English preoccupation in Europe saved this country from disaster.

The War of 1812 was fought on land and sea. On land, the United States suffered a series of almost uninterrupted defeats. At sea, American warships—among which were the *Constitution*, the *United States*, the *Essex*, and the *Hornet*—won a number of notable victories. American privateers also took more than 1,300 prizes, and the United States Navy captured 165 more. Despite these accomplishments, the United States lost the war at sea. By 1814, the British navy had practically destroyed the American merchant marine and navy, and blockade had seriously hurt the American economy.

At first, the initiative on land lay with the United States. As long as the British were tied down by the war in Europe, they were forced to limit their military activity in North America to holding operations. In 1812, Great Britain had only 5,000 soldiers in Canada, and until Napoleon was defeated there was no way by which she could reinforce them. In contrast to the United States' population of almost 8,000,000 there were only 500,000 Canadians, many of whom were French-Canadians who had no desire to risk their lives defending the British Empire. Despite these favorable conditions, American armies were unable to make any appreciable gains in Canada in 1812.

The American effort to drive the British out of Canada during the first phase of the war was seriously hamstrung by New England. Her merchants and shippers stubbornly refused to support a conflict that, as they insisted, was not of their making. Their spokesmen in Congress condemned the invasion of Canada, fought conscription, and tried by every means to defeat the Administration's loan bills and tax projects. Outside the halls of Congress, they were equally vehement in their opposition. Individuals, the press, town meetings, and state legislatures contemptuously referred to "Mr. Madison's War" and described it as "unjust," "ruinous," and "unconstitutional." Federalist bankers tried to prevent the sale of government bonds. To quote Henry Adams: "Probably New England lent to the British Government during the war more money than she lent to her own." New Englanders even helped provision the British fleet operating off the coast and the British armies in Canada. The British were careful not to alienate these "allies" in New England; throughout the war, no part of this region was blockaded by the British navy.

No other section was as opposed to the war as New England, but there was little agreement about either the conduct or objectives of the war in the South and the West. Although the War Hawks were

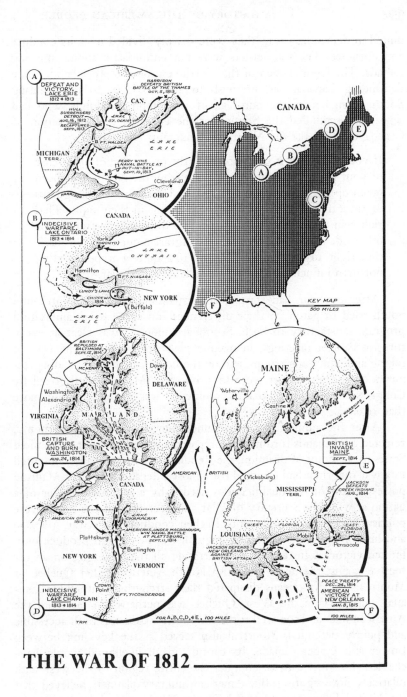

THE WAR OF 1812

united in demanding war, they were sharply divided over its conduct and purposes. The southerners were not enthusiastic about annexing Canada. The frontiersmen of the Northwest, on the other hand, while demanding Canada, had no wish to add territory to the planting South. Even before the outbreak of war, John Randolph, who had repeatedly reminded the South that the conquest and annexation of Canada would make the North preponderant, warned:

> If you go to war, it will not be for the protection of or defense of your maritime rights. Gentlemen from the North have been taken up into some high mountain and shown all the kingdoms of the earth; and Canada seems tempting in their sight. That rich vein of Genesee land . . . is said to be even better on the other side of the lake than on this. Agrarian cupidity, not maritime right, urges the war . . . It is to acquire a preponderating northern influence that you are to launch into war.

After the war had started, the expansionists of the North and South tried to patch up their differences and agree to an annexation program satisfactory to both. Sectional animosity was clear at every turn—in cabinet meetings, in making plans for financing the war, in raising and equipping troops, and on the field of battle. These disagreements on the war effort were so strong that Madison, authorized by Congress to appeal for 50,000 volunteers, was unable to raise more than 10,000.

After the administration had undermined the national economy, rejected all demands for military preparedness, and brought the United States to the point of disunion, the Republican leaders finally consented to a war that they had opposed for almost a decade. President Madison possessed few of the qualifications needed by a successful leader of a nation at war. His Secretary of War and Secretary of the Navy were political hacks and incompetents. In their conduct of the war, Madison and his colleagues adopted a strategy that at best could produce only limited victories. Instead of concentrating all their energies on an offensive against the heart of British North America—either Quebec or Montreal—the Americans dissipated their strength by attacking Canada's periphery in the West. Quebec was perhaps too far from the American lines and too well fortified, but Montreal was both accessible and poorly defended. Montreal also served as the key link between Lower and Upper Canada. Its capture in all likelihood would have enabled the Americans to conquer the entire region to the west with relatively little fighting. But American military planners believed that the United States should attack in the West, where the inhabitants were expected to rally to the support of an invading army. At most, this strategy would have resulted in the acquisition of only relatively small areas of British territory rather than the conquest of Canada.

Mismanagement, lack of adequately trained administrators, and poor leadership prevented even minor American victories in the West. The American campaign plans for 1812 called for twin offensives against Canada through Detroit and Niagara. On July 12, William Hull, the Governor of Michigan Territory, marched an American force out of Detroit and began the invasion of Upper Canada. After advancing only a few miles, rumors of British troop concentrations in the area frightened him back to Detroit, where he was surrounded by a British army of regulars, militiamen, and Indians led by Major-General Isaac Brock. On August 12, Hull surrendered without a fight. Brock then rushed his troops to Niagara and defeated another American force under Stephen Van Rensselaer at Queenstown Heights (October 13, 1812). Meanwhile, Major-General Henry Dearborn, who was stationed at Plattsburg, was preparing an expedition against Montreal. He did not set out, however, until late November; and when he reached the Canadian border after a twenty-mile march, he halted and then marched back to Plattsburg. American militiamen refused to fight on foreign soil, and Dearborn was afraid of a reportedly larger British force in the region. The projected offensive against Montreal came to nothing. By the end of 1812, the Americans had won no victories and had been forced to relinquish some land to the British in the West.

The American campaigns in 1813 were somewhat more successful, but they had little effect on the over-all course of the war. On September 10, 1813, a small fleet on Lake Erie under the command of Captain Oliver Hazard Perry defeated the English at Put-in-Bay. Perry's exploit and his colorful announcement of the victory ("We have met the enemy, and they are ours, two ships, two brigs, one schooner, and one sloop") were enthusiastically received by the American people, but the battle did not prove to be a prelude to the successful invasion of Canada. Less than a month after the battle of Put-in-Bay, Americans operating out of Detroit under William Henry Harrison defeated the British at the Thames River (October 5, 1813). Harrison was able to recoup Hull's losses, but his army only nibbled at the fringes of Canada. At the same time, the British managed to fight off the American attacks in the vicinity of Niagara. After taking York (Toronto) in April, 1813, an American force led by Dearborn was compelled to withdraw, and at the end of December the British captured Fort Niagara. The projected campaign against Montreal turned out to be as much of a fiasco as that of the preceding year.

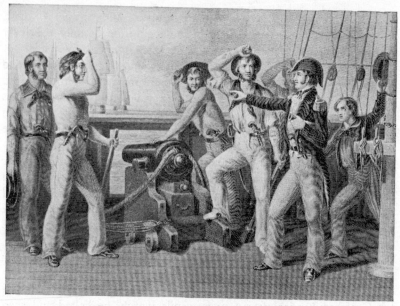

"Ready!"   "All Ready, Your Honor!"

Perry at Lake Erie

In 1814, the entire character of the war in America was changed by Napoleon's defeat in Europe. The British were able for the first time to contemplate bringing their full power to bear on the struggle in the New World. They therefore planned to attack the United States at four major points—Plattsburg, Washington, New Orleans, and Maine. The campaign against Plattsburg was entrusted to Sir George Prevost and an army of 14,000. After reaching the fort, which was held by approximately 4,000 Americans, Prevost decided to delay his attack until the arrival of a supporting fleet on Lake Champlain. But when the British ships were defeated in a battle off Plattsburg Bay by an American flotilla under Captain Thomas Macdonough, Prevost marched his troops back to Canada without risking a battle that he probably could have easily won. The failure of the Plattsburg campaign deprived the British of an unparalleled opportunity to cut off New England from the rest of the United States.

Despatching a small part of their navy of nearly 1,000 various warships into Chesapeake Bay, the British were able to capture, but not hold, the capital of the United States. The British marched into Washington on August 24, 1814, a few hours after it had been evacu-

The British at Washington, 1814

ated by the officials of the government. The attack on Washington was designed to demoralize the American people rather than to prepare the way for a full-scale invasion. After burning the city's public buildings, the English retired to their ships and transports. A similar raid on Baltimore proved less successful. The British were repulsed by Fort McHenry's guns and by recruits gathered to defend the city.

The New Orleans campaign, like that against Washington, was undertaken, not to conquer territory, but to teach the Americans a lesson. The British hoped that by taking New Orleans they could create discontent among southwestern farmers who would no longer be able to use the Mississippi for the export of their surplus commodities. The British plan, however, miscarried. Two weeks after peace had been concluded at Ghent—but before news of it had reached America—the British were overwhelmingly defeated at the battle of New Orleans (January 8, 1815). American militiamen led by Andrew Jackson, who had already distinguished himself as an Indian fighter, barricaded themselves behind bales of cotton and mowed down the British regulars. The battle of New Orleans could have been prevented by modern communications; still the victory at New Orleans was the most notable American success of the war. The battle made Jackson the outstanding American hero of a war that was memorable for the lack of American foresight and heroism.

The British won their most important victory in America in Maine. After landing on September 1, 1814, at the mouth of the Penobscot River, they captured the town of Castine and advanced without opposition up the Penobscot Valley to Bangor. The inhabitants in the northeastern section of Maine took an oath of allegiance to the King, and the entire region was placed under British control. Inhabitants of the coastal regions, instead of trying to drive out the invaders, appeared to welcome the arrival of the British. New England ships that had previously traded with the British at Halifax now sailed for Castine with goods for their country's enemies. In the relatively short period from September, 1814, to the end of the war, American ships calling at Castine paid out £13,000 in duties to the royal customs officials at the Maine port.

Harsh Tidings from Hartford

New England's response to the British invasion of Maine accurately reflected the section's aversion to the war and to the Madison administration. In September, 1814, Massachusetts and Connecticut withdrew their militia from federal service. In the following month, the Massachusetts legislature issued an invitation to her neighboring commonwealths to send delegates to a convention "for the purpose of devising proper measures to procure the united efforts of the commercial states, to secure them from further evils." Five states—Massachusetts, Connecticut, Rhode Island, New Hampshire, and Vermont—responded, and the delegates assembled at Hartford on December 15, 1814.

What action the convention would take was problematic. For more than ten years states' rights and secession had been freely discussed in New England. Less than a week before the Hartford Convention assembled, Daniel Webster, speaking in the House of Representatives against a proposed federal conscription law, stated:

> The principles of the bill are not warranted by any provision of the Constitution . . . not connected with any power which the Constitution has conferred on Congress. . . . The Constitution is libelled, foully libelled . . . An attempt to maintain this doctrine upon the provisions of the Constitution is an exercise of perverse ingenuity to extract slavery from the substance of a free government.

Webster's exposition reflected the spirit of commercial New England. In the Hartford Convention, the radical members were eager for secession. They were outnumbered, however, by moderates, whose opinion prevailed. After scolding the Administration and threatening nullification if conscription were used, the Convention recommended seven amendments to the Constitution. Collectively these amendments, if adopted, would have excluded the slaves from the count in determining state membership in the House of Representatives, made the admission of new states impossible without a two-thirds majority of Congress, prohibited all embargoes of more than sixty days, prevented a declaration of war without a two-thirds majority in Congress (except in case of invasion), and put an end to the monopoly of the presidency by Virginians.

In both the West and South, press and platform denounced the Hartford Convention. The Richmond *Enquirer* wrote:

> No man, no association of men, no state or set of states has a right to withdraw itself from this Union of its own accord: . . . The majority of the states which form the Union must consent to the withdrawal of any one branch of it. Until that consent has been obtained, any attempt to dissolve the Union or to obstruct the efficacy of its constitutional laws is Treason—Treason to all intents and purposes.

Apparently the *Enquirer* had forgotten the Kentucky and Virginia Resolutions. Events in 1860 would revise this stand and make Virginia appear even more intransigent than the men of Hartford in defense of states' rights.

Good News from Ghent

Any possibility that the New England states might secede from the Union was removed early in 1815 with the announcement of peace between the United States and Britain. The Treaty of Ghent, which ended the War of 1812, was the culmination of a series of negotiations that went back to the first months of the war. Soon after the outbreak of hostilities, negotiations were undertaken for ending the war. As early as September, 1812, the Tsar had proposed to John Quincy Adams, the American representative at St. Petersburg, that Russia serve as a mediator between Great Britain and the United States. The Tsar's move was not disinterested. The end of the war in America would permit Britain, which was now Russia's ally, to concentrate all its energies on the defeat of Napoleon. In March, 1813, Madison accepted the Russian offer and nominated John Quincy Adams, James A. Bayard, and Albert Gallatin to serve as the American representatives at the peace talks. The British, however, balked at the idea of Russian mediation. But when the Tsar renewed his proposal, officials in London indicated that they were willing to deal directly with the American negotiators. Madison agreed to the British plan and appointed two additional commissioners, Henry Clay and Jonathan Russell, the American minister to Sweden. Because of the numerous proposals and counterproposals, as well as the relative slowness of trans-Atlantic communications, the American and British delegates did not convene at Ghent until August, 1814. Both sides had spent almost as much time trying to end the war as to win it.

After prolonged negotiation, the representatives at Ghent were forced to realize that they would have to settle for a peace without victory, for neither nation was in a position to press its demands. The Americans saw no point in continuing what in fact was a losing war, and the British were uneasy about events in Europe during and after the final days of Napoleon. Twenty years of war and high taxes had not prepared Englishmen for more fighting in America. Many of them, in fact, were hoping that a free and friendly America would become England's best customer. A harsh peace might not serve English industry well. The English government at the time, however, was not dominated by or immediately responsive to commercial or industrial interests. The final decision about the struggle in America and the conditions of peace was to be made by men who had fought Napoleon, particularly the Duke of Wellington. Probably his decision not to press the issue in America to final victory turned England from war toward peace and the peace from revenge toward leniency.

The Treaty of Ghent merely made provision for the cessation of hostilities, the release of prisoners, the restoration of conquests by both sides, and the termination of Indian hostilities. No reference was made to neutral rights, the impressment of American seamen, or the effect on American commerce of blockades, seizures, and confiscations. Nor was any mention made of the control of the Great Lakes, Indian territories, the fisheries, or the navigation of the Mississippi. From the point of view of the expansionists, the document was, as Clay labeled it "a damned bad treaty," but news of its completion was joyously received by an exhausted administration and by the people of the nation.

Although the Treaty of Ghent removed none of the causes of the war, it nevertheless marked a turning point in the history of the United States' relations with Europe. In the years after 1815, the United States was able to settle most of its outstanding difference with Great Britain, force the Spanish out of Florida, and formulate an over-all policy to govern the relations between the nations of the Western hemisphere and those of the Old World. The American Revolution had severed America's political ties with Great Britain, but it was not until the conclusion of the War of 1812 that the United States' independence was fully secured. Following the Treaty of Ghent the American people were able for the first time since their nation's establishment to devote their major energies to domestic rather than foreign problems. To contemporaries, the War of 1812 was viewed as a series of blunders and misfortunes; to students of American history, it stands as a second war of independence.

For the next hundred years relative peace in Europe freed America from the dilemmas she had faced from 1789 to 1815. The coming century of European quiet would strengthen America's belief that she had succeeded in isolating herself from the Old World. When the next world war began in 1914, it was extremely difficult for Americans to realize that their century of fruitful isolation had been less an act of choice than a stroke of chance.

FOR SUPPLEMENTARY READING

Many of the books cited at the end of Chapter 10 are pertinent for the events connected with the War of 1812. To these, students should add R. H. Brown, *The Republic in Peril: 1812* (1964); H. L. Coles, *The War of 1812* (1965); P. C. T. White, *A Nation on Trial: America and the War of 1812* (1965); and J. W. Pratt, *Expansionists of 1812* (1925) an influential latter-day analysis of the causes of the war. Be sure, however, also to consult A. L. Burt, *The United States, Great Britain and British North America* (1940); and B. Perkins, *Prologue to War . . . 1805–1812* (1961) and *Castlereagh and Adams* (1964). I. Brant, *James Madison: Secretary of State 1801–1809* (1953) and *James Madison: The President 1809–1812* (1956), are attempts to lift Madison's reputation. There is a convenient but thin collection of Madison's writings in Saul Padover, *The Complete Madison* (1953).

For a restatement of accepted views, consult George Dangerfield, *The Era of Good Feelings* (1952). Two good studies on the major problems leading to the war are J. F. Zimmerman, *Impressment of American Seamen* (1925), and L. M. Sears, *Jefferson and the Embargo* (1927).

The most recent history of the war is F. F. Beirne, *The War of 1812* (1949). On the war at sea, A. T. Mahan, *Sea Power in Its Relation to the War of 1812* (2 vols., 1919), has the merits of a classic. Andrew Jackson's role in the war can be found in Marquis James, *Andrew Jackson: The Border Captain* (1933). On the War Hawks, use first C. Eaton, *Henry Clay and the Art of American Politics* (1957), and C. M. Wiltse, *John C. Calhoun: Nationalist, 1782–1828* (1944).

Two good books on New England during the war are Henry Adams (ed.), *Documents Relating to New England Federalism* (1877), and S. E. Morison, *The Life and Letters of Harrison Gray Otis* (2 vols., 1913). The peace negotiations are well analyzed in S. F. Bemis, *John Quincy Adams and the Foundations of American Foreign Policy* (1949).

America Moves West

URING the twenty-five years after the War of 1812, the West played an increasingly important role in the history of the American people. By 1840, the Indians had been forced to relinquish their lands east of the Mississippi, millions of acres of land on either side of the Ohio were producing huge crops of corn and grain, and the Old Southwest had been converted into the leading cotton-growing region of the world. In the Far West the fur industry had risen and declined and a whole tier of new states had been established west of the Mississippi. The vast territory stretching from the Appalachians to the Rockies tempted and beckoned countless easterners and Europeans. Some of these went west because of their love of adventure and the unknown. Still others went to escape the restrictions and injustices of eastern or Old World society. But most of those who turned to the West traveled for the opportunity "out there" that promised independence and success. To the struggling eastern farmer, dissatisfied tradesman, religious dissenter, or ambitious young lawyer, the West was a "promised land."

Settling the Old West

The center of American population has steadily moved westward. Shortly before the American Revolution, the first groups of settlers reached the crest of the Appalachians. Like millions to come after them, the wild magnificence of the lands beyond inspired a curious blend of idealism and venality. By 1810, what is known as the Old West had a population of more than one million. By 1820 this had more than doubled, and by 1830 there were nearly four million settlers beyond the Appalachians. In less than ten years after 1810, six new western states were admitted to the Union: Louisiana (1812), Indiana (1816), Mississippi (1817), Illinois (1818), Alabama (1819), and Missouri (1821). Between 1820 and 1830, Kentucky gained 22 per cent in population, Louisiana 41 per cent, and Tennessee and Ohio 61 per cent each. But the rate of increase in younger states was even more phenomenal: Mississippi gained 81 per cent, Missouri 109 per cent, Indiana 133 per cent, Alabama 142 per cent, and Illinois 185 per cent. Between 1810 and 1830, the never ending migration westward had taken more than two million people out of the seaboard states. By 1840, the West had a population in excess of six million.

People generally moved westward in parallel lines. Tennessee and Kentucky, for instance, were settled by Germans and Scotch-Irish from the piedmont regions of Virginia and the Carolinas. With the invention of the cotton gin and the tremendous demand for cotton, the coast planters pushed into the interior counties of the old southern states. Unable to compete, the wealthier free farmers who sensed future profits and prestige bought slaves and adopted the plantation system; others sold their lands and migrated. The supply of cheap good land in Kentucky and Tennessee, however, was quickly exhausted, and the younger generation, together with the new arrivals from the eastern communities, settled in southern Ohio, Indiana, Illinois, Missouri, and the Gulf states.

The population of the Gulf states came almost entirely from the Old South. Many of the independent upcountry yeomen went to this section, but it was even more alluring to the planters of Virginia, the Carolinas, and Georgia. Excessive cultivation of tobacco and failure to employ scientific methods of rotation and fertilization had exhausted much of the soil in such eastern regions as Virginia by the end of the eighteenth century. The competition of Kentucky-grown tobacco, the embargo, the War of 1812, droughts, ravages of insect pests, and the burden of old debts added to farm and plantation distress. The Southwest, with its abundance of virgin land, seemed to promise economic salvation. The region also attracted thousands of Carolina and Georgia planters in search of new cotton lands. Before 1840, cotton culture had spread from Georgia to Texas, and a new South had been created. Like the farmers of the Northwest, the Gulf-state planters, with few exceptions, were nationalistic and expansionist. As aggressive exploiters of

Stage Wagon in the West

the soil under the plantation system, they perfected slavery as a commercial system.

While southern planters and backcountrymen were occupying the lower Mississippi Valley, middle staters and New Englanders, supplemented by German immigrants, were pushing westward. Central Ohio, Indiana, and Illinois were largely colonized by people from New York, Pennsylvania, and New Jersey. From Massachusetts and Connecticut an almost endless procession of Yankees moved northward into Maine, New Hampshire, and Vermont, and then westward. By 1812, they had occupied the western shore of Lake Champlain, the St. Lawrence Valley, the greater part of central, western, and southern New York, northeastern and northwestern Pennsylvania, and northeastern Ohio. They also planted colonies in New Jersey, eastern Pennsylvania, and southern Ohio. After the War of 1812, many New Englanders settled in southern Michigan and Wisconsin. Between 1830 and 1840, thousands of immigrants from southwestern Germany occupied the more sparsely populated sections of the states north of the Ohio. Among them were a large number of able, intelligent men who exerted a powerful influence upon intellectual life in the Old Northwest.

No area of the country was free from the pull of the West. Every county and probably every town became familiar with the stories, rumors, and reports of some promised land to the west. The decision to leave "the old place," the sale of encumbering possessions, the final loading of horses and wagons, and the round of farewells and promises to write were familiar to both Yankees and Southerners. The movements west powerfully affected the image of America as a place of great restlessness and as an eternal beginning. They fed a belief that somewhere in the dark fields of the republic there lay one big chance that justified the hardships and pain involved in settling the land, in trying its richness, and, after failure, in starting in again over the horizon.

Wagons and Waters Westward

From whatever section the eager traveler came, his journey west was not an easy one. Before the opening of the Erie Canal in 1825, the majority of settlers went overland. Some traveled by stagecoach or wagon, others on horseback and some on foot. Morris Birkbeck depicted this overland movement as he journeyed along the National Road through Pennsylvania in 1817.

> We are seldom out of sight as we travel on this grand track, towards the Ohio, of family groups, behind and before us. . . . A small waggon (so light that you might almost carry it, yet strong enough to bear a good load of bedding, utensils and provisions, and a swarm of young citizens,—and to sustain marvellous shocks in its passage over these rocky heights) with two small horses, sometimes a cow or two, comprises their all; excepting a little store of hard-earned cash for the land office of the district; where they may obtain a title for as many acres as they possess half-dollars, being one-fourth of the purchase money. The waggon has a tilt, or cover, made of a sheet, or perhaps a blanket. The family are seen before, behind, or within the vehicle, according to the road or the weather, or perhaps the spirits of the party. . . . A cart and single horse frequently affords the means of transfer, sometimes a horse and a packsaddle. Often the back of the poor pilgrim bears all his effects, and his wife follows, naked-footed, bending under the hopes of the family.

Fortunately for the emigrant, there was more than one route to the western country. Before 1825 the New Englanders either pushed over the Berkshires to Albany and then along the valley of the Mohawk

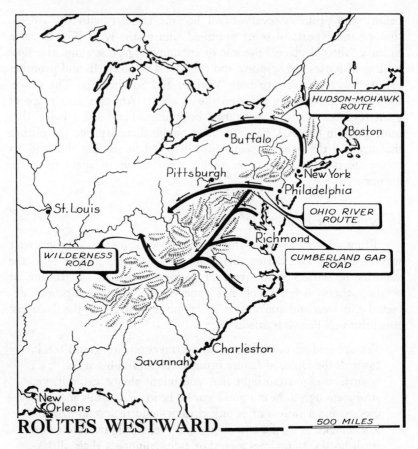

ROUTES WESTWARD _____ 500 MILES

and the Genesee Turnpike to Lake Erie, or crossed the Hudson farther
to the south and moved over the Catskill Turnpike through southern
New York to the upper waters of the Allegheny. From this point,
many floated down to Pittsburgh on lumber rafts. Most of the emigrants from the middle states went west by way of the old Philadelphia-
Lancaster-Pittsburgh road, built by General Forbes during the French
and Indian War. By 1830, the greater portion of these 350 miles of
highway had been turnpiked. The most important route extended
from Baltimore and Washington up the valley of the Potomac to Cumberland and then over the National Road to Wheeling on the Ohio.
This route, following in part Braddock's line of march to the Mononga-
hela, also connected with Pittsburgh; over it passed many Virginians
from the uplands and the Shenandoah Valley to the Ohio country.
Emigrants from southern Virginia and North Carolina generally went
up the Roanoke to the Great Divide, where they either turned to the

northwest or to the southwest and continued through the Cumberland Gap and along the wilderness road into Kentucky or into the valley of the Tennessee. From South Carolina the principal route extended through the Saluda Gap into eastern Tennessee. Two main routes converging at Fort Mitchell stretched from central Georgia into southern Alabama and Mississippi.

Supplementing these overland routes were the numerous natural waterways. Once the settler reached the Ohio or its tributaries, he usually went by water, a journey made easier with the introduction of the steamboat on the rivers of the West after 1811 and the completion of the Erie Canal in 1825. With the exception of Lake Erie, the Great Lakes were little used as emigrant highways before 1840. The first Lake Erie steamer was not built until 1818, and the first steamboat did not reach Chicago until 1832. After the War of 1812, an increasing number of easterners went to the West by way of New Orleans and from there up the Mississippi and its branches by steamer.

Settling in Beyond the Alleghenies

Whatever the route and however diverse their origins, at their destination all settlers had to translate their ambitions into fact. Peaceable Indian relations, title to land, ready money, a system of credit, and an adequate market for agricultural produce were among the more important needs of all pioneers who settled beyond the Alleghenies. Without organized states in the new regions, the settlers lived only under federal law, but if the authorities in Washington failed to provide the kind of help that was desired, the westerners were prepared to take the law in their own hands. The newness and rawness of the country, the distance from settled communities and "law and order," invited self-help, improvisation, and open violence. Although many Europeans romanticized the West as the home of noble savages, the Americans who lived there often thought of it as a land of sin.

However fierce the conflicts among whites, the struggle with the Indians was ceaseless and severe. Between 1815 and 1840, Indian titles in practically all the territory east of the Mississippi were extinguished. For a time the old practice of driving the tribes toward the west prevailed. Finally, in 1825, John C. Calhoun, President Monroe's Secretary of War, worked out a different, if not entirely satisfactory, policy. "One of the greatest evils to which they [the Indians] are subject," he said, "is the incessant pressure of our population which forces them from seat to seat." As a remedy, Calhoun urged that the Indians be given permanent homes in the Great Plains beyond Missouri. His recommendation was accepted, and during the next fifteen years the tribes were transferred to their new home, far west of the frontier.

The removal of the Indians created new problems. In the Northwest in 1832 an attempt by the Sac and Fox tribes, under their chief Black Hawk, to regain ceded land in western Illinois and southwestern Wisconsin led to a frontier war in which the Indians were decisively defeated. In the Southwest, however, the Indians, who were protected by constitutional guarantees, were dislodged only after a strenuous contest. Here the Creeks, Cherokees, Choctaws, and Chickasaws had ceded large tracts of territory between 1814 and 1830, but they still retained control of well over 33,000,000 acres in Georgia, Alabama, Tennessee, and Mississippi. That 50,000 "inferior" people should monopolize such extensive territory seemed preposterous to the land-seeker and to the states in which the Indians resided, particularly Georgia. For forty years Georgians considered the presence of these independent Indian nations within the state's boundaries a menace and an obstacle to progress. They repeatedly urged that the federal government acquire title to these lands so that they could be opened up for settlement.

A treaty, which ceded all Creek lands in Georgia, had been approved by a few Creek chiefs in 1825. It was subsequently repudiated by the majority of the tribe as fraudulent and unrepresentative of the will of the Creek nation. After careful investigation, President John Quincy Adams concluded that the Creeks were right and directed that a new treaty be negotiated. Meanwhile, Georgia, in spite of the threats and remonstrances of the federal government, insisted upon its right to survey the lands ceded under the original treaty. The ensuing controversy, in the course of which Georgia threatened to resist the authority of the national government, was adjusted when in 1826 and 1827 the Creeks signed new treaties extinguishing their claims to their Georgian territory.

The contest between the state of Georgia and the Cherokees resulted in still another defeat for the Indians. By a revision of their tribal constitution in 1827, the Cherokees revealed their determination to remain a sovereign community within the boundaries of Georgia. Late in 1828, the state legislature, without treaty action or consent of the federal government, annexed the Cherokee lands to five adjacent counties. The annexation statute further directed that after June 1, 1830, all laws of the Cherokee nation should be null and void and its citizens subject to the jurisdiction of the state. The tribal leaders protested to Washington, but President Adams took no action.

When Andrew Jackson became President (1829), he at once took steps to settle the difficulty. Through Secretary of War John H. Eaton, the Cherokee representatives were informed that they must either "yield to the operation of those laws which Georgia claims, and has a right to extend throughout her own limits," or else settle beyond the Mississippi. This policy was substantially reiterated by Jackson in his annual messages of 1829, 1830, and 1833. Justice and humanity, he said, required that the southwestern tribes be saved from destruction, a fate that surely awaited them if they remained islands in a white population or if they were sent "from river to river and mountain to mountain." He therefore proposed that they move west of the Mississippi, where ample territory would be set apart for them. If they chose to remain, however, they had to submit to the laws of the state in which they lived.

The Indians refused to accept either of Jackson's alternatives. In *Worcester vs. Georgia* (1832), a test case before the United States Supreme Court, Justice Marshall held that the Cherokees were still a nation within whose territory "the laws of Georgia can have no force, and which the citizens of Georgia have no right to enter but with the assent of the Cherokees themselves, or in conformity with treaties and with the Acts of Congress." But Georgia ignored the ruling of the Court, and Jackson is reported to have said: "John Marshall has made his decision; now let him enforce it." Finally, in 1835 the Cherokees yielded, and the majority moved to the West and joined their fellow tribesmen who were already settling in the territory set apart for them by Congress. From 1827 to 1837, more than a hundred Indian treaties, most of them treaties of cession, were concluded.

No less important to the westerner than the Indian question was the problem of acquiring valid title to his land. Although the Harrison Land Act of 1800 had been designed to meet the needs of all settlers in the region, it clearly benefited those least in need of government assistance. Taking advantage of the measure's deferred payment plan, thousands of bona fide settlers purchased large holdings, expecting to sell part to incoming emigrants at a profit and to keep the remainder for themselves. Speculators bought immense tracts on credit that they in turn disposed of on a credit basis, but in 1817 the government announced that it would accept payment in specie only. By 1820 more than $21,000,000 was due the government for unpaid installments. Even before the Panic of 1819, many settlers and speculators fell behind in their payments, and in desperation they appealed to the government for relief. For a time Congress arranged credit extensions, but in 1821 it passed a general act enabling those who had not completed their payments within the prescribed time to surrender their unpaid-for land and apply any payments already made toward the cost of the land that they retained. The government also remitted all interest arrears on unpaid accounts.

While Congress was engaged in relieving the overburdened land debtor, it proceeded to abolish the credit system. By the Land Act of 1820, the public domain was to be sold in 80-acre tracts, for cash, and at a minimum price of $1.25 per acre. Many eastern businessmen denounced the act. Only higher land values in the West, they maintained, would keep taxes low, check the drain of population westward, and prevent higher wages in the East. Speculators, against whom the change of policy was largely directed, also objected to the new system. The settler, however, was aided by the act, for he was no longer tempted by a credit system to purchase beyond his available capital.

Instead of buying land, many pioneers simply became unauthorized dwellers, or squatters, on government domain, hoping that Congress would at some future time legalize their actions and allow them to pay for their land at the minimum price. In spite of the opposition of eastern congressmen, seventeen such special "pre-emption" acts were passed before 1840. The following year Congress, at the instigation of Thomas Hart Benton, enacted a general Pre-emption Law. By its terms, the head of a family, a man over twenty-one years of age, or a widow had the right to settle on 160 acres and to purchase them subsequently, free from competitive bids, at the minimum government price.

Even if he could make his land claim valid against changing government policy, frontier violence, and knavery, the western pioneer was always confronted by the problem of inadequate currency and credit. He needed money to cover the cost of the trip to the West, to make payments on his land, and to provide for himself and his family until his farm had become self-supporting. The first pioneers used barter or rude mediums of exchange, such as a given weight of furs, grain, or tobacco. As population increased and trade developed with the Spanish at New Orleans, some Spanish silver began to circulate on the frontier. But because of its unfavorable balance of trade with the East, the West was unable to accumulate an adequate supply of hard money. With the outbreak of the War of 1812, trade relations with Europe were interrupted, and the West was forced to depend exclusively upon the East for manufactured goods. What little currency the region did possess was then drained to the East to pay for these products. Western banks, even when honestly run, were forced to suspend specie payments and to issue unsecured paper currency to meet the demand for money.

When peace came in 1815, there was an unprecedented wave of prosperity in the West. In their eagerness for more land, farmers mortgaged their property and bought more manufactured goods. To satisfy the greater demand for ready money, state and private banks multiplied, and the western country was flooded with paper currency unprotected by specie reserves. There was scarcely a western state legislature that did not charter a crop of new banks; by 1818, Kentucky had fifty-nine and Ohio twenty-eight. In Zanesville, Ohio, thirty kinds of paper money were circulating in 1817, not to mention the cheapest paper, the "shinplasters," ranging in face value from $.03 to $2.00, that were issued by city and village authorities, internal improvement and manufacturing companies, merchants, and tavern keepers.

In 1818, the directors of the second Bank of the United States—an institution chartered by the federal government in 1816 and which up to then had neglected to control carefully the specie of the country—issued instructions virtually compelling state banks to redeem their notes in specie or to close their doors. Western bankers, in response, pressed their debtors. Mortgages were foreclosed, produce prices fell, and land values declined. Western farmers and merchants attributed the hard times to the second Bank of the United States. "All the flourishing cities of the West," Thomas Hart Benton said, "are mortgaged to this money power. They may be devoured by it at any moment. They are in the jaws of the monster!" From its inception, the bank had been regarded by those westerners impatient with limits on speculation and on local banks as an undemocratic, monopolistic institution, the creature of the moneyed East. In 1816, by constitutional provision, Indiana attempted to prevent the establishment within its limits of any bank not chartered by the state; two years later Illinois followed this example.

Pacified Indians, clear title to his land, and easy money and credit would still leave the western settler with his greatest problem, an adequate market for his products. The widely scattered western population was more than 95 per cent agricultural. Western "cities," as yet small and few in number, consumed only a small portion of the surplus grain and livestock of the western farm. Before the opening of the Erie Canal and the era of railroading, lack of adequate cheap transportation over the Appalachians made it difficult for the westerner to ship his surplus products to the markets of the eastern seaboard. Although many turnpikes were built before the first quarter of the nineteenth century, most of them were located in the East. In any event, freight charges over the Cumberland Road and other improved eastern highways were prohibitive for bulky and heavy commodities like flour and grain. The maximum price for western wheat before 1825 was about $.75 a bushel, while the cost of transporting it overland from Pittsburgh to Philadelphia was approximately $1.50 a bushel. Even Virginia farmers residing less than a hundred miles from the tidewater complained in 1818 that it took "one bushel of wheat to pay the expense of carrying two to a seaport town." What was true of wheat also applied to corn and other farm produce.

To overcome this handicap, the farmers of western New York and northern Ohio sent their produce by water to Quebec and Montreal. Others, not so fortunately located, turned their crops into whisky or raised livestock, both of which were less expensive to market. Until about 1820, the main highways leading from the West to the East were crowded with droves of cattle and hogs on the way to market from the Ohio Valley. It was estimated that Kentuckians annually drove more than 100,000 hogs to the East, and other thousands to the plantations of Virginia and the Carolinas. From the valley of the Ohio came droves of mules and horses for the southern planter. In the decade from 1820 to 1830, livestock valued at more than $2,000,000 per year passed eastwards through the Saluda and Cumberland Gaps to the Old South.

Because of these limited and costly shipping facilities, the western farmer became an outspoken advocate of internal improvements. Through his spokesmen in and out of Congress, he urged the federal government to tie the West to the East with turnpikes, canals, and railroads. Henry Clay spoke for the westerner when in 1824 he complained that Congress had done "everything on the margin of the ocean but nothing for domestic trade; nothing for the great interior of the country."

Before 1825, the bulk of the surplus products of the West reached the markets of the East and Europe by way of the Mississippi. Down the "father of the waters" and its tributaries floated all kinds of craft loaded with furs, hay, flour, grain, hemp, livestock, tobacco, whisky, and lumber. In 1822, three years before the opening of the Erie Canal, it was estimated that more than $3,000,000 worth of agricultural produce reached New Orleans from the Ohio Valley alone. Even in 1830, after the Erie Canal had been opened, approximately $28,000,000 worth of produce from the Mississippi basin was reshipped from New Orleans to the markets of the East and the Old World.

The Fur Trails of the Far West

For almost forty years after the purchase of Louisiana, the fur trade was the most lucrative business west of the Mississippi. The pioneer farmer could still find an abundance of good land east of the river, and the mineral treasures of the mountains in the distant West were as yet undisclosed. As in other frontier areas, it was the trader and trapper, rather than the official explorer, who first found and established the principal trails over which settlers and commerce subsequently moved. Even Lewis and Clark in their journey up the Missouri sometimes met the descending pirogues of trappers and hunters, loaded with furs, on their way to St. Louis, the center of the fur trade.

Before the close of the first quarter of the nineteenth century, the bulk of the fur trade was controlled by a few powerful companies. As early as 1670, the Hudson's Bay Company had secured a monopoly of the trade of the Hudson Bay region. Following the French and Indian War, the old French trade of the St. Lawrence, Great Lakes, and beyond fell into the hands of a small group of Scottish merchants of Montreal, who in 1783 organized the Northwest Company. A third concern, the Mackinaw Company, operated mainly in what are now the states of Minnesota and Wisconsin.

While a few Americans made small abortive efforts to capture parts of this trade, John Jacob Astor took active steps to obtain control of the entire fur trade of the continent. Born in 1763 of poor parents in the village of Waldorf, near Heidelberg, Germany, Astor worked in his father's butchershop until he was sixteen. Then he ran away to London and four years later came to America. Here he exchanged his small store of merchandise for furs, and returning at once to London, he disposed of them at a profit. With this success he entered the fur business, and by the end of the eighteenth century he had amassed about a quarter of a million dollars and was regarded as America's leading entrepreneur. As soon as Astor realized that the Louisiana territory was rich in furs, he formulated plans for a gigantic commercial undertaking, a monopoly of the fur trade of the entire West. The key to this scheme was the creation of a transcontinental trans-Pacific trade route. A chain of posts, built at strategic points, was to extend from St. Louis to the Pacific, with its western terminus at the mouth of the Columbia. Goods for the Indian trade were to be sent from New York to St. Louis and Mackinaw, or around Cape Horn to the post on the Columbia. Furs collected at the latter point were to be conveyed in Astor's ships to Chinese ports, where they were to be traded for tea, spices, and silks and other textiles that would bring large profits in the New York market. Astor also planned to develop a coastal trade on the Pacific. Posts east of the Rockies were to be supplied from St. Louis and were in turn to send their furs there.

To execute this plan, Astor incorporated the American Fur Company for $1,000,000, with a charter from the state of New York, and the Pacific Fur Company, a $400,000 subsidiary of the American Fur Company. He then organized two expeditions to the Columbia, one by sea and the other by land. The *Tonquin*, a small vessel of some 290 tons, sailed from New York in 1810. After considerable delay, it reached the mouth of the Columbia, and there in 1811 a trading post called Astoria was established. The overland expedition left St. Louis in March, 1811, along the old Lewis and Clark route and arrived at Astoria early in 1812. During the winter of 1812, Astor's men enlarged and improved the post; launched a small schooner, christened the *Dolly* in honor of Astor's wife; and made preparations to open up the rich fur country. In May another ship, the *Beaver*, arrived from New York with clerks and other employees and an ample cargo. For almost two years the Astorians spread their trade over an area bounded by the Continental Divide on the east, the headwaters of the Willamette on the south, and Thompson River (in British Columbia) on the north. When the War of 1812 broke out, the fur trade, which had been one of the chief spoils of the colonial wars, was again an issue. Astor, knowing that the British Northwest Company would try to capture Astoria, asked the American government for protection for the post. In response, the government prepared to send a warship to the mouth of the Columbia, but at the last moment it canceled the order. News of the war between England and America reached Astoria in January, 1813. On October 23, Duncan McDougall, temporarily in charge, sold the post and property to the Northwest Company for a fraction of their value. A week later a British naval vessel arrived, and on December 12 its captain took possession of all the territory and rechristened the post Fort George. Although Great Britain restored the post to the United States after the war, Astor did not renew his enterprise on the Pacific coast.

Forced out of the Oregon country, Astor concentrated his efforts on the trade east of the Rockies. He first prevailed on Congress to pass an act of 1816 by which foreigners were excluded from participating in the fur trade of the United States except in subordinate capacities under American traders. As a result of this act, the Northwest Company was compelled to dispose of its interests in the United States to the American Fur Company. Then, by inducing Congress to abolish the United States agencies in the area for trading with the Indians, Astor was able to eliminate government competition. Finally, in 1822 he established the western department of the American Fur Company, with headquarters in St. Louis. This department supervised all operations on the Missouri and the lower parts of the Mississippi and the Illinois, while a northern department had charge of the region of the Great Lakes and upper Mississippi.

Even within this more restricted area, the American Fur Company met competition. Foremost among its rivals was the Rocky Mountain Fur Company, organized in 1822 by a group of St. Louis traders. The valuable beaver catches and the prosperity of the new organization aroused the interest of Astor's company, which at once sent its agents and traders to compete for the wealth of the territory. Cutthroat competition resulted, but the company with the greater financial resources eventually triumphed, and in 1834 the Rocky Mountain Fur Company dissolved. It is estimated that during its short career it shipped approximately half a million dollars' worth of beaver packs to St. Louis.

The men of the Rocky Mountain Company opened up the country drained by the sources of the Platte, Green, Yellowstone, and Snake rivers; they discovered the Great Salt, Utah, and Sevier lakes; they named the Sweetwater River, Independence Rock, Jackson Hole, and the streams flowing into the Green River and Great Salt Lake; they discovered South Pass and other routes over the mountains. "They were," in the words of H. M. Chittenden, "the first to travel from Great Salt Lake southwestwardly to southern California, the first to cross the Sierras and the deserts of Utah and Nevada between California and the Great Salt Lake, and the first, as far as is known, to travel by land up the Pacific coast from San Francisco to the Columbia." * When the government undertook to explore the Far West, it sought the services of such men as Kit Carson and Jim Bridger, who, like the other members of the Rocky Mountain Company, knew the land and who had blazed new trails to the Pacific.

At the same time that the Astor interests were attempting to destroy the Rocky Mountain Company, they were successfully monopolizing the fur business in the territory between the Great Lakes and the Missouri. Here their principal opponent was the Columbia Fur Company, a young concern composed for the most part of men of French descent. Although this company was capitalized at only $16,000, it was estimated that its competition meant an annual loss of

---

* H. M. Chittenden: *The American Fur Trade of the Far West* (New York: J. P. Harper, 1902), Vol. I, p. 306.

at least $10,000 to the American Fur Company. After considerable negotiation, the Columbia Fur Company was persuaded to unite with the older concern. Lesser rivals in the field were bought off or eliminated by trickery or violence.

By 1830, the American Fur Company thus controlled practically all of the American trade, but large profits in furs were beginning to disappear. Men like Astor realized that the fur yields of $500,000 a year that were typical of the early 1830's could not last forever. The beaver meadows were nearing exhaustion, and on a visit to London in 1834 Astor noted that silk was displacing beaver in the manufacture of hats. A few months later he retired from the fur business; the great company that he had done so much to create survived for several years, but its business steadily declined. Its agents had opened the trails into the trans-Mississippi country for the settlers who were to follow. Their feverish search for pelts from forest and stream was soon matched by the farmers bold attacks on the virgin soil.

The Middle Border Moves Westward

While fur traders opened the lands of the Far West, planters, farmers, ranchers, and miners were pushing the frontier line of settlement beyond the Mississippi. In the territory of Orleans—the name given by Congress in 1804 to that part of the Louisiana Purchase that lay to the south of the thirty-third parallel—planters from the older states added thousands of cleared acres of rich cotton and sugar lands to those already held by French and Spanish settlers. Some of the newcomers also produced wheat, corn, sweet potatoes, and melons and other fruits. By 1810, the territory had more than 76,000 people, and two years later it was admitted into the Union as the state of Louisiana. Although two thirds of the new state was swamp and pine barren, its population more than doubled during the next decade. The minerals of the Missouri region to the north had attracted a considerable number of settlers from the South and elsewhere. In the vicinity of the sources of the Big and St. Francis rivers lay a valuable mineral region 3,000 square miles in area, rich in lead, and containing in addition silver, zinc, iron, black manganese, alum, and saltpeter. By 1820, more than a thousand men were employed in the highly lucrative lead-mining industry. Numerous salt works and new farms and plantations also did profitable business.

The population of the territory increased from 20,000 to more than 60,000 between 1810 and 1818. St. Louis was no longer a frontier post, but became an important commercial center of nearly 4,000 people; smaller towns on either bank of the Missouri were growing rapidly. Ambitious leaders quickly organized a movement for statehood, and in 1818, Congress was asked to divide the territory into two parts, the upper to be admitted as the state of Missouri and the lower to be organized as Arkansas Territory. This petition brought on a national political crisis that resulted in the famous Missouri Compromise, by which Maine was admitted as a free state and Missouri as a slave state.*

Arkansas, to the south of Missouri, remained a frontier region for a longer time. Settlement was retarded by the malarial swamps fringing the west bank of the Mississippi and by the uncertainty of title to the soil, much of which had been taken under Spanish grants that had not yet been passed upon by the government of the United States. According to the census of 1810, Arkansas' population numbered only 1,062. During the next ten years, however, the number of inhabitants multiplied to more than 14,000, an increase of more than 12,000 persons for the decade. New settlers continued to arrive, and between 1830 and 1835 the region's population more than doubled. To the rich alluvial valleys of the White, Washita, Arkansas rivers, and to the bottom lands of the Red River—all well adapted to the cultivation of tobacco, corn, and cotton—came slaveholding planters from the East. A number of small farmers and grazers pushed into the hill country only to be crowded out by the planters. Long hot summers, abundant rainfall, a comparatively inexhaustible soil, and navigable rivers made eastern Arkansas into part of the planting kingdom. From the outset, despite the diversity of the territory, representatives of the planting class dominated the government. Largely through their efforts, the territory was admitted as a slave state in 1836.

East of the Mississippi and far to the north, the broad expanse later included in the states of Michigan and Wisconsin became a part of the Middle Border. Before 1805, when the lower peninsula of Michigan was cut off from Indiana and organized as a separate territory, practically the only white men in Michigan were French-Canadians who occupied the trading post of Detroit and the surrounding country. For a time the hostile attitude of the Indians and the War of 1812 effectually checked all efforts at settlement. By 1818, however, the war was over, and the federal government had concluded the first of a series of treaties wiping out all Indian land titles in the Lower Peninsula. Many easterners—particularly New Englanders and New Yorkers— seized the opportunity to obtain cheap and fertile government land and moved into the territory. By 1819, the population was sufficiently

---

* See below, pages 403–5.

large to enable the territory to send a delegate to Congress. In less than half a dozen years the southern tier of counties was transformed into a miniature New England with its township system and its social and religious institutions. The opening of the Erie Canal in 1825 further stimulated settlement, and when the census of 1830 was taken, important settlements had already been planted in the Saginaw Valley. Indian outbreaks, cholera epidemics, and land speculators of the early 1830's failed to retard the movement into the territory.

Michigan's rapid growth soon led to a movement for statehood. In 1832, the question of forming a state government was submitted to popular referendum and carried by a large majority. Three years later, a state constitution was drafted and approved; but a boundary, dispute with Ohio caused Congress to postpone admission. For two years, Michigan occupied the anomalous position of not being in the Union but of exercising sovereign powers within the limits of federal jurisdiction. After months of dickering, Congress agreed to admit the state if it would accept the region known as the Upper Peninsula in lieu of the territory in dispute with Ohio. Ignorant of the fact that the Upper Peninsula contained rich copper and iron deposits, a convention at Ann Arbor in September, 1836, rejected the proposal. After the delegates had returned home, a small unauthorized group of men convened at Ann Arbor in December, 1836, and voted to accept the terms of Congress. Without examining the credentials of the committee, Congress admitted Michigan on January 26, 1837.

The territory of Wisconsin grew even more rapidly than Michigan. For nearly two centuries, French explorers, missionaries, and trappers were the only white men in the region. During the French and Indian War, Wisconsin *habitants* and *voyageurs* with their Indian allies sacrificed themselves for a losing cause. Even after the Union Jack had been raised over the territory, the Indians, led by Pontiac, struggled to overthrow British dominion. When in 1816 American troops took possession of Wisconsin, the country was still French in form and spirit. The first Americans to migrate to the territory were fur traders, who competed with the British for the control of the fur industry. They were followed by emigrants from Virginia, Kentucky, Tennessee, and Missouri, who were attracted by chances for mining. As early as 1811, it was reported that the Indians in what is now southwestern Wisconsin had "mostly abandoned the chase, except to furnish themselves with meat, and turned their attention to the manufacture of lead." In 1810, the Indians in this region smelted 400,000 pounds of metal, exchanging most of it for goods from American and Canadian traders. Twelve years later, accounts of the richness of the lead mines

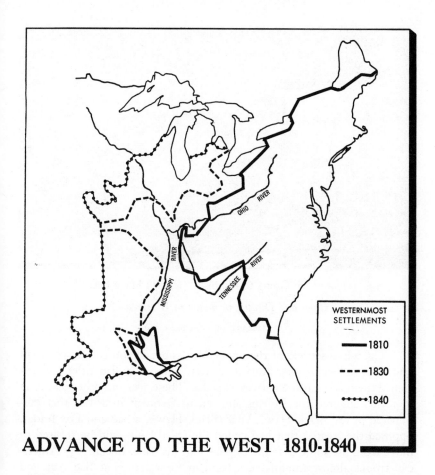

ADVANCE TO THE WEST 1810-1840

WESTERNMOST
SETTLEMENTS

——— 1810

- - - - 1830

•—•—•1840

along the upper Mississippi appeared in St. Louis papers. Men came on
foot, by boat, and on horseback, and by 1827 some easterners and a few
Europeans began to arrive. Soon southwestern Wisconsin had a population of more than 10,000. Despite the fact that most of the miners followed the crude and wasteful methods of the Indians, more than one
million pounds of lead were produced in 1828. Old Indian trails were
converted into highways over which long caravans of ox-hauled ore
wagons carried the product to the nearest river port for shipment to
St. Louis and New Orleans, or to the lake front for shipment to eastern
markets. The industry grew so rapidly that it soon overshadowed the
fur trade, and for a time Wisconsin ranked as one of the leading mining
sections of the country. The rush to the Pacific coast gold fields in
1849, however, coupled with unfavorable tariff legislation and the lack
of adequate transportation facilities, led to its decline.

(*right*) "I'm Going to Illinois!" (*left*) "I Have Been!"

Hopes and Disappointments in Western Life

[LIBRARY OF CONGRESS]

The white settlers of the upper Mississippi region ruthlessly swept aside the Indian miners. Squatters often ignored Indian titles and enriched themselves at the natives' expense. These acts and other irritating incidents angered the Indians and led to frequent disorders that culminated in the Black Hawk War. Black Hawk, a Sac and Fox leader, opposed the treaties that had ceded the tribal lands, and he refused to move from his home near the cemetery of his tribe. But in 1832 American troops almost annihilated a band of his warriors at Bad Axe and made Black Hawk a prisoner. Few patriot leaders of any nation have voiced their sentiments more eloquently than did Black Hawk when he said: "I loved my village, my cornfields, and my people. I fought for them."

The Black Hawk War advertised the broad valleys and the fertile prairies of Wisconsin and extinguished the old impression that it was a "Dismal Swamp." The farmers' sons among the volunteers who fought against the Indians hoped to stake out claims along the war's line of march after the Indians were beaten. In the East, publishers sold thousands of guidebooks and pamphlets purporting to describe the natural attractions of the territory. Emigrants from New England and New York soon moved into the region. Thousands came from the middle states by way of the Ohio, while others came by the Mississippi or overland by prairie schooner. Nearly a decade later, streams of Old

World immigrants began to pour into Wisconsin, especially thousands of discontented Germans. Some had gained a knowledge of the territory through books, pamphlets, and newspaper accounts published in their homeland; others were advised in America to make it their objective. "In New York," wrote a German settler of 1848, "every hotel-keeper and railroad agent, every one who was approached for advice, directed men to Wisconsin." Scandinavians, Dutch, Swiss, Irish, Poles, and Belgians soon followed in the footsteps of the Germans. By 1848, when the territory came into the Union as a state, it had a population of well over 200,000. Even before admission, its leading towns were commercial centers; every community had its school and church, and a bill establishing the University of Wisconsin was passed by the first territorial legislature in 1836.

Southwest of Wisconsin were the rolling, grass-covered prairies of Iowa, a region of unusual fertility interspersed with wooded areas. Only a handful of whites had settled in the territory when the Black Hawk War occurred. But in 1832 the so-called Black Hawk purchase by the government of almost six million acres lying west of the Mississippi and north of the Des Moines stimulated the entry into that region of thousands of settlers who had impatiently waited for the removal of the Indians. Canal boats, lake and river steamers, and long lines of prairie schooners bore New Englanders, New Yorkers, and Ohioans to the trans-Mississippi country. The vanguard rushed for the lead-mining district about Dubuque, but the later arrivals soon discovered that the rich alluvial soil of the prairies offered its own rewards.

Four years after the Black Hawk purchase, the population of Iowa numbered more than 10,000. In 1838, when the population was nearly 23,000, a territorial government was organized, and by 1840 more than 43,000 persons had settled in the territory. When the territory became a state in 1846, many towns were prosperous centers. Iowa City, a hundred miles west of the Mississippi, had seven general stores, twelve lawyers, and two weekly newspapers, and was the seat of the recently founded state university, Iowa City College, and a "female academy." Of all the Middle Border communities, perhaps none was more characteristic of New England than Iowa, for its institutions closely resembled those of the older seaboard society with which the majority of its pioneers were acquainted.

The only other state in the Middle Border to enter the Union before the Civil War was Minnesota. Home of the Chippewa and the Sioux, Minnesota remained a wilderness throughout most of the prewar period. Like other sections of the Great Lakes country, it had been explored by French traders and missionaries, but aside from a few

French posts, there were no settlements in the region until the nineteenth century. Both the Northwest Company and the American Fur Company had agents in Minnesota, but neither company was primarily interested in making permanent settlements. As late as 1837, when the native tribes ceded the large strip of territory between the St. Croix and the Mississippi, the number of whites and half-breeds living apart from the Indians was probably not more than 500 or 600, and it was not until the early 1850's that settlers—most of whom were drawn from the Middle Atlantic states—entered the region in appreciable numbers. Organized as a territory in 1849, Minnesota became a member of the Union in 1857.

The Frontier as a Civilization

Like other western states, Minnesota was first opened by the hunter and trapper who then gave way to the farmer and townsman. The settler had to face the Indian problem, conflicts over land policy, and the need for cheap routes to markets. In all these respects, the "frontier experience" of Minnesotans was close to that of settlers elsewhere. Whether there was a common frontier life and influence beyond this in all the new areas is understandably a question of great importance in American history. All Americans believe that the frontier has had deep effects on our national development, but it has been very difficult for historians to agree about what those effects have been.

The general problem of the frontier in American history was given wide scholarly consideration after 1893, when Frederick Jackson Turner addressed the annual meeting of the American Historical Association on "The Significance of the Frontier in American History." Turner believed that the "existence of an area of free land, its continuous recession, and the advance of American settlement westward explain American development." He argued that the source of the distinctive features of American life was the West. There the former easterner or immigrant settler was so changed by his environment as to become the real American, uniquely individualistic, opportunistic, nationalistic, and democratic. The frontier, with its free land and invitation to "try again," also worked as a "safety valve" by providing an escape for easterners in hard times. It weakened America's ties with Europe, created a distinctive American nationality, spawned American democracy, furthered the territorial expansion of the United States, and served as the seedbed of American radicalism.

The wide scope of the Turner thesis is both its most appealing feature and its most serious defect. Turner seldom backed up his general statements with an adequate array of facts, and he frequently neglected to define key words. He never made exactly clear what he meant by "frontier," and his failure to specify to which of the numerous American frontiers he was referring often weakened his analysis. In claiming the frontier as the source of democracy, he could hardly have been alluding to the southern frontier's devotion to the slave system, or to the cliques and rings of greedy men who early took control of the politics of most new states, The word "democracy" at times seemed to mean little more to Turner than a kind of devil-take-the-hindmost squatter sovereignty. Turner also consistently overlooked the numerous democratic advances that originated in the East and the important European contributions to the American democratic tradition. Many of the major reforms of the pre-Civil War period were first espoused by easterners who in turn were intellectually indebted to the experiences of men in various European countries. In an analysis of the growth of Americanism, furthermore, how could the occupant of an isolated shack in Ohio in 1800 be said to be more American than a Rhode Island farmer or a Philadelphia mechanic in the same year?

Turner was probably weakest in analyzing the frontier origins of American individualism. It undoubtedly required individualism of a high order to establish a home in the wilderness, but in many respects it was equally individualistic for an easterner—or an Englishman, for that matter—to risk his wealth on a new business enterprise, to espouse an unpopular reform, or to invent and apply a labor-saving device. Americans, East and West, were individualistic—a fact that can probably best be explained by the nation's expanding economy on the land as well as in the towns. Individualism also implied for Turner an admirable impatience with the status quo and the desire to take risks for oneself, but, great as its achievements were, such individualism did set man against man in a ruthless battle for prestige and success and caused a ceaseless mauling of our rich natural resources. Practically, this individualism released enormous energy, but with it came also the violence, vendetta, and viciousness of the frontier that writers such as Mark Twain have recorded in books like *Huckleberry Finn* and that are the constant themes of the "Western" movie.

Turner's hypothesis of frontier individualism, whether moral or immoral, conflicted with his theory that the westerners strengthened the power of the central government by their insistent—and often successful—demands for cheap land, improved transportation facilities, elimination of the Indians, and favorable currency policies. If the westerners came to Washington with their most pressing problems—as they did—it seems reasonable to conclude that they were individualists only when it suited their convenience. In this respect, they were not unlike eastern manufacturers lobbying for higher tariffs or eastern shippers seeking subsidies for the American merchant marine.

Turner's theories about the influence of the frontier upon expansion, cultural isolation, and discontent in the East have been modified, but not disproved, by subsequent historical research. Abundant evidence exists of the westerner's desire for continental expansion and of his ability to create incidents that helped to make expansion a possibility.* There is also little doubt that the farther a pioneer lived from the seaboard, the less was his cultural dependence on Europe. Before the development of a national network of railroads, inadequate transportation often weakened, if it did not entirely eliminate, Europe's influence on the daily life and thoughts of the frontiersman. Paradoxically, however, as the flow of western products increased, the westerners' dependence on overseas markets to take their surpluses likewise increased.

The theory that the frontier was a safety valve for discontent in the East has undergone frequent revisions ince 1893. Some of Turner's earlier students argued that the free land of the West drew off underprivileged urban workers, but further research has demonstrated that the city poor were prevented from moving West by the cost of the trip and that most emigrants were farmers. Most of these, moreover, paid for their land, for the available free land was too poor, or too far from road, stream, or railroad to attract a man seeking a fresh start. It has been suggested, however, that those farmers who went West might otherwise have gone to the city to increase economic pressures there; to this extent, the frontier was of real importance as a safety valve.

Perhaps the most serious deficiency of Turner's analysis was his failure to emphasize the numerous ways in which the West resembled the East. Interested only in contrasts, he ignored the many things that the two sections had in common. The southern frontier corresponded to the Old South in many ways, and the institutions of many communities in the Great Lakes region closely resembled those of the New England towns from which most of their settlers had been drawn. Analysis of the first constitutions of western states shows them to imitate in major characteristics the constitutions of the areas from which the settlers came. A study of western magazines also gives the impression that the new settlers often wished to emulate the eastern culture they had recently left.

---

* It would probably be impossible to prove any connection between the existence of the frontier and overseas expansion, although many historians have seen a relationship between the passing of the frontier and the overseas imperialism of the 1890's.

Toward a Western Culture

In the number and excellence of its schools the West matched the East in aspiration but not in accomplishment. The western commonwealths had ideals of statewide democratic education. Ohio's first constitution in 1802 forbade the passage of any law depriving citizens of equal rights in any educational institution endowed in whole or in part by funds derived from government land grants, and Indiana's first constitution required the legislature to provide for "a general system of education, ascending in a regular gradation from township schools to a state university, where tuition shall be gratis and equally open to all."

Shortage of funds made it impossible for frontier communities to provide educational opportunities equal to those of the East so that in the early years of frontier life, eastern education was probably more attractive. As early as 1825, however, the West did have numerous academies, seminaries, colleges, and embryonic universities. In fact, of the sixty-odd institutions of higher learning in the entire country in 1830, twenty-eight were west of the Alleghenies, and they had a total student enrollment of approximately 1,400. Many of these were started by religious denominations, and nearly all were handicapped by lack of money and proper equipment. Transylvania University at Lexington, Kentucky, was exceptionally influential in shaping the culture of the frontier. It was founded as a seminary in 1783 and became nominally a university in 1798–9. By 1828, after slow growth, the university had a college of liberal arts and schools of law and medicine, a student body of more than 400, and a staff that included some of the most eminent teachers and scholars of America. Miami University at Oxford, Ohio, was probably the second most influential institution of higher learning west of the Alleghenies before 1840. Despite the location of these schools in the West, however, it would be difficult to say in what way their curricula were distinctively different from or superior to those of eastern schools and academies.

The West slowly attempted to create and spread a distinctive popular culture. An increasing number of western printers turned out periodicals and magazines, books, and newspapers. Western novelists like James Hall and Timothy Flint recorded and dramatized the problems and possibilities of the early western settlements. Despite the calls of leading citizens for a real western culture, study of the "western mind" before 1850 shows little intellectual distinction or originality in most places and shadows of the East in the rest.

Of all the influences shaping the moral and intellectual outlook of the westerners, none was more important than religion. Living as they

Perils of Western Life: The Wolf Attack

did in crude circumstances, cut off from the richness and diversity of
an established culture, anxious for something "spiritual" to lift them out
of the drab dullness or sordid dangers of their life, the western settlers
found the circuit preacher and camp meeting welcome relief or release
from loneliness and isolation. Long before the voice of the political
spellbinder was heard beyond the mountains, pioneer preachers had
penetrated into the wilderness. In rude log churches or at camp meetings, they moved souls by their warnings of the eternal damnation and
everlasting hell fire that awaited the ungodly. Travelers journeying to
the West during the first quarter of the nineteenth century were impressed with the number of religious sects with which they came in
contact. Timothy Flint, for example, observed in 1814 that "a circulating phalanx of Methodists, Baptists, and Cumberland Presbyterians, of Atlantic missionaries, and of young élèves of the Catholic theological seminaries, from the redundant mass of unoccupied ministers,
both in the Protestant and Catholic countries, pervades this great
valley."

   Given the simple life and humble beginnings of most settlers and
the distances between farms and settlements, it was appropriate that an
uncomplicated "faith of the heart," direct and quick in its appeal, and
without elaborate organization or strong ministerial control, should

appeal most to frontier people. Although there were numerous varieties of Protestant sects, the Methodists, Baptists, Disciples of Christ, and Presbyterians were the most active religious groups. Conducted either by an itinerant circuit riding "minister" or in crude church buildings, the services were overwhelmingly "enthusiastic." The minister prayed and exhorted his listeners to come to Christ. Folk hymns and public confession also played important roles in converting hardened or ignorant hearts to the Word of God. Dating back to the days of the Great Awakening and earlier, this form of religious life continued to be an immense influence in rural life in the West and East even after "fancier" churches and more sober services appeared with the passing of frontier conditions.

Evangelical Protestantism gave color and tone to the American West that are difficult for today's citizen to appreciate. It sharpened the sense of individual responsibility and fostered a strong sense of evil at work in the world. Given the temptations of frontier life, it was a helpful strengthener of conscience. Setting a premium on the folk virtues of simplicity of character and directness of person, it tended to reinforce many of the qualities of an individualistic and egalitarian society. Unfortunately, at times it also nurtured that hostility to "book learning" and intellectual discipline to which Americans have been unusually susceptible. It tended to make moral choice too simply black and white, and it created the illusion that goodness of heart and folk nostrums could put right all the world's problems. The evangelical faiths contributed to rural America's failure to understand or to cope successfully with a modern world that resisted responding to preachers' panaceas against the "Devil's plots" or temptations.

During the nineteenth century, the rural East and frontier West were closer to each other in religious life and general outlook than either was to the more cosmopolitan centers of Boston, New York, or Charleston. Even in these coast cities, very few citizens had access to the higher goods of the spirit. Of course, as new areas were settled, real regional differences between East and West emerged, and it would be foolish to maintain that there was no difference between the frontier and the seaboard. One was an essentially primitive society, whereas the other was relatively civilized. Still, with passing years, the West increasingly resembled the East. Every part of the United States was at one time in its history a frontier, and there seems little ground for assuming that this experience left a deeper impression on the West.

The most important effects of the West upon the course of American history were economic, political, and psychological. A vast region of farms and plantations, the West provided industry with raw materials, gave businessmen a larger market for their manufactured goods and surplus capital, increased the amount of American exports, and stimulated the construction of new transportation facilities. The addition of western states to the Union also upset old sectional balances and was responsible for the emergence of new political alliances. Whether it was different from the East or not, the frontier nourished belief in new beginnings. It helped enlarge the endless American search for success, which the size and richness of the continent had always promised but seldom gave completely or unambiguously to any man.

FOR SUPPLEMENTARY READING

The famous "Turner thesis" about the influence of the frontier can be found in F. J. Turner, *The Frontier in American History* (1920), and in R. A. Billington (ed.), *Frontier and Section* (1961) (Pb), a selection of Turner essays. The literature on Turner's ideas is very large, but a start can be made in George R. Taylor's pamphlet, *The Turner Thesis* (1949). Another of Turner's works, *The Rise of the New West* (1906), is a general history of this period. On the history of the former Northwest territory, start with A. H. Kohlmeier, *The Old Northwest* (1938); T. D. Clark, *Frontier America* (1959); and R. A. Billington, *The Far Western Frontier 1830–1860* (1956). The southern frontier is the subject of E. Dick, *The Dixie Frontier* (1948).

On land policy and problems use R. M. Robbins, *Our Landed Heritage* (1942). On the fur trade the most informed, if sprawling, study is H. M. Chittenden, *The American Fur Trade of the Far West* (3 vols., 1902).

For American expansion during the period, the best work is S. F. Bemis, *John Quincy Adams and the Foundations of American Foreign Policy* (1949). On the Missouri Compromise use G. Moore, *The Missouri Controversy, 1819–1821* (1953). The early chapters of W. H. Goetzman, *Exploration and Empire* (1965), have special appeal.

Two newer approaches to the frontier influence in America are M. E. Curti, *The Making of an American Community* (1959), and R. C. Wade, *The Urban Frontier . . . 1790–1830* (1959).

13

An Era of Mixed Feelings

THE HISTORY of the United States from the end of the War of 1812 to Andrew Jackson's election to the presidency in 1828 provides a study in contrasts. For a brief period after the war, a spirit of unity and nationalism seemed to have carried the day, but its triumph was more apparent than real. By the 1820's, divisive interests were everywhere in the ascendancy and were largely responsible for the destruction of the Federalist and Republican parties and the emergence of new political organizations that more accurately reflected the temper of the times.

Clearing Accounts with Europe

The years after the War of 1812 provided the United States with the opportunity to settle most of its outstanding disputes with the nations of the Old World. Europe needed time to recover from more than two decades of revolution and war, and its people had no desire to embark on new adventures in America. Within a short time, American diplomats had succeeded in settling their differences with the British on the Canadian-American border, in forcing Spain to relinquish control over East Florida, and in formulating a doctrine that warned Europe against attempting to interfere in the affairs of the Western hemisphere. While Europe was at war, American foreign policy had been forced to conform to the pattern of European power politics. After the War of 1812, the United States was able to pursue a course that was conditioned more by events in America than by developments abroad.

In the period that immediately followed the Treaty of Ghent, the United States and Great Britain were able to resolve a number of potentially dangerous diplomatic disputes to the satisfaction of both nations. When the war ended, each country had naval forces on the Great Lakes, and there was always the possibility that an incident between the two fleets might lead to a major conflict. To prevent a future battle, both countries in 1817 accepted the Rush-Bagot Agreement, which provided for the demilitarization of the Great Lakes. The Rush-Bagot Agreement was followed by the Convention of 1818, which settled the old fisheries and boundary questions. American fishing rights in Canadian waters were restricted, but not altogether prohibited. At the same time, the northern boundary of the Louisiana Purchase was fixed to run along the forty-ninth parallel from the Lake of the Woods to the Rocky Mountains. The Oregon country, to which both nations laid claim, was placed under joint occupation for a ten-year period.

While American diplomats were successfully concluding their negotiations with the British, expansionists were demanding that the United States take advantage of Spain's misfortunes in both the New and Old Worlds by seizing East Florida. Between 1814 and 1819, there were renewed American complaints about Indian raids, smuggling, and the escape of Negro slaves. Spain, rocked by disturbances at home and open rebellion in South America, was unable to control the inhabitants of Florida. Matters came to a head late in 1817. As a result of fresh Indian raids, a punitive expedition under General Andrew Jackson entered Florida. Jackson captured St. Marks and Pensacola; hanged Alexander Arbuthnot and Robert Ambrister, two British subjects who were charged with complicity in the Indian attacks, and virtually established American sovereignty over the entire northern part of the Spanish province.

Jackson's invasion of Florida threatened to disrupt the United States' relations with both Great Britain and Spain. The British, however, withdrew their protests after it had been made clear that Arbuthnot and Ambrister had been engaged in illegal activities in Florida; but the dispute with Spain was not settled until 1819. Jackson returned in triumph to Tennessee, and in every section Americans greeted the news of his exploits with unrestrained enthusiasm. But Jackson had many enemies in the Monroe administration, and for some time it seemed likely that the government would disavow him. Congress rejected resolutions condemning Jackson only after a long debate. Every member of Monroe's cabinet except Secretary of State John Quincy

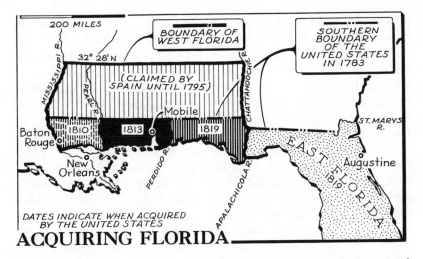

ACQUIRING FLORIDA

Within the map:

200 MILES

BOUNDARY OF WEST FLORIDA

SOUTHERN BOUNDARY OF THE UNITED STATES IN 1783

32° 28' N

(CLAIMED BY SPAIN UNTIL 1795)

MISSISSIPPI R.

PEARL R.

CHATTAHOOCHIE R.

Mobile

Baton Rouge

1810

1813

1819

ST. MARY'S R.

New Orleans

EAST FLORIDA 1819

Augustine

PERDIDO R.

APALACHICOLA R.

DATES INDICATE WHEN ACQUIRED BY THE UNITED STATES

Adams favored the payment of reparations to Spain, and Secretary of War John C. Calhoun thought that Jackson should be censured for insubordination. But Adams, who was probably supported in his stand by an overwhelming majority of the American people, eventually won over his colleagues. The United States refused either to indemnify Spain or to apologize for Jackson's foray. Instead, Adams assumed the diplomatic offensive. In a note that condemned Spain for its inability to maintain law and order in Florida, he demanded that Spain punish the Spanish officials in Florida and pay the United States the costs of Jackson's expedition. Adams's note was a thinly disguised ultimatum, warning the Spanish that if they did not give up Florida, the United States would take it from them. With more than enough troubles both at home and in Latin America, the Spanish government had no alternative but to yield.

After some delay, Spain accepted the inevitable. In 1819, the Spanish minister at Washington signed a treaty ceding the Floridas to the United States in exchange for $5,000,000, the sum due American citizens for damages to their commerce by Spanish authorities during the Napoleonic wars. The two powers also agreed to a western boundary for the Louisiana Purchase, a line extending from the mouth of the Sabine River toward the northwest and eventually due west to the Pacific.

Monroe's Famous Doctrine

The danger of conflict with Spain had helped clarify the need for a general American position on the role of the Old World states in the politics of the Western hemisphere. President James Monroe in his annual message to Congress on December 2, 1823 set forth a sweeping statement of future policy. Known as the Monroe Doctrine, the message on foreign policy consisted of two separate passages in the presidential message. In one part of his address, Monroe expressed his opposition to further European colonization in the New World; in the other, he took a stand against interference of the major powers of Europe in the recently established Latin American republics.

The passage opposing colonization was directed primarily against Russia, which at the time claimed the northwestern American coast north of the fifty-first parallel. In 1821, the Tsar had issued a ukase forbidding foreign vessels from coming within a hundred miles of Russian America. He had thus both claimed authority over the high seas and revealed that Russia was intent on extending its territorial holdings in North America. Although most Americans at that time had little or no interest in the Pacific Northwest, Secretary of State John Quincy Adams, a confirmed nationalist, was not prepared to stand by while Russia threatened what he considered American interests and rights. Adams protested to the Russian minister in Washington. "I told him [Adams later wrote] . . . that we should contest the right of Russia to *any* territorial establishment on this continent, and that we should assume . . . the principle that the American continents are no longer subjects for *any* new European colonial establishments." In his annual message of 1823, Monroe merely rephrased Adams's remarks when he said: "The occasion has been judged proper for asserting that the American continents, by the free and independent condition which they have assumed and maintained, are henceforth not to be considered as subjects for future colonization by any European powers."

Although this passage in the Monroe Doctrine was to play a significant role in the subsequent history of the United States, it had no appreciable effect on Russian-American relations in the 1820's. In the negotiations between the United States and Russia in 1824, Russia agreed to fix its southern boundary in North America at 50°40'. The Russian decision to withdraw above the fifty-first parallel was not due to the warning of the American President. Harassed by domestic troubles and owning enough territory in Europe, Asia, and North America to take care of all its needs in the foreseeable future, the Tsar's government saw no reason for antagonizing the United States in the Pacific Northwest. The policies of other nations were also not affected by Monroe's statement at the time. Without exception, the European powers either ignored it or indicated that they would not abide by it if their interests

James Monroe

otherwise dictated. The European response to Monroe's pronouncement on non-colonization was summed up by a French newspaper that wrote:

> Mr. Monroe, who is not a sovereign, has assumed in his message the tone of a powerful monarch, whose armies and fleets are ready to march at the first signal . . . He has prescribed to the potentates of Europe, the conduct which they will observe under certain circumstances, if they do not wish to incur their own disgrace . . . Mr. Monroe is the temporary President of a Republic situated on the east coast of North America. This republic is bounded on the south by the possessions of the King of Spain and on the North by those of the King of England . . . By what right then would the two Americas be under its immediate sway from Hudson's Bay to Cape Horn?

The second section of the Monroe Doctrine, dealing with the possibility of European intervention in established American governments, grew out of the United States' fear that the nations of the Old World were planning to restore to Spain her former American colonies. Following Napoleon's downfall, Austria, Prussia, Russia, and France had formed a series of alliances that were designed to prevent revolution and to insure the preservation of the status quo. In 1821, Austrian troops suppressed uprisings in Italy; two years later, French troops restored Ferdinand to the throne of Spain; and there were repeated reports that the powers would soon dispatch an expeditionary force to Spanish America to reconquer Spain's lost provinces. Of the European nations, only Great Britain opposed the policies of the Quadruple and Holy Alliance. Now that the leading nations of the Continent were allied, it was impossible for England to pursue her traditional balance-of-power policy; furthermore, if Spain regained her New World territories, English merchants and manufacturers would lose the profitable trade that they had already built up with the new Latin American republics. The plans of the Holy Alliance appeared particularly menacing to the United States. The return of Catholic and autocratic Spain to the Western hemisphere was viewed as a threat to American democracy and to the territorial integrity of the United States.

In August, 1823, George Canning, the British Foreign Secretary, suggested to Richard Rush, the American minister in London, that Great Britain and the United States act jointly to prevent intervention by the Holy Alliance in Latin America. When Rush relayed this proposal to his government in Washington, Monroe enthusiastically endorsed it. Only Secretary of State Adams opposed the British plan. Sensing that there was no actual danger of European intervention in the New World, Adams thought that the United States should pursue an independent policy. He realized that the British fleet would prevent the reconquest of Spanish America, so there was no reason why the United States should not make a unilateral statement. The United States could then take all the credit, while the British navy in any case, could be counted upon to do whatever work was needed to uphold the American position. Convinced by the force of Adams's logic, Monroe, in his annual message, warned the Holy Alliance to stay out of Latin America. He called the extension of the different political systems of Europe to America a danger to "our peace and safety." While declaring no intention of interfering with existing colonies in the New World, Monroe practically guaranteed the independence of freed states in the Western hemisphere from European intervention. As for American interests in Europe, in prophetic words, the President added: "Our policy in regard to Europe, which was adopted at an early stage of the wars which have so long agitated that quarter of the globe, nevertheless remains the same, which is not to interfere in the internal concerns of any of its powers . . ."

Although the members of the Holy Alliance did not subsequently intervene in Latin America, their decision cannot be attributed to Monroe's announcement, but to their weakened condition following the Napoleonic wars and—as Adams suspected—to the power of the British fleet. Nevertheless, the Monroe Doctrine symbolized an important change in America's relationship with the Old World. Washington, John Adams, and Jefferson had voiced similar sentiments long before 1823, but it was Monroe who had been able to make them an accepted formal part of American policy. For almost a century after Monroe's declaration, the United States was to concentrate on domestic and New World events and largely ignore developments in Europe. Although the Monroe Doctrine did not cause this change in policy, it made it formal and gave it the aura of being a first principle. If the War of 1812 was the second War of Independence, the Monroe Doctrine was a second Declaration of Independence.

Strong Union, Safe Contracts, and John Marshall

The vigorous foreign policy pursued by John Quincy Adams and James Monroe during Monroe's two terms as President had a parallel in domestic affairs in Chief Justice John Marshall's numerous decisions emphasizing the supremacy of the nation over the states. Born on the frontier, partly self-educated, Marshall's early life resembled Thomas Jefferson's. But there was little other resemblance between the two men. After serving as a soldier during the Revolution—taking part in the siege of Norfolk and four major battles—Marshall opened a law practice in Richmond, Virginia, and became a member of the state legislature. Appalled by the weakness of both the Continental Congress and the Congress of the Confederation, he became an outspoken and enthusiastic Federalist, working for the ratification of the Constitution and voting with his fellow Federalists as a member of Congress. He was later one of the three American commissioners who conferred with the XYZ delegates in France, and in 1800 was appointed Secretary of State by John Adams. In February, 1801, he became Chief Justice of the Supreme Court, a position that he held until his death in 1835. Long after the Federalist party had disappeared, Marshall continued to hand down decisions that Alexander Hamilton would have favored. He proved as determined in his opposition to Andrew Jackson in the 1830's as he had to Thomas Jefferson thirty years earlier.

John Marshall contributed more to American constitutional development than any other jurist. A forceful man with a domineering personality, he was able to influence the views of a majority of his colleagues on the Court throughout his entire term as Chief Justice.

Taking a broad view of the Constitution, he made it a flexible instrument of truly national government. By establishing the precedent for judicial review in *Marbury vs. Madison* and by upholding the rights of the Court, Marshall almost singlehandedly made the Supreme Court a major branch of the government. His rulings constantly reflected his beliefs that the United States was a nation rather than a mere collection of states, that the federal government had certain clearly defined powers that could neither be impaired nor abrogated, and that the property rights of the individual must be upheld against breach of contract. He had learned his economics from the founders of the Federalist party, and his rulings indicate that he was an exceptionally able student.

Marshall's decisions all have an air of finality that reveal both the strength of his convictions and his deep-seated belief that he fully understood the intentions of the authors of the Constitution. Once he had made up his mind about any question, he was able to substantiate his conclusions with an argument in which each point seemed to lead logically—and even inevitably—to the next. His opponents were shown to have based their arguments on false hypotheses. Marshall constantly searched for the general principle involved in a case rather than for particulars that might require a pragmatic judgment. His logic, in an age given to the rule of generalities, seemed impeccable. John Randolph's despairing cry over one of Marshall's decisions was: "All wrong, all wrong, but no man in the United States can tell why or wherein."

Marshall made what is generally considered his most brilliant exposition of his theories on the nature of the Constitution and the supremacy of the national government in *McCulloch vs. Maryland* (1819). In response to the pleas of local business groups irritated by the power of the second Bank of the United States to restrict currency and credit and to set the pace of the banking business, the state of Maryland had taxed the notes of a branch of the Bank at Baltimore. Maryland based part of its case on the doctrine that the Constitution was "an act of sovereign and independent states," and that what was obnoxious to the states was illegal. But to Marshall nothing was further from the truth. "The government of the Union . . . ," he said in his decision, "is emphatically . . . a government of the people. In form and substance it emanates from them. Its powers are granted by them, and are to be exercised on them, and for their benefit." The people had "in express terms decided" that the "Constitution and the laws of the United States which shall be made in pursuance thereof . . . shall be the supreme Law of the Land." Under the "necessary and proper" clause of the Constitution, Congress had the right to establish a bank to fulfill its explicit powers over currency and commerce. Marshall declared: "We admit, as all must admit, that the powers of the government are limited, and that its limits are not to be transcended. But . . . let the end be legitimate, let it be within the scope of the Constitution, and all means which are appropriate, which are plainly adapted to that end, which are not prohibited, but consist[ent] with the letter and spirit of the Constitution are constitutional. . . ."

Having established the right of the federal government to create a bank, Marshall then turned to the question of the constitutionality of the Maryland tax. After pointing out that "the power to tax involves the power to destroy" and that "the power to destroy may defeat and render useless the power to create," Marshall concluded: "The States have no power, by taxation or otherwise, to retard, impede, burden, or in any manner control, the operations of the constitutional laws enacted by Congress to carry into execution the powers vested in the general government. This is, we think, the unavoidable consequence of that supremacy which the Constitution has declared."

Marshall's decision caused an uproar. Smaller bankers and their allies were temporarily frustrated in attempts to destroy the national bank. To men like John Taylor of Caroline and George Mason of Virginia, Marshall's words seemed to mark the final undoing of the Constitution of 1787. They claimed that Marshall had altered the intentions of the fathers of the Constitution. In effect, he gave the federal government the power to withdraw from state jurisdiction any subject in any field in which powers were shared. Since Congress had created a bank under, in part, its taxing powers, no individual state could use its tax power to restrict the national purpose. The Constitution had become the supreme law of the land at the expense, it was feared, of local liberty and individual rights.

Marshall's decision in *McCulloch vs. Maryland* contains his most comprehensive statement on the supremacy of the federal government but he emphasized the same point in a number of other rulings. In *Cohens vs. Virginia* (1821), a case that concerned the attempt of Virginia to prevent the sale of tickets for a lottery established by Congress, the Chief Justice again made clear that under the Constitution the United States was far more than a federation of states. In Marshall's words: "The constitution and laws of a State, so far as they are repugnant to the Constitution and laws of the United States, are absolutely void. The States are constituent parts of the United States. They are members of one great empire—for some purposes sovereign, for some purposes subordinate." Four years later, in *Gibbons vs. Ogden* Marshall's broad interpretation of the Constitution's commerce clause supplemented the decision in *McCulloch vs. Maryland* and measurably strengthened

John Marshall

[BOSTON ATHENAEUM]

the power of the federal government over the states. The case dealt with a New York state grant to a syndicate of a steamship monopoly on New York waters, including trade on the Hudson between New York and New Jersey. Even though the grant was a contract between New York and private individuals, Marshall declared the monopoly illegal on the ground that Congress's "power over commerce with foreign nations and among the several states" was "complete in itself."

The bank case had given the federal government supremacy in conflicts over shared powers. *Gibbons vs. Ogden* withdrew completely from the states power over any subject, like commerce or trade, with which, by its nature, Congress alone was fit to deal. Marshall's decision meant that no local law or rule could stand in the way of Congress on a matter of national interest and that the powers of the national government had to match the size of the economy.

Like the power of judicial review invoked in *Marbury vs. Madison*, the national power to block state laws announced in these famous decisions would not be really felt until after the Civil War. Marshall had, nevertheless, paved the way for a full use of national power. Future generations could call on the Court either to undo state attempts to regulate business practices, or to uphold federal regulation of commerce whose scope had grown beyond the power of the states.

Marshall's work on behalf of federal supremacy was supplemented by the work of Joseph Story, a Supreme Court Justice from 1811 to 1845, who shared Marshall's nationalist views. Story handed down two decisions on the supremacy of the federal government that deserve to rank with those of Marshall. In *Martin vs. Hunter's Lessee* (1816), Story affirmed the Court's authority to reverse state court decisions in cases that involved rights guaranteed by the Constitution. In *Martin vs. Mott* (1827), Story ruled that a state had to transfer its authority over its militia to the national government when it was ordered to do so by the President.

Marshall was as anxious to safeguard the property rights of individuals as he was to prevent the states from assuming the powers of the federal government. In *Fletcher vs. Peck* (1810) and *Dartmouth College vs. Woodward* (1819), Marshall upheld the sanctity of contract by refusing to permit states to withdraw grants that had been made to groups of individuals. In *Fletcher vs. Peck*, the issue before the Court was Georgia's repeal of its land grant to the Yazoo companies. Despite the corruption that attended the grant and despite the fact that Georgia's claim to the lands in question was at best tenuous, Marshall ruled that the repeal by the Georgia legislature of its original grant to the companies was contrary either to the "general principles which are common to our free institutions" or to the "particular provisions of the Constitution of the United States." In the Dartmouth College case, which involved New Hampshire's rescinding a charter that had been granted to the college before the Revolution by the royal government, Marshall declared that the state had exceeded its authority, for the Constitution provides that the "Legislature of a State shall pass no act 'impairing the obligation of contracts.' "

John Marshall remained a defender of national power until the day he died. His decisions on the sanctity of contracts revealed the Federalist disposition to place property rights above the power of legislatures or of the popular will. Safely removed from the daily struggles of party politics, Marshall was safe on the Court and continued to uphold the Federalist concept of the Union long after the death of the party and most of its members. His great contribution to his and our times was his insistence that the Constitution was a product of the people rather than of the states: that the powers of the federal government were clearly superior to those of the states and that they must grow in accord with national needs.

Rough-and-Tumble Politics

In 1815, American political life was still largely under the influence of John Marshall's contemporaries, the generation of impressive men who had freed the republic from England and had governed it since the first days of independence. Within a generation after the Treaty of Ghent, the last of these men died. A new excitement swept through American politics and fresh energy was released in business life. Clay, Webster, Calhoun, Van Buren, men who were to control American politics until the eve of the Civil War, came into their own. The republic was to face a variety of problems that required novel political programs and produced new parties and political alignments.

The period after 1815 was not an era of good feelings. Men at the time had, at best, decidedly mixed sentiments about what political position to adopt or support. The struggle to establish new political alliances involved bitter strife throughout the country as well as in Congress. At Washington, men like John Marshall and John Quincy Adams tried to uphold Federalist notions of the government's responsibility for guiding national development against the demands of vigorous local and small business interests. Young merchants, bankers, lawyers, and farmers were impatient with established traditions and privileges. They wanted either *laissez faire* or a government more favorable to their needs than to those of older established interests. They wanted more democratic parties so that their voice could be heard in drafting political programs and choosing candidates. The generation that came to maturity about 1815 was impatient with the aristocratic rhetoric of superiors and inferiors, of one's station in life and its duties, of the need for confidence by the poor and humble in wisdom of the rich and well-born. These "men on the make" wanted their place in the sun and a voice in their destiny. After 1815, the nation debated what program could bring the new, energetic interest groups together and wondered about what men would fill the places once held by Washington and his generation.

The new politicians who rose to power after the War of 1812 represented a wide array of interest groups. They acted as brokers on behalf of their clients, arranging the best deal possible. They soon learned that compromise to their disadvantage on one issue could be made up some other time on some other matter. Although politicians at Washington fought for and identified themselves with what they alleged to be the best interests of their districts, states, or sections, they also helped blunt the force of those interests in the process of legislative compromise. The daily give and take of politics and the constant traffic in jobs and favors were powerful influences against intransigence. One might even say that lack of principle among many politicians often helped avoid final fights over issues like the tariff or slavery, which, pressed to the limit, could bring government to a halt or the Union to disaster.

Beyond the influence of the need to compromise and of the claims of expediency was the temptation of higher office. No one at Washington could know for sure when the call to higher office might come. It was essential for the ambitious politician to keep all doors open, to make many friends and few enemies, to steer a course favored back home but compatible with the interests of powerful political friends elsewhere. What was most needed was the chance to identify with or create some fresh issue that would please constituents and promise, at the same time, a national reputation.

These were features of the American political system that began to take shape early in the nineteenth century. Every representative and senator had to learn many lessons in order to survive politically. As literacy spread in the nation, as access to distant regions became easier through internal improvements, and as newspapers grew in number and influence, a more exciting political atmosphere was created. The pace of political maneuver also increased. Issues came and went more quickly. Reputations were more easily made and unmade. Secrecy and calm deliberation become more difficult. The generation after 1815 was, in fact, creating the basic characteristics of the American party system.

The old pattern of political life was also disturbed by the entrance of many states into the republic. These provided new issues or revived old ones like internal improvements and an adequate national banking system. The growth of new groups and fresh interests in the older areas of the Union also made political life more complicated. The increase in manufacturing, the greater diversity of farms, the decline of old crops and the appearance of new ones, the growing numbers of small artisans and mechanics anxious for businesses of their own, the clamor of an incredible array of reformers seeking this law or that—all these features of life in the older states increased the complexity of American national life and made demands on politicians used to an easier, more isolated, or more anonymous legislative or executive routine at Washington.

If the growth of new states, new economic interests, and new so-

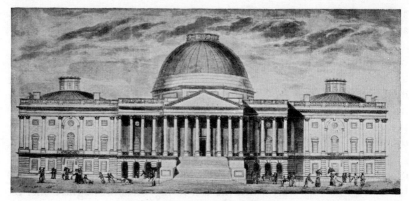

The Capitol in the 1820's

cial ideals were not enough to challenge the patrician political system inherited from the generation of 1776, changes in the electorate helped increase the threat. Between 1790 and 1828, in both old and new states, formal suffrage requirements were lowered. No one section or party can be clearly identified with this process. Western states drafted their voting rules at about the time they entered the Union. Lacking settled traditions and without strong class distinctions, the relatively few first residents in the West tended to ask lower requirements for voting than reformers in the East were able to obtain, but the differences between East and West were not dramatic.

In the older areas the suffrage laws had been liberalized in a see-saw struggle in which each party attempted to capture political power by drawing in previously disfranchised voters. Slowly, most of the potential electorate obtained political rights, and each party increasingly tried to identify itself with the cause of the common man. Some scholars are prepared to claim American suffrage was near-democratic by 1776; yet fierce fights and competitive bidding to lower legal requirements for voting were recurrent in the period after independence was achieved.

Those white males who could vote by 1776 had either fulfilled the property and religious qualifications or were able to vote in spite of the law. Where many men voted illegally, there arose fights after 1776 to guarantee in law what had become a fact. In older states like Massachusetts and New York, the struggle for a more democratic franchise was partly to prevent the old controlling interests from using the law to restrict former supporters who now threatened to desert the old élite for new political leaders. A wide suffrage by 1776 was, of course, no guarantee that as new areas of settlement opened or as population increased the right or practice of voting would keep pace. Large numbers of men were at times kept from voting by law or trickery after 1776. Vote reform was thus often an answer to a decline in the legal or actual suffrage. Very often the demand for democracy in the suffrage included complaints against malapportionment, insufficient polling places, or election frauds. People who had the legal right to vote or who had previously been permitted to vote sometimes found that their legal or practical right was being frustrated. The spread and use of political rights in the early years of the republic also followed the changing curve of political enthusiasm. Exciting elections always brought more legal and illegal voters out than dull contests did.

In this complex growth of political democracy, the legal requirements for voting had been steadily lowered by 1828 in both eastern and western states. Most political factions, whether aristocratic or democratic in their rhetoric, had helped establish more egalitarian rules and practices. Even more important than the growth in voting rights, however, were the experiments with newspapers, pamphlets, speeches, meetings, handbills, provocative symbols, and harsher and irresponsible attacks on opponents, through which, when necessary, the legally larger electorate could be aroused.

Most of the party leaders who took over from the older Jeffersonians and Federalists after 1815 were involved in these electoral changes. A more easily aroused electorate, one quicker to sound its voice or to take its revenge, considerably increased the difficulty of political maneuver in an era when the establishment of new states and the rise of fresh and vigorous interest groups had raised the stakes in the political game. The role of the banks, the effects of tariffs, internal improvements, slavery in new states, became more thorny issues than they had been because of the greater variety of interest groups that now had a voice in shaping national policies.

Triumphant Federalism and Moribund Federalists

In the years immediately after the Treaty of Ghent, the Jeffersonians were to take over the once-despised Hamiltonian program, and the Federalists sank into oblivion, deprived of even their policies. In the election of 1816, the Federalists did not even bother to nominate a candidate. James Monroe, Madison's Secretary of State and the third Virginia planter in succession selected by the Jeffersonians as their party's standard bearer, received 183 electoral votes, while Rufus King, with 34 votes, was supported only by Connecticut, Massachusetts, and Delaware. Four years later, in the elections of 1820, all but one electoral vote was cast for Monroe.

The extent to which the Jeffersonians had been Federalized was revealed with the adoption of bills establishing the second Bank of the United States and increasing existing tariff rates. Difficulty in financing the War of 1812 without a national bank (the first Bank's charter had expired in 1811) suggested future trouble in conducting the government's fiscal business. President Madison, the former anti-Federalist, signed a bank charter bill in 1816 that was a Federalist measure in all essentials. It provided that one fifth of the new bank's $35,000,000 capital was to be subscribed by the government and that five of its twenty-five directors were to be appointed by the President of the United States. The other twenty directors were to be elected by stockholders resident in the United States. In the hope of forcing other banks to rely on specie payment or of cutting them out of business, provision was made that all notes and deposits had to be paid in specie. The bank was at least potentially in a position to control the national currency. No person could refuse the bank's notes, and all notes circulated by the bank were receivable for payments due the United States. All government receipts were to be kept in the bank or in any of the branches that it had authority to establish. In return for an exclusive twenty-year charter, the bank was to transfer, free of charge, government funds from place to place in the United States and to pay into the federal treasury $1,500,000. Congress was also given the power to inspect the books of the bank, and if violations were found, to compel the bank to show cause why its charter should not be forfeited.

Despite the Federalist character of this bank, with its strong national powers, the bank bill was not passed by either a party or sectional vote. Of the seventy-one House members opposing the measure, thirty-eight were Federalists and thirty-three Republicans. Henry Clay strongly favored the new bank, excusing his earlier opposition to the first bank on the ground that he had had doubts about its constitutionality, that the bank had been interested in politics, and that his state legislature had instructed him to oppose its recharter. John C. Calhoun, no less nationalistic at this time than Clay and envisioning South Carolina's need for the bank, also championed the bank. Daniel Webster, spokesman for commercial New England, opposed the bank for fear that it would cut into the profits of Boston bankers. John Randolph, fully loyal to the ideals of an agrarian republic, asserted that "every man present in the House or out of it with some rare exceptions" was "either a stockholder, president, cashier, clerk or doorkeeper, runner, engraver, papermaker, or mechanic in some other way to a bank." The whole banking business, he concluded, was little more than a swindle.

The vote on the tariff of 1816, which raised the existing rates on cotton cloth, woolens, bar iron, and other commodities, also failed to reveal any clear-cut party cleavages. Although it was opposed by many eastern commercial and shipping interests, the bill received the support of representatives from all sections of the country. The new tariff was criticized by John Randolph on the ground that it would be injurious to the South; but it had been recommended to Congress in the first place by President Madison, a Virginian. John C. Calhoun, originally a voice of the small-farmer, backcountry region of South Carolina and an ardent nationalist, supported the manufacturers. A tariff, he argued, would "form a new and most powerful cement, far outweighting any political objections that might be urged against the system." The indomitable southern leader, not yet converted by the plantation interests, believed, like many of his colleagues, that the South might also become a manufacturing section.

This aura of agreement and of nationalist enthusiasm that touched men who were to be bitter rivals in only a few years was deceptive. In the country at large, political waters were muddy. Although the second Bank of the United States had had congressional supporters from all sections in 1816, it was not long before the rapidly expanding rural regions of the South and West, angry at the bank's controls over currency, were protesting against the policies of what they considered a grasping financial monopoly. Between 1816 and 1819, Ohio, Kentucky, Tennessee, Maryland, North Carolina, and Georgia followed the example already set by Indiana and Illinois in imposing heavy taxes upon branches of the national bank. Ohio and Tennessee levied a tax of $50,000, and Kentucky $60,000. In 1819, however, Chief Justice Marshall in *McCulloch vs. Maryland* held that the act chartering the bank was constitutional and emphatically asserted that the states had no constitutional power to tax the bank's branches. This ruling was bitterly resented in the West. The land boom of 1816—19 had collapsed partly because of the sudden decision of the bank to tighten credit. In 1821, the legislature of Ohio, after reaffirming the Virginia and Kentucky Resolutions, passed an act practically outlawing the Bank of the United States in the state. Kentucky was equally hostile toward the lair of the "moneyed aristocrats."

The states west of the Alleghenies were not content with mere opposition to the bank. Practically every western state took positive steps to relieve its debtor class. Kentucky, Tennessee, Illinois, and

Missouri, for instance, enacted replevin and stay laws that granted debtors an extension of time in satisfying executions of foreclosure. "People's banks" were chartered, and the sale of debtors' lands to pay debts was forbidden unless it brought three fourths of the value set upon it by a board of appraisers who were usually neighbors and themselves debtors.

Opposition to the Bank also arose in the East. Well established private bankers resented the national Bank's inroads on their business. Some of these were able to come to terms with the Bank; others fought its power. More speculative and smaller bankers were irritated at the Bank's growing effective controls over shady or marginal credit and over currency operations. Many small potential businessmen began to see the Bank as a symbol of monopoly and government favoritism. New York banking groups resented the location of the Bank's headquarters at Philadelphia because of the drain of specie collected or earned in New York customs to the smaller city. As the 1830's were to show, the power of the Bank created much hostility throughout the country that a skillful politician might be able to exploit.

The question of federal-financed internal improvements produced political alignments different from those created by the bank issue. When President Madison recommended a number of internal improvements to Congress in 1816, his proposals were enthusiastically endorsed by nationalists, manufacturers, importers, western farmers, speculators in western lands and those interested in old and new internal improvement companies. Madison's suggestions, however, were overshadowed by John C. Calhoun's proposal that the $1,500,000 paid by the second Bank of the United States as the price of its charter, together with the dividends on the bank's stock owned by the United States, should be set apart as a fund for building roads and canals. In making this proposal, Calhoun said: "Let us bind the republic together with roads and canals."

After protracted debate, the so-called Bonus Bill embodying Calhoun's ideas on the subject passed both houses of Congress by a narrow margin, but it was vetoed by Madison on the ground that it was unconstitutional. The vote in both houses had sectional features. New England, fearing that the West was depopulating the East and that the admission of additional agrarian states would further undermine the economic and political power of the commercial Northeast, was overwhelmingly opposed. The middle states were most in favor of the measure because the chief eastern markets on trade routes from the West lay in those areas, and middle state merchants had much to gain in supplying and buying from the trans-Appalachian region. The South

*Vote on "Bonus Bill" in House of Representatives,
February 8, 1817*

	FOR	AGAINST
New England	6	34
Middle States	47	19
South	22	23
West	11	8
	86	84

was neatly split on the question. Interests nearer the seaboard were not anxious to establish easier access to the interior, because that would open up new, competing farms, and might pave the way for a whole system of improvements that would have to be paid for by higher taxes. Even the West was divided, fearing or hoping, as the case might be, that new areas would be brought under settlement or cultivation, or that the roads and canals would favor one part of the West and not another, or that eventually improvements would have to be paid for by the public.

The Fire Bell in the Night

Further evidence of the complexity of interests at work in the postwar period was provided by Missouri's application for admission to the Union in 1818. When the bill for statehood was reported to the House of Representatives, James Tallmadge of New York decided to offer an amendment that forbade the further introduction of slavery into the new state and provided that all children of slaves born in the state after its admission should become free at the age of twenty-five. Tallmadge's desire to curry favor with party leaders in New York may very well have been involved in his decision. If the amendment carried, it would mean that most of the Louisiana Purchase territory would be closed to slavery and that slavery would be confined within the states where it already existed. It would mean, furthermore, that the South would almost at once be deprived of its equality with the North in the Senate. In the North, the amendment was supported by hundreds of resolutions adopted by mass meetings and state legislatures. In the larger cities, committees of correspondence were appointed to carry on a campaign against the admission of new slave states. Citing the clause in the Constitution that reads, "New states may be admitted by Congress into the Union" as proof that Congress had authority to prescribe the terms of a state's admission, Senator Rufus King of New

York pointed to Ohio, Indiana, and Illinois as having been admitted under restrictions regarding slavery imposed by the Ordinance of 1787.

The northern motives for opposition to slave state status for Missouri were mixed. For some men, undoubtedly, the principle of the restriction of slave territory was at stake. This did not imply belief that slavery ought to be abolished where it existed and, even less, belief in the equality of white and black races. But for most of the Northern politicians, the question turned on whether the diverse interest groups in the North who were constantly striking bargains with each other in Congress could afford to introduce new votes in the Senate and House that might go against them on issues like higher tariffs, cheaper public lands, and internal improvements.

Just as northern interests closed ranks against Missouri, southerners did the same on the other side. The South declared that the amendment was a violation of the constitutional rights of the states. In reply to King, Senator William Pinkney of Maryland asserted that the Union was composed of free and equal states and that Congress consequently had no power to restrict Missouri's freedom of action about its own problems. Thomas W. Cobb of Georgia warned that passage of the amendment would mean dissolution of the Union, and Jefferson likened the debate on the measure to a fire bell in the night. "In the gloomiest hour of the Revolutionary War," he stated, "I never had any apprehensions equal to those which I feel from this source."

Although the Missouri bill passed the House by a vote that closely followed sectional lines, it was defeated in the Senate. The question was brought up again in the new Congress of 1819–21, and a way out of the dilemma was presented: the eastern counties of Massachusetts— now known as Maine—applied for separate statehood, with the approval of the parent state. The Senate then proposed that both Maine and Missouri be admitted concurrently and that each be free to determine the status of slavery within its borders. Practically speaking, this solution meant that Maine was to be admitted as a free state, while Missouri would be slave. Since there were eleven slave and eleven nonslave states, such an arrangement would preserve the political balance of the Union. For a time the Missouri opponents in the House were unyielding, but, after six weeks of debate, they agreed to a compromise proposed by Senator J. B. Thomas of Illinois. By its terms, both Maine and Missouri were to be admitted without any restriction as to slavery; the remainder of the Louisiana Purchase north of the parallel 36°30′, the southern boundary of Missouri, was to be forever free.

Although those in and out of Congress who debated the Missouri

THE NEW STATES AND
THE MISSOURI COMPROMISE

question emphasized slavery and constitutional questions, neither was the basic issue. Slavery at the time was not yet heatedly defended nor attacked, and constitutional arguments were used as rationalizations. The heart of the matter was the struggle of diverse interest groups and political men for the votes of new states. Political leaders from both the older sections realized that the West especially held the key to future political power in the national government. If the Louisiana Purchase were opened or closed to slavery, the South's or the North's chances for dominating the federal government would be immeasurably increased.

Tempests Over the Tariff

GOODS COMING IN - HAVE ↑
IMPORT DUTIES ∴ MID-WEST
PRODUCE → MKT.

Of all issues, the tariff revealed most about the conflict of interests in the United States after 1816. In the Northeast, opinion was divided. The tariff was opposed by the section's shippers and merchants, but it found enthusiastic supporters among the rising but still small class of manufacturers. In their repeated requests for higher protective duties, the manufacturers were generally supported by farmers in the middle states. The West held the balance of power and was split on the issue. Since the end of the Napoleonic Wars, some farmers had no longer

why South not for.

been able to count on a foreign market for their products, and many hoped that the protected development of American industry would expand their home market. In the South, opposition to the tariff soon became almost universal. As the region turned increasingly to the production of cotton, it was compelled to export to the other sections and to Europe much of what it grew and to import much of what it consumed. Under the circumstances, the southerners concluded that a higher tariff would only increase the prices of practically everything that it bought either abroad or in the North.

Two years after the adoption of the tariff of 1816, the duty on all manufactured iron was increased. In 1819, the duty of 25 per cent on cotton and woolens was extended to 1826 instead of being reduced to 20 per cent, as provided in the Tariff of 1816. In 1820, Congress drafted a new bill containing even higher rates. This bill, known as the tariff of 1820, passed the House but failed in the Senate by a margin of one vote.

Vote of House of Representatives on Proposed Tariff of 1820

	FOR	AGAINST
New England	18	17
Middle States	55	1
South	5	49
West	12	10
	90	77

Again, eastern commercial and shipping interests, believing that a high tariff would diminish their trade, refused to support the measure. Daniel Webster was their principal spokesman, and in a speech in Faneuil Hall he declared:

I feel no desire to push capital into extensive manufactures faster than the general progress of our wealth and population propels it. I am not in haste to see Sheffields and Birminghams in America. It is the true policy of government to suffer the different pursuits of society to take their own course and not to give excessive bounties or encouragements to one over another.

Although enough manufacturers in the Northeast favored the tariff to split that section's vote, the commercial East had the backing of an almost solid South. Southern leaders like Calhoun, who had favored protection in 1816, now opposed it. With increased demand for plantation products, visions of southern factories and southern industrial centers had quickly vanished. Cotton culture, thanks largely to the spinning jenny and the cotton gin, was too profitable to be abandoned, and increasingly it took the South's capital and energy. Since two thirds of the southerners' staple products were shipped to Europe, they saw no reason why they should support a policy that was aimed at their principal customer, Great Britain, and that forced them to pay higher prices for their manufactured goods. To the southern planter, the tariff question had by 1820 come to mean, as John Randolph had said, "whether you, as a planter, will consent to be taxed in order to hire another man . . . to set up a spinning jenny."

Despite the defeat of the tariff bill of 1820, the manufacturers and middle states farmers continued their campaign both in and out of Congress. With corn and wheat falling in price and flour expensive, western farmers joined forces with the eastern protective interests. They flooded Congress with memorials and petitions. Henry Clay, stressing the "home market" argument, declared that Europe could not continue to consume the surplus of the American farm and that the time had therefore come to exclude European manufactures in order to strengthen the buying power of the home manufacturer. Nevertheless, bills for higher rates, introduced in the House in 1821 and 1823, were not adopted. On the eve of the presidential election of 1824, a tariff carrying higher duties was squeezed through Congress.

Vote of House of Representatives on Tariff of 1824

	FOR	AGAINST
New England	15	23
Middle States	60	15
South	1	57
West	31	7
	107	102

This tariff provided increased protection for manufacturers of wool, iron, hemp products, lead, glass, and cotton bagging. The duty on silk, linens, cutlery, spices, and other articles was also increased. The 25 per cent minimum duty on cotton and woolens was increased to $33\frac{1}{3}$ per cent (but the increase in rates for woolens was largely nullified by a 15 per cent advance in the rates for raw wool). The rate on hammered iron, which was used extensively by shipbuilders, fixed at $.45 per hundredweight in 1816 and subsequently advanced to $.75 by special act in 1818, was now raised to $.90.

In the debate on the bill, New England commercial and shipping interests struggled desperately against New England manufacturers, Pennsylvania ironmasters, and Kentucky hemp growers. The South labeled the measure as specious and outrageous, "a combination of the few against the many," "of the wealthy against the poor." The tariff seemed to be a tax on southern planters to protect northern manufacturers. In reply, Henry Clay, then Speaker of the House and spokesman of the protectionists, declared that "Dame Commerce" was "a flirting, flippant, noisy jade," and if the United States were governed by fantasies about low tariffs it would "never put off the muslins of India and the cloths of Europe." The most dramatic feature of the vote on the tariff of 1824 was that the bulk of the new western votes went solidly for protection.

The tariff of 1824 was unsatisfactory to the woolen manufacturers, who objected to the duty on raw wool. Despite a campaign of meetings, memorials to Congress, and circulars, the woolen men lost their fight in 1826.

The protectionists now redoubled their efforts. Representatives of manufacturing concerns and interested politicians met at Harrisburg, Pennsylvania, in the summer of 1827. One hundred delegates from thirteen of the twenty-four states outlined a plan for increased protection. High duties were recommended not only for wool and woolens, but for iron, flax, hemp, cotton, and glass. The delegates to the convention were particularly interested in woolens, and the recommended increases were dramatic. These recommendations were embodied in a memorial to Congress and in an address to the people.

Fear and anxiety grew in the South. Dr. Thomas Cooper, President of the College of South Carolina, stated: "There is not a petty manufacturer in the Union . . . who is not pressing forward to the plunder; who may not be expected to worry Congress for permission to put his hand into the planter's pocket . . . to force on us a system which will sacrifice the South to the North, which will convert us into colonies and tributaries." In various sections of South Carolina, resolutions were passed denying the constitutional right of Congress to enact a protective tariff. The landed interest of the South was becoming more bitter and more determined. In the North, the once powerful voice of the commercial and shipping aristocracy was already growing weaker. The capital and energy of the East steadily, and with increasing rapidity, shifted from ship to factory. On the South, therefore, would fall the brunt of the future battle in the struggle against the "new rich."

Raising New Party Banners

The shifting pattern of national interests was directly responsible for the disintegration of the old parties and the establishment of new ones. No single section could by itself control the central government, and parties had to be worked out on the basis of intersectional alliances. Such alliances were difficult to achieve, because no two sections were in agreement on all the major issues of the day and no one section was unified on all issues. By the mid 1820's, a number of political leaders had worked out plans for establishing a successful political coalition. John C. Calhoun, the emerging leader of the Old South, hoped to unite the voters of his region with those of the Southwest. Henry Clay of Kentucky was seeking to form an alliance between the more prosperous farmers of the West and the industrial groups of the Northeast. Martin Van Buren of New York, the most important rising politician of the Middle Atlantic states, thought that a Northeast–Southeast combination would prove successful. As long as Daniel Webster of Massachusetts remained allied with the old Federalist commercial elite, he found it difficult to unite his New England supporters with political groups elsewhere.

The new parties that eventually emerged under President Andrew Jackson in 1828 were built on the wrecks of their predecessors. The Federalists, first of the old parties to disappear, were particularly hard hit by the rise of the Western states. Very few Federalist programs had ever been designed to appeal to the voters of the backcountry regions. By 1816, the Federalists faced other insurmountable obstacles. The party was identified with the New England opposition to the War of 1812 and the disastrous Hartford Convention. As the Republicans cut off patronage to them and adopted virtually every part of their program, the Federalists were deprived of the jobs and much of the platform on which they could base their opposition. Although small pockets of Federalist voters remained in various sections of the country, the party had ceased to influence national politics by 1820.

Despite its landslide victory in the election of 1820, the Republican party was little more than a collection of factions, each of which drew its strength from particular sections and groups. Although this factionalism was less apparent during "the Era of Good Feeling," it came to the surface in the election of 1824.

As in the past, the congressional caucus of the Republican party nominated the party's candidate for the presidency. William Crawford, the choice of the caucus, was a southerner. He satisfied neither the ambitions nor the interests of the voters in the other sections of the coun-

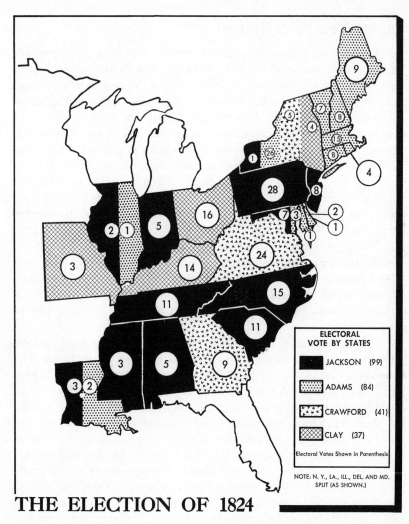

ELECTORAL VOTE BY STATES

	JACKSON	(99)
	ADAMS	(84)
	CRAWFORD	(41)
	CLAY	(37)

Electoral Votes Shown in Parenthesis

NOTE: N. Y., LA., ILL., DEL. AND MD. SPLIT (AS SHOWN.)

THE ELECTION OF 1824

try. The Northeast and West put forward their favorite candidates through resolutions passed by state legislatures. The Tennessee legislature nominated Andrew Jackson; Kentucky selected Henry Clay; and Massachusetts named John Quincy Adams. Although all four candidates were nominally Republicans, they represented particular rather than party interests. No candidate was able to pick up sufficient votes outside his own section, and none received the necessary majority in the electoral college. Jackson—high man, with ninety-nine votes—had drawn most of his strength from the West and the South. Adams's eighty-four votes came largely from the Northeast, while Crawford, with forty-one electoral votes, was a candidate of the Old South. Clay, who ran a poor fourth, had lost out all along the line because of his attempt to cut across sectional lines. Although Clay received considerable support in the Ohio Valley, he trailed each of the other candidates in their respective sections.

The failure of any candidate to achieve a majority threw the election into the House. It was anticipated that Jackson, with the highest number of votes would be elected, but Clay directed his followers to vote for Adams. The union of the Clay and Adams forces assured the New Englander's election. When Adams made Clay Secretary of State, the Jacksonians immediately accused the two men of a "corrupt bargain." Although they were unable to substantiate their charge, the Jackson men nevertheless insisted that Clay had supported Adams in the House in return for a promise that he would be given the top cabinet post.

The Second Adams

The new president, John Quincy Adams, the son of John Adams, had devoted most of his life to the service of his country. He had had the most distinguished public career of any man of the age. At fourteen he was secretary to the American representative to Russia, and at twenty-seven he was a diplomat in his own right. In 1808, after serving five years in the Senate, he resigned because of the Massachusetts legislature's opposition to the embargo. In 1809, having shifted from the Federalist to the Republican party, he was named minister to Russia. Five years later, he was a member of the American peace commission at Ghent, and in 1815 he was made the United States representative in London. From 1817 to 1825, he compiled an outstanding record as Secretary of State. A widely read, scholarly man, Adams, like his father, possessed a demanding conscience and a cold demeanor. Although a more skillful politician than the first Adams, he was no match for his opponents during his term as President. Dedicated to the highest ideals of public service, ambitious in his plans for a greater Union, fantastically self-disciplined, this brilliant man was to reap disaster as President.

With Adams's accession to the presidency, new party coalitions began to take definite shape. During his administration, Adams failed to win over the voters who had supported his rivals in the election of 1824. In his first annual message, Adams advocated that the federal government encourage manufacturing and agriculture, construct additional highways and canals, improve the nation's harbors, strengthen the militia and navy, and establish a national university, military schools, and an

Clay of Kentucky

observatory. Adams's policies attempted to unite interests in the North-east with the voters in the Ohio Valley who supported Henry Clay.

Although Adams's personality was altogether unlike that of Clay, who was a warmhearted, friendly extrovert, the two men had common political objectives. Clay had served in the House since 1811. He was the most skillful Congressional politician of his day. Shrewd, handsome, and energetic, he was destined, despite repeated efforts, to be a President-maker rather than a President. Since 1816, he had based his hopes for political success on his so-called American System. Calling for internal improvements and a high tariff, the American System was designed to appeal to the interests of the Middle West and Northeast. It envisaged the federal government taking a firm leadership over national economic development. The plan was appealing for Adams, who conceived of the presidency as a stewardship for preserving and expanding the economic and cultural riches of the country. Adams joined forces with Clay and to a large extent made the American System the administration's program. He was in effect laying the groundwork for an all-Northern political organization that soon became known as the National Republican party. Despite its sectional character, the National Republican party was opposed by many northerners who thought that its principal objectives were incompatible with demands for an end to government intervention in economic life, low taxes, and freer play to local and individual interests. John Quincy Adams was caught in the strong American ebb tide away from the Hamiltonian and mercantile state.

To southern leaders, Adams's policies meant only increased taxes to provide funds that would be spent to benefit other sections. Most westerners viewed Adams's program as a device for aiding the already powerful business interests of the Northeast, while small businessmen, artisans, and mechanics in the East suspected paternalism and government meddling on behalf of established interest groups. These diverse opposition groups represented a majority of the nation's voters, but they were powerless as long as they remained unorganized. Andrew Jackson's supporters now conducted a vigorous campaign to place their hero at the head of these anti-Adams forces. Their numbers were increased by the addition of Calhoun's backers when Calhoun was promised the vice-presidency on the Jackson ticket for 1828. The intersectional alliance was finally completed when Martin Van Buren's followers joined the Jackson camp. It was these three groups—western Jacksonians, southern supporters of Calhoun, and Van Buren's New York State machine (which was known as the Albany Regency)—that formed the nucleus of what was soon to be known as the Democratic party.

Adams's reputation rested largely on his proved ability in diplomacy, yet even his most important venture in foreign policy as President helped his opponents. In 1825, the United States was invited to send delegates to Panama to attend a Latin-American congress organized by Simon Bolivar to discuss ways to force Spain to recognize her former colonies in the New World. Adams opposed the idea on the ground that it might involve the United States in attempts to secure the independence of Puerto Rico and Cuba. Clay, the Secretary of State, who considered himself an authority on Latin-American affairs, thought otherwise. He eventually convinced the President. On December 26, 1825, Adams asked the Senate to confirm the nominations of two delegates to attend the Panama conference. The critics of the administration immediately turned the question into a party issue and made it an

The Second Adams

excuse for attacking the President's conduct of foreign policy. The confirmation of the appointments was so delayed that the American delegates did not arrive in Panama until after the congress had ended. Adams's opponents in Congress had succeeded in embarrassing the President over what otherwise would have been a routine matter.

An Implacable Opposition

Throughout Adams's entire administration, the "corrupt bargain" both embittered the friends of Jackson and gave them their most effective campaign weapon. By harping on this theme, they were able to convey the impression that Jackson, the choice of the majority, had been cheated out of the presidency by a minority candidate of upper-class background. Jackson was put forward as a man of the masses who was responsive to the popular will, and Adams was pictured as the representative of a small but powerful moneyed group. Although Jackson was a member of the controlling oligarchy in the state of Tennessee and probably wealthier than Adams, in the popular mind he became the champion of the rising spirit of democracy. By making Jackson's name virtually identical with majority rule and equal rights, his supporters were able to make a particularly effective appeal to the new electorate in both the new and old states.

The groups supporting Jackson represented such diverse economic and sectional interests that there was no single issue on which they could all agree. They were united in their opposition to Adams and in hunger for the presidency, but they had little else in common. To win, Jackson had to capture the votes of both the West and the South. The southerners liked Calhoun for Vice-President more than they trusted Jackson's rhetoric of the will of the majority. Westerners approved of Jackson for the very reasons that the planters distrusted him. As a hater of banks, a popular military hero of western origins with a seeming simple and direct manner, and an opponent of aristocracy, Jackson was viewed by many westerners as the symbol of the age.

The Jacksonian supporters completed their preparations for the election with the tariff of 1828—a measure that some of them hoped would fail to be adopted and that John Randolph described as referring "to manufactures of no sort or kind, but the manufacture of a President of the United States." A higher tariff on raw materials as well as on manufactured goods, so ran the scheme, would appeal strongly to both the middle states and the West. The duties on various types of iron were raised from 10 to 25 per cent, while those on hemp were increased from $35 to $45 a ton. Higher rates were also provided for the product of greatest importance, raw wool. It was confidently expected that New England manufacturers would oppose such a tariff and join with the South in defeating it. The iron-mongers of Pennsylvania, the hemp growers of Kentucky and the South, in general, would be relieved. Adams would be discredited if he signed or vetoed the bill, and the election of Jackson would be practically assured. Much to the chagrin and disappointment of its authors, enough New England votes existed to carry the bill. Even Webster, who for years had been the eloquent spokesman of maritime and commercial New England and who had opposed the tariff of 1824, voted for the 1828 measure. In four years, the economic winds of that region had shifted, and the Massachusetts leader trimmed his sails accordingly. Manufacturing New England apparently reasoned that a tariff with objectionable features was better than no tariff at all.

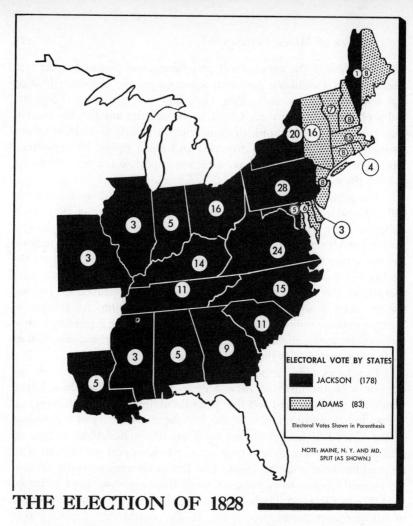

ELECTORAL VOTE BY STATES

■ JACKSON (178)

▨ ADAMS (83)

Electoral Votes Shown in Parenthesis

NOTE: MAINE, N. Y. AND MD.
SPLIT (AS SHOWN.)

THE ELECTION OF 1828

When Adams signed the so-called Tariff of Abominations, he greatly increased the South's opposition to the Administration in Washington. From Chesapeake Bay to the mouth of the Mississippi, "northern despotism" was assailed. Flags flew at half-mast; protest meetings passed resolutions; and newspapers, editors, preachers, college professors, and public officials, contrasting the prosperity of industrialized New England with the depression then current in the South, urged retaliation and nullification. John C. Calhoun, under strong pressure at home and anxious to ingratiate himself further with South Carolina's ruling groups, now understood more clearly than ever before that the interests of the South faced the opposition of the industrial capitalists of the North. Calhoun presented to the legislature of South Carolina his famous *Exposition and Protest*, in which he asserted that the Tariff of Abominations was unconstitutional, sectional, and destructive to the liberty, prosperity, and happiness of the South, and must therefore be destroyed. The states, he maintained, had created the national government and were therefore ultimate judges of its power and authority. If any state deemed a federal act unconstitutional, it might forbid its execution within the limits of the commonwealth; and if supported in its action by three fourths, or more, of the states of the Union, the law in question would become null and void. Like earlier New England and southern protests against national "usurpation," this interpretation of the Constitution was not a disinterested political philosophy. Its purpose was to afford the free-trade South an avenue of escape from the "abominable" tariff burdens imposed by "despicable" northern manufacturers.

Despite the failure of the Democrats' tariff strategy, Jackson, a great popular hero, won a decisive victory in the heated and sordid election of 1828. Adams was sabotaged on the patronage within the administration; he had already lost control of Congress in 1826. Still, Adams and Rush, the two candidates who headed the National Republican ticket, gained majorities in almost all of New England, in those counties in New York state where New Englanders predominated, in the Western Reserve in Ohio, in Kentucky and the southern portions of Indiana, Illinois, and Ohio where there was a strong demand for internal improvements, and in some remaining strongholds of Federalism in southern New Jersey, Delaware, and Maryland. Against this alignment Jackson carried the South, the West, and Pennsylvania. In winning by 178 electoral votes to 83 for his opponents, Jackson had successfully combined several appeals. He won the South largely because Adams's policies were identified with the North and with opposition to states' rights. The West voted for Jackson because he had been "cheated" in 1824, and because he was both a westerner and a "democrat." In the Middle Atlantic states Jackson received many votes from the "middling" class that opposed the control of the government by an aristocratic minority. By managing to be many things to many people, Jackson did more than win an election, for the patterns of party politics and national party leadership that he developed after 1828 have survived basically unchanged to the present day.

FOR SUPPLEMENTARY READING

An attractive general history is George Dangerfield, *The Era of Good Feelings* (1952). On John Quincy Adams, start with S. F. Bemis, *John Quincy Adams and the Foundations of American Foreign Policy* (1949); Allan Nevins (ed.), *The Diary of John Quincy Adams* (1951); and A. Koch and W. Peden (eds.), *The Selected Writings of John and John Quincy Adams* (1946). Students might well read also Max Weber, "Politics as a Vocation," in H. Gerth and C. W. Mills, *From Max Weber: Essays in Sociology* (1947) (Pb).

On John Marshall and the Marshall Court, read A. J. Beveridge, *The Life of John Marshall* (4 vols., 1916–19); E. S. Corwin, *John Marshall and the Constitution* (1919); and C. B. Swisher, *American Constitutional Development* (1943).

There is no one book that really does justice to the story of the transformations of American politics in the generation 1808–28, but some idea of the complexity of events can be obtained from D. R. Fox, *The Decline of Aristocracy in the Politics of New York* (1919) (Pb); M. Ostrogorski, *Democracy and the Organization of Political Parties* (2 vols., reissued 1964); C. Williamson, *American Suffrage From Property to Democracy* (1960); S. Livermore, Jr., *The Twilight of Federalism . . . 1815–1830* (1962); R. P. McCormick, *The Second American Party System: Party Formation in the Jacksonian Era* (1966); D. H. Fischer, *The Revolution of American Conservatism* (1965); R. V. Remini, *Martin Van Buren and the Making of the Democratic Party* (1959); and C. S. Sydnor, *The Development of Southern Sectionalism, 1819–1848* (1948).

For understanding the new politics, take special note of T. P. Abernethy, *From Frontier to Plantation in Tennessee* (1932), but compare it with C. G. Sellers, *James K. Polk: Jacksonian, 1795–1843* (1957); R. P. McCormick, *The History of Voting in New Jersey* (1953); C. M. Wiltse, *John C. Calhoun, Nationalist* (1944); and C. McCarthy, *The Anti-Masonic Party* (1903). Examine the relations between local discontents and party politics.

On the Monroe Doctrine, the primary authority is D. Perkins, *A History of the Monroe Doctrine* (1955). On other aspects of foreign policy see S. F. Bemis, *The Latin American Policy of the United States* (1943) and his general *Diplomatic History*. An excellent group assessment is in A. Rappaport (ed.), *The Monroe Doctrine* (1964).

Essential economic background is found in C. P. Nettels, *The Emergence of a National Economy, 1775–1815* (1962).

PART IV

ENERGIES OF
DEMOCRACY

[THE NEW YORK HISTORICAL SOCIETY]

14

Jacksonian Democracy

ANDREW JACKSON was a colorful, strong-willed, astute, dynamic individual who profoundly influenced the course of American civilization. But Jackson's powerful personality should not obscure the fact that he was the product as well as the maker of his times. A large part of his political genius—and he was an astonishingly skillful politician—lay in his ability to sense the direction in which public opinion was moving even before the people themselves were aware of where they were heading. He had few, if any, superiors in gauging the popular will, and his well-merited reputation for leadership lay, not in his ability to institute new movements, but in the skill with which he placed himself at the head of existing trends and gave them both direction and verve. As the successful ruler of a democracy, he neither formulated nor followed the national will; instead he was its most influential and accurate spokesman.

Jackson Rides a Rising Tide

Andrew Jackson was born in the backcountry of South Carolina in 1767. He fought in the American Revolution when he was little more than a boy. At twenty he began the practice of law in the North Carolina frontier, and a year later he moved to Nashville, Tennessee, where he became successively public prosecutor, a member of the

United States Senate, and a judge of the state's supreme court. On numerous occasions, Jackson interrupted his political career and law practice to take up arms against the enemies of his country. In March, 1814, at the head of a band of Tennessee frontiersmen, he decisively defeated the Creeks at Horseshoe Bend; in January, 1815, he won his great victory at New Orleans; and in 1818, he led his famous expedition into East Florida. In 1823, when he was again elected to the Senate, he seemed to many Americans in all sections to be a typical product of the nation's frontier. A self-made man and Indian fighter, who believed in action instead of words, he possessed all the qualifications of a western folk hero.

In the years before he became President, Jackson gave little indication that he was to become the champion of the majority in an "age of the common man." Although his eastern opponents considered him crude and uncouth, the fact remains that he was a member of the upper class in Tennessee, and he shared the views of the well-to-do in his community. Jackson moved from an early start in land speculation and a varied trade (including slaves) to cotton-planting. He was a hard-money man, antimonopolist, and an enemy of banks. But, being a very shrewd and energetic rather than a learned man, Jackson possessed few deeply reasoned positions on economic affairs. His "ideas" were often only intuitions. At their worst, however, they more closely resembled sudden irritations and outbursts, rather than logical and informed opinions. Thoughts about public policy and the dictates of private animosities often overlapped in Jackson's career. Whatever their basis, his early opinions have been well described by Professor Wilfred E. Binkley: "It was with the eyes of the great and not the petty planter that Jackson had come to view public issues. The Hermitage was one of the finest mansions of the West and as the domicile of a Democrat it was to amuse the Whigs of the 1830's no less than did Hyde Park the Republicans of the 1930's."

Although Jackson's name is invariably associated with democracy, he was responsible for none of the major advances in popular government during the first third of the nineteenth century. In Tennessee, he consistently opposed attempts to break the control of the state by rich men. In the nation, however, in the 1820's, the undemocratic caucus system for presidential nominations gave way to party conventions; the first group to substitute a party convention for nomination by legislative caucus was the Anti-Masons.

The Anti-Masonic party was the short-lived product of an otherwise unimportant incident in up-state New York. In 1826, a certain William Morgan of Batavia, New York, who had published a pamphlet that purported to reveal the secrets of the Masonic order, disappeared and was never seen again. Many people—particularly those in the rural districts—assumed that he had been kidnapped by Masons who objected to his pamphlet. Because many Masons held prominent positions in the government and because the Masons were a secret society, the protest against Morgan's disappearance developed into a political movement opposed to the control of the government by Masonic leaders in particular and secret organizations in general. Being a secret clique with set requirements for membership, the Masons could be made to appear antidemocratic. The Anti-Masons proposed that candidates for office should be chosen democratically, in the open, by the voice of the people's delegates. True to their own principles, the Anti-Masons held a national convention in 1830, and in the following year at another convention they nominated candidates for the campaign of 1832. The Anti-Masonic party was a haven for every variety of dissatisfied political leader. It was strongest in western New York and Pennsylvania and in the rural sections of New England. Its principal leaders were Thurlow Weed and William H. Seward of New York and Thaddeus Stevens of Pennsylvania. In the mid-1830's, it was swallowed up by the Whigs, but not before both the National Republicans in 1831 and the Democrats in 1832 followed their lead and called nominating conventions.

At the same time, the selection of presidential electors by state legislatures was abandoned for a system of direct election. As with other democratic political changes, the states, not Jackson's Administration, were responsible for the change. The formal expansion of the suffrage had also been the direct result of state action, not of Jackson's or his supporters' leadership. Most new western states entered the Union with provisions for universal manhood suffrage. In the East, Connecticut in 1818, New York in 1821, and Virginia in 1830 liberalized suffrage laws and provided for the popular election of most state and local officials.

The rising belief in majority rule and equal rights had been skillfully exploited by eager politicians, and by 1828 the old religious and property barriers to manhood suffrage had largely disappeared. In spite of the fears and protests of the landed and commercial interests and their spokesmen, Fisher Ames, James Kent, and Daniel Webster, the suffrage had been extended to all white males over twenty-one. Because of population growth, new techniques for arousing the electorate, and the greater excitement and democracy in political life, between 1828 and 1848 the number of voters trebled. With their votes needed by the politicians, the unpropertied mechanic and factory worker now regularly cast their ballots alongside the dignified clergyman and conservative capitalist. The effect of these changes is evident from Kent's comment in 1835:

> There never was such misrule. Our Tory rich men are becoming startled and alarmed at our downhill course. My opinion is that the admission of universal suffrage and a licentious press are incompatible with government and security to property, and that the government and character of this country are going to ruin. This suffrage is too great an excitement for any political machine. It racks it to pieces, and morals go with it. It is probable England is going the same way. We are becoming selfish, profligate, crazy . . .

Although Jackson deserves no credit for the various steps taken to democratize American government, he identified himself with those developments as President, and as "Old Hickory" came to symbolize them. He was also quick to recognize the significance of the major economic changes within the United States. America was entering a period of unrestrained economic individualism. Just as the people believed that the aristocracy should give way to popular rule in government, they also thought that economic privilege should give way, not to economic equality, but to equality of opportunity. The opening of the West, development of the nation's transportation system, growth of industry, and expansion of agriculture provided almost limitless chances for profits, which the mass of small businessmen, artisans, and mechanics thought should be available to all who had the initiative and ability to get them. In the course of Jackson's administration, on both national and state levels, the Democratic party took up the cause of the "man on the make." Jackson did not attack the Bank of the United States because he was opposed to financial institutions as such, but, as he put it, because he was opposed to a privileged financial institution that was thwarting economic individualism.

The key doctrines of Jacksonian democracy thus came to be majority rule and economic individualism. These concepts were not peculiar to the West, as some historians have stated. Nor, as some students have contended, was Jacksonian democracy the exclusive product of eastern working-class radicalism, for the working class was relatively small, scattered, and comparatively unorganized when Jackson was President. His principal supporters came from the middle class of every section—small farmers, small businessmen, and artisans. They had already been given the vote, and they had used it to place a great popular hero in the White House. They now asked that he act in their interest and that they be permitted to get ahead without interference from others. If Jackson was their political hero, Adam Smith was their economic idol.

Jackson's appeal as a nationalist should also not be overlooked. His military experience—among other things—had made him a thorough-going patriot, and in domestic affairs he gradually abandoned his belief in states' rights and tended to view the nation as a single unit rather than as an alliance of states or a combination of sections. In his conduct of American foreign policy, he guarded American rights as jealously as had any of his predecessors, and in his defense of the Union against the attacks of the states, he was as much of a nationalist as any Federalist.

Jackson and the Democratic Party

When Jackson assumed the presidency on March 4, 1829, the Democratic party was an unstable association of three major sectional blocs—the northeastern Democrats led by Van Buren, the southern supporters of Vice-President Calhoun, and Jackson's western followers, whose principal spokesman in Congress was Senator Thomas Hart Benton. These diverse and often conflicting groups had been brought together behind a soldier-hero in the campaign of 1828 by a series of ingenious alliances. But as soon as they had achieved their immediate objective with the election of Jackson, they began to fight over the spoils of victory. Each faction hoped to dominate the administration, and each in turn learned that Jackson could not be dominated. Despite the fact that he was the head of what amounted to a coalition government, Jackson repeatedly demonstrated that he would smash the coalition rather than let any part of it take over the control of his administration.

Jackson's use of the spoils system was one of the few measures of his administration that was approved by all the factions within the party. Although Jackson did not invent the spoils system—it went back to Washington and was used in many states, and in England as well—and although he never made the wholesale removals of which the opposition accused him, his handling of the patronage nevertheless clearly indicated that he thought no individual had a special right to hold public office. Other Presidents on occasion dismissed their political opponents from government service; but Jackson both institutionalized this practice and declared it a positive good. It was the contention of the Jacksonian Democrats that federal positions in the past had been monopolized by an unrepresentative minority. To break this hold of the "aristocracy" on the government, they proposed that officeholding be placed on a rotating basis, reasoning that if majority rule meant filling elective offices with the representatives of the majority, appointive positions should be filled in the same way. To observe that the spoils system produced administrative inefficiency and even corruption while aiding the party in power—and it most certainly did so—is to miss the point. To the Americans of the 1830's, the spoils system was just one more method by which the majority increased its control over the nation's governmental machinery.

The results of the spoils system were as important as its manifestations. By holding out to loyal party workers the prospect of a steady income, it provided a new incentive for party loyalty and encouraged the development of a group of professional politicians whose only job was to work for the party's victory. Under such circumstances, political parties tended to become permanent institutions, for they now contained vested interests whose livelihood depended on the party's success. Thus the spoils system was more responsible than any other factor for the creation of the modern American political party; and, despite civil-service reforms, it still provides much of the cement that holds together each of the two major parties.

Jackson's cabinet appointments, as well as his distribution of the lesser offices in the government, revealed his desire to reward the various rival groups that had supported him in the election of 1828. Jackson was careful, however, not to bring many really powerful figures into his cabinet. The Northeast was represented in the cabinet by Secretary of State Martin Van Buren of New York; the Calhoun wing by Secretary of the Treasury Samuel D. Ingham, Secretary of the Navy John Branch, and Attorney General John M. Berrien; and the West by Postmaster General William T. Barry and Secretary of War John H. Eaton, both from Kentucky. While the cabinet accurately reflected the sectional basis of the party, its members with the exception of Van Buren were mediocre. Although Jackson described the cabinet as "one of the strongest . . . that has ever been in the United States," he seldom consulted its members; instead, he relied almost exclusively for advice on a small group of friends that were known collectively as the "kitchen cabinet." Consisting of William B. Lewis, Amos Kendall, Duff Green, and Isaac Hill, the kitchen cabinet helped Jackson formulate policy, kept him informed on trends in public opinion, and assumed most of the responsibility for the distribution of the patronage. All four members of the kitchen cabinet had worked for Jackson's election in 1828; three of them, significantly, were newspaper editors. All were in some way associated with the government; two held posts in

the Treasury Department, a third was awarded the government printing contract, and the fourth became a member of the Senate in 1831.

The cabinet not only provided Jackson with little assistance; it
soon became a source of considerable embarrassment. Two months before Jackson's inauguration, John J. Eaton married Margaret O'Neale,
the attractive widow of a navy paymaster and the daughter of a Washington tavernkeeper. The cabinet wives, led by Mrs. Calhoun, disapproved of the match, and Peggy, whose charms were conceded by
even her enemies, found herself ostracized by Washington society.
Jackson, whose own wife had often been slandered before her death in
1828, rushed to Peggy's defense, and at a special cabinet meeting called
to discuss the "Eaton trouble," he described her as "chaste as a virgin."
But the female rulers of Washington society thought differently and
continued to refuse to accept her socially. The administration was soon
split into two factions, the anti-Eaton forces led by Calhoun and the
pro-Eaton group headed by Van Buren, a widower.

The Eaton tempest in the administration teapot was more serious
than it appeared on the surface, for it revealed a sharp sectional cleavage within both the party and the government. While Mrs. Calhoun
may have objected only to the Secretary of War's choice of a wife,
her husband also objected to an administration that made no move to
take care of the needs of the South. Calhoun was well aware that
Jackson and Van Buren agreed on many other points besides Mrs. Eaton's morals. The Tariff of Abominations was still on the statute books.
Calhoun made no effort to conceal his belief that the time was fast
approaching when the southern states would be forced to put into
practice the principles that he had advanced in his *Exposition and Protest*. The West also had reason to be dissatisfied with the President's
attitude toward internal improvements. When Congress in May, 1830,
authorized federal purchase of some of the stock of the Maysville road
in Kentucky, Jackson, following Monroe's precedent, vetoed the
measure on the ground that the turnpike project was local in character,
although at the same time he tried to cover himself by implying he
supported interstate improvements. To both westerners and southerners
it appeared that Jackson had sold out to the East and that Van Buren
had taken over the management of the government.

Conflicting sectional interests divided Congress as well as the
executive branch of the government. Senator Samuel A. Foot of Connecticut, who, as a spokesman for a section that feared it would soon
be depopulated by emigration westward, proposed a resolution calling
for restrictions on government land sales in the West. After Benton on

Daniel Webster

January 13, 1830, had attacked the resolution as inimical to western interests, Senator Robert Y. Hayne of South Carolina and Daniel Webster began a debate that was to last more than a week. As the debate progressed, the Foot resolution was lost in a discussion of the nature of the Union. To Hayne, who followed closely Calhoun's reasoning in the *Exposition and Protest*, the Union was a league of sovereign states, a league that the states had created and that they therefore could dissolve. Webster, whose views were now similar to those of John Marshall, attacked Hayne's position on practical, constitutional, historical, and patriotic grounds. Neither man convinced the other, but Webster had the last word in a peroration that has since been recited by countless members of every generation of American school children:

While the Union lasts we have high, exciting, gratifying prospects spread out before us, for us and our children. Beyond that I seek not to penetrate the veil. God grant that in my day, at least, that curtain may not rise! God grant that on my vision never may be opened what lies behind! When my eyes shall be turned to behold for the last time the sun in heaven, may I not see him shining on the broken and dishonored fragments of a once glorious Union; on States dissevered, discordant, belligerent; on a land rent with civil feuds, or drenched, it may be, in fraternal blood! Let their last feeble and lingering glance rather behold the gorgeous ensign of the republic; now known and honored throughout the earth, still full high advanced, its arms and trophies streaming in their original lustre, not a stripe erased or polluted, not a single star obscured, bearing for its motto, no such miserable interrogatory as "What is all this worth?" nor those other words of delusion and folly, "Liberty first and Union afterwards," but everywhere, spread all over in characters of living light, blazing on all its ample folds, as they float over the sea and over the land, and in every wind under the whole heavens, that other sentiment, dear to every true American heart,—Liberty and Union, now and forever, one and inseparable!

Although the two men had little else in common, Jackson shared Webster's views on the Union, and soon after the debate had ended, he publicly challenged the stand of the Southern states' rights spokesmen. At a party dinner held on April 13, 1830, to commemorate Jefferson's birthday, the President replied to a series of speeches by southerners on state sovereignty with the toast: "Our Federal Union—it must be preserved!" Vice-President Calhoun answered immediately with: "The Union—next to our liberty the most dear! May we all remember that it can only be preserved by respecting the rights of the states and distributing equally the benefits and burdens of the Union." These remarks fully revealed the irreconcilable nature of the conflict within the administration. In May, 1830, the President precipitated an open break by demanding to know why Calhoun as a member of Monroe's cabinet had urged that Jackson be censured for his Florida expedition. When Jackson refused to accept Calhoun's explanation, the rupture was complete. Within a year, Calhoun had resigned the vice-presidency and had entered the Senate to lead the dissident southerners against the administration tariff program.

Soon after the break with Calhoun, Jackson was able to clear up the Peggy Eaton affair and to rid the cabinet of Calhoun's supporters. When Van Buren and Eaton, in an attempt to relieve the President of further embarrassment, withdrew from the cabinet, Ingham, Branch, and Berrien were forced to follow suit. To fill these vacancies, Jackson made Edward Livingston of Louisiana Secretary of State, Lewis Cass of Michigan Secretary of War, Roger B. Taney of Maryland Attorney General, Louis McLane of Delaware Secretary of the Treasury, and Levi Woodbury of New Hampshire Secretary of the Navy. Both Eaton and Van Buren were rewarded for their loyalty; the former was named governor of Florida, and the latter was appointed minister to England. But the Senate by a single vote cast by Vice-President Calhoun refused to confirm Van Buren's nomination. The opposition's victory, however, was short-lived, for events were soon to demonstrate that Benton was correct when he stated that the Senate had "broken a minister and elected a Vice-President."

By 1831, Jackson had fundamentally altered the character of the party that had taken over the control of the government two years earlier. He had driven the rival southerners from the administration, and, at the same time, he had maintained a delicate balance between the West and the Northeast. The West could count on the President's support for its campaigns against the Indians, its demands for internal improvements (as long as they were not local in character), and its requests for a reduction in the sales price of the public lands. Jackson, however, was not a prisoner of the West, for he had also vetoed the Maysville Road bill, maintained the Northeast's strength in his cabinet, and made Martin Van Buren the crown prince of the Administration. Jackson, of course, was a westerner who had a deep affection for the region where he had lived and prospered. He was also a politician who knew that he had to have the support of the Northeast as well as the West to stay in power; yet as a nationalist, he refused to permit the interests of any section to take precedence over those of the nation.

Disunion Postponed

Although Jackson entered the presidency as a firm believer in states' rights, during his administration he established himself as one of the country's staunchest supporters of the Union. When South Carolina openly defied the federal government in 1832–3, he called the state's bluff and let it be known that he was willing to resort to force to uphold his principles. Then, confounding those who had repeatedly criticized him for his hot-headed impetuosity, he accepted a compromise that left the situation much as it had been before South Carolina had acted. By skillfully blending threats and diplomacy, Jackson was able both to preserve the Union and to assert the right of the majority to govern the minority.

The conflict between the administration and South Carolina had its origins in the tariff of 1828. As part of a section that exported what it produced and imported what it consumed, South Carolina was inevitably penalized by any increase in duties. But many New Englanders, including woolen manufacturers and consumers of molasses, also objected to the Tariff of Abominations. Several woolen manufacturers declared that they could manufacture to better advantage under the tariff of 1816 than under that of 1828. Some northerners and westerners also believed that some concession was due the South. These men could point to the fact that the revenues of the government were piling up beyond all expectation. This was sufficient evidence to many that tariff reduction was possible. Memorials and petitions, the majority begging for the elimination of the more objectionable features of the 1828 tariff, began to flood the desks of congressmen. Little, however, was done. Efforts to reduce the duties on iron, hemp, flax, cotton, woolens, and indigo met with failure. Some slight progress was made in 1830 when, as a partial cure for the surplus revenue, some duties were reduced.

Meanwhile, in the South the declining price of cotton convinced the planters that they were increasingly at the mercy of the manufacturers. Leading South Carolinians felt that the time had arrived for state action, but Calhoun counseled delay in the hope that the new Congress, which was to assemble in December, 1831, would give relief. In preparation for the renewal of the struggle, both protectionists and anti-protectionists held national conventions in the summer of that year. As soon as Congress met, a number of opinions and proposals were advanced. Clay, restating the principles of the American System, stood adamant for the continuation of high protection. McDuffie of South Carolina advocated a general *ad valorem* duty of 12½ per cent on all goods subject to import tax, and the abolition of specific duties. McLane, Secretary of the Treasury and spokesman for Jackson, recommended a 17 per cent reduction of the average rate of duty including reductions of the duty on raw wool, and on manufactured woolens, and the abolition of most of the system of minimum duties. John Quincy Adams, now in the House, reported a measure from the Committee on Manufactures that, with a few changes, became the tariff of 1832. It virtually removed the features of the tariff of 1828 that were objectionable to the manufacturers and the commercial East but it did not help the South. It abolished the minimum system of valuation, in-

Calhoun

creased the duty on manufactured woolens and placed a tax on woolen yarn. Wool costing less than eight cents a pound was admitted free; duties on hemp and iron were reduced.

In the opinion of the more radically discontented southerners, the tariff of 1832 added insult to injury. The planters had waged another battle against the "new rich" and again had lost; they now turned to what they believed to be their only recourse—nullification. In November, 1832, Calhoun, Hayne, and their followers called a special convention in South Carolina. Despite the strenuous efforts of a Unionist minority, they passed a nullification ordinance that stated "that the tariff law of 1828, and the amendment to the same of 1832, are null, void, and no law, nor binding upon this State, its officers, or citizens," and that they were not enforceable after February 1, 1833, unless modified to relieve the aggrieved party. If the federal government should attempt to enforce its authority within the boundaries of the state, such action would result in immediate war. State officers were to be required by oath to support the ordinance, and no case arising under it was to be appealed from a South Carolina court to the courts of the United States. The rest of the South, aggrieved though it was, hesitated to follow, and the radical South Carolinians stood alone.

When Jackson heard the news of South Carolina's action, he declared that he would meet it "at the threshold and have the leaders arrested and arraigned for treason." Probably with Calhoun in mind, Jackson added that he was ready to "hang every leader . . . of that political or social position." A warship and a fleet of revenue cutters were sent to Charleston Harbor; the federal forts in the harbor were reinforced; and Jackson in a proclamation issued on December 10, 1832, called South Carolina's plan of nullification "incompatible with the existence of the Union, contradicted expressly by the letter of the Constitution, unauthorized by its spirit, inconsistent with every principle on which it was founded, and destructive of the great object for which it was formed." But, at the same time, he urged South Carolina to reconsider its stand. When in January, 1833, he asked Congress to enact a "Force Bill" that would grant him full power to use the army and navy to enforce collection of revenue duties in the nullifying state, he also frankly stated that in his opinion the tariffs of 1828 and 1832 were unjust and should be lowered.

This policy of moderation was followed shortly afterward by the introduction of the Verplanck bill, an Administration measure that proposed a sweeping tariff reduction of 25 per cent. Manufacturers in great alarm quickly protested; Webster and John Quincy Adams professed to see in it the utter ruin of the industrial East. In his diary Adams said that Jackson had "cast away all the neutrality which he had heretofore maintained upon the conflicting interests and opinions of the different sections of the country, and surrenders the whole union to nullifiers of the South and the landrobbers of the West." Clay at heart probably shared a similar opinion, but the picture of his veteran political enemy, Jackson, at the head of troops coercing South Carolina was too much for him. After a conference at Philadelphia with the industrial leaders of the East, at which he was apparently told to use his own judgment, he hurried to Washington, where he entered into negotiations with Calhoun. The result was the Compromise Tariff of 1833. In its final form it provided for a general reduction over a nine-year period of all duties exceeding 20 per cent; the measure applied to specific as well as to *ad valorem* duties. Another liberal provision included the enlargement of the free list.

Vote of House of Representatives on Tariff of 1833

	FOR	AGAINST
New England	10	28
Middle States	24	47
South and Southwest	75	2
West	10	8
	119	85

On March 1, 1833, Congress passed both the Force Bill and the Compromise Tariff. Ten days later, South Carolina's convention withdrew the ordinance of nullification and in a final gesture of defiance voted to nullify the Force Bill. And there matters stood. The South had a lower tariff, and the Unionists had blocked secession. Still the issue remained, for the problems raised by South Carolina's stand had been postponed rather than solved.

In one sense the struggle between South Carolina and the federal government was a conflict between state and nation in which Jackson championed the Union. But even more it was a contest between majority and minority rule. South Carolina and Calhoun had demanded not only that the minority be guaranteed certain basic rights but also that it be permitted to call the tune for the majority. Faced with this problem, Jackson, although offering compromise, took his stand at the head of the majority. In so doing, he placed principle above party loyalty. His action antagonized a large bloc of Southern voters, many of whom withdrew from the Democratic party. Jackson, in alienating an important segment of his party, had adhered to his principles, reaffirmed his right to popular leadership, and had piloted the Union with a skillful hand through one of its most trying crises.

Settling Scores with England and France

Jackson, a nationalist in foreign as well as domestic affairs, demonstrated that the technique of threat and compromise that he had used in the tariff dispute could be employed as effectively against European nations as against American nullifiers. The first President since John Adams who had not previously served as Secretary of State, Jackson made up for lack of experience by the vigor, tact, and adroitness with which he defended American rights abroad. His forthright approach to the nation's foreign problems has been called "shirt-sleeve" diplomacy; but, regardless of what it is called, the fact remains that it was successful. Although Jackson's conception of American foreign policy was based on national rather than sectional considerations, the East rather than the West was the principal beneficiary of his diplomacy.

Jackson's most notable accomplishment in foreign affairs was the solution of a problem that had vexed all his predecessors. Since the Revolution, American vessels had been either partially or completely excluded from the British West Indian trade. The fact that many American vessels smuggled with the West Indies did not make the legal restrictions less obnoxious. On taking office, Jackson informed the British that the change in administration in the United States was sufficient cause for removal of the restrictions on the trade. In his annual message of December, 1829, he referred to Great Britain as "alike distinguished in peace and war" and as a country with which the United States could "look forward to years of peaceful, honorable, and elevated competition." He then induced Congress to grant him the authority to open the ports of the United States to the British as soon as Americans were given access to the British ports in the West Indies. At the same time he had Van Buren prepare a "communication . . . for Congress recommending a non-intercourse law between the United States and Canada, and a sufficient number of cutters commanded by our naval officers and our midshipmen made revenue officers, and a double set on every vessel." Jackson had used every conceivable weapon in his diplomatic offensive, and in October, 1830, the British gave way. In the future, American ships were permitted to participate in every phase of the West Indian trade except that between the islands and Great Britain.

In his efforts to settle the French spoliation claims, Jackson used much the same techniques that had proved so successful in his negotiations with the British. These claims, which grew out of French attacks on American commerce during the Napoleonic Wars, had never been paid despite repeated American demands. The issue was further complicated by the French contention that the United States had failed to live up to the most-favored-nation tariff provision in the 1803 treaty for the Louisiana Purchase. In his message of December, 1829, Jackson stated that the spoliation claims might lead to a "collision" between the two countries; but a year later, after Louis Philippe had become King of France, he substituted flattery for veiled threats and congratulated the new ruler on the fashion in which his accession to power had reflected the "paramount authority of the public will." Largely because of Jackson's efforts, the French on July 4, 1831, accepted a treaty in which they agreed to pay American citizens 25,000,000 francs in six annual installments. The treaty also provided that the United States would pay 25,000,000 francs to cover the claims against American damage to French shipping, that France would drop its protests concerning the treaty of 1803, and that the United States would reduce its duties on French wines.

Although the treaty went into effect in February, 1832, the French failed to pay their first installment on the agreed date. In an address to Congress in 1834, Jackson accused the French of a breach of faith and proposed reprisals against French property in the United States. The French replied by severing diplomatic relations with the United States and demanding that the President apologize. Although Jackson insisted that the "honor of my country shall never be stained by an apology from me for the statement of truth and the performance of duty," he did go so far as to say that "any intention to menace or insult the Government of France" was "unfounded." The French were satisfied, and in 1836 they paid the United States the first four installments of the spoliation claims.

The record reveals that Jackson was a nationalist both at home and abroad. His defense of the Union in the conflict with South Carolina was worthy of John Marshall, and his conduct of American foreign policy was as spirited and skillful as that of John Quincy Adams during Monroe's administration.

The Great Bank War

Of the major events during Jackson's administration, none better illustrates his adherence to the concepts of both majority rule and economic individualism than the struggle over the second Bank of the United States. Long before Jackson became President and throughout most of the Bank's history, its policies had been vigorously opposed in both the South and the West. Less than three years after its establishment, the bank had been justifiably held responsible by many for helping precipitate the Panic of 1819 and the ensuing depression. Although agricultural distress, the inability of American manufacturers to compete against the heavy importation of European goods, the lax and fraudulent methods of the state banks, and overspeculation in western lands were all in some measure responsible for the advent of hard times, the Bank's loan policy also contributed to the disaster. After two years of laxness and maladministration, from 1818 to 1820 the second Bank of the United States reduced its loans from $41,000,000 to $31,000,000. It also curtailed its note circulation from about $8,400,000 to about $3,500,000. It thus virtually forced the state banks to reduce their excessive and in some cases questionable issues from $100,000,000 in 1817 to $45,000,000 in 1819. Partial suspension of specie payments followed, accompanied by widespread business failures. The federal government, despite retrenchment, found it necessary to contract loans to cover deficits in both 1820 and 1821.

The South and West, where the effects of the Bank's contraction policy were especially felt, were extremely antagonistic. Only the action of Chief Justice Marshall in *McCulloch vs. Maryland* (1819) and *Osborn et al. vs. The Bank of the United States* (1824), which declared attempts by states to tax the Bank out of existence to be unconstitutional, saved the institution from the wrath of these sections. Even so, the Bank might have gone to the wall as a result of its own practices had not Langdon Cheves, a conservative South Carolina businessman, been put in charge in March, 1819. Although Cheves was sometimes inept, he undoubtedly enabled the Bank to weather the storm. Under the presidency of Nicholas Biddle, a Philadelphia financier who was Cheves' successor, the second Bank of the United States prospered and expanded its operations. Improved means for controlling the twenty-nine branches of the Bank were devised; balances due from the state banks were collected; discounts were increased; and a surplus was accumulated. From 1816 to 1831 the dividends on the bank's stock averaged 5 per cent. Of the $14,700,000 cash in the Bank's vaults in 1829, nearly half was specie. Potentially, the Bank could dictate to the entire American economy.

Neither conservative management nor expansion of the Bank's operations had any effect on the opposition. Even before the close of the 1820's, eastern mechanics, despite their dependence on financial stability, were coming to believe that the Bank was a tyrannical monopoly controlled by the rich and the well-born. The continued opposition of the South and West was in large measure caused by the fact that the notes of the Bank of the United States drove from circulation the notes of the shaky state banks and the shady or competing private banks of both sections. Politicians, farmers, and speculators—inflationists all—therefore denounced the Bank. Many were fully aware that, although the greater part of the Bank's stock was owned in the East, most of its profits came from the West and the South. Of the Bank's shares outstanding in 1828, New England held 20,853, New York 46,638, Pennsylvania 70,763, Maryland 34,262, and South Carolina 35,495. Only 19,815 were held in the remaining southern states, and 1,804 in Ohio, Indiana, Illinois, Kentucky, and Tennessee combined. The foreign holdings totaled 40,412 shares. The circulation of the Bank's notes, on the other hand, was largest in the dissatisfied sections.

In the Northeast, where their circulation was smaller and where the notes of the state banks were generally better secured, the antagonism to the Bank centered in the New York financial community, which was jealous and angered over Philadelphia's power to divert so much needed cash and banking profits away from the nation's chief port. The people of the West and South believed that they were compelled to pay tribute to eastern and foreign interests for the money they needed to buy land, make internal improvements, and engage in speculative enterprises. Opponents in the East objected to the Bank's near financial monopoly and superior position over competing banks.

More damaging to the Bank, perhaps, than the claim that it worked economic hardship on the farming sections of the country was the accusation that it discriminated against the followers of President Jackson and that certain of its branches had used their influence to defeat him in the election of 1828. There were also open charges that the Bank had subsidized members of Congress and that under the leadership of Biddle the supporters and beneficiaries of the Bank were engaged in a nationwide campaign to discredit its enemies. These allegations were partly true. For example, Daniel Webster, who was legal advisor and a branch director on the payroll of the Bank, once wrote to Biddle: "If it be wished that my relation to the Bank should be continued, it may be well to send me the usual retainer." Biddle, knowing that Jackson was unsympathetic toward the Bank, went out of his way at first to win Jackson's favor, after himself voting for Jackson in 1828. Only after failing in this effort and after the Bank war began did he seek to break the backbone of the political opposition by sharply contracting the Bank's loans. Before Jackson declared open warfare on the Bank, there is practically no evidence that the institution deliberately discriminated against his followers; on the contrary, it was almost illegally solicitous about keeping its opponents quiet with loans and favors.

In his first message to Congress, Jackson mildly attacked the Bank on the ground that it was both unconstitutional and monopolistic. Against Biddle's judgment, the question of rechartering the Bank was dragged into the campaign of 1832; the National Republicans referred to it as "a great beneficent and necessary institution." To make doubly certain that this issue would not be overlooked in the campaign, Biddle was induced to petition Congress for a renewal of the Bank's charter four years before it expired. Congress, confident that the need for the Bank and its good, honest work was self-evident, acted favorably on the request. On July 10, the eve of the presidential campaign, Jackson vetoed the measure. In the message that accompanied the veto, he pointed out that the capitalists of the northeastern states were growing rich at the expense of the people of the West and South. "Many of our rich men," he said, "have besought us to make them richer by act of

The Second Bank of the United States at Philadelphia

Congress. By attempting to gratify their desires, we have in the results of our legislation arrayed section against section, interest against interest, and man against man, in a fearful commotion which threatens to shake the foundations of our Union." To those who cited Supreme Court decisions in defense of the Bank, Jackson replied that the Court was only one branch of the government and that the "authority of the Supreme Court must not . . . be permitted to control the Congress or the Executive when they are acting in their legislative capacities." Although Biddle might declare that Jackson's statement was "really a manifesto of anarchy such as Marat or Robespierre might have issued to the mob," events were to demonstrate that Jackson was speaking for a majority of his countrymen.

The political and constitutional implications of Jackson's stand were fully as significant as his economic views. In defying both Congress and the Court, he championed what he sensed to be the will of the people. Jackson's veto message built a bridge between the presidency and the American people that gave him a degree of authority enjoyed by none of his predecessors. Jackson discovered that a president backed by a majority of the voters possessed power far greater than that granted to him by the Constitution. The majority was virtually unrepresented on the Supreme Court. In Congress the effectiveness of that majority was often dissipated by sectional rivalries; but in a President like Jackson it had a leader who could transform its latent strength into an effective force for shaping the government's policies. Although Jackson's discovery was ignored by many of his successors in the White House, others—notably, Abraham Lincoln, Theodore Roosevelt, Woodrow Wilson, and Franklin D. Roosevelt—adopted it as a guiding principle in their conduct of the nation's affairs.

Because the National Republicans had made the Bank virtually the only issue of the campaign of 1832, the voters were given an unexampled opportunity to either approve or reject administration policy. The first candidate in the field was William Wirt, who was chosen by the Anti-Masons in September, 1831, at the first national nominating convention in the nation's history. The National Republicans, following the precedent set by the Anti-Masons, selected delegates who convened at Baltimore and nominated Henry Clay. Although Jackson's nomination was a foregone conclusion, the Democrats, too, held a convention, which went through the formality of choosing Jackson and then named Van Buren as his running mate. Because Jackson wished to create the impression that Van Buren was the overwhelming choice of the party, he had the convention adopt a rule that no candidate could be nominated unless he received two thirds of the votes of the delegates. With Jackson's support Van Buren more than met this requirement. After 1844 the two-thirds rule remained a regular feature of Democratic conventions until it was repealed a century later at the instigation of Franklin D. Roosevelt.

The outcome of the election revealed that Jackson had not misinterpreted the temper of the voters. With 219 electoral votes, Jackson carried seventeen states and lost only Vermont, Massachusetts, Rhode Island, Connecticut, Delaware, Maryland, South Carolina, and Kentucky. Vermont gave its seven votes to Wirt, South Carolina cast its eleven votes for John Floyd of Virginia, while Clay received the forty-nine electoral votes of the other anti-Jackson states. The popular vote was 687,502 for Jackson to 530,189 for Clay. The soldier hero of 1828 had now created an image of himself as the champion of democracy.

Jackson interpreted the results of the election of 1832 as a mandate for the continuation of his anti-Bank program. The institution had worked for his defeat, and the President was therefore more convinced than ever that it should be destroyed. All his personal rancor and dangerous irritability were aroused. "I long for . . . repose on the Hermitage," he wrote in 1833. "But until I can strangle this hydra of corruption [the Bank] I will not shrink from my duty." To perform

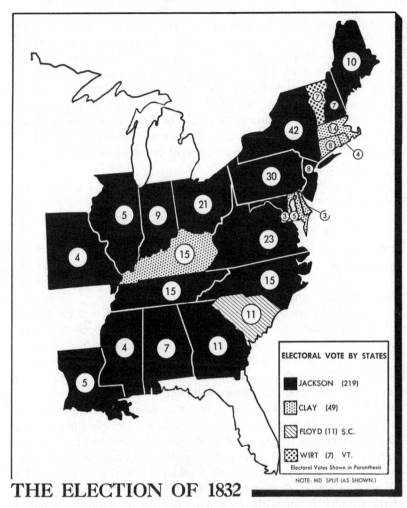

ELECTRICAL VOTE BY STATES

■ JACKSON (219)

▨ CLAY (49)

▨ FLOYD (11) S.C.

▨ WIRT (7) VT.

Electoral Votes Shown in Parenthesis

NOTE: MD SPLIT (AS SHOWN.)

THE ELECTION OF 1832

what he considered his duty, Jackson decided to take advantage of a provision in the Bank Act that authorized the Secretary of the Treasury to withdraw the government's deposits whenever he thought such action was warranted by the condition of the Bank. But at this point the President encountered an unexpected difficulty. Secretary of the Treasury McLane refused to order the removal of the deposits. Jackson thereupon made McLane Secretary of State and named William J. Duane of Philadelphia his successor. But Duane also refused to cooperate, and in September, 1833, he was supplanted by Roger Taney. Taney, a Maryland man, had a long-standing hatred of the Bank, and he immediately put the President's policy into effect. The government's incoming funds were placed in state banks, or "pet banks" as they were called by Jackson's opponents. The opposition complained bitterly that Jackson's action was both unconstitutional and inexpedient, and in New York State the opposition to the Jacksonians, sensing the power of the antimonopoly and "equal rights" issues now charged Jackson with government favoritism. The Senate, at Clay's instigation, adopted a resolution censuring the President. But Jackson ignored these complaints, and Benton, the bank's bitterest and oldest foe, was able to induce the Senate to remove the motion of censure from the record of its proceedings.

In 1836, the second United States Bank came to an end as a national institution. Biddle, however, at enormous cost, secured a charter from Pennsylvania. Greatly restricted in its activities and hard hit after 1837, the Bank went to the wall in 1841. Fifteen years were spent in liquidating its affairs; creditors were paid in full, but the shareholders lost everything. Biddle was indicted for conspiracy to defraud the other shareholders, but the indictment was quashed. In 1844, he died, poverty-stricken and broken-hearted.

Closely associated with the dispute over the Bank was the contest that developed during Jackson's second administration between the advocates of a "hard" currency and those who favored "soft"—or, in this instance, paper—money. Although Jackson had enjoyed the support of the West in his attack on the Bank of the United States, the same section, which was overwhelmingly inflationist, was opposed to his demand for hard money. Despite the fact that Jackson had destroyed the only institution in the country that had checked irresponsible or inflationary movements by state and local banks, Jackson and his principal advisers firmly believed that unrestricted paper issues by banks produced a speculative upswing in the business cycle that was inevitably followed by panic, depression, and hard times for the great majority of the people. In line with the general distrust of economic privilege that characterized the times, the Jacksonians objected to the power that the right to issue small notes gave the banks over the nation's economic system. In an effort to curb the steady flow of paper emanating from the banks, Congress, at the instigation of the administration, passed a series of laws in 1834 to increase the supply of gold coins in circulation and to ban notes of small denomination.

Because of the refusal of the states to follow the lead of the federal government, the administration's attempts to check the speculative boom that developed after 1834 had little success. As soon as the restraining hand of the second Bank of the United States was removed a new crop of local and state banks sprang up, many with little capital or specie. Between 1829 and 1837, their number increased from 329 to 788, their note circulation grew from $48,000,000, to $149,000,000, and their loans rose from $137,000,000 to $525,000,000. With easy credit (often encouraged by the "pet banks"), a mania for internal improvements and speculation in western land set in. Never, contemporaries declared, had the country been so prosperous. Even the treasury was filling up, and in 1835, upon the extinction of the entire national debt, Congress voted to distribute the mounting surplus in the treasury among the states, nominally in the form of a loan, but in reality as an outright gift. Much of this money promptly went into more internal improvements. Suddenly, there occurred a number of disturbing events: the final destruction of the Bank of the United States, the disastrous New York City fire of 1835, and bad harvests in the same year. The bubble burst in July, 1836, when Jackson issued his famous "Specie Circular" requiring that all public lands be paid for in specie or in notes of specie-paying banks. On top of this step came pressure from English creditors, more bad harvests, credit contraction, and a money stringency. On May 10, 1837, the New York banks suspended specie payment, and in a few days the banks in every important city in the country followed suit; the unprecedented overexpansion of credit gave way to the nation's worst depression up to that time.

Jackson's second term had ended before the crash. He left the presidency convinced of the wisdom of his policies. In his farewell address, he reviewed and reaffirmed his stand on economic individualism, sound money, internal improvements, foreign policy, the destruction of the Bank of the United States, and the preservation of the Union. To the end, he held to his faith in majority rule and to his fears of the effect of the concentration of economic power on American democracy and individualism. Soon after he retired to the Hermitage, he wrote to a friend: "It is now plain that the war is to be carried on by the monied aristocracy of the few against the Democracy of numbers; it is the plan of the prosperous to make the honest laborers hewers of wood and drawers of water to the monied aristocracy. . . ."

Four Years of Martin Van Buren

Jackson's forthright policies had alienated as well as attracted large blocs of voters. Many westerners had been antagonized by the Maysville Road veto and the administration's hard-money policies. Those southerners who subscribed to Calhoun's views on states' rights had withdrawn from the Democratic party because of the tariff dispute with South Carolina. There were also Americans in every section of

the country who had no use for the egalitarian rhetoric and democratic features of the Jackson Administration. As the leader of the opposition, Henry Clay hoped to weld these disparate groups into a majority party that would put his American System into effect. In 1834,
Clay's party had changed its name from National Republican to Whig
in an effort to symbolize opposition to what its members claimed was
the "reign of King Andrew." At the same time, the party had assumed
the character that it was to retain until its death in the 1850's. In the
South the Whigs could count on the support of the large planters; in
the Northeast the national party was generally backed by the business
interests and many farmers; and in the West it tended to attract the
more well-to-do farmers, who hoped that Clay's program of internal
improvements would bring them better markets. The Whigs were
strongest in the cotton belt of the Deep South, in New England, and
in the Ohio Valley. Although locally Whigs appealed to a wide diversity of interests and supported measures like general incorporation acts
in order to steal Jacksonian thunder, nationally in the late 1830's they
were identified by the Jacksonians as descendants of the Federalists, a
party of privilege.

The Democratic party drew its principal strength from the "middling" classes of the Northeast, the small farmers in the South, and
those corn and hog farmers of the West who had not been alienated
by Jackson's program. Jackson had ruled over these groups with a
firm partisan hand, and through his control of the party machinery he
was able to have Martin Van Buren of New York selected as his
successor.

On the surface, Van Buren seemed everything that Jackson was
not. Known as "the Little Magician" because of his prowess as a politician, he was something of a dandy who never would have been mistaken for a frontiersman or Indian fighter. He owed his rise to national
power to the Albany Regency's control over the Democratic party in
New York State, his ability as a political organizer, his loyalty to
Jackson, and his faith in democracy in a democratic age. A fastidious
dresser who liked good food and good wine, he was accused by his
opponents of being nothing more than a wily politician who used unscrupulous methods to achieve his objectives. Actually, he was neither
more nor less of a politician than the other party leaders of the day.
Van Buren, in short, was a good Jacksonian Democrat, who looked like
the stereotype of a Whig.

Van Buren's victory in the election of 1836 can be attributed to
prosperity, to the willingness of many voters to support a candidate
endorsed by Jackson, and to the disorganized state of the opposition.

Van Buren, "The Little Magician"

The Whigs were so riddled by factionalism that they did not even bother to hold a convention. Instead, by nominating a number of local candidates, they tried to have the election thrown into the House, where it was thought that Van Buren could be beaten. But this strategy failed, for Van Buren, with 170 electoral votes, had a clear majority over William Henry Harrison's 73, Hugh L. White's 26, Daniel Webster's 14, and the 11 votes cast by South Carolina's nullificationists for William P. Mangum. An unusual feature of the election was that no vice-presidential candidate received a majority, and for the only time in the nation's history the choice was made by the Senate, which selected Richard M. Johnson of Kentucky.

Van Buren unfortunately took office two months before the onset of a severe and protracted depression. By September, 1837, nine tenths of the nation's factories had closed. Real estate values tumbled, and internal-improvement projects came to a standstill or were abandoned. Banknote circulation fell from $149,000,000 in 1837 to $59,000,000 in 1843, and loans from more than $525,000,000 to less than $255,000,000. Bank failures were an everyday occurrence; New York City alone had 250 business failures in two months. Even banks organized and run by

"*July 4th, 1837, 61st Anniversary of Our Independence*": Satirizing the Panic of 1837

the states, as in Mississippi, Tennessee, Alabama, Arkansas, and Florida, were forced to close. Almshouses and poorhouses were filled to over-flowing. The winter of 1838 was exceptionally bitter, and many suf-fered from starvation and exposure. Many states repudiated their public debt, and incensed foreign investors like Charles Dickens were slow to return to the American market with their much needed capital.

Although he had no responsibility for the events leading up to the Panic of 1837, Van Buren was held culpable by many Americans for the ensuing hard times. Van Buren could do little to alleviate the im-pact of the depression. Any attempt by the government to check the downward swing of the business cycle would have required some aid to the nation's business classes. To Van Buren, a good Jacksonian, such a policy was out of the question; the new President was convinced that the principal task facing his administration was to prevent private groups from controlling the nation's finances. Jackson had devised no constructive alternative for the Bank of the United States, and it re-mained for his successor to find a method both to safeguard the gov-ernment's funds and to prevent the recurrence of an inflationary spiral generated by unrestricted issues of paper money. Yet any attempt to use private banks for this purpose would bring on charges of monopoly and favoritism from political opponents. The Jacksonian ideal of no national government intervention in the economy had come home to roost. Van Buren, accordingly, proposed an independent-treasury sys-tem that would consist of a series of subtreasuries or vaults for the storage of federal funds. Such an arrangement would enable the govern-ment to handle all its monies through its own officials. Since the sub-treasuries would issue only specie and secured treasury notes, this system would tend to limit the expansion of paper currency. No one could accuse the government of unfair favors to private banks.

The Whigs, who were able to agree on little else, were united in their opposition to Van Buren's proposal for an independent treasury. Henry Clay predicted that the plan would reduce all property values by two thirds, and John Quincy Adams said: "As to the sub-treasury— Bedlam seems to me the only place where it could have originated. . . . A Divorce of Bank and State! Why a divorce of Trade and Shipping would be as wise. . . ." Philip Hone, a New York Whig, thought the idea the "most mischievous in its tendency that had ever been presented to the American people," and the *Boston Atlas* stated that it "aimed at the interests of the country a blow, which if it do not recoil upon the aggressor, must be productive to the country of lasting mischief, per-haps of irretrievable anarchy." Many conservative Democrats shared these views, and in Van Buren's own state of New York, the Albany Regency was split over the issue.

The vehemence with which the Whigs attacked the subtreasury proposal was matched by the enthusiasm with which it was received by many of the more radical groups in the Northeast. Throughout Jackson's administration, his financial policies had been wholeheartedly supported by a number of so-called Workingmen's parties, many of whose leaders were comfortably off. The most prominent of these parties was a branch of the New York State Democratic organization known as the Loco-Focos. This group got its name in 1835 when the local conservative Democrats in New York City tried to break up a meeting by turning off the lights in the hall. The radicals were prepared for such an emergency; when the lights went out, they continued the meeting with candles that they lit with matches called loco-focos.

Within a short time Loco-Focoism had become synonymous with radicalism in general and with the demands of the pro-Jackson enthusiasts in the Northeast in particular. In local politics it was the Loco-Focos who converted the Democratic party to equal rights ideals after Jackson had shown the way in the Bank war of 1832. Because Van Buren's insistence on hard money and on the separation of banking and government seemed logical conclusions to the program inaugurated by Jackson, both friends and foes of the Administration identified his subtreasury proposal with Loco-Focoism. And they were right, for Van Buren more than any other president before the Civil War was a representative of the more radical elements in the Northeast.

The Subtreasury bill did not become law until the last year of Van Buren's administration. Although it was passed by the Senate in 1837 and in 1838, it was defeated on both occasions by the House of Representatives. It was not approved by both branches of Congress until 1840. Regardless of the economic theory of the independent-treasury system, its political significance is unmistakable: a semi-independent government agency rather than private groups would now regulate the nation's finances, and—in the words of Frederick Jackson Turner—the "so-called 'money power' [would have] . . . to operate more or less *sub rosa* instead of being an integral part of the government."

Van Buren was able to put his Loco-Foco theories into effect on only one other occasion. By issuing a proclamation authorizing a ten-hour day for laborers in federal shipyards, he became the first President in the nation's history to adopt a policy that was designed specifically to aid the workingman.

Jackson's Coalition Loses Power

Throughout Van Buren's four years in the presidency, the Whigs waged a relentless campaign against him and his administration. He was blamed for the Panic of 1837, accused of appointing corrupt officials, and charged with turning the government over to a small group of unrepresentative radicals. Northern audiences were told that he was too friendly to the South. Southerners were told that he had blocked southern expansion by refusing to annex Texas, which, after achieving independence in 1836, had applied for admission to the Union. In the West, Van Buren was pictured as an effete, pleasure-loving easterner. In the East, he was described to conservatives as more of a Jacksonian Democrat than Jackson. Many voters apparently accepted these criticisms at face value, for in the depression year of 1838 the Democrats lost control of both branches of Congress. But in that same year Calhoun made uneasy peace with Van Buren in order to re-establish connections with a national party.

In the campaign of 1840 the Whigs paid the Jacksonian Democrats the high compliment of emulation. Nominating their own soldier-hero William Henry Harrison, they proclaimed him a man of the people and a rough and ready defender of popular rights. Harrison, who had little in common with Jackson except his record as an Indian fighter and his substantial financial position, was hailed as a typical westerner. Shortly before the election, he predicted that most people would vote for him "on the same grounds as they supported General Jackson." In an effort to capitalize on the South's dissatisfaction with the Democratic program, the Whigs gave second place on their ticket to John Tyler, a Virginian and a firm believer in states' rights. The Democratic convention renominated Van Buren, announced that the party would stand on its record in office, and left the selection of a vice-presidential candidate to their "fellow-citizens in the several states."

During the campaign the Whigs succeeded in obscuring all the issues and in creating the impression that the "hero of Tippecanoe" was a Jackson-like figure who lived in a log cabin and loved the common man's drink, hard cider. Actually Harrison lived in a large and comfortable house in Ohio and never showed any particular preference for hard cider. In innumerable campaign parades, the Whig marchers shouted "Tippecanoe and Tyler, too," and carried banners inscribed:

> Farewell, Dear Van
> You're not our man
> To guide the ship
> We'll try old Tip

The New Look of Whiggery, 1840

Whig campaigners wore coonskin caps, and no Whig rally was complete without a log cabin, barrels of cider, and pictures showing Harrison in a rustic setting. While all the homey and simple virtues of the frontier were attributed to Harrison, Van Buren was depicted as wallowing in urban luxury, and a famous campaign song contrasted Van Buren lounging on "his cushioned settee" drinking wine from "his coolers of silver" to Harrison on his "buckeye bench" sipping some of the apparently inexhaustible supply of hard cider. The outcome of the election revealed the success of the Whigs' tactics and the impact

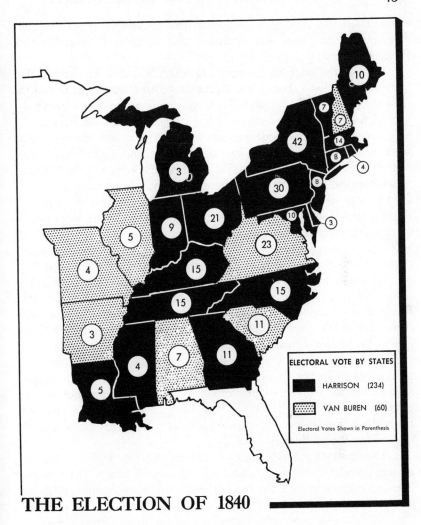

ELECTORAL VOTE BY STATES

◼ HARRISON (234)

▦ VAN BUREN (60)

Electoral Votes Shown in Parenthesis

THE ELECTION OF 1840

of the depression. Harrison defeated Van Buren by an electoral vote of 234 to 60 and a popular vote of 1,275,016 to 1,128,702.

The Whigs had only a brief time in which to enjoy their triumph, for after a month in office Harrison died. Clay, who had expected to dominate Harrison, now had to contend with Tyler, who immediately demonstrated that he was more a southerner than a Whig. An opponent of a high tariff, a third Bank of the United States, and internal improvements, and a defender of states' rights and nullification, Tyler had no use for any part of Clay's American System. The result was a virtual stalemate. Although Clay controlled majorities in both houses of Congress, he could not command enough votes to override the President's veto.

Despite the conflict between the executive and legislature, the Whigs were able to abolish Van Buren's substitute for the Bank and to raise the tariff. Both Clay and Tyler were opposed to Van Buren's financial program, and in August, 1841, Congress, with the President's approval, repealed the Independent Treasury Act. But the two men were unable to agree on new financial controls, and Tyler vetoed two bank bills enacted by Congress. Despite his principles, however, Tyler was compelled by the treasury's need for additional revenue to accept Clay's proposal for an increase in tariff duties. In August, 1842, he signed a new Tariff Act. Under the terms of this bill, rates were raised to approximately the same level as in the tariff of 1832. Tyler would accept no other part of the Whig program. The only other significant measures adopted during his administration were the Pre-emption Act of 1841 and a Bankruptcy Act that was subsequently repealed. Even before the end of Tyler's first year in office, the breach between the President and his party was complete. After Tyler's veto of the second bank bill, every member of his cabinet except Secretary of State Daniel Webster resigned, and a caucus of Whig congressmen issued a statement announcing that "those who brought the President into power can no longer, in any manner or degree, be justly held responsible or blamed for the administration of the executive branch of the government." Even this act was not enough for Clay. He resigned from the Senate in protest—no doubt in the hope that he would be drafted for the presidency in 1844.

The deadlock in the Whig party did not interfere with the conduct of foreign affairs. Foreign policy was one area in which Tyler might hope to make a record for himself and earn renomination. Webster also sensed the possibility of achieving national renown and, possibly, the presidency through an outstanding foreign policy. Before Webster resigned as Secretary of State in 1843, he and Lord Ashburton, the British minister to the United States, were able to settle a number of disputes that threatened the friendly relations of the two countries. Both men were ideally suited for their task. Webster had met Ashburton on a visit to England in 1839 and had been enthusiastically received by English leaders. Ashburton, a personable businessman and politician, had visited America on numerous occasions, was married to an American, and had as much respect for the United States as Webster had for England. Their negotiations were facilitated by Tyler's coop-

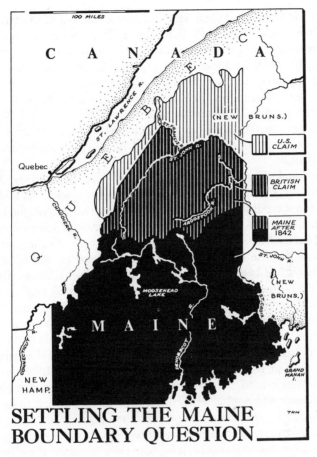

SETTLING THE MAINE
BOUNDARY QUESTION

eration and the determination with which he supported Webster's
position.

One of the most vexing problems confronting Webster and Ashburton concerned an incident that grew out of the attempt of some
Americans in the northern part of the country to aid the rebels in the
Canadian insurrection of 1837. On December 29, 1837, a small group of
Canadian volunteers retaliated against the interventionists by crossing
the Niagara River and sinking the *Caroline*, an American steamship
that had been used to supply the rebels. The United States immediately
demanded reparations, but Lord Palmerston, the British foreign minister, refused to consider the American claim. The dispute was further
complicated in 1840, when a Canadian named McLeod boasted in a
New York City tavern that he had killed an American during the at-

tack on the *Caroline*. When McLeod was arrested and placed on trial for murder in a New York State court, Palmerston threatened war and demanded the Canadian's release on the ground that a soldier performing his military duties could not be charged with murder. Just when it appeared that both sides would use force to resolve their difficulties, developments on both sides of the Atlantic made a peaceful settlement possible. Palmerston was succeeded as Foreign Secretary by the more conciliatory Lord Aberdeen; McLeod was acquitted by a New York jury; and Webster accepted Ashburton's apologies for the *Caroline* affair.

By concluding a mutually satisfactory agreement on the location of the boundary between Maine and New Brunswick, Webster and Ashburton were able to liquidate a controversy that had plagued Anglo-American relations for more than half a century. Commissions appointed under both the Jay Treaty and the Treaty of Ghent had done little to clarify the dispute. A boundary proposed by the King of the Netherlands had been rejected in 1831 by the United States. By 1838, people on both sides of the border were prepared to take matters in their own hands. Maine and New Brunswick called out their militia. Congress appropriated $10,000,000 for the defense of American rights and authorized the President to issue a call for 50,000 volunteers. But no lives were lost in the so-called Aroostook War. General Winfield Scott, serving as Van Buren's special representative, was able to arrange a truce in March 1839. Neither side, however, abandoned its claim, and both Webster and Ashburton realized that the matter had to be settled once and for all. Under the compromise they devised, the United States received a little more than half the 12,000 square miles in dispute. This division gave the Americans less than they thought they deserved. Partly to assuage their feelings Ashburton agreed to the United States's claim to approximately 200 square miles of land at the source of the Connecticut River and accepted a minor adjustment of the northern boundary in the vicinity of Lake Champlain. For a time it seemed likely that both Parliament and the Senate would refuse to approve the proposed boundary line between Maine and New Brunswick. But a 1782 map in the British foreign office convinced Parliament of the validity of the American claim, while a different map of the same year, which was in Webster's possession and which tended to substantiate the British position, had a similar effect on the Senate.

The Webster-Ashburton negotiations almost broke down over the problem of suppressing the slave trade. The British, who had freed the slaves in their colonies in 1833, were making a strenuous effort to eliminate the slave trade and wished to stop and search suspected slave ships. The Americans, fearing that the right to search would quickly be converted into the right to impress, refused to grant the British this privilege. Because of the American stand, slavers, regardless of nationality, flew the American flag to prevent interference by the British. In 1841, the controversy grew worse when the ship *Creole*, which was transporting slaves from Virginia to New Orleans, put in at the British Bahamas after the slaves on board had mutinied and killed a white passenger. The British officials at Nassau had executed the murderers but had set the other slaves free. Despite the strained relations caused by the *Creole* affair, the matter was amicably settled by an exchange of notes in which it was agreed to turn the question over to a mixed claims commission. Meanwhile, the larger problem of the control of the slave trade was resolved by a provision in the Webster-Ashburton Treaty that called for the armed patrol of the African coast by British and American vessels. The treaty went into effect in 1842; it was the most important development in Anglo-American relations in the three decades preceding the Civil War and a notable accomplishment of an otherwise undistinguished administration.

By the early 1840's, the national issues around which Jacksonian democracy had taken shape had declined in importance. The control of the Democratic party continued to turn largely around the New York–Charleston axis, the followers of Van Buren in uncomfortable alliance with the friends of Calhoun. Within a few years, Americans were to turn their attention from the economic issues of the 1830's to the question of the territorial expansion of the United States and to the sectional dispute engendered in large part by the slavery controversy.

FOR SUPPLEMENTARY READING

The book that started the present wide interest in Jacksonian politics is Arthur Schlesinger, Jr., *The Age of Jackson* (1945). Some sense of various alternative interpretations can be obtained from reading Richard Hofstadter, *The American Political Tradition* (1948) (Pb); Oscar and Mary Handlin, *Commonwealth* (1947); Marvin Meyers, *The Jacksonian Persuasion* (1957); J. W. Ward, *Andrew Jackson, Symbol for an Age* (1955); F. J. Turner, *The United States, 1830–50* (1935); T. P. Abernethy, *From Frontier to Plantation in Tennessee* (1932); H. C. Syrett, *Andrew Jackson* (1953); G. Van Deusen, *The*

Jacksonian Era 1828–1845 (1958); Lee Benson, *The Concept of Jacksonian Democracy: New York As a Test Case* (1961); and R. V. Remini, *The Election of Andrew Jackson* (1965).
from Parton's longer classic work.

The freshest view of Jackson and the spoils system is L. D. White, *The Jacksonians* (1954). On the bank war, use T. P. Govan, *Nicholas Biddle* (1959); B. Hammond, *Banks and Politics in America* (1957); and George R. Taylor's pamphlet, *Jackson vs. Biddle* (1949). On the nullification controversy, start with W. W. Freehling, *Prelude to Civil War: The Nullification Controversy in South Carolina* (1965), and C. M. Wiltse, *John C. Calhoun: Nullifier, 1829–1839* (1949). Supplement these with Hofstadter on Calhoun in *The American Political Tradition*. Older views of the organization of the Whig opposition to Jackson are in E. M. Carroll, *Origins of the Whig Party* (1925), and G. R. Poage, *Henry Clay and the Whig Party* (1936).

The biographies for this period are numerous. See especially S. F. Bemis, *John Quincy Adams and the Union* (1956); C. M. Fuess, *Daniel Webster* (2 vols., 1930); W. N. Chambers, *Old Bullion Benton* (1956); C. B. Swisher, *Roger B. Taney* (1935); C. G. Sellers, *James K. Polk: Jacksonian, 1795–1843* (1957); J. A. Garraty, *Silas Wright* (1949); *The Autobiography of Martin Van Buren* (1918); and, for Jackson himself, J. S. Bassett, *The Life of Andrew Jackson* (2 vols., 1911), and R. V. Remini (ed.), *The Presidency of Andrew Jackson* (1967) (Pb), from Parton's longer classic work.

Over-all, the most exciting and fruitful study of the United States in Jackson's time is Alexis de Tocqueville, *Democracy in America* (2 vols., 1946) (Pb).

15

Americans at Work

THE GREAT GROWTH of American agriculture and industry after 1815 was made possible in large part by the expansion of the nation's transportation system. During the fifty years preceding the Civil War, old roads were improved and new ones constructed, a network of canals was built, and a system of railroads was established. While these developments stimulated and facilitated domestic commerce and farming, a flourishing overseas trade provided Americans with foreign products and with markets for their surplus goods. Confronted with an ever larger market, American businessmen built factories and shops to supply the country with its needs and thereby created a whole new range of national economic and political problems.

Roads Westward

At the close of the Revolutionary era, American domestic trade was relatively unimportant. Aside from local merchandising, practically all domestic commerce in 1790 consisted of the exchange of imported wares for the surplus agricultural produce from the inland regions east of the Appalachians. Thousands of dollars worth of imported goods were annually turned over to hinterland farmers by Philadelphia merchants in payment for meat, grain, flour, and lumber. Goods from abroad largely paid for the products that reached the wharves of New

York from the Hudson, Mohawk, and Connecticut valleys. Farmers from the upper Chesapeake Bay regions and from the extensive territory drained by the Susquehanna looked to Baltimore as a market for their products and a source of supply for their needs. In the South, European agents continued to exchange their goods for tobacco, rice, and flour.

As population increased and people began to move into the trans-Allegheny country, the need for adequate inland transportation facilities became more urgent. At first an effort was made to solve the problem by transforming the old Indian trails into earth roads, but these dirt roads were described by travelers as "execrable," "savage," "shameful," "infamous," "tedious," and "wretched." The rapidly growing western trade led to a remarkable era in improved road building, in which Pennsylvania took the lead. In 1792, the Philadelphia and Lancaster Turnpike Company was chartered to build a road connecting the head waters of the Potomac and Ohio rivers, and within two years it had completed a sixty-two-mile pike at a cost of $465,000. The Lancaster Pike, an almost instant success, became one of the leading thoroughfares for those headed for the Ohio country, enhanced land values, and brought to merchants of Philadelphia a rich trade from one of the most fertile agricultural regions in America. The traffic over it was so great that its nine tollgates, located on the average about seven miles apart, turned in a revenue that enabled the company to pay dividends running as high as 15 per cent.

News of the success of the Philadelphia–Lancaster enterprise soon reached other sections of the country, and the next twenty or thirty years brought great activity in road building. Because long poles with pikes were swung across the road at toll houses to bar advance until payment had been made, these improved toll roads were called turnpikes. Turnpikes and turnpike companies became leading topics of conversation and offered fine opportunities for private investment. Lotteries and local county and state aid were other sources of capital. Pennsylvania chartered 86 companies, and by 1832 the state had more than 2,000 miles of improved highways. Approximately 180 turnpike companies were formed in New England by 1810, of which New Hampshire chartered 20 and Vermont 26. Connecticut built nearly 800 miles of hard-surfaced roads. By 1811, New York had chartered 137 companies whose combined capital totaled $7,500,000; these companies constructed about 1,400 miles of road. From Baltimore three turnpikes westward were constructed. The western farmer discovered that the absence of turnpikes into the trans-Allegheny country made it impossible for him to share in the profits coming from the heavy English imports of American foodstuffs during the Napoleonic Wars when the average price of a barrel of American flour nearly doubled. He vigorously demanded that the federal government take steps to remedy this situation. Manufacturers in search of cheaper raw materials and widening markets united with the westerners in agitation for internal improvements.

The Great National Road

Although the purchase of Louisiana and the opening of the Mississippi eased the western farmer's problem, the agitation for better connections between the East and the West did not subside. Many people argued that the government should either build roads and canals or help finance private undertakings. By 1805, an arrangement for Congress to spend 5 per cent of the profits from the sale of lands in new states for roads had produced $12,600. In March of the following year, Congress voted to construct a road from Cumberland, on the Maryland side of the Potomac, to Wheeling, on the Virginia side of the Ohio. Among those who enthusiastically advocated the new road was Albert Gallatin, Jefferson's Secretary of the Treasury. In a letter to Jefferson, Gallatin called attention to "The immense importance of that road as part of a great western travelling road and principally as the main communication for the transportation of all the foreign or Atlantic articles which the western states consume and even for the carriage of western flour and produce to the Potomac." By 1817, after several delays, the eastern portion of the road was opened, and in 1818 the full 130-mile stretch from the Potomac to the Ohio was completed. Its extension further westward was opposed by many easterners, but the road was continued to Columbus, Ohio, in 1833, then due west through Richmond, Indianapolis, and Terre Haute, Indiana, until it reached Vandalia, Illinois, in 1852. Henry Clay of Kentucky was the principal champion of the road, and between 1806 and 1838 he supported more than thirty federal acts to aid it. By 1836, Congress had turned the road over to the states through which it ran.

For nearly two decades, the Cumberland (or National) was one of the leading arteries to the trans-Allegheny empire. A person could now go from Baltimore to Wheeling in three, instead of eight, days. Property along the route rose in value, and villages multiplied in number and population. The road was also the main route for emigrants. For merchant and pioneer farmer it afforded a long hoped for avenue between the East and the West over which merchandise and western farm products of all kinds could be shipped at greatly reduced costs.

THE NATIONAL ROAD

The success of the Cumberland Road further stimulated interest in internal improvements of all kinds, and between 1815 and 1830 numerous turnpike and canal companies were organized. Many were designed for purely local projects; others were interstate in character. Nearly all companies hoped that they would be financially assisted by government. While some were disappointed in this expectation, many received public aid. The practice of granting federal appropriations for road building, however, was halted for a generation when President Jackson in 1830 vetoed the Maysville Road bill, a measure providing for a sixty-mile turnpike from Maysville to Lexington, entirely in the state of Kentucky. The veto shifted the burden of highway construction to the states, towns, and counties which, after 1840, were to try the cheaper but less satisfactory plank roads.

The Maysville veto was a severe blow for all those who were in any way interested in building roads for improving communication or for speculation. Western farmers were especially hard hit, for the younger commonwealths considered themselves too poor to vote adequate funds for road making. Private toll companies still functioned on the roads, ferries, and bridges but, with the coming of the steamboat and the railroad, they ceased to be profitable ventures. Taking the country as a whole, the roads, aside from the turnpikes, were abominable, and Charles Dickens did not seriously exaggerate when in 1842 he described American roads as "a series of alternate swamps and gravel pits."

Steamboats on the Rivers

Waterways were more important than roads in the development of early American domestic commerce; on the principal rivers and their tributaries there were no tolls to pay and no oxen, mules, or horses to feed or wagons to repair. Rapids, falls, treacherous currents, headwinds, and, occasionally, low water were the main drawbacks. With the exception of New England, where the fall line is near the coast, the great region east of the Mississippi contains many navigable streams. Since roads were poor or altogether lacking, many farmers, particularly those of the trans-Allegheny region, were virtually compelled to depend on these streams to get their surplus produce to market.

The use of rivers for transportation was practically revolutionized by the steamboat. Before 1800, a number of Americans experimented with the use of steam to drive boats. In 1786, John Fitch attained a speed of three miles a hour on the Delaware with a boat driven by twelve mechanically operated upright oars. Subsequent models had more power and greater speed. Though Pennsylvania, Delaware, New York, New Jersey, and Virginia granted him the sole right to operate steamboats on their waters, Fitch's attempt in 1790 to make regular trips between Philadelphia, Bordentown, Trenton, and Wilmington proved unprofitable.

Robert Fulton, however, made steam navigation a success. In 1801, while living abroad, Fulton met Robert R. Livingston, the American minister to France. Both were interested in the possibilities of the steamboat, and together they studied the attempts at steam navigation that had been made on either side of the Atlantic. Fulton came to the conclusion that a powerful and well built engine was indispensable to success. Through Livingston's influence he succeeded in inducing the British government to allow a Boulton and Watt engine to be shipped to America. This engine he installed in the *Clermont*, a 160-ton sidewheeler, which in August, 1807, completed a round trip between Albany and New York City in 62 hours.

In 1803, Fulton, Livingston, and their associate, Nicholas Roosevelt, obtained exclusive control of the navigable waters of New York State. Private steamboat companies soon introduced service up and down other rivers, including the Mississippi. In 1824, John Marshall's decision in *Gibbons vs. Ogden*, breaking Fulton's monopoly on the Hudson, ended state control of navigable rivers carrying interstate commerce and opened the way for increased steamboat traffic on inland waters. By 1820, sixty steamboats were in operation on the Mississippi and its tributaries. Twenty years later, the number had multiplied to over 400, and by 1860 to more than 1,000.

Steamboat transportation on the Great Lakes developed more slowly, for until the completion of the Erie Canal in 1825, the whole Lakes region was outside the range of navigation and settlement. After the Erie and Ohio canals were built, however, the Lakes trade grew

Fulton's Clermont *on the Hudson*

rapidly; the tonnage, only 3,500 in 1820 had increased to 75,000 in 1840 and to 470,000 in 1860.

Although steamboats on the western waters were able to reduce the time from New Orleans to Pittsburgh from one hundred to thirty days, to cut the cost of transportation in half, and to expand the market for both farmer and merchant, they operated under most trying conditions. Natural perils to navigation, poor construction, weak engines, fires, explosions, and collisions took a heavy toll. Fairly accurate records indicate that by 1850, 1,070 vessels, representing a total cost of $7,100,-000, had been lost with human casualties of 2,269 killed and 1,881 wounded. The diarist Philip Hone concluded that steam had become a "substitute for war in the philosophical plan of keeping down the superabundance of the human race, and thinning off the excessive population of which political economists have from time to time expressed so much dread." Between 1822 and 1860, the federal government appropriated more than $3,000,000 for the removal of traffic hazards to steamboats on the Mississippi, Ohio, Missouri, and Arkansas rivers.

Despite the fact that the National Road and the steamboat facilitated settlement of the trans-Allegheny country and materially aided both farmer and merchant, they did not solve the transportation problem. Farmers in western New York, northern Ohio and Indiana, and other sections of the country remote from the national pike or a navigable stream continued to demand better communications with the East. Even those north of the Ohio, who could make use of the Mississippi and its tributaries, complained of the long, roundabout, and hazardous route by which their commodities reached the seaboard or

European markets. A shorter, more direct, and cheaper route between the Atlantic coast and the trans-Appalachia was still urgently needed. Not until New York State built the Erie Canal, connecting Lake Erie with the Hudson River, was this need met.

Canal Fever

Plans for canals in America antedated the Revolution, and before the close of the eighteenth century a number of short local canals around rapids or falls or between important towns had been built or were under construction. But not one of these linked the East with the West. Although a major waterway had been visualized by Washington, Robert Morris, Albert Gallatin, and many others, it was not until the British blockade had put an end to coastwise shipping that discussion of the project was revived. The continued high cost of sending merchandise overland from the Atlantic coast towns to the West caused the merchants of the Ohio country to wonder if it would not be more profitable to buy their imported goods from New Orleans rather than from Boston, New York, Philadelphia, and Baltimore. Far-sighted Easterners feared that they would be deprived of western markets, and that East and West might drift apart commercially and politically.

As early as 1784-5, New Yorkers began to plan major canals to prevent New York City from losing the produce of the interior to New Orleans and Montreal. Opposition by tax payers and federal refusal of aid frustrated efforts for twenty years. But, in 1817, the state of New York, thanks to Governor De Witt Clinton, finally undertook the task alone. The $7,000,000 estimated as the cost of building the two waterways was borrowed on the credit of the state, and was to be financed in a variety of ways, including lotteries, taxes, and tolls.

Actual construction of the Erie Canal was entrusted to small contractors. The first strip of the Lake Erie–Hudson River waterway—the fifteen-mile stretch between Rome and Utica—opened in 1819. Four years later, boats could pass from Rochester into the waters of the Hudson River at Albany, and in 1825 a triumphant fleet headed by the *Seneca Chief* made its way from Lake Erie to New York Bay, where, on November 4, Governor Clinton pronounced these words as he poured a cask of lake water into the sea to symbolize "the marriage of the waters."

This is intended to indicate and commemorate the navigable communication which has been accomplished between our Mediterranean Seas and the Atlantic Ocean, in about eight years, to the extent of more than four hundred and twenty-five miles, by the wisdom, public spirit, and energy of the people of the State of New York; and may the God of the Heavens and the Earth smile most propitiously on this work, and render it subservient to the best interests of the human race!

The original Erie Canal was 363 miles long and cost between $7,000,000 and $8,000,000. So great was the traffic, however, that the tolls during the first nine years more than covered the cost of construction. During its first year, when it was operated only part of the season, the tolls equaled one seventh of its original cost. The financial returns to the state from the Erie Canal were small in comparison with its far-reaching economic, social, and political effects. The canal served as a highway for the entire western Lakes district. The time required for freight shipments from Buffalo to New York was reduced from twenty to six days, and the cost from $100 to $8 a ton. Grain, lumber, pot- and pearl-ashes and other bulky products that formerly had gone by river or pike to Baltimore, Philadelphia, Montreal, and New Orleans were now sent eastward at greatly reduced rates. In 1835, ten years after the canal opened, nearly 868,500 barrels of flour from western New York, and 268,000 barrels from states farther west passed over the new route. By 1846, the arrival of wheat and flour at Buffalo had surpassed that at New Orleans. Western farm products increased rapidly in volume and in some sections doubled or trebled. Land values rose correspondingly. The canal also served to lower the prices of eastern manufacturers in the West; New York City, where real and personal property rose from $70,000,000 in 1820 to $125,000,000 in 1830, was transformed from a market town for the Hudson Valley into the leading metropolis of America. By 1850, it had outstripped Philadelphia, Boston, and Baltimore in both population and wealth. The Lake towns of Buffalo, Cleveland, Detroit, Milwaukee, and Chicago now developed with amazing rapidity and by 1850 were challenging each other for supremacy in the West.

The Erie Canal also increased economic specialization. Eastern farmers, particularly those of New England, who were handicapped by poor soil, were now unable to compete with the farmers of the West. Eastern potatoes, for example, which had sold readily for seventy-five cents a bushel before the opening of the canal, were rapidly replaced by western-grown potatoes at half that price. The production of transportable farm produce was increasingly left to the trans-Allegheny; and an ever increasing number of New England

Lockport on the Erie Canal

[NEW YORK PUBLIC LIBRARY]

farmers left their stony hillsides for rising mill towns or swelled the growing streams of pioneers headed westward. Many of the emigrating farmers, as well as nearly all of the Germans and Irish who went West, made use of the canal packet boats, which covered the distance between Albany and Buffalo in four and a half days.

The success of the Erie Canal at once intensified demand for canals in other seaboard states. Boston, Philadelphia, Baltimore, and, to a lesser extent, Charleston, took immediate steps to improve their transportation facilities with the West. A Massachusetts venture to link Boston's markets with the eastern end of the Erie Canal by water failed. Although a Philadelphia to Pittsburgh series of canals and portage railways costing $10,000,000 never seriously rivaled the Erie route, it enabled Philadelphia to retain a share of the trade that otherwise would have gone to New York. Baltimore also sought to tap the West with the Chesapeake and Ohio Canal along the Potomac, and by a tunnel under the mountains. The project, begun in 1828, was never completed.

The large-scale projects that were designed to join the Atlantic with the Middle West were supplemented by a number of smaller canals. In the Northeast, most of these were built as feeders to the main canals or as outlets for the anthracite coal district of eastern Pennsylvania. In the Middle West, with its great distances, lack of roads, and

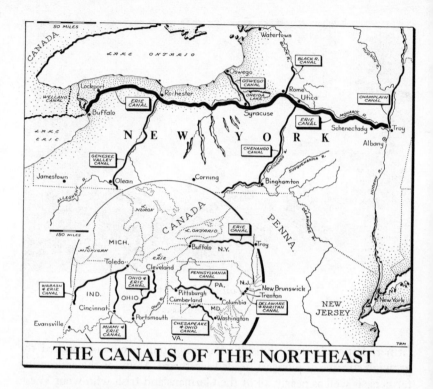

THE CANALS OF THE NORTHEAST

desire for better transportation facilities, the most important of the canals were those that, by joining the Great Lakes with the Ohio and Mississippi systems, provided continuous inland water communication to either New York or New Orleans. Of the major sections, only the South failed to build canals on a large scale. In the states south of Maryland and the Ohio River, mountainous terrain more often than not made canal construction difficult, if not impossible.

Before 1850, nearly 3,200 miles of canals were built in the United States. The principal burden of financing this major undertaking was borne by the states, which by 1840 had spent $200,000,000 on internal improvements. To raise this sum the states had to borrow, and the state securities were generally regarded as first rate investments; but because America lacked enough liquid capital to float all the state bond issues, it was necessary to turn to the Old World for financial aid. It was estimated in 1839 that American states and corporations owed European creditors at least $200,000,000. Englishmen had invested more than $110,000,000 in American stocks. In addition to borrowing money, several states—notably Ohio, Indiana, and Illinois—received generous grants of saleable land (consisting of alternate sections from a strip five miles wide on either side of the canals) from the federal government. Few internal improvements were built from money raised by taxation.

The Triumph of the Railroad

The craze for canals had scarcely reached its height before all existing systems of inland transportation were challenged by the railroad. Long used in English mines, quarries, and manufacturing plants, where the cars were propelled by gravity or by men and horses, the railway along an inclined plane was introduced into the United States during the opening decade of the nineteenth century. At the same time, engineers, realizing that steam might be used to propel wheeled vehicles as well as boats, were experimenting on both sides of the Atlantic. In 1829, the *Rocket*, a locomotive built by the Englishman, George Stephenson, hauled a train weighing thirteen tons over the Liverpool-Manchester railway at an average speed of fifteen miles an hour.

In the two generations after Independence, a number of American experiments with steam-driven vehicles and railroads were made. In 1826, a group of Baltimore citizens started planning a railroad to the West to keep for Baltimore its share of the trans-Allegheny trade. The project was received with considerable favor, and in April, 1827, the Baltimore and Ohio Railroad Company was incorporated. On July 4, 1828, the day that President John Quincy Adams turned the first shovelful of dirt for the Baltimore and Ohio Canal, Charles Carroll, the last surviving signer of the Declaration of Independence, turned the first soil for the new railroad. By the end of 1828, a fourteen-mile stretch was opened for traffic; four years later, the line had been completed to about seventy-three miles west of Baltimore. In South Carolina, New York, Pennsylvania, and Massachusetts, other railroad lines were soon being built, and by 1840 the railway mileage of the country totaled 2,818 miles. Nearly all the roads, however, were short lines that served purely local needs.

For half a century or more, the railroad promoters struggled to overcome the ignorance and prejudice of the public, the opposition of vested interests, and a variety of mechanical and engineering obstacles. Few Americans in 1820 knew anything about railroads. As late as 1823, the editor of a leading Pennsylvania newspaper, when asked by a correspondent: "What is a railroad?" was unable to answer and suggested that "perhaps some other correspondent can tell." Far more difficult to overcome than the ignorance and distrust of the public was the hostility of the vested interests in turnpike, plank-road, bridge, steamboat, canal, and stagecoach companies; state governments; tavern keepers; and even farmers who thought that the new means of transportation would seriously impair the market for horses, hay, and grain. Opposition of the turnpike and canal companies was especially strong where the railroad was a prospective competitor. The promoters of the Boston and Worcester Railway, for example, found their chief opponents in the owners of the stage lines and those dependent upon them, and the canal interests in New York State hampered the railroads in every way possible. Along the Erie Canal, mass meetings demanded that railroad competition should not be allowed to affect the receipts of the canal, and the legislature in 1833 prohibited any railroad in the state from carrying freight. In 1844, an amendment permitted the railroads to haul freight during the periods when canal navigation was suspended; but not until 1851 were the restrictions on railroad freight from Albany to Buffalo removed. Railroad companies in other states experienced similar opposition. The Baltimore and Ohio Railroad met a powerful adversary in the Chesapeake and Ohio Canal Company, and the Pennsylvania Railroad was compelled by its charter to pay a tonnage tax of $.005 per mile. Many of the competing concerns were rivals not only for business, but for capital as well.

Sharp curves and steep grades, poor roadbeds, iron-covered, wooden, or stone rails, and a variety of gauges all made rail travel uncomfortable, discontinuous, and often unsafe. After unsuccessful experiments with imported English locomotives, American engineers began to build their own. The *Best Friend of Charleston*, the *West Point*, the *Tom Thumb*, the *DeWitt Clinton*, and the *York*, the first American-built locomotives for practical use, were wood-burners without cabs. The original passenger cars were little more than highly ornate, brightly painted stagecoach bodies placed on flanged wheels. They were unsurpassed for discomfort. Almost immediately, however, they began to be superseded by longer cars with seats on either side of a central aisle and doors at the ends. Both locomotives and cars were at first equipped with brakes like those of a stagecoach, heavy blocks of wood that were pressed against the rim of the wheels by hand and foot levers.

Despite these handicaps, railroad construction grew steadily, and by 1860 more than 30,000 miles had been built. Almost three quarters of this mileage was in the Northeast and in the Old Northwest. From 1850 to 1860, there was an enormous expansion in railway mileage and the beginning of the consolidation of short independent lines into great trunk lines. In 1851, the New York and Erie, the first trunk line to join the Atlantic coast and the Middle West, was finally completed to Dunkirk on Lake Erie. In the North, the famous New York Central, Pennsylvania, Baltimore and Ohio, and Boston and Albany systems began to take shape. By 1854, Charleston, Savannah, and Atlanta had direct connections with the Northwest, and over this route quantities of western meat and grain were shipped to the eastern cotton belt. Two years before the outbreak of the Civil War, Richmond had been connected by rail with Memphis, Nashville, and Chattanooga.

Beyond the Alleghenies, where by 1850 only about 1,000 miles had been constructed, railroad mileage in the next ten years multiplied more than tenfold. Towns and cities on the Great Lakes were united with those on the Ohio and Mississippi rivers, and the entire section connected with the western terminals of the eastern roads. Chicago beat its rival St. Louis to become the great railroad center of the Middle West. In the region south of the Ohio, by 1860 approximately 8,000 miles had been built between the Ohio and the Gulf.

What available capital the United States had when railroads first appeared was largely tied up in turnpikes, canals, farms, and commerce. Because the railroad was new and untried, many persons were reluctant to give it financial support. Nevertheless, more than $1,250,000,000 was invested in railroads in the three decades preceding the Civil War. American farmers and merchants, inspired by the prospect of quicker and cheaper transportation and higher land values, donated lands for roadbeds and stations or subscribed to stock in the new companies. Bankers were generous subscribers as soon as it became evident that railroads were profitable ventures; and, with the decline of whaling and shipping, much of New England's capital was reinvested in manufactures and railroads. Railroad promoters induced press and pulpit to give publicity to the elaborate prospectuses. They opened subscription books along the routes, they made house-to-house canvasses, and they held public subscription meetings. "It is almost impossible," ran an account in the early 1830's, "to open a paper without finding an account of some railroad meeting. An epidemic on this subject seems nearly as prevalent throughout the country as the influenza." Europeans, especially the French and Germans, were heavy investors in American railroad securities.

Railroad promoters were also able to obtain substantial aid from towns, counties, cities, states, and the federal government in the form of gifts of money or land, stock subscriptions, and guarantees for the whole or part of a railroad's securities. In 1853, the railroad debt of Wheeling amounted to $55 per capita; that of Pittsburgh, $34; of New Orleans, $23; and of Philadelphia, $20. By 1858, Milwaukee had sub-

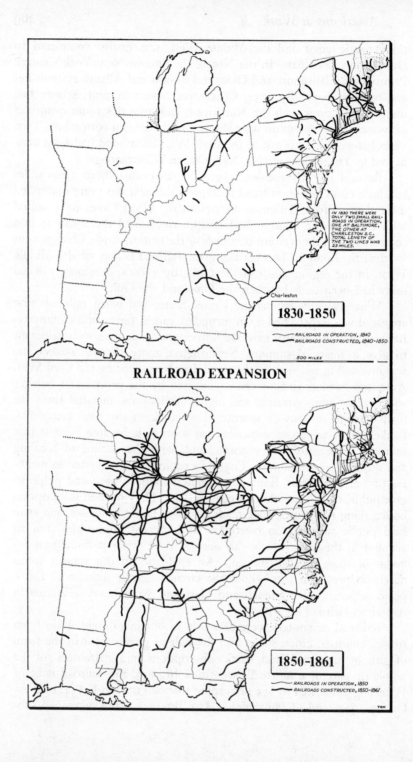

IN 1830 THERE WERE
ONLY TWO SMALL RAIL-
ROADS IN OPERATION,
ONE AT BALTIMORE,
THE OTHER AT
CHARLESTON, S.C.
TOTAL LENGTH OF
THE TWO LINES WAS
23 MILES.

Baltimore

Charleston

1830-1850

RAILROADS IN OPERATION, 1840
RAILROADS CONSTRUCTED, 1840-1850

500 MILES

RAILROAD EXPANSION

1850-1861

RAILROADS IN OPERATION, 1850
RAILROADS CONSTRUCTED, 1850-1861

sidized railroads to the extent of $1,614,000. Many southern states were liberal stock subscribers; Virginia, for example, subscribed more than $21,000,000 before the Civil War. Massachusetts and Ohio were the only northern states that gave the railroads aid through stock subscriptions.

States in every section lent or granted money to the railroads both for the actual costs of construction and for subsidiary expenses. Massachusetts advanced $40,000,000 to the Great Western and $3,600,000 to the Boston, Hartford and Erie. New York gave aid to nine railroads to the extent of over $8,000,000. Georgia endorsed bonds of the Macon and Brunswick to the amount of $2,550,000. Federal aid to the railroads was extended in the form of land grants and tariff remission on rails. During the ten years 1832–42, rails were released from duty, thus reducing their cost by as much as $20 a ton. Congressional land grants on a lavish scale began in 1850, when the state of Illinois, largely through the efforts of Stephen A. Douglas, received 2,700,000 acres from the national government to be used for the Illinois Central. Subsequent grants totaling 31,600,842 acres were made to nearly a dozen states by the end of 1860.

Railroad operation, as well as general communication, was enormously facilitated by the invention of the telegraph. From the days of Benjamin Franklin, men on both sides of the Atlantic had experimented with electricity and its possible use in transmitting messages. In 1837, an English inventor patented an electro-magnetic telegraph. Meanwhile, the American, Samuel Finley Breese Morse, whose talents ranged from portrait painting to medicine, was also at work. Utilizing information from various sources, Morse had also succeeded by 1837 in making his apparatus practical. Without means of his own and unable to attract private capital, he sought government aid. With the help of Amos Kendall and other friends, he finally induced Congress to appropriate $30,000 for the construction of a line from Baltimore to Washington. Two years later, when a private company opened a line between New York and Philadelphia, the feasibility of the telegraph was assured. Telegraph lines soon connected the leading towns of the Northeast. By 1860, the country east of the Rockies had been linked together by about 50,000 miles of telegraph.

Home and Foreign Trade

As a national market was opened by the canals and railroads, the nature and methods of trade were transformed. The variety and volume of commerce increased; trade routes lengthened; and trains and boats took the place of wagons and carts. Local trade and barter through the peddler, town merchant, and general store, gave way to national trade for cash.

In the West and South, instead of depending on visiting river flatboats for supplies, farmers and plantation owners sold their crops and made their major purchases through agents at places like New Orleans. Corn, wheat, pork, and whisky from the Ohio Valley and large supplies of cotton, sugar, molasses, and tobacco from the states on the lower Mississippi helped to increase the trade and wealth of New Orleans. By 1850, its total annual trade was just under $100,000,000, of which cotton accounted for almost half.

As the population of the northeastern United States and of western Europe grew and the East-West railroads supplemented the Great Lakes and the Erie Canal in the 1850's, the farmers of the upper Mississippi Valley became less dependent on New Orleans or on their former large markets in the plantation South. After 1850, nearly all the surplus produce of the Ohio River country went to the East by railroad and, even more, by the Erie Canal. In 1820, western produce formed 58 per cent of the commodities coming to New Orleans, but by 1860 it totaled only 23 per cent.

While domestic trade by land grew rapidly, American overseas commerce, although increasing in volume, experienced a series of cyclical fluctuations. By far the greater portion of the total volume of domestic commerce during the half-century preceding the Civil War was carried by ship along the coast. New England vessels made their way down the coast, stopping at ports from New York to New Orleans. From the South they brought back cargoes of the great staples and cheap food that had come down the Mississippi to New Orleans. Every pound of cotton for New England's mills came by sailing vessels.

Because of favorable legislation at home and disturbed conditions in Europe, American foreign shippers enjoyed unparalleled prosperity from 1790 to 1807. In 1807, the value of American exports totaled about $108,000,000, and imports $138,000,000. Yankee merchantmen were seen increasingly in European and West Indian ports and also sailed the waters of the Far East.

American commercial expansion during these early years faced the serious obstacles of the Barbary Pirates and the English and French wartime restrictions. The effects of the Embargo and Nonintercourse Acts were even more devastating. But neither restrictive legislation nor the War of 1812 completely drove American commerce from the high seas. England, Spain, Canada, and the West Indies continued to receive American grain and cotton through American smugglers.

The Docks of New York

[NEW YORK PUBLIC LIBRARY]

Soon after the Treaty of Ghent had been signed, American exports of wartime surpluses of cotton, flour, grain, tobacco, and lumber rose from less than $7,000,000 in 1814 to $52,000,000 in 1815, and to more than $93,000,000 in 1818. During the years immediately following the War of 1812, largely because of English "dumping," imports rose from about $13,000,000 in 1813 to $121,750,000 in 1818.

During the last months of 1818, there were numerous indications that the country was heading into a severe depression; foreign trade rapidly declined, and for twelve years continued in the doldrums. Every Atlantic port complained about the dullness of the import trade. Export business fared somewhat better.

For half a dozen years after 1830 there was however, a marked improvement in overseas trade, due, in part, to a number of reciprocal trade treaties that were negotiated, particularly one that opened England's colonial trade to our ships. Exports and imports, mostly to northern Europe, more than doubled in value between 1830 and 1836.

The Panic of 1837 destroyed these gains, and it was not until 1846 that foreign trade began to rise to new levels; but between 1846 and 1860 overseas tonnage more than trebled, particularly in American agricultural commodities. Much of this trade went through New York City. With its excellent harbor, its water connections with the agricul-

The Flying Cloud, *Greatest of the Clippers*

tural West, its growing population, and its varied industry, New York was by 1830 already the warehouse.of the New World. It had surpassed Philadelphia and was drawing away the trade of Baltimore, Savannah, and Charleston. Boston alone among the New England ports hung on, but ultimately much of its trade was also transferred to New York. In the South, Mobile and New Orleans enjoyed a profitable export trade, but their import business was negligible.

The clipper ship was also responsible in part for the rapid development of American shipping during the late 1840's and early 1850's. With a fair breeze in its great expanse of sail, the clipper was more than

Imports and Exports by Decades

YEAR	TOTAL EXPORTS	TOTAL IMPORTS
1800	$ 70,972,000	$ 91,253,000
1810	66,758,000	85,400,000
1820	69,692,000	74,450,000
1830	71,761,000	62,721,000
1840	123,609,000	98,259,000
1850	144,376,000	172,510,000
1860	333,576,000	353,616,000

The Great Western *Steamship Reaches New York, 1838*

[NEW YORK PUBLIC LIBRARY]

a match for a steamship. Many clippers made more than 300 miles a day. On her maiden voyage in 1851 Donald McKay's *Flying Cloud* broke all records with a day's run of 374 miles and covered the distance from New York to San Francisco in 89 days. Between 1851 and 1855, during the "clipper fever," construction of clippers more than doubled; but by 1850 it was already evident that steam tonnage would soon replace wooden sailing vessels on the seas.

After a number of trials with steam in the 1820's, a group of British businessmen organized the Great Western Steamship Company in 1836. Its vessel, the *Great Western,* a steam-driven side-wheeler, made the voyage from Bristol to New York in April 1838 in fourteen and a half days. Englishmen quickly organized other companies after this and other successes. Heavily subsidized by the British government, these companies were soon in a position to drive the American clippers from the seas.

Despite grants of more than $1,000,000 a year by Congress in the 1840's to American steamship companies, in 1858 Congress practically abandoned the entire steamship subsidy because of southern opposition. The Panic of 1857, the destruction of two principal vessels, and the sale of the remaining American vessels to English companies left the British in complete control of the trans-Atlantic steamship service; still, American steam service to the Pacific coast continued even without a subsidy.

The relative decline of the American merchant marine was also a result of the increasing transfer of American capital from commerce to manufacturing, internal improvements, mining, and land speculation after 1815. The Civil War alone did not cause the decline in the American merchant marine. The decline had previously set in; the war merely gave it added momentum as it speeded America further along the road to industrial supremacy.

An Expanding Commercial Agriculture

As American commerce grew and as railroads and canals steadily brought the West closer to the seaboard, farmers and plantation owners occupied the lands opened up for settlement. In the two generations before the Civil War, a growing population and improved transportation provided the farmer with an ever larger market, and farming in all sections of the country thus moved generally in three directions: toward greater production of a wide variety of crops, toward further commercialization of the land and more active involvement in a monied round of life, and toward slow but steady growth in the size of larger farms and plantations at the expense of the smaller farmer.

At the close of the War of 1812, farming was little different from that of pre-Revolutionary days. Cheap land, scarcity of labor, inadequate transportation, and limited credit tended to discourage those who were inclined to adopt new techniques. During the next thirty years, however, the position of the farmer in the American economy was fundamentally altered. Northern farmers, for example, were able to dispose of their produce in the rapidly expanding markets of the Northeast. In 1790, this region had only three urban communities of more than 8,000 people, but in 1840 there were thirty-three with a combined population of nearly 1,000,000.

Despite a large expansion in private and governmental aid to farmers and in the availability of expert advice which would have enabled the farmer to make the most of his opportunities, the temptations of the larger market and poor habits of husbandry were too powerful to overcome. There occurred little wiser planning of the economy of the farm, and the abuse of the soil continued to arouse agricultural experts. By 1860 both northern and southern farmers had become so overwhelmingly commercialized and so insensitive to the consequences of their reckless exploitation of the soil that the stage was already set for the grave farm crisis that set in after the Civil War.

The Land and Staples of the South

The South embraces approximately one million square miles, and includes the vast region sweeping south from Chesapeake Bay westward to San Antonio, Texas, and up the Mississippi Valley to Arkansas, the greater part of Tennessee and Kentucky, and portions of Missouri. Physiographically, this vast expanse contains several fairly distinct sections, each with its own soil and irrigation problems and with its distinctive crops.

Much of the region, with the exception of the mineral-rich Appalachians and the tropical southern tip of Florida, has summers lasting from six to nine months. The growing season is so long that in some areas three crops of vegetables can be raised in a year. Because of the extreme heat and the tendency of the abundant rainfall to run off instead of soaking in, shallow-rooted vegetation easily parches. By comparison with the North, the greater part of the South is ill-suited for grass and grain, with the exception of rice, which is artificially watered. Consequently, although large numbers of cattle roamed the isolated "piney woods" and other isolated areas of the pre-Civil War South, the section did not specialize in livestock, and the absence of natural manures, in turn, made maintaining the fertility of the soil for farming more difficult.

The pre-Civil War South was not a land of large plantations, but a region of farms interspersed with fairly localized plantation areas. Only in the cotton counties of the Mississippi Delta was the small landowner relatively unknown; elsewhere in the South many small proprietors lived on the "thinner" lands adjacent to the plantations. Most of the planter holding were located in the tobacco areas about Chesapeake Bay and in central Kentucky, in the sugar area of Louisiana, in the rice and cotton regions of South Carolina, and in the Gulf South. Comparatively few plantations were to be found in the piedmont and Appalachian valleys and almost none in the "pine barrens" and hill country. These were predominantly farm areas and are often referred to as the farmers' South in contrast to the tidewater, or planters' South.

Before 1860, nine tenths of the South's landowners were small proprietors. The farmers always outnumbered the planters in every southern state. Cultivating from fifty to a hundred acres or more with methods similar to those of the planters (but rarely owning slaves), living in a small and poorly furnished house, the farmer managed by hard work to make ends meet, to give his children at least a minimum of schooling and a good dose of evangelical piety, and sometimes to send a son or daughter to a denominational college.

Although few of them were slaveholders, the majority of the farmers feared that the abolition of slavery would release an unmanageable and dangerous mass of semihostile Negroes. An intense Negrophobia, perhaps more than any other fact, helps to explain why the

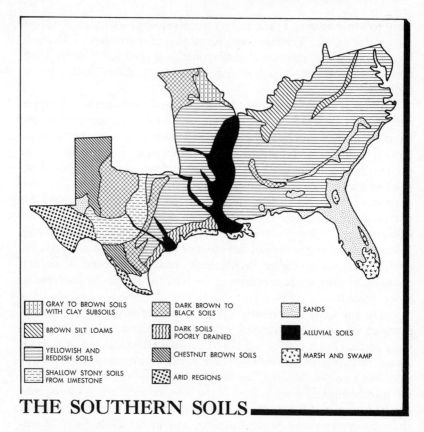

GRAY TO BROWN SOILS
WITH CLAY SUBSOILS

BROWN SILT LOAMS

YELLOWISH AND
REDDISH SOILS

SHALLOW STONY SOILS
FROM LIMESTONE

DARK BROWN TO
BLACK SOILS

DARK SOILS
POORLY DRAINED

CHESTNUT BROWN SOILS

ARID REGIONS

SANDS

ALLUVIAL SOILS

MARSH AND SWAMP

THE SOUTHERN SOILS

farmer was not more antagonistic toward the planter on the slave and race issues.

Plantations varied greatly in size, ranging from three or four hundred acres to holdings of five or six thousand acres or more. Great estates were the exception rather than the rule; the average plantation consisted of about a thousand acres. Several planters, of whom Nathaniel Heywood and Samuel Hairston were typical, owned vast tracts, but in few cases did their tracts comprise a single plantation. Heywood owned fourteen rice plantations, a cotton plantation, a considerable tract of pine woodland, and nine residences in Charleston. Hairston's properties consisted of many plantations lying in the piedmont along both sides of the Virginia-North Carolina boundary. From colonial times to the outbreak of the Civil War, such staple-growing planters tended to increase the size of their holdings by acquiring adjacent farms. The great Mississippi plantation of Joseph and Jefferson Davis was made up of dozens of small farms whose owners were forced to move elsewhere.

Most of the smaller plantations and even a few of the larger ones were managed directly by their owners, who, in so far as possible, undertook the entire work of supervising the plantation's many activities. In general, however, the large plantation was managed by a hierarchy strikingly similar to that of the factory with its general manager, superintendents, and foremen. At the top, in charge of a group of plantations, was a steward, over each plantation an overseer, and at the head of each slave gang a foreman or "driver." Both stewards and overseers received full detailed instructions from the planter and were paid increasingly as time passed with a fixed wage, a house, and partial food supply. In some cases a Negro foreman virtually managed the plantation, and on some of the larger ones the overseer had slave-gang bosses or "slave drivers," whose business it was to see that the slaves performed their tasks. Since these "drivers" were relieved of physical work and could inflict punishment on those under them, they were often mistrusted and disliked by both master and slave. On the whole, the closer a white southerner was to supervising slaves, the less was his prestige in southern society.

Although the great majority of southerners did not own slaves, this did not keep them from raising the staple crops usually associated with the slave system. General farming was carried on in some southern areas—notably the Shenandoah Valley and the Bluegrass country—and wheat and corn were grown as main crops in some areas of Maryland, Virginia, and North Carolina, but by far the greater portion of the South's tillable land was devoted to the great commercial staples: tobacco, rice, sugar cane, and cotton. Each was produced in more or less irregularly defined and sometimes overlapping zones. The heart of the tobacco country lay in an area including southern Maryland, Virginia east of the Blue Ridge, northern North Carolina, northern and western Kentucky, northwestern Tennessee, and the eastern and north-central counties of Missouri, all of which had a growing season averaging six months. Rice, with a growing season of nine months, was concentrated along the coast of the Carolinas and Georgia and in the delta of the Mississippi, and sugar cane, with a similar season, was concentrated in Louisiana and about Galveston, Texas. The cotton belt, with seven- to nine-month summers, extended more than 1,000 miles from Albemarle Sound on the North Carolina coast to San Antonio and varied in width from 200 miles in Carolina and Texas to 600 or 700 miles in the Mississippi Valley.

Tobacco culture in the South before 1840 had changed little since colonial times, and at the opening of the nineteenth century, tobacco still occupied first place among the southern staples; more than one half of the total southern population was engaged in, or dependent upon, its cultivation. Its supremacy, however, soon came to an end. From 1800 to 1840, the production of southern tobacco was increasingly unrewarding, while profits from cotton rose steeply. But after 1840 the tobacco industry took on new life. The introduction of charcoal heat for curing tobacco and of new varieties of leaf helped the South regain its former European markets. During the decade 1850–60, tobacco production increased 115 per cent.

Rice culture was confined to a more restricted area than that of tobacco. Because of the need for an abundant supply of fresh water, the flood plains on the tidal course of a fresh water stream near the coasts were selected for the crop. Four fifths of the annual crop came from the coastal regions of South Carolina and Georgia. Long before 1850, American rice culture was greatly improved by both seed selection and cultivation. While many planters successfully made systematic efforts to keep up the fertility of their rice soils, others, by repeated cropping practically ruined their acres for further production. Both crop and land were sometimes destroyed by floods or by salt water driven inshore by hurricanes. Output depended on acreage, soil fertility, and season; in 1850, it totaled more than 245,000,000 pounds, the maximum crop produced in the pre-Civil War period, but production declined considerably between 1850 and 1860.

Climatic conditions narrowly confined the profitable production of cane sugar to southern Louisiana and to the southeastern coast of Texas. The first commercially successful crop of sugar in Louisiana was produced on a plantation near New Orleans in 1796. By 1858 the 1,328 cane-growing plantations in Louisiana and Texas produced about 368,000 hogsheads of sugar. Tens of thousands of slaves on hundreds of sugar plantations performed work in the cane fields that was much more arduous that that required by cotton and tobacco.

Of all the southern staples, cotton was in many respects the simplest to produce. Seeded in April and harvested after late August, the size of the cotton crop was governed by harvesting capacity. A laborer could plant and cultivate about twice as much cotton as he could pick. It was customary, therefore, for many cotton growers to supplement their cotton with other crops, especially corn, sweet potatoes, peanuts, cowpeas, and small grain. On a well-managed farm or plantation, a full-time hand was expected to care for from six to ten acres of cotton and from eight to ten acres of corn or its equivalent

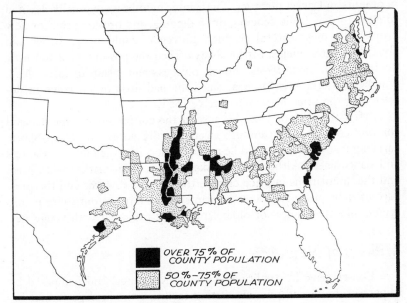

THE COMMON AREAS OF SLAVERY AND COTTON

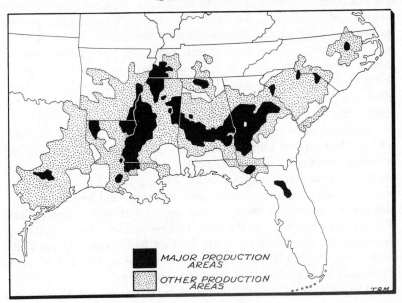

MAJOR PRODUCTION AREAS

OTHER PRODUCTION AREAS

TRM

in peanuts and sweet potatoes. The winter months were usually devoted to clearing new lands, fencing, ditch digging, and breaking soil for new crops. The most careful planner, however, could never be certain about his cotton yields, for he always faced the possibility of too little or too much rain, frosts, insect ravages, and plant diseases. And, whether his crop was large or small, he had little or no voice in determining the price he would receive for it.

After the War of 1812, because of the cotton gin and the demand for raw cotton, cotton culture swept rapidly across the Deep South, carrying many small and middle range farmers into the ranks of planters and slaveowners. Although the risks of the cotton market were great and the fluctuations in price erratic, the possible rewards and the pressure of debt pushed the cotton planters and farmers onto virgin soils which, like the owners of older lands, they exploited with vengeance.

Millions of New Acres

Conservative by tradition, without experience, and hampered by imperfect credit and poor marketing facilities, the average farmer before 1840 was hesitant to abandon the familiar paths of self-sufficiency. After 1840, however, the area of land under cultivation in the North was considerably enlarged by the settlement of comparatively large numbers of farmers in the West. By 1840, the westward moving farmers had reached the eastern fringe of the prairie. Many of them held back from pushing beyond this point, for the prairie country, though extremely fertile, was unwooded, hard to turn with a plow, and without stones for houses. The plains afforded no protection from wind and storms, and, aside from rivers and occasional springs, the prairie settler had to rely upon hand-dug wells for his water supply.

Increased immigration, however, and the taking up of available land, pushed settlers into the timberless area. By 1850, farmers had occupied practically all the prairie lands east of the Mississippi that were not in the hands of speculators. During the 1840's, also, higher prices for western wheat, corn, beef, and pork and better farm implements permitting the farmer to sow and harvest more extensive fields of grain put a premium on the level, treeless prairie. The railroads that connected the grass country with the East had opened up profitable markets for western farmers, enabling them to bring fuel and materials for fencing and building from the timbered regions.

The addition of a vastly increased farm acreage and higher town wages during the twenty years preceding the Civil War greatly aggravated the farm labor problem in both East and West as young men from eastern farms went in ever larger numbers to the West. Undoubtedly, this labor shortage would have been even more keenly felt had it not been for the continued development and introduction of a great variety of improved farm tools and machinery. By the 1850's, tens of thousands of factory-produced steel plows proved extremely valuable to Mississippi Valley farmers confronted with sticky soil. Double harrows with finer teeth set closer together, grain drills and seeders, mowers, hayrakes, and horse-drawn reapers and threshers were either invented or improved before 1860, and were widely adopted by American farmers. In larger perspective, the reaper and thresher were to the North what the cotton gin was to the South. Together with the railroads, they brought an enormous increase in farm production. The wheat crop of the United States doubled in one generation. At the same time, the centers of most agricultural and livestock production moved steadily westward. By 1860, the West had greatly increased its acreage of oats, hay, and potatoes, although the East still led in the production of these crops. Western states became the suppliers of the nation's meat, hides, and wool, and shared honors with the East in dairying. Only in truck farming did the East remain in the lead.

The Farmers' Problems

The western farmer, like the southern staple-grower, was heedless in his exploitation of the soil. Cheap fertile land, lack of capital, the development of better tools and harvesting machinery, and better transportation facilities and markets were conducive to extensive rather than intensive agriculture. With some exceptions, little or nothing was done to prevent soil exhaustion or to increase productivity per acre. Year after year, the western farmer plowed his quarter-section and seeded it to wheat as the southern grower put out his cotton or tobacco, unaware that each succeeding crop further deteriorated his soil. When yields at last began to decline, he blamed the weather, poor seed, and wrong sowing time.

Agricultural expansion in the West, moreover, brought hardship to the eastern farmer. His labor force steadily declined as his sons went West to farms of their own or into higher-paying city jobs. For a generation before 1840 (that is, since the opening of the Erie Canal and the beginning of steamboat transportation), he had faced increasing competition from the West. The westerner could undersell the easterner in pork, wheat, flour, wool, beef, butter, cheese, and potatoes. The establishment of through railroads between the East and the West during the 1840's and 1850's sharpened the competition, and eastern farmers faced economic disaster. New England was especially hard hit; its wool growers and cattle raisers for example, were virtually forced out of business.

There were those who clearly foresaw that the East could not hope to compete in the production of commodities that could be successfully transported from the West. William Buckminster of Massachusetts spoke prophetically when he wrote in 1838: "The times are changed and we must change with them. We cannot now, as formerly, raise much grain for the market . . . Let them [the western states] supply our cities with grain. We will manufacture their cloth and their shoes. Our artisans may eat bread from the West—we will supply them with what cannot be brought from a distance."

Although some refused to accept this point of view and grumbled about what they termed their hard luck, the majority of New England farmers and those in the middle states who suffered from the competition of the West either lapsed back into self-sufficiency or raised perishables for local markets. The growing network of railroads in the East brought formerly isolated areas near to the markets. The long-lasting eastern lead in truck gardening and fruit raising and good showing in the dairy industry were very favorably affected by the spreading railway net.

American farmers could have adjusted even more successfully than they did to changing market conditions had it not been for the fact that they were backward as businessmen. Despite the vast amount of expert advice made available to the farmer, consistent leadership was lacking. The exodus to the cities and to the West·had deprived the eastern farmer not only of traditional crops and labor, but of valuable leadership. What farmers most needed were brains. "Wit, ingenuity, shrewdness, tact," one observer said, "seem to gravitate, all of them, into other pursuits, into cities, into shops, into courts, into pulpits: and the dullest of the sons takes the farm. I dislike to say it. I dislike to say it all the more because it is so true."

Want of leadership was not the only difficulty; most farmers were without business training and experience. Few had more than the rudiments of common schooling. About the workings of the economy they knew almost nothing. Sales and purchases, often in foolish amounts, were made largely through the country store. Often the victims of sharp practice, farmers believed that all businessmen were tricksters to be avoided as much as possible.

Lack of capital and credit also severely handicapped the farmers. The overwhelming majority of farmers, instead of investing their surplus in diversified crops, new seed varieties, improved livestock, or labor-saving devices, used what profits they made to enlarge their houses or to buy more land or slaves. With little or no control over prices, returns from their surplus produce often did not furnish them with adequate working capital even for wise investment. They were thus virtually compelled either to borrow funds or to employ only half as much labor as they could have profitably used and to get along without fertilizers and much-needed machinery. The results were summarized in the *New England Farmer*: ". . . thus he passes his life continually pinched for the want of a little money, incessantly harassed by duns, and once in a while appalled by a tap on the shoulder, though gentle it may be, of the practiced hand of the constable."

Banks were not interested in financing short and unreliable farm loans in the North, and few farmers made use of bank credit. Many farmers feared and distrusted bankers more than any other businessmen. "A farmer should shun the door of a bank," the *New England Farmer* warned, "as he would the approach of the plague or cholera." The country store was practically the only source of northern farm credit.

The farmers' injuries and losses from dependence upon the country merchant resulted in part from imperfect marketing facilities. Most produce was disposed of to the country store or to specialized salesmen. Frequently, farm produce in the North passed through four or more middlemen before reaching its ultimate destination. Because the same price was usually paid for a product, whatever its quality, there was little incentive for farmers to improve their products, although middlemen, by refusing to pay "top prices" for what they asserted to be second-class crops, strengthened the repeated plea of the farm journals for better commodities. Most farmers, hard pressed by creditors and worried over false rumors about prices, were not in a position to hold their produce for more favorable quotations.

In the South, the machinery for marketing cotton did not differ essentially from that employed in the marketing of tobacco during the colonial period. By far the greater proportion of the crop ultimately moved through the four great export towns of Charleston, Savannah, Mobile, and New Orleans. The greater part of the cotton was consigned to factors or cotton brokers who were often agents of northern investors and who served both as high-charging commission merchants and as bankers who extended sought-after credit and loans for purchasing lands and slaves. Their interest charges ran from 8 to 12 per cent and often higher. Often, the factor required the planter to consign to him his entire crop, and to guarantee to pay a penalty if the crop fell below a stipulated number of bales. In addition to commissions and interest on advances, there were many other marketing charges, such as freight, storage, insurance, draying, weighing, sampling, and bale repairage. All things considered, the cost of marketing a bale of cotton ranged from $2.50 to $4.00, depending largely upon location, producing territory, and ultimate place of consumption. Although several southern states attempted to establish banking systems to lighten the planter's huge debt and charge burden, most credit for the planters came through the factors or brokers.

The southern grower, like farmers elsewhere, was usually victimized by existing market arrangements. Cotton brokers had special facilities, not enjoyed by the planters, for obtaining information about cotton acreage and market and shipping conditions. Southern cotton producers believed that brokers and other middlemen enjoyed unfair advantages, and rumors that combinations of leaders were cornering or otherwise influencing or controlling the market often created great discontent among the planters. Credit institutions, particularly the Bank of England, were accused of influencing cotton prices adversely for the planter.

It is impossible to ascertain the extent to which the imperfect credit and marketing facilities in North and South affected the steady increase in farms and plantation mortgages, but the available evidence indicates that at least one third of all eastern farms were mortgaged and that a high mortgage indebtedness was constant in the South. The relation between credit and marketing opportunities, on the one hand, and farm tenancy, on the other, is even more difficult to trace. That some farms in every section of the nation were worked by tenants, mostly for a share of the crop, is certain. From one fourth to one third of all the farms in Warren County, New Jersey, are reported to have been operated by tenant farmers in 1843. The Wadsworth estate, comprising nearly forty square miles of the Genesee Valley in New York State, was worked entirely by tenants. There was also tenancy west of the Alleghenies, and in growing degree in the South.

Although the tendency in both North and South was for the large land owner and the tenant to squeeze the middle sized farmer between them, on the whole, American farms, with the exception of the few but powerful plantations, were small. In 1860 there were in the free states, excluding California, only 525 farms of more than 1,000 acres. The average size of all farms in 1860 was 199.2 acres, of which 79.8 were improved land. With the advent of industrialization and western competition, much poor land, which at the beginning of the century had been under cultivation, was permitted to return to timber and bush.

Before the Civil War, despite grave problems, the American farmers enjoyed prestige and power as the chief producing class and "bulwark of the republic." This favored position did not stop the growth of complaints against the ever more remote and impersonal market forces over which farmers and plantation owners had few controls. Whether plantation and slaveowners or hundred-acre men, most farmers compared themselves favorably with the "moneybags" with whom they were compelled to deal, failing to realize how their own eagerness for profits severely qualified their pretensions to being the creators of a "Greek democracy" or innocent Jeffersonian yeomen.

The Stimulus of a National Market for Industry

This rapid expansion of the American transportation and communications system opened all the settled parts of the nation not only to the farmers but to a small but ambitious industrialist group. Although the growth of industry in England in the early nineteenth century made for the creation of the railroads, in the United States the so-called Transportation Revolution inspired the expansion of the factory system.

In 1790, the United States was not a manufacturing nation. Before the Revolution the abundance of land, sparse population, relatively high-priced labor, lack of capital, and restrictive legislation by England had hindered manufacturing. During the War of Independence, however, Americans began to manufacture articles that formerly had been imported in large quantities. Certain industries closely connected with the war, such as the making of powder and firearms, were enlarged, and the output of household manufactures increased. With the conclusion of peace, however, these enterprises were in large part destroyed by the British, who flooded the United States with cheaper goods. "Let the dispute with America be settled as it may," an English pamphleteer wrote in 1782, "while their wool continues inferior to ours, they [the Americans] must from interest, the strongest tie of friendship, deal with us. Interest is more binding than any treaty of commerce."

Despite British efforts to monopolize her new industrial techniques, attempts were made to introduce the new processes into the United States as early as 1775, when Samuel Wetherill, Jr., a Quaker merchant of Philadelphia, together with number of his fellow townsmen, founded the United Company of Philadelphia for Promoting American Manufactures. During the next quarter of a century, similar organizations were established in several other cities, but actual experiments undertaken in various towns in Massachusetts, Connecticut, and Rhode Island failed either partially or completely.

While these experiments were in progress, announcement of premiums for cotton machinery, offered by American societies interested in promoting manufacturing in the New World, came to the attention of Samuel Slater, who was in charge of the manufacture of machinery in an English cotton factory. Slater sailed secretly for the United States. Landing in New York in 1789, he accidentally got in touch with Moses Brown, member of the famous commercial family of Providence, who wanted to improve cotton manufacturing. Slater went to Providence, where, with the aid of a local carpenter and a blacksmith and working from memory, he succeeded in building two carding machines and a water frame of twenty-four spindles. With Brown's financial backing, he opened the first successful cotton factory in the United States in 1790.

Although numerous small cotton mills were erected during the early 1790's, at the opening of the nineteenth century only fifteen factories were in operation, and all of these were in New England. The demand for American agricultural produce and a prosperous commerce made it far more profitable for the United States to import manufactured goods than to produce them. But as soon as Britain and Napoleon began to molest neutral shipping, American commerce fell off rapidly; farmers were unable to market their produce, and imports of foreign manufactured goods declined. Cut off from the imports of Europe, Americans were forced to make their own commodities, and capital went into manufacturing. As in Revolutionary days, home manufacture became a patriotic duty. States, counties, municipalities, and societies organized to encourage manufactures, offered bounties and premiums, or bought stock in new manufacturing concerns. In 1810, Albert Gallatin, in a report to the House of Representatives, stated that the United States was manufacturing sufficient quantities of woolen, leather, and other goods to supply the needs of the entire population. Among those manufactures firmly established and supplying all or a greater part of the needs of home consumption were iron goods, textiles, hats, paper, malt and liquors, gunpowder, and window glass.

Although the factory system had thus secured a foothold in the United States by the end of the War of 1812, the new industries faced a severe test in the years immediately following the conflict. Scarcely had peace been declared before British merchants and manufacturers, anxious to empty their overstocked warehouses and regain their American markets, began again to export enormous quantities of goods to the Western world. Imports which totaled only $13,000,000 in 1813, mounted to $147,000,000 in 1816. Between 1815 and 1820, each inhabitant of the United States consumed imported goods averaging $13.50 as against $2.50 per capita for the years 1810–14. In the face of this competition and of the rising price of raw materials by the reopening of the European market, American textile manufactures were prostrated. In 1816, there were nearly 150 mills in operation in the mill district of Rhode Island; a year later, all but the old Slater mill were closed. Cheap foreign goods had put them out of business.

Neither foreign competition, however, nor the period of world economic depression from 1816 to 1820 could permanently destroy American manufactures. New factories equipped with more modern machines were soon built. At first the textile machinery in the United States had been for carding and spinning only. In 1814, however, Francis Cabot Lowell, Harvard graduate and son of a New England lawyer, with the assistance of Paul Moody, a mechanic, perfected a power loom, which was installed in a factory at Waltham, Massachusetts. This new machine which differed markedly from its English predecessors, made it possible to combine spinning and weaving under one roof. In the next decade, new looms and carding machines strengthened the position of American textile firms. In 1846, Elias Howe patented the sewing machine, although it did not come into general use either in home or in factory until the Civil War.

Considerable technical advance was also made in the manufacture of primary metals and metal products. The first improvement in the extraction of iron was made in 1830 by successfully melting iron ore with anthracite coal. The old blast furnace was replaced by the so-called hot blast about 1840. By 1855, anthracite smelting had replaced charcoal smelting in the production of pig iron. Bituminous coal and coke were little used for this purpose until the Civil War. In 1851, William Kelly, a Kentucky ironmaster, independently discovered the same method devised by Bessemer in England of decarbonizing molten metal by forcing air through it. By that time, the nation's furnaces were producing approximately 600,000 tons annually. At the same time, nails, tacks, bolts, files, wire, screws, spikes, chains, firearms, and other metal articles formerly produced by hand were now manufactured by machines. Largely as the result of the efforts of Eli Whitney and Simeon North, the principle of interchangeable parts was being very widely employed in the manufacture of clocks, firearms, and certain kinds of machinery. In originality, variety, and efficiency, American machine tools surpassed those of Europe.

Until the middle of the nineteenth century, water power drove practically all the mill machinery in America. Although some early textile machines were run by hand or horsepower, these were the exception rather than the rule. By 1830, New England's streams were harnessed to nearly their full capacity. Soon after 1800, steam began to be used in those sections where water power could not easily be obtained, and in such industries as glass manufacturers, bleacheries, and print works, where heat was required. According to the 1830 census, 57 out of 161 plants in Pennsylvania and almost the entire Middle West relied on steam power; in Rhode Island, on the other hand, only 4 out of 132 textile mills used steam.

Although before 1860 wood was the principal fuel employed for generating steam power, by 1860 coal was of prime importance to the whole industrial economy. Anthracite had been tried in forges as early as 1769, but its inefficient use and the ample supply of wood restricted its spread. After 1812, when wood became scarce near the larger Atlantic coast cities, factories turned to bituminous or soft coal which had been discovered near Richmond, Virginia, about 1750. Between 1820 and 1830, better grates and furnaces, the expanding smelting industry, and the increasing use of steam for manufacturing and transportation stimulated the demand for coal. The total output of coal rose from less than 50,000 tons in 1820 to more than 14,000,000 tons in 1860. American consumption of foreign coal also rose and reached an average of 235,000 tons a year between 1850 and 1860.

These improvements in the manufacture of textiles and iron and in the development of power were characteristic of the progress made in every branch of industry during the first half of the nineteenth century. Although most factories were small, practically all of them were quick to seize upon new ideas and devices that promised to increase their efficiency. Some conception of the remarkable accomplishments of American inventors may be gained by examining the records of the Patent Office. From 1790 to 1810, the number of inventions patented annually averaged 77; in 1830, they numbered 544; by 1850, the number had risen to 993; and ten years later to 4,778. During this period, the United States granted more patents than England and France combined. Testifying before a parliamentary committee in 1841, a witness said: "I apprehend that the chief part . . . [of the] new inventions . . . have originated abroad, especially in America."

The effects of the application of machinery to manufacturing are revealed in part by the census returns. By 1840, American manufacturers were valued at slightly under $500,000,000; twenty years later the figure was nearly $2,000,000,000. The number of men working in manufacturing establishments having an output valued at $500 or more increased from 791,000 in 1840 to 1,311,000 in 1860. Of the many growing American industries, textiles were easily pre-eminent. More than 5,235,000 cotton spindles were in operation in 1860, more than double the number in 1840. At the outbreak of the Civil War, approximately 1,900 wollen mills were turning out products valued at over $68,865,000,

The Mills of Lowell, Massachusetts

[WORCESTER ART MUSEUM]

a more than threefold increase over 1840. During the same period, silk manufacture increased from almost nothing to an amount valued at $6,500,000.

Manufacturing was concentrated in two areas, or mill zones, one along the Atlantic coast of the northeast and middle states, the other in the trans-Allegheny. New England produced in 1860 two thirds of all the nation's cotton goods. Although Philadelphia, with its 200,000 spindles, and with another 200,000 in tributary districts, was still the leading individual textile center in 1860, Massachusetts could boast of Lowell, Fall River, New Bedford, and a score of lesser textile towns. The general pre-eminence of the Northeast in manufacturing can be suggested by comparing it with the South. In 1860, the value of the southern cotton-goods production was only about $8,000,000, as compared with nearly $80,000,000 for New England and over $26,000,000 for the middle states; the city of Lowell alone had more spindles than the entire South.

Behind the Atlantic coast mill zone there developed a second industrial "belt" extending westward from a line running roughly from Utica, New York, to Harrisburg, Pennsylvania. By 1860, this zone produced few textiles but shared honors in iron production with the coastal zone. It took in farm products and sent out flour, liquor, packed meats and farm supplies, such as cordage, and bagging and agricultural machinery. After 1840, however, the larger farm machines came from the Middle West. In 1847, Cyrus H. McCormick, son of a Virginia piedmont farmer, in partnership with others established a plant at Chicago to manufacture the automatic reaper for which he had taken out his first patent in 1834. Three years earlier, at Racine, Wisconsin, Jerome I. Case had laid the foundation of what eventually became the greatest thresher works in the world. At the outbreak of the Civil War, Ohio and Illinois led all other states in the production of agricultural machinery, while New England retained its lead in the small hand tools such as spades, hoes, forks, and rakes.

The Owners and the Workers

By 1830, the growing scope of American industry and the increased size of individual businesses had led the visiting Frenchman, Alexis de Tocqueville, to predict that any future American aristocracy was likely to be drawn from the manufacturers. In America, as elsewhere, with the spread of industry came greater rationalization in production, more impersonal relations—more often than not antagonistic—between employers and workers, and numerous complex problems in industrial discipline and in the use of leisure that endure to this day. The factory system, in short, brought a new culture to America.

In the past, manufacturing had been almost entirely either a handi-craft or domestic industry. Production had been on a small scale and entailed many risks in relation to supply of materials, control over mar-kets, and demand for products. The artisan, whether merchant, master, or journeyman, had enjoyed considerable independence. He had been his own capitalist, the cost of his tools and buildings had been nominal, and he had manufactured for a limited but familiar market. In conse-quence, his supply of raw materials and finished products had been measured by immediate needs. Often working side by side, owners and workers were in personal touch with each other to discuss problems and to share news about the business and community.

By 1850, the older methods of production, although still wide-spread in isolated areas were being supplanted by the factory system. In New England, the textile factory had practically put the old-fash-ioned spinning-wheel out of business. Young men, instead of becoming apprentices, usually became owners or operatives of the new machines. Many craftsmen, farmers, small merchants, retired shippers and sons of shippers had by this time amassed considerable capital and made reputa-tions either as manufacturers or as merchant-capitalists. Their factories turned out large quantities of goods formerly produced by inexpensive hand tools in the home or shop. The ever opening continent and in-creasing population enormously expanded their markets. Better banking facilities, profits from foreign trade, and the eagerness of Old World investors for the higher rate of overseas interest enabled the American manufacturer to secure capital for expansion.

Many early factories were managed or supervised directly by their entrepreneur-owners. They were small establishments competing with household manufactures. In 1815, for example, half of the 167 cotton mills of Rhode Island ran less than 500 spindles each; in 1840, the aver-age number of spindles per mill for the entire United States was still only 2,000, as compared with 5,000 twenty years later. Most early mills were owned by individuals, families, partners, or joint-stock companies. The corporate form of control did not become general until after 1815, and even then it was for many years chiefly confined to New England. Of fifty woolen mills in 1833, thirty-four were operated on an individual or partnership basis.

As early as 1820, however, there was a marked tendency for larger concerns to buy up their lesser rivals. In addition to these amalgama-tions, there were numerous alliances not unlike the post-Civil War "gentlemen's agreement." State authorization for incorporation was unnecessary, and the sale of corporate securities expedited the raising of capital funds. Shares in the joint-stock companies were usually in small denominations; stock ownership was, as a rule, concentrated in the hands of a few. With the rapid expansion of the factory unit, the acquisition of wealth, and the concentration of power, the owner retired from immediate control, and his place was taken by a paid manager or supervisor. The owner's connection was represented by his investment, usually in the form of stocks and bonds. Often he had little or no knowledge of conditions in the factory. As a shareholder and a businessman, he was primarily concerned with dividends and profits; whatever interest he may have had in his workers was, as a rule, secondary.

Although in the minority, the new industrialists, like their English compeers, challenged the political leadership and social prestige of the commercial and landed aristocracy. It was a challenge by the "new rich" to the "old rich." From 1825 on, the new leaders of industry were increasingly represented in both local and national politics by lawyers who safeguarded the industrial *bourgeoisie*. Members of the new money class, at first frowned upon by the older aristocracy, eventually gained admission to political power and to polite society as well.

The industrial workers were in striking contrast to the industrial capitalists. The competition for labor, which was always scarce in America, and the sparseness of population made it difficult for the early millowners and mine operators to secure workers. A few of the New England textile factories employed skilled foreign artisans from Great Britain and Ireland, but the number of these was small. Of 612 workers at Fall River in 1826, for example only 38 were foreigners, and these appear to have been employed in the more responsible positions. Foreigners were not a majority of the mill population in the Fall River district or in other New England mill towns until the 1850's. America's factory labor supply had to be recruited at first from the native population.

Before 1860, many factory workers came from farmers' families. Many farmers' sons and daughters sought employment in factories to help a struggling father pay off a mortgage on a hillside farm, to obtain a little extra money, to help send a brother to school, or to escape from what they regarded as the narrow horizon of farm life. Frequently the entire family permanently left the farm, and in other cases men took factory jobs in the winter months and spent only the summers in farm work.

Very young children constituted the principal labor supply in the early textile plants. Samuel Slater's first nine operatives were seven boys and two girls, all under twelve years of age. In the opinion of many people, including Alexander Hamilton, factory employment of children added to both the family income and the nation's wealth. It could free the community from the expense of caring for orphans and paupers who now could be taught proper habits of work that would make them God-fearing, industrious citizens. Where parents were reluctant to allow their children to be employed in a factory, the owners sought pauper apprentices. Dejected in countenance, broken in spirit, mentally and physically stunted, and denied the pleasures of childhood or opportunity for even the most rudimentary education, these children became increasingly unfit for employment as the size, complexity, and weight of machinery increased. From 1800 to 1860, although children constituted from two to three fifths of the total number of factory hands, the age level continued to rise.

Among the first adults to be employed in the cotton and woolen mills, many were women. According to testimony before the House Committee on Manufactures in 1828, 41.4 per cent of the employees in the seven largest woolen mills in the country were women; four years later, the woolen plants of Massachusetts employed 49 per cent women, as against 42 per cent men. The percentage of women employed in cotton mills was considerably higher. Of the 6,000 operatives employed in the Lowell cotton mills in 1836, 5,000 were reported to be "young women from seventeen to twenty-four years of age, the daughters of farmers from the different New England states." As with the children, the hiring of women slowly declined with expansion of industry; still, women probably constituted about one fifth of the total labor supply of manufacturing industries in 1860, and increasing numbers of women shifted to jobs in mercantile establishments.

Whether man, woman, or child, the life of the factory worker was at best one of narrow, blighting routine. He labored an average of from twelve to fifteen hours a day for a wage that ranged from $1.00 to $6.00 a week. If he happened to be employed in a factory on the basis of piecework, the hope of obtaining a living wage induced him to work long hours. As late as 1849, Dr. Josiah Curtis in a report given before the American Medical Association stated that there was not a state prison or a house of correction in New England where the hours of labor were so long, hours for meals so short, and ventilation so much neglected as they were in the cotton mills of that section. Frequently the worker's house was also owned by his employer. If he tried to organize, he was liable under the English Common Law to arrest and punishment for conspiracy. Without capital reserve or extended credit, his only asset was his labor, and this he sold on terms arranged by the employer. Although his over-all standard of living rose under the factory system, the instabilities of the labor markets, the anonymity and restlessness of town life, and the boredom and unceasing close routine of the factory made the farm with all its limitations seem in retrospect a better existence.

The children employed in the factories were even worse off than adult workers. Children, like women, received less pay than men for equal work. A committee of the Massachusetts legislature investigating child labor in 1825 found that the time of employment was "generally twelve or thirteen hours each day excepting the Sabbath," and "this left little opportunity for daily instruction." In 1836, Massachusetts ruled that all children under fifteen years of age must have at least three months' schooling a year. Four years later, similar action was taken by Rhode Island. The first legislation prohibiting child labor was enacted in 1848 by Pennsylvania; it forbade the employment of children under twelve years of age in textile factories.

In a few cases women workers enjoyed better than average conditions. In 1835, Harriet Martineau, the English reformer, favorably portrayed the life of the factory operative in Waltham where a paternalistic scheme had been put into effect to attract young women. She concluded:

> The people work about seventy hours per week, on the average. The time of work varies with the length of the days, the wages continuing the same. All [appear] . . . well dressed . . . The health is good; or rather [as this is too much to be said about health anywhere in the United States] it is no worse than it is elsewhere.
>
> These facts speak for themselves. There is no need to enlarge on the pleasure of an acquaintance with the operative classes of the United States.

But Miss Martineau's picture, although perhaps not overdrawn for the mills she described, was not representative of the general run of American textile plants. Even the so-called Waltham system that she had observed had its drawbacks, chief of which was the blacklist. If an operative was dishonorably discharged, the employer made a record of that fact and forwarded the name to other employers. A few states attempted to remedy the worst evils of employment by legislation, but advances in this direction were exceedingly slow. Here and there a humanitarian raised his voice in protest against the existing system; the worker, he asserted, was at least entitled to a shorter day, a higher wage, healthier conditions of employment, and a better home.

The Workingmen Organize

The American labor movement originated among skilled artisans seeking to become businessmen themselves. Between 1783 and 1825, isolated local societies of printers, shoemakers, carpenters, and other "mechanics" tried to protect themselves against inferior competing workers, long hours, and low pay by strikes or "turnouts," as they were then called. The English common law against conspiracy, the traditions of economic individualism, public fear of higher prices, hostile employer organizations, and charges of un-Americanism were all used to frustrate the efforts of the workingmen. In 1825, Boston employers claimed that a successful carpenters' strike would create "a spirit of discontent and insubordination to which our native mechanics have hitherto been strangers." In 1827, the Mechanics' Union of Trade Associations was organized in Philadelphia. This organization was the first city central union and resulted directly from the failure of a strike of journeymen carpenters who sought a ten-hour day. It led to the first workingman's party in 1828. The leaders of the smaller operators of the city apparently realized that all trades must cooperate if strikes were to be won and workingmen's demands respected.

A period of rising prices and inflated currency preceding the Panic of 1837 aroused the artisan and mechanic. The cost of living rose nearly 70 per cent in less than three years, but wages trailed. Employers, stimulated by mounting prices and the "tastes of unusual profits," often drove the workers through a long working day to increase production. In an effort to remedy unsatisfactory conditions, the workers turned to trade unionism and its principal weapon, the strike. From 1834 to 1837, 150 labor societies and trade unions were established in Boston, New York, Philadelphia, and Baltimore. Women formed unions of their own. Eleven cities formed central labor unions. During these years, a few crafts made crude attempts to organize national trade unions. In 1834, some thirty delegates, from six industrial cities, assembled in New York City and organized the National Trades' Union, the first national labor organization of its kind in the Western World. Subsequent conventions were held in the next three years. Like the Jacksonian loco-focos with whom it was closely allied, the National Trades' Union declared itself in favor of a system of free, universal education, demanded that public lands which were being acquired by speculators be retained by the government for actual settlers, deplored the conditions of children employed in textile factories, advocated a ten-hour day, and opposed special privilege for a "favored few." The union membership of the six industrial centers of the nation in 1834 totaled approximately 26,250. So great was the impact of the inflation that two years later it had risen to 300,000.

Labor, however, did more than organize and hold conventions. It made use of its principal weapon—the strike. Of the 173 strikes in the United States between 1833 and 1837, 103 were for higher wages and 26 for a ten-hour day; every organized group went on strike. Factory workers who up to this time had played little part in the labor movement, now began to agitate feebly, and strikes took place in Connecticut, New Jersey, and Massachusetts. In the eyes of the courts, strikes were still illegal, and not until 1842, in *Commonwealth vs. Hunt*, was it ruled that workers had at least a legal right to organize and to adopt peaceful measures to accomplish their ends.

Although many of the new unions were wiped out by the Panic of 1837, the trade-union movement nevertheless provided the principal impetus for the agitation that resulted in the establishment of the ten-hour day. By 1835, the original movements for the ten-hour day had assumed nationwide proportions with parades, circulars, mass meetings, and strikes. In 1840, President Van Buren extended the ten-hour rule to all employed by the national government. The unions next made serious efforts to obtain state legislation for a ten-hour day. In the 1840's, New Hampshire and Pennsylvania took limited steps toward the ten-hour day, but the Massachusetts legislature successfully resisted petition after petition and urged labor to seek spiritual improvement for the inner man instead.

In the decade preceding the Civil War, there was a marked decline in the interest of organized labor in both politics and reform; but national craft unions of printers, machinists, and hat workers, among others, were formed. These small unions demonstrated at least the feasibility of a national labor movement and revealed an increasing desire among skilled workingmen to restrict entrance to their trades and to exact better terms from employers.

Fundamentally, however, the growth of a mass labor movement in which workers accepted permanent roles as wage-earning employees was impossible as long as the American workingman looked on his job merely as the first step to becoming a businessman in his own right. Before 1860, the American workers' image of himself was basically that of a small entrepreneur. On the farm, in commerce, and in industry, actual opportunity seemed to show the validity of this image and the workingman's criticisms were seldom directed against the assumptions of the American business creed of hard work and success. What he protested against, rather, were the failures of the system as it was to give him the opportunity to show his mettle or to gain the rewards appropriate to his talents.

FOR SUPPLEMENTARY READING

The best general study of the American economy in the era before the Civil War is G. R. Taylor, *The Transportation Revolution 1815–1860* (1951). On the era of road-building, use J. A. Burrenberger, *Turnpikes* (1931), and A. B. Hurlburt, *Paths of Inland Commerce* (1920). On the water routes, read L. D. Baldwin, *The Keelboat Age on Western Waters* (1941), and L. C. Hunter, *Steamboats on the Western Rivers* (1949). The canal era is studied by C. Goodrich, et al., *Canals and American Economic Development* (1961), and N. Miller, *The Enterprise of a Free People . . . 1792–1835* (1962). The key role of government in the development of internal transportation is stressed in L. Hartz, *Economic Policy and Democratic Thought, Pennsylvania 1776–1860* (1948), and C. Goodrich, *Government Promotion of American Canals and Railroads 1800–1890* (1960).

On American railroads, four good studies on railroad building are: E. C. Kirkland, *Men, Cities, and Transportation* (2 vols., 1948); P. W. Gates, *The Illinois Central Railroad and Its Colonization Work* (1934); T. C. Cochran, *Railroad Leaders, 1845–1900* (1953); and above all, A. Fishlow, *American Railroads and the Transformation of the Ante-Bellum Economy* (1965).

R. G. Albion, *The Rise of New York Port 1815–1860* (1939), and S. E. Morison, *The Maritime History of Massachusetts 1783–1860* (1921), are classics about American commerce after 1815. On ocean commerce, start with R. G. Albion, *Square Riggers on Schedule* (1938), and A. H. Clark, *The Clipper Ship Era 1843–1869* (1910). On the Far Eastern trade, F. R. Dulles, *The Old China Trade* (1930), has priority.

The two leading works on American agriculture are P. W. Bidwell and J. I. Falconer, *History of Agriculture in the Northern United States 1620–1860* (1925), and L. C. Gray, *History of Agriculture in the Southern United States to 1860* (2 vols., 1933). A recent work by Paul Gates, *The Farmers' Age, Agriculture 1815–1860* (1959), is a most impressive synthesis of more recent scholarship.

W. E. Dodd, *The Cotton Kingdom* (1919), and U. B. Phillips,

Life and Labor in the Old South (1929), have reputations as classics but are now out of date in some respects. A. O. Craven, *Edmund Ruffin, Southerner* (1932), and H. J. Carman, *Jesse Buel, Agricultural Reformer* (1947), have much information on farm problems in the South and North. E. E. Edwards, "American Agriculture–The First 300 Years," *Yearbook of Agriculture* (1940), is a general analysis by a meticulous scholar. The American mystique about the soil is brilliantly analyzed in H. N. Smith, *Virgin Land* (1950) (Pb).

Early industrialization can be studied in V. S. Clark, *History of Manufactures in the United States 1607–1928* (3 vols., 1929), and R. M. Tryon, *Household Manufactures in the United States 1640–1860* (1917). A general survey is T. C. Cochran and W. Miller, *The Age of Enterprise* (1942). On the textile industry, use C. F. Ware, *The Early New England Cotton Manufacture* (1931), and A. H. Cole, *The American Wool Manufacture* (2 vols., 1926). A. Nevins, *Abram Hewitt, with Some Account of Peter Cooper* (1925), and J. Mirsky and A. Nevins, *The World of Eli Whitney* (1952), are good studies of two early entrepreneurs. Technology, science, and their effects are the subjects of J. A. Kouwenhoven, *Made in America* (1948); Roger Burlingame, *March of the Iron Men* (1938); and J. W. Oliver, *History of American Technology* (1956).

On labor, a general survey is P. Taft, *Organized Labor in American History* (1964). The classic work is J. R. Commons (ed.), *History of Labor in the United States* (4 vols., 1918–35). N. J. Ware, *The Industrial Worker, 1840–1860* (1924), specializes in this period.

On the general impact of industrialization on American society, read E. W. Martin, *The Standard of Living in the United States in 1860* (1942); Vera Shlakman, *Economic History of a Factory Town* (1935); J. S. Davis, *Essays on the Earlier History of American Corporations* (2 vols., 1917); L. H. Jenks, *The Migration of British Capital to 1875* (1927); and W. B. Smith and A. H. Cole, *Fluctuations in American Business, 1790–1860* (1935).

Two works of first importance in understanding the sociology of industrial life are W. W. Rostow, *The Process of Economic Growth* (1952), and H. A. Williamson and J. A. Buttrick, *Economic Development: Principles and Patterns* (1954).

16

An Age of Idealism

IN 1800, the population of the United States was 5,300,000; by 1860, the census showed more than 31,400,000 Americans. The gross area of the nation when Jefferson came to power was 892,000 square miles; when Lincoln arrived in Washington for his inauguration in 1861 he was President-elect of a nation of more than 3,000,000 square miles. According to the best estimate, American national wealth in 1800 was approximately $2,400,000,000, but by 1860 this figure had increased nearly sevenfold to $16,160,000,000. In 1800, only one American city had a population in excess of 50,000 and there existed only 33 urban centers with a population of more than 2,500. On the eve of the firing on Fort Sumter, there were over 392 towns and cities with at least 2,500 people, and the total urban populace had increased nearly twenty times over that of 1800 to more than 6,200,000. At the turn of the century America had no railroads, and only 23 miles of railroad existed in the United States in 1830; more than 30,000 miles of tracks were in operation at the outbreak of the Civil War.

Generations later, in reflecting on this vast growth in national size and power the philosopher George Santayana observed that America had been the greatest civilization of idealists the world had ever known. No culture that he could recall had so continuously and thoroughly believed that the harsh and stubborn world would ultimately give way before man's will and dreams. The strong, willful quality of American life in the period 1815–60 was most apparent in the growing attraction of a money-making ethos; yet, as Santayana remarked, even monetary success, although deprecated by moralists as mammon worship, was usually taken by Americans as a heroic victory of the individual and as further proof of the special fortune decreed by God for the United

States. On the other hand, the pride, the sense of power, the hunger for success of Americans were constantly in conflict with a demanding moral code whose principal source lay in evangelical Protestantism. The themes of man's sin and redemption, of making right prevail in one's heart or in the world's conduct, played against the demands aroused by the tempting abundance of a continent. Thus, the desire to make one's life as powerful as the size and fecundity of the American land suggested it might be, was ever in conflict with the Christian wish to make life pure and just. The ceaseless warnings about wicked worldliness, overweening pride, and indulgence of the flesh that Americans heard from their parents and ministers, made more intense a long waged war between the Word of God and the world of man. This conflict between the Christian desire for inner purity and an equally strong hunger for worldly rewards greatly influenced the sense of life of most Americans in the nineteenth century. Together, Christian piety and desire for the dollar produced a character that was impatient, even reckless, about any limits on life. Although immensely practical, Americans at the same time were liable to be grandiose in their schemes of spiritual or social redemption. Primed for earth-shaking achievements, they invited the frustration, despair, and other bitter fruits of a victory never quite gained. Having made an investment in life that only a 90 per cent return might have satisfied, even the extraordinary rewards that America seemed to offer the plain man were often insufficient to fulfill his dreams.

Wiping out the Past

When the astute young Frenchman Alexis de Tocqueville visited the United States in 1831, he quickly understood that the energetic Americans were leading the world toward a new culture whose coming marked the destruction of the age-old foundations of European life. Although Americans increasingly thought of themselves as being blessedly free from the Old World, throughout the nineteenth century, as Tocqueville implied, they were always involved in Western culture.

By the 1830's, for example, American abolitionists, loco-focos, and others had taken the Declaration of Independence of 1776 as an invitation to create a new order of human affairs throughout the world, and Americans generally greeted the popular uprisings in Europe between 1820 and 1848 as essentially the same kind of struggle as they had made against George III in 1776. Frenchmen like Condorcet and LaFayette and Americans like Jefferson and James Monroe had prepared the way for the belief that the "spirit of '76" and the ever active French ideals of 1789 were essentially the same. The revolutions were taken as setting both Europeans and Americans on the road to equality. Tocqueville warned Europe that the tides of democracy could not be stopped, although perhaps they could be controlled, and that the American passion for equality should be studied, the better to understand the future of Europe.

During the nineteenth century in Europe and America industrialization and the ideals of 1776 and of 1789—Liberty, Equality, Fraternity—transformed Western life. From a relatively inflexible hierarchical society of orders and estates, stations and duties, Europeans moved toward the ideals of equality before the law, regardless of one's class, and the career open to talent rather than to high birth. For centuries before European society had had an official religious basis with established churches, but in the century after Waterloo previous tendencies to secularization and to freedom of worship became dominant, blunting the intellectual strength of religion and increasingly reducing the question of religious affiliation to largely a private matter. In economic life, as the potentialities of the factory and machine were slowly realized in Europe, the age-old threats of scarcity, permanent poverty, and misery began to be lifted. Indeed, it was the promise of the industrial system that made socialists like Karl Marx promise the working classes that they had nothing to lose but their chains. Because America was so far along the road to the egalitarian, secular and affluent society of the future, Tocqueville believed the United States had lessons for all Europeans. Tocqueville's purpose was to study the new society and to appraise its weaknesses and strengths. The observations and reflections in his masterpiece, *Democracy in America*, added up to the most impressive sociology of democratic life that had yet or has since been made. Although an aristocrat, Tocqueville understood and appreciated the attractions of democracy or "equality of conditions." He was frightened, however, that in liquidating the traditional social restraints of church, crown, and class, the Americans and Europeans, hungry for the promises of the new democratic age, would create a "tyranny of the majority" far worse than the injustice of the aristocracy of the *ancien régime*.

The Holy Nation

Among those forces in America that Tocqueville believed would work against democratic absolutism was the Christian religion. He thought that the idea of man's sinfulness and the sense of human limitations taught by orthodox Christianity would tend to remind democrats that they were not, after all, gods and that there was Divine recompense for those who acted too pridefully or too arrogantly in life. Although Tocqueville was full of praise for how Americans had strengthened the attractions of Christianity by making religion a private choice rather than official public creed, he underestimated the forces that were weakening religious restraints on democratic enthusiasms.

During the first three generations after 1789, American religious life underwent several notable changes. Starting with great Methodist revivals in the 1780's, evangelical ministers and preachers made a largely successful counterattack against public profession of rationalist ideas and enlightened religion. The Protestant ministers were even more effective in checking religious indifference. In many coastal cities and in the more pietistic backcountry, the call to redemption from sin and a change of heart toward one's fellow man evoked powerful enthusiasms and energy that were eventually poured into innumerable schemes for reforming American society. Although the so-called Protestant Counter-Reformation was not strong enough to kill completely benign or rationalist theories of man, in many sections of the country it did put rationalism and deism, with their great faith in man's reason, on the defensive. It was not until the 1830's that the rationalist doctrines of the eighteenth century enlightenment came again into wider circulation. At the same time American thinkers came under the influence of less rationalistic but equally optimistic faiths of the heart derived from the thought of Europeans such as Jean Jacques Rousseau, Immanuel Kant, Samuel Taylor Coleridge, and others of the so-called romantic school. Often an American raised with a Calvinist view of man would revolt against what he took to be its repressive features and transfer his religious enthusiasm to one or a succession of more liberal creeds. Whether sentimental or rationalist in their basis the optimistic Christian faiths such as Universalism or Unitarianism differed from the Calvinism of the older sects, but both optimists and pessimists about the chances for man's redemption continued to share concern about perfecting his character and making right prevail. Both religious "liberals" and "conservatives" also tended to argue for their particular scheme of redemption in a glowing and absolute manner. The fervor and sweeping promises for the future in the hellfire and brimstone harangue of the backwoods Methodist preacher and in the speech of a learned Bostonian like Theodore Parker in full revolt against the Calvinist tradition were very similar despite doctrinal differences.

Parker said that men needed a religion of reason and good works ". . . to heal the vices of modern society, to revolutionize this modern feudalism of gold, and join the rich and poor, the employer and the employed in one bond of human fellowship . . . to break down the walls between class and class, nation and nation, race and race—to join all classes into one nation, all nations into one great human family." Compare Parker's words with an orthodox sermon and the common mood of certainty, of deliverance, and of redemption is apparent. It was evident, said one Calvinist writer, "that some will be finally rejected from the Kingdom of Heaven and it is probable that it will be a part of their punishment to see those who were their former companions enjoying that blessed state, from which they are excluded by their own folly and sin. The punishment and tortures of condemned spirits will be increasing to all eternity. How tremendous and overwhelming is the thought that the suffering of one soul will be greater than the united suffering of all in the universe for millions of ages."

If Tocqueville hoped that either the sense of sin in pronouncements of the orthodox or the idea of the magnificence of God in an enlightened theology like Parker's would temper ill-considered democratic enthusiasms by teaching men that "it is only by resisting a thousand petty selfish passions of the hour that the general and unquenchable passion for happiness can be satisfied," he was mistaken. The absolutist visions of imminent deliverance in American religious life not only reinforced the willful qualities in American character but strengthened the notion that popular democracy and republican institutions were themselves sanctioned by God. Although Americans believed in a God-given fundamental moral law transcending man-made rules or human ambitions, they very easily tailored the Word of Heaven to the demands of the world and endowed Manifest Destiny or slavery or the rights of property with Godly sanctions.

Diversity and Dissension in American Religion

The power of religion as a check on American materialism or egalitarianism was limited not only by the power of the gospel of success and by trimming Christianity to fit the world's needs, but also by the continuing fragmentation of American Protestantism into many small doctrinal and doctrinaire sects. In the generation before the Civil War, for the most notable examples, both the Baptist and Methodist national organizations split into northern and southern wings over the slavery issue. This split was, however, one of the more dramatic schisms in a long history of quarrels that dated back to the days of the colonial settlers.

During the second quarter of the nineteenth century, America continued to be a land of religious dissension. Protestants increasingly were arrayed against Catholics, as well as Protestants against Protestants. Fervid individualism, the failure of existing church organizations to shepherd their flocks carefully, disagreement over questions of theology or church organization, the new streams of population pouring in from Ireland and western Germany were largely responsible for the religious upheavals of these years.

Everywhere in the United States, but particularly west of the Alleghenies, new doctrines and new ceremonies were attracting adherents. Many of the new denominations had names resembling that of a parent religious group but qualified by a word or phrase that indicated a cause for secession. Among the Baptists, there were the regular Baptists, Seventh-day Baptists, Free Baptists, Free-will Baptists, General Six Principle Baptists, Seed-in-the-Spirit Predestinarian Baptists, and at least three Negro Baptist bodies. Among the Methodists there was similar confusion. In addition to the regular organization of the Methodist Episcopal Church, ultimately divided into the Church North and the Church South, there were the Methodist Church, New Congregational Methodist Church, and Independent Methodist Church. The Negro Methodists worshipped by themselves and formed at least six major denominations of their own. The Presbyterian Church was less divided, but even some of its divisions were superficially perplexing —for instance, the distinction between the Presbyterian Church in the United States and the Presbyterian Church in the United States of America.

The growing pluralism of American religious life can also be suggested by mentioning just a few of the other important sects. In addition to a half dozen types of Adventists there were the United Society of Believers (or Shakers, as they were generally called), the Rappites, the Dunkers (or German Baptist Brethren), the Quakers, Mormons, Moravians, Schwenkfelders, Campbellites, Universalists, and the many varieties of Mennonites, including the Amish and the Old Amish. With the coming of the Scandinavian and German immigrants in the 1850's, even more sects were added.

The Adventists in many respects exemplified the so-called millennialist strain among the lesser religious groups. They had their immediate origins in 1831, when William Miller, an earnest New England farmer of Baptist background, began to warn the people of the United States that the end of the world was at hand. Evangelists had been preaching this idea for some time, and it was only when Miller set the second coming of Christ for sometime in 1843 that he began to attract widespread interest. In 1839, he was invited to preach in the leading

Baptist church in Boston, and he soon had calls from many large churches in all parts of the country. Journals such as the *Signs of the Times* in Boston, the *Midnight Cry* in New York, and the *Philadelphia Alarm* propagated the new gospel. As the time approached for the supposed end of the world, great meetings were held in churches, tents, public buildings, fields, and groves. At dawn on March 21, 1843, Miller's followers—variously estimated at from 50,000 to 1,000,000—gathered in graveyards and on housetops, hilltops, and mountainsides. Some were in white robes; others wore their best clothes. One white-gowned convert climbed a tree at the final hour, tried to fly away, and broke his neck. The failure of the Lord to appear nearly prostrated Miller. His followers decreased, but all did not desert him. In 1845, he perfected a loose organization known as the Adventists. The following year, the Seventh Day Adventists separated from the main body over the question of observing as the Sabbath the seventh day, Saturday, instead of Sunday.

The challenge to accepted opinions and practices, the threat to established churches and well set ministers, and the general disruption of community life were recurrent causes for the unpopularity of sects like the Millerites. Denunciation often gave way to physical attacks on the new religionists and their leaders, but none of the Protestant sects suffered so much for their "heresy" as did the Mormons. The fate of no other group revealed so clearly the accuracy of Tocqueville's comments on the intolerance and touchiness of Americans on creeds uncongenial to the majority. Their story also shows the risks minorities had to take in a pluralistic society without settled or authoritative religious traditions.

The Church of Latter Day Saints, as the Mormon Church is called, was founded in 1830 by Joseph Smith at Palmyra, New York. Smith proclaimed that an angel had directed him to a cave on a hillside where he had found concealed a number of golden plates bearing strange inscriptions. These records, which Smith asserted he alone could translate, formed the basis of *The Book of Mormon*, the holy book of the sect. Smith became the first head of the church, and "revelations" from time to time gave him complete control over the moral, temporal, and spiritual welfare of its members. His persuasive personality, his claim of direct revelation, and the mystic and authoritative nature of the new religion soon won Smith thousands of converts. In Great Britain, to which the movement soon spread, Mormon preachers gained more than 4,000 converts in the course of three years. Mormonism, with its miracles, signs, and revelations, and its promise of a new Zion, drew many who were discontented with the members or practices of an older religious group or who were simply, as was often the case, in search of religious novelty.

From the outset the Mormons encountered opposition and persecution. The prophet and his followers moved from New York to Kirtland, Ohio, in 1831, where the flock remained only a short time before marching on to Independence, Missouri, the place selected for the permanent site of Zion. Yet, after two years of peace and prosperity, the Latter Day Saints again became embroiled with the non-Mormon inhabitants, and in 1833 the sect sought refuge in Clay County, Missouri, where, far removed from its persecutors, it founded a semi-socialistic community. Only a few years elapsed, however, before southern pioneers began to surround the colony. Hostility quickly developed, for neither the new faith nor the socialistic organization of the community appealed to the frontier farmers. Friction and mutual animosity, resulting in systematic and bitter persecution, culminated in 1838 in the wholesale expulsion of the Saints from Missouri. Taking refuge in Illinois, they purchased the abandoned frontier village of Commerce and in 1840 rechristened it Nauvoo. By thrift and by hard work they acquired new farms, manufactures, and wealth. New disciples arrived every month from the eastern states, England, Scandinavia, and the Germanies, and in a comparatively short time Nauvoo had a population of approximately 15,000. But in 1843 a new revelation sanctioned polygamy. Whatever erotic attraction the thought of having several wives may have had, the ostensible purpose of Mormon polygamy was to prevent the sect from dying out. Added, however, to Smith's alleged political intrigues and to the charges that the Mormons were harboring cattle thieves, counterfeiters, and other criminals, the new marriage rule led to turbulence within the community and to renewed hostility from the outside. In the following year, Smith and his brother Hyrum, who had been jailed by the authorities, were seized by a mob and murdered.

Smith was succeeded by Brigham Young, a man of remarkable energy and gifted leadership. Under his direction, the Nauvoo population, with 3,700 wagons, 30,000 cattle, large flocks of sheep and poultry, a number of hogs, and "all manner of tools, machinery, and materials deemed serviceable in the colonization of a wilderness," migrated to Council Bluffs, Iowa, during the spring and summer of 1846. Early in the next year, Young, with a company of picked men, set out in quest of the long-sought haven where there would be no chance of molestation. After a long journey, Young staked out the site of what proved to be the Mormons' permanent home on the tableland overlooking

Great Salt Lake in Utah. At the time, the region lay within Mexican territory, but the following year it was ceded to the United States. Late in September, 1847, the first division of the main body, numbering 1,553 men, women, and children, arrived; others followed, and by 1850, Utah had a population of more than 11,000.

Under Young's directing genius, the colony soon became a great cooperative community with an intelligently diversified economy. Of all the more extreme sects that were born in America in the years before the Civil War, the Mormons had struggled longest and with greatest pain against the hostile majority, and few achieved such material success to reward their perseverance.

The Fear of Rome

The fate of America's growing Roman Catholic population was another notable case of how faith in democracy and Christianity combined to the disadvantage of minorities, especially as the older American Protestant denominations grew continuously in size after 1800. From 1800 to 1850, the Presbyterians increased from 40,000 to 500,000, the Baptists from 100,000 to 800,000, and the Methodist Episcopal Church in all its branches from 65,000 to more than 1,250,000. This increase in numbers helped solidify the convictions of many citizens that the benefits of American life were intended principally for Protestants. With the growth in the size of the Roman Catholic population in the 1840's and 1850's, the long standing but latent anti-Catholicism of an intensely Protestant population was stirred up by bigots and demagogues. If anything was needed to show Tocqueville that religion would not always act as a brake on democracy, but might indeed inflame its self-righteousness, the rise of Nativism in the 1850's would amply serve that purpose.

The growing strength of Roman Catholicism in the United States came from the great waves of immigrants that reached American shores from Europe after 1830. Between 1820 and 1830, less than 500,000 foreigners, principally English, Welsh, Scots, German, and Irish, came to America. From 1830 to 1850, however, nearly 2,500,000 immigrants were added to a population that increased altogether from slightly less than 13,000,000 to over 23,000,000. More than 2,700,000 additional foreigners arrived during the decade preceding the Civil War to enjoy the higher paying jobs, cheap farms, and political refuge from oppression that they believed they could find in America. Many objected to the newcomers, but many businessmen, sensing greater profits and needing unskilled labor, welcomed them.

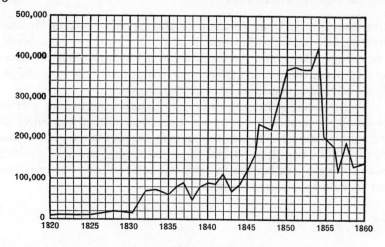

Immigration, 1820–60

[BASED ON U. S. CENSUS REPORTS]

Between 1830 and 1860, economic distress and political upheaval set in motion an especially large German migration to the New World. In 1847, 50,000 Germans entered the United States, and by 1860 more than 1,000,000 had arrived, but, unlike the more numerous Irish, many Germans who landed on this side of the Atlantic had a little money, and several of them had had considerable experience in politics, business, and the professions in their native land. Most of them also were Protestants, and, although they were not unequivocally welcomed, their wealth, their Protestantism, and the decision of the majority to go beyond the Alleghenies for farms and, often, communities of their own eased their acceptance into American society. They became prosperous farmers in the new West or formed an important group in the small but growing cities of Cincinnati, Louisville, St. Louis, and Milwaukee.

Although other immigrants of the time included French-Canadians, Dutch, Belgians, and Swiss, no group was larger, more impoverished, or more ill-treated than the Irish. Poverty and devastating famines during the 1840's drove hundreds of thousands of them to America. With the failure of the Irish potato crops in 1845, hundreds died of starvation, the unburied dead lying where they fell with their mouths stained green from the weeds and thistles eaten in desperation. Of those who survived, 1,500,000 migrated to America before 1860. Like earlier immigrants from the British Isles, a few of the better educated went directly into business; but the great majority settled in groups in the cities and villages of the industrial Northeast, where as unskilled laborers they were eagerly sought by mill owners and builders of canals, railroads, and other enterprises. In the cities Irish girls soon displaced the native born as domestic servants.

With the influx of Irish immigrants into the United States, the Catholic Church grew so rapidly that it soon seemed a threat to many Protestants. Although Irish Catholics had migrated to the United States in small numbers since colonial times, not until the 1840's was there such a mass immigration of Roman Catholics. The new arrivals largely accounted for the increase in the number of American Catholics from 600,000 in 1820 to 3,500,000 in 1850. The Irish were so heavily concentrated in New England that Theodore Parker commented on the Massachusetts census returns for 1855: "Suffolk County is 'County Cork'; Boston is a young Dublin."

Many native Protestants, alarmed especially by the rapid growth of the Catholic Church but generally hostile to most foreigners, opposed the newcomers in a variety of ways. In 1834, anti-Catholics burned the Ursuline convent in Charlestown, Massachusetts; the next year S. F. B. Morse's *Foreign Conspiracy* attacked the Catholic Irish in America; and in every large city there were occasional anti-Catholic demonstrations. Nativist agitators roused their countrymen by pointing out that the squalid sections of cities, where many immigrants lived, were breeding places of vice and crime. Protestant Americans were terrified as they beheld the "hordes" of Catholics building churches, establishing convents, and organizing parochial schools. Patriot ministers like Lyman Beecher exhorted their fellow citizens to guard against the dark designs of the "revolutionaries" who were streaming to America intent on overturning the nation's government and cherished institutions. Politicians opposed to a liberal land policy tied it to the fear of the immigrant and declared that free or cheap land would invite to America "the bandit of the Apennines, the mercenary Swiss, the hungry loafer of the cities of the Old World, the offal of disgorged jails, penitentiaries, and houses of correction of foreign countries."

As a result of this widespread clamor against the immigrant, a nationalistic organization known as the Supreme Order of the Star-Spangled Banner, or the Sons of the Sires of '76, was formed in New York in 1850. An oath-bound fraternity, made up of members descended from at least two generations of American ancestors who had never been members of the Catholic Church, this organization pledged itself to put none but native Americans in office and in every other way possible to "preserve America for Americans." "In every city, town and hamlet," said the president of this organization, "the danger has

Immigrants Arriving in New York (Harper's Weekly)

been seen and the alarm sounded. And hence true men have devised this order as a means . . . of advancing America and the American interest on the one side, and, on the other, of checking the stride of the foreigner or alien, of thwarting the machinations and subverting the deadly plans of the Jesuit and the Papist." Because members, when asked about the order, invariably replied, "I don't know" or "I know nothing," they were dubbed "Know-Nothings" and their social and political organization the Know-Nothing party. These fanatics and unprincipled politicians made common cause in the early 1850's. In many parts of the country Know-Nothing or Native American parties began to appear. In Massachusetts in 1854, Nativists elected a governor and practically the entire legislature. In New York, they elected forty members to the state legislature and they helped elect a governor and some members of the legislative body of Pennsylvania. They also elected a few Know-Nothings to Congress from the same states. The following year Know-Nothing governors were elected in Massachusetts, Connecticut, Rhode Island, New Hampshire, California, and Kentucky. The Know-Nothings also controlled the legislatures of all these states with the exception of New Hampshire. In Texas, New York, and Maryland, where there were no gubernatorial contests, Know-Nothing state tickets triumphed. In New Hampshire, Maryland, and Tennessee, the legislatures were controlled by a fusion of Whigs and Know-

Nothings, and the legislatures of New York, Virginia, Georgia, and Louisiana boasted strong Know-Nothing minorities. Know-Nothing candidates were also elected to Congress and to many municipal offices.

Despite these startling successes, between 1854 and 1856 the movement began to decline as the slavery controversy became more heated. The platform of the American party (as the national nativist group was called) declared in the presidential campaign of 1856 that Americans must rule America; that no state or territory could admit to suffrage or political office any except native citizens unless previously naturalized under federal law; that twenty-one years' residence for naturalization should be required; and that there should be no union of church and state, no state interference with religion, and no religious oaths for office. With Millard Fillmore as its standard bearer in the election of 1856, the American party won nearly 1,000,000 votes. It had gained phenomenal success in the two previous years partly because numerous Democrats and Whigs, dissatisfied with the policies and leadership of their respective parties, had voted the Know-Nothing ticket as a protest; but inefficient leadership, little legislative achievement, the prominence of the slavery issue, the birth of the Republican party, and the need for more cheap labor in a rapidly expanding country were rocks upon which the Know-Nothings foundered.

Despite such anti-Catholic agitation and social pressures against Protestant dissenters, American public policy became more tolerant before the Civil War. Laws that discriminated against Catholics, Jews, and atheists in the exercise of the franchise and in officeholding were gradually abolished in the states. The polygamy of the Mormons might offend the moral fastidiousness of the nation, and the fear of papal machinations might produce fanatical organizations, but most Americans could worship without interference. The same multiplicity of creeds that created uncertainty about one's identity and invited sectarian struggle also prevented a long run predominance of any one denomination and reduced the opportunities for religious persecution. Many examples may be cited of brutalities caused by religious bigotry, such as the hounding of the Mormons; yet if one recalls the sixteenth and seventeenth centuries in Europe and America's colonial period, it is clear that by the eve of the Civil War religious intolerance had remarkably declined in the United States.

The agitation against the Catholics and the Mormons revealed a conception of American life very often found in other political and social movements. Although America once was a wonderful country—this reasoning ran—something had gone wrong with its machinery, and renovation and restoration were called for. There was derived from this a sense of two Golden Ages, the America that had been and the America that could yet be. Both had their source in sheer nostalgia and in a secularized image of America as a Christian Paradise, given by God to man, lost by his sin or by the sins of his children, but to be restored by reconversion to the truth and redeemed by the self-discipline and inflexible righteousness of converts to the true American faith. Most American reform movements were at times affected by this image and consequently took on the characteristics of a crusade. They were filled with missionary idealism, were led by masters and apostles, worshiped their own hierarchy of saints or holy figures, and promised redemption to all who heeded their word. The combination of reverence for a perfect past with high hopes for a purer future makes it difficult to judge the reformers of the generation after 1830. Many men who denounced the spread of slavery, for example, may have been more concerned to keep the American West white-man's country in the future than to grant Negroes equality. Rabid opponents of the Catholics would declare that America was planned as a Protestant country, that aliens had corrupted the new Eden, and that restrictions on Catholics would restore America to its birthright; thus men who were seriously and deeply concerned about crime and poverty in Boston or New York and who wished to improve their communities were misled to believe that the "one thing needful" was to circumvent Catholic power and all would be refreshed, restored, and renewed.

The Common School Revolution

Although many of the reforms in the period after 1830 that are associated with the rise of Jacksonian democracy seemed radical to contemporaries, the reformers themselves often shared the conviction that some alien ideal or wicked group had taken the republic from the road laid out by the founding fathers; reform work was thus not radical but restorative. It was, for example, the realization that free elementary education might be used to save the old republican ideals that assured the success of the common school movement.

When it was first proposed that tax-supported common schools be established in order to prepare all American children to enjoy their birthright of equal opportunity, opposition arose at once on the grounds that public schools were too expensive, that they usurped parents' prerogatives, and, most of all, that they were likely to breed radical "leveling" tendencies or religious infidelity. Very quickly, however, as wealthy men and ministers began to understand that public instruction could be used to blunt the threats of rising egalitarianism and irreligion, the opposition against free public education diminished. Instead there began the perennial American debate over the "aims of education" for a finer future and "the failures of the schools" to preserve the American heritage of the golden past.

The most bitter early fight took place over the place of religion in public education. All those interested in education agreed that its main objectives should be character training and intellectual achievement and that "character" could only be attained when children learned certain absolute principles of morality and righteousness. Given the tendency of most men of the age to think of religious and moral instruction as mutually interdependent, the intense concern about the danger of a secular education is understandable. Theodore Dwight, Jr., one of the most active opponents of secular education, claimed, "To separate . . . religious, moral, and intellectual instruction is to tear sound education limb from limb." Despite many such protests, full sectarian teaching was judged to be incompatible with publicly supported education, and only a vague Christianity found its way into public school textbooks before 1860.

By the eve of the Civil War, inspired by the faith that education could both preserve the past and save the future, most states outside the South had at least accepted the principle of tax-supported publicly controlled schools. By 1850, for example, the country already had 80,000 elementary schools with 90,000 teachers and nearly 3,500,000 students. The enthusiasm for education also inspired the beginnings of the second phase of the American educational revolution, the growth of the high school, for by 1860 there were hundreds of public high schools in operation in the northern states. However great the crudeness of most schoolhouses and poverty of instruction, the nation was well on the way to guaranteeing every child as much public instruction as he wanted.

From its beginnings the education revolution tapped the American fervor for redemption. Since it is in the schools that the power of ideas and the appeal for a better future have their strongest claims on individuals, American reformers have generally been enthusiastic about the possibilities of education and zealous about conditions in the schools. Horace Mann, the nation's outstanding educational leader before the Civil War, set the universal theme: "Educate, only educate enough, and we shall regenerate the criminal and eradicate vice; through the schools we shall teach mankind to moderate their passions and develop their virtues; let us but conquer the world of knowledge that is lying at our doors, and then, and then only shall we be able . . . to 'ring out the false and ring in the new.'"

Mann's great effort was just a small part of the general ferment that came with the growing enthusiasm for education. He served as the first secretary of the Massachusetts board of education, and in 1839 he secured the first state-supported American normal school, at Lexington, Massachusetts. Six years later, he organized a state association of teachers in Massachusetts. He also established teachers' institutes, advocated compulsory education as a bar to child labor in factories, studied the educational value of physiology and hygiene, supported the introduction of instruction in music, sought ways to help defectives and delinquents, and insisted that women should have equal privileges with men in the schools. Mann's activities soon attracted nationwide attention; his reports were eagerly read, and other states began to emulate Massachusetts. By 1849, fourteen states had superintendents of education, and a number of the larger urban communities had appointed city superintendents.

At the same time that Mann was leading his crusade, American education started to acquire its impressive administrative apparatus and its many journals. Henry Barnard of Connecticut, who was trained at Yale and in Germany, helped found the American Association for the Advancement of Education and became its first president in 1855. He also established the *American Journal of Education* and edited it for more than a quarter of a century. Countless teachers were indebted to him for his translations of the writings of the European theorists of education, Comenius, Rousseau, and Pestalozzi. Like Mann, he was interested in arousing a professional spirit among teachers, and his and Mann's work was promoted by the efforts of a group of able women including Catharine Beecher, Mary Lyon, Elizabeth Peabody, Emma Willard, and her sister, Mrs. Almira Phelps. Unfortunately, despite this great flurry of activity, the results were intellectually meager and common school education gave millions of citizens little more than mere literacy.

Even advocates of modern scientific and humanistic subjects for college students were able to make only slight improvements in American education. Although many new colleges and universities were also established after 1815, they served thin intellectual fare. Some of these, particularly in the South and West, were state institutions, but the larger number were small denominational colleges that were controlled by a narrow and sectarian clergy.

Whatever aspirations to reform and intellectual excellence existed in higher as well as lower education were frustrated by lack of money, books, and trained teachers. Many of the new denominational colleges began with a subscribed capital fund of less than $10,000, and several colleges lived in continual financial crisis. College libraries were generally inadequate and little used by students. At Dartmouth, for example, the library was open one hour a week, and a fee was collected for each book borrowed. With the exception of a few brilliant teachers like Francis Wayland of Brown and Mark Hopkins of Williams, American faculties were mediocre. Among the handful of first-rank scholars, however, was Benjamin Silliman, who occupied the first chair of chemistry and natural history at Yale. He founded the first American scientific periodical, wrote one of the earliest scientific textbooks in the United States, and was among the first Americans to examine from a scientific viewpoint the Biblical account of the creation. Joseph Henry was another outstanding scientist who taught at Princeton from 1832 to 1846, served as the first director of the Smithsonian Institution, and conducted important experiments in electromagnetism. At the South Carolina College, Francis Lieber produced several pioneer works in political science and was perhaps the most renowned American scholar in this field. At Harvard alone, the oldest and best of the American universities, the traditions of intellect were well served by a number of able professors. George Bancroft, Joseph G. Cogswell, Edward Everett, and George Ticknor—all of whom had graduated from Harvard and studied in Germany—made Harvard the nation's outstanding center for the study of history and the humanities. In the sciences, the Swiss-born Louis Agassiz, who joined the Harvard faculty in 1846, introduced the laboratory method in zoology, and shattered traditional geological concepts with his glacial theory.

The place of the universities in American life at this time showed the general problem of American education. The universities, like the best private secondary schools, were among the few American institutions still trying to maintain a classical European tradition, while most Americans, as Tocqueville observed, were enthralled with the idea of breaking down historically sanctioned restraints on individualism. The universities, consequently, were in an anomalous position. Like all schools, they had to teach a body of learning that was known and already mastered by the teachers, but the major energies of their society were increasingly turned against the stable and the static in intellectual as well as in social life. As the instability and uncertainty of life in a culture so committed to innovation became painful, Americans hoped that the schools would "safeguard the perilous future"; yet, at the same time, they seemed to doubt that their new purposes could be served in practice, by the traditions of Western learning. Requiring from education, as from other reforms, quick, dramatic and easily grasped results, they became increasingly impatient with the demand-

The University of Virginia

[NEW YORK PUBLIC LIBRARY]

ing discipline by which real intellectual excellence is attained; further-more, nourished by egalitarian, pragmatic, and evangelical hostility to learning, the schools were asked to prepare students for "real life" rather than for philosophic or "fancy" speculation. As a result, at the very beginnings of its educational revolution, American society, al-though dependent on producing the best ideas to make good on its promise of happiness for all, developed strong tendencies to denigrate genuine intellect and civilized thought.

The Passion for Purity

The controversies about the nature and directions of American education were part of a large variegated reform enthusiasm that swept over the United States between 1820 and 1860. Although the only satisfactory explanation of the cause of these reform movements lies in an analysis of the lives of the individual reformers, the sources of their rhetoric and their image of America can be discussed in general terms.

The growth of industry and the commercialization of national life, the egalitarian enthusiasm, the changes in political institutions, the rise of new political and social elites—in sum, the dismantling during the age of Jackson of the institutions of the late eighteenth century—created many conflicts in the minds of Americans between images of what the nation had been and what it might become. With the general social dislocation after the War of 1812, men and women went into many reform movements that promised to set the country right. Why they chose any one reform, such as temperance or the peace movement, de-

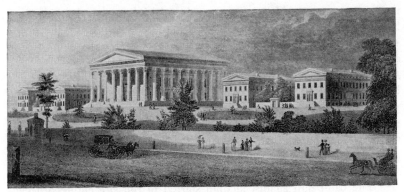

Girard College for Orphans, Philadelphia

pended on the circumstances in each case. Whatever their individual motives, the ideas that attracted them were drawn principally from two sources, the Declaration of Independence and the Gospel's admonition to love one's fellow men. Jeffersonian idealists often joined hands with representatives from every religious denomination to sponsor orphan and insane asylums, temperance crusades, prison reform, and the abolition of slavery. In the 1830's, the radical workingmen of loco-foco democracy joined the campaigns and sought free public education, the end of imprisonment for debt, mechanics' lien laws, and the reform of militia systems. By 1840, there were few phases of American life that had not been held up to some ideal standard by the nation's reformers.

The reform leaders were drawn from every group and section of the country, but the more famous were members of the middle and upper classes in New England. With the growth of commerce and industry in New England, many members of the region's older families saw the gradual destruction of long-standing family privileges and prerogatives. Some accepted the new order and became factory lords or merchant princes; others became scholars and intellectuals, living in a world that they inhabited but had not made; and still others became reformers seeking to restore the lost golden age or to build a new one.

Before the abolititionists captured the major energies behind the reform impetus, the most successful reform crusade was temperance. For generations European travelers in the United States had been appalled at the enormous American thirst for alcohol. Whether American consumption in fact exceeded that of lower class Europeans at home, to whose habits the foreign traveler in America might be less sensitive, is a moot question. Whatever the criteria of excessive drinking, in a hard-working, unstable, competitive society, liquor, being cheap and easy to come by or to make from grains at the back door, was an anodyne and tranquilizer. The family still was as much a feature of rural American life as the omnipresent saloon was of the city. Although liquor was often a social menace, destroying individual lives and weakening or wrecking family ties, the absolutely disciplined man and morally righteous community that the temperance crusaders envisioned as the result of their work were almost more frightening to contemplate than the weak but human drunkard who abused or neglected his wife and children.

The campaign against alcohol started in the late eighteenth century, largely as a health measure. After 1800, as religious reformers increasingly determined to make America into God's land and looked about for signs of sin and corruption, few common habits seemed more noxious than drinking. Starting out, like most other reform movements, in scattered localities and then growing in numbers and organization as it captured the popular imagination, the temperance and "teetotaling" movement formally became a national body, the American Temperance Union, in 1826. When this society gave way to its successor, the United States Temperance Union in 1833, there were between 2,000 and 3,000 groups fighting for the redemption of America by restricting or abolishing the use of alcohol.

Long before the ballyhoo of the presidential election of 1840, these groups had staged mass meetings and parades, printed millions of pieces of hortatory literature ranging from handbills to full length novels, poems, and plays, and, in general, had used much of the apparatus that was soon to become conventional in American political campaigns and crusades.

Although there was a range of opinions within the temperance movement that led to internal dissension and charges of "heresy" by one group of the faithful against another, the temperance fervor caught on, and, like other reform movements, it ceased to be a social movement and became political. Overzealous idealists and expedient politicians soon made common cause and convenient alliances. In the intensely evangelical American society of the age, the simple analysis of social ills offered by the temperance and prohibition leaders, when coupled with the politician's promise of laws for the deliverance of the individual and the nation, made war on "demon rum" a useful political device. Since the anti-alcohol campaign gave moments of grandiose pseudo-spirituality to a people generally preoccupied with narrow and crass material pursuits, it seemed admirably to serve the American passion for moral purity. It made weak people feel moral and small men feel powerful.

As the temperance movement gained strength it became more militant in its tone, more absolute in its demands, and more sweeping in its promises. One temperance song of the 1840's, *Take Courage*, can only suggest the high hopes that the campaign aroused:

> From the mountain top and valley
> See! the banner streaming high!
> While the sons of freedom rally
> To the widow's lonely cry,
>   Sisters weeping
> Bid us to the rescue fly.
>
> Could we hear the mother pleading,
> Heaven relief will quickly send;
> Can we see our country bleeding,
> Still refuse our aid to lend?
>   No! dread monster,
> Here thy triumph soon shall end.

In 1854, the mountain of propaganda against the evils of drink was topped by T. S. Arthur's famous work *Ten Nights in a Barroom*, which was quickly dramatized and became almost as popular as *Uncle Tom's Cabin*. Besides the sinful aspects of tippling liquor, the temperance advocates emphasized the injurious effects of alcohol on the body and working efficiency, and the long trail of sorrowing mothers living in dirty, gloomy houses with wan and ragged children who were neglected or terrorized by besotted fathers.

At first the political program of the prohibitionists called for licensing systems, heavy taxes, and quantitative restrictions on sales of liquor, but since these let too many sinners slip through the nets, laws were soon sought against the manufacture and sale of intoxicants except for medicinal purposes. Paradoxically, however, the consumption of liquor began to decline as the temperance movement achieved its most notable political successes. In 1846, the Maine legislature, led by Neal Dow, passed the first law in America that prohibited the sale of liquor as a beverage. The law proved difficult to enforce, and in 1851 it was supplanted by another, which, under the name of the Maine Liquor Law, became a model for all similar legislation. By 1856, thirteen northern states had laws that were intended to control the sale of intoxicants, but no state below the Mason and Dixon line prohibited the sale of liquor. In most states, however, prohibition remained a continuous con-

PROGRAMME OF THE TEMPERANCE CONVENTION,

MIDDLETOWN, Oct. 26, 27, 1841

Tuesday, 26th. The Connecticut Temperance Society will commence its Annual Meeting in the North Cong. Church, at 2 o'clock P. M. Hon. Chief Justice WILLIAMS, President. The Society will proceed immediately to the appointment of Committees, and as far as time will permit, will hear reports of the Delegates from County and local Societies.

Tuesday Evening.—ANNUAL REPORT of the State Society, and several Addresses at the North Church.

Wednesday Morning.—A TEMPERANCE PROCESSION will be formed on the South Green, under the direction of LINUS COE, Esq. Chief Marshal, aided by Messrs. Wm. S. Camp, John L. Smith, Edward Treadway, J. H. Morrow, Charles W. Newton, Geo. E. Taylor, and Norman Smith, Assistant Marshals.

ORDER OF PROCESSION.

Chief Marshal, and Aid, on Horseback.
Music.
Sabbath Schools, and other Children and Youths.
Connecticut Temperance Society and Visiting Strangers.
Washington Temperance Societies.
Faculty and Students of Wesleyan University.
Citizens.
Assistant Marshal on Horseback.

The Procession will form in the above order, at 10 o'clock A. M. and passing through William, Broad, Washington and Main streets, will return to the south Green.

Sabbath Schools and other children and youths, will repair to the South Congregational Church, and be addressed by Nathan Crosby, Esq. Secretary of the Mass. Temperance Union, and Commander in Chief of the Mass. Cold Water Army, and by several other Gentlemen.

All others will repair to the Methodist Church, and be addressed by Messrs. Pollard and Wright of Baltimore, and other distinguished laborers in the cause.

Wednesday Afternoon, and also in the *Evening,* the Meetings of the State Society will be continued in the North Church, to hear addresses, and discuss important Resolutions.

The "Hurrah for bright Water," and other Temperance Music, to be sung, and the Temperance Hymn Books to be used in these meetings, may be obtained at the Bookstore of Luke C Lyman, opposite the Post office, where Delegates, and visiting strangers will record their names, and be directed to accommodations.

Temperance Poster

troversy. Laws were passed, repealed, and passed again as the prohibition forces continued their work throughout the nineteenth and into the twentieth century.

Although not all reform movements aroused as much enthusiasm or involved as much intervention in private lives as did prohibition, it did demonstrate certain common themes in an age when, as Ralph Waldo Emerson remarked, man seemed born for reform. Like other reforms, temperance and prohibition had their sources in social dislocation and evangelical piety; they grew from local to national proportions; they used themes of sin and redemption and created a crusade atmosphere; they passed from a social to a political phase and were exploited by the politicians and men too quick to equate their own vision of righteousness with the happiness or well-being of their fellow citizens. The temperance movement, starting as early as it did, also acted as a school in reform techniques that former temperance leaders carried over into later crusades.

The Rights of Women

Less spectacular than temperance reform, but far more revealing about the deep changes underway in the status of persons in America was the gradual emancipation of women. Down to the nineteenth century, the dominant American attitude was that the woman's place was in the home. Abigail Adams' ready wit and energy might be charming, but she shone chiefly as John Adams' clever wife. An education beyond elementary school was not regarded as necessary or even advisable for women. The aim of a girl's training was to fit her for marriage, housekeeping, and rearing children. After marriage, she subordinated herself to her husband; under the common law, her property belonged to him, and in turn he was responsible for her conduct and well-being. Any desire to enter into activities accessible to men was ridiculed and deplored as unladylike and even as immoral. Frances Wright, Lucy Stone, Elizabeth Cady Stanton, Lucretia Mott, Margaret Fuller, and other feminists were regarded either as cranks or as dangerous fanatics.

But the loosening of traditional restraints that so impressed Tocqueville about America also affected the position of American women. Speaking of the difficult position of parents of girls in the unsettled conditions of American democracy Tocqueville said, "As they could not prevent her virtue from being exposed to frequent danger, they determined that she should know how best to defend it, and more reliance was placed on the free vigor of her will than on safeguards which have been shaken or overthrown."

The first passing of age-old restrictions on women came in their education. Numerous girls' seminaries, departments for girls in many academies, and the first public high schools for girls (intended largely to supply teachers), were established before 1830. In 1833, when Oberlin College, founded by liberal Congregationalists, opened its doors, it was as a coeducational college; Antioch followed its example in 1853; and in 1858 the University of Iowa became the first state university to admit women.

In many of these schools subjects stressing domestic training, social usefulness, and moral and religious ideals were gradually supplemented by studies calculated to further mental discipline and intellectual enjoyment. The growing demand for women teachers in the lower schools was also providing more careers for women. Women had rarely taught during the eighteenth century, but by the end of the first quarter of the nineteenth century they were increasingly sought as teachers, both because men were more involved in business life and because the woman teacher seemed a fitter substitute for the mother. Many private seminaries, normal schools, and public high schools contributed thousands of women to the nation's teaching staff.

These better educated women soon demanded that they be granted the same rights as men. Education awakened women to their social and civil subservience, and jobs as teachers gave a little more economic independence to many of them. Women began to make modern careers for themselves in professions formerly monopolized by men. In 1849, Dr. Elizabeth Blackwell received the first medical diploma given to a woman in America. She began practice in New York City in 1850, but the prejudice against her led her to establish a private dispensary that in 1857 became incorporated into the New York Infirmary and College for Women, a hospital conducted entirely by women. In 1869, she returned to England, the country of her birth, and in 1875 she became professor of gynecology in the newly established London School of Medicine for Women.

The most outspoken champion of women's rights was Margaret Fuller. As editor of the *Dial*, as a reviewer for Horace Greeley's *Tribune*, and in many other ways she identified herself with various reforms. In 1845, she shocked the prim element of America with her book *Woman in the Nineteenth Century*, an apology for the efforts of women to emancipate themselves from man-made customs. Going beyond a discussion of equality of economic opportunity and of political rights for women, she discussed sexual morality, marriage, and prostitution. No less scandalous was her theme, "I have urged on Woman independence of Man, not because I do not think the sexes mutually needed by one another, but because in Woman this fact has led to an excessive devotion, which has cooled love, degraded marriage, and prevented either sex from being what it should be to itself or the other."

Despite the agitation of feminists, the movement for the liberation of women from civil and political restraints made relatively little progress in the period before 1860. Mississippi in 1839 was the first state to grant women control of their own property after marriage, and by 1850, six other states had adopted similar legislation. In 1848, the first women's-rights convention was held at Seneca Falls, New York. It was led by women who had been denied a voice at an antislavery convention. The delegates issued a manifesto in language similar to that of the Declaration of Independence, asserting the right of women to share equally with men all economic, political, legal, and educational advantages.

Despite their failure to win their rights, a number of gifted women demonstrated that women could do as good work as men on political and social disorders, and that effective reforms did not always require the authoritarianism and love of self-righteousness of some of the temperance and other reform leaders. Foremost among such women was Dorothea Lynde Dix (1802–87). Following positions as a teacher in Boston and Worcester, she discovered her life's work in 1841, when she became a Sunday-school teacher in the East Cambridge House of Correction. Here she found feeble-minded and insane people mixed with criminals. In 1840, there were only eight insane asylums in the United States, and the insane, who were regarded as willful, perverse, or depraved, were imprisoned and often harshly and brutally treated. For two years Miss Dix quietly investigated the condition of the insane in jails, almshouses, and houses of correction in the state of Massachusetts. In 1843, influential men presented her *Memorial to the Legislature of Massachusetts,* which called attention to "the present state of insane persons confined within this commonwealth, in cages, closets, cellars, stalls, pens! Chained, naked, beaten with rods, and lashed into obedience!" At the same time, Miss Dix wrote letters to the press in an attempt to arouse public opinion. One immediate result was an increase in the size of the Worcester Insane Asylum.

Miss Dix worked indefatigably for the enlargement of existing hospitals for the insane and the establishment of new ones. Between 1845 and 1852, she was largely responsible for the founding of state hospitals in more than a dozen states in the North and South and even at Halifax, Nova Scotia. She also worked diligently for the passage by Congress of an act that would allocate funds from the sale of the national domain for the care of the insane. The bill passed both houses of Congress only to be vetoed by President Pierce. It would be difficult to point to a greater benefactor of mankind in the nineteenth-century United States than this frail woman who devoted the vigor of a sound mind to the welfare of unsound ones.

Villages of Holiness

In no movement did the sense of social dislocation of the Jacksonian period and the redemptive mood of the nation's evangelical heritage reveal themselves more clearly than in the utopian experiments of the generation before the Civil War. The utopians sought what in logic seemed a paradox and in practice an impossibility, a high-spirited individualism in harmony with general social needs.

Although there were many different types of special communities established to fulfill the utopian hope for a life cleansed of the taint of commercial competition, all the utopian reformers believed that man could become perfect, but that first society—and specially competitive industrial society—needed fundamental reorganization. Among these utopian reformers were Theodore Parker, Margaret Fuller, Horace Greeley, Albert Brisbane, Parke Godwin, Robert Owen, and Frances Wright. Practically all the important utopians were New Englanders making a strong ethical protest against the harshness and meanness produced by the growth of industry.

The American utopians were all at least partly influenced by European reformers. In France, Charles Fourier, Saint-Simon, and Etienne Cabet had devised elaborate schemes for social reorganization that they believed would substitute harmony, the brotherhood of man, and cooperation for greed, conflict, and misery. In Scotland, Robert Owen claimed that his model community demonstrated that humaneness rather than exploitation could be the guiding principle in the management of a factory. As a group, the utopians differed from the later Marxists in emphasizing voluntary individual cooperation rather than deliberately exacerbated class warfare and forcible expropriation; furthermore, as Marx's own scornful remarks about the utopians revealed, they believed that an appeal to ideals, when joined with effective demonstration of the practicality of cooperation, would persuade men to abandon their competitive practices.

Few of the European reformers had a more profound effect on the early American utopians than Robert Owen, manager and afterward owner of a large cotton mill in the squalid, poverty-stricken factory town of New Lanark, Scotland. Owen raised wages, restricted drinking, built adequate homes, enforced strict sanitary rules, established a school system, and opened stores where the workers could obtain supplies at a reduction of 20 per cent from previous prices. In less than a dozen years, the town became a model community, famed for its temperateness, cleanliness, and the happiness of its workers. An American visitor to New Lanark wrote, "There is not to be found in any part of the world, a manufacturing community, in which so much order, good government, tranquillity, and rational happiness prevail." Owen, however, was a benevolent despot who constantly drifted off into irrelevant speculation. Unfortunately also for his coming experiment in America, he had highly unorthodox views about religion and marriage. Owen condemned the individualism, competition, and greed upon which he believed business society was based. The main object of society, he declared, should be the happiness and economic equality of all, rather than the enrichment of the few and the impoverishment and degradation of the many. Anxious to put his ideas into practice, Owen in 1825 purchased the settlement that had been established by some German Rappites at New Harmony, Indiana. "I have come to this country," he said in his opening address to his colony, "to introduce an entire new state of society; to change it from an ignorant, selfish system to an enlightened social system which shall gradually unite all interests into one and remove all causes for contest between individuals." Despite Owen's lofty ideals, New Harmony was anything but harmonious. After three years, during which Owen's tendency to abstraction, his heterodox moral ideas, and the many freaks attracted to New Harmony worked against its success, the community came to an end.

Etienne Cabet, a French civil servant and reformer, also thought that America would be an ideal proving ground for his theories. Soon after an active role in the French Revolution of 1830, he became an exile in England, where he came under the influence of the Owenites. When he returned to France in 1839, he had reached the conclusion that communism offered the only solution for the conflict of wealth and poverty, and a year later he published his program in a romance, *Voyage en Icarie*. Cabet's efforts to found an Icarian community in America met with indifferent success. His first colony on the Red River in Texas did not prosper, and in 1849 he moved to the deserted Mormon village at Nauvoo, Illinois. Subsequently, smaller Icarian settlements were made in Missouri, Iowa, and California.

Although the French utopian Charles Fourier never migrated to the United States, he had the greatest effect on the later American utopian movement of the 1840's. His program, called Phalanstery, was an elaborate plan for communal living. Unlike Owen, Fourier had no ideas about religion or marriage that would upset a highly moralistic people. He believed that society should be divided into groups, or phalanxes, of about 1,500 persons, who were to live and work together cooperatively. Since free play for human interests and abilities was necessary to human happiness, each person entering a phalanx was to do work that suited his tastes and desires.

Fourierism soon attracted the enthusiastic attention of Albert Brisbane, son of a well-to-do New York landowner. In 1840, Brisbane published his *Social Destiny of Man; or, Association and Reorganization of Industry*, which was largely a reprint of the more striking passages of Fourier's works. The book, rather than Fourier's own ideas, met with instant success and won many converts. In 1841, Horace Greeley gave Brisbane a column in his newly begun *New York Tribune* and, in an effort to interpret Fourier's principles for the American public, entered into a long debate with Henry J. Raymond, then editor of the *Courier and Enquirer* and later of the *New York Times*. Nature, Greeley declared, had ruled that every man should appropriate as much of the earth as he could cultivate and improve, but this rule had been violated under industrialization by the selfish few. He wanted to put the world right by using Fourier's Association, a more rational social system. Greeley stated:

> By Association I mean a social order which shall take the place of the present township, to be composed of some hundreds or some thousands of persons who shall be united together in interest and industry for the purpose of securing to each individual the following things: (1) an elegant and commodious house; (2) an education complete and thorough; (3) a secure subsistence; (4) opportunity to labor; (5) fair wages; (6) agreeable social relations; (7) progress in knowledge and skill.

Greeley found an enthusiastic supporter for his scheme, Parke Godwin, associate editor of the New York *Evening Post*. Godwin contended:

> Blind competition tends to the formation of gigantic monopolies in every branch of labor; it depreciates the wages of the working classes; it excites an endless warfare between human arms and machinery and capital—a war in which the weak succumb; it renders the recurrence of failures, bankruptcies, and commercial crises a sort of endemic disease; and it reduces the middle and lower classes to a precarious and miserable existence.

Godwin's book *Democracy, Pacific and Constructive* became the best of the contemporary studies on Fourierism. Charles A. Dana, afterward editor of the *New York Sun*, and George Ripley, literary editor of the *Tribune*, were others who accepted Fourier's basic principles.

The Unitarian leader William Ellery Channing, though not a member of the "inner circle," showed sympathy during the last years of his life for the Associationists, as the disciples of Fourier were called. With such influential publicists, Fourierist ideals spread quickly during the economic upset of the early 1840's. The association ideal struck at the new business class and rising social leaders for their venality and avarice and gave those defeated by new business leaders the satisfaction of seeming spiritually superior to the moneygrubbers. The Fourierists' claims for human dignity, their call to general spiritual and material progress, their emphasis on cooperation and a more intimate and fraternal society suggested a new era for mankind. For intellectuals, then as now, the proclamation of a new, more moral politics, when linked with the belief that men of ideas were to be the instruments of a universal disinterested justice, had a powerful appeal.

Between 1840 and 1850, more than forty communistic projects, most designed along Fourierist lines, were launched in America. Many were short-lived, but some, notably the Brook Farm experiment, attracted considerable attention. In 1841, a group of about twenty intellectuals including Ripley, Dana, and, for a while, Nathaniel Hawthorne, the novelist, took over a 200-acre dairy farm near Boston for the purpose of substituting "a system of brotherly co-operation for one of selfish competition." They proposed ". . . to impart a greater freedom, simplicity, truthfulness, refinement and moral dignity to our mode of life." The Brook Farm enthusiasts became Fourierists in 1843 and fixed a uniform rate of compensation for all labor, established a maximum working day of ten hours, and provided free education, medical care, and library facilities. All persons were to be employed according to their taste and ability. Dances, music, and literary and scientific discussions were arranged for leisure hours. But Brook Farm was no more successful than the other collectivist communities. At its top strength it had only about 100 inhabitants, including several people with great gifts. Their general impracticality, however, and the faddish nature of the retreat for many of the idealists soon took their effects. In 1846, a fire destroyed the nearly finished phalanx building, and in a few months the experiment was only a memory.

Without exception, the American communistic enterprises failed. They were often founded with little or no preparation, and frequently without capital. The majority of the members were unskilled for farming or small crafts. Internal dissension over religion and other controversial matters created disharmony. To most Americans dedicated to private ownership, the reformers were either lunatics or dangerous radicals whose doctrines, if accepted, would wreck society. American society was individualistic, and collective or communistic systems were alien to its temper.

To Set All Men Free

Of all the reform movements in antebellum America, none attracted as much attention, produced as much acrimony, and had as much effect on the nation's politics as the antislavery crusade. Before the invention of the cotton gin, it had seemed likely that slavery would gradually disappear in the South as it had in the North, and during the first decades of the nineteenth century the most active antislavery groups were in the southern and the middle states, but in New England, interest in the slavery question was largely academic and theoretical. The early antislavery reformers were influenced by the work in England of Thomas Clarkson and William Wilberforce, who finally succeeded in 1807 in inducing Parliament to prohibit the slave trade.

Church groups also took an active part in the first stages of the antislavery crusade. In 1812, the Methodist General Conference voted that a slaveholder could not continue as a local elder. The Presbyterian General Assembly in 1815 recommended the education of slaves as a preparatory step toward emancipation. Certain Baptist congregations refused to admit slaveholders to membership; and the Quakers, relying on their fundamental doctrine that God reveals His Spirit to all persons, remained adamant in their opposition to slavery in any form. As time went on, however, and as the antislavery crusade became more militant and cotton culture and slavery became entrenched in the South, the slavery issue disrupted some of the larger denominations. In 1844, the issue of whether a Methodist bishop could hold slaves led to the organization of the Methodist Episcopal Church South. In the same year, the Baptists also divided over the question of whether a slaveowner might become a missionary. In 1853, the Presbyterians split on the question, one faction refusing membership to any slaveholder.

While the churches were registering opposition to slavery, antislavery agitators like Benjamin Lundy and James G. Birney were busily engaged in organizing antislavery societies. By 1830, more than a hundred such organizations were providing centers of discussion and were issuing addresses, memorializing legislatures, protecting Negroes, and sustaining antislavery publications. In 1832, the New England Anti-Slavery Society was organized in Boston. The next year a national organization, known during the later years of its life as the American Convention for Promoting the Abolition of Slavery and Improving the Condition of the African Race, was formed in Philadelphia. Both organizations carried on active propaganda and were instrumental in keeping the antislavery discussion alive.

Before 1830, schemes for colonizing American slaves were more attractive than plans for abolition, and colonization societies were organized with the intention of ultimately ridding the country of a Negro population. Of these, the most important was the American Colonization Society, formed at Washington in 1817. Aided by state auxiliaries, county and city societies, and by state and federal appropriations, in 1822 the American Colonization Society planted a Negro settlement called Liberia on the west coast of Africa. Distance and unhealthful environment, however, combined with savage neighbors and the desire of most free Negroes to remain in the United States, practically ruined the scheme. In the ten years 1820–30, the society, though it spent $100,000, transferred fewer than 1,200 persons, and the greater number of these died within a few years after reaching their new home. This poor showing disheartened many of the society's supporters, and the organization soon declined in importance.

Until about 1830, the crusade against slavery was, on the whole, marked by an absence of bitterness, not because the arguments against it differed from those of later date, but rather because the earlier abolitionists hoped that their objectives might be achieved through a quiet campaign of education and the peaceful evolution of the South away from slavery. Lundy, a pious Quaker, and Birney, a former slaveholder, carried on their work in a spirit of moderation, appealing to reason rather than to prejudice or passion. With the emergence, however, of the democratic idealism of the 1830's, and with the growing use of slaves for cotton culture in the South, the movement assumed a more belligerent form. Men of the stamp of William Lloyd Garrison and George Bourne, ignoring the constitutional and legal guarantees surrounding slavery, militantly and uncompromisingly demanded immediate and unconditional emancipation. In an address "To the Public," published in the first number of his antislavery paper, the *Liberator*, which appeared in Boston on January 1, 1831, Garrison apologized for ever having "assented to the popular but pernicious doctrine of *gradual* abolition," and declared that he would "strenuously contend" for the immediate emancipation and enfranchisement of the entire slave population. He wrote:

> I will be as harsh as truth, and as uncompromising as justice. On this subject, I do not wish to think, or speak, or write, with moderation. No! No! Tell a man whose house is on fire to give a moderate alarm; tell him to moderately rescue his wife from

the hands of the ravisher; tell the mother to gradually extricate her babe from the fire into which it has fallen—but urge me not to use moderation in a cause like the present. I am in earnest—I will not equivocate—I will not excuse . . . —AND I WILL BE HEARD!

Garrison and his followers were heard. Abolitionist orators shocked a public dedicated to white supremacy, if not to slavery, with loud and violent speeches. Northern businessmen, particularly financiers and manufacturers interested in cotton, denounced them as half-crazed fanatics determined to destroy the sacredness of private property and undermine the Union itself. Most colleges as well as many churches also opposed the abolitionists. Even political leaders like Van Buren and Cass decried the movement as an agitation that threatened to upset the political status quo. The meeting places of the abolitionists were frequently attacked, even sometimes burned; abolition orators were hissed, stoned, and tarred and feathered. Garrison himself was dragged through the streets of Boston and narrowly escaped with his life. Officials of Philadelphia treated the abolitionists virtually as outlaws.

In spite of the notoriety of Garrison's activities in New England, it was in the Old Northwest that the abolitionist movement attracted the largest number of supporters. In those parts of the Northwest that had been settled by New Englanders, antislavery sentiment was far more widespread than in comparable areas in the East. In Theodore Weld, whose abolitionism was based on the Gospels, the western abolitionists possessed a leader who did far more to arouse grass roots opposition to slavery than did Garrison or any other easterner. A skillful organizer and expert publicist, Weld probably won over far more northerners than did Garrison to abolitionism, but he was also more responsible than any other individual for the establishment of an antislavery bloc in Congress. Western abolitionists, like those of New England, often aroused considerable hostility. In Cincinnati the office of the *Philanthropist*, an abolitionist paper, was gutted, and desperate efforts were made to kill its editor, James G. Birney. At Alton, Illinois, Elijah Lovejoy, preacher and publisher of an abolition paper, was killed by a mob, and his printing press was destroyed.

As the antislavery crusade gained momentum in the North it died out in the South. Garrison's denunciation of slavery as "a damning crime" was enough to cause resentment; but on top of this was his sweeping characterization of the southern people:

We would sooner trust the honor of the country and the liberties of the people in the hands of the inmates of our peniten-

RAFFLE

Mr. Joseph Jennings respectfully informs his friends and the public that, at the request of many acquaintances, he has been induced to purchase from Mr. Osborne, of Missouri, the celebrated

DARK BAY HORSE, "STAR,"

Aged five years, square trotter and warranted sound; with a new light Trotting Buggy and Harness also, the dark, stout

MULATTO GIRL, "SARAH,"

Aged about twenty years, general house servant, valued at *nine hundred dollars*, and guaranteed, and

Will be Raffled for

At 4 o'clock P. M., February first, at the selection hotel of the subscribers. The above is as represented and those persons who may wish to engage in the usual practice of raffling, will, I assure them, be perfectly satisfied with their destiny in this affair.
The whole is valued at its just worth; fifteen hundred dollars; fifteen hundred

CHANCES AT ONE DOLLAR EACH.

The Raffle will be conducted by gentlemen selected by the interested subscribers present. Five nights will be allowed to complete the Raffle. BOTH OF THE ABOVE DESCRIBED CAN BE SEEN AT MY STORE, No. 78 Common St., second door from Camp, at from 9 o'clock A. M. to 2 P. M. Highest throw to take the first choice; the lowest throw the remaining prize, and the fortunate winners will pay twenty dollars each for the refreshments furnished on the occasion.
N. B. No chances recognized unless paid for previous to the commencement.

JOSEPH JENNINGS.

Grist for the Abolitionist Mills: A Horse and a Human Being

tiaries and prisons, than in their hands for safe keeping. . . . They ought not to be allowed seats in Congress. No political, no religious co-partnership should be had with them, for they are the meanest of thieves, and the worst of robbers. We should as soon think of entering into a compact with the "convicts" at Botany Bay and New Zealand. . . . We do not acknowledge them to be within the pale of Christianity, of republicanism, of humanity.

Such statements naturally aroused the hostility of the South. Alarmed by the Nat Turner insurrection (1831), which resulted in heavy destruction of property and loss of life, the section took immediate steps to protect itself against every possible antislavery onslaught. The militia in several southern states was reorganized, and special statutes to prevent and to suppress uprisings and to curb slavery discussion were enacted. Attempts were made to close the mails to abolitionist books and newspapers, and abolitionists were threatened with drastic punishments if they dared set foot on southern soil. In 1836, a gag rule preventing the consideration of antislavery petitions was pushed through the House of Representatives. The free states, under threat of economic boycott, were requested to prohibit publication of abolitionist literature, to silence abolitionist orators, and to suppress abolitionist societies. After a long fight in the House of Representatives, led by Congressman John Quincy Adams, the gag rule was removed.

Despite opposition, the movement for abolition gained in strength and intensity. The abolition press, filled with editorials and illustrations depicting the reputed horrors of slavery, increased in circulation; state legislatures and Congress were bombarded with antislavery petitions, and antislavery organizations rapidly multiplied from hundreds to thousands. Increasingly, abolitionists, particularly those who were churchgoers and members of philanthropic societies, assisted slaves to escape along the "Underground Railroad" to places of safety in the North or over the border to Canada, but in doing so they probably drew off some of the Negroes best suited to lead the slaves of the South when and if they were freed.

At no time, however, did the abolitionists become more than a small, vexatious, militant minority. Despite the fact that they had justice on their side, their predominant call for immediate abolition ignored the fact that, for better or worse, slavery was the basis of a long-developed way of life in the South. Only the most skillful and delicate handling of the problem could free the slaves and prevent social turmoil, if not race war. Although the abolitionists pricked America's guilty conscience, their absolutism and self-righteousness made more difficult what was already an incredibly complex problem.

As time passed, antislavery became a powerful disruptive influence in American life. It became clear that freedom of speech, press, assembly, petition, and other basic rights of all Americans were tied up with the question of the future of the Negro. Whether or not one believed in immediate abolition, attacks on the abolitionist leaders showed that there was more at stake in the great national debate over slavery than the freedom of Negroes, for the wish to discuss even that question by 1840 everywhere involved the already guaranteed freedoms of whites.

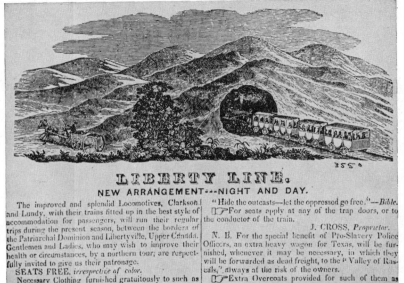

LIBERTY LINE.

NEW ARRANGEMENT---NIGHT AND DAY.

The improved and splendid Locomotives, Clarkson and Lundy, with their trains fitted up in the best style of accommodation for passengers, will run their regular trips during the present season, between the borders of the Patriarchal Dominion and Libertyville, Upper Canada. Gentlemen and Ladies, who may wish to improve their health or circumstances, by a northern tour, are respectfully invited to give us their patronage.

SEATS FREE, *irrespective of color.*

Necessary Clothing furnished gratuitously to such as have "*fallen among thieves.*"

"Hide the outcasts---let the oppressed go free."---*Bible.*

☞For seats apply at any of the trap doors, or to the conductor of the train.

J. CROSS, *Proprietor.*

N. B. For the special benefit of Pro-Slavery Police Officers, an extra heavy wagon for Texas, will be furnished, whenever it may be necessary, in which they will be forwarded as dead freight, to the "Valley of Rascals," always at the risk of the owners.

☞Extra Overcoats provided for such of them as are afflicted with protracted *chilly-phobia.*

The Latest in Railroads in the 1840's

By the 1840's, abolitionists were strong enough in areas all over the North to make demands on local politicians. Sometimes an outright abolitionist leader, like the famous Illinois preacher Peter Cartwright, would be nominated for Congress. More often a less dangerous stand for "free soil," or no further extension of slavery, would be the moderate response to abolitionist demands. It was "free soil" rather than abolition that eventually brought North and South into conflict. As free soil or abolitionist leaders in the North found themselves holding the balance of power between rival regular party candidates they proved themselves capable of forcing the major parties to take some stand on the slave question and thereby helped convert a principle espoused by a small minority into one that eventually involved all Americans in a choice that meant war.

The Highest Flights of Idealism

The abolitionists shared with other reformers of their time a sense of certainty about their purposes and a conviction about the highness of their motives, but of all the movements towards purity of spirit in the age of Jackson, none was as intellectually impressive as the work of the New England transcendentalists. Never an organized movement and lacking any authoritative full formal statement of their creed, the transcendentalists sought the realization of what they took to be the best potentialities of human nature. Churches for centuries had preached a similar doctrine, but the transcendentalists argued that churches were more interested in ritual than in spirit and more concerned with dogma than with man. To the transcendentalists, man was spiritually self-sufficient, and his being a microcosm of divine goodness permitted him to lift himself above his immediate limiting environment. They believed that a moral law was incarnate in man that transcended the laws of society and that man could better his spiritual lot in this world by striving to live on a high plane of idealism beyond the conventions of contemporary society.

Transcendentalism was an outgrowth of New England's religious past, for it drew heavily on both Puritanism and Unitarianism. From the Puritans the transcendentalists inherited their concern with morality and their concept of the individual's responsibility to God. From the Unitarians they inherited their rejection of original sin and predestination and their belief in the perfectibility of man; in fact, many of them at one time had been members of the Unitarian Church. The successive steps from Calvinism to Unitarianism to transcendentalism were important chapters in New England's religious history. The Calvinists believed in predestination, an anthropomorphic vengeful God, considered Jesus divine, and worshiped "God in three persons." The Unitarians insisted that there was but a single loving God, that Jesus instead of being divine was the perfect "Son of Man," and that all men were capable of salvation. Transcendentalists, on the whole, rejected the idea of God's "personality" and thought of Him as an impersonal force that worked in conjunction with the moral law. Because Unitarianism, itself an example of rationalist religion of the eighteenth century, had become formalized and decorous (Ralph Waldo Emerson called it "corpse-cold") and because it seemed to be doing nothing to preserve New Englanders from the taint of getting and spending, the transcendentalists withdrew from the Unitarian church and began to preach lay sermons to men of all faiths.

The transcendentalists were influenced by the romantic movement in Europe as well as by New England's religious past. Emerson maintained that, although he and the members of his group disagreed on many points, they "agreed in having fallen upon Coleridge and Wordsworth, and Goethe, then on Carlyle, with pleasure and sympathy." Like the German and English romantics, the American transcendentalists modified or rejected certain notions of the eighteenth-century enlightenment. They believed, on the whole, that reason was not self-sufficient. They claimed that nature was more complex and changing than simple and static. Its truths, moreover, could be apprehended intuitively and then ratified by reason. They accepted the deists' concept of a natural law, but they insisted that it was incapable of a mechanistic interpretation and was subordinate to the moral law. The transcendentalists also shared the romantics' concern for individuality, for the fact that did not "fit," and they deplored the stultifying effects of the new industrialism on efforts to achieve ideal self-realization.

As a group, the transcendentalists had little cohesion and were seldom if ever in full agreement. Emerson was undoubtedly the best known, but others included Henry David Thoreau, who was Emerson's neighbor in Concord; Margaret Fuller; Bronson Alcott, a teacher, writer, and the founder of his own utopian community at Fruitlands; and Theodore Parker, the Unitarian minister who had broken with leaders of his church but who continued to preach to large audiences in Boston. If the transcendentalists can be said to have had an organ of opinion, it was the *Dial*, which was edited by Margaret Fuller. To a certain extent Brook Farm was also an attempt to carry some of their theories into practice, but Emerson, Parker, and Thoreau did not participate in the experiment.

Ralph Waldo Emerson (1803–82) studied at Harvard, served as a Unitarian minister, and subsequently withdrew from the church. In 1836, he outlined his transcendentalist philosophy in his first book, a small volume entitled *Nature*. He wished to formulate a philosophy that would encompass God, the soul of man, and nature and thus establish the "original relation" of man to the universe. Having rejected materialism (for it denied both man's soul and God), he turned to mysticism, pantheism, and idealism. But each of these in varying degree slighted the world of nature. The idealist regarded nature as the mere product of mind; the pantheist slighted nature, for he believed that nature was only the expression of an almighty power, and the mystic ignored nature. But to Emerson, nature was an immediate reality that held the key to both man and his universe; mind and nature were one. He wrote:

In the woods we return to reason and faith. . . . Standing on the bare ground,—my head bathed by the blithe air and uplifted into infinite space,—all mean egotism vanishes. I become a transparent eyeball; I am nothing; I see all; the currents of the Universal Being circulate through me; I am part or parcel of God.

This view implied immediate communication with God without church or creed, the essential "spirituality" of all being, and a belief in the fullest self-reliance.

If man were to realize completely his potentialities, Emerson believed, he must become "man thinking"; and in a Phi Beta Kappa address at Harvard in 1837 he described the road to this goal. The present state of society, he complained, was "one in which the members have suffered amputation from the trunk, and strut about so many walking monsters,—a good finger, a neck, a stomach, an elbow, but never a man." Under the circumstances, the tradesman was "ridden by the routine of his craft . . . the priest becomes a form; the attorney a statute-book; the mechanic a machine; the sailor a rope of the ship." If the scholar wished to avoid a similar fate—if he wished to become man thinking—he had, first, to be aware of nature and to "settle its value in his mind." Secondly, he must know the "mind of the Past"; but in coming to know it he must guard against letting books become his master. Man thinking "must not be subdued by his instruments. . . . When he can read God directly, the hour is too precious to be wasted in other men's transcripts of their readings." Action, although subordinate, was essential, and without it "thought can never ripen into truth." All of these ideals were attainable for the man who realized that "the world is nothing, the man is all; in yourself is the law of all nature; . . . in yourself slumbers the whole of Reason; it is for you to know all; it is for you to dare all."

Emerson believed all men could achieve self-realization by pursuing the goals similar to those he had set for scholars. In his essays "Self-Reliance" and "The Over-Soul"—both published in 1841—he sought to convince his readers that God had given them the power to transcend both their environment and their times. "Man," he wrote, "is timid and apologetic; he is no longer upright; he dares not say 'I think,' 'I am,' but quotes some saint or sage." To such men Emerson said: "Insist on yourself; never imitate . . . [A] great man is a unique." Happiness and strength were to be found neither by lamenting the past nor by hoping for the future but by "living with nature in the present, above time." The self-reliant man recognized that "nothing is at last sacred but the integrity of . . . [the] mind"; he was guided by intuition or "that gleam of light which flashes across his mind from within"; he understood the limits of the church and the limitlessness of man; and he sought to live according to the dictates of the Over-Soul, the universal spirit of which both man and nature were the expression, and which provided the universal moral law that made it possible for all men to live in harmony with nature.

Emerson understood that few men were capable of heeding his sermons and that those who did would be branded nonconformists and whipped by the world "with its displeasure." He once wrote in his journal that he had been "writing and speaking what were once called novelties, for twenty-five or thirty years, and [I] have now not one disciple. Why?" Perhaps the answer lay in the fact that he gave a counsel of perfection. Or perhaps it lay in his requirement that each man form a party of one rather than become his or any other man's disciple. When Emerson, for example, observed the reformers of the age, he admired their mission but also shrewdly observed:

> The reforms have their high origin in an ideal justice, but they do not retain the purity of an idea. They are quickly organized in some low, inadequate form, and present no more poetic image to the mind that the evil tradition which they reprobated. They mix the fire of moral sentiment with personal and party heats, with measureless exaggerations, and the blindness that prefers some darling measure to justice and truth. Those, who are urging with most ardor what are called the greatest benefits of mankind, are narrow, self-pleasing, conceited men and affect us as the insane do. I think the work of the reformer as innocent as other work that is done around him; but when I have seen it near, I do not like it better. It is done in the same way; it is done profanely, by management, by tactics, and clamor. It is a buzz in the ear.

Of all the transcendentalists Henry David Thoreau (1817–62) came closest to approximating Emerson's concept of the self-reliant individual, who kept clear of "movements" and "campaigns." In *Walden*, Thoreau's account of the two years he spent in a cabin at Walden Pond, he sought to understand life rather than to escape it— to find, as it were, his essential self, beyond the pettier claims of culture. Thoreau exemplified and tried to justify intellectually the American will to cast off the limits on life imposed by institutions. In *Walden* he wrote,

> I went to the woods because I wished to live deliberately, to front only the essential facts of life, and see if I could not learn what it had to teach, and not, when I came to die discover that I had not lived. I did not wish to live what was not life, living is so dear; nor did I wish to practice resignation, unless it was quite necessary. I wanted to live deep and suck out all the marrow of life, to live so sturdily and Spartan-like as to put to

rout all that was not life, to cut a broad swath and shave close, to drive life into a corner, and reduce it to its lowest terms, and, if it proved to be mean, why then to get the whole and genuine meanness of it, and publish its meanness to the world; or if it were sublime, to know it by experience, and be able to give a true account of it in my next excursion.

Walden was not merely a tract for the times, but a notable contribution to what Lionel Trilling has called "the mystique of the self," the drama of the individual in the modern world who consciously strives to understand the nature and uniqueness of his identity. Although the limitations of American society were probably less weighty for most men than they were for Thoreau, and although one may find traces of merely sentimental hankering for simplicity in his call back to "fundamentals," he never suggested that every individual should leave society and take to the woods. Instead, he tried to show how his sojourn at Walden Pond had fulfilled his own particular needs. He did not urge every man to accept his way of solitude and self-sufficiency, but he believed that every thinking man should both recognize the need to find his best self and attempt to fulfill it.

Like many reformers of his time, Thoreau had little use for the forces that were transforming New England. "Trade," he said, "curses everything it touches; and though you trade in message from heaven, the whole curse of trade attaches to the business." Nevertheless, Thoreau himself was not a professional reformer. He was too much an individualist to believe in the efficacy of such cooperative experiments as Brook Farm. "I came into this world," he declared, "not chiefly to make this a good place to live in, but to live in it, be it good or bad." For church and state in their daily compromises and limitations he had only contempt.

When Thoreau believed that taxes collected by the federal government during the Mexican War were helping to spread slavery, he went to jail rather than pay them. His vigorous and indignant, but intellectually confused analysis of this experience in *Resistance to Civil Government* became one of the important texts in the modern argument for the supremacy of conscience over the claims of state and society. Whatever the logical or practical difficulties in Thoreau's assertion that "any man more right than his neighbors constitutes a majority of one," his appeal to a morality and law beyond convention was one culmination of the transcendentalist belief in the potential divinity of all men. Like other transcendentalists, Thoreau thought that human personality was not defined solely by historical circumstances but had sanctions for its holiness beyond what he considered the profane tampering or petty claims of government and society.

The Democratic Skeptics and a Democratic Faith

Whether religious reformers, rationalist crusaders, or transcendental idealists, the Americans who contributed to "freedom's ferment" before the Civil War had created an unprecedented image of man's immanent power to effect whatever change in life he put his mind to. The redemptive visions of the age aroused great expectations, but the luxuriant optimism, the air of moral certainty, and the mood of absolutism in the public rhetoric of the time helped obscure many of life's tragedies, ironies, and ambiguities and covered over the venality and coarseness of many acclaimed public achievements. Whatever deference had to be paid to the actual complexity of the world and to the weight that wickedness and sorrow carried in it was outweighed for many reformers by the conviction that some ideal good was so near fruition that doubt about its coming seemed a sin and resistance to it an insult to the dignity of man.

It is all the more striking therefore that in the best American writers in the generation before the Civil War there runs a strong current of skepticism about the "bent" of American life. Like most artists with a special sense of life, many American writers felt "alienated" from their society, but their alienation, joined as it was with fine talent, rather than denying them insight or making their works remote or abstruse, provided the psychological conditions for a notable flowering of letters. Within a generation of Tocqueville's visit of 1831, a number of writers had given evidence against his claim that democratic society would be incapable of great flights of literary or poetic imagination. The best works of writers like James Fenimore Cooper, Nathaniel Hawthorne, and Herman Melville were not, however, celebrations of democracy but criticisms of its material and spiritual defects. Although essentially democratic in their own ideals, these men were wary, if not dismayed, about the form that American aspirations and ambitions often took.

In the nineteenth century the most common subject for serious writers in America and Europe was the individual's struggle for self-realization. In the more settled area of the United States, where hurly-burly Jacksonian individualism was in conflict with an older, previously accepted social order, many themes bearing on the question of self-realization seemed ready-made for writers. But, however old and settled the East was, it lacked the color and seemingly inexhaustible variety of roles, social types, and situations that a thousand-year history had supplied to European novelists. As Henry James was to observe a half-century later, "The flower of art blooms only where the soil is deep, . . . it takes a great deal of history to produce a little literature, . . . it needs a complex social machinery to set a writer in motion." The United States of the 1840's did not lack a past, but it did not have a profound sense that the past set any limits on human endeavor. The past was conceived not, as it was in Europe, as a barrier to self-realization, but rather as a constant invitation to a better future. The notable events of American history—the first Puritan migration, the Declaration of Independence, and the constant passage to the frontier—were all construed as breaks with history. With these events in mind, men of the early nineteenth century looked upon America as something still to be made rather than something already finished.

Living in a society in which traditionalism was weak and codes of manners and morals more uniform than diverse, American writers tended to explore the worlds of symbol, myth, and allegory rather than the classic theme of the European novel, the conflict of the self and society. The two greatest American novels of the age, Hawthorne's *Scarlet Letter* and Melville's *Moby Dick*, were elaborate studies of the psychology of individuals, not conceived with the complexity that reflects life as we commonly experience it but rather as symbolic representations of various moral ideas and principles. In the classic American novel that took shape in the Jacksonian period there is little attempt to supply the reader with what he may want to know about the family, class, education, religion, business, and ordinary habits of the major characters. One constantly misses what one finds in the European novel of the same time—a strong sense of society and its multitude of claims and effects on the individual. One finds instead the elaboration of situations in which character tends to become idealized and often merely serves a plot that veers toward morality play, melodrama, or pastoral idyll.

American novels and stories often deal with people and events in which there is a strong play of contrasting principles and feelings without either sign or certainty of mediation by the long-matured forces of society. The rules of social life as we commonly know them are weak or suspended. Leading characters are often shown in pursuit of some distant ideal, in the grip of an obsession, or in a situation of isolation that is accentuated by a sense of the vast rawness of America's continental setting; often, too, these characters seem mythic in size.

The most widely read American writers of the period after 1830 did turn out hundreds of sentimental novels that took their cues from popular European fiction. But the chief characters of these stories were puppets or caricatures of Americans. Their difficulties were defined with inexpert simplicity, and the end of the tale brought everything back sanely and safely to the main channels of workaday experiences. Most of these widely read American writers of the 1830's and 1840's are now forgotten names, but the lions among them have become part of the American schoolhouse heritage. Henry Wadsworth Longfellow, John Greenleaf Whittier, James Russell Lowell, and Oliver Wendell Holmes were the leading writers from New England; W. C. Bryant and Washington Irving were the most important of the New York literati; and W. G. Simms and W. Grayson were two of the most popular southern writers. Although these men occasionally produced a poem or story with some claim to genuine distinction, they were essentially minor talents exploiting subjects and themes congenial to the tastes of the polite reading public: domestic scenes, nostalgic tales, and conventional moral lessons.

Like the greater writers of the age, however, these men had to contend with limits imposed by public taste. Excessive admiration for English authors, evangelical warnings against the corrupting influence of fiction "which leads the mind to impossible things," and genteel considerations of delicacy, refinement, and idealism all stood between what was predominantly a youthful, vigorous, colloquial, rough-and-tumble America and the writing of books that caught the true spirit of the country. While an impressively rich folk literature and small mountains of cheap trash appealed, then as now, to the mass imagination, "good taste" and the demand for moral and psychological certainties about the world in decorous plots consigned the more experimental writer, along with the vulgar hack, to anonymity or to the future. Few things ever threaten the nurture and prestige of genuine literary talent more than an enforced concern for "Literature." When, as in "the sentimental years" 1830–60, it had to be "the best literature," the strain on the writer already irritated by the demand for conventional subjects and style was oppressive. Against James Russell Lowell's remark, "Let no man write a line that he would not have his daughter read," one must juxtapose the determination of a writer like Herman Melville to strike through "the paste-board mask of life" and the frank sexuality and vigorous verse of Walt Whitman.

That a writer's limitations are not, however, to be accounted for by his tradition or culture or even by the nature of his aspirations, but ultimately by the extent of his talent and imagination, is well illustrated in the works of the first of the greater American novelists, James Fenimore Cooper (1789–1851). Cooper was a well-born and wealthy New

Yorker who lived in Europe for years. He caught the appeal of Europe's old culture with its almost limitless possibilities for the artist's imagination. Despite this appeal and his Federalist background, Cooper was for most of his life a democrat struck by the contrast between the highness of American aspirations, the fullness of America's will, and the lowness of their usual forms: money-making, social envy, and petty party politics.

Cooper is said to be the first major American novelist, which means that his critics have sensed in him a degree of talent commensurate with the breadth of his imagination; yet in more than thirty novels, Cooper's language, full of poses and inflated phrases, and his faults in characterization and plot prevented him from exploiting fully his one great gift, his grasp of what was at stake in the American passion for life. This insight is best embodied in his famous "Leatherstocking Tales": *The Pioneers* (1823), *The Last of the Mohicans* (1826), *The Prairie* (1827), *The Pathfinder* (1840), and *The Deerslayer* (1841). These books are a myth-like account of the life of Natty Bumppo, an idealized frontiersman whose virtues of masculinity, honor, and natural piety toward all forms of life are constantly threatened by the advances of civilization into the wilderness. Although Natty is reminiscent of the influential literary image of the simple "noble savage," and innately moral "natural man," he is particularly American in his relentless determination to define without interference the conditions of his existence. His vision of self-sufficiency and fullness of life checked only by a self-imposed code epitomizes the incessant and contradictory American lust for experience and desire to remain innocent, unscarred, and untainted by life. As Natty grows older, he constantly moves away from the compromises, evasions, and corruptions of civilization. Starting as a youth in the forests of frontier New York about 1740, he travels westward and finally dies, more than sixty years later, in a golden sunset somewhere 500 miles west of the Mississippi.

Cooper had attempted to create a Homeric myth about an archetypal figure of the American past who stands, like all primeval fathers, as an eternal judge of what the world has become since his time. Great descriptive passages about the American landscape strengthen the reader's sense that a cosmic drama is being enacted on this continent; but, despite the magnificence of Natty's aspiration, the implication is that Natty and his noble Indian friends are doomed. Cooper's ideal civilization was one in which aristocratic gentlemen and Natty Bumppoes share power. However, the spread of settlement over the continent did not give power to such men but to the low and mean and envious who lacked Natty's piety about man and nature. Cooper was so distressed by what seemed to be the low fulfillment of American aspirations that he increasingly rejected American society, and he seemed to suggest that solitude and death in the wilderness were preferable to the association and corruption of society.

Cooper used a number of themes that were to recur in many later American writers down to F. Scott Fitzgerald and William Faulkner. There is the conflict between the noble self-reliant innocent striving for a fulfillment that perhaps no foreseeable culture could provide; there are the account of the betrayal of a great dream and the figures of the killers of the dream. Cooper also exemplified an American belief that the cause of personal failure does not lie in excessive demands on life by a hero but more in what a corrupting society does to a vigorous innocent. In Cooper's image of America's golden age, man casts off the restrictions of law and convention and tries to define all the conditions of his existence alone. Natty Bumppo saves himself from the savagery that his rejection of culture seems to imply by devising, under the pressure of necessity and the demands of his essentially good instincts, a personal code of honor and heroism. From Natty Bumppo, or "Leatherstocking," there descends a long line of similar American heroes, including Twain's Huckleberry Finn and F. Scott Fitzgerald's Gatsby, who exemplify the idealism against which American society seems in conspiracy.

Nathaniel Hawthorne (1804–64) was constantly preoccupied with characters held by some private obsession or seeking their fulfillment on a transcendent or ideal plane. Unlike Cooper or the transcendentalists (with many of whom he was friendly), Hawthorne exposed the evil consequences of breaking "the magnetic chain of humanity" which he believed set imperfect but necessary limits on human beings. Hawthorne's best known works were *Mosses from an Old Manse*, *The Marble Faun*, *The House of Seven Gables*, and *The Blithedale Romance*. His greatest work, *The Scarlet Letter* (1850), was both a brilliant examination of various types of responses to a sin and a warning to Americans about the possible costs of a search for an ideal existence.

In the opening part of the novel Hawthorne speaks of the old customhouse at Salem, Massachusetts (where he himself had been an appointee before political changes deprived him of his job). He implies that in days deep in the colonial past when the customhouse was new men took moral issues much more seriously than in nineteenth-century America, where people refused to recognize or accept all the implications of moral choice. This opening sets the stage for the story of Hester Prynne, a vigorous and beautiful woman who, unhappy in an arranged marriage to a man she does not love, has come to Massachusetts with the first generation of settlers. Hester's story is in part the tale of what happens to a powerful individual with long-frustrated desires for love and life when confronted with the possibilities of a new world.

Keeping her lover's name a secret, Hester has committed adultery with one of the most exemplary of the leaders of the Puritans, the Reverend Arthur Dimmesdale, and eventually has a child by him. For her crime against God and society and for refusing to name her lover, Hester is publicly humiliated and condemned to wear a scarlet letter "A" on the breast of her clothes to identify her as an adulteress. The story of Hester's sin and expiation tells of the conflict between society, convention, authority, and law (or "Europe") and will, pride, individuality, and passion (or "America"). It has also remote and vague theological overtones of the struggle of a person with an "inner light" against a religion (Calvinism) that takes only conduct as a sign of salvation or damnation.

Although Hester accepts her shame at first, she is too strong to accept the status of a mocked sinner for long. Slowly, brooding on her badge, she begins to justify and even to glorify her sin as a legitimate act for freedom for herself and for all women whom society has frustrated. She dreams of a new life in the "wilderness" and of finding a freedom no man or woman has ever known before. The abstraction and nobility of her ideal hides from Hester her baser motives of revenge and vindication. Eventually she determines to propose escape to Dimmesdale, whom she has never revealed as her lover but whose conscience is increasingly tortured by conflicting duties to himself, to Hester, to their daughter Pearl, to the community that so defers to him, and to God.

It is Pearl, the child, who suggests the impossibility of Hester's obsession. Pearl knows no father (the traditional source of law and authority), and her isolation as a result of her mother's sin has made her into a wild creature who seems only half human. The child has become a warning of what the mother's dream and unwillingness to accept the consequences of her adultery may lead to. The more Hester's will for freedom and escape to an ideal existence increases, the wilder Pearl becomes, the less womanly Hester grows, and the more the scarlet letter seems to glow. At a chance meeting in the forest, Dimmesdale is temporarily overwhelmed by Hester's dream of escape and agrees to her plan. Hester tears the letter from her dress and lets down her hair, which she has bound up for years, thus suggesting that their decision will bring the fulfillment of the passion that she and Dimmesdale have been denied by society. But when she calls Pearl, the child refuses to come and points to the scarlet letter on the ground. The implication is that before her parents can possess and control Pearl, Hester must accept her sin. Only when Hester puts up her hair and pins on the scarlet "A" does Pearl approach her.

Hester's dream is finally frustrated by the arrival of her husband, Roger Chillingworth. All his humanity has been drained from him by the knowledge of Hester's infidelity and pride in her sin and, gruesomely, he sets out to watch and speed Dimmesdale's death by insinuating himself into his household as a physician for the minister's strange ailments. Chillingworth tells Hester that she will never escape him or the consequences of her crime. Dimmesdale weakens, but before he dies he finds the strength to admit publicly that he was Hester's lover.

The collapse of her scheme for escape, and the sobering effects of her lover's death, make it possible for Hester to rejoin "the magnetic chain of humanity." As the years pass Hester becomes a nurse and helper of the ill and distressed, and is able to raise Pearl as a lovely woman who eventually achieves a happy marriage. As the rigors of the days of the oligarchy decline and Hester's good deeds bring her fame, she becomes a respected woman. By resisting the temptations of abstract intellect and by accepting the consequences her choices in life have set for her, Hester gains what happiness she can.

Insofar as his masterpiece is a criticism of American life Hawthorne was warning contemporaries about the dangers of the American fullness of will, excessive pride, and overly intense idealism. In judging the conflict between Hester and society he makes it clear that when two competing absolutes (Hester's vision and Puritan law) confront each other directly, the chances of mutual accommodation are extremely limited. Neither society nor the individual can make absolute demands on the other; both must learn to accept the imperfections that are the price of a tolerable humanity.

Similar themes interested Hawthorne's friend Herman Melville (1819–91), a New Yorker by birth. Soon after writing two popular, if misunderstood, novels about the attractions and dangers of pagan life in the South Seas, *Typee* (1846) and *Omoo* (1847), Melville published his masterpiece, *Moby Dick* (1851), regarded by some critics as the greatest American novel. Despite much unevenness, it has epic proportions, a complexity of conception, beauty of descriptive passages, and seriousness of theme not found elsewhere in American fiction.

Taking one of the more heroic American industries, whaling, as his background, Melville tells the story of a Promethean but misguided figure, Captain Ahab, who has lost a leg to an albino whale, Moby Dick. In pursuit of revenge, which he disguises to himself as an attempt to vindicate men's dignity against a cruel nature, Ahab develops an awesome self-sufficiency that shuts away from him all who do not share his vision and that eventually destroys him. In the words of Newton Arvin, Ahab's fixation is an extreme assertion of "the ruinous individualism of the age," reckless, incapable of true insight, and over-confident about the certainty of its ideals.

While the transcendentalists spoke principally of ideal or iso-lated self-realization, Melville, like Hawthorne, worried about aliena-tion for the sake of an ideal from the common human purposes that bind fallible humans together. Starbuck, Ahab's first mate, under-stands Ahab's desire to assert himself pridefully against a force of na-ture that has maimed him. But Ahab believes the whale is a monstrous personal enemy of humanity and a symbol of the Universe's hostility to man; Starbuck, seeing the whale only as a dumb animal, knows that Ahab's search for him is falsely heroic, "blasphemous," and mad.

Ahab's search ends in death; he and his ship are destroyed in a final attempt to kill Moby Dick. Ahab's sense that his suffering and pain can be explained, that there is some final resolution of the seemingly endless contradictory play of life and death in man's existence, is never vindi-cated. No ideal or deity resolving all man's dilemmas really exists or is knowable. Man moves between the polar opposites of life and death. He has great powers of mind, will, and imagination but is checked by the limits of humanity and of his own gifts. For happiness one must abjure absolutes (although Melville was never as much at ease with skepticism as Hawthorne was) and seek those transitory instances of love, shared purposes, and friendship that life may offer.

Neither Melville nor Hawthorne had a "program" to present as an alternative to those things that they criticized in American life, but against the rigidity and absolutism of many contemporaries they did maintain an image of a more flexible and more compact humanity. They did not, however, elaborate any formal theory of fraternity. Whatever hopes they had for democratic comradeship were modified by the idea that love and fraternity were not inherent in the nature of things but came to men by chance or had to be snatched from life.

Walt Whitman (1819–92) had a less skeptical faith in the possi-bilities of human association, and he has become famous for a mystique of democratic fellowship that was first expressed in his volume of po-etry, *Leaves of Grass* (1855). Whitman's image of democratic life was, however, different from what admirers have generally made it to be. He was considered the typical American, and, indeed, he often pre-sented himself as such; but he said:

I give you fair warning before you attempt me further,
I am not what you supposed, but far different.

George Santayana was correct when he said that Whitman "is regarded
as representative chiefly by foreigners, who look for some grotesque
expression of the genius of so young and prodigious a people."

When Whitman first published *Leaves of Grass* he seemed to be a
dangerous radical glorying in filth and smut and with no conception
of the nature of poetry, although there were a few exceptions to this
view, notably Emerson. The adverse judgments have since been
transformed into a regard for Whitman as a great liberator of human
sexuality, as well as the "spokesman of the common man." There is
some validity in this view of Whitman, but both the facts of his life
and some less often noticed but ever recurring ideas in his poems make
it difficult to accept the later flattering assessment at full value. It is
true, as Whitman's critics charge, that his ideas are often absurd and
philistine, and his conception of a poem is difficult to define. However, poems like "As I Ebb'd with the Ocean of Life" and "When
Lilacs Last in the Dooryard Bloom'd" show a control of technique as
well as profundity of idea radically at variance with views of him as
the happy-go-lucky spokesman of a vigorous democracy or as a
simple rhymester with pretensions to being a serious poet. Although
Whitman did at many moments play roles as court poet of popular
democracy or as jolly innocent reveler in the immediately sensual, he
is often greatest as a poet when he is most skeptical about the ration-
ality or comprehensibility of the universe, which he describes as:

> Withdrawn far, mocking me with
>   mock-congratulatory signs and bows,
> With peals of distant ironical laughter
>   at every word I have written,
> Pointing in silence to these songs, and
>   then to sand beneath.

If Whitman at other times could "merge" with life and seemed
to abolish all individuality in some cosmic and optimistic notion of fraternity, he also described himself in ways that strongly suggest alienation from experience and detachment from life. If he loved life, he was
equally in love with death, with purity, and purification.

Whitman has often been acclaimed as the poet of the democratic
future, a utopian visionary of a new unambiguous order of life for
man and woman. However, judging by his best known political essay,

Democratic Vistas (1871), Whitman's image of America was more complex than this. On the one hand, the liberal strain in him leads to belief that for America all things are possible, that history sets no limits on the future of the United States. On the other hand, he believes that all that America needs to know was given in 1776; the future holds no new truths but exists merely to permit men to work out ideas already known. In the American future a cleansed republic will renew an old heritage rather than find a new image of itself. Recurringly, Whitman's call for freshening old democratic ideals and restoring America's freedom and exhilaration has been taken by critics so as to obscure what may be called his conservatism. Just as death and passivity play against life and vitality in Whitman's cosmology, so do present and past, conservatism and radicalism, figure in his politics.

If democracy is taken to mean a way of life in which one general moral or religious truth is shared by all men, then Whitman does not fit the role of the prophet of such a democracy. He was consciously full of contradictions, just as American culture was in his day—and as it has remained, whatever simpler castings have been made of it. Like Hawthorne and Melville, he thought of America as too diverse, too rich in contrasting possibilities to be forced in any one direction or to be content with only one vision of life, however noble. Better perhaps than the tendency of many Americans in the years before the Civil War to insist on simple standards of belief and behavior for their fellow citizens was the tendency of mind and feeling implied in Whitman's words:

> Do I contradict myself?
> Very well then I contradict myself,
> (I am large, I contain multitudes).

FOR SUPPLEMENTARY READING

The one full study of the reform movements, although too simple in analysis, is A. F. Tyler's *Freedom Ferment* (1944). Studies on the religious basis of reformism are C. C. Cole, Jr., *The Social Ideals of the Northern Evangelists 1826–1860* (1954); T. L. Smith, *Revivalism and Social Reform in Mid-Nineteenth Century America* (1957); E. S. Bates, *American Faith* (1940); and J. Smith and A. L. Jamison (eds.), *Religion in American Life* (4 vols., 1961).

Foreign views of America other than Tocqueville's can be sampled in Allan Nevins (ed.), *American Social History as Recorded by British Travellers* (1931), and Oscar Handlin, *This Was America* (1949).

On individual reformers and reform movements, read A. Bestor, *Backwoods' Utopias* (1950); W. Merrill, *Against Wind and Tide* (1963); H. S. Commager, *Theodore Parker* (1936); G. H. Barnes, *The Anti-Slavery Impulse, 1830–1844* (1933); and W. Cross, *The Burned-Over District* (1950). Recent important re-evaluations of abolition are D. Donald, *Lincoln Reconsidered* (1956), and M. Duberman (ed.), *The Antislavery Vanguard* (1965). On slavery, consult L. Filler, *The Crusade Against Slavery, 1830–1860* (1960); D. C. Dumond, *Antislavery: The Crusade for Freedom in America* (1961); and D. B. Davis, *The Problem of Slavery in Western Culture* (1965).

On the Mormons, a good work is R. B. West, *Kingdom of the Saints* (1957). The literature on immigration begins with the works of M. L. Hansen, *The Immigrant in American History* (1940) and *The Atlantic Migration* (1940). Students should also read Handlin's *The Uprooted* (1951), and G. M. Stephenson, *A History of American Immigration, 1820–1924* (1926).

On outstanding writers, excellent general studies are R. Chase, *The American Novel and Its Tradition;* M. Bewley, *The Complex Fate* (1952) and *The Eccentric Design* (1959); and Yvar Winters, *Maule's Curse* (1938). For the link between folk culture and the more formal literary imagination, use C. Rourke, *American Humor* (1931) (Pb). A brilliant study of the literary mind before the Civil War is F. O. Matthiessen, *American Renaissance* (1941).

Two important works on education after 1820 are S. L. Jackson, *America's Struggle for Free Schools* (1941), and R. Hofstadter and W. Metzger, *The Development of Academic Freedom in the United States* (2 vols., 1955). On art and artists, read J. T. Flexner, *That Wilder Image* (1962), and N. Harris, *The Artist in American Society . . . 1790–1860* (1966); O. W. Larkin, *Art and Life in America* (1949).

17

──────────────────────

>>>->>>->>>->>>->>>->>>->>>->>>

──────────────────────

Continental Expansion

THE SAME MOTIVES that inspired Englishmen to seize India and to settle in Australia, Frenchmen to acquire Algeria, and Spaniards to plant their flag on the soil of Cuba and the Philippines drove Americans during the nineteenth century first into the trans-Appalachian country and then into the territory beyond the Mississippi. Missionaries and fur traders were followed by pioneers, gold-seekers, speculators, and businessmen. Ignoring national boundaries, American settlers did not hesitate to push into foreign-held lands with the confident conviction that their government would support their invasion. Nor did their government disappoint them, for by 1850 the United States territory of 1789 had been trebled, and the nation's western boundary had been pushed to the shores of the Pacific.

Manifest Destiny

By 1840, many Americans had reached the conclusion that the United States was destined to assume control over all of North America. Their country seemed to be entrusted with a mission to spread democracy and liberty, and they could think of no better way to carry out this mission than to have their government take over the entire continent. Convinced of the superiority of the United States, the expansionists argued that this nation could not shirk its responsibility to provide the "less fortunate people" in neighboring countries with the "blessings of American freedom and democracy." The imperialists were so certain that it was the "Manifest Destiny" of the United States to expand that they found it difficult to believe that either Englishmen or Mexicans in North America could think otherwise; if foreigners were not prepared to accept American rule peacefully, the expansionists were ready to impose it on them by force.

"Manifest Destiny"—the term used to describe the American expansionist spirit of the 1840's—was characterized by a bumptious enthusiasm and naive nationalism. Its proponents claimed that the United States had the world's best government, that its people were better off than those of any other nation, and that its expansionist designs were sanctioned by both divine and natural law. The expansion of the United States seemed not only universally desirable but inevitable. European nations were said to be imperialistic for selfish reasons, whereas the United States was expanding for the benefit of all mankind. In fact, Manifest Destiny was in many ways similar to the general philosophy of imperialism: it was justified by forces beyond the control of the expansionists; it was advanced as a doctrine that would uplift both the conquerors and the conquered; and its advocates were utterly lacking in either self-restraint or sense of humor. The following statement, made by a speaker at the New Jersey Democratic State Convention in 1844, is a typical example of imperialistic oratory in this period:

> Land enough—land enough! Make way, I say for the young American Buffalo—he has not yet got land enough; he wants more land as his cool shelter in summer—he wants more land for his beautiful pasture grounds. I tell you, we will give him Oregon for his summer shade, and the region of Texas as his winter pasture. Like all of his race, he wants salt too. Well, he shall have the use of two oceans—the mighty Pacific and the turbulent Atlantic shall be his . . . He shall not stop his career until he slakes his thirst in the frozen ocean.

The growth of Manifest Destiny in the 1840's was partly due to the widespread fear of British power in North America. The United States and Great Britain had occupied Oregon jointly since 1818, and after the Texas war of independence in 1836 the British repeatedly tried to use the Texan republic to their advantage. A southern expansionist spoke for Americans in every section when he said "Some people talk as though they were affeered of England. . . . Haven't we licked her twice and can't we lick her again? Lick her! Yes; jest as easy as a b'ar can slip down a fresh peeled saplin'." Many expansionists argued that the extension of American democracy was the only way to thwart the spread of British "autocracy" in the New World. In this respect, Manifest Destiny was a reaffirmation of the principles announced by James Monroe in 1823.

Sectional controversy also fostered enthusiasm for expansion. By the 1840's, many political leaders thought that any regions subsequently obtained by the United States would in all likelihood determine the outcome of the contest that was developing between the North and the South over the control of the federal government. New territories would eventually be carved into states whose representatives would upset the old political balances by allying themselves with either the North or the South; and the section that could count on the support of these new states would be in a position to dictate the nation's tariff, land, banking, and slave policies. Under the circumstances, some southerners wished to acquire more slave territory, and men in the North were equally determined to add free territory to the nation. Each section opposed the expansion of the other, but both favored some form of expansion. As a result, there were very few people in the United States during these years who did not advocate the acquisition of more land.

Americans in Oregon

The Oregon country was a region larger than the combined area of New England, New York, and Pennsylvania. Before the Lewis and Clark expedition or the founding of Astoria, France, Spain, Russia, and England had all laid claim to this territory. The French claims, based on voyages of seamen between 1763 and 1779 and on the possession of Louisiana, were surrendered to the United States with the purchase of Louisiana in 1803. Spain's title, also founded on explorations of her seamen, passed into American hands through the treaty of 1819. Russia's claims were based upon the expeditions of Vitus Bering, a Danish explorer in the service of the Tsar, and on the operations of fur merchants who had organized the Russian-American Fur Company at the close of the eighteenth century. By a treaty with the United States in 1824, however, Russia had renounced all claim to the territory south of latitude 54°40′.

England's original claim to the Oregon country was based on the voyage of Sir Francis Drake, who in 1579 supposedly anchored his ship, the *Golden Hind*, in Oregon waters. Two centuries later—during the American Revolution—the British admiralty sent Captain James Cook to explore the northwest coast of America and to find, if possible, the long-sought northwest passage. In 1778, Cook anchored off Nootka,

Vancouver Island, where he obtained a few otter skins that were subsequently disposed of in Canton, China, at fabulous prices. The Spanish, however, were also interested in this region, and in 1789 Spanish war vessels seized two British merchantmen in Nootka Sound. War was averted by the Nootka Sound Convention of 1790, which provided that neither nation was to interfere with the activities of the other in the region. Two years later, Captain George Vancouver reached Oregon with instructions to explore the Pacific coast from the thirtieth to the sixtieth parallel. In the course of this expedition he discovered and named Puget Sound, circumnavigated the island that bears his name, explored the coast of British Columbia, and named Mount Baker. In addition to these voyages and explorations, the British claim was strengthened by the overland expeditions of the Northwest Company.

America's title to the Oregon country rested substantially upon the same basis as England's—exploration and trade. American independence had scarcely been recognized before Yankee merchants and shippers had begun to push into the Pacific. In 1784, the *Empress of China*, a New York merchantman, had entered Canton Harbor, and other American vessels had soon followed, but all had been handicapped by the fact that the goods that they brought were much less in value than those they obtained. To remedy this, a group of Boston merchants decided to combine the fur trade of the Pacific with the Far Eastern trade. Two vessels, the *Columbia* and the *Lady Washington*, under command of Robert Gray and John Kendrick respectively, left Boston in 1787 with cargoes of blankets, knives, iron bars, copper pans, and trinkets that were to be exchanged with the Oregon Indians for furs. Both vessels reached the Nootka Sound region the following year, and in the fall of 1789, Captain Gray sailed for China with a cargo of furs. He returned home by the Cape of Good Hope in 1790 and in a few months was again on his way to the Pacific. In 1792, while engaged in exploring the coast south of Vancouver, he discovered and named the Columbia River. The government at the time paid almost no attention to his discoveries; but it was eventually indebted to him and to Captain Kendrick for its claim to the Oregon territory.

Few other Americans displayed any interest in Oregon during the first quarter of the nineteenth century. In 1818, representatives of Great Britain and the United States attempted to divide the territory and to establish a definite boundary from the Rockies to the Pacific. Because the British insisted on the line of the Columbia River, while the Americans were committed to the forty-ninth parallel, no division was effected; but the two countries agreed to a joint occupation for ten years. Theoretically, the citizens or subjects of either country were to enjoy equal rights to settle or to trade in any part of the country; but, in reality, the Americans were practically excluded from the territory by the Hudson's Bay Company, which had absorbed Astor's old rival, the Northwest Company. The American fur interest, acting through a Virginia Representative, John Floyd, and Senator Thomas Hart Benton of Missouri, attempted without success to secure relief from Congress. But many representatives from the older states argued that the annexation and occupation of Oregon would decrease land values in the East, cause high wages, and restrict development of manufactures. Others declared that the Rocky Mountains formed a natural boundary for the United States on the west and that the "most prolific mind" could not picture a time when territory up to this boundary would be densely populated; they believed that seizure of the Oregon territory by any nation would be a blessing for the United States. In 1827, after another futile effort to reach an agreement on the boundary, the joint occupation was renewed for an indefinite period, each nation retaining the right to terminate the treaty at a year's notice.

Several easterners made attempts in the 1830's to colonize Oregon or to open it for trade, but their efforts failed. More important than their efforts to settle Oregon was the work of the missionaries. According to legend, in 1831 representatives from two Indian tribes that lived beyond the Rockies came to St. Louis to ask that Christian missionaries be sent to teach their people. Whether this request was real or fanciful, an account of it was published in the eastern press and attracted the attention of the Methodists and Presbyterians. The Methodist Missionary Society voted $3,000 to carry the Gospel to the Indians. Additional funds were raised by Methodists, and in 1834 a band of missionaries set out with an expedition of settlers. Instead of settling among the Indians, they established a mission on the east side of the Willamette, about sixty miles from its mouth. Following the example of the Methodists, the Presbyterians also sent out missionaries, who, under the leadership of Dr. Marcus Whitman and two preachers, made settlements in the upper Walla Walla Valley. Other Protestant sects, and Catholics as well, soon had missionaries on the spot, and by 1840, Oregon had an American population of at least 400. All of these pioneers settled south of the Columbia, partly because they felt that they were on what would ultimately become American territory, but more especially because of the fertile agricultural soil. The territory north of the Columbia River, the boundary proposed by the British, was heavily wooded, and there American settlement was strenuously opposed by the Hudson's Bay Company.

The efforts of the missionaries aroused additional interest in the

THE OREGON CONTROVERSY

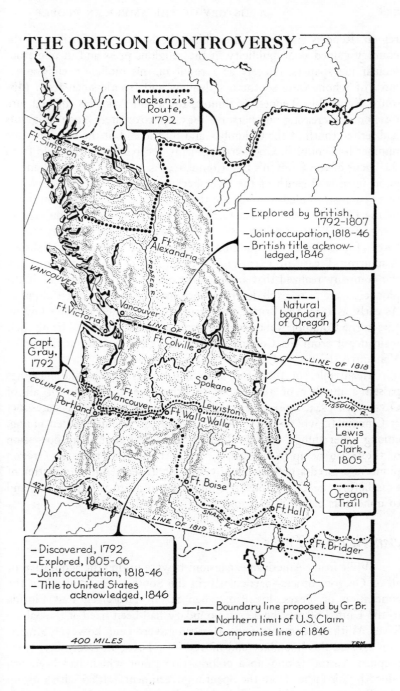

Mackenzie's Route, 1792

Ft. Simpson
54° 40' N

—Explored by British, 1792-1807
—Joint occupation, 1818-46
—British title acknowledged, 1846

Ft. Alexandria

FRASER R.

VANCOUVER I.

Ft. Victoria

Vancouver

LINE OF 1846

Natural boundary of Oregon

Capt. Gray, 1792

Ft. Colville

LINE OF 1818

COLUMBIA R.

Spokane

Portland

Ft. Vancouver

Lewiston

Ft. Walla Walla

MISSOURI R.

Lewis and Clark, 1805

Ft. Boise

42° N

SNAKE R.

Ft. Hall

Oregon Trail

LINE OF 1819

Ft. Bridger

—Discovered, 1792
—Explored, 1805-06
—Joint occupation, 1818-46
—Title to United States acknowledged, 1846

——I—— Boundary line proposed by Gr. Br.
— — — Northern limit of U.S. Claim
• • • • Compromise line of 1846

400 MILES

T.R.M.

region. Reports and letters describing the beauty and fertility of the country gained wide publicity in the religious press and in numerous secular newspapers. Largely as a result of this publicity, emigrants—most of whom were southern uplanders and frontiersmen from Missouri, Kentucky, Tennessee, Illinois, Iowa and Arkansas—moved into Oregon in increasing numbers. By 1845, approximately 6,000 emigrants had settled south of the Columbia, and by the end of the next year the number had doubled. Upon arrival, many received generous help from the agent of the Hudson's Bay Company. As numbers increased and as good farm land south of the river became scarcer and less accessible, this generosity failed to convince the Americans that the region north of the Columbia was British territory. The Joint Occupation Agreement of 1818, renewed in 1827 for an indefinite period, was still in force (for the boundary question had been omitted from the Webster-Ashburton Treaty of 1842) and as the influx of strangers continued, the company realized that armed resistance would be necessary if the pioneers were to be excluded from the territory north of the Columbia. As early as 1839, the British, anticipating a battle and running low on furs in the Columbia valley, considered the advisability of shifting their main depot from the Columbia River to a new location at the tip of Vancouver Island, and in 1845 this change was made.

Meanwhile, in the East, state legislatures and public meetings passed a number of resolutions favoring the acquisition of all of Oregon. In 1843, representatives from six Mississippi Valley states met at Cincinnati, where they adopted a series of resolutions demanding, among other things, that the United States take immediate possession of the territory up to latitude 54° 40'. At the same time the Oregon pioneers created a provisional government. It seemed only a matter of time before the United States would have to go to war with England to uphold its claims to Oregon.

Americans in Texas

While many American expansionists were urging the acquisition of all of Oregon, others—particularly in the South—were demanding the annexation of Texas. In 1819, when Spain transferred East Florida to the United States, the Texan boundary had been fixed at the Sabine River. With the consent of the Mexican government, however, Americans crossed this boundary and moved into Texas. In December, 1821, Stephen Austin, taking up a colonization grant which had been obtained by his father from the Spanish government, settled with a group of followers on the banks of the lower Brazos. A year later, this grant was confirmed by the new government in Mexico. In 1825, the state of Coahuila and Texas enacted a colonization law which invited foreigners to enter the region, guaranteed them security of person and property, and assured them the right to choose and to follow any calling. They had to swear to obey the federal and state constitutions and to observe the Catholic faith.

When this law was passed, Austin's colony was prospering, and men who had unsuccessfully sought grants at an earlier period soon took advantage of the opportunities offered by the new law. In a short time, an area approaching the present size of Texas had been blocked out, and by 1830 approximately 20,000 Americans had crossed the border. The majority of these came from Kentucky, Tennessee, Mississippi, and Louisiana, but the population also included settlers from all parts of the United States.

The rapid increase in the number of Anglo-American settlers alarmed the Mexican officials. It soon became evident that the newcomers, instead of becoming good Mexicans, were retaining their American ways and were developing political consciousness. Quarrels between the natives and the Anglo-Americans increased; and as early as 1826 settlers unsuccessfully attempted to establish an independent republic within Texas. Following the Fredonian Rebellion—as this uprising was called—the Mexican government stopped further immigration into Texas. All pending land contracts were suspended; foreigners were forbidden to enter the northern borders unless provided with passports from Mexican officials; heavy duties were levied upon all imported goods; and troops were dispatched to enforce the collection of these duties.

Americans in Texas protested against these restrictive measures, and in 1833 they petitioned for their repeal. Since the United States had ratified a treaty in April, 1832, which conferred upon the citizens of each country the right to reside and to remain in the territories of the other, the Mexican government repealed the law forbidding American immigration; but otherwise the petitioners gained nothing. In 1835, the Mexican congress, at the instigation of General Santa Anna, who had made himself dictator of Mexico, enacted a series of laws abolishing the federal constitution of 1824, and a military governor was sent to rule the territory. Many Texans, however, openly defied the Mexican authorities; and by 1836 a movement for self-government had been converted into a war for independence. The struggle was short. On March 2, 1836, Texas issued a declaration of independence; fifty-three of the sixty signers were Americans the majority of whom came from the slave states.

Four days after the announcement of Texas' independence, 5,000 Mexicans successfully concluded a thirteen-day siege of the Alamo mission in San Antonio. But all of the Alamo's 188 defenders preferred death to surrender, and "Remember the Alamo" soon became the battle cry of the Texas rebels. Three weeks later, more than 300 American volunteers under James Fannin were captured and murdered at Goliad. Within a month, however, the Texans, under the leadership of Sam Houston, a former Governor of Tennessee and close friend of Andrew Jackson, rallied and won the war at the battle of San Jacinto (April 21, 1836). This decisive victory marked the end of Mexican domination over Texas, and the region was at once organized as a separate republic with Houston at its head.

The new republic did not, however, desire to remain an independent nation. As early as 1833, Houston, who had then been in Texas only two months, wrote Jackson that nineteen-twentieths of the population favored annexation to the United States; three years later, when the question was submitted to popular referendum, there was hardly a dissenting vote. The majority of the Texans were Americans, and annexation would afford them greater stability and the liberties guaranteed by the Constitution of the United States. The Texans also believed that annexation would prevent Mexico from attempting to regain the lost province.

Many Americans thought it advisable to annex the new republic without delay. They argued that annexation not only would add to the United States' wealth, resources, and power, but that it would also prevent the development of a formidable and even dangerous rival on the southwestern frontier. Unless Texas were annexed, they maintained, it might become an unfriendly state or enter into an alliance with England. In either event, it might seize all northern Mexico, drain the South of its slaves, outstrip the United States in the production of cotton, injure American commerce and manufactures, and involve the United States in difficulties with foreign powers.

In the South, representatives of the newer cotton states believed that Texas presented an unparalleled opportunity for extending the area of cotton cultivation in response to world demand and for increasing the power of the slave states in the federal government. Other planters, however, worried about the competition from new cotton lands, the pressure on slave prices, and the effects on business of a national political conflict over Texas. Yet the rapid growth of population in the North had led to a corresponding increase in northern political strength that could only be offset by the admission to Congress of additional representatives and senators from the South. On the political question of guaranteeing southern strength southerners were more united than they were on the economic advantages of Texas' admission.

The role of the South's political leaders was the most important influence in determining how the South spoke about Texas. Of all the southern leaders, Calhoun was among the first to recognize the importance of Texas to his section. Calhoun had withdrawn from the Democratic party after the nullification struggle with Jackson and for some years had remained a man without a party; but Texas presented him with a chance to improve both his own and his section's political fortunes. In Calhoun's mind, the acquisition of Texas would add to the political and economic strength of the South, and the inevitable northern opposition to annexation would force the South to unite and to present a common front against its opponents within the Union. Calhoun would be able to offer this new issue to his restless constituents and party rivals. Like President Tyler, who had succeeded William Henry Harrison in the Vice-President's post, Calhoun was looking for a program he could use in bargaining for the Presidential nomination in 1844. Texas was a fruitful issue, given the general fervor for Manifest Destiny, and seemed an ideal issue for Calhoun to be associated with. Calhoun believed that he was the obvious choice to lead a united South in its struggle with the North. He therefore became one of the most outspoken advocates of the annexation of Texas and eventually made common cause with President Tyler.

Throughout the North, opposition to annexation was vociferous. Antislavery agitators and the antislavery press condemned it as a slaveholders' conspiracy that would embroil the nation in a war with Mexico. William Ellery Channing, the famous Unitarian reformer, said:

> I trust indeed that Providence will beat back and humble our cupidity and ambition. I now ask whether as a people we are prepared to seize on a neighboring territory to the end of extending slavery? I ask whether as a people we can stand forth in the sight of God, in the sight of nations, and adopt this atrocious policy? Sooner perish! Sooner our name be blotted out from the record of nations!

Six or eight slave states as large as Kentucky, the opposition asserted, could be carved out of Texas, and the South would then control the nation. A number of northern states presented formal protests to Congress, and William Lloyd Garrison, the Boston abolitionist, called upon the North to secede rather than acquiesce in the annexation of Texas as a slave state.

Fearful of provoking a political storm and remembering the Mexican threats of war, President Jackson, though personally favoring annexation, thought it advisable to delay action when Texas first sought statehood. He did, however, recognize the independence of Texas. Van Buren continued Jackson's policy by refusing to press the issue of annexation.

The Texans, refused at first by the United States, turned to Europe for support. England quickly recognized the advantages of an independent Texas that would serve as a barrier to further American expansion to the south, relieve English textile firms of their dependence on American cotton, and provide English manufacturers with a market. Britain recognized Texas's independence and concluded treaties of commerce and amity with the new republic. Texas obtained similar concessions from France.

Texan success in treating with England worried American leaders who favored annexation. When Tyler succeeded Harrison as President, he re-opened negotiations for the acquisition of the Lone Star Republic by the United States. Secretary of State Daniel Webster toyed with the idea of working to annex Texas, but, fearing the political opposition in his home state of Massachusetts, he resigned the office. His successor in 1843, Abel Upshur, was killed in a naval explosion, and Tyler turned to a sympathetic Calhoun. In 1844, the President submitted to the Senate an annexation treaty that had been drafted by Secretary of State Calhoun. In North and South, resolutions, memorials, and petitions were circulated. Thomas Hart Benton of Missouri asserted that while the measure was under discussion, the State Department, White House, and Senate lobbies were crowded with speculators in Texas land and holders of depreciated Texas bonds, all of whom were working for ratification. Yet when the vote was taken, the treaty was rejected thirty-five to sixteen. Tyler's unpopularity, northern fear of increasing the political power of the South, the split in southern ranks, and the opposition of leaders like Clay and Webster (now converted to the opposition by the abolitionists in his home state) explain its defeat.

Adding the Stars for Texas and Oregon

Both the Texas and Oregon questions played a major role in the presidential campaign of 1844. The Whigs unanimously nominated Henry Clay, and in an effort to avoid a difficult issue, they did not even mention Texas in their platform. The Democrats, on the other hand, paired Oregon and Texas in an attempt to gain the support of both the slavery and antislavery groups and, at the same time, to capitalize on the powerful expansionist sentiments in every section of the country. The Democratic platform therefore supported the United States title to all of Oregon and demanded the "reannexation of Texas," on the ground that under the treaty of 1803 Texas had been part of the Louisiana Purchase and that it had been "disannexed" by the treaty of 1819. Van Buren had been the leading preconvention candidate for the Democratic nomination, but he was outmaneuvered by those Democrats urging return of the "two-thirds rule" for nomination at the 1844 Convention. This re-adopted rule put a powerful minority of pro-Texas speculators and rising politicians into a strategic position. As a consequence, the delegates passed over the New York leader and nominated James K. Polk of Tennessee, a dark horse, Jackson's favorite, and an avowed expansionist.

Manifest Destiny was the principal national issue in the campaign of 1844. Polk repeatedly emphasized the desirability of acquiring Oregon and Texas. Clay, in an attempt to win the support of both friends and opponents of expansion, shifted like a weather vane. Polk won a sweeping victory; he carried many western and southwestern states, was able to win New York, and the Democrats gained a large majority in Congress. His election seemed a mandate for Manifest Destiny.

Tyler interpreted the election as a popular endorsement of the annexation of Texas. Now interested in safeguarding the South's interests and in keeping Texas away from England, Tyler laid the question before Congress after his treaty had been defeated in the Senate. He suggested that Congress annex Texas by a joint resolution, which would require only a majority vote of both houses, and in 1845 Congress acted. The joint resolution admitted Texas to the Union on an equal footing with the original states. Not more than four additional states could be formed out of its territory, and then only with its consent. The territory was to assume its own debt, but the resolution explicitly stated that any disputes that might arise over the Texas boundary were to be settled by the United States.

Following the adoption of the joint resolution by Congress, England renewed its efforts to prevent the union of Texas and the United States. For a time, English leaders had thought that annexation would be forestalled by a Whig victory in the election of 1844; but when Polk defeated Clay, Lord Aberdeen, the British Foreign Secretary, decided that only British diplomacy could preserve Texas' independence. Accordingly, in May, 1845, a special British representative induced the Mexican government to recognize Texan independence. But the British and the Mexicans had delayed too long. Congress had already acted, and to most Texans, Mexico's belated recognition seemed a poor alternative to the advantages that they could obtain as citizens of the United States. In the summer of 1845, a convention of Texas delegates voted almost unanimously to join the United States; and in December, 1845, Texas entered the Union as a slave state.

Because the Texas question was virtually settled when Polk assumed office on March 4, 1845, he immediately turned his attention to the problem of Oregon. American expansionists, who were demanding "all Oregon or none" had made "fifty-four forty or fight" their war cry. But Polk did not have to be goaded. He agreed with the stand on Oregon expressed in the Democratic platform, and he had repeatedly attacked the British claim for the territory north of the Columbia. In his annual message of 1845, he urged Congress to adopt measures that would insure the American right to all of Oregon, and he recommended that Great Britain be notified that the United States planned to end the joint occupation at the end of a year, stating:

> At the end of the year's notice, should Congress think it proper to make provision for giving that notice, we shall have reached a period when the national rights in Oregon must either be abandoned or firmly maintained. That they can not be abandoned without a sacrifice of both national honor and interest is too clear to admit of doubt.

After months of debate, Congress on April 27, 1846, adopted a resolution embodying the President's recommendation.

Despite the bluster of the expansionists and the threats of Polk, the United States did not want to precipitate a war in the Northwest. Polk was already deeply involved in a dispute with Mexico, and he knew that armed conflict with Great Britain would delay—if not prevent—him from carrying out his plans for the acquisition of New Mexico and California. The British, beset by internal difficulties, also wished to avoid war. The dispute over the repeal of the corn laws had produced a serious division in England; and British manufacturers wanted to prevent any development that would deprive them of American markets and raw materials. Largely because of these considerations and because of Aberdeen's determination to settle the question peacefully, the British offered a compromise plan to the United States. Although Polk was reluctant to abandon the American claim to all of Oregon, he agreed to submit the British proposals to the Senate before taking action. The Senate advised acceptance, and on June 15, 1846, the treaty was signed. The forty-ninth parallel became the boundary from the Rockies to the sea; Great Britain, however, retained the whole of Vancouver Island and the right to navigate the Columbia. Possible war with Great Britain was averted, and all but the more rampant expansionists were satisfied.

The population of Oregon continued to increase, especially after Congress in 1850 passed the Donation Land Act, which granted land on liberal terms to previous settlers and to those who settled in Oregon before 1854. In 1859, the present state of Oregon was admitted to the Union.

Americans in New Mexico and California

In New Mexico and California, as in Oregon and Texas, an advance guard of American settlers and traders prepared the way for eventual annexation. In 1800, the territories of New Mexico and California, which had been organized by Spain as defensive barriers against England and Russia, were separated from the advancing American frontier by more than 1,000 miles of desert and mountains. At this time, the people of the United States were almost totally ignorant of these regions.

Slowly, however, American trade with the region expanded, but after 1835, sixteen years after the Spanish territories had been ceded to an independent Mexico, a drastic increase in Mexican taxes and duties enraged all Americans who in any way benefited from the trade. The Mexican policy tended to make expansionists and annexationists out of all those it affected adversely.

The history of the relations between Americans and Mexicans in California followed a similar pattern. During the last quarter of the eighteenth century, Spanish padres had established a string of missions from San Diego to Sonoma to bring the Catholic faith and Spanish civilization to the natives on the coast. The choice lands of the territory were pre-empted by Spanish laymen. But California was not to remain a land of missions and farms. Yankee traders, whalers, and merchants trickled into California. The merchants settled in the coast towns. By becoming naturalized, adopting the Catholic faith, and marrying Spanish women, they ingratiated themselves with the Californians and soon became trusted, influential citizens. Deserting sailors, mechanics, trappers, and adventurers joined the new communities or took up farms.

Although the number of American settlers increased yearly, in 1840 there were less than 400 of them in a total population of between 5,000 and 6,000. But tales of wandering trappers and newspaper accounts of California's "cloudless skies" and fertile soil were arousing the imagination of Americans everywhere. Companies of emigrants were soon on their way westward, and by 1845, 700 Americans were in California.

A few went by the Santa Fe route, but the majority followed the more direct route by way of Great Salt Lake and the Carson and American rivers. Some settled in the coast towns, but by far the larger number built homes and marked out farms in the valley of the Sacramento or its tributaries. Many were befriended by John A. Sutter, a man of German-Swiss extraction, who arrived in San Francisco in 1839. Sutter became naturalized and received a grant of land along the American River, where he built an elaborate establishment including a fort, blacksmith shop, distillery, tannery, gristmill, and carpenter shop. In addition to 4,000 cattle, 2,000 horses, and as many sheep, he owned extensive orchards, vineyards, and grain fields.

As the number of American settlers in the province increased, however, the Mexican authorities began to fear that California might become a second Texas. "Even now," Sir George Simpson wrote from California in 1842, "the Americans only want a rallying point for carrying into effect their theory that the English race is destined by 'divine right' to expel the Spaniards from their ancient seats. . . ." As early as 1829, rumors reached Mexico City that Americans were plotting to seize the port of San Francisco. The following year, the California authorities were instructed that the Russian and American settlers together must not exceed one third of the population. Shortly afterward, orders were issued compelling every foreigner to justify his residence in the country under penalty of fine or imprisonment. Finally, in 1843, Santa Anna, once more in violation of the Mexican treaty with the United States, issued an edict forbidding all immigration into California. Any foreigner without a passport was denied legal status and the right to purchase land. The American representative at Mexico City secured the repeal of this edict, only to have a similar one issued in 1845. But neither edicts nor land decrees could prevent prairie schooners from climbing the mountain passes or pioneers from pre-empting lands along the Sacramento.

Prelude to War

Polk entered office in 1845 as an expansionist who was determined that the United States should acquire New Mexico and California. He pushed his plans forward almost immediately. The United States had claims against Mexico that had been reduced from an original $5,000,000 to $2,000,000 by an agreement between the two countries; these represented the accumulated business losses of American citizens over a long period of years. After the first three installments, a total of $300,000, had been paid, the Mexican payments ceased. Meanwhile, the disputable Texas-Mexico boundary was as yet unadjusted. The Texans wanted to establish the boundary at the Rio Grande but from the Mexican standpoint, all of Texas was still a part of Mexico, and the Sabine River was still the boundary between the United States and Mexico.

Encouraged by the Mexicans, in November, 1845, Polk sent John Slidell to Mexico City with instructions to settle both the boundary and indemnity questions. Slidell was ordered to uphold the American position in the boundary dispute, to offer to assume the United States' claims against Mexico, and to pay Mexico as much as $25,000,000 if she would cede the disputed territory and both New Mexico and California. But when Slidell reached Mexico, he found the country in political upheaval: "Every morning it looked for a revolution and every night for a mutiny." When it was learned that he had been sent to Mexico to acquire New Mexico and California, Mexicans accused the United States of having stolen Texas and of plotting the further dismemberment of the republic. Angry patriots and politicians demanded war. Under such circumstances, the tottering Herrera government did not dare to receive the American minister.

Even before Slidell had been dispatched on his mission, Polk and his cabinet had prepared for a conflict. In June, 1845, they sent General Zachary Taylor, with a small defensive force, to protect the "historic" western boundary of Texas. Taylor barely entered the disputed territory, however, and waited at Corpus Christi on the south side of the Nueces. Only after Polk had received word that Slidell had been rejected by Herrera's government did he send Taylor toward the Rio Grande. In January, 1846, Taylor took up a position near the mouth of the Rio Grande. Meanwhile, the American fleet in the Pacific was reinforced by vessels from the Mediterranean and East Indian squadrons; and Thomas O. Larkin, wealthy Monterey merchant and United States Consul in California, was told that, although the administration would not attempt to detach California from Mexico by force, it would welcome any move that the people of that province might make toward independence. He was further instructed to stir up a "spontaneous" revolt among the Californians against Mexico and to induce them to seek annexation to the United States.

Polk, who had patiently tried peaceful negotiations, received news of Slidell's final rebuff and the bellicose statements of the Mexicans. On April 7, 1846, the Cabinet decided to lay the matter before Congress, pointing out that Slidell had not been received and that the claims of American citizens were as yet unsatisfied. Slidell returned and saw the President on May 8. He told a story of Mexican insults and duplicity. Polk decided to ask the Cabinet for war, and on the following day the Cabinet decided on war if Mexico attacked. News arrived that evening that a detachment of General Taylor's army had been defeated in a skirmish with the Mexicans on the north side of the Rio Grande. In his message to Congress, the President declared:

> The grievous wrongs perpetrated by Mexico upon our citizens throughout a long period of years remain unredressed . . . The cup of forbearance had been exhausted even before the recent information from the frontier of the Del Norte [Rio Grande]. But now after reiterated menaces, Mexico has passed the boundary of the United States, has invaded our territory and shed American blood upon the American soil.

The Mexican government had first encouraged and then refused to receive an American envoy or to listen to his propositions. "War exists," said Polk, "notwithstanding all our efforts to avoid it, exists by the act of Mexico herself." Nowhere in Polk's message was there any mention that the boundary was a disputed boundary, or that the territory upon which blood had been spilled was disputed territory. As to the responsibility for precipitating the war, both nations seemed eager for a clash, but Mexico had attacked first. As long as Mexico insisted that the United States had no right to annex Texas and the United States contended that it had such a right, war was a real possibility.

Marching through Mexico

Polk's war message swept all before it. Congress, voting overwhelmingly for war, authorized the President to raise a volunteer army of 50,000 men and placed at his disposal $10,000,000. Polk decided to draw most troops for the war from the states nearest Mexico. Of the nearly 70,000 volunteers who enlisted, at least 40,000 were from the southern and western states, whereas the more distant, more populous, and wealthier North furnished only 8,000. Opposition to the struggle developed quickly in the North, even though many northern congressmen had voted for hostilities. Some denounced it is an unwarranted attack on a smaller and weaker nation; some opposed it because they were Whigs and Polk was a Democrat; still others objected to it because they believed it would lead to the annexation of more slave territory. James Russell Lowell spoke for the last group in his *Biglow Papers*:

> They may talk o' Freedom's airy
> Tell they're pupple in the face,—
> It's a grand gret cemetary
> Fer the barthrights of our race;
> They jest want this Californy
> So's to lug new slave-states in
> To abuse ye, an' to scorn ye,
> An' to plunder ye like sin.

From the outset, the American conduct of the war was hampered by the President's fear that Taylor and General Winfield Scott, both of whom were Whigs, would be able to make political capital out of their exploits in the field. Polk, remembering how Jackson's and Harrison's military reputations had appealed to the voters, was in the awkward position of wanting the Whig generals to win battles without winning glory. Taylor, who was instructed to march south on Mexico City, was compelled to wait two months for adequate supplies and his army of 6,000 did not begin its advance until August, 1846. Despite lack of training and the difficulty of the terrain, Taylor's troops reached Monterrey on September 21, and after a three-day battle, the Mexicans surrendered. But when Taylor permitted the enemy forces to evacuate the town after its surrender, Polk believed that the American commander had violated his express orders. Taylor's popularity at home, however, made his removal inexpedient. He resumed a slow march southward, giving Santa Anna time to gather a force of approximately 20,000 to repel the invaders. The two armies met at Buena Vista (February 22–23, 1847), and again the Americans, who were outnumbered three to one, defeated the Mexicans.

Following Taylor's failure to capitalize on his victory at Monterrey, Polk had decided to alter the over-all American strategy by having an army under Scott's command invade the eastern coast of Mexico. Scott, who was placed in charge of all American troops in Mexico, landed with a force of approximately 12,000 at Vera Cruz on March 9, 1847. After occupying the city, he proceeded inland along the route that Cortez had taken to Mexico City more than 300 years earlier. At Cerro Gordo Pass, his way was blocked by an army that Santa Anna had gathered after the battle of Buena Vista. By using a mountain road discovered by Captain Robert E. Lee, Scott's troops were able first to outflank and then to inflict a disastrous defeat on the Mexicans. Although the road to Mexico City was now open, Scott was forced to halt at Puebla for recruits to replace the volunteers whose terms of enlistment had expired. In mid-August Scott resumed the advance and

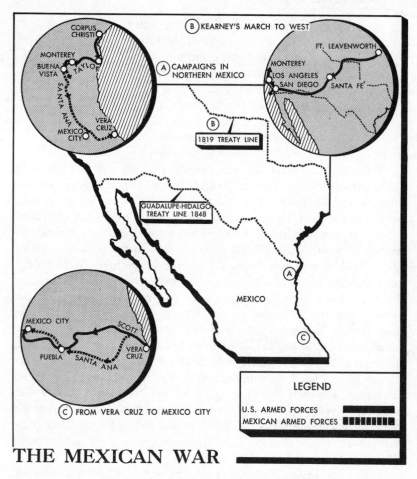

B KEARNEY'S MARCH TO WEST

A CAMPAIGNS IN
   NORTHERN MEXICO

CORPUS
CHRISTI

FT. LEAVENWORTH

MONTEREY
BUENA
VISTA   TAYLOR

MONTEREY
LOS ANGELES
SAN DIEGO   SANTA FE

SANTA ANA

VERA
CRUZ

MEXICO
CITY

B 1819 TREATY LINE

GUADALUPE-HIDALGO
TREATY LINE 1848

MEXICO

A

C

MEXICO CITY

SCOTT

PUEBLA   SANTA ANA

VERA
CRUZ

C FROM VERA CRUZ TO MEXICO CITY

LEGEND

U.S. ARMED FORCES
MEXICAN ARMED FORCES

THE MEXICAN WAR

encountered no opposition until he met and defeated the Mexicans at Contreras (August 19). In the next three and a half weeks Scott fought his way to the gates of Mexico City, and on September 14, 1847, the Americans entered the Mexican capital.

The Stars and Stripes on the Pacific

While Taylor's and Scott's troops were defeating Santa Anna's armies in Mexico, other Americans were conquering New Mexico and California. In August, 1846, Colonel Stephen W. Kearny at the head of an army of Missouri volunteers captured Santa Fe. After establishing a territorial government for New Mexico, Kearny sent south the larger part of his force under Colonel A. W. Doniphan's command to join

Taylor in Mexico, while he set out with 300 dragoons for California. When Kearny reached his destination, he found the revolt in California in full progress. Larkin, who had been ordered to conciliate the Californians and "to arouse in their bosoms that love of liberty and independence so natural to the American continent," had carefully and adroitly carried out his instructions. At the same time, John C. Fremont, the ambitious son-in-law of Thomas Hart Benton, was taking a leading part in the rebellion. In company with Kit Carson and about 100 men, Fremont had set out in 1845 to find the best route to the Pacific south of Oregon. No sooner had he arrived in California, however, than his actions had aroused the suspicions of the Mexican officials, who had ordered him to leave the country. He had then retreated to Oregon. Apparently gambling on the chance that by this time hostilities had broken out between the United States and Mexico, Fremont soon returned to California, where rumors had begun to circulate that the Mexican authorities were planning to drive Americans out of the country. The alarmed settlers prepared to revolt, and on June 15 they proclaimed California an independent republic. On July 7, the American flag was raised over Monterey, and a proclamation was posted that California was annexed to the United States. For a short time, the native Californians fought against the American forces, commanded by Colonel Kearny, Commodore Robert F. Stockton, and Fremont. But the odds were too great, and by the autumn of 1846, California had been conquered. With the entrance of Scott into Mexico City in September, 1847, the war was virtually over. Mexico, defeated and torn by internal dissension, was powerless.

How much of the conquered republic the victor would take and on what terms was the question that now divided the people of the United States. Speculators in quest of new lands for investment, manufacturers thinking of extending their markets, planters and planter-politicians eager to enlarge slave territory, and antislavery men anxious for a free Mexico to hem in the slave South, favored total annexation. "Destiny beckons us," said Secretary of State James Buchanan, "to hold and civilize Mexico." Many other politicians agreed with him. The *New York Sun* wrote:

> God has not made a more magnificent land than Mexico. We welcome . . . the whole press of the Union to share our admiration. Let them repeat it until it becomes a common theme, and we shall see the Aztec and the American eagle clasping wings, and our Yankee boys swapping knick-knacks with the Americanized Rancheros for gold.

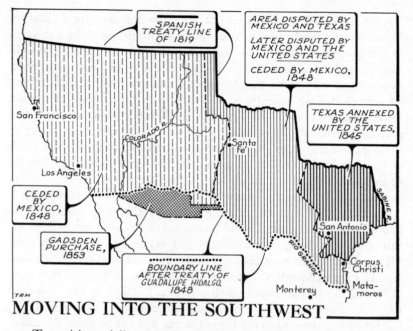

MOVING INTO THE SOUTHWEST

To anti-imperialists these demands were "wicked and uncalled for." To despoil Mexico of a foot of territory would constitute, they declared, a greedy and shameless act. Antislavery opponents of the acquisition of all Mexico were outspoken in their protests; yet, Calhoun who had deprecated the war, now feared that the acquisition of more territory might precipitate a slavery crisis. He offered a resolution to the effect that to incorporate Mexico into the Union would be inconsistent with the avowed object for which the war was fought, in "conflict with the character and genius" of our government, and "in the end subversive of our free and popular institutions."

But the wishes of neither imperialist nor anti-imperialist prevailed. The treaty of peace signed at Guadalupe Hidalgo on February 2, 1848, was a compromise. Mexico ceded New Mexico and California—an area of more than one half million square miles—to the United States. She recognized the annexation of Texas by agreeing to the Rio Grande as the boundary between the two nations. In compensation for the loss of territory, she received $15,000,000, and the United States assumed the claims against Mexico held by American citizens. Polk had indeed "conquered a peace."

By concluding what Polk regarded as too soft a treaty, the American envoy, Nicholas P. Trist, had actually ignored instructions to return to Washington. Although furious, Polk feared that the new Whig majority in the House of Representatives would refuse more war funds. Regretfully he accepted the Treaty of Guadalupe Hidalgo, and Congress approved its terms.

Trist had received last minute instructions to include the entire Gila River Valley (now in Southern Arizona) in the ceded territories. This region contained the lowest passes of the Rocky Mountains and was thus the best railroad route between the southern United States and the Pacific. Though Trist failed to obtain the desired territory, it was acquired five years later through the negotiations of James Gadsden, a South Carolina railroad president, for $10,000,000. Thus another slice of Mexican territory, amounting to 54,000 square miles, was added to the United States' domain.

Golden California

Less than two weeks before the Treaty of Guadalupe Hidalgo was signed, James Marshall, while engaged in building a sawmill for John A. Sutter in the Sacramento Valley, discovered that the region was rich in gold. Despite Sutter's efforts to keep the matter a secret, the news spread quickly, and people rushed to the new mining country. Settlements were completely deserted; homes, farms, and stores abandoned. Ships deserted by their sailors crowded the Bay of San Francisco, soldiers deserted wholesale; churches were emptied; town councils ceased to sit; merchants, clerks, lawyers, and judges and criminals everywhere, flocked to the foothills. By the middle of the following summer rumors of the new El Dorado had reached the East. At first people were skeptical, but all doubt was removed when in September an official communication reached Washington that there was "more gold in the country drained by the Sacramento and the San Joaquin rivers than would pay the cost of the late war with Mexico a hundred times over."

Nothing could be more calculated to appeal to cash-conscious Americans than easy gold. The effect of this report, published in all the leading newspapers of the country, was phenomenal. California became the topic of excited conversation; visionary stories stirred artisan and banker alike. Boys and men, rich and poor, abandoned the farm, drygoods counter, workshop, bank, or lawyer's desk, for the "Golden West." The fortune hunters poured into California by ship around Cape Horn, by the way of the Isthmus of Panama, and overland across the plains.

The first of these routes was extremely popular during the winter months. Between December 14, 1848, and January 18, 1849, more than 125 vessels left eastern and southern ports for the Pacific coast. In Feb-

The San Francisco Post Office during the Gold Rush

[NEW YORK PUBLIC LIBRARY]

ruary, 1849, alone, approximately 150 vessels loaded with "Forty-niners" from New England and the middle states set sail for San Francisco. In a few weeks, it was almost impossible to book passage to California.

The impatient and the reckless chose the shorter Isthmus route, and people paid as much as $1,000 for steerage tickets from Panama to the Golden Gate. The rise in traffic soon led to demands and proposals for either a railroad or a canal across the Isthmus. In 1846, expansionists had negotiated a treaty of amity and commerce with New Granada (after 1863, known as the "United States of Colombia," and after 1886, as the "Republic of Colombia"), which gave the United States a right of way across the Isthmus. Two years later, the treaty was ratified. At once a group of American capitalists began constructing the much talked-of railway.

At the same time, another American company was authorized by the Nicaraguan government to build a canal across Nicaragua. After this corporation, which, under the leadership of Cornelius Vanderbilt, had failed to interest English capital in the project because a preliminary survey indicated that the plan was not feasible, a Vanderbilt subsidiary obtained from Nicaragua the monopoly of a route that combined land and water travel across Nicaragua. The mutual fear of England and the United States that the other would gain control of the practicable routes cross the Isthmus resulted in the Clayton-Bulwer Treaty (1850). Eng-

By Sea to 'Frisco

land and the United States agreed to join in promoting the construction of a ship canal by the Nicaraguan route. Neither was ever to "obtain or maintain for itself any exclusive control over the said ship canal," or "assume or exercise any dominion . . . over any part of Central America." Both governments also agreed to guarantee and protect the neutrality of the canal unless there should be "unfair discriminations" or oppressive exactions in its management. By Article VIII, the same principle of neutrality was extended to every means of transit that might be constructed across any part of the Central American isthmus. From the standpoint of the expansionists, the Clayton-Bulwer Treaty was far from satisfactory. In large measure, it nullified the concessions obtained from New Granada in 1846 and prevented United States' exclusive control over any transit project across the Isthmus.

The majority of "forty-niners" did not go via Panama but overland from the Mississippi Valley. Many were already experienced pioneers who earlier had migrated from other regions. The three principal routes started in New Orleans, Fort Smith, Arkansas, and Independence, Missouri.

These overland journeys usually required about five months— months filled with anxiety and suffering. On the plains, the Indians and the buffalo herds were a constant menace. Water was scarce, and the supply of grass for cattle and horses was undependable. Some began the trip with insufficient supplies; others set out overburdened with personal

belongings. Wagons frequently mired in crossing streams, were demolished in mountain passes, or rolled against breast-high sagebrush. The trail across the desolate desert was soon strewn with the mementos of lost hopes: broken wagons and skeletons of cattle, horses, and men. Yet, in spite of all difficulties, between 20,000 and 30,000 people crossed the Rockies during the summer and autumn of 1849.

To these Americans, to Mexicans, Peruvians and Chileans, to ex-convict Australians, and to Chinese and Malayans—to all these, as well as to Old World speculators, California seemed the promised land. Before the middle of January, 1849, five mining and trading companies with an aggregate capital of £1,275,000 were chartered in London. Similar companies were organized in Paris. Some 4,000 impecunious Frenchmen were transported to California, but many Frenchmen came on their own initiative; still others deserted the ships dispatched to California by Paris and Bordeaux merchants.

California's population in 1850 was almost 100,000, a tenfold increase in two years. Of this number, about 20 per cent were foreigners, and more than 70 per cent were Americans from all sections of the nation. Although the Chinese had totaled only 791 in 1850, a year later their number exceeded 4,000. Places like Stockton and Sacramento did not exist in 1848. By 1850, they were thriving towns. The population of San Francisco in the course of a few years mounted from a few hundred to 35,000.

There had been other gold rushes in American history, but none had matched this. Every mining camp and town was infested with middlemen who in contrast to most of the miners, soon grew rich. Horses that cost $20 sold for $200, and cattle that had been bought for $6 were sold for from $100 to $200. Flour sold for between $1.50 to $5.00 a pound, and pork from $1.20 to $4.00 per pound; boots brought $20 a pair. Land in San Francisco and Sacramento sold for $1,000 an acre. Merchants and transportation company agents usually succeeded in concealing the pitiable stories of the thousands of men who annually returned from the mines broken in health and penniless by sedulously circulating reports of "lucky finds," "fabulous strikes," and sudden wealth.

Agitation for California's admission to the Union had begun as early as 1847. Two years later, the provisional Governor of California issued a proclamation calling a constitutional convention. More than two thirds of the forty-eight delegates were under forty years of age, and most had not been in California very long. The clause in the state constitution prohibiting slavery caused a long and bitter debate on the floor of Congress, but California was finally admitted as a free state in 1850.

By 1850, however, the country had already been debating for four years the fate of the territories that had been Mexican. Both North and South had looked to California's new congressmen for support in the struggle for the control of the national government. The question of whether California should be admitted to the Union as a slave or free state intensified sectional conflict and contributed to the tragic drama that was to culminate in civil war.

FOR SUPPLEMENTARY READING

R. A. Billington, *The Far Western Frontier 1830–1860* (1956), is a comprehensive recent history of the era of expansion. This should be read along with N. A. Graebner, *Empire on the Pacific* (1955); A. Weinberg, Manifest Destiny (1935); and F. Merk, *Manifest Destiny and Mission in American History: A Reinterpretation* (1963).

Two works by J. H. Smith should be consulted: *The Annexation of Texas* (1911) and *The War With Mexico* (2 vols., 1919). O. A. Singletary, *The Mexican War* (1960), is good and brief. The war issue is debated in R. E. Ruiz, *The Mexican War: Was It Manifest Destiny?* (1963).

Bernard DeVoto, *The Year of Decision: 1846* (1943), is a well-known study of the start of the Mexican War, but too censorious of Polk. Allan Nevins has edited the Polk diaries under the title *Polk: The Diary of A President, 1845–1849* (1952). C. G. Sellers, *James K. Polk, Continentalist, 1843–1846* (1966), has much fresh material, and R. Seager, *And Tyler Too* (1963), supplies a long-missing study.

On Oregon questions, start with O. O. Winther, *The Great Northwest* (1947), and Francis Parkman's fine work, *The Oregon Trail*, originally *The California and Oregon Trail* (1849). On California there is a good general history, J. W. Caughey, *California* (1953). Most helpful on understanding the revolt of the Californians against Mexico is A. Nevins, *Fremont, Pathmaker of the West* (1955).

The politics of the 1840's still need a historian, but excellent partial studies do exist. Of these, the first volume of A. Nevins, *The Ordeal of the Union* (1947), starts with the end of the Mexican War. For the earlier crisis of 1844–45, be sure to read J. C. N. Paul, *Rift in the Democracy* (1951), and J. D. P. Fuller, *The Movement for the Acquisition of All Mexico, 1846–1848* (1936).

PART V

... THAT THAT NATION MIGHT LIVE

18

→≫-≫-≫-≫-≫-≫-≫-≫

The Making
of Sections

ALTHOUGH the United States has always been a heterogeneous society, strong differences of interests and of ideals have fortunately produced only one civil war. Despite the great diversity within both the North and the South and regardless of the strong ties of language, religion, and common ancestry, after 1830 the North and South drew apart steadily. The lines dividing the sections were never clear-cut and the sections were never really united. Nevertheless, by 1850 the South gave its allegiance to a social ideal that differed radically from that of most northerners. Regardless of whether public controversy at any time happened to center on tariff rates, territorial expansion, or public-land policy, all questions eventually became involved with slavery as a moral and political issue and on that issue North and South drifted ever further apart. Repeatedly, disputes and conflict were settled by peaceful means; but as bitterness increased, the possibility of compromise diminished. By 1860, there were influential and respected leaders in both the North and South who believed that further concessions were out of the question. Although few responsible citizens in either section professed a desire for war, no one was able to devise a formula that would both preserve peace and satisfy North and South alike.

The Sectional Economies

Although both North and South at first depended for subsistence in large measure upon agriculture, the North soon began to achieve an economic diversification that added to its wealth and influenced every phase of its civilization. The change from a purely agricultural to an agricultural-manufacturing-commercial system, which had become marked by 1840, was even more noticeable twenty years later.

Instead of engaging extensively in commerce and manufacturing, the South's greatest investment went into the production of the great staples—rice, cotton, tobacco, and sugar. By 1860, the planting South stretched from Maryland to the Rio Grande and as far up the Mississippi Valley as Kentucky and Missouri. Over 400,000 square miles were devoted primarily to the production of cotton. Between 1840 and 1859, the annual production of 500-pound bales quadrupled, and the value of cotton exports increased from about $15,000,000 to nearly $300,000,-000. The crops of sugar and tobacco, as well as hemp, rice, and other agricultural products, also grew in size.

Since the staples yielded annual returns of $300,000,000, it was natural that southern leaders should regard agriculture as the section's main source of strength and prosperity. "Cotton is King" became the slogan of southern statesmen and politicians. On the South, they declared, rested the prosperity of the nation, and indeed of the whole industrial world; for the South furnished the bulk of exports and thus provided the basis for American credit abroad. From its fields came the cotton for the textile plants of England, France, and America, employing millions in capital and hundreds of thousands of hands. With its staples, the South was able to purchase provisions and manufactured goods, whose production, sale, and transportation gave employment to northern farmers, laborers, shippers, and merchants. "I rejoice," John B. Floyd said in a speech in New York, "that the great staples of the South are the chief means by which your commerce is fostered, and your mechanics and artisans kept constantly at work." Jefferson Davis expressed the same sentiment in addressing a Boston audience in Faneuil Hall when he said: "Your interest is to remain a manufacturing, and ours to remain an agricultural people. Your prosperity, then, is to receive our staple and to manufacture it, and ours to sell it to you and buy the manufactured goods." George Fitzhugh, urging the South not to abandon agriculture wrote: "For fifty years, she [the South] had been more usefully, more industriously, more energetically and more profitably employed than any people under the sun. Yet all the while she had been envying and wishing to imitate the little truck patches, the filthy, crowded, licentious factories, the mercenary shopkeeping, and the slavish commerce of the North."

Despite these arguments, many southern leaders saw the growing economic disparity between the South and North. In their opinion, the South, with comparatively few manufactures, little mining, and restricted banking capital, was virtually a colony of the North; without a merchant fleet of its own, its cotton, rice, and tobacco had to be shipped in either English or northern vessels. Practically all foreign goods for southern consumption entered through northern ports. Northern factories supplied an increasing portion of the cloth, hats, and farm tools of the South, and northern bankers furnished the money with which to buy more land and more slaves. These leaders believed that northern merchants and bankers were prospering at the expense of the planter.

The economic dependence of the South on the North underlay much sectional rivalry. Southerners were envious and alarmed at the material growth of the North. The southern statistician Thomas P. Kettell calculated in *Southern Wealth and Northern Profits* that the North obtained annually millions in profits from manufacturing for the South, carrying its commerce, and acting as its banker. It was natural, therefore, that southerners should resent being in what they termed a state of "degrading vassalage." Southerners were humiliated by the contrast made by every foreign traveler between the backward, agrarian South and the wealthy populous North with its towns and cities, its efficient transportation facilities, its manufactures and mines, its commerce, its superior agricultural methods, its homes, its shops, its places of amusement, its schools and colleges, its newspapers, and its literature and art.

Half Slave, Half Free

The basic economic differences between the North and South need not have ended in armed conflict. On the contrary, the economies of the two sections were complementary rather than conflicting, for each concentrated on the production of what the other needed; and history is replete with examples of agrarian and commercial-industrial regions living side by side in peaceful cooperation. Down to the Civil War, the plantations drew much of their food supply from the Northwest. The economic relationship between the Northwest and the Northeast, on the other hand, was not unlike that between the South and the North. The Northwest, as a predominantly agrarian section, could also complain of northeastern control over credit, transportation, and marketing facilities.

There was then more than an economic division between North and South; what set the South off from the rest of the nation was that it alone adhered to the slave system.

By 1850, most northerners thought of the South, too simply, as a slave society with only three classes: slaveowners, slaves, and "poor whites." Despite better information supplied by observers like F. L. Olmsted, the simpler image persisted. Had the North realized the actual complexity of southern society, it would have been apparent that the South was, socially and politically, far from being "solid," and that with skillful maneuver, the ground could have been cut out from under the feet of the more intransigeant spokesmen who represented themselves as *the* South during the 1850's.

Firmly established at the top of southern society was the planter oligarchy, consisting largely of cotton magnates. This group owned extensive tracts and many slaves and included in its ranks many millionaires. These planters, however, numbered only three or four thousand out of a total southern population of approximately nine million in 1850, but they monopolized the wealth of the entire section. Individual "leading" families had much prestige, based largely on the capital they controlled. Capable, conservative, and usually well informed and widely traveled, these oligarchs controlled the life of their communities. Such unquestioned economic and social supremacy in the hands of an able leisured class naturally brought with it considerable political influence, which, throughout the South at least, amounted to virtual domination.

More numerous and less wealthy than the great planters were the middle-class farmers and well-to-do townsmen. The landowners with five to twenty slaves differed markedly from their wealthier and more aristocratic neighbors. They often devoted more attention to general farming than to the production of staple crops. Less given to lavishness than the more affluent planters, usually for want of money, they were equally as much stout defenders of the South and its institutions. The merchants and professional men of the towns were associated with both the planters and middle-class farmers in business and social life, sharing many of their interests and their point of view. The chief ambition of the man of the middle was to rise into the ranks on top and the fact that many leading southern "aristocrats" were themselves only one generation removed from humble or middling circumstances stimulated their competitiveness.

Small farmers, white mechanics, and lesser tradesmen made up the bulk of southern society. Comparatively poor—for few of those who owned land had slaves, and many had neither—the members of this group closely resembled in family traditions, religious opinions, and

"The Shadows," New Iberia, Louisiana

household arrangements the artisans and middle-class farmers of the North. Some aspired to be wealthy planters, but more, although envious of the rich, were content to keep from slipping down the economic scale. In religion, by far the greater number were Baptists, Methodists, or Presbyterians, and in politics they subscribed to Jacksonian doctrines of individualism. Many were as enthusiastic in their support of slavery and sectionalism as those whose benefits from both had been materially greater. From the ranks of the yeomanry came many plantation overseers, professional men, and political leaders.

The "poor whites," inhabitants of the unproductive pine barrens between the tidewater and piedmont regions, were in many respects the most unfortunate people in the South. Termed collectively "white trash" but known locally as "sand hillers," "crackers," "tar heels," "hill billies," "red necks," "wool hats," "rag tails," "bob tails," "clay eaters," and by other names as well, they were the lowliest of the whites. The planter's monopoly of the staple markets and the better lands as well as lack of free capital had practically forced these people from their original holdings on to worthless tracts that yielded a bare subsistence. The poor white often lived in a one-room log cabin chinked with clay and straw; a few rickety chairs, a long bench, a dirty bed or two, a skillet, a rude cupboard, a rifle, and a spinning wheel were its principal furnishings. One or two ramshackle outbuildings housed dogs, horse, cow, pigs, and poultry. On the small clearing surrounding his home, the poor white raised a little corn, a few pumpkins, and perhaps a small quantity of garden truck. His scanty crops were supplemented by hunting and sometimes by fishing. Although the poor white often owned cattle, he let them roam about in the nearby woods. The lack of adequate transportation to markets turned the cattle into a mere paper asset. Lank, angular, sallow-complexioned, a victim of fever and hookworm, addicted to tobacco and strong drink, the poor whites were listless, uncouth, and shambling. Few could read and fewer could write; they were ignorant and superstitious. Frances A. Kemble in her *Journal* characterized them as "the most degraded race of human beings claiming an Anglo-Saxon origin that can be found on the face of the earth." Even the slaves, toward whom they were bitterly hostile, scorned them.

Not all southern Negroes were slaves. Over the years, there arose in the South a class of freed Negroes. By 1790, the number of freedmen in southern states exceeded thirty thousand, and by 1860 it was more than a quarter of a million. Free Negroes were most numerous in Maryland, Virginia, North Carolina, Kentucky, and Louisiana. Elsewhere the stringency of the laws about their status and the high price of slave labor tended to reduce their numbers. The free Negroes varied greatly in character and in talent. At one extreme were those who owned considerable property, including slaves; at the other were vagabonds who could scarcely gain a livelihood. Many freedmen were mere squatters on waste lands or abandoned farms, where they tilled a few acres on their own account, and when occasion offered, worked for the whites at a wage. Like the poor whites, the free Negroes were considered outcasts of southern society and, with some exceptions, were "regarded with distrust bordering on apprehension." The majority were penniless. Few were educated, and most of the southern states denied them formal schooling; other restrictions curtailed their freedom of movement and economic activity. In most southern states, free Negroes had to register before a county court and in some cases to give bonds for their good behavior. In some states they were even required to wear badges showing registry number, name, and occupation. They were usually required to have licenses for peddling and other forms of merchandising and were forbidden certain jobs. Sometimes free Negroes were fraudulently re-enslaved; kidnapping freedmen to sell them as slaves was common. A few voluntarily converted themselves into slaves, and the rest lived an increasingly precarious existence as the defense of slavery became more intense.

At the bottom of southern society were the slaves, who constituted approximately 90 per cent of the Negro population of the South. Divided into "house hands" and "field hands," for the most part, slaves were concentrated in the rice-cotton-, and sugar-producing areas. During the first half of the nineteenth century, the total slave population more than doubled; but the increase was far greater in the newer states of the Southwest than in the Old South.

Despite the large numbers of slaves, slave ownership in the South was not widespread. Probably not more than 400,000 of the more than 7,000,000 Southern whites in 1860 were slaveholders; and of these, 277,000 owned fewer than ten slaves apiece. Allowing five persons to a family, nearly 5,000,000 Southerners did not possess slaves and had no direct investment in slave labor.

The Slave System

By 1850, plantation labor was almost entirely slave. Before the closing of the African slave trade in 1808, the native slave supply was augmented by slave cargoes from across the sea. Even after the passage of the prohibitory legislation, there was considerable smuggling that was not checked until Congress in 1820 declared maritime slave trade to be piracy. To what extent smuggling went on after that date is unknown, but that it did not cease entirely is certain. Some authorities place the number of illicit importations between 1808 and 1860 as high as 270,000. In 1808, the United States had about 1,000,000 slaves; upon these, their descendants—and whatever Negroes were smuggled in— the planters depended for their labor supply.

The closing of the African slave trade, combined with the exhaustion of the soils of parts of Maryland and Virginia, the production of tobacco at smaller cost in the trans-Appalachian region, and the production of cotton on a large scale in the Gulf states, tended to stimulate interstate traffic in slaves. The older planting East, unable to compete with the newer plantation sections, turned to the profitable business of supplying the Gulf-state planters with slaves. Many slaves were carried from the older regions to the new by migrating farmers and planters who sold them and used the proceeds for new homesteads. By far the greater part of the traffic between Virginia and the lower South, however, was conducted by firms specializing in this particular business.

GROWTH OF NEGRO POPULATION IN THE SOUTHERN STATES, 1810–60

STATE	1810	1820	1830	1840	1850	1860
OLD SOUTH						
Maryland	145,000	147,000	155,000	151,000	165,000	171,000
Virginia	423,000	462,000	517,000	499,000	526,000	549,000
North Carolina	179,000	219,000	265,000	268,000	316,000	361,000
South Carolina	200,000	265,000	323,000	335,000	394,000	412,000
Georgia	107,000	151,000	220,000	283,000	384,000	465,000
LOWER SOUTH						
Florida			16,000	26,000	40,000	62,000
Alabama		42,000	119,000	255,000	345,000	437,000
Mississippi	17,000	33,000	66,000	196,000	310,000	437,000
Louisiana	42,000	79,000	126,000	193,000	262,000	350,000
Texas					58,000	183,000
Arkansas		2,000	5,000	20,000	47,000	111,000
Tennessee	45,000	82,000	146,000	188,000	245,000	283,000
Kentucky	82,000	129,000	170,000	189,000	220,000	236,000
Missouri	4,000	10,000	25,000	59,000	90,000	118,000

PER CENT INCREASE OVER 1810

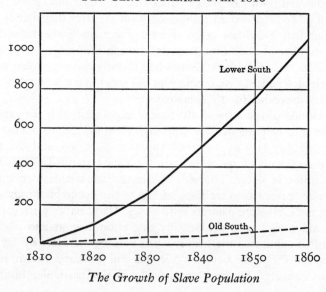

The Growth of Slave Population

Each of these had its assembling headquarters, field agents, selling agency and auctioneers, and perhaps a vessel or two for transport along the coast. The peak of the long-distance traffic was reached in 1835, when it was estimated that dealers and emigrating owners had carried 120,000 slaves out of Virginia alone. After 1840, the declining price of cotton and the renaissance of Virginia's agriculture checked the southward trade slightly.

Masters were understandably eager to dispose of slaves who were indolent, unruly, or suspected of misdemeanors, and frequently those who were beginning to lose their vigor and vitality. The dealers, on the other hand, preferred "likely Negroes from ten to thirty years old" —men who had been "drivers" or who were artisans, women who were comely or expert in some domestic art, and laborers of either sex who were physically strong. Dealers assembled their purchases in private stockades, public jails, taverns, and warehouses. Those slaves not shipped in vessels along the coasts or by river steamers were sent overland in coffles and often were disposed of to planters and townsmen along the way. Prices in the long run steadily rose but within the longer period varied from year to year and from locality to locality. Slave prices were governed in large measure by staple prices. At the beginning of 1837, when cotton was selling at $.13 a pound in New York City, an able-bodied Virginian field hand sold for as high as $1,100. In 1845, when cotton reached the low-water mark of $.05 a pound, an able-bodied slave brought only $500.

Of all the Southern whites the slave trader was the most despised; even in the South he was, as a rule, socially ostracized. In 1860, D. R. Hundley of Alabama wrote:

> Preeminent in villainy and a greedy love of filthy lucre stands the hard-hearted Negro trader . . . Although honest and honorable when they first go into the business, the natural result of their calling seems to corrupt them; for they usually have to deal with the most refractory and brutal of the slave population, since good and honest slaves are rarely permitted to fall into the unscrupulous clutches of the speculator . . . Ah! Messrs. Stock-Brokers of Wall Street—you who are wont to cry up your rotten railroad, mining, steamboat and other worthless stocks—for ingenious lying you should take lessons from the southern Negro trader.

Closely related to slave trading was slave hiring, which was common in all southern states. When confronted with financial reverses or with the opportunity for profit, the slaveowner gladly rented his chattels to others. Many thousands of slaves were annually rented as household servants for private families, boarding houses, and hotels. Even larger numbers were hired to work in fields, forests, mines, and on construction jobs. Merchants, mechanics, contractors, drovers, and others hired slaves as helpers. Small farmers, unable to buy a slave, frequently hired one for part time. Slaves were hired out either directly by the owner or through an agent. Those who hired them succeeded temporarily to the owner's authority over, and obligations to, the slave. Although treatment accorded the slave varied, it was always to the interest of the owner to see that his property did not suffer physical injury.

To carry on the work of the plantation, the slaves were divided according to strength and ability into classes: field hands, carpenters, blacksmiths, bricklayers, house servants, and the like. The two accepted methods of slave labor were piece work, or the task system, and time work, or the gang system. The former was most used on the rice coast of South Carolina and Georgia, where the small plots formed by the drainage ditches made it extremely easy to divide up the work. The individual plot assigned to each field hand each morning constituted his or her task for that day, and when it was completed, the slave had at his disposal such time as remained. Usually the more difficult tasks were assigned to those who were best fitted to perform them. The possibility of an hour or two of leisure at the end of the day made for diligence and speed and insured accomplishment, for drivers saw to it that the work was well done.

On the tobacco, short-staple cotton, and sugar plantations, the gang system prevailed. The workers were divided into gangs of varying numbers, each of which was paced and supervised by a driver. Any worker who failed to keep up with the driver was liable to punishment. On several estates the whip was frequently used, but many planters thought that the best results were obtained when other incentives were employed. On many plantations where the gang system was used, the hours of labor were from sunrise to sunset. Some planters, however, thought it advisable to divide the long day with a midday recess of from one to three hours. The gang system probably reached its maximum efficiency in the black-belt territory along the Mississippi, where the plantation system was more highly commercialized than in the older South.

Control of the slave was based on physical force, regulated by statutory law, and modified by such schemes of nonviolent control as individual masters found practicable. Although many planters sought to rule their slaves by kindness and affection rather than through fear, others relied chiefly on severe punishments for disobedience or infractions of any sort. State laws forbade slaves to assemble, carry arms without a permit, or fish in certain waters. Theft, arson, assault, rape, murder, resisting legal arrest, and conspiracy to rebel were punishable by death. Fear of insurrection, which became greater after the Nat Turner insurrection of 1831, caused most of the southern states to guard against the movement of slaves, especially at night; they passed curfew laws and laws forbidding Negroes to leave their plantation without written permission of the master or his representative and they enforced these rules by means of patrols. All minor delinquencies, though punishable by the courts, were usually taken care of privately by the owner of the slave; but sometimes mild-tempered masters and mistresses sent the guilty one to the local jail to be whipped by the jailer. Whipping or flogging was meted out for lesser offenses. Brutal floggings were not unknown, and lynching tended to increase. Slaves were sometimes punished for no offense, and mutiny and desertion frequently resulted. How many runaways there were can never be exactly ascertained. Newspaper advertisements indicate that the number was not small. Often runaways were caught and brought back only to abscond again. Sometimes, when the private punishment was unduly severe, the person inflicting it was hailed into court. At other times, the slave would take the law into his own hands by setting fire to his oppressor's house, or by killing him.

The effect of slavery on the planter's profits is a question on which few historians agree. On the one hand is the indisputable fact that slaves worked for nothing beyond their subsistence. On the other hand are the numerous economic risks involved in the use of slave labor: weak slave children might be born; a slave might be temporarily or permanently incapacitated; and in old age the slave was likely to become an economic burden. Again, losses might be incurred through disease, theft, flight, or accident. A bolt of lightning, for example, killed twenty slaves on one plantation, and on another a poisoned well carried off a whole gang and reduced its owner to bankruptcy. At other times, smallpox and fever epidemics swept one third or more of a plantation's slave population into their graves in the course of a few weeks. The problem was further complicated by the fact that in the fifteen years preceding the Civil War the average price of field hands approximately doubled, while the price of cotton fluctuated with shifts in supply and demand in the world market. Although this rise in the cost of slaves produced a corresponding rise in the value of the planter's property in slaves, it also made it that much more difficult for a planter to add to his supply of workers. The increase in slave prices worked the greatest hardship on small owners who lacked the money to purchase slaves at the higher prices. Unlike the large planters, who could count on their labor force being increased by slave births, the small planters frequently owned only male slaves. All things considered, it seems reasonable to conclude that there was a direct ratio between the size of the plantation and the profitableness of slavery.

The Peculiar Institution

Regardless of the effect of slavery on the planter's profits, there can be no doubt that it victimized the South as a whole. The yeomanry and more prosperous farmers found competition with large-scale production difficult and were encouraged to buy or hire slaves at excessive cost. Furthermore, the leading whites tended to believe that work, especially manual labor such as slaves had to do, was beneath them; and this attitude helped discourage immigration and was demoralizing to the poor whites. Even more important, southern capital, tied up in land and slaves, was not available for investment in the industries that were rapidly creating wealth in the North.

Around slavery was built, not merely the southern economy, but the entire structure of southern civilization. After 1830, slavery was thought to be absolutely essential to the southern race system as well as to prosperity; consequently, southern spokesmen with few exceptions defended it as right and shaped their policies to secure both the protection and extension of "the peculiar institution," as it was called. Certainly slavery was the most dramatic difference separating the sections during the pre-Civil War period.

In defending slavery, the southerners pointed out that slavery was sanctioned by the ancient Greeks and Romans, that it was legalized by the Jews, and that it was even approved by some of the fathers of the medieval Church. England had formerly sanctioned villeinage, and Locke had permitted slavery in his model constitution for the Carolinas. To precedent was added the argument of scriptural authority. Did not the Tenth Commandment forbid man to covet "his manservant, or his maidservant," and were not the Jews allowed to buy bondmen or bondmaids? "If his master have given him a wife, and she have born him sons or daughters; the wife and her children shall be her master's." Passages from the New Testament were also frequently quoted in defense of slavery. "Let every man abide in the same calling wherein he was called." "Servants, be obedient to them that are *your* masters according to the flesh, with fear and trembling, in singleness of your heart, as unto Christ." And, again, "Let as many servants as are under the yoke count their own masters worthy of all honour." Similar Bibli-

Family Worship on a Plantation (Harper's Weekly)

cal passages were often repeated as undeniable proof that slavery was right and proper.

Another argument, formulated by Thomas R. Dew, president of William and Mary College, was based on the theory that slavery was part of the natural order of things: Men are not equal; some were designed to be without property and to toil in the fields while others were to manage and direct; Furthermore, said President Dew,

> The exclusive owners of property ever have been, ever will and perhaps ever ought to be the virtual rulers of mankind . . . It is the order of nature and of God that the being of superior faculties and knowledge and therefore of superior power should control and dispose of those who are inferior. It is as much in the order of nature that men should enslave each other as that other animals should prey upon each other.

This statement, which first appeared in 1832, soon became the prevailing philosophy of the South. Six years later, it was re-emphasized by Chancellor William Harper, of the South Carolina Supreme Court, in his work entitled *A Memoir on Slavery*: "To constitute a society a variety of offices must be discharged from those requiring the very lowest degree of intellectual power to those requiring the very highest."

Harper held that the lowest class in society—the slaves—should be trained only to labor and be kept in a state of ignorance: "If there are sordid, servile, and laborious offices to be performed, is it not better that there should be sordid, servile, and laborious beings to perform them?" James H. Hammond of South Carolina declared that "God created Negroes for no other purpose than to be subordinate 'hewers of wood and drawers of water'—that is, to be the slaves of the white race."

Of course, slavery was also defended on the ground that it was economically profitable. Dew, though admitting that Virginia and Maryland were too far north for the advantageous employment of slave labor, never lost an opportunity to point out the profits that these slave-breeding states derived each year. "It is, in truth, the slave labor in Virginia," he wrote, "which gives value to her soil and her habitations; take away this, and you pull down the Atlas that upholds the whole system; eject from the State the whole slave population, and the Old Dominion will be a 'howling wilderness'." Other Southern spokesmen, like Edmund Ruffin of Virginia, defended slavery by stressing the economic importance of large-scale scientific agricultural production, the advantage of purchasing supplies in large quantities, and the savings possible through specialization of labor and the elimination of conflicts between capital and labor.

Many southerners also asserted that slavery had universal advantages. It was said to be socially beneficial to the whites because it improved their manners, created higher respect for white women and provided them with leisure for cultural pursuits, and fostered kindliness and affection. Slavery was beneficial to Negroes, they argued, because it rescued them from savagery, brought them to Christianity and the influences of civilization, taught them "habits of regular and patient industry," relieved them of care for themselves and their offspring, saved them from jungle diseases, and afforded them opportunity for comfort and happiness. Finally, the planter contended that slavery was a national benefit because every part of the Union shared in the fruits of slave labor. "Upon the South as upon the strong arm of a brother," said B. F. Stringfellow, "so as long as Negro slavery exists, the North can rely; it will furnish materials for its workshops, a market for its manufactures, wealth to its capitalists, wages to its laborers."

The Growth of the North

Like the South, the North was a large complex of regions and interests, bound together increasingly by leaders chosen by the dominant political factions in the northern states. As the diverse interests of the North seemed threatened by the maintenance or growth in the power of southern states at Washington, the northern political spokesmen and press increasingly referred to "a northern way of life," contrasting it with that of the slave states.

The northern states, like the South, suppressed dissent and defied the federal courts when it suited their purposes over the slavery issue, but such events were less frequent than below the Mason and Dixon line. Though the predominant population of small farmers and small businessmen believed like the South, in white supremacy they genuinely feared the expansion of slavery. Some thought that slavery was a positive wrong, but most agreed that it degraded or competed with white labor. Consequently, "Free soil" became as much a crusade in the North as the defense of slavery, was in the South, and southerners were depicted as a cruel and alien people lowering America's prestige in the world by maintaining the blight of slavery.

As northerners sensed that a narrow construction of the Constitution was useful to the slaveowners' argument, they became more receptive to views of the Constitution as a document that had to grow and change with the times. To Calhoun's and other southerners' claims that the founding fathers of 1787 had not given the national government the specific powers it was assuming in the slavery controversy, northerners answered that the nation of the 1850's was not the same country it had been in 1787. During the search for a moral basis for northern claims against the South, leaders like Lincoln went back beyond the Constitution to the ideas about equality and the people's rights in the Declaration of Independence. These phrases were used to justify limits on the expansion of the slave states. The pursuit and capture of former slaves on northern soil, the fights over the admission of new states in the 1850's, certain decisions of the Supreme Court were all interpreted as parts of a southern plot to extend slavery indefinitely, to destroy the "freedom-loving" North, and to block the satisfaction of northern interests in tariffs, public lands, and railroads.

As slavery became more entrenched in the South after 1830, northern opposition increased. The repressive efforts of the proslavery group, particularly against the right of petition and freedom of the press, quickened the zeal of the abolitionists and won converts to the cause of free soil. Northerners and westerners who had been at least outwardly indifferent to the slavery controversy now began to accept the abolitionists' statements that slavery was inhuman and that the "slavocracy" was bent on curtailing the white man's liberty. The South, on the other hand, angered by abolitionist attacks, became more dogged in its defense of slavery and in its attitude toward the North. To the extremists of both sections—the Garrisons, the Phillipses, the Yanceys, the Quitmans—belongs the responsibility for making the problem of slavery a great moral issue.

Slavery Becomes a Permanent Political Issue

Although abolitionism produced endless and heated controversies, actual abolitionists were few and much despised. It was not until the slavery question was transformed into a political issue that it threatened to disrupt the Union. The slavery controversy became a permanent feature of national party politics with the debate in Congress over the antislavery petitions of the 1830's. At first these petitions dealt only with slavery in the District of Columbia, but within a short time they touched on every aspect of the subject and were so numerous that they threatened to interfere with the conduct of the ordinary business of Congress. In an effort to solve this problem, and at the same time to avoid committing itself on slavery, Congress in 1836 adopted a resolution stating that all such petitions should be laid on the table without debate.

The so-called gag rule, which had been sponsored by southern members of Congress, raised questions concerning the conduct of the government and the fundamental rights of its citizens. No one realized this fact more clearly than John Quincy Adams, who had been a member of the House of Representatives almost since the end of his presidential term. He consistently opposed the resolution until its repeal in 1844. Historians have been unable to agree on Adams's reasons; but, whether he was motivated by his opposition to slavery or by a desire to discredit the administration, the fact remains that his militant stand brought the slavery question out into the open. Many politicians who would have preferred to remain silent on such a controversial matter had for the first time to stand up and be counted. Slavery had become a political issue, and it was to remain one until the Civil War.

Most of the antislavery petitions had originated in the Old Northwest, a section in which there was a strong abolitionist movement and a widespread conviction that the South was gaining greater control of the national government. The gag rule confirmed this conviction, and the antislavery groups, disgusted with the indifference of the Whigs and the Democrats, thought that there was no other alternative to establishing their own party. The Liberty party, which entered the campaign of 1840 with James G. Birney, a southern abolitionist, as its presidential candidate, was thus more than an antislavery movement; it was also a product of belief in the Northwest that the South dominated the established parties. In 1840, Birney polled only 7,069 votes; four years later, he received 62,300 votes. Despite the poor showing of the Liberty party in both elections, subsequent events were to demonstrate that it had raised the most dangerous issue of the age.

The reluctance of either the Whigs or Democrats to take a clear-cut stand against slavery can be attributed to their trans-sectional character. With supporters in the North and the South, both parties wished to play down an issue that threatened to split them along sectional lines and on which compromise would be most difficult. Eventually, however, the problems arising from westward expansion forced them to consider the slavery issue.

Long before the crusade against slavery had assumed a militant character, the planter aristocracy had realized that the security of slavery as well as their economic and political control of the South depended on prosouthern votes in Congress. Some planters thought that the new lands were needed for additional acreage and for replacing fields that had been cropped to exhaustion. Others feared the competition from new plantations. But politically, all planters could agree that it was of utmost importance to have territory from which new slave states might be carved to balance the admission of new free states. Southern leaders were aware that once the political balance between the two sections was destroyed, the South would be practically at the mercy of the more populous North when there was legislation to be passed about tariffs, bounties, ship subsidies, internal improvements, banking, and currency.

Slavery and the Territories

The thousands of emigrants who had passed beyond the Alleghenies into the Mississippi Valley had laid the foundations of a slaveholding Southwest and a free Northwest. Both sections were alike in that they were frontier communities, but the culture of one included plantations and slave labor, while that of the other had family-sized farms tilled by freemen. The growing southern commitment to slavery was matched by the opposition of the rising antislavery sentiment in the North. As the two frontiers advanced, it was almost inevitable that sooner or later a struggle for territorial, and consequently political, control would arise between the North and South.

The question of the expansion of slavery was extensively debated in Congress at the time of the Missouri Compromise, but not until the age of Manifest Destiny did it again become an issue that threatened the Union. It will be remembered that many but not all southern leaders enthusiastically supported the annexation of Texas and the acquisition of the Mexican cession. A sufficient number of slave states was to be carved from the two areas to counterbalance all the new free-soil commonwealths in prospect for many years to come and enable the South to retain its grip upon the federal government indefinitely. Throughout the North, on the other hand, antislavery people viewed the future with despair. "No living man," said John Quincy Adams, "will see the end of slavery in the United States!" With the election of Polk to the presidency in 1844, the Democrats became the first of the two major parties to suffer from this association of the slavery and expansion issues. Many northerners suspected that the acquisition of Texas and the Mexican War were parts of a thinly disguised plot to add more slave states to the Union, and others were offended by the Oregon Compromise. Van Buren's failure to support the annexation of Texas—an effort to avoid sectional divisions over slavery and expansion—had cost him the Democratic nomination in 1844, and his wing of the party in the North was therefore unfriendly to Polk and to the South. Polk's patronage policies and his cabinet choices, particularly the selection of the skillful Robert Walker, who had blocked Van Buren in 1844, for the Treasury and for Secretary of War William Marcy, one of Van Buren's principal New York rivals, angered the "Little Magician." Accordingly, he and his followers broke with the administration.

Economic issues began to divide the Democratic party along sectional lines. The Bill providing for the re-establishment of the Independent Treasury system in 1846 was a party measure that was approved by all good Democrats in every section; but the administration's tariff program, although also favored by the commercial East, was interpreted as reflecting the interests of the party's southern members. The man responsible for the general tone of the tariff was Secretary of the Treasury Walker, an admirer of Richard Cobden and an advocate of free trade. In a famous report of December 3, 1845, Walker laid down six principles that pointed to a substantial reduction of the tariff. The tariff act of 1846, which incorporated Walker's proposals, was adopted only after Vice-President George Dallas's vote had broken a tie in the Senate. Many northern Democrats—including Dallas—who voted for the Walker tariff had to subordinate the interests of their constituents to the demands of party loyalty. Largely to assuage these groups, Congress adopted a pork-barrel bill that provided for federal expenditures on river and harbor improvements in those parts of the North where Democratic opposition to the tariff of 1846 was strongest. But Polk vetoed the bill, and northern Democrats were more convinced

James K. Polk

[LIBRARY OF CONGRESS]

than ever that the South controlled the executive branch of the government.

By 1846, the northern Democrats were in open revolt. The center of the rebellion was Pennsylvania, a Democratic stronghold and the most protectionist state in the Union. The controversial Wilmot Proviso was introduced by a congressman from that state who was both a free soiler and worried about what issues would most affect his political future. In August, 1846, when the war with Mexico was only a few months old, President Polk asked Congress for an appropriation of $2,000,000 to be used to negotiate for peace. When the bill was on its way through Congress, David Wilmot, as spokesman for the disgruntled northern Democrats, moved the following amendment:

> Provided, that as an express and fundamental condition to the acquisition of any territory from the Republic of Mexico by the United States, by virtue of any treaty which may be negotiated between them, and to the use by the Executive of the moneys . . . appropriated, neither slavery nor involuntary ser-

vitude shall ever exist in any part of said territory except for crime, whereof the part shall first be duly convicted.

The language of the Proviso was unmistakable: slavery was to be for-ever excluded from any territories acquired from Mexico. When Wil-mot, running for re-election, won seemingly on the basis of the popularity of his Proviso, politicians everywhere took warning.

The effect of the Proviso upon the country was not unlike that of the Tallmadge Amendment almost thirty years before. In the North, hundreds of Wilmot Proviso Leagues were formed; in the South, mass meetings and conventions denounced the proposal. Resolutions of ten free states endorsing the measure were met with condemnatory resolu-tions from slave states. Radicals in North and South used it as a theme for preaching disunion. A contemporary, writing for the *Nineteenth Century*, declared that the measure had aroused "more noise in the land than any other since the bank question. It has been discussed in Congress, in the newspapers, on the stump, at the street corners, all over the whole country . . ." Although accepted by the House, the Proviso was twice defeated by the Senate; its rejection, however, by no means settled the question of slavery extension.

Compromise in 1850

In the election of 1848, both the major parties did their best to obscure the issues that had been raised by the Wilmot Proviso. Al-though Polk had tried to please all groups in his party and had tried to settle all outstanding issues, he left office with his party badly split and northern and southern Democrats even more suspicious of each other. The Democrats nominated a northerner who argued that the slavery question should be ignored, and the Whigs, who had con-sistently opposed Polk's policies, selected a southern slaveowner who had no discernible opinions on any public question. The Democrats made Lewis Cass of Michigan their candidate, because they thought that his location would appeal to the dissatisfied Westerners in the party and because he had proposed a policy—"squatter sovereignty"—that would take the problem of the expansion of slavery out of Congress (where it had split the Democratic party) and leave it to the decision of the voters in each of the territories. The Whigs made Zachary Taylor of Louisiana their standard bearer because he stood for nothing in the minds of the voters except the glories of Mexican War victories. One Whig politician, in explaining his party's choice, said: "We must mix up a little humbugging with our glorious Whig creed, before we can expect a victory, and General Taylor's *military fame* is about the best we can make use of at present."

With both major parties skirting the slavery issue, the Free Soil party held its first convention in 1848 and nominated Martin Van Buren for the presidency. The Free Soil party, like most third parties, was a catchall for idealists and disgruntled regular party politicians. It was made up of abolitionists, members of the anti-Administration, or Barnburner, faction of the Democratic party in New York, Liberty party men, and those Whigs who because of their refusal to abide by their party's decision to repudiate the Wilmot Proviso were known as "Conscience Whigs." Despite the presence of some abolitionists among the Free Soilers, the party's principal objective was not the end of slavery, but the prevention of slave expansion into the territories. The party's motto was "Free Soil, Free Speech, Free Labor and Free Men," and its platform, reflecting the various interests temporarily roosting in the new party, called for river and harbor improvements, free land for settlers on the public domain, and a protective tariff. Twelve years later, the Republicans were to elect Abraham Lincoln on much the same platform.

Although the Free Soilers did not carry a single state, the 291,263 votes polled by Van Buren were probably decisive in determining the outcome of the election. By drawing votes from Cass in several key northern states, the Free Soilers undoubtedly made possible Taylor's victory. The new party also elected thirteen of its members to the House of Representatives. If nothing else, the election of 1848 demonstrated that the Democrats and Whigs could not indefinitely ignore the slavery issue, since its vote getting potentialities had now been demonstrated in closely balanced key states.

The outcome of the Mexican War was responsible for reviving sectional conflict. Congress could not put off making a decision on the status of slavery in the territories granted the United States under the terms of the Treaty of Guadalupe Hidalgo. Key leaders in the North were increasingly convinced that only free soil could solve this problem, whereas southern intransigeants were equally certain that their section's future required the government's protection of slavery in the new possessions. Although neither of the sections was united, the more strident voices made more of an impression than their numbers warranted. "In the presence of the living God," Robert Toombs said, "if by your legislation you seek to drive us from the territories of California and New Mexico, I am for disunion." South Carolina declared that the day had come for the southern states to join "in resisting the application of the Wilmot Proviso at any and all hazards." The Virginia legislature asserted that the adoption and attempted enforcement of the measure would force the people of the state to accept one of two courses: either "abject submission to aggression and outrage" or "determined resistance at all hazards and to the last extremity." Seventy southern members of Congress drafted an address to their constituents in 1849 in which they assailed the antislavery forces and urged the South to unite. In the North every free-state legislature, except that of Iowa, passed resolutions declaring that Congress had power to prohibit and should prohibit slavery in the territories; several states wanted slavery abolished in the District of Columbia, and many enacted legislation compelling state officials to protect runaway slaves, or at least forbidding them to give aid to slaves' pursuers.

As sectional lines tightened and threats of secession became more numerous, the break-up of the Union seemed imminent. It was clear that if a national catastrophe was to be averted, some satisfactory solution to the question of slavery in the new Southwest must be quickly found. Among the various suggestions made, in addition to the Wilmot Proviso, were proposals for the extension of the Missouri Compromise line to the Pacific; admission of slavery to the territories on the ground that it could not be legally prohibited; and application of the principle of "squatter sovereignty" or "popular sovereignty," as it was afterward renamed by Stephen A. Douglas. This doctrine rested on the assumption that it was the right of the settlers in any territory to decide the fate of slavery or any other institution within their borders not forbidden by the federal Constitution.

Since no one of these solutions was acceptable to everyone, the Union was in jeopardy, but neither the North nor the South was united enough to permit its more militant defenders free play. The elder statesman Henry Clay came forward with his famous compromise resolutions. California, whose population had made a phenomenal increase because of the gold rush, was to be admitted as a free state; the slave trade, but not slavery, was to be abolished in the District of Columbia; Congress was to enact a more effective fugitive slave law; Texas was to relinquish its claim to disputed New Mexican territory in return for which the federal government would assume the Texas debt contracted before annexation; Congress was to have no power to interfere with the slave trade between slave states; and the territories of Utah and New Mexico were to be created with the provision that either, or any part of either, might be admitted to the Union "with or without slavery as their constitution may provide at the time of their admission." In short, the doctrine of popular sovereignty rather than the Wilmot Proviso was to apply to the remaining territories of the Mexican cession

Washington in the 1850's

[NEW YORK PUBLIC LIBRARY]

at the time their citizens sought statehood. Clay, an old man of seventy-three, made a passionate plea for sectional conciliation. "At this moment," he said, "we have in the legislative bodies of this capital and in the states twenty odd furnaces in full blast, emitting heat and passion and intemperance and diffusing them throughout the whole extent of this broad land." It was a time, he declared, for mutual sacrifice and for both sections to support his compromise scheme in order to restore concord, harmony, and peace."

The enfeebled Calhoun, eager to protect the voting power of the planting South, opposed Clay's plan as being both unconstitutional and ineffectual. The North, he asserted, was responsible for the present crisis, for it had upset the equilibrium of the sections by excluding slavery from about three fourths of the territory added to the original states. It had driven the South toward secession by enacting protective tariffs and other measures favorable to the northern businessman and detrimental to the southern planters. The Union could be saved, not by compromises, but by granting the South its full measure of justice; equal rights in acquired territories, return of fugitive slaves, suppression of all antislavery propaganda, and the restoration of political equilibrium between the two sections by constitutional amendment.

Webster stood with Clay in defense of the resolutions. In answer to Calhoun's charge of northern aggression, he pointed out that the South had dominated the politics of the country for three fourths of its national history. On the other hand, he condemned the Wilmot Proviso; geography and climate, he said, had settled "beyond all terms

Constitutionalist

Clay - Webster - Unionists

no legal precedent for secession

of human enactment" that slavery could not exist in New Mexico or California. "I would not (try) . . . to reaffirm an ordinance of nature, nor to re-enact the will of God. And I would put in no Wilmot Proviso for the (sake) . . . of a taunt or a reproach." To the dismay of the antislavery faction, he denounced the abolitionists and declared that the South was right in its charge that the North had failed to respect the laws regarding the return of fugitive slaves. Like Clay, he believed that secession could never be accomplished peacefully, and that if it were accomplished, it would not solve the problems that were then distracting the country. His entire speech was a fervent appeal for tolerance between the sections, for the upholding of the Constitution, and, above all, for the perpetuation of the Union. Webster's stand was denounced by the great majority of the antislavery voters; some openly accused him of sacrificing his conscience and truckling to the slave interests to win the presidency. James Russell Lowell referred to his "mean and foolish treachery." "He is a man," said Emerson, "who lives by his memory; a man of the past, not a man of faith and hope. His finely developed understanding only works truly and with all its force when it stands for animal good; that is, for property." Horace Mann characterized him as "a fallen star! Lucifer descending from heaven!" Theodore Parker said that he knew of "No deed in American history done by a son of New England to which I can compare this but the act of Benedict Arnold. The only reasonable way in which we can estimate this speech is as a bid for the presidency." And John Greenleaf Whittier undoubtedly expressed the thoughts of thousands in his *Ichabod*:

> Let not the land once proud of him
> Insult him now,
> Nor brand with deeper shame his dim,
> Dishonored brow.

But those who denounced Webster's action apparently failed to comprehend that the adoption of Clay's resolutions would cut the ground from under the feet of the southern extremists, strengthen the hand of southern moderates, and postpone secession perhaps long enough to enable the North to outstrip the South more completely in man power and material resources. In justice to Webster, it should be noted that his "treachery" existed only in the minds of the abolitionists. Webster, who had never been an abolitionist, could hardly be accused of treachery to them.

William Seward of New York and Salmon P. Chase of Ohio were principal spokesmen for northern Free Soil forces. Both denied that the

Constitution recognized chattel slavery and demanded that it be excluded from the territories. Seward, voicing his opposition to all legislative compromises because he thought they were "radically wrong and essentially vicious," asserted that there was "a higher law than the Constitution," which forbade slavery. These prophetic words soon became the slogan for all opponents of slavery. If the "higher law" was to prevail, then the South should be compelled, by force if necessary, to agree to it.

On April 18, 1850, after weeks of debate, Clay's original measures were, in effect, voted down by being referred to a Senate committee of thirteen, of which Clay was chairman. Senator Stephen A. Douglas of Illinois did the lion's work in reformulating the proposals and on May 8, the committee reported the resolutions in the form of five bills. Around these a tempest raged for weeks; finally they were passed as separate measures by both houses but only a handful of Senators voted for all the bills. Meanwhile, Taylor had died in July, 1850, and had been succeeded by Vice-President Millard Fillmore of New York. Fillmore, who at one time had been considered a representative of the antislavery forces, had emerged from the crisis of 1850 a strong Union man, and in September of that year he signed all the measures that had been adopted by Congress.

All but the extremists approved what came to be called the Compromise of 1850. "The Closing of the Drama," "The Country Saved," "Most Glorious News from Washington," were typical newspaper headlines announcing the passage of the acts. Businessmen, who believed that the agitation had upset normal conditions, welcomed the settlement as an omen of "better times." Enthusiastic meetings endorsing the Compromise and sponsored by tradespeople were held in Boston, New York, Philadelphia, and other northern centers. The majority of the southern planters who had not favored disunion acquiesced, but southern political leaders felt that they had been defeated. The advance in cotton prices and the general upward trend of business in the early 1850's momentarily helped southerners to forget their economic grievances against the North. Most politicians, anxious to be rid of a troublesome problem that was already disrupting party ranks, gave it their unqualified support, and within a year or so the Acts of 1850 achieved their reputation as brilliant compromises.

The respite proved short-lived. New causes of friction indicated that neither the problem of slavery nor sectional rivalry had been finally disposed of. An immediate source of controversy was the Fugitive Slave Act. Designed in the interests of the planter, this law vested the federal government with almost unlimited powers for the appre-

CAUTION!!

COLORED PEOPLE
OF BOSTON, ONE & ALL,

You are hereby respectfully CAUTIONED and advised, to avoid conversing with the

Watchmen and Police Officers of Boston,

For since the recent ORDER OF THE MAYOR & ALDERMEN, they are empowered to act as

KIDNAPPERS
AND
Slave Catchers,

And they have already been actually employed in KIDNAPPING, CATCHING, AND KEEPING SLAVES. Therefore, if you value your LIBERTY, and the *Welfare of the Fugitives* among you, *Shun* them in every possible manner, as so many *HOUNDS* on the track of the most unfortunate of your race.

Keep a Sharp Look Out for KIDNAPPERS, and have TOP EYE open.

APRIL 24, 1851.

After the Fugitive Slave Act

hension and return of runaway slaves. The alleged fugitive was denied trial by jury, could not summon witnesses or testify in his own behalf, and was liable to capture even though he might have escaped years before the statute was enacted. Any federal official, moreover, charged with the apprehension and return of fugitive slaves might, if he feared a rescue, summon the aid of any person. Heavy penalties were to be inflicted on any official who failed to perform his duty and on those who harbored or aided in the escape of a fugitive. Under this law, "slave-catching" and "man-hunting" were brought close to every northerner, and hundreds of thousands of people who had formerly been moderates, or at least indifferent to the slave question, now became hostile to the whole system of slavery. On the other hand, the violations of the law embittered many southerners and strengthened the appeal of those who had threatened that failure to enforce it would mean disruption of the Union. The response of both sections to the Fugitive Slave Act revealed that the Compromise of 1850 had dealt with the surface, not the roots, of the issues that were threatening to disrupt the Union.

FOR SUPPLEMENTARY READING

Start with C. S. Sydnor, *The Development of Southern Sectionalism 1819–1848* (1948), and follow with A. O. Craven, *The Growth of Southern Nationalism 1848–1861* (1953). On Southern society, read A. M. Schlesinger, Sr.'s edition of F. L. Olmsted, *The Cotton Kingdom* (1953); U. B. Phillips, *Life and Labor in the Old South* (1929); K. M. Stampp, *The Peculiar Institution* (1956); F. L. Owsley, *Plain Folk of the Old South* (1949); R. Shugg, *Origins of Class Struggle in Louisiana 1840–1875* (1939); W. J. Cash, *The Mind of the South* (1941) (Pb); W. R. Taylor, *The Old South and the American National Character* (1961); R. C. Wade, *Slavery in the Cities: The South 1820–1860* (1964); and C. G. Sellers (ed.), *The Southerner as American* (1960).

How northerners set themselves off from the South can be studied in H. R. Floan, *The South in Northern Eyes 1831–1861* (1958), and A. C. Cole, *The Irrepressible Conflict 1850–1865* (1934). See R. N. Current, *Daniel Webster and the Rise of National Conservatism* (1955), for the changing northern conception of the Union, as well as P. Nagel, *One Nation Indivisible . . . 1776–1861* (1964). The southern response is studied in C. Eaton, *The Mind of the Old South* (1964).

On the politics of the early 1850's, use A. Nevins, *The Ordeal of the Union* (2 vols., 1947). On the crisis of 1850 itself, read H. Hamilton, *Prologue to Conflict* (1964); C. M. Wiltse, *John C. Calhoun, Sectionalist* (1951); and G. F. Milton, *The Eve of Conflict* (1934).

19

→»-→»-→»-→»-→»-→»-→»

Political Collapse
of the Union

IN THE EARLY 1850's, the North and the South were actually regions with great inner diversity, but the control of political life in each section was in the hands of a small group of politicians who seemed to speak for or to represent "The South" or "The North." These were the men who made the fateful choices leading to civil war.

The March of the Free Soil Men

The election of 1852 was the last presidential contest before the Civil War in which politicians in both major parties sought to avoid rather than face the issues that were splitting the nation into two hostile sections. The Whigs, who hoped that once again they would be able to win with a military figure, nominated General Winfield Scott. The Democrats, who had suffered most from the events of the preceding decade, were confronted by the difficult task of selecting a candidate who would be acceptable to all factions—Southerners, Unionists, and Free Soilers. Some old-line Democrats thought that Cass should be given another chance; the southerners favored James Buchanan of Pennsylvania; the western wing of the party wanted Senator Stephen A. Douglas of Illinois; the New Englanders backed Supreme Court Justice Levi Woodbury. Woodbury died, however, before the convention met, and the New Englanders shifted their allegiance to Franklin Pierce, a relatively unknown politician and lawyer from New Hampshire.

Pierce's anonymity was his greatest asset, but it still took forty-nine ballots to choose the Democratic candidate. The Free Soilers nominated John P. Hale of New Hampshire.

Because Pierce had not committed himself on any of the major issues of the day, he was acceptable to all the Democratic factions. Although the New York dissidents of 1848 returned to the party to support him, even the southerners felt that he was safe on the slavery issue. Scott, on the other hand, proved an inept candidate. Although he came from Virginia, many southerners thought that he was allied with the Conscience Whigs of the North. In addition, despite the fact that his military career was more illustrious than that of either Harrison or Taylor, he never captured the imagination of the voters. The result was that a variety of local issues were pre-eminent, and Pierce swept the election. With 254 electoral votes to 42 for his opponent, he carried every state but Massachusetts, Vermont, Kentucky, and Tennessee.

With the election of 1852 behind them, the Democratic politicians looked forward to four years of peace and harmony. They had defeated the Whigs by ignoring the issues, and they now planned to enjoy the fruits of their victory by avoiding any questions that threatened the status quo. But the issues would not remain dormant, and within a short time proposals for a transcontinental railroad revived the conflict between North and South over the expansion of slavery in the territories.

Soon after Pierce had taken office, Secretary of War Jefferson Davis announced his plan for a transcontinental railroad that would follow an all-southern route and have its eastern terminus in Memphis, Tennessee. This proposal, unacceptable to the northerners, was countered by another railroad project, advanced by Senator Stephen A. Douglas of Illinois. A dynamic individual with his eye on the White House, Douglas was closely associated with powerful railroad and real estate interests in Chicago. The railroad suggested by Douglas was to extend from Chicago through Nebraska and Wyoming to the Pacific coast. Although this route went through territory that contained few inhabitants and some of the highest mountains in the United States, Douglas selected it in the hope that it was central enough to be acceptable to both the North and the South.

Before a railroad could be constructed, the territories through which it would pass had to be organized by the federal government. Douglas, chairman of the Senate Committee on Territories, wanted to settle the issue of slavery in the territories and to make a bid for the Democratic Candidacy in 1856. He drew up a bill that called for the formation of two territories—Kansas and Nebraska. In an effort to

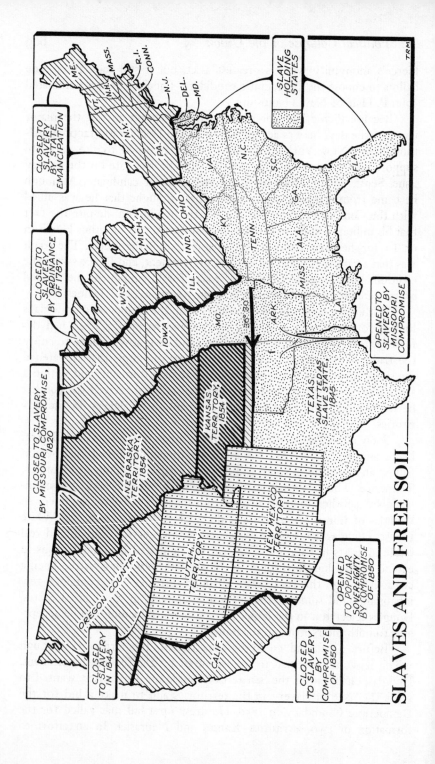

SLAVES AND FREE SOIL

SLAVE HOLDING STATES

CLOSED TO SLAVERY BY STATE EMANCIPATION

CLOSED TO SLAVERY BY ORDINANCE OF 1787

CLOSED TO SLAVERY BY MISSOURI COMPROMISE, 1820

OPENED TO SLAVERY BY MISSOURI COMPROMISE

CLOSED TO SLAVERY IN 1848

OPENED TO POPULAR SOVEREIGNTY BY COMPROMISE OF 1850

CLOSED TO SLAVERY BY COMPROMISE OF 1850

ME.
VT.
N.H.
MASS.
R.I.
CONN.
N.J.
DEL.
MD.
N.Y.
PA.
OHIO
MICH.
IND.
ILL.
WIS.
IOWA
MO.
VA.
N.C.
S.C.
GA.
FLA.
KY.
TENN.
ALA.
MISS.
ARK.
LA.

36°30'

TEXAS ADMITTED AS SLAVE STATE, 1845

KANSAS TERRITORY, 1854

NEBRASKA TERRITORY, 1854

NEW MEXICO TERRITORY

UTAH TERRITORY

OREGON COUNTRY

CALIF.

TRM

avoid the slavery issue, Douglas incorporated in the act a provision stating that the question of slavery would be left to the inhabitants of each of the territories—a provision that in effect repealed the Missouri Compromise, for states north or south of the 36° 30' line would no longer be automatically free or slave. Douglas's measure, however, could not be adopted without the support of southern congressmen, who refused to vote for it unless it specifically repealed the Missouri Compromise. Popular sovereignty was not enough. Douglas agreed to their demand, and when the Kansas-Nebraska Act was adopted in 1854, it contained provisions for both popular sovereignty and the repeal of the Missouri Compromise.

The sections in the Kansas-Nebraska Act dealing with slavery provided northern antislavery politicians with a clear-cut issue on which they could attack both the administration and Douglas. The first man to take advantage of this situation was Salmon P. Chase, a Democratic senator from Ohio, whose "Appeal of the Independent Democrats in Congress to the People of the United States" offered northerners a platform on which they could unite to oppose the alleged southern plans for the expansion of slavery. This statement, which was signed by several antislavery men in various parties in Congress, was printed in nearly every free-state newspaper and was widely circulated in pamphlet form. Declaring that the Kansas-Nebraska Act "menaced the freedom of our institutions" and "the permanency of our union," it warned that the bill would transform all the western territories into "a dreary region of despotism, inhabited by masters and slaves." It stated that the bill was "an atrocious plot to exclude from a vast unoccupied region immigrants from the Old World and free laborers from" the East. Regardless of the truth of these charges—and historians have been unable to agree on this point—there can be no doubt that the "Appeal" accurately reflected the widespread dissatisfaction in the North over the seeming southern control of the government.

Other northerners were alarmed by the administration's program of expansion. In his inaugural address, Pierce had practically announced that he was an apostle of manifest destiny and that he desired to carry out the expansionist program inaugurated by Polk. One of his first acts was to send James Gadsden to Mexico to purchase a strip of land adjacent to the United States so that an American railway line might be built along the Gila River to the coast. At the time, the *New York Herald* asserted that Gadsden had been secretly instructed to acquire the Mexican states of Chihuahua, Sonora, and Lower California.

Next, on the advice of his Secretary of State, William L. Marcy, Pierce in 1854 instructed Pierre Soulé, a Louisiana expansionist who

ORGANIZING KANSAS AND NEBRASKA

NEBRASKA TERRITORY 1854

KANSAS TERRITORY 1854

UTAH TERRITORY 1850

MINNESOTA TERRITORY 1849

WISCONSIN 1848

IOWA 1846

ILLINOIS

MISSOURI 1821

NEW MEXICO TERR. 1850

TEXAS

INDIAN TERRITORY

ARKANSAS

MISSOURI COMPROMISE LINE OF 1820 36° 30'

had been sent to Spain the previous year, to purchase Cuba, which between 1848 and 1854 had been invaded by several filibustering expeditions supported by prominent southerners. The Spanish government, however, refused to sell, and Soulé finally withdrew to Belgium, where he was joined by James Buchanan and John Y. Mason, American ministers to Great Britain and France respectively. The three then drafted the Ostend Manifesto. After declaring that geographically Cuba was a part of the United States, this startling statement recommended that if Spain refused to sell, the United States should "by every law, human and divine" seize Cuba by force. Although Marcy repudiated the sentiments expressed in the Manifesto, the mere knowledge that such a recommendation had been made excited the antislavery factions.

The events of the first two years of Pierce's administration marked an important turning point in the sectional controversy that preceded the outbreak of the Civil War. An increasing number of northerners had come to view the South as an obstacle to national progress. In both sections, the central question was not slavery itself, but its expansion to the West. In the North, fear of slave expansion was largely responsible for the formation of the Republican party. This party, which originated in the Old Northwest in the aftermath of the Kansas-Nebraska Act, was a manifestation of both the moral fervor and the economic and political discontent that pervaded that area. These feelings were made articulate by many local politicians whose crusading zeal and sense of righteous indignation sent people flocking to meetings throughout the Old Northwest to protest the Kansas-Nebraska Act. These rallies were attended by many disaffected Whigs and Democrats. Although those who gathered at such places as Ripon, Wisconsin, and Jackson, Michigan, referred to themselves as Republicans, most of them did not realize that they were participating in the formation of a new party. The product of a popular upheaval and of assorted political discontents, the Republican party was a disaffected politicians' party, a reform party, and a party whose main plank was opposition to the extension of slavery.

Despite the power of Chase's appeal to free soil sentiment in causing the formation of the Republican party, the nation's political party lines had already been disturbed before Chase's call by the rise of nativist political groups after 1852. In some parts of the country the Republican party was brought into existence as a counterweight to the successful inroads of nativism on regular party ranks. By 1854, the Know-Nothings * had demonstrated their prowess as vote-getters in the South as well as the North. Scott's overwhelming defeat in 1852 had made many politicians, particularly the defeated Whigs, in both sections turn to the American party. Southerners, realizing that cutting off the flow of immigrants to the North would help maintain the South's political strength and happy for a party that was not Democrat and not Whig, were understandably attracted to the American party. The view of nativist Southerners was succinctly expressed by one planter who said: "The mistake with us has been that it was not made a felony to bring in an Irishman when it was made piracy to bring in an African." In the North, the nativists were able to capitalize on both the fears and the prejudices of American-born Protestant workers and farmers. In 1854, the Know-Nothings swept the Massachusetts election and joined with the Whigs to win control of Pennsylvania's government; and they held the balance of power in the new House of Representatives. In Ohio, they provided nine out of the ten nominees on the Republican slate in the election of 1855.

The political situation was still further confused by the presence of two other parties. There were the Prohibitionists, who had exhibited unexpected strength in a number of state elections. Maine, under the leadership of Neal Dow, had adopted state-wide prohibition in 1851, and in the next two years Rhode Island, Michigan, Vermont, and Wis-

* See Chapter 16, p. 512.

Ripon, Wisconsin. "We went in . . . Whigs, Free Soilers, and Democrats. We came out of it Republicans."

consin followed suit. Although the Prohibitionists never formed a national political party, they played an influential role in shattering traditional political allegiances in many states, and their endorsement was often sought by the candidates of the other parties. In the years before 1854, therefore, traditional party allegiances had been broken by many splinter groups.

In the midterm elections of 1854 there were as many as five separate tickets in some states. When the final returns were in, it was found that the Democrats had lost, but no one could be sure who had beaten them. Although the opposition groups appeared to outnumber the Democrats, they could accomplish little until they could agree on a positive program with which to oppose the administration. This problem, however, was soon solved by developments in the newly organized territories, and within two years "bleeding Kansas" and "free soil" had helped sweep the various factions together and make the Republicans the second largest political party in the nation.

The Fight for the Territories

Kansas and Nebraska were opened up for settlement in 1854. Some people from Missouri had already moved into Kansas, and many more followed after the territory was formally organized. The Missourians brought few slaves with them, but practically all of them favored the extension of slavery in the territories. They were not to have Kansas to themselves, however, for the region also proved very attractive to men who were descendants of New Englanders, and who were determined that Kansas would be a land neither of slaves nor of plantations. A small direct New England emigration was aided by the New England Emigrant Aid Company, founded by Eli Thayer of Worcester, Massachusetts, to assist antislavery men who wished to settle in Kansas.

Within a few months, the Missourians had established the towns of Atchison and Leavenworth along the Missouri River, and the Free Soilers had set up communities at Topeka and Lawrence farther to the west. It was not long before the two groups were fighting a miniature and sporadic civil war over conflicting land claims which locally had little to do with the slavery issue. The Missourians banded together in "Protective Associations"; the free groups were armed with Sharps rifles, or "Beecher's Bibles," as they were called after Henry Ward Beecher had said that they could be a "greater moral agency" in Kansas than the Bible.

Meanwhile Andrew H. Reeder, an antislavery Pennsylvania Democrat, had been appointed Governor of Kansas by Pierce. He reached the territory in 1854 and immediately began buying up large blocs of land in the hope of making a speculative profit. In November, a proslavery territorial delegate was elected to Congress with the help of 1,600 inhabitants from Missouri who crossed the border into Kansas on election day. The following March, a similar influx of Missourians resulted in the selection of a proslavery legislature. When the legislature met at Pawnee, the site of one of Reeder's more prominent speculative ventures, it refused to seat the antislavery members, passed a bill over the Governor's veto to move the capital to Shawnee Mission, adopted a slave code similar to that of Missouri and petitioned Pierce to remove the governor. When Reeder, who made no attempt to conceal his antislavery views, refused to resign, the President accepted the legislature's advice and dismissed him. Meanwhile the free-state groups refused to recognize the territorial legislature, drew up their own constitution, and established an antislavery government.

When other expedients failed, the inhabitants of Missouri and Kansas used violence to achieve their objectives. On May 21, 1856, a band of "border ruffians" from Missouri sacked the free-state capital at Lawrence, burned many of the town's buildings, and destroyed all its newspaper offices. At this point John Brown, a fanatical—and perhaps, insane—abolitionist, who was also involved in Kansas land strug-

The Massacre at Lawrence, Kansas

gles decided that it was his duty to punish the friends of the South for the "sack of Lawrence." On May 24, Brown and six followers murdered five proslavery men in the so-called Pottawatomie Massacre. In all, 200 people—one of whom was a son of Brown—lost their lives in "bleeding Kansas," and more than $2,000,000 worth of property was destroyed in the course of the conflict. Yet, by 1860, after years of such bloodshed, the census revealed that there were only two slaves in Kansas. Clearly, the issue was not slavery, but rather the question of whether the disputed area would, after admission to Congress, be friendly to the interests of the North or South.

While free and slave-state groups struggled in Kansas for control of the territory, representatives of the North and South debated the issue in Congress. On May 19, 1856, Senator Charles Sumner of Massachusetts, an outspoken abolitionist and leading Republican, stated the radical northern view in a long and savage philippic that he entitled "The Crime against Kansas." After accusing the South of "the rape of a virgin Territory, compelling it to the hateful embrace of slavery," Sumner launched into a bitter and very personal attack on Senator Andrew P. Butler of South Carolina. Three days later—and two days before the Pottawatomie Massacre—Preston Brooks, who was Butler's nephew and a member of the House from South Carolina, attacked Sumner while he was at his desk in the Senate and beat him with a cane until he was unconscious. Sumner, who retired from the Senate for three years, became a martyr throughout the free states. In the South, Brooks was hailed as a hero by leading "fire-eaters."

The struggle in Kansas more than any other event was responsible for making the Republicans the leading opposition party out of the many political groups that had bid for power in the early 1850's. Republican leaders throughout the North made countless speeches denouncing southern tactics in Kansas, and Republican papers such as the Chicago *Tribune* gave their readers detailed—and often biased—accounts of events in the territory. Kansas had become the battleground of the sections, and the Republicans made full use of Kansas as an example of the results of the southern determination to extend slavery to the territories.

When the Republicans gathered at Philadelphia in 1856 for their first national nominating convention, the party had assumed the character it was to retain until the Civil War. Consisting of ex-Democrats as well as ex-Whigs, Germans as well as nativists, workers as well as farmers, and abolitionists as well as Free Soilers, its only unifying principle was the determination of its members to prevent the extension of slavery to the territories. It was a party that appealed economically to small producers. Ideologically, it was a reforming—or even crusading—party. And geographically, it was a party that found its greatest strength in the New England zone of settlement that stretched from Vermont and Massachusetts across upstate New York to the upper Northwest bordering on the Great Lakes.

The Republicans' candidate in 1856 was John C. Fremont, whose outstanding asset was his "availability." Known to Americans as an explorer and soldier, he was a colorful figure who had done nothing to antagonize any of the factions that made up the Republican party. As a famous man and a political nonentity, he was an ideal candidate for a new party that was made up of many diverse groups. To oppose Fremont, the Democrats passed up Pierce and Douglas because of their close identification with the unhappy events of the preceding four years and gave the nomination to James Buchanan of Pennsylvania. The remnants of the Know-Nothing party, which had given way to the greater appeal of the free soil issue, made ex-President Fillmore their candidate. During the campaign, Buchanan, whose service as minister to England had kept him out of most of the sectional controversies of the Pierce administration, was put forward by the Democrats as a safe and sane statesman who would refrain from any rash acts that might split the Union. The Republicans, in contrast, campaigned as a strictly sectional party; their slogan was "Free Soil, Free Speech and

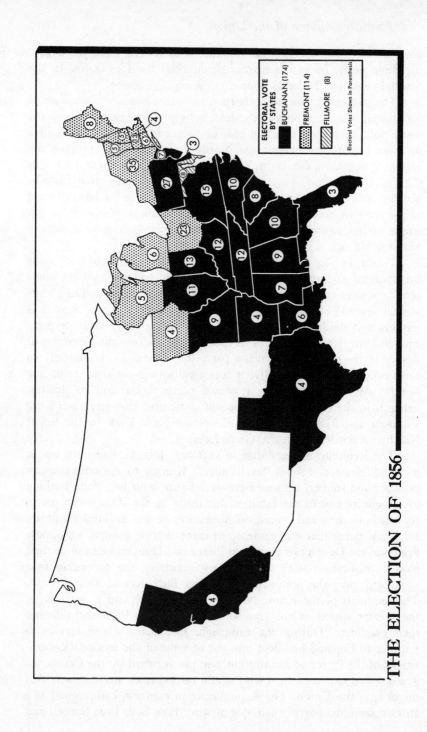

ELECTORAL VOTE BY STATES

BUCHANAN (174)
FREMONT (114)
FILLMORE (8)

Electoral Votes Shown in Parenthesis

THE ELECTION OF 1856

Fremont" and their principal issue, "Bleeding Kansas." The outcome of the election seemed to indicate that a majority of the voters still put the preservation of the Union before all other considerations, for Buchanan received 174 electoral votes to 114 for Fremont and 8 (from Maryland) for Fillmore. On the other hand, Fremont had carried all but five northern states, and if he had won in Pennsylvania and Illinois, the Republicans would have triumphed.

The Fight Thickens

When Buchanan became President in 1857, his backers believed that, as a northerner who wished to save the Union at all costs and who had serious doubts about the constitutionality of interference with slavery, he would be able to hold the Union together by playing down any issues that threatened to split the sections. But events had reached the stage at which they could no longer be controlled by Buchanan. Any action he took would be judged friendly to one section or the other. Leading southerners insisted on the extension of slavery to the territories; the most vociferous northerners were equally determined that slavery should be barred from the territories; and both sides were increasingly convinced that further compromise would soon be out of the question. As a result, Buchanan, instead of narrowing the chasm that separated North and South, was not even able to hold his own party together.

Two days after Buchanan's inauguration on March 4, 1857, the Supreme Court entered the slavery controversy with its decision in the case of *Dred Scott vs. Sandford*. Scott, a slave held by Dr. John Emerson, an army surgeon, had been taken by his master first into the free state of Illinois and then into the northern part of the Louisiana Purchase where slavery was forbidden by the Missouri Compromise. In 1838, both master and slave returned to Missouri. After Emerson's death in 1843, Scott brought suit in a Missouri court for his liberty on the ground that his residence in free territory had automatically made him a free man. In the trial court, Scott won, but the state's supreme court, to which the question was carried, ruled against him. Meanwhile, Mrs. Emerson became the wife of Dr. C. C. Chaffee of Springfield, Massachusetts, a Know-Nothing and an abolitionist. To allow Scott to bring the case into the United States District Court, the Chaffees sold him, his wife, and children to Mrs. Chaffee's brother. J. F. A. Sanford of New York. In this court Scott won. After a long period of litigation the case finally came before the federal Supreme Court. The first question that the Court had to decide was whether or not Scott was a citizen. If not, the case would presumably be dismissed for want of jurisdiction, and the Court would not be called upon to pass on the more important question of his freedom. The majority opinion, handed down by Chief Justice Roger B. Taney, declared that since no state had had Negro citizens at the time the Constitution was adopted, that document was intended to apply only to white men. Scott was, therefore, not a citizen and could not bring suit in the federal courts. Here the case would have ended, but Taney and his associates, hoping that an *obiter dictum* backed by the courts would materially assist in putting an end to the slavery controversy, went on to argue that Congress had no authority to deprive any person of his property, in whatever form, within the domains of the United States. Congress, consequently, had no power to prohibit slavery in the territories, and the Missouri Compromise had from the day of its enactment been null and void. Justice Curtis of Massachusetts, who with Justice McLean of Ohio dissented from the majority opinion, argued that Negroes had been citizens in 1787 and since; he denied Taney's contention that Congress had no right to prohibit slavery in the territories; and he asserted that the Missouri Compromise had been constitutional until repealed in 1854, and the Scott's residence on free soil had made him free.

Instead of settling the slavery problem, the decision merely increased sectional hostility. The South was jubilant, for the nation's highest court had recorded its opinion that Congress had no power to prohibit slavery in the territories. Such action by Congress would now require constitutional amendment, for which the necessary majorities were at the time unobtainable. Slavery was now a domestic institution that, under the Constitution, the federal government was bound to protect, and could neither prohibit or destroy. Antislavery leaders, on the other hand, stressing the fact that five of the nine judges came from slave states, declared that the decision was further proof that the slave interests were strengthening their hold on every branch of the federal government. For the newly organized Republican party, whose basic principle was the restriction of slavery extension in the territories, the decision was a challenge. "We know," said Abraham Lincoln, "the Court that made it has often overruled its own decisions, and we shall do what we can to have it overrule this." Horace Greeley, writing in the *New York Tribune Weekly*, declared that the decision was "entitled to just so much moral weight as would be the judgment of a majority of those congregated in any Washington bar-room."

The sectional animosity engendered by the Dred Scott decision was heightened by the effect of the Panic of 1857 on both the North and the South. Caused by overexpansion and unsound banking policies and resulting in widespread misery and hardship, the panic was used to illustrate the arguments of both disunionists and unionists. A free and independent South, fire-eaters argued, would forever put an end to the danger of panics for which this section was in no way responsible. The South was not injured as much by the financial crash as were the West and North. In the South, there had been less expansion and less speculation; and large crops and good prices in the years immediately following the panic enabled the section to recover rapidly. Many northern businessmen were convinced that only close future ties to the South would give them the markets that had helped pull them out of the depression of 1857. They favored appeasing the South. Other northerners attributed the severity of the depression to southern political tactics. They believed that only some form of federal aid to business and a homestead act could restore prosperity, but that this program was blocked by the efforts of southern congressmen. Some of the southern leaders interpreted the role of southern markets in the revival of northern business as a future weapon, to be used to force the North to accede to southern demands. The economic ties between North and South, it was pointed out, were too close to permit "fanatics" to split the union. The more zealous southerners, however, urged their states to recognize that "cotton was king" and that the South could do more for itself economically by declaring its independence than by remaining in the Union.

The split illustrated by the different responses within the two sections to the Panic of 1857 was still further widened by the government's tariff, land, and expansionist policies during Buchanan's administration. Despite the demands of northern protectionists for an increase in customs duties, Congress in 1857 lowered rather than raised the tariff in an act that reduced the rates for all dutiable schedules and greatly enlarged the free list. When Congress three years later, over the objections of the South, adopted a homestead act that provided for the disposal of the public domain to actual settlers at $.25 an acre, Buchanan vetoed the measure. If any further proof were needed of the charge that the Administration was prosouthern, it was furnished by Buchanan's expansionist plans and the wholehearted fashion in which they were endorsed by the inhabitants of the slave states. Southerners, who had closely watched the late filibustering expeditions against Nicaragua led by William Walker of Tennessee, approved the President's statement in 1858 that all Central America would become a part of the United States in the natural course of events. They also endorsed his program for the acquisition of a part of northwestern Mexico in return for $10,000,000 from which were to be deducted claims of citizens of the United States against Mexico. When Mexico rejected this office, Buchanan—again with southern approval—recommended that the United States assume a protectorate over northern Mexico; and in 1859, he asked Congress for authority to send an expeditionary force for the ostensible purpose of collecting debts and restoring order. Congress, however, was too much agitated by other issues raised by slavery to heed the President's request, and his proposals came to nothing.

Once again, as in Pierce's administration, Kansas both dramatized and intensified the issues dividing the North and South. In June, 1857, an election was held in Kansas to choose delegates to a convention for the purpose of drawing up a constitution to submit to Congress when the territory applied for statehood. Because the election was sponsored by the southern groups in Kansas, the free-state inhabitants refused to participate in it, and only proslavery delegates were chosen for the convention. In the following October, the delegates convened at Lecompton and drew up a constitution that protected slavery in Kansas. Instead of permitting the voters to pass on the entire document, the convention decided to submit only the slavery clause for ratification; because the constitution contained other provisions dealing with slavery, the result would make Kansas a slave state regardless of how its people voted. Once more the free groups refused to vote, and the Lecompton Constitution was overwhelmingly adopted. Meanwhile, in an election for a new territorial legislature, the free-state supporters won their first victory; for Robert J. Walker, the territorial Governor, disqualified the proslavery returns in two precincts in which the number of votes cast exceeded the number of inhabitants. The free-state majority in the new legislature voted to have the entire Lecompton Constitution submitted to the electorate. Only the free-state men participated in this election, and the constitution was almost unanimously rejected. A comparison of the two referendums on the Lecompton Constitution indicates that the free-state men easily outnumbered their opponents. In the first election, 6,226 votes were cast for the slavery clause; in the second, 10,226 votes were cast against the Lecompton Constitution.

Throughout the struggle in Kansas, Buchanan sided with the slave-state groups. In November, 1857, Walker resigned, and in February of the following year, Buchanan requested Congress to admit Kansas as a state under the Lecompton Constitution. In taking this stand, Buchanan openly defied Stephen A. Douglas, the most powerful northerner in the party and the administration's likely heir. Douglas had staked his whole political career on a popular sovereignty principle that was now being ignored by both the slave-state interests in Kansas and the President. Douglas thus had no alternative but to reject the Le-

Douglas, "The Little Giant"

compton Constitution and to insist that Congress pass an enabling act providing for an election under federal supervision. But Buchanan refused to change his position, and, in an interview with Douglas at the White House, he pointed out that he was still President and that the Illinois senator would have to abide by the administration's decision. When Buchanan appealed to history and mentioned that Jackson had known how to handle recalcitrant congressmen, Douglas is reported to have replied: "Mr. President, Andrew Jackson is dead."

Despite Douglas' break with the administration, Buchanan's plan for admitting Kansas as a slave state was approved by the Senate. But in the House it was blocked by a combination of Republicans and northern Democrats. At this point, however, the open rupture of the Democratic party was prevented—or at least postponed—by a compromise measure known as the English Bill (May 4, 1858). If the Kansans would accept the Lecompton Constitution as a whole, the state would get less land than the Lecomptonites asked for. If they rejected Lecompton, they would have to wait until they had a larger population before applying for statehood with a new constitution. On August 2, 1858, the inhabitants of Kansas rejected the Lecompton Constitution, in part due to the smaller land grant, by a vote of 11,300 to 1,788. As a result, Kansas stayed out of the Union until 1861.

The Emergence of Lincoln

Although the English Bill permitted the Democratic party to remain outwardly intact, it did not end the split between Douglas and the administration. Despite the South's opposition to popular sovereignty—southerners believed it a device that would make not only Kansas but all the territories free—Douglas would not retreat from his original stand, and he emphasized it repeatedly during his campaign for re-election to the Senate in 1858. To oppose Douglas, the Illinois Republicans selected Abraham Lincoln, a Springfield lawyer and one of the most prominent members of the party in the state. Born in Kentucky in 1809, Lincoln had lived as a boy in both Indiana and Illinois. When he was only twenty-three, he was a candidate for office, and during his campaign he displayed—according to Albert J. Beveridge—the "vagueness and dexterity . . . of the natural politician, a type which he was to become, excepting only Jefferson, the supreme example." Before he was thirty, Lincoln had become one of the leading members of the Whig delegation in the Illinois legislature. He was a good Whig, on friendly and highly profitable terms with Illinois business interests, and there is no evidence that he had publicly expressed any strong feelings about slavery in these years. During the Polk administration, Lincoln was elected to the House of Representatives; but when he joined the other Whigs in opposing the Mexican War, he was not returned to Washington for a second term by his bellicose constituents in Illinois. Although he served as a Republican elector in 1856 and was given some support for the party's vice-presidential nomination in the same year, he was still more of an ex-Whig than a Republican.

In his speech accepting the senatorial nomination of the Illinois Republicans in June, 1858, Lincoln outlined a program that was broad enough to appeal to all the northern Republicans. Arguing that "a house divided against itself cannot stand" and that "this government cannot endure, permanently half slave and half free," he asserted: "Either the opponents of slavery will arrest the further spread of it, and place it where the public mind shall rest in the belief that it is in the course of ultimate extinction; or its advocates will push it forward till it shall become alike lawful in all the States, old as well as new—North as well as South." After a recital of the events of the preceding three years, Lincoln declared that, if the South's hold on the government was not broken, it would be only a matter of time before there would be "another Supreme Court decision, declaring that the Constitution of the United States does not permit a State to exclude slavery from its limits." Therefore, he concluded, the voters of Illinois had a moral duty to defeat a man like Douglas, who, despite his opposition to the southern Democrats, was willing to countenance the spread of slavery if it was approved by the people in the territories.

In the famous Lincoln-Douglas debates, which highlighted the Illinois senatorial contest of 1858, Lincoln refused to be pinned down to any definite program of action by his Democratic opponent. At the same time, he was able to compel Douglas to make a number of admissions that set Douglas further apart from the southern wing of the Democratic party. Particularly damaging to Douglas was his stand on the Dred Scott decision. When Lincoln at the debate in Freeport asked if the people in a territory could exclude slavery, Douglas was placed in the position of having to repudiate either the Supreme Court ruling or his own version of popular sovereignty. In answering this question Douglas stated—in what came to be known as the "Freeport Doctrine" —that, regardless of how the Supreme Court decided the question, the people of a territory "have the lawful means to introduce it (slavery) or exclude it as they please, for the reason that slavery cannot exist a day . . . unless it is supported by local police regulations." To the militant southerners this answer seemed little better than heresy, while to many northerners it appeared to express the views of a man who was willing to subordinate moral considerations to political expediency.

Although the Republican vote in Illinois exceeded that of the Democrats, the legislature was controlled by the Democrats, and it selected Douglas as the state's Senator over Lincoln. In going down to defeat Lincoln gained a national reputation and demonstrated to his party the type of strategy that would produce a victory in 1860. Knowing that the North could outvote the South, he sought to avoid any issues that threatened the unity of the free states and to dissociate the Republican party from such extremists as the abolitionists. He stated that the country was menaced by a plot to extend slavery to the territories and even to the free states and maintained that every northerner had an obligation to support a party that was seeking to check the growth of slavery in the West and the power of the slavocracy in Washington. Slavery presented more than a moral problem, for Lincoln insisted that every free worker suffered from its presence. Lincoln thus shrewdly played to the white workers' fear of Negro competition. His conclusion was inevitable; if the existence of slavery was detrimental to all free men, then all free men must oppose its expansion. Here, in short, was a platform on which all the anti-Administration groups in the North could unite.

The Clouds Lower

The succession of dangerous events during Buchanan's administration came to a climax in John Brown's raid on Harper's Ferry, Virginia, in 1859. Disappointed with the Republican party because it refused to adopt an abolitionist program and obsessed with the idea that he had been divinely ordained to exterminate slavery, Brown resolved to stir up a slave insurrection and levy war against the slaveholding South. He succeeded in enlisting the interest and the support of prominent northern abolitionists, including Gerrit Smith, Theodore Parker, Thomas Wentworth Higginson, and George L. Stearns, who, with others, contributed $4,000 to the enterprise. With a band of twenty-one followers, three of whom were his own sons and five of whom were Negroes, he seized the government arsenal and rifle pits at Harper's Ferry on Sunday night, October 16, 1859. A few Negroes were set free, but the hoped-for insurrection did not materialize, and the following morning armed men from the surrounding countryside quickly hemmed in the invader. Late Monday evening, Colonel Robert E. Lee arrived with a small detachment of United States marines, and the next morning Brown and his surviving followers were captured; ten of his band had been killed and four had escaped. Brown was indicted for conspiracy, murder, and treason, found guilty, and publicly hanged on December 2, 1859.

Brown's small raid with its abrupt ending had profound consequences. Southerners charged the Republicans with responsibility for the deed. Even Stephen A. Douglas openly declared that it was his "firm and deliberate conviction that the Harper's Ferry crime was the natural, logical, inevitable result of the doctrines and teachings of the Republican party." Jefferson Davis characterized it as "the invasion of a State by a murderous gang of abolitionists bent on inciting slaves to murder helpless women and children." In the free states, Brown was hailed as a martyr. Instead of his lawlessness, antislavery people remembered his fortitude and his high purpose. On the day of his execution, funeral bells were tolled and memorial services were held throughout the North. Addressing a Boston audience, Ralph Waldo Emerson referred to Brown as "that new saint than whom none purer or more brave was ever led by love of men into conflict and death—the new saint awaiting his martyrdom, and who, if he shall suffer, will make the gallows glori-

John Brown

ous like the Cross." The divisive effects of John Brown's raid were also reflected in Congress. Members of both houses were too excited and too embittered to listen to reason. Altercations were an everyday occurrence on the floor of the House, where a long-drawn-out contest for the speakership followed; bitter personal attacks led to challenges and to duels, and the unchecked hisses and applause from the galleries added to the confusion. Many even feared bloodshed. "The members on both sides," wrote Senator Grimes of Iowa, "are mostly armed with deadly weapons, and it is said that the friends of each are armed in the galleries." This statement was corroborated by another senator, who declared that "every man in both Houses is armed with a revolver—some with two—and a bowie-knife."

While politicians in and out of Congress were wrangling over the slavery issue, propagandists in both North and South were adding still more fuel to the fires of sectional controversy. In the North, pulpit, press and platform seemed to compete with each other in condemning slavery and the South. Horace Greeley, owner and editor of the *New York Tribune*, denounced slavery and slaveholders in his columns. During the 1850's, the circulation of the *Tribune* increased fivefold; throughout the free states, where most of its subscribers lived, it wielded unprecedented power as a molder of public opinion. The *Tribune*, in turn, set the pace for the *New York Times*, the Springfield *Republican*, and lesser antislavery sheets. More sensational than the newspapers was Harriet Beecher Stowe's *Uncle Tom's Cabin*, which appeared in book form in 1852. This novel, although not depicting the South as completely depraved, caught the attention of millions of people for its more brutal passages. Three hundred thousand copies were sold the first year, and the story was soon dramatized and played in every northern city and town. Enraged southerners denounced it as a hideous distortion of the truth, but it made a lasting impression on the North, particularly on the countless thousands of boys who were to be voters in 1860 and who were to hear Lincoln's call for volunteers. Less important than Mrs. Stowe's work in shaping the sentiment of the two regions was Hinton Rowan Helper's *The Impending Crisis of the South: How to Meet It*. Helper, a small farmer of North Carolina, denounced slavery as fatal to the interests of the middle and lower whites of the South. It was his thesis that if these classes were to prosper, if the South were to advance, if the region were ever to develop a varied commerce and industry and to enjoy the same degree of cultural progress as the North, then slavery must go. In the eyes of the leading spokesmen of the South, Helper was a traitor, and northern endorsement of his book, a malicious and unpardonable insult.

The South also had its propaganda after 1850. The North was painted as a land of "poverty, crime, infidelity, anarchy, and licentiousness." Every southern youth was taught to regard northerners as vulgar and depraved people "reeking with irreligion, blasphemy, and radicalism." James De Bow, an eminent editor defined "Yankees" as a "species of the human race who foster in their hearts lying, hypocrisy, deceit, and treason." Calhoun's *Disquisition on Government* was studied in southern colleges, and appeals were made to forego the use of Northern literature. One proslavery leader wrote:

> So long as we use such works as Wayland's *Moral Science* and the abolitionist geographies, readers, and histories, overrunning as they do with all sorts of slanders, caricatures, and blood-

thirsty sentiments, let us never complain of their use of that transitory romance [*Uncle Tom's Cabin*]. They seek to array our children by false ideas against the established ordinances of God.

The Election of 1860

When the Democrats gathered in April, 1860, for their convention in Charleston, South Carolina, for the first time in their history they were forced to face the fact that they would be unlikely to agree on a nominee. The southerners arrived at the convention determined to reject any platform that failed to provide for federal protection of slavery in the territories. The most important group of northerners was equally convinced that the party could not survive unless it endorsed the principle of popular sovereignty and nominated Douglas for the presidency. Both groups had compromised for the last time, and both thought that the conflict in their party was irreconcilable. Of the thirty-three states represented in the convention, fifteen were slave and eighteen free; but among the latter, two states—Oregon and California—voted with the South. The platform committee, which consisted of one representative from each state, presented a report advocating Federal protection of slavery in the territories, and the convention, voting by delegates rather than by states, defeated the proposal. Rather than accept this decision, most of the delegates from eight southern states withdrew from the convention. The remaining delegates then made an unsuccessful attempt to select a presidential candidate. Douglas was unable to obtain the required two-thirds vote, and after ten days of balloting the convention broke up.

The Democrats reconvened at Baltimore on June 18, only to discover anew that the issues dividing them could not be compromised. Within a few days, the delegates had formed two conventions. The northerners nominated Douglas on a platform of popular sovereignty. The southerners selected John C. Breckinridge of Kentucky and reaffirmed their demand for the federal protection of slavery in the territories. Meanwhile, representatives of the defunct Whig and American parties had formed the Constitutional Union party. Meeting at Baltimore in May, they nominated John Bell of Tennessee for President and Edward Everett of Massachusetts for Vice-President. In their platform, the members of the new party condemned "the creation and encouragement of geographical and sectional parties" and recognized "no political principle other than the Constitution of the country, the Union of the states, and the enforcement of the laws."

The entry of four political parties into the selection enhanced the role of small groups of well-organized militants in both North and South. Holding as they did the balance of power, by playing their hands shrewdly they could force into intransigency the more moderate politicians who feared that failure to appease the militants would result in the loss of local power. The Democratic schism also virtually insured a Republican victory in 1860. The delegates to the Republican convention at Chicago nevertheless were careful to draw up a platform that appealed to every major interest group in the free states. The poor in both the East and West were promised free homesteads, and within a short time "Vote yourself a farm" had become one of the Republican's most effective campaign slogans. A tariff plank was included in an effort to win the support of northeastern industrialists, while internal improvements were provided for by a demand for a transcontinental railroad to be constructed with federal assistance. While the platform condemned popular sovereignty and "threats of disunion," it denied "the authority of Congress, of a territorial legislature, or of any individuals to give legal existence to slavery in any territory of the United States."

The Republicans' choice of a candidate also revealed a desire to conciliate all the factions in the party. For some months before the convention, it was generally thought that Seward would receive the nomination. But Seward, who had been in public life for many years, had committed himself on too many issues to be acceptable to all the groups in the party. He was opposed by the ex-Know-Nothings because he had been on good terms with the Catholics during his term as Governor of New York State, and he had made too many outspoken attacks on slavery. When it became apparent that Seward could not obtain the nomination, the delegates turned to the favorite sons of the various northern states—Simon Cameron of Pennsylvania, Edward Bates of Missouri, Caleb Smith of Indiana, Abraham Lincoln of Illinois, and Salmon Chase of Ohio. Of these, only Lincoln was acceptable to the party's major factions, for he alone had not antagonized the abolitionists, the groups opposed to the extension of slavery, the Know-Nothings, the immigrants, the prohibitionists, the ex-Whigs and the ex-Democrats. Lincoln's nomination by the Republican delegates on the third ballot marked the triumph of availability and excellent political management.

Throughout the campaign of 1860, the Republicans made repeated appeals to northern workingmen and businessmen. They warned the white supremacist workingmen that slavery threatened to deprive them of their livelihood; Republican orators asked: "How can the free laboring man ever get two dollars a day when a black slave (now) costs his master only ten cents a day?" Their efforts to win the support of the

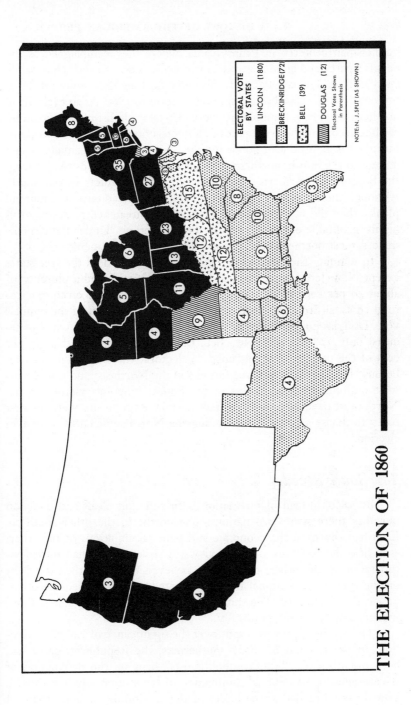

ELECTORAL VOTE
BY STATES

■ LINCOLN (180)

▦ BRECKINRIDGE (72)

▤ BELL (39)

▥ DOUGLAS (12)

Electoral Votes Shown
in Parenthesis

NOTE:N. J. SPLIT (AS SHOWN)

THE ELECTION OF 1860

businessman centered in Pennsylvania, where they campaigned as the people's party and emphasized the tariff exclusively. Nevertheless, while many iron producers in Pennsylvania voted for Lincoln, it is doubtful that businessmen as a class backed the Republicans in 1860. As an exclusively northern party, the Republicans were viewed with distinct suspicion by the businessmen who were part of an intersectional economy. Northern manufacturers produced goods for the South, northern bankers loaned money to the South, northern railroad men shipped goods to and from the South, and northern merchants sold their products in the South. Although these groups might approve the Republican tariff and railroad planks, they did not approve of a party that threatened to destroy this highly profitable economic alliance of the sections. Under the circumstances, most northern businessmen did not vote for Lincoln.

In winning the election of 1860, Lincoln carried all the free states except New Jersey and received 180 electoral votes and a plurality of about 40 per cent of the popular vote. Breckinridge received 72 electoral votes, all from the slave states, but only 18 per cent of the popular vote. Douglas polled more than 29 per cent of the popular vote but secured only 12 electoral votes. Bell, though receiving less than 13 per cent of the popular vote, obtained 39 electoral votes. Lincoln had won because free workers and free farmers in the Northeast and the Northwest outnumbered the voters in the South. Lincoln's victory in the North must be attributed to the fact that the Republicans were the first party to devise a formula for uniting the North sufficiently to win an election.

The South Secedes

By 1860, instead of one nation with common ideals and common purposes there were two nations: one northern, the other southern. Each had thwarted the economic and political ambitions of the other; each held diametrically opposite views of slavery; each had hurled vituperation at the other; each firmly believed that the other was bent on the ruin of its sectional rival; each hated and mistrusted the other; yet, as the election of 1860 showed, the sections were not united about what course to follow politically.

The southern press was split over the significance of Lincoln's election. In the opinion of many southerners, the Republican party had been organized by "Yankee abolitionists" bent on the destruction of slavery and on the political subjugation of the section where it existed. Lincoln was branded as the leader of the abolitionists, a compatriot of Garrison; and his election on a platform calling for internal improvements, a protective tariff, and a railroad to connect the Northwest with the Pacific was regarded as conclusive evidence that the worst was about to happen. "With Lincoln," said the Richmond *Examiner*, one of the South's leading newspapers, "comes something worse than slang, rowdyism, brutality, and all moral filth; something worse than all the rag and tag of western grog-shops and Yankee factories . . . With all those comes the daring and reckless leader of Abolitionists." Lincoln's opposition to the acquisition of additional slave territory and his statement that the Union must become all free or all slave were emphasized as proofs that slavery was to be everywhere abolished. It was this feeling in part that prompted the governor of South Carolina to advise the South Carolina legislature on the eve of the election of 1860 to be prepared for any emergency "in view of the probability of the election to the presidency of a sectional candidate by a party committed to the support of measures which, if carried out, will inevitably destroy our equality in the Union, and ultimately reduce the southern states to mere provinces of a consolidated despotism, to be governed by a fixed majority in Congress hostile to our institutions and fatally bent upon our ruin." Many conservative southerners believed that a Republican administration would mean more abolitionist agitation, more runaway slaves, more personal-liberty laws, more John Brown raids, more likelihood of unfriendly federal legislation. Secession and independence, the militants argued, seemed to afford the only avenue of escape from impending evils. Any doubt about Lincoln's course was as effective as the alleged certainties about his plans to oppress the South, for the fire-eaters also used Southern doubts to good advantage.

Nevertheless, the election of 1860 had shown that the South was divided on what path to take to protect its interests. None of the candidates had campaigned for secession, although there was a common feeling that Breckenridge was the man favored by southern intransigents. At any time in the South before 1861, actual secessionists and "fire-eaters" were in a minority. Unfortunately, the breakdown of the two party system in the election of 1860 accentuated the role of these determined and skillful minority groups in rushing the South toward secession, and the indecision of a majority of Southerners aided their cause.

In the months after Lincoln's election, the old holders of power in the South had to choose between a policy that would save the Union and one that meant deferring to the more irresponsible small groups that threatened to throw their votes against the controlling political elite if they dared consider compromise. Faced with the choice of compromising to save the Union or of losing their places as political leaders in their home states, most of the southern moderates capitulated.

On December 20, 1860, a South Carolina convention formally repealed the state's ratification of the Constitution of the United States and the subsequent amendments and adopted an ordinance of secession from the national government. By February 1, 1861, Mississippi, Florida, Georgia, Alabama, and Louisiana had also left the Union; Texas soon followed. Of the remaining eight slave states, four—Virginia, North Carolina, Tennessee, and Arkansas—with fewer slaves and a larger non-slaveholding population than the lower South, delayed until after the bombardment of Fort Sumter and Lincoln's call for troops. Then they too severed their connection with the Union. The other four—Deleware, Maryland, Kentucky, and Missouri—though having less at stake in slavery than the states of the cotton belt, nevertheless contained powerful secessionist factions and were saved to the Union largely by the prompt and vigorous action of the federal authorities. In the mountainous counties of northwestern Virginia, inhabited mostly by nonslaveholding people of Scotch-Irish and German ancestry whose social and economic interests did not always accord with those of the tidewater planters, the sentiment for the Union was strong. When Virginia voted to secede, the mountaineers dissented, and, aided and abetted by the federal government, they set up the new state of West Virginia, which was admitted to the Union in 1863.

No sooner had the states of the lower South withdrawn from the Union than steps were taken to form a southern confederacy. A congress of delegates from the six cotton states meeting at Montgomery, Alabama, on February 4 organized a *de facto* government under the name of the "Confederate States of America." For President it selected Jefferson Davis, a West Pointer, who had served as Secretary of War in Pierce's cabinet and later as Senator from Mississippi, and who represented the conservative planter class. Alexander H. Stephens of Georgia, who had attempted to delay and defeat secession, was chosen as Vice-President. The Constitution of the Confederacy closely resembled the more famous document drafted at Philadelphia in 1787. There were, however, some notable differences: Congress could not grant bounties, levy protective tariffs, or subsidize internal improvements except as an aid to navigation. A duty could be laid on exports only with the consent of a two-thirds vote of both houses. Congress was bound to protect slavery in all territories and could enact no law denying or impairing the right of property in slaves. Despite the agitation before secession for restoration of the slave trade, the document prohibited the importation of slaves, possibly as a gesture for European sympathy. An executive budget was provided for, and the President, who was limited to a single six-year term, could veto any item in an appropriation bill. Congress

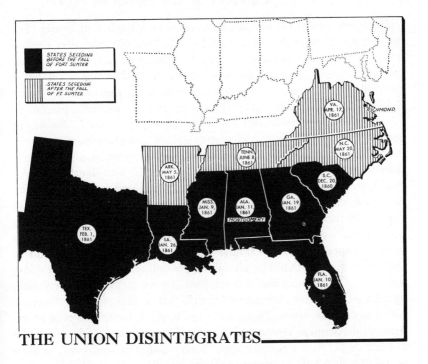

THE UNION DISINTEGRATES

could grant seats to the heads of executive departments on the floor of either house, where they were to enjoy the privilege of discussing any measure pertaining to their department.

The southern states were urged to withdraw from the Union for a number of reasons. The most important argument, perhaps, was that with Lincoln's election the South would never again be able to regain its political power in the federal government. Between 1850 and 1860, three free states, California, Minnesota, and Oregon, had been taken into the Union, while not a single slave state had been admitted. Efforts to secure slave territory in the Caribbean regions for future states had been unsuccessful, and topography and climate assured that no additional slave states would be formed in the existing territorial domain, except perhaps in New Mexico. The rapidly developing Northwest, now more securely linked by social and economic ties with the East than with the South, could no longer be counted upon for political support. The old political balance, in short, had been upset, and the ability of the South to safeguard and promote its interests had been curtailed. Under such circumstances, secession seemed to many the only alternative to subjection.

For many southerners who advocated secession, the Republican triumph also meant the loss of office and with it the loss of money. For half a century or more, southerners had filled the administrative departments of the federal government and had occupied many of the offices in the army, navy, and diplomatic service. With Lincoln at the helm, all would be changed; southerners would be ousted in favor of "Black Republicans" who would draw the salaries and distribute the patronage.

Southern spokesmen also urged the dissolution of the Union on the ground that such action would protect slavery and promote the material property of the South. The slave states, they asserted, had for generations been exploited economically by the North. The South, they declared, paid more than its share of the taxes, suffered from a deficiency of capital, and was forced, for as long as it remained in the Union, to depend on the North for manufactured goods. Once it declared its independence and set up a separate republic, its economic difficulties would disappear. The discriminatory tax burden would cease; direct trade with Europe could be established; manufacturing would develop; the African slave trade could be revived; a great southern confederacy, including Cuba, Santo Domingo, Mexico, and perhaps, Central America, could be created; internal commerce and banking facilities would be expanded; mechanical arts would flourish; immigrants would pour in—in a word, as *De Bow's Review* said: "Every industrial and every professional pursuit would receive a vivifying impulse." Avowed secessionists held that it was next to useless to advocate the diversification of southern industry as long as the Union continued. "Direct trade with the customers of the South in Europe," said the Charleston *Mercury*, is an impossibility . . . Norfolk, Charleston, Savannah, Mobile, are only suburbs of New York."

Less tangible, but nevertheless influential, in creating support for secession was the spirit of southern nationalism. The vast majority of the southern people loved their homeland. As children they had been taught to respect local institutions and to devote their lives to the well-being of their respective states. With many, the state took sentimental precedence over the Union. It was in part this patriotic fervor that led southern men and women to preach or accept secession when they believed that their civilization was endangered by the ascendancy of the North. It was this spirit that caused them to resent the constant denunciation of the South and of slavery by politicians, press, and pulpit in the North. It was this same attitude that impelled Robert E. Lee to resign his commission in the United States Army and to offer his services to the Confederate forces. Southern radicals appealed to this local pride and patriotism when, in their campaign for secessionist converts, they declared that "every Yankee had hated every Southern citizen from the day of his birth." The South, they insisted, was in reality already a nation and possessed population and resources sufficient to enable it to take its place among the nations of the earth.

Following the example of the Second Continental Congress, several of the secession conventions—apparently for the purpose of influencing public opinion at home, in the border states, in the North, and in Europe—adopted formal declarations of grievances. These documents, almost without exception, stressed the violation of the Constitution by the North. Rejecting the northern theory that the Constitution was an agreement of the people and that the United States was therefore an indestructible Union from which no state could withdraw, the secessionists followed Calhoun's interpretation and asserted that the Constitution was a mere compact among sovereign states and that the Union under it was an alliance that the states could dissolve. The northern states, they contended, had violated the Constitution by the passage of personal-liberty laws, by antislavery legislation, and by elevating to the presidency a candidate of a sectional party hostile to slavery. One declaration went so far as to declare that the North had overthrown the Constitution and had transformed the republic into a "consolidated democracy" in which the South was a hopeless minority. All the secessionist leaders agreed that inasmuch as the Southern states had entered the Union voluntarily under the "Constitutional compact," they were now at liberty to leave it.

More significant than constitutional considerations, however, was the fact that southern leaders who advocated secession often contended that cotton was "King." As early as 1830, the southern states had become formidable competitors of the other cotton-producing areas of the world, and ten years later they had practically monopolized the world's production. In the years 1849–51, more than a million bales of American cotton were exported annually to Great Britain. Of a total importation into Great Britain of nearly 4,800,000 bales for the two-year period 1859–60, approximately 4,000,000 bales came from the South. At the same time, these states shipped large quantities to the North and to continental Europe. The importance of cotton in the economic system of the world led southerners to argue that secession would be peaceful. They reasoned that northern industry would be paralyzed without cotton and without a southern market, and that the North in consequence would be unable to wage war. Even should war follow, they felt reasonably sure that England and France, rather than suffer an interruption of their cotton supply would at once recognize the South as a separate nation, conclude favorable commercial treaties with it, and come to its assistance with military and naval forces. Beyond doubt, the idea that the South held the key to the world's economy exerted a powerful influence on those who advocated secession.

The secessionist leaders also hoped that the Ohio Valley states would come to their support. In southwestern and central Kentucky, slave labor was used on a fairly extensive scale, and many families in other parts of the state were closely allied by blood or friendship to the planting kingdom. The southern parts of the states of Ohio, Indiana, and Illinois, settled mostly by southerners, were still connected with the South by commercial ties. Although slavery was legally forbidden in these three states, it nevertheless existed under the guise of voluntary servitude, a system of slave contract labor. For these reasons, disunionist leaders had dreams about allies in the Ohio Valley states that were never to be realized.

Sentiment for disunion in the South was strongest in the cotton states and in the larger tobacco-growing areas of Virginia. The propertied, mercantile, and financial elements of the towns protested for a time against secessionist agitation but were with some exceptions finally converted to the cause. A number of southerners opposed it on principle, others on grounds of expediency. Alexander H. Stephens of Georgia, who had already been elected Vice-President of the Confederacy, counseled against secession as a remedy for "anticipated aggressions." Lincoln's election, he declared, was not sufficient reason for leaving the Union:

> The President of the United States is no Emperor, no Dictator —he is clothed with no absolute power. He can do nothing unless he is backed by power in Congress. The House of Representatives is largely in a majority against him . . . In the Senate he will also be powerless . . . Why, then, I say, should we disrupt the ties of this Union, when his hands are tied—when he can do nothing against us?

But the secessionists had grown too strong to be halted. Two weeks after Stephen's plea for delay he wrote: "I am daily becoming more and more confirmed in the opinion that all efforts to save the Union will be unavailing. The truth is our leaders and public men . . . do not desire to continue it on any terms. They do not wish any redress of wrongs; they are disunionists *per se,* and avail themselves of present circumstances to press their objects." Three days later he wrote: "I . . . fear it is too late to do anything . . . the people are run mad. They are wild with passion and frenzy, doing they know not what."

The War Begins

In the North, word that the southern states had seceded was received with mingled emotions. Throughout the section, the burning question was whether the "wayward sisters" should be compelled to return to the fold or should be allowed to go their way in peace.

Chief among those who were willing that the South should leave the Union unmolested were the radical abolitionists, some of whom had advocated secession unless slavery was abolished. Garrison and Phillips rejoiced that the southerners and their "nefarious institution" had left the Union. Greeley in the columns of the *New York Tribune* said:

> If the cotton states shall become satisfied that they can do better out of the Union than in it, we insist on letting them go in peace . . . Whenever a considerable section of our Union shall deliberately resolve to go out, we shall resisit all coercive measures designed to keep them in. We hope never to live in a republic where one section is pinned to the residue by bayonets.

Whittier expressed the same opinion in verse:

> They break the links of Union; shall we light
> The flames of hell to weld anew the chain
> On that red anvil where each blow is pain?

A second group willing at first to see the southern states leave the Union peacefully consisted of numerous northern businessmen—manufacturers, merchants, and bankers. Much as these interests desired to see the Union kept intact, they feared that any coercive measure to preserve it would result in war and in the confiscation of the estimated $200,000,000 that the South owed to the North in 1860. The apprehension of such a catastrophe had caused the banks of Washington, Baltimore, Philadelphia, and Pittsburgh to suspend specie payment and had caused a panic on the New York stock market. In some of the larger commercial centers of the North, the money interests declared that the abolitionists were responsible for the country's plight. "It is sad," Nathan Appleton of Boston wrote, "to see this powerful, glorious nation, in the midst of an unparalleled prosperity, shattering itself into fragments, and all out of an impracticable idea, a nonentity, connected with the institution of slavery." In Boston, a mob, composed for the most part of businessmen, raided an antislavery meeting that had assembled to commemorate the anniversary of John Brown's death. In New York, the mercantile interests were outspoken in their condemnation of the abolitionists as well as of any plan that entailed the use of force to compel the seceded states to acknowledge federal authority. Fernando Wood, the mayor, went so far as to suggest that the city declare its independence and thus save its trade. However, as war neared, business sentiment in the North began to favor coercion of the South to save the investments they had originally thought secession would not threaten.

Although Buchanan did not condone secession, he made no move to prevent the withdrawal of the southern states from the Union. In his annual message, delivered on December 3, 1860, before a single southern state had seceded, he attributed the crisis in the South to the radicals and abolitionists in the North. Although maintaining that secession was unconstitutional, he made it clear that he did not think that the federal government should employ force to preserve the Union. Repeatedly, he argued that the dispute could be ended by compromise, but the kind of settlement that he recommended invariably required the North (which, whatever else it had done, had not seceded) to do all the compromising. He urged, for example, the adoption of a constitutional amendment that would assure the southerners the return of their runaway slaves and that would guarantee slavery not only in the states where it already existed, but also in all the territories. Buchanan, however laudable his intentions in an admittedly difficult situation, often gave the impression that he was totally unaware of the outcome of the election of 1860.

Buchanan's only attempt to uphold the rights of the Union was his unsuccessful effort to defend federal property in Charleston harbor. Following South Carolina's secession, Major Robert Anderson, who was in command of the federal troops in the region, evacuated nearby Fort Moultrie and transferred the garrison to Fort Sumter, which was located on an island at the harbor's entrance. Although Anderson had to have reinforcements to maintain his position, Buchanan for some time hesitated to make any move that might offend South Carolina. But on January 5, 1861, the President ordered 200 soldiers to be sent to Fort Sumter on the *Star of the West*, a merchant vessel. When this ship approached Charleston harbor, it was fired on by shore batteries, and it returned to New York without completing its mission. Buchanan made no further attempt to aid Anderson.

While Buchanan was doing nothing to check the secession movement, a number of other politicians were drawing up conciliatory proposals designed to save the Union. Of these, the most important were the Crittenden Plan and the Virginia, or Peace Convention, Plan. The Crittenden scheme, drafted in December, 1860, and named after the senior Senator from Kentucky, provided, among other things, for six constitutional amendments: (1) The Missouri Compromise line was to be re-established. In the territories north of the line, slavery was to be prohibited, and south of it slavery was to be recognized and protected. Any state, however, formed out of territory on either side of the line, however, was to be admitted with or without slavery as its constitution might prescribe. (2) Congress was to have no power to abolish slavery in places under its exclusive jurisdiction but situated within the limits of a slave state. (3) Congress was to have no power to abolish slavery in the District of Columbia so long as it existed in Maryland and Virginia. In addition, it had to have the consent of the people of the district and furnish just compensation. (4) Congress was forbidden to interfere with the domestic slave trade. (5) Owners of fugitive slaves were to be paid full value by the Federal government when arrest of fugitives was prevented or rescue made. (6) The Constitution was never to be amended so as to affect the above provisions or to interfere with slavery in any of the slaveholding states.

The Virginia, or Peace Convention, Plan, which was sponsored by leading Virginians, was the product of more than a month's labor by 150 delegates from 21 of the 33 states of the Union. The proposals of the conference, which convened in Washington on the same day that the delegates from the seceded states assembled at Montgomery to form a southern confederacy, did not differ markedly from the Crittenden scheme. Provision was made, however, that with some exceptions no new territory should be acquired unless by treaty ratified by four fifths of all the members of the Senate.

Despite strong popular support, both the Crittenden and the Virginia Plans faced insurmountable obstacles. The militant leaders, both North and South, did not want compromise. President-elect Lincoln, who was rapidly becoming the acknowledged leader of the faction that was determined to preserve the Union without the extension of slavery, opposed the Crittenden Plan as no longer pertinent to the situation as it existed, and because it permitted future extension of slavery. In his inaugural address, he declared that the Union was much older than the Constitution, that no state could lawfully depart from it of its own volition, that the ordinances of secession were legally void, that acts of violence to uphold them were insurrectionary or revolutionary, and that he would enforce the laws of the country to the fullest of his ability; he thus virtually served notice on every man and woman in the land that the Union would be preserved by force if necessary. His entire address, though couched in kindly and sympathetic language, was an ultimatum that recognized neither secession nor compromise.

Lincoln was a nationalist and a Unionist, and, like Andrew Jackson,

The President-Elect; 1860

[MESERVE COLLECTION]

he refused to be intimidated by southern threats. He did not want war, but he preferred it to the destruction of the American nation. When he entered office, he tried to refrain from making any overt move that would impel the border states to join the Deep South in secession. At the same time, if war came, he wished to have it started by the South rather than the North.

Although the seceding states had obtained or seized federal forts, post offices, and customhouses throughout the South, it was Fort Sumter, rather than any one of a hundred or more other places, that became the symbol of the conflict between the government of the United States and the South. Because Anderson was running out of supplies, the question facing Lincoln could not be postponed. If the President did not send a relief expedition to Fort Sumter, the South, the North, and the entire world would conclude that his administration was willing to countenance rebellion. On the other hand, if he attempted to aid Anderson's beleaguered forces, it would mean war. Despite the objections of most of his cabinet and of General Winfield Scott, Lincoln on April 4, 1861, decided to send supplies only to Fort Sumter but arms to Fort Pickens at Pensacola, Florida. Lincoln hoped that his strong stand at the less threatened post in Florida would impress those northerners demanding a strong stand and would dissuade southern hotheads about starting war. On the other hand, the attempt only to provision Sumter would appease northern moderates and, with advance notice to the Governor of South Carolina, Lincoln hoped, not provoke South Carolina to fight. The first expedition accomplished its mission, and Fort Pickens remained in northern hands throughout the war; but the success of even the limited Sumter expedition was prevented by South Carolina's decision to force the issue. On April 11, General P. G. T. Beauregard, acting on orders from the Confederate cabinet, which had to placate radicals in South Carolina and Montgomery, invited Anderson to surrender. He agreed, but his message did not reach Beauregard before Charleston shore batteries began the bombardment of Fort Sumter. The next day, April 13, Anderson surrendered and transferred his troops to the northern relief ships, which had arrived but had not participated in the engagement. On April 15, Lincoln issued a call for the militia of the loyal states and ordered Congress to convene in special session on July 4. The Civil War had begun.

FOR SUPPLEMENTARY READING

The outstanding recent general works on the politics of the 1850's are by A. Nevins, *The Ordeal of the Union* (2 vols., 1947) and *The Emergence of Lincoln* (2 vols., 1950).

Two studies of the party system have much importance: R. F. Nichols, *The Disruption of American Democracy* (1948), and J. A. Isely, *Horace Greeley and the Republican Party* (1947). D. Donald, *Charles Sumner and the Coming of the Civil War* (1960), is also excellent for its details on the pressures on the professional politicians.

On the Kansas-Nebraska Act, start with G. F. Milton, *The Eve of Conflict* (1934), and contrast this view with the controversial interpretation of P. O. Ray, *Repeal of the Missouri Compromise* (1909).

On the complex history of the Kansas troubles, the two most important works are P. W. Gates, *Fifty Million Acres* (1954), and J. C. Malin, *John Brown and the Legend of Fifty-Six* (1942). There is a decent resumé of recent scholarship in A. Nichols, *Bleeding Kansas* (1954).

On foreign affairs during the 1850's the most relevant books are B. Rauch, *American Interest in Cuba, 1848–1855* (1948), and E. S. Wallace, *Destiny and Glory* (1957).

The Dred Scott Case has its best analyst in V. Hopkins, *Dred Scott's Case* (1951), and an excellent examination from a different point of view in C. B. Swisher, *Roger B. Taney* (1935).

Besides Nevins' study of Lincoln's growing prominence, read H. V. Jaffe, *Crisis of the House Divided* (1959), and W. E. Baringer, *Lincoln's Rise to Power* (1937). J. G. Randall attempts to rehabilitate part of Buchanan's low reputation in the early chapters of *Lincoln the President*, Vol. I (1945). P. G. Auchampaugh presents a view of Buchanan's fears and naive legalism in *James Buchanan and His Cabinet on the Eve of Secession* (1926). Add to this P. S. Klein, *President James Buchanan* (1962).

The closer one gets to the secession crisis itself, the more voluminous the literature. D. L. Dumond, *Southern Editorials on Secession* (1931), and H. C. Perkins, *Northern Editorials on Secession* (2 vols., 1942), should be studied along with O. Crenshaw, *The Slave States in the Presidential Election of 1860* (1945). R. H. Luthin, *The First Lincoln Campaign* (1944), tells much about the sources of Lincoln's strength, and D. M. Potter, *Lincoln and His Party in the Secession Crisis* (rev. ed., 1962) (Pb), is a good account. The same months are brilliantly, if too partisanly, analyzed by K. M. Stampp, *And the War Came* (1950). Business pressure in the North in 1860–61 is dealt with by P. Foner, *Business and Slavery* (1941), and secession demands in the South in R. A. Wooster, *The Secession Conventions of the South* (1962).

One aspect of the history of secession has been virtually neglected.

The home state pressures of a rising yeomanry on southern politicians at Washington can be assessed from reading relevant portions of R. Shugg, *Origins of Class Struggle in Louisiana, 1840–1875* (1939); H. R. Helper, *The Impending Crisis of the South* (1857); R. von Abele, *Alexander H. Stephens* (1946); and L. A. White, *Robert Barnwell Rhett* (1931).

A number of excellent essays also throw light on the long crisis of the Union. Among these are C. V. Woodward's contribution on John Brown's raid in D. Aaron (ed.), *America in Crisis* (1952); R. F. Nichols, "The Kansas Nebraska Act: A Century of Historiography," *Mississippi Valley Historical Review*, Vol. XLIII (Sept. 1956); and H. K. Beale, "What Historians Have Said About the Causes of the Civil War," in Social Science Research Council, *Theory and Practice in Historical Study* (1946). Historians debate these causes in N. A. Graebner (ed.), *Politics and the Crisis of 1860* (1961). A. O. Craven sums up years of work in *Civil War in the Making, 1815–1860* (1959).

The full texts of the most famous debates in the period are now available in P. W. Johannsen (ed.), *The Lincoln-Douglas Debates of 1858* (1965).

20

>>>->>>->>>->>>->>>->>>->>>->>>

Civil War

T HE CIVIL WAR was the first modern war. The vast numbers of
men involved, the close connection between the military establishments and the civilian economies, the enormous sums of
money that were required to maintain the contending military
machines, and the intensity of feeling aroused by the conflict, all combined to make the Civil War a precursor of the global wars of the twentieth century. During the conflict, no American could escape its effects;
and if the War Between the States—to use the southern term—was not
total war, it was only one step removed. If nothing else, the Civil War
demonstrated that in a long, drawn-out modern struggle, no part of a
nation's life could hope to escape the touch of fire.

Raising the Armies

At the outset of the Civil War, the states of the Confederacy with
a population of 8,700,000, including nearly 3,500,000 slaves, were opposing twenty-two states with a population of approximately 23,000,000.
With the admission of Kansas in 1861 and West Virginia in 1863, the
ratio of population, slaves excluded, was about five to one. Only
two slave states ranked among the eight most populous states of the
Union in 1860, and one of these—Missouri—did not join the Confederacy. Even if the Confederacy had been able to carry with it Missouri,
Kentucky, Delaware, Maryland, and West Virginia, the addition of
the combined population of these five states (totaling 3,600,000) would
still have left the South numerically inferior to the North.

In wealth, as well as population, the North enjoyed marked superiority. Its real and personal property was valued at $11,000,000,000,

as compared with $5,370,000,000 for the South; the valuation of its farm lands alone totaled $4,800,000,000, or more than two and a half times that of the Confederacy. Its banking capital of approximately $330,000,000 was more than seven times that of the South. Most important of all, in its factories, mines, railroads, and ships, the North possessed a supply of developed material resources and industrial techniques from which to obtain the weapons of war and to which the agrarian South could oppose no adequate counterpart.

The crisis of Fort Sumter found both sides unprepared for war. Neither had a first-class army, or the munitions and other supplies with which to equip one. The small regular army of 18,000 was widely scattered, and few of its officers had seen action except against the Indians; many West Point graduates had left the service to engage in some civilian pursuit.

In raising armies, North and South each employed both the volunteer system and conscription. In the spring of 1861, when patriotism in both sections was running high and when only Robert E. Lee and a few others perceived that the struggle would be long and bitter, both central governments called for short-term volunteers. The response at first was so great that neither government had sufficient arms and equipment for all. Many recruits were sent to organization camps, where, dressed in the clothes they had worn at home and drilling with broomsticks as muskets, they prepared for the front. In a few months, however, enthusiasm gave way to disillusionment. Every day it became increasingly evident that both sections were in earnest and that the conflict would be much longer and more destructive of human life than had been at first anticipated. Many of those who had had a taste of war had grown tired of it and failed to re-enlist at the expiration of their terms of service; others, perceiving the opportunities for high wages or large profits at home, refused to shoulder a musket and share the hardships and dangers of army life. Under these circumstances, both sections resorted to bounties to stimulate enlistments.

The two central governments—and the states, counties, and municipalities as well—employed the bounty system. The federal government inaugurated the practice in July, 1861, by offering $100 to every volunteer, an amount subsequently increased to $302 for recruits and $402 for veterans. The sums offered by the states and the smaller political units of each section varied greatly, but in comparison with the grants of the central governments, they were considerable. In addition to bounties, the volunteer who served as a private received clothes and rations and $13 a month until May 1, 1864, when his pay was increased to $16. The bounty system soon led to the crime of "bounty jumping".

For a man to enlist and desert eight or ten or even a dozen or more times was not uncommon. Immigrants in many instances proved easy victims for unscrupulous agents. All told, the federal government paid $300,000,000 for bounties, and $286,000,000 more was expended by the northern states and municipalities for the same purpose.

Before the war was two years old, the authorities in Washington and Richmond began to realize that voluntary enlistment, even when stimulated by bounties, could not be relied upon to furnish the numbers necessary to keep the armies up to strength. Accordingly, both sections were forced to the only remaining expedient; conscription. In this move the Confederacy was first. On April 16, 1862, President Davis signed a conscription act that called to the colors every able-bodied white male between the ages of eighteen and thirty-five. This law was supplemented by the act of September 27, 1862, which extended the age limit to forty-five. Exemptions were provided for the physically unfit, and for all Confederate and state officials, teachers, preachers, keepers of apothecary shops, hospital officials, newspaper proprietors, persons employed in transportation and important war industries, and overseers on the larger plantations. Before 1863, exemption could also be gained by supplying a substitute. The pressure to fill the depleted ranks of the army toward the close of the war was so great that the Confederate Congress in March, 1865, provided for the service of slaves, each state to furnish its quota, which was not to exceed one quarter of its slaves.

In the North, the first step in the direction of conscription was taken on August 4, 1862, when Lincoln ordered a draft of 300,000 militiamen through the agency of the states. The result was disappointing, for only about 87,000 soldiers were obtained. After protracted debate, Congress on March 3, 1863, passed a conscription act that formed the basis for all future drafts. By its terms, all able-bodied male citizens or alien declarants between the ages of twenty and forty-five if unmarried, and twenty and thirty-five if married, were enrolled in the forces of the United States and made subject to military duty at the President's call unless exempted for certain specified reasons. The law further provided that each draft should be apportioned among the several enrollment districts and that the names should be drawn by lot. In districts where the required quota was raised by voluntary enlistments, no draft was to be made. High public officials, teachers, preachers, criminals, and men who were the sole support of dependent families were the principal classes exempted. Any drafted man, however, could escape service by furnishing an acceptable substitute or by paying the government a fee not to exceed $300.

The conscription acts angered the people of both sections, and their results were far from satisfactory to the governments. In the South, defenders of states' rights, like Robert Barnwell Rhett and Vice-President Stephens, asserted that the Confederate government in enacting the conscription laws had exceeded its authority and that the laws were unconstitutional. Acting on this assumption, Governor Joseph E. Brown of Georgia refused to permit them to be carried out in his state. In North Carolina, where opposition was even more bitter, the legislature at the suggestion of Governor Zebulon B. Vance not only drafted a formal protest against the policy of conscription, but later passed a law, in direct contravention to the act of the Confederate Congress, that exempted millers, blacksmiths, and others from military service. It is impossible to ascertain how many able-bodied Southern men escaped military service by claiming to belong to the exempted classes, but it is known that many physicians were bribed to issue certificates of disability, that apothecary shops sprang up overnight, and that many who had never thought of doing so before became preachers or teachers. In 1864, General John S. Preston of the Confederate Bureau of Conscription declared that "from one end of the Confederacy to the other every constituted authority, every officer, every man and woman, is engaged in opposing the enrolling officer in the execution of his duties."

In the North, opposition to conscription was equally widespread. Exponents of states' rights, Quakers and other conscientious objectors, "copperheads"—that is, those who wanted immediate peace at any price—and those who distrusted the government for any reason whatsoever asserted that the Conscription Act was unconstitutional, contrary to the traditional policy of the nation, and the work of a "military despotism." The provision of the act that allowed a man to evade service by furnishing a substitute or by paying $300 into the federal treasury was denounced by the laboring classes and others of limited means as a scheme favoring the well-to-do in "a rich man's war and a poor man's fight." In several states—notably Pennsylvania, Ohio, Indiana, Illinois, Iowa, Wisconsin, New Jersey, and New York—the draft was forcibly opposed and in some instances the enrollment officers were murdered.

In New York City, the first draft under the law was accompanied by four days of rioting. When the lists of conscripts were published on Sunday, July 13, 1863, nearly all those on the lists were mechanics and laborers of foreign birth, some of whom were on strike and whose places had been filled with Negro strike-breakers. The resumption of drawings the next day was the signal for revolt. Mobs destroyed conscription offices; robbed Unionists in the streets and pillaged and burned their homes; attacked the residence of the mayor; and burned out the

"Horatio Seymour of New York Helps Enforce the Draft," 1863

office of the *New York Tribune.* Negroes, as well as abolitionists, were blamed for having caused the war and the draft, and the mob attacked them furiously. Some were shot, others were beaten to death, and a number were hanged from trees and lamp posts. An orphan asylum for Negro children was sacked and burned. Business was almost completely paralyzed, and not until troops had raked the streets with cannon and howitzers and had arrested many of the ringleaders was order restored. It was estimated that at least a thousand people were killed or wounded and that property was damaged to the extent of $1,500,000. Similar disturbances, but on a much smaller scale, occurred in several other cities.

Authorities differ as to the number of officers and men in the armies during the war. Some contend that from 1,200,000 to 1,400,000 served under the Confederate flag; others maintain that this figure is too large.

The Union enlistments numbered 2,898,304, but these included bounty jumpers and others who enlisted more than once. The total number was probably in the neighborhood of 2,675,000, an estimate that includes more than 100,000 Negroes recruited from the seceded states and 54,000 whites from the Confederacy, of whom 31,000 came from Tennessee.

Supplying the Armed Forces

In equipping its armed forces, the Confederacy was greatly handicapped in comparison with the North. Before the war, the South had done little to develop its rich deposits of coal and iron. It had purchased nearly all its iron goods and railroad materials in the North. Iron was so scarce that during the war the suggestion was made that the Confederate government make a public appeal for broken or worn-out plows, plow points, hoes, spades, axes, broken stoves, and household and kitchen utensils. When hostilities began, the South had no adequate factories for the production of clothing, boots and shoes, and other necessary supplies. Despite these deficiencies, the Confederacy managed to equip its armies in some fashion until the very last month of the war. The government seized, either directly or through the states, practically the entire stock of arms, ammunition, and machinery stored in the federal forts and arsenals within the seceded states. In addition, small amounts of war equipment were acquired from several of the southern governments, especially from Virginia and South Carolina, which had purchased considerable stores of arms and ammunition before the ordinances of secession were passed. Part of this material had come from abroad and part from the North. Only a few days before the firing on Fort Sumter began, Confederate agents placed large contracts for munitions with northern firms; and throughout the war, supplies of arms and ammunition were smuggled through the northern lines. Another—and in some respects the most important—source was Europe, particularly England. Through Caleb Huse, leading Confederate purchasing agent abroad, the South bought millions of dollars worth of guns, ammunition, and machinery; Europe supplied approximately one half of all the small arms used by the Confederate armies. Supplies of all sorts were also salvaged from the battlefields or obtained from northern prisoners of war. The Confederacy also set up its own blast furnaces, although they were greatly inferior to those of the North; and it established foundries and produced heavy ordnance and some small arms. It erected numerous powder mills, which produced almost enough ammunition to supply the wants of the armies, although at times there was a scarcity of saltpeter. Textile factories and tanneries also multiplied in number and in output, but they were unable to meet the demands of both the public and the army.

The problem of feeding the Confederate armies caused even greater concern than equipping them. During the first year of the war, there was no serious difficulty, for crops were abundant and of excellent quality. By the autumn of 1862, however, conditions had changed. A severe drought had cut the grain supply, money was rapidly depreciating, prices rose precipitously, and transportation facilities were not functioning properly. Realizing the danger, both the central and state governments brought pressure to bear on the planters by legislation and by appeal to grow less cotton and more wheat and corn, and the press, planters' conventions, and other agencies carried on an aggressive campaign for food production. As a result, cotton acreage diminished, and that devoted to cereals increased. But even though crop yields for 1863 were above normal, the situation did not improve. Vicksburg had been taken and the Texas granary had thus been cut off; transportation facilities were more demoralized than ever; and farmers refused to accept Confederate currency in return for their products. Meanwhile, the Confederate Congress on March 23, 1863, passed an impressment act authorizing army officers to seize any property anywhere in the Confederacy "for the good of the service." During the following month, it imposed a tax of one tenth in kind on agricultural products.

Like the Conscription Act, both measures were condemned by many southerners. The Supreme Court of Georgia ruled that the compensation clause of the Impressment Act was unconstitutional and void, and the Georgia legislature declared that through the execution of the law citizens had been "greatly harassed, defrauded, and wilfully wronged." Resolutions passed by other state legislatures complained of the law in similar terms. Even General Lee, who thought that impressment was necessary, admitted that it was "very objectionable in many ways—and not calculated to bring out fully the resources of the country." Though both tithe and impressment were probably unavoidable, they undoubtedly lessened production of foodstuffs. The increasing loss of southern soil to the federal armies in 1863 and 1864 also constantly reduced the food-producing area on which the Confederacy had to depend for its sustenance; and some regions, though not occupied by northern forces, were so devastated that they were almost useless to the South for food production. With the growing scarcity of food, it became increasingly difficult to supply the armies with even the usual rations.

Defective transportation as well as lower production of food supplies undoubtedly contributed to the difficulty of feeding the southern armed forces during the latter part of the war. As early as 1863, the Confederate Secretary of War complained about the "dilatory and irregular transportation on the railroads." Cut off from their former source of equipment and without labor or materials with which to make repairs, the southern railroads steadily deteriorated. The government's attempts to provide through traffic by combining short lines were often frustrated by towns apparently more concerned with saving their transfer business than with feeding the army. Supplies destined for the army piled up along railway lines, and during the last two years of the war the Confederacy suffered not so much from lack of food as from a defective system of distribution. While Sherman's army found plenty of food in Georgia, Lee's soldiers were almost starving in Virginia.

The North, with its ever increasing number of factories, overflowing granaries, superior transportation system, and larger credit, experienced fewer of the difficulties with which the South had to contend in equipping and rationing its troops. At the outset of the war, it is true, the North was as unprepared as its rival, and like the South, it turned at once to European manufacturers for arms and other supplies. During 1861, the fortunes of war turned in no small degree upon the ability of the two contestants to secure the necessary munitions from the Old World. According to the report of the United States Ordnance Officer for the fifteen months ending June, 1862, the federal government purchased 726,000 rifles from European makers and only 30,000 from American manufacturers. Several northern states, including Ohio, Connecticut, and Massachusetts, also placed orders in Europe for arms.

Northern dependence on Europe soon ended, and by the second year of the struggle, foreign contracts for war materials ceased. Stimulated by the greatly increased demand and by the remarkable opportunity to make enormous profits, dozens of private concerns turned to the production of war materials: new iron plants were constructed, munition factories were enlarged, and machine shops were transformed into gun factories. Some materials were also manufactured by the federal government; 3,000 men employed at the armory at Springfield, Massachusetts, turned out 1,000 rifles a day. The government might also have engaged in the manufacture of cannon and projectiles had the opposition of private interests not been so strong. Government clothing factories, meat-packing establishments, and laboratories for the manufacture of drugs and medicines were set up despite the efforts of those who did not favor such forms of government enterprise. Not all of the northern war material was of first-class quality, however. Unscrupulous businessmen, more intent on riches than service to their country, amassed fortunes by selling inferior goods to the government. Supposedly all-wool uniforms and overcoats for which the government paid excessive prices turned out to be made of old rags chopped into pulp and pressed into a species of cloth called "shoddy." Such large quantities of shoddy shoes, hats, stockings, and the like were sold to the government that "shoddy" became a popular synonym for fraud and corruption, and profiteers were soon labeled the "shoddy aristocracy."

In sharp contrast to their rivals, the federal troops seldom suffered for want of rations or for lack of adequate means of transporting goods and supplies to the front. Throughout the war, the agricultural output of the North steadily increased despite the drain on its manpower made by the armies in the field and the new mines of the Far West. Immigrants, eastern laborers, and women and children turned to farm labor, and by using such labor-saving devices as the drill, reaper, and thresher, they kept the granaries full. Other agricultural products, including meat and vegetables, were maintained at the pace set by the grain crops. The railroads and waterways, though often taxed to their capacity in serving both the army and the public, were immeasurably superior to those of the Confederacy, and were better used. Unprecedented quantities of rations and equipment moved with remarkable celerity from the northern commercial centers to the army depots behind the lines.

The armies of both belligerents suffered severely from lack of modern medical and surgical facilities. Knowledge of medicine and of the rules of hygiene had made little advance since the days of the Revolution. Thousands died of typhoid fever and other diseases. Careful estimates indicate that more than half the deaths in all the armies were caused by typhoid and pneumonia. Anesthesia—nitrous oxide gas, ether, and choroform—had been introduced and was employed to some extent in the federal armies; frequently, however, the Confederate forces were entirely without it. Antiseptic surgery had not yet been developed, and the surgeons were inadequately trained for handling the enormous burden thrust upon them. There were also no trained nurses, although thousands of self-sacrificing women like Clara Barton left their homes in the North and South to risk their lives as army nurses.

The lot of the soldier was made easier by the enormous amount of relief work carried on by the noncombatant population. Hostilities had no sooner begun before women in every part of the North began to organize Ladies' Aid Societies to make bandages, shirts, underwear, towels, blankets, and other supplies. In New York City some fifty or sixty of these groups under the leadership of Dr. Elizabeth Blackwell formed the Women's Central Association for Relief. Largely as a result of the efforts of this body, the federal government approved the creation of the United States Sanitary Commission in June, 1861. Although this national organization supplemented the work of the United States government in caring for sick, needy, and wounded soldiers and their dependent families, it was supported entirely by private contributions. Most of the local relief societies immediately affiliated with the Sanitary Commission, although some continued to act independently and to devote their energies to the troops recruited from their own communities. Measured in dollars and cents, the services the Sanitary Commission rendered to the soldiers in camp, on the battlefield, and in the hospitals were estimated at close to $35,000,000. After the battle of Gettysburg, the Commission distributed $75,000 worth of food and clothing among the wounded. During the months of May and June, 1864, it spent $515,-000 for battlefield service in Virginia. It sent thousands of bushels of potatoes, onions, and cabbages, as well as other vegetables, to scurvy-threatened areas. It also provided hospital care, surgeons, convalescent camps, and soldiers' homes.

The work of the Sanitary Commission was supplemented by that of the United States Christian Commission, which was organized in November, 1861, under the auspices of the Young Men's Christian Association to promote "the spiritual good of the soldiers and, incidentally, their intellectual improvement and social and physical comfort." In addition to carrying on evangelical work, it established free reading rooms in the camps, where the soldiers had access to religious literature, periodicals, and county and state newspapers and could find writing tables, stationery, and free postage stamps. It even furnished food and succor to the wounded after battle, and many men undoubtedly owed their lives to the Commission's prompt and benevolent action.

Although the South had no such central body as the Sanitary Commission, innumerable state and county relief associations, such as the Central Association for the Relief of South Carolina Soldiers and the Hospital Aid Association of Virginia, carried on in more restricted fashion much the same type of work. Similarly, the Bible Society of the Confederate States functioned in somewhat the same way as the Christian Commission. It distributed Bibles and religious tracts, conducted camp services, and comforted the wounded and diseased.

Unless the Confederate soldier owned land, the lot of his family bordered on the tragic. Faced with high prices and a depreciated currency, deprived of medicines and other necessities, and living in constant fear of being driven from their shelters by an invading army or a pitiless landlord, these families led a precarious existence. Their desperate circumstances undoubtedly account in part for the large number of desertions from the Confederate ranks, especially during the latter half of the war.

From Bull Run to Vicksburg

The military strategy of both belligerents was conditioned by the resources that they had at their command. At the beginning, the advantage of leadership rested clearly with the Confederacy. Many of the reputedly best officers of the United States Army cast their lot with the South. Jefferson Davis, a West Point graduate, veteran of the Mexican War, and Secretary of War during Pierce's administration, knew intimately the capacities of most of the prominent army officers, of both the North and South. The leading Southern generals occupied commands of importance from the outset. Robert E. Lee, who declined the informally tendered command of the Union forces in favor of a commission in the Army of Virginia; Joseph E. Johnston, considered by some as the equal of Lee as a military leader; energetic, versatile "Stonewall" Jackson; and the talented Albert Sidney Johnston were the most brilliant of the Confederate leaders. The deaths of A. S. Johnston and Jackson before the military crisis of the war had been reached impaired the effectiveness of the southern armies in the field.

In contrast to the Confederacy's success in assigning men of competence to responsible posts was Lincoln's desperate quest for capable generals. Before the end of the war, the Union had its share of outstanding generals, but not one was recognized at the beginning. Before Ulysses Grant, William T. Sherman, and Philip Sheridan emerged as the leaders to whom the major operations would be entrusted, Lincoln dolefully fumbled with a series of commanders of the main Union army operating in Virginia—McClellan, Pope, McClellan again, Burnside, Hooker, and Meade. Some, if not all, of them were competent division or even corps commanders, but they failed lamentably in the formulation and execution of major operations that required skill in strategy as well as in tactics. Not until 1863 were Grant and Sherman revealed as the men able to lead the Union troops to ultimate victory. Before then, the activities of Union generals seldom did more than to provid a colorful background for the deft handling of the Confederate force by Lee, with the able assistance of Jackson.

Throughout the war, one of the North's most important assets was its naval supremacy. On April 19, 1861, Lincoln proclaimed a blockade of all enemy-held ports in an effort to deprive the South of the goods that it had to import to survive. Although at the time the Union navy consisted of only ninety ships, most of which were obsolete, the fleet was steadily expanded until there were approximately seven hundred vessels participating in the blockade at the end of the war. As the blockade grew in effectiveness, shortages of civilian and military goods in the South increased proportionately. The blockade thus made a major contribution to the ultimate defeat of the Confederacy. The Union navy also supported the northern armies in the "river war" in the West and won important victories at Port Royal, South Carolina, in 1861, at New Orleans in 1862, at Mobile in 1864, and Wilmington in 1865.

The South's naval efforts were confined to raids on northern shipping on the high seas and to an attempt in 1862 to break the blockade with an ironclad named the *Virginia*. Constructed by placing on the captured *U.S.S. Merrimac* armor plate made from railroad rails, the *Virginia* on March 8, 1862, sank two Union warships and damaged three others in an engagement at Hampton Roads. But on the following day the Union navy was able to meet this challenge with the *Monitor*, an ironclad that consisted of little more than a revolving gun turret on a floating platform. At the end of the day's fighting, neither vessel had been able to cripple the other, and the battle of the ironclads ended in a stalemate. The following month, however, the Confederates sank the *Virginia*—or *Merrimac*, as it was generally known despite its change in name—to prevent it from being captured by the Union forces.

The land warfare of the Civil War falls into two distinct phases. Until the summer of 1863, the North was able to accomplish little or nothing on the Virginia front, although Union armies in the West won a number of significant victories. In 1864–5, however, the North held the initiative as Grant struck at Lee in Virginia and Sherman devastated large areas of the Deep South. During the entire war, the immediate objective of the Union was the capture of Richmond, but the North's over-all strategy called for an "anaconda movement" in which the South would be encircled and crushed. Lee, for his part, hoped that an invasion of the North would induce the northern public to abandon the war. After Gettysburg, Lee's strategy was calculated to inflict such terrible losses upon the Union forces that a war-weary, disheartened North would give up the struggle.

In the opening weeks of the war, most northerners supposed that the Union army would capture Richmond within a short time and that the war would be over in a matter of months. "On to Richmond" became the northern war cry, and in early July, Lincoln, despite the advice of Scott, ordered General Irvin McDowell to begin an advance on the Confederate capital. After a five-day march, McDowell's 30,000

The Ironclads in Battle at Hampton Roads, Virginia

troops came into contact with approximately 24,000 Confederates under Beauregard at Bull Run, a creek. On the first day of battle at Bull Run (July 21), the Federals had the advantage; but on the following day, when General Joseph E. Johnston arrived with reinforcements for Beauregard and General Thomas J. Jackson earned his nickname "Stonewall" by holding his ground against repeated northern attacks, the tide of battle turned, and the Union troops were routed. As they fled in confusion, their way was impeded by numerous social and political figures from Washington who had come to watch what they thought would be a decisive Union victory. For a time it was feared that Beauregard would capture Washington, but heavy rains checked his advance, and the capital was saved.

Following the Union defeat at Bull Run, George B. McClellan succeeded McDowell as commander of the Army of the Potomac. McClellan, who had seen some action in western Virginia during the first months of the war, was a superb administrator and immediately set to work to drill and reorganize the Union troops. By October he had a well-trained force of 100,000 men; but, despite the pressure of both Lincoln and public opinion in the North, he refused to undertake an offensive against the 50,000 Confederates under Johnston's command until he considered his army ready. Throughout the winter of 1861-2, McClellan, who in November had been made commander in chief of all Union forces following Scott's resignation, remained in winter quarters while Congress and the Union press ranted against his dilatory tactics. The repeated announcements of "all quiet along the Potomac" accurately described the situation and infuriated those northerners who had expected a short and glorious war.

In March, 1862, after Lincoln had given specific orders for an advance, McClellan began to transfer his army to the peninsula that lies between the James and York rivers; and by May 1 he had assembled 112,000 men at Fortress Monroe. By slow stages, he pushed forward, until at the end of the month his advance guards were less than five miles from Richmond. Then, on May 31, Johnston attacked at Seven Pines in a two-day battle that proved indecisive. Johnston, however, was wounded, and Lee was named commander of all the "armies in eastern Virginia and North Carolina." Lee immediately began preparations for an offensive. On June 18, J. E. B. Stuart at the head of 1,200 men was sent on a reconnoitering expedition that was to take him clear around the entire Union army, and Jackson was recalled from the Shenandoah Valley, where his troops had inflicted a series of severe defeats on much larger federal forces in this region. On June 26, Lee began the attack that inaugurated the Seven Days Battles (Mechanics-

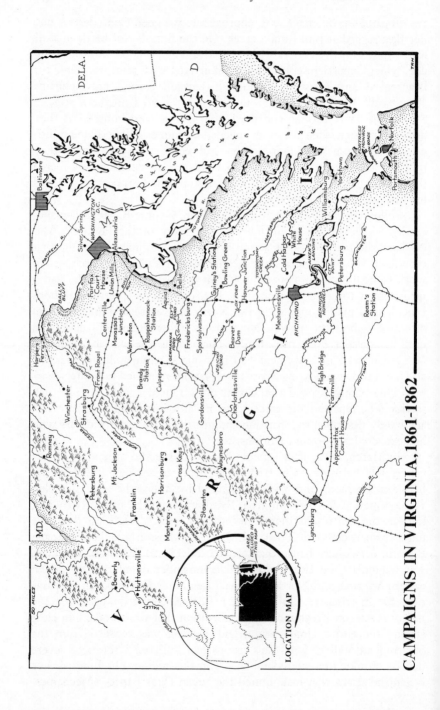

CAMPAIGNS IN VIRGINIA, 1861-1862

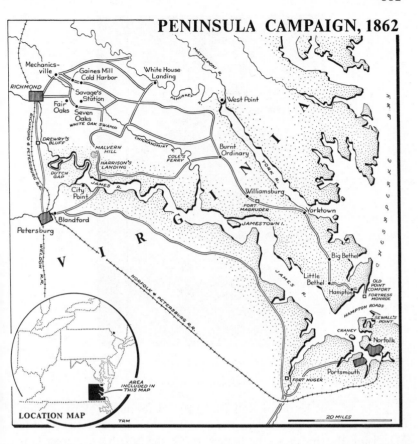

PENINSULA CAMPAIGN, 1862

ville, June 26; Gaines Mill, June 27; Savage Station, June 29; Frayser's Farm, June 30; and Malvern Hill, July 1). At the end of the week-long struggle, Confederate casualties were twice as large as those inflicted on the Union army, but McClellan had been compelled to retreat twenty miles to Harrison's Landing on the James. McClellan then proposed that he cross the James and approach Richmond from the south. But this plan was vetoed by General Henry W. Halleck, who had now been named general in chief. McClellan was removed and ordered to Aquia Creek on the Potomac; and General John Pope, who had served in the West, assumed command of the "Army of Virginia" on the Rappahannock. Lee attacked Pope at the end of August, and in the second battle of Bull Run (August 29–30, 1862) a Confederate army of 48,000 overwhelmingly defeated a federal force of 75,000. Lee's losses were only 9,000 in contrast to Pope's 16,000, and once again Washington was saved from capture by torrential rains that made the roads impassable.

George B. McClellan

[NATIONAL ARCHIVES]

The second battle of Bull Run marked the nadir of the Union's military fortunes, and before the North could recover, Lee invaded Maryland. By this move, he hoped to cut the North's east-west communications, find a new source of supply for his army, and weaken the northern desire to continue the war. After crossing the Potomac near Leesburg, Virginia, he sent part of his army under Jackson to capture Harper's Ferry while he advanced with the remainder toward Hagerstown. But McClellan, who had been restored to his command after Pope's defeat at Bull Run, learned of these plans after one of Lee's orders had been intercepted. Lee, nevertheless, had time to reunite his army and take up positions on Antietam Creek. In the ensuing battle of Antietam (September 17), McClellan was able to check Lee's northern advance. Both sides, however, claimed a victory, and, because McClellan made no move to press his advantage, Lee was able to recross the Potomac without interference on September 19.

Despite repeated requests from Lincoln, McClellan did not cross into Virginia until October 26. But Lincoln had already lost his patience with McClellan, and on November 5, he dismissed "Little Mac"

Thomas "Stonewall" Jackson

[NATIONAL ARCHIVES]

and replaced him with General Ambrose Burnside. Within a month, the Union armies were again on the march. Lee, however, had established his army in entrenched positions at Fredericksburg on the south side of the Rappahannock. At noon on December 13, 1862, Burnside's troops crossed the Rappahannock and began a frontal assault on the Confederate fortifications on the hillside. For the rest of the day, the southerners mowed down the advancing Federals in a great slaughter in which Burnside's losses totalled 12,600 to 5,300 for the Confederates. Two days later Burnside retired across the river, and on January 25, 1863, he was replaced by General Joseph ("Fighting Joe") Hooker.

By April, 1863, Hooker had 130,000 men across the Rappahannock, and once again the Union forces were advancing along the short—but seemingly endless—road to Richmond. As in the past, it was Lee who picked the time and place of the decisive battle, and on May 2, he launched his attack in a wooded area of thickets and underbrush known as the "Wilderness." While part of the Confederate army under Jackson rolled back Hooker's right flank west of Chancellorsville, another force under Lee drove against the Union troops from the east. After

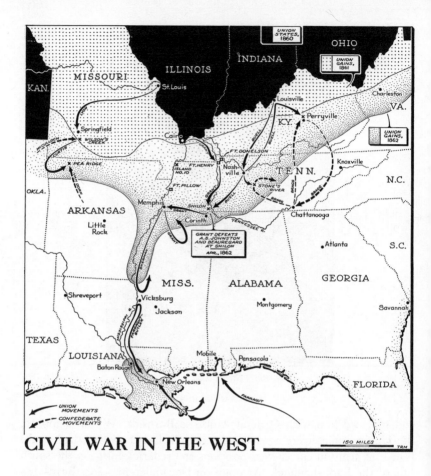

CIVIL WAR IN THE WEST

150 MILES

three days of fighting, the Union army was forced to withdraw despite its two-to-one numerical superiority. Lincoln still had not found a general who could outthink and outmaneuver Lee. Chancellorsville was one of Lee's most brilliant victories, but it was also one of his costliest, for on May 2, Jackson was wounded, and eight days later he died.

It was in the West rather than in Virginia that the Union armies under the leadership of General Ulysses S. Grant demonstrated their fighting ability during the opening years of the war. A graduate of West Point and veteran of the Mexican War, Grant had resigned from the regular army in the 1850's to avoid being courtmartialed for drunkenness. At the outbreak of the Civil War, he had assumed command of an Illinois regiment, and within a few months he had risen to the rank of brigadier-general. Despite the objections of Halleck, who in November, 1861 had been placed in charge of all the Union forces in the West,

Grant drew up plans for an offensive against the Confederate positions in northeastern Tennessee. On February 6, 1862, he won his first victory when Fort Henry surrendered after a bombardment by Union gunboats commanded by Commodore Andrew Foote. A week later, he made an unsuccessful attack against Fort Donelson; but when the Confederates attempted to fight their way out of the trap into which Grant had maneuvered them, they were repulsed, and on February 15, Grant accepted the "unconditional and immediate surrender" of the fort's 12,000 defenders.

Because Halleck did not permit Grant to follow up his victory at Fort Donelson, General Albert Sidney Johnston was able to assemble a Confederate force of approximately 40,000 at Corinth on the Tennessee-Mississippi border. In the early spring, Grant began to advance on Corinth; but before he reached his objective, he was attacked by Johnston near Pittsburgh Landing. In the two-day battle of Shiloh (April 6–7, 1862), in which both sides claimed a victory, Johnston was killed, Grant was caught napping, and the Union forces made no attempt to interfere with the withdrawal of the Confederates to Corinth. Halleck then assumed personal command of Grant's army, and on May 30, 1862, he occupied Corinth without a battle. Although the Army of the West was relatively inactive for the remainder of the year, by July 1 the navy under Admiral David G. Farragut had captured New Orleans, Baton Rouge, and Natchez. Meanwhile, Halleck was transferred to Washington to be general in chief, and Grant was placed in charge of all the Union forces in western Tennessee and northern Mississippi.

Farragut's victories had given the North control over all of the Mississippi except the region around the Confederate stronghold at Vicksburg. Grant was determined to capture Vicksburg at any cost. Defended by 30,000 Confederates under General J. C. Pemberton, Vicksburg was inaccessible from the river because of the high bluffs on which it rested, while on the north it was guarded by extensive swamps and bayous. Grant at first tried to take it from the north with a force of 30,000 led by General William T. Sherman and then by digging a canal to divert the course of the Mississippi; but when both these attempts failed, he decided to cross the river below Vicksburg and attack the city from the southwest. By May 1, his army was on the east bank of the Mississippi sixty miles below Vicksburg. In the next three weeks, Grant met and defeated the Confederates on five different occasions and then bottled Pemberton up in Vicksburg. After two frontal assaults against the city had failed, Grant besieged Vicksburg until July 4, when Pemberton surrendered. Many historians have attributed Grant's victory to bull-headed determination rather than military genius; but, re-

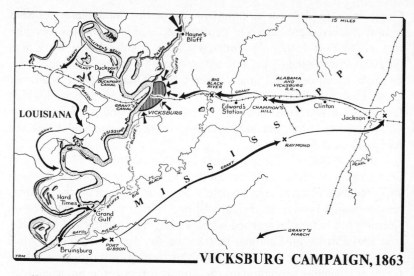

VICKSBURG CAMPAIGN, 1863

gardless of how his ability is assessed, he deserves the principal credit for placing the entire Mississippi in Union hands and for cutting off the Southwest from the rest of the Confederacy.

From Gettysburg to Appomattox

The fall of Vicksburg coincided with Lee's defeat at Gettysburg. Desiring to capitalize on the North's war weariness, Lee had decided in early June to invade Maryland and Pennsylvania. Crossing the Potomac near Harper's Ferry on June 25, 1863, he reached Pennsylvania before the end of the month. Although Hooker thought that Lee's invasion of the North presented the Union with a priceless opportunity to take Richmond, he was instructed by Lincoln to keep his army between the Confederate force and Washington. But on June 28, Hooker resigned after a disagreement with Halleck, and General George G. Meade took over his command. Three days later, advance units of the Confederate and Union forces met outside Gettysburg in the opening skirmishes of the most important battle of the Civil War. In the fighting during the remainder of the day, the federal troops were forced to give ground along the entire line, and on the morning of July 2, they had only a precarious hold on Cemetery Ridge, while the Confederates were gathering in full strength on Seminary Ridge a mile away. On the second day of the battle Lee had hoped to outflank the Union forces with a dawn attack on Little Round Top at the southern extremity of Meade's position; but General James Longstreet delayed his offensive until four o'clock in the afternoon. By then it was too late, for the

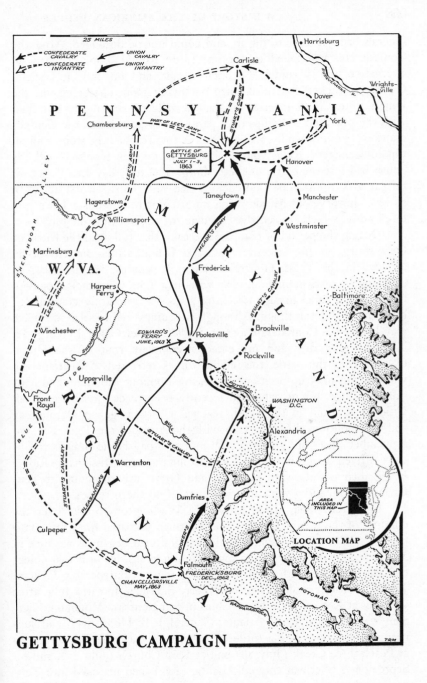

GETTYSBURG CAMPAIGN

federals had had time to dig in, and could not be dislodged. After the Confederates had failed to capture Little Round Top, Lee had no alternative but to launch a frontal assault, and on July 3, General George E. Pickett led 10,000 men on their famous charge against the Union center. Moving across the shallow valley separating the two lines with the precision of troops on a parade ground, most of the Confederates were cut down by artillery fire. A few reached the stone wall on top of Cemetery Ridge, but Pickett's charge was repulsed, and the South had lost the battle of Gettysburg. The next day Lee began his retreat to Virginia. The Confederacy had suffered the worst defeat in its brief history, but Meade made no attempt to annihilate Lee's battered army, which crossed the Potomac for the last time on July 13.

During the period of comparative calm that followed the battle of Gettysburg on the eastern front, the Union armies undertook an advance in the West. General William Rosecrans, having occupied Chattanooga on September 9, 1863, without a fight, was attacked on September 19 at Chickamauga Creek by a Confederate army commanded by General Braxton Bragg. Although Rosecrans' right and center gave way before the Confederate assault, the left under General George H. Thomas stood firm and prevented a complete rout of the Union troops. After the battle, the federal forces retreated to Chattanooga, while Bragg took up positions on nearby Lookout Mountain and Missionary Ridge. Grant, who had recently been placed in charge of all Union operations in the West, reached Chattanooga on October 23 and was soon joined by Sherman with the Army of the Tennessee. On November 23, Grant attacked, and in a two-day battle Bragg's troops were driven from both Lookout Mountain and Missionary Ridge. Bragg then withdrew to Georgia, and Grant was promoted to lieutenant-general and given command over all northern forces.

In March, 1864, Grant arrived in Washington to take over the conduct of the war in Virginia, and Sherman prepared for a drive into the Deep South from Tennessee. When Sherman began his advance in May, 1864, at the head of 100,000 Union veterans, his principal objective was Atlanta. With an army of only 53,000 Confederates, General Joseph Johnston could at best only delay Sherman. In early July, after victories at Resaca, New Hope Church, and Kenesaw Mountain, Sherman was within sight of Atlanta. General J. B. Hood, who had succeeded Johnston, made a futile effort to turn back the federal troops at Peach Tree Creek (July 20) and at Ezra Church (July 28), and on September 2 Sherman entered Atlanta. Hood then marched into Tennessee, where he was overwhelmingly defeated by Thomas at Nashville on December 15-16.

William T. Sherman

Sherman, after burning Atlanta, set out for the sea in mid-November with 60,000 troops. Living off the country and destroying the property that could be of any conceivable value to the Confederacy, Sherman more than made good his boast that he would "make Georgia howl." By December 10, Sherman had reached Savannah, and within two weeks he was able to present the city to Lincoln as a Christmas gift. Turning northward in February, he entered South Carolina, where his army repeated the tactics that it had perfected on its famous march to the sea.

While Sherman was laying waste to large areas in the Carolinas, Grant at the head of more than 100,000 men was fighting the final Union campaign against Lee in Virginia. The forces of the war's two leading generals met for the first time in the Wilderness on May 5–6, 1864, and Lee handled Grant in much the same fashion that he had Hooker a year earlier. Although Union losses were 18,000, Grant immediately resumed his advance, and at Spotsylvania Court House he lost another 12,000 men in a five-day battle (May 8–12). Nevertheless, once more Grant pushed forward, and on June 3, 1864, his army suffered its most crushing defeat of the campaign at Cold Harbor. In a month, Lee, with a force that was half the size of Grant's, had deprived the Union commander of the services of approximately 50,000 soldiers.

Following the battle of Cold Harbor, Grant crossed the James, and Lee dug in at Petersburg. After Union troops had been repulsed in a

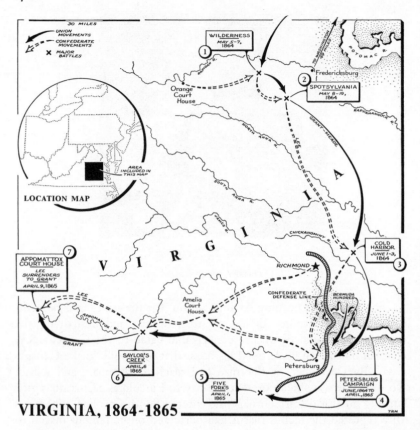

VIRGINIA, 1864-1865

four-day attack (June 15–18), Grant settled down to a siege. Grant could afford to wait, for he was confident of Sherman's ultimate success in the Deep South, and he knew that his own army would never want for either supplies or men. Lee's forces, on the other hand, consisted of approximately 40,000 ragged and often barefooted soldiers who were short of both food and ammunition and whose ranks were daily depleted by desertions. At the end of July, Grant's army tried unsuccessfully to dislodge the Confederates by mining a 510 foot tunnel, while Lee hoped that General Jubal A. Early's exploits in the Shenandoah Valley would force the Federals to send a major part of the army attacking Petersburg to the defense of Washington. At one point, Early was only five miles from the Union capitol, but Grant sent General Philip Sheridan to the valley with a force that was many times larger than Early's. With victories at Winchester (September 19), Fisher's Hill (September 22), and Cedar Creek (October 19), Sheridan destroyed all Confederate resistance in the Shenandoah and so devastated

Robert E. Lee

[LIBRARY OF CONGRESS]

the region that "a crow flying over the country would have to carry his own rations."

By February, 1865, Lee's position had become desperate. Grant had begun to extend his lines south of Petersburg, Sherman was on his way north, and the underfed, poorly clothed Confederate troops were suffering untold hardships in the frozen trenches. A month later, when Sheridan rejoined Grant, the Confederate situation became even more hopeless. On April 2, after an attack the day before at Five Forks had failed, Lee led his 30,000 veterans on their last retreat. Moving westward from Petersburg and Richmond, Lee's men halted on April 4, only to learn that the expected provisions had not arrived. For four more days the half-starved, exhausted remnants of a once-glorious army struggled on, with Grant in close pursuit. But on April 9, Lee, realizing that his army could neither retreat nor fight, surrendered to Grant at Appomattox Courthouse. Under Grant's terms, officers and men of the Confederate army were released on parole. The Union commander also permitted the Confederate artillerymen and cavalrymen to keep their horses for use on their farms. On April 26, Sherman accepted Johnston's surrender in North Carolina.

Financing the War

The Civil War, like all wars, was expensive. The total cost in money was about $5,000,000,000 for the North and $3,000,000,000 for the South; or, together, three or four times the estimated value of all the slaves in the Confederacy. Neither side was prepared at the outset to meet this enormous financial strain, and before the conflict was over, both sections were forced to resort to nearly every known expedient to obtain necessary funds.

When Lincoln issued his first call for volunteers in 1861, Secretary of the Treasury Salmon P. Chase was confronted with a virtually empty treasury and an income insufficient to meet the ordinary expenses of government. Chase recommended that revenue for ordinary expenditures, for interest on the public debt, and for a sinking fund to extinguish the debt be raised by taxation and that the expenses of the war be met entirely with borrowed funds. In view of the economic strength of the North, this policy was a blunder, but Chase apparently feared that any great increase in taxes might cause businessmen to become hostile to the war and the administration. Chase, who opposed high taxes on democratic principles, also believed that the war would be short. Although receipts from taxation increased enormously as the war progressed, they were still greatly overbalanced by the amount obtained from loans.

Taxation took various forms, of which one of the most important was the tariff. When Lincoln took the oath of office, the United States was very nearly on a free-trade basis. Under the tariff of 1857, duties on many articles had been lowered and the free list had been enlarged. The income of the federal government, which had averaged more than $68,-000,000 annually during Pierce's administration (1853-7), had dropped to $46,500,000 in 1858; during the next three years, deficits had accumulated to the amount of $50,000,000, and the government had been compelled to resort to borrowing to pay its bills. To balance the budget and to afford more adequate protection for "home interests," the Republicans, under the leadership of Justin Morrill of Vermont, succeeded in securing the adoption of a tariff measure in March, 1861, which it was thought would increase the revenues of the government and insure moderate protection to American manufactures. This law was revised in 1862 and again from time to time until finally, by the act of 1864, the average rate of duties on all imports was advanced to 47 per cent, the highest in the history of the country up to that time. This measure, enacted to help pay for the war and to protect the northern manufacturer from foreign competition and thus to enable him to pay heavy internal taxes, marked the beginning of a new tariff policy under which manufacturing was to become more profitable than ever before.

Coincident with the increase in tariff rates, in 1862 Congress passed a sweeping internal revenue law. Guided by the principle that it was better to impose moderate duties upon a large number of goods than excessive duties upon a few, its framers provided for a variety of taxes, including levies upon liquor and tobacco, manufactures and manufactured products, auction sales, carriages and yachts, billiard tables, railroads, steamboats, and ferry boats, meat, banking institutions and insurance companies, advertisements and inheritances, and upon salaries and pay of officers in the service of the United States. The law also provided for an elaborate system of stamp duties and licenses for occupations. Its far-reaching character was summarized by a critic who said that it imposed a tax upon virtually

> every article which enters into the mouth, or covers the back, or is placed under the foot; upon everything which is pleasant to see, hear, feel, smell, or taste; upon warmth, light and loco-motion; upon the sauces which pamper man's appetite and the drug that restores him to health; upon the poor man's salt and the rich man's spice.

No industry and no occupation escaped taxation, and in 1864 the rates were increased. It was a new experience for a country that had been free from internal taxation for more than a generation. To what extent these taxes were passed on to the ultimate consumer has never been ascertained. The tax on incomes, although it came under the category of internal revenue, was something quite new in American taxation. First levied in 1861, it authorized a 3 per cent tax on incomes above $800. In 1862 and again in 1865, the law was amended to tax all incomes between $600 and $5000 at 5 per cent and above $5000 at 10 per cent. From the outset, there was considerable opposition to this tax, and the inadequate machinery for enforcing it made evasion easy. The greater part of the revenue derived from it, moreover, was not received until the war was over.

The government embarked on a policy of large-scale borrowing in the summer of 1861, when Congress authorized the Secretary of the Treasury to borrow not more than $25,000,000. To float such a loan was not easy. There was only a small amount of gold in the country, and commercial concerns naturally competed for it with the government. Many of those who had money were reluctant to lend it, for northern victory was not yet certain. Early reverses suffered by the federal troops and the unfriendly attitude of Great Britain and France made the outlook extremely dubious. Despite these and other handicaps, Chase, with the assistance of a group of New York, Philadelphia, and Boston bankers, succeeded in obtaining $150,000,000 in 1861 on three-year notes bearing 7.3 per cent interest, and in disposing of $50,000,000 worth of twenty-year 6 per cent bonds. But the cost of the war averaged $2,000,000 a day, and the funds from these first loans did not last long. The money had scarcely been received before Chase requested additional funds, and from the beginning of 1862 until the close of the war, the government borrowed repeatedly. Many bonds were sold to the banks at a rate below par, to be resold by them to the public at a profit. Jay Cooke, a Philadelphia banker who was allowed a commission of .005 per cent on all bonds sold up to $10,000,000 and .0375 per cent on all sums above that amount, organized a country-wide system for disposing of them. In less than a year, this experienced banker and his 2,500 agents, by appealing to the patriotic duty of every person to buy a bond, sold $400,000,000 worth of "five-twenties." All these loans lacked uniformity. Some were sixty-day loans, and others, like the "ten-forties," were redeemable at the option of the government in from ten to forty years; some bore compound interest, others did not; some were paid for in gold, others in paper money; some carried the express stipulation that they should be redeemed in coin, others made no mention of the medium of redemption.

Because of the rapidly mounting military expenditures, the inadequacy of the tax receipts, and the inability of the treasury at times to dispose of its bonds except at a great discount, the government was forced early in the war to issue paper money. The first issue of $150,-000,000, authorized by the Legal Tender Act of February, 1862, was followed by another $150,000,000 in June of the same year. Two more issues were authorized in January and March, 1863, for $100,000,000 and $50,000,000 respectively. Of the $450,000,000 thus authorized, $431,000,000 was outstanding in June, 1864. All this currency was in the form of non-interest-bearing notes, unsupported by specie reserve, and dependent for ultimate redemption upon the good faith and the future financial solvency of the government—in short, a forced loan, without interest, from the people. These "greenbacks" were made receivable at face value and constituted legal tender for all debts except duties on imports and interest on the public debt, which were to be payable in coin. Following the northern victories at Gettysburg and Vicksburg, the sale of government bonds increased, and no paper money was issued for the remainder of the war.

As soon as it became known that the government was contemplating the use of paper money, opposition arose. Metropolitan papers, with few exceptions, denounced the proposal as dangerous and contrary to every principle of sound finance. Morrill of Vermont spoke of it as "a measure not blessed by one sound precedent and damned by all." Bankers and their representatives hastened to Washington, where they sought to induce the government to adopt some other policy. But the demand for greenbacks was too strong. The bankers and their spokesmen were branded as "usurers" and "note shavers," and the greenbacks' supporters asserted that the government should free itself from the grip of the "money monopoly."

The vicissitudes of war, the abundance of the greenbacks, speculators' manipulations, and the fact that the paper currency was not only too plentiful but was not full legal tender, caused violent fluctuations in its value, with a marked trend toward depreciation. In January, 1862, $1.00 in paper currency was worth $.98 in gold, but twelve months later its value had dropped to $.69. In the summer of 1864, it reached the low point of $.39, and at the close of the war it stood at $.67. Depreciation quickly led to an increase in the premium on the precious metals and to a rise in commodity prices. Though in many instances workingmen's wages increased, they lagged behind the cost of living.

With the rise in the premium on precious metals, silver coins disappeared from circulation. In desperation, cities and business establishments issued their own paper money and metallic substitutes. Congress in July, 1862, authorized the use of postage stamps, but this inconvenient medium was replaced in March, 1863, with fractional paper currency, or "shinplasters," as they were commonly called. Before the war was over, $50,000,000 of these non-interest-bearing paper notes had been authorized. Issued in denominations as low as three cents, they proved a most serviceable addition to the currency of the country.

Northern finances were also directly affected by the establishment of the National Banking System. For a number of years before the outbreak of the war, there had been a growing sentiment that Congress should enact a national currency law that, among other things, would regulate the banking business of the country. Several arguments in favor of such a law were advanced. In the first place, its advocates declared that it would make for uniformity and standardization of currency. On January 1, 1862, there were approximately 1,500 banking institutions in the United States that enjoyed the power to issue banknotes. Chartered under the laws of twenty-nine different states, possessing different privileges, and subject to different restrictions, they issued a variety of currency differing widely in quality and in amount. In some states, boards of bank commissioners made frequent and thorough examinations; in others, such boards did not exist or existed in name only. More than 7,000 different kinds of banknotes circulated in addition to thousands of counterfeits and altered notes. Some of these notes had adequate security behind them; many had little or none. The substitution of national banknotes for the paper issues of the state banks, it was argued, would provide the country with a standardized currency. Secondly, national control was advanced as a guarantee of a more evenly distributed currency. Currency issued by the state banks was subject to violent contractions and expansions. As the majority of the state banks were located in the older settled regions of the country, the East enjoyed a larger banknote circulation than did the West. New England in 1862, for example, had a note circulation of $50,000,000, whereas Ohio, with a population three fourths as large, had a circulation of only $9,000,000. A third important argument was that the establishment of national control would strengthen the spirit of nationalism, obtain for the government the more cordial backing of the business interests, and enable the federal treasury to market its bonds to better advantage. In helping to float the early bond issues, the state banks had obtained substantial profits. A properly drafted national banking act, it was argued, would relieve the government of the necessity of making bad bargains with these private institutions. The state banks did not favor the proposed legislation, and when it was recommended by the Secretary of the Treasury in 1861, they were able to prevent it. An act of 1863, however, together with an amending act of 1864, provided for the organization of national banking associations. Each association was required to buy federal bonds to the extent of one third of its capital (the minimum capital was fixed at $50,000 for places under 6,000 population, $100,000 for places not exceeding 50,000, and $200,000 for larger cities) and to deposit them with the Treasurer of the United States as security for circulating banknotes that it might issue up to 90 per cent of the market value of the bonds it owned. Interest on the bonds was to be paid to the banking association depositing them, and the government guaranteed the ultimate redemption of the banknotes. Provision was also made for national supervision of the entire system. The slowness with which the state banks accepted the new system caused Congress in 1865 to levy an annual tax of 10 per cent on all state banknotes. This law had the desired effect, and by the end of 1865 there were 11,582 national banks with over $400,000,000 capital, possessing $440,000,000 of government bonds and circulating notes amounting to $213,000,000. Except for its failure to furnish an elastic currency capable of expanding and contracting in response to the needs of trade, the National Banking Act accomplished the results expected of it.

Funds for the Confederate war chest were derived from sources similar to those of the North. When the war broke out, the Confederacy at once seized about $1,000,000 belonging to the Washington government—practically all the money in the branches of the United States Mint and in the customhouses in the South. To conserve its specie supply and to harass the North, it also enacted a law in 1861 prohibiting the payment of private debts to northern creditors and directing that such debts be paid into the Confederate treasury. Additional revenue to finance the war, it confidently expected, would be derived in part from the sale of cotton, tobacco, and other southern staples. But when the northern blockade quickly and effectually shattered this plan, the South was forced to turn to taxation, loans, and paper money.

Acting reluctantly on the recommendation of C. G. Memminger, Secretary of the Treasury, the Confederate Congress in August, 1861, levied a direct tax of .005 per cent on all property except Confederate bonds and money. There were certain exemptions—for instance, for the property of religious, charitable, and educational institutions. In accordance with the Confederate constitution, the tax was apportioned among the states. As in the days of the Revolution, the states either refused to act or raised their respective quotas by issuing bonds or paper money, and only Texas made any effort to raise the necessary amount by means of taxation. After the direct tax on property had proved unsatisfactory, the Confederate legislature adopted an internal revenue measure in 1863 that provided for excise duties on naval stores, salt, liquors, tobacco, and other produce payable in kind. Although the rates for both direct and indirect taxes were increased during the last years of the war, it is impossible to estimate the exact effect of the increase in tax rates on southern finances.

From the beginning of the struggle, the South resorted to borrowing to finance its military program. As early as February, 1861, the Secretary of the Treasury was authorized to float a $15,000,000 8 per cent bond issue that effectively drained the southern banks of most of their specie. This loan was followed by a number of bond issues payable in produce, which gave the government possession of considerable quantities of cotton, tobacco, sugar, naval stores, and other commodities. These staples were used as security in floating a $15,000,000 bond issue in Europe in 1863, which netted the Confederacy only about $6,250,000. In addition, the states of the South issued bonds for war purposes.

Because of the meagerness of its credit resources, the South was compelled to rely chiefly on issues of irredeemable paper money. Printings followed one another in rapid succession, until by 1864 more than $1,000,000,000 of Confederate treasury notes were in circulation in addition to the varied assortment of paper currency issued by states, municipalities, banks, factories, railroads, turnpike and insurance companies, and other private concerns. As in the North, postage stamps and "shinplasters" added to the profusion of fiat money. In less than six months after the first issue, this unsecured paper began to depreciate. In March, 1861, $1.00 in gold would exchange for $1.00 in paper; in March, 1862, for $1.30; in March, 1863, for $4.10; in March, 1864, for $22; in March, 1865, for $61; during the last days of the war, Confederate paper money was worthless.

Europe and the War

Throughout the war, the leaders of both sections were aware that the outcome of the struggle might depend on the attitude of Europe. If the federal government could successfully cut off southern commerce with the outside world, and if, while preventing the exchange of southern staples for European manufactured goods, it could also avoid provoking foreign nations to diplomatic or military intervention, it could be more certain of ultimate victory. If the Confederacy, on the other hand, could secure European recognition and military aid, the chances were stronger that it would win. Consequently, many policies of the rivals throughout the war were framed in the light of their probable effect on the major European powers.

Nothing was perhaps more influential in deciding the fate of the Confederacy and in shaping European sentiment than the enforced economic isolation of the South. The war was only a few days old when President Lincoln on April 19, 1861, issued a proclamation blockading the ports of the Confederacy. Within a remarkably short time, the South found it difficult to market its tobacco and cotton or to obtain adequate supplies and manufactures from abroad. Cotton exports, which amounted to $202,000,000 in 1860, fell to $42,000,000 in 1861, and $4,000,000 in 1862. Ordinary commodities, like salt, tea, coffee, soap, matches, and drygoods, became extremely scarce. The conveniences and comforts of life to which the well-to-do were accustomed were difficult to obtain. Southern newspapers were forced to decrease their size and in some instances were printed on brown wrapping paper of home manufacture.

The effect of the blockade on Europe, while not as disastrous as on the South, was, nevertheless, important. Great Britain in 1861 had 2,650 cotton factories that housed more than twice as many spindles as all the other European nations combined. At the time the blockade was proclaimed, England was overstocked with raw cotton, and cotton manufactures were a glut on the market. Manufacturers therefore welcomed the decrease in cotton importations, for it enabled them to dispose of their finished goods on hand at high prices. Part of England's oversupply of cotton was even reshipped to America during the early months of the war at prices considerably in advance of the original cost. By the end of 1862, however, England and France were confronted with a cotton famine. English importations from America declined from 2,580,700 bales in 1860 to 1,841,600 bales in 1861, and to less than 72,000 bales in 1862. Cotton mills were forced to close, and half a million operatives who were thrown out of work became dependent on public and private charity. Similar conditions prevailed in the cotton-manufacturing districts of France. In one department, more than a hundred thousand laborers, forced into idleness, had to depend on alms for subsistence. Bankers who loaned money and businessmen who had sold supplies to the Confederacy on a cotton security basis became alarmed as the blockade tightened and cotton importations fell off. Cotton manufacturers and affiliated banking and commercial interests began to urge the recognition of the Confederacy and the breaking of the blockade.

Apart from the questions of cotton supply, markets, and the blockade, leading figures in government circles in Great Britain and other leading European states were inclined to favor, or at least to sympathize with, the South. The aristocracy of the Old World rejoiced at the prospect of the permanent disruption of the powerful Western democracy. The English privileged classes feared that a northern victory would strengthen the democratic movement in England. The upper classes of Europe looked upon the southern planter as an aristocrat with whom they had much in common. Many Europeans, like Napoleon III, also thought that the disruption of the United States would nullify the Monroe Doctrine and open up new opportunities for the European acquisition of American territory.

Fortunately for the North, the pressure of these powerful influences was counterbalanced by others. The people of Europe were far from unified in sentiment or in policy toward the American struggle. Although the British aristocracy and Napoleon III openly favored the South, they distrusted each other, and this fact was in some measure responsible for their failure to agree on any common plan of action. Napoleon on more than one occasion proposed that the two nations cooperate in mediating between the warring sections, but each time Great Britain objected. Napoleon was unwilling to intervene alone, because he was afraid intervention would mean war with the North and partly because he feared that if such a war broke out, Prussia, Russia, Austria, Sardinia, and possibly Great Britain would promptly take advantage of his distraction.

The British rejection of the French proposals, however, was due not so much to mutual distrust as to lack of unanimity in Great Britain itself and to the course of events in America. The majority of the English aristocracy—as well as of the manufacturers and the commercial class, whose interests were adversely affected by the blockade—strongly sympathized with the South. Whatever moral compunctions these groups may have entertained respecting slavery were apparently subordinated by their strong sympathy for the cotton planter and by their desire for profits. A minority of the ruling class and the leaders of five or six million unenfranchised wage earners did not share this sympathy and unreservedly sided with the North. In their opinion, the South was fighting for the institution of slavery. Throughout the war, John Bright, Richard Cobden, William Forster, John Stuart Mill, Thorold Rogers, and many others actively campaigned in favor of the North. Antislavery societies were formed, hundreds of meetings addressed, and tons of literature distributed. Although the majority of the meetings were held in London and in the great manufacturing districts about Manchester, no part of England or Scotland was neglected. To counteract pro-northern efforts, James Spence, William Lindsay, and other southern propagandists staged mass meetings and drafted giant petitions. Both Federal and Confederate sympathizers used slush funds freely among the poverty-stricken industrial workers of England. To what extent the unenfranchised English worker influenced his government is difficult to say.

That neither England nor France nor any other European nation recognized the Confederacy as an independent state was probably most affected by military events in America. In the late summer of 1862, when Great Britain and France were inclining toward intervention, McClellan checked Lee at the battle of Antietam. Lord Palmerston, the British Prime Minister, who had been expecting a great southern victory, at once expressed doubt whether the moment was ripe for

European overtures or recognition. Proposals for immediate action soon gave way to hesitation and cautious delay. Less than a year later, Vicksburg fell, and Lee was turned back at Gettysburg. These victories ended, or at least indefinitely postponed, any plans for recognizing the South.

Another event that kept Europe neutral was the announcement of emancipation. Antislavery sentiment was particularly strong in England, and many Englishmen found it difficult to support the North as long as Lincoln insisted that the federal government had no intention of abolishing slavery. But Lincoln's emancipation proclamations (September 22, 1862, and January 1, 1863), and the growth of the subsequent movement for widespread emancipation, removed many doubts about the purpose of the war and strengthened the position of those who favored the North.

The dependence of Great Britain on northern wheat during the greater part of the war, some claim, helped strengthen the chance for English neutrality. By 1860, the United Kingdom had become a great wheat-importing country. Wheat imports, which had averaged only 900,000 quarters for the decade 1830–40, increased to 5,030,000 quarters for 1850–60. Most of this imported grain came from the United States, Russia, Germany, and France. A succession of crop failures at home during the three-year period 1860–2 made it necessary for Great Britain to import nearly one half its wheat supply. Largely because of short harvests, the wheat-producing regions of continental Europe, Egypt, and South America were unable to meet this demand; consequently, Great Britain had to turn to the wheat-growing states of the North. Some notion of Great Britain's dependence may be gained from the fact that the wheat exports of the United States mounted from 17,500,-000 bushels in 1860 to 53,000,000 bushels in 1861 and to 62,000,000 bushels in 1862. America's wheat, moreover, was most needed at the very time when there was an oversupply of cotton. In the industrial centers, Bright, Forster, and others stressed the possibility of a wheat famine if England and the United States should go to war. It is difficult to determine to what extent, if any, the British government was influenced by this consideration. There is some reason to believe that the threat of a wheat famine was Union propaganda. Certainly it was not discussed in Parliament or by the cabinet. With few exceptions, the British press ridiculed the idea, and the *Times* pointed out that without wheat shipments to England, the United States would have been unable to pay for its tremendous purchases of war materials in Europe during these years.

Northern diplomacy ably helped to keep Europe neutral. In Charles

Francis Adams, son of John Quincy Adams, the North had a minister at the Court of St. James admirably suited by education, family, and character for the difficult tasks of war time. With a keen intellect, possessing a wide knowledge of European affairs, and renowned for his calm judgment, Adams was particularly fitted to deal with the British government. Diplomatic representatives of high caliber were also sent to the continental countries.

The most obvious reason for England's failure to intervene was war income. British cotton manufacturers and those interested in the linen and woolen industries obtained large profits. English profits in linens alone had mounted to nearly $100,000,000 by 1865. Another business that prospered during these years was the munitions industry. Exclusive of clothing, tents, shoes and leather goods, Great Britain sold the American belligerents approximately $100,000,000 worth of war supplies. Blockade runners and shipbuilders became increasingly aware of the advantages of neutrality as the profits rolled in. At the same time, the American merchant marine was practically driven from the seas, and its business fell largely to England.

Europe Aids the Confederacy

Failure to recognize the South as a sovereign nation, however, did not prevent both England and France, and to a much lesser extent Spain, from actions favorable to the Confederacy. By issuing a proclamation of neutrality, each recognized the South as a belligerent. Both Great Britain and France allowed their ports to be used as bases of operation against northern commerce. Confederate raiders like the *Alabama* and the *Florida*, built and equipped in British harbors, destroyed northern shipping worth millions of dollars. At first, the North protested in vain against this open infringement of neutrality, and not until after the Union victories of 1863 and Adams' forceful warning to the British Foreign Office that the "escape" of any more vessels destined for the Confederate service would be an act of war did the British government take steps to enforce its neutrality obligations.

The *Trent* affair at the start of the war came closer than any other event to causing an open rupture between Great Britain and the North. In 1861, the Confederacy sent James M. Mason and John Slidell to England and France respectively to work for southern recognition. Eluding the blockade at Charleston, they reached Havana and took passage for Liverpool on the British steamer *Trent*. When one day out from Havana, the *Trent* was stopped by the *San Jacinto*, an American man-of-war commanded by Captain Charles Wilkes, and the Confederate commissioners and their secretaries were taken off by force and carried to Boston, where they were held as prisoners. Wilkes had acted "without orders," but the news of his exploit was received by the people of the North with enthusiasm. The press proclaimed him a hero, and the House of Representatives gave him a vote of thanks for his "brave, adroit, and patriotic conduct." Great Britain viewed the matter differently. A neutral vessel sailing from one neutral port to another had been held up on the high seas and "searched." Forgetting the War of 1812, the English denounced Wilkes' action as an affront to the nation. An American living in London at the time wrote Seward that "there never was within memory such a burst of feeling as has been created by the news of the boarding of the *Trent*. The people are frantic with rage, and were the country polled I fear 999 men out of a thousand would declare for immediate war. Lord Palmerston cannot resist the impulse if he would." The British government under threat of war demanded the instant release of the commissioners and an apology. The navy, arsenals, and dockyards were put on a war footing, and 8,000 soldiers were hurried off to Halifax to the tune of "Dixie." Fortunately for the Federal government, the British demand was softened, and by the time it reached the United States—there being no cable or wireless—public anger on both sides had cooled. Since Wilkes' action ran counter to America's traditional policy regarding the freedom of the seas, it seemed wise to yield, and on December 26, Lincoln ordered the release of the detained commissioners. By this action, the United States ended what for a time looked like a fairly certain prospect of armed aid and recognition for the South.

Napoleon III, to whom neutrality obligations meant even less than they did to the British Ministry, supported the British in the *Trent* affair; at the same time, he sanctioned the construction of Confederate commerce-destroyers in French shipyards, indirectly assured the Confederate agents that such vessels might be fitted out in French ports, and sought to set up a puppet regime in Mexico. Victimized by foreign investors, mismanagement, and revolution, Mexico had accumulated during the years preceding the outbreak of the Civil War a foreign debt of more than $80,000,000. Of this amount, she owed English bankers $69,000,000, French $9,000,000, and Spanish a much smaller amount. Unable to collect their debts, the creditor banks appealed to their respective governments for assistance. After some delay, during which the three powers concerned endeavored without success to induce the United States to join them in intervening in Mexican affairs, in 1861 they seized Vera Cruz and other coast towns. But when Napoleon, who hoped to re-establish a French empire in the New World, suggested the capture of the Mexican capital and the reconstruction of the Mexican government—a procedure contrary to the original agreement of the allies—the British and Spanish withdrew. Backed by a Mexican faction composed for the most part of clericals, the French captured Mexico City and set up a monarchy with Maximilian of Austria, brother of Francis Joseph, as Emperor.

Before the coming of the French, the Confederacy had cultivated the friendship of the Mexicans and had formulated various schemes for gaining ultimate control of Mexican territory. Consequently, there was reason to believe that the Confederates would redouble their efforts to secure French recognition and that they would also seek an alliance with the Maximilian government. Many northerners, citing the Monroe Doctrine, wanted the federal government to take immediate action. Aware that such a policy might lead to a war with France at a time when the United States was conducting a far more important struggle, Seward at first refrained from any mention of the Monroe Doctrine and tactfully notified Napoleon that the American people were not in sympathy with his Mexican project. After Appomattox, however, in more peremptory language he insisted that the French withdraw. Napoleon, faced by domestic opposition and danger from the Prussians and realizing that the United States was now in a position to press its demands, yielded as gracefully as possible. Soon after the withdrawal of the French troops, the Emperor Maximilian fell into the hands of Juarez, the deposed Mexican President, who had waged constant warfare against the European invaders with arms and munitions quietly supplied by the North. All pleas for clemency for Maximilian were unavailing, and in June, 1867, the Hapsburg Prince, who knowingly or unknowingly had been the tool of Napoleon, met death before a firing squad.

Spain also had visions of enlarging her American empire. In 1861, she annexed the Dominican Republic, comprising the former Spanish portion of the island of Santo Domingo. Three years later, she became involved in a war with Peru, largely on the pretext that Peru had refused to reimburse certain Spaniards for alleged injuries sustained during the Peruvian wars for independence. She also seized the Chincha Islands, although the Spanish government emphatically denied any intention of acquiring them permanently. The United States protested in both instances but was powerless to do more while the Civil War lasted. With the termination of war, Spain withdrew from both territories, although her dispute with Peru was not settled until years afterward.

The North at War

Although the first year and a half of the war was accompanied by hard times, the Northern economy was on the whole greatly stimulated by the struggle. At first business slackened, mills closed, and many persons began to shift about in search of a livelihood. The *New York Tribune* in August, 1862, commented on "our paralyzed industry, obstructed commerce, our over-loaded finances, and our mangled railroads." But this state of affairs was only temporary. By the autumn of 1862, the business cycle had begun to swing upward, aided by the bumper crops of 1861 and 1862, the foreign demand for foodstuffs, and government purchases of war material.

Depression gave way to renewed industrial activity and to an unprecedented period of money making. The northern output of coal, iron, copper, salt, and the precious metals for the years 1861-5 surpassed all previous records. Twenty-one million tons of coal were mined in 1864 as against 13,000,000 tons in 1860. The pig iron output of 821,000 tons for 1860 increased to 1,014,282 tons in 1864. Petroleum production rose from almost nothing in 1859 to 128,000,000 gallons in 1862, and during the last two years of the war the North exported a total of 60,000,000 gallons. New deposits of iron, copper, and salt were opened up in Michigan, and new mines in the West greatly augmented the supply of gold and silver. Lumber production kept pace with mining; the output of the lumber camps in Maine, New York, and the Great Lakes region was the largest in the history of the industry. The farms of the North increased in number and yielded more than ever before. The wheat production of the loyal states in 1862 was greater than that for the entire Union in 1859. Wool production increased from 60,000,000 pounds in 1860 to 142,000,000 pounds in 1865. Throughout the North the evidence was the same: more acreage, larger flocks, and greater output.

The remarkable increase in northern manufactures during the war constitutes another index of northern prosperity. The manufacturer not only provided for the needs of the people at home but supplied clothing, arms, ammunition, cannon, wagons, and medical stores for the northern armies. New factories were built or old ones remodeled and enlarged, new machines and new processes were introduced, and new fortunes were amassed. The woolen industry was typical: during the war the number of carding machines increased from 3,000 to 5,000, and the annual consumption of wool mounted from 85,000,000 to more than 200,000,000 pounds. Government contracts, currency inflation, and high protective tariffs helped create high prices and enormous profits. A few industries, however, notably the manufacture of cotton cloth, suffered as a result of the war.

The wartime prosperity of the North was also obvious in greatly increased commercial activity. Banks and insurance companies flourished, and money at reasonable rates was easy to obtain. The large and profitable trade of the South, lost by secession, was more than compensated for by business expansion in the North and West. After 1862, commercial failures were astonishingly few in number, and the liabilities involved were small. Everywhere boards of trade and chambers of commerce carried on campaigns for advancing the business interests of their respective towns and of the country as a whole. Trade conventions and trade excursions were numerous, and few merchants complained.

Other evidence of the North's industrial prosperity during the war was furnished by added transportation facilities and increased shipments of both raw material and manufactured goods. New railway lines were built, and the formation of trunk lines, previously begun, was continued. Freight tonnage on many roads, including the Illinois Central, Erie, and Pennsylvania, increased by 100 per cent. Shipments by water were even larger than those by land. During the second year of the war, the number of Great Lakes vessels entering and clearing from the port of Buffalo was five times that of the best previous year. In the same year, the Erie Canal carried a tonnage greatly exceeding that of the Erie and New York Central railroads together. The western rivers and canals also did an excellent business. On the other hand, the American merchant marine suffered. In 1860, foreign trade to the value of $507,000,000 was carried in American vessels; in 1864, the traffic was only $184,000,000. Capture or fear of capture by the *Alabama* and other Confederate cruisers, the transfer of vessels to the government for transport service, the inability of American shipowners to compete with subsidized foreign vessels, and the movements of American capital away from ocean transportation caused the decline of American ocean shipping during the war.

The wartime prosperity of the North led to extravagance and luxurious living. Speaking of the unprecedented number of recently acquired fortunes, the New York *Independent* in June 25, 1864, wrote:

Who at the North would ever think of war if he had not a friend in the army, or did not read the newspapers? Go into Broadway and we will show you what is meant by the word extravagance. Ask Stewart about the demand for camels' hair shawls, and he will say "monstrous." Ask Tiffany what kind

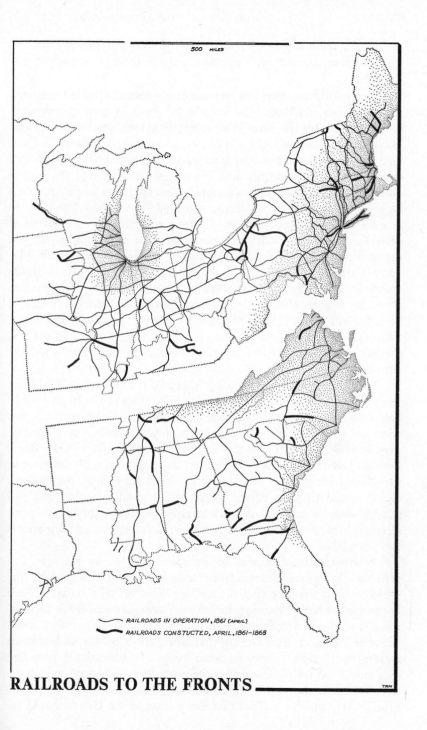

500 MILES

RAILROADS IN OPERATION, 1861 (APRIL)
RAILROADS CONSTUCTED, APRIL, 1861-1865

RAILROADS TO THE FRONTS

TRM

of diamonds and pearls are called for. He will answer "the prodigious; as near hen's egg size as possible; price no object."

Northern prosperity was not uniformly spread. The laboring and salaried classes and those who lived in less favored rural communities were hard hit by the war. Wages lagged behind commodity prices. Many families were reduced to poverty, and industrial unrest was common by 1863. "In many manufactories," the Springfield *Republican* said in 1864, "whose profits have been augmented beyond the wildest dreams of their owners, wages are only from twelve to twenty per cent higher than they were before the war, and there is absolute want in many families while thousands of young children who should be at school are shut up at work that they may earn something to eke out the scant supplies at home." If the worker quit, his place was filled by a newly arrived immigrant or his duties were performed by some labor-saving device. Faced with this situation, he could either join the army, try to go to a midwestern farm or to the mines of the Far West, or keep his job and try to improve it by joining a labor organization. Strikes were frequent and sometimes successful. At the close of the war the laborer, though better off financially than in 1863, was worse off than in 1860.

Many northern municipalities, in spite of the war and its problems, started numerous improvements during the years 1861–5. In practically every northern city new dwellings, hotels, business houses, schools, and churches were erected. In Philadelphia, approximately 7,200 building permits were issued during the last three years of the war. Portland, Boston, Lowell, and New Haven erected city halls; Brooklyn and Cleveland built new courthouses; New York City built twenty-three churches and Chicago fifteen. Many cities installed water, gas, and sewage systems and fire-alarm telegraphs, while twenty-seven built streetcar lines. A number opened new parks and improved their streets and sidewalks.

Northern education was not seriously affected by the war. Except for the decreased attendance caused by enlistment and by the withdrawal of southern students, college life went on as usual. Fifteen institutions of higher learning, including Vassar, Cornell, Bates, Swarthmore, and the Massachusetts Institute of Technology, were founded between 1861 and 1865. During the same period, private endowments totaling more than $5,000,000 were raised for educational purposes. The movement for federal aid for the promotion of agricultural education, begun in the 1850's, culminated in 1862 in the passage of the Morrill Act, which provided that every state in the Union should receive 30,000 acres of public land for every congressional representative it had in 1860 or might have at the time of its admission. At least 90 per cent of the gross proceeds of the grant were to be used for the endowment, support, and maintenance of at least one college for instruction in "such branches of learning as are related to agriculture and the mechanic arts." Under this act, the states received 10,400,000 acres of land, an area about equal to the state of Maryland. Private and professional schools flourished during the war, and the lower grades of the public schools, in spite of the demand for child labor, were filled. Low salaries and the need for men in the army and in the business and professional worlds resulted in the replacement of men by women teachers. As with wages, the scale of salaries increased somewhat during the war, but in 1865 there were still hundreds of teachers receiving less than $1.00 a day.

The South at War

The South was a striking contrast to the North. Hemmed in by the blockade, overridden by armed forces, and without fluid capital or a well-established industrial order, the majority of its people suffered privations. The decrease in the supply of commodities that had formerly been obtained from the North or from abroad led to strenuous efforts to produce them at home. Salt works were established in Virginia, North Carolina, Texas, Louisiana, and Alabama. Small, poorly equipped factories for turning out boots and shoes were set up here and there. Cotton mills backed by state subsidies were also put in operation in Georgia, South Carolina, and Alabama. Other manufactures, including hats, blankets, hosiery, candles, lamp black, printers' ink, glass, matches, and pottery, were also established, but it is doubtful if any of these industries got beyond the experimental stage, largely for want of capital, necessary machinery, and skilled labor.

During the war, southern transportation steadily deteriorated. Compared with the North, the South had few railroad systems and no trunk lines. Of the 9,283 miles in operation in 1861, approximately 3,000 miles soon fell into the hands of the Federals. The roads that were not captured or destroyed often were in need of repairs and new equipment. The consequent slow movement of goods retarded manufacturing, isolated many rural sections, and seriously impaired the fighting efficiency of the armies. Passenger travel was dangerous, and the mails were irregular and long delayed.

Under such circumstances, many merchants were ruined. Tradesmen in the larger centers benefited from blockade running, for adventurous businessmen and others who had capital soon realized that evading the blockade afforded rare opportunity for profits. Swift, narrow, side-wheel steamers loaded with cotton frequently slipped through the blockade squadron and made their way to Bermuda, Nassau, or Havana, where they exchanged their cargoes for army equipment, tea, soap, fabrics, medicines, liquors, wines, and other European merchandise. Wilmington and Charleston were the chief ports of entry on the return trip. Some trade was also carried on with Europe by way of Mexico. Commerce between the two warring sections also went on throughout the struggle, either illicitly or under quasi-authority.

Like the North, the South had its *nouveaux riches*. Men without a dollar at the beginning of the war accumulated fortunes. Others who were already well-to-do grew richer. "The greed for gain now so prevalent in the southern Confederacy," a journalist wrote in 1863, "is more wicked and infamous than the same vile passion in Yankee hearts." In the same year, Jefferson Davis wrote: "The passion for speculation has seduced citizens of all classes from a determined prosecution of the war to a sordid effort to amass money." Still others spoke of "the insatiable thirst for gain and speculation." Luxury and extravagance naturally followed. Richmond and Charleston were crowded with prosperous parvenus. Theaters were well patronized, and dances, dinners, and receptions were common occurrences. In February, 1864, the Confederate Congress prohibited the importation of foreign luxuries, but this had little effect on those who were out to show and to spend.

The mass of the southern people, however, went without many of the everyday necessities of life. As in the North, those with fixed incomes or salaries found it extremely difficult to make ends meet. By 1863, after the transportation system had begun to disintegrate, many parts of the South were impoverished. Only the rich had tea and coffee. Salt was so scarce in Alabama that the "earthen floors of smoke-houses, saturated by the dripping of bacon, were dug up and boiled." Calicoes and homespuns replaced velvets and silks. Practically every household became a workshop for making wearing apparel. In communities where commodities were available, the person of ordinary means frequently could not pay the high prices. The systematic devastation of southern territory by northern troops during the last years of the war made the problem of securing food, clothing, and shelter still more difficult.

Civil liberty in both sections was considerably restricted during the war. In the North, President Lincoln, as Commander in Chief of the armed forces of the United States, performed acts that in the minds of many persons were of doubtful constitutionality, even in wartime. Among these were the suspension of the privilege of the writ of *habeas corpus*, the authorization of arbitrary arrests, and the abridgment of freedom of speech and of writing. The writ of *habeas corpus* was first suspended in Maryland in 1861, when it was felt that a majority of the Maryland legislature would vote for secession. Several members were accordingly arrested on the charge of plotting treason and imprisoned without benefit of the writ. They at once appealed to Chief Justice Taney of the United States Supreme Court, who ruled that they had committed no crime against the civil law. Lincoln, however, ignored the ruling, and the prisoners were not released. Military arrests were made in all parts of the North, the most notorious being that of Clement L. Vallandigham of Ohio, leader of the "Copperheads," a name given to a powerful group of northerners who opposed the war. On September 24, 1862, Lincoln issued a proclamation suspending the writ of *habeas corpus* throughout the Union and ordering the arrest of all persons discouraging enlistment or guilty of any other "disloyal practice." Hundreds of arrests followed in all parts of the North, and the victims were jailed without a hearing or sentenced by military courts without a jury. This action aroused widespread opposition, and Congress passed a law generally known as the *Habeas Corpus* Act of 1863. It empowered the President to suspend the writ, but no arrested person could be kept in prison more than twenty days unless indicted by a grand jury. Lincoln virtually ignored this act, however, and military arrests of civilians continued to the end of the war. Even the press did not escape; the New York *World* and the Chicago *Times* were among the newspapers temporarily suppressed. The civil courts were powerless to assert their authority, although in 1866 the Supreme Court in the case of *ex parte Milligan* ruled that the constitutional rights of a person accused of crime could not be set aside either by the President or by the Congress in any part of the country where there was no need for military rule and where the regular courts were "in the proper and unmolested exercise of their jurisdiction."

In the South, the central government exhibited greater regard for the liberty of the individual. Unlike Lincoln, the President of the Confederacy never assumed that he had the right to suspend the writ of *habeas corpus;* and when in 1862 he declared martial law and suspended the writ in certain disaffected areas, he acted under the express authorization of his Congress. In the secession states, martial law was not used as effectively and harshly as it was in the North, and yet it met with powerful resistance. In North Carolina it was bitterly denounced, and the Supreme Court of the state went so far as to issue writs of *habeas corpus* to persons arrested and held by Confederate authority. The Georgia legislature in 1864 unanimously provided that a justice of any court who refused to grant a writ of *habeas corpus* should be subject to a fine of $2,500. Sensing the strength and determination of the opposition, the Confederate Congress gradually curtailed the President's sweeping use of the martial law power. Finally, in 1864, after protracted debate, it refused to accede to his request for a renewal of the privilege. Except when requested by the Confederate authorities to refrain from publishing dispatches that might aid the enemy, the southern newspapers were entirely without censorship or control.

Wartime Politics

Throughout the Civil War, Lincoln had to contend with four distinct political groups in the North: the conservative Republicans, radical Republicans, War Democrats, and Copperheads. The conservative Republicans, who comprised the bulk of the party, viewed the war simply as a struggle to preserve the Union. The radical Republicans, whose leaders were Thaddeus Stevens of Pennsylvania, Charles Sumner of Massachusetts, Benjamin Wade of Ohio, and Zachariah Chandler of Michigan, considered the war primarily a crusade against slavery. The War Democrats, although critical of the Lincoln Administration backed the northern war effort. The Copperheads opposed both the Union cause and Republican rule. The key to understanding Abraham Lincoln's leadership lies in his efforts to gain the support of all these groups except the Copperheads, while at the same time seeking to prevent any one of them from dominating either him or the government. To maintain this coalition, Lincoln agreed with the conservative Republicans that the war was being fought to preserve the Union, for this war aim was endorsed by the War Democrats as well as the conservatives, and the radical Republicans also approved of it, although they believed that it did not go far enough.

The make-up of the cabinet reveals a great deal about Lincoln's political strategy and the nature of the Republican party. Secretary of State William H. Seward was an ex-Whig leader from New York, Lincoln's chief rival for the Republican nomination at Chicago, and, as the war progressed, spokesman for the party's conservative wing. Balancing Seward's conservatism was the near-abolitionist Secretary of the Treasury Salmon P. Chase, an ex-Democrat from Ohio and another unsuccessful candidate for the Republican nomination in 1860. Lincoln's first Secretary of War, Simon Cameron, the boss of the Republican machine in Pennsylvania, and Secretary of the Interior Caleb Smith of Indiana were both appointed because of deals arranged by Lincoln's political managers before his nomination. Attorney General Edward Bates of Missouri and Postmaster General Montgomery Blair of Maryland provided the border states with representation in the administration. In addition, Bates was closely allied with the "American" faction of the party, while Blair was a member of a family that for years had been identified with Jacksonian democracy. Secretary of the Navy Gideon Welles knew nothing about naval affairs, but he was an ex-Democrat and the only New Englander in the cabinet. Regardless of the ability of the members of Lincoln's cabinet, they all possessed certain clearly recognizable political assets. In the aggregate, they represented every section and every faction that had given any support to the Republican party. When corruption in the War Department compelled Lincoln in January, 1862, to remove Cameron and make him minister to Russia, Edwin M. Stanton, a War Democrat who had served as Attorney General under Buchanan, became Secretary of War. With Stanton in the cabinet and McClellan who was also a Democrat, at the head of the Union armies, the management of the northern war effort was largely in the hands of Democrats. Lincoln thus could make the leaders of rival groups in and out of his party share responsibility for major decisions.

Lincoln's difficulty in maintaining what amounted to a coalition government was illustrated by an incident that occurred during his first month in office. On April 1, 1861, Seward, who was confident of his ability to dominate both the President and the administration, sent Lincoln a memorandum entitled "Some Thoughts for the President's Consideration." After stating that the government was "without a policy, either domestic or foreign," Seward proposed that the United States declare war against Spain and France. This move, the Secretary of State argued, would solve the sectional crisis, for the South would undoubtedly return to the Union to help in a war against a foreign enemy. In conclusion, Seward suggested that he be entrusted with the management of this program. Instead of dismissing or reprimanding Seward for this preposterous proposal, Lincoln politely rejected it. By adopting this course, he not only avoided an open break with the party's outstanding conservative, but he also made it clear that he, not Seward, was responsible for the formulation of the government's policies.

Despite the Seward incident, Lincoln's principal troubles arose over his relations with the radicals rather than with the conservatives in his party. The radicals in Congress made their influence felt by the Committee on the Conduct of the War, which was formed by the House and Senate in the first year of the war. Representing Congress's legitimate interest in war policies and dominated by men who wanted a vigorous prosecution of the war, punishment for the South, and rapid emancipation or abolition dominated by radicals, the committee investigated every aspect of the war effort. It sought to impose its strategic concepts on the Union military leaders, complained of McClellan's dilatory tactics, supported those generals who shared the radical views on the slavery question, and repeatedly criticized Lincoln's attitude toward the war and his conduct of the nation's military affairs. In one sense, the activity of the Committee on the Conduct of the War was an accurate indication of the determination of the radicals to convert the war into a crusade against slavery; in another it reflected the desire of many congressmen to deprive the President of the war powers granted to him by the Constitution; and in still another, it provided one more example of the civilian's deep-seated conviction that he knows more about the conduct of war than professional soldiers do. Despite recurrent tension between Lincoln and the radicals, the President cooperated with them on a number of matters and by skillful maneuvers prevented the group from coalescing against the administration.

The results of the midterm elections of 1862, which provided the free state voters with their first opportunity to pass on the administration's program, gave Lincoln little encouragement. The Democrats carried five more northern states than in 1860, including Lincoln's own state of Illinois, and if the South had been in the Union, the Republicans would have lost the election. The Democratic gains in part reflected the dissatisfaction with events in the field and the widespread opposition to Lincoln's proclamation suspending the writ of *habeas corpus*. The preliminary Emancipation Proclamation, moreover, which was issued on September 22, 1862, seemed to the conservatives to go too far, while the radicals complained that it did not go far enough. In sum, in trying to retain the support of all the loyal groups, Lincoln had ended up by completely satisfying none of them.

The results of the election and the continued military reverses led to a new radical attempt to direct the policies of the Lincoln administration. Accordingly, a group of radical senators called on the President and urged him to make "such selections and changes [in the cabinet] . . . as will secure to the country unity of purpose and action." Seward, realizing that he was the principal target of the radical attacks, sought to save the President from further embarrassment by offering to resign. But when Lincoln conferred with the committee a second time, he arranged the meeting so that all the members of the cabinet except Seward were present. Chase, although in constant touch with the members of the committee and the leading radical in the cabinet, was thus placed in a position where he felt forced, however reluctantly, to state "that the cabinet were all harmonious." "The upshot of the whole matter," in the words of Professor James G. Randall, "was that Chase as well as Seward resigned; Lincoln promptly refused to accept either resignation; and the crisis passed with a 'milder spirit' prevailing, the cabinet continuing as before, the senators somewhat chagrined, Chase embarrassed, and the President holding the tricks."

Lincoln's ability to outmaneuver the radicals could not obscure the fact that their stand on the slavery question was threatening to disrupt both the Republican party and the administration. As the war progressed, it also became increasingly clear that Lincoln could not indefinitely postpone taking a stand on this issue. He had been elected on a platform calling for the restriction, but not for the abolition, of slavery. Congress, on July 22, 1861, had passed a resolution stating that the war was being waged, not to overthrow slavery or interfere with the rights or the established institutions of the South, but to preserve the Union; and Lincoln was in accord with this resolution. Nevertheless, the President privately, as well as many others besides the abolitionists, believed that slavery was wrong and that it ought to be abolished. Despite his personal convictions on the question, despite the innumerable petitions and suggestions for emancipating the slaves, and despite the denunciations hurled at him by the gifted abolitionist leader, Wendell Phillips, and others, Lincoln remained adamant throughout 1861. For his inaction and for what seemed to many his wavering policy, Lincoln had numerous reasons. Basically a conservative who took only the minimal position forced on him by circumstances, Lincoln said that his policy was "to have no policy." He believed that neither he nor Congress had any authority under the Constitution to emancipate a single slave, and he feared that if such action were taken it would lead to the secession of the four border states. Furthermore, he knew that many northern soldiers who had enlisted to save the Union would not have enlisted to free slaves.

By the spring of 1862, circumstances had changed. Throughout the Confederacy, Negroes were being used for military purposes: they produced food for the soldiers, served as teamsters in the army, and helped to construct entrenchments. Many prominent northerners believed that drastic action should be taken to put an end to this source of southern military strength. Hundreds of escaped slaves flocked into the camps of the northern armies, and their presence raised a number of embarrassing questions. Were they contraband property, and, if so, should they be confiscated? If not, should they be returned to their masters in accordance with the Fugitive Slave Act? Then, too, the antislavery extremists or radical element of the Republican party, daily growing stronger and more influential, insisted that slavery be forever ended. Finally, certain northern leaders believed that perhaps the best way to prevent foreign intervention and to strengthen the cause of the North would be to favor widespread emancipation. Consequently, the administration began to modify its course. On April 10, 1862, Congress voted to extend financial aid to any state that might adopt gradual emancipation. Within a week, it enacted another law providing for compensated liberation of the slaves in the District of Columbia. Two months later, on June 19, the Republican majority swept slavery forever from the federal territories, despite the fact that Chief Justice Taney still lived and that the Dred Scott decision had supposedly settled the question of slavery for all time. This action was followed on July 17, 1862, by the passage of the Second Confiscation Act.

Meanwhile, Lincoln, aware of changing conditions and of the growing northern sentiment in favor of emancipation, had decided that slavery had to go but wanted it to disappear peacefully and with as little rancor as possible; for he had grave doubts that the two races could live peacefully together in freedom, and he did not believe in full equality between the black and white races. Accordingly, he formulated a program providing for gradual emancipation, full compensation to owners, and colonization of the freedmen in Liberia or Latin America. But this proposal came to nothing. The border-state leaders, with whom Lincoln pleaded for its adoption, rejected it as infringing the constitutional right to hold slaves and as being financially impracticable. Abolitionists condemned it as a scheme for "enriching thieves and robbers!" Chagrined by his failure to effect gradual abolition, Lincoln concluded that if the Union were to be saved, the time had arrived for him to emancipate the slaves by proclamation. Basing his authority for such action on the war powers of the Constitution, he read the draft of a proclamation of emancipation to his cabinet on July 22, 1862, just ten days after his last futile meeting with the representatives of the border states. On the advice of Seward, however, he laid it aside until the North achieved a notable victory on the field of battle. Antietam afforded the desired opportunity, and on September 22, 1862, a preliminary proclamation declared that all slaves in any part of the Confederacy in rebellion against the United States on January 1, 1863, should be forever free. This limited proclamation did not apply to the four border states or to those parts of the Confederacy under the control of the federal armies. It "freed" only those slaves in areas where the federal government could not enforce its will; i.e., behind Confederate lines.

The preliminary proclamation provoked various responses. Some antislavery Radicals, dissatisfied because Lincoln did not free all the

Lincoln's Cabinet with the Emancipation Proclamation (Left to right, sitting: Stanton, War; Lincoln; Welles, Navy; Seward, State; Bates, Attorney General. Standing: Chase, Treasury; Smith, Interior; Blair, Postmaster General.

slaves, continued to attack him. The proslavery groups both North and South professed to see in the proclamation the menace of Negro equality and social demoralization. In England, although liberal leaders and working class people welcomed the proclamation, others regarded it as an effort by the administration to incite a servile war. It was received with apprehension and contempt by the press. On the Continent, much the same feeling prevailed.

Lincoln, though greatly perturbed by the opposition to the preliminary proclamation and by the fact that his party lost more than thirty seats in Congress in the fall elections of 1862, did not alter his course. In his message of December, 1862, he said: "Without slavery the rebellion could never have existed; without slavery it could not continue." On January 1, 1863, he issued a second proclamation that confirmed the first and announced that the former slaves would be received into the armed forces of the United States. Thereafter the movement for emancipation gathered headway. Between 1863 and 1865, Missouri, Tennessee, Maryland, and parts of Louisiana, Arkansas, and Virginia abolished slavery by state action. Emancipation was completed on December 18, 1865, with the ratification of the Thirteenth Amendment, which forbade slavery and involuntary servitude anywhere in the United States or in territory subject to its jurisdiction, except as punishment for crime.

The Emancipation Proclamation did not end Lincoln's troubles. As the election of 1864 approached, there again seemed no way to prevent a split in the party. Despite Chase's presence in the cabinet, his supporters were working openly for his nomination for the presidency. Even some conservative Republican leaders opposed Lincoln's nomination. More damaging to party unity was the nomination of John C. Fremont at a radical convention held in Cleveland in May, 1864. Despite these developments, the Republican convention was dominated by administration supporters. In order to gain votes and to appear nonpartisan, the party was renamed the Union Party. Lincoln was unanimously renominated, and Andrew Johnson, a War Democrat of Tennessee, was named the party's vice-presidential candidate. The Democrats selected General McClellan as their candidate and adopted a "peace plank" which referred to the war as "four years of failure." But, since both McClellan and his Democratic supporters also thought that the Union should be preserved at all costs, their position was not unlike that of the Republican or Union party.

Throughout a large part of the campaign, it seemed likely that Lincoln would be defeated. In order to win the election, Lincoln used his patronage powers ruthlessly. He had soldiers who could be spared sent home to vote, and Nevada was brought into the Union in order to get its electoral votes. Two developments shortly before election day insured Lincoln's victory. On September 22, Fremont dropped out of the campaign, and news of Sherman's entrance into Atlanta convinced even the most dubious northerners that the collapse of the Confederacy was only a matter of time. Although Lincoln's popular majority over McClellan was only 400,000, he carried every free state but New Jersey, Kentucky, and Delaware, and the electoral vote was 212 for Lincoln to 21 for McClellan.

The election of 1864 was in a very real sense a vindication of Lincoln's policies. He had held the Republicans together, and he had retained the support of a majority of northerners despite defeats in the field and factionalism in his party. At times he appeared to be the only political leader in the North who realized that the preservation of the Union required the united efforts of all those who were fighting the South. The Civil War had, among other things, transformed Lincoln from an ambitious, evasive, local politician in quest of a job into a national leader and statesman.

On April 15, 1865, six days after Lee's surrender, Lincoln was assassinated by John Wilkes Booth. The shock occasioned by the President's death was exceeded only by the extent to which friends and foes of the fallen leader vied in praising him. Lincoln died a martyr, but he was more than that; as Americans increasingly came to appreciate his humility, his contribution to the preservation of their nation, his magnanimity, and his ability to laugh at himself while sympathizing with others, they made him a symbol of all that they treasured most in their nation's history.

End and Beginning

The Civil War marked, but did not necessarily cause, the conclusion of one era and the beginning of another in the history of American civilization. In the years following the conflict, the United States was to return to those pursuits that have preoccupied its citizens until the present day. With the elimination of the menace of disunion, the American people increasingly devoted their energies to developing industry, exploiting the country's mineral deposits, expanding its transportation facilities, and building up its financial power.

A decade before Fort Sumter, the United States had been a commercial and farming civilization; twenty years after Appomattox, it was being transformed into an industrial society. Although large numbers of Americans still depended on agriculture for a livelihood, it was the industrialist and financier rather than the farmer who shaped the course of national policy, controlled the country's economy, and set the standards by which their fellow citizens lived and thought. This transformation was to be symbolized by the growth of the city. Although millions of Americans continued to live in rural areas, it was in the city that the culture of postbellum America was developed and then imposed upon the rest of the country.

Although Americans for years after the Civil War continued to glorify the exploits of the individual, the fact remained that the individual steadily lost out to the institutions that he had created. Individualism was still a basic tenet of the American creed, but in an age of big business, big government, big labor, and big agriculture, the kind of individualism that had been expounded by Jefferson and Emerson could serve no other function than to remind Americans of a past that they could never recapture, however much they idealized it. The Civil War had been fought to solve problems that had grown out of an earlier age; but it paved the way for the emergence of those institutions and ideals that today are still very much a part of American life.

FOR SUPPLEMENTARY READING

The best one-volume general study of the Civil War is David Donald's revision of J. G. Randall, *The Civil War and Reconstruction* (1961). A short sketch is A. Barker, *The Civil War in America* (1961). Randall was the most authoritative Lincoln scholar of our time. His four volumes on Lincoln's presidency are *Lincoln the President* (1945–55). There is also an excellent selection of essays by Randall in *Lincoln the Liberal Statesman* (1947). The best one-volume study of Lincoln is B. P. Thomas, *Abraham Lincoln* (1952). Carl Sandburg's *Abraham Lincoln* (1954) is a one-volume edition of his leading work on Lincoln as folk hero. No student should fail to read the works by two of Randall's best students—D. Donald, *Lincoln Reconsidered* (1956), and R. N. Current, *The Lincoln Nobody Knows* (1963) (Pb) and *Lincoln and the First Shot* (1965).

On the North during the war, use P. W. Gates, *Agriculture and the Civil War* (1965), and E. D. Fite, *Social and Economic Conditions in the North During the Civil War* (1910). Relatively short but good histories of the southern nation are C. Eaton, *A History of the Confederacy* (1954); C. P. Roland, *The Confederacy* (1960); and F. E. Vandiver, *Basic History of the Confederacy* (1962).

The military histories of the war are staggering in number. The dramatic works of Bruce Catton—*Mr. Lincoln's Army* (1951), *Glory Road* (1952), *A Stillness at Appomattox* (1954), and *This Hallowed Ground* (1956)—are predominantly studies of the Army of the Potomac. There still does not exist any single well-scaled general study of the northern armies, but students may use T. H. Williams, *Lincoln and His Generals* (1952). For the southern armies, use D. S. Freeman, *R. E. Lee: A Biography* (4 vols., 1934–35), abridged in one volume by R. H. Lee (1961), and *Lee's Lieutenants* (3 vols., 1942–44). F. Vandiver, *Rebel Brass* (1956), is an important analysis of the southern command. For the life of the soldiers, use H. S. Commager, *The Blue and the Gray* (2 vols., 1950), and B. I. Wiley, *The Life of Johnny Reb* (1943) and *The Life of Billy Yank* (1952). Special studies with obvious interest are B. Quarles, *The Negro in the Civil War* (1953), and D. T. Cornish, *The Sable Arm: Negro Troops in the Union Army, 1861–65* (1958). A fine military historian, J. F. C. Fuller, has written a book that comprehensively evaluates the chief generalships of the war: *Grant and Lee* (rev. ed., 1957). The military in politics is debated in G. McWhinney (ed.), *Grant, Lee, Lincoln, and the Radicals* (1966).

Two books that should be used first on wartime diplomacy are E. D. Adams, *Great Britain and the American Civil War* (2 vols., 1925), and F. L. Owsley, *King Cotton Diplomacy* (rev. ed., 1959).

Wartime politics and personalities other than the generals are the central themes of T. H. Williams, *Lincoln and the Radicals* (1951); H. J. Carman and R. Luthin, *Lincoln and the Patronage* (1943); D. Donald's edition of Chase's diaries, *Inside Lincoln's Cabinet* (1954), and *The Diary of Gideon Welles* (3 vols., 1911). For southern politics, use B. J. Hendrick, *Statesmen of the Lost Cause* (1939); F. L. Owsley, *States Rights in the Confederacy* (1925); R. W. Patrick, *Jefferson Davis and His Cabinet* (1944); H. Strode, *Jefferson Davis, Confederate President* (1959).

There is no agreement on the reasons for southern defeat, but reviews of the possibilities are B. I. Wiley, *The Road to Appomattox* (1956), and D. Donald (ed.), *Why the North Won the Civil War* (1960).

The future of the Negro at the time is analyzed in B. Quarles, *Lincoln and the Negro* (1962) and J. M. McPherson, *The Struggle for Equality: Abolitionists and the Negro in the Civil War and Reconstruction* (1964).

There remain to be set off by themselves three recent general works on the war: A. Nevins, "The War for the Union," 2 vols. to date—*The Improvised War 1861–1862* (1959) and *War Becomes Revolution* (1960); Bruce Catton, "The Centennial History of the Civil War" (3 vols., 1961–65)—*The Coming Fury, Terrible Swift Sword,* and *Never Call Retreat;* and Edmund Wilson, *Patriotic Gore* (1962), a remarkable study of intellectuals' responses to the war.

The Legacy of Civil War

THE CIVIL WAR, which was fought to preserve the Union, helped to undermine the economic and social foundations on which the antebellum Union had rested. After the war, the South was reduced to the status of a conquered province, and the North was transformed by a revolution that subordinated the farm to the factory and supplanted the standards of an agrarian society with the mores of an industrial civilization. By 1877, when the last northern troops were withdrawn from the defeated South, it was clear that the North had won more than a military victory. Although farmers still comprised the single largest element in the population, the United States had become an industrial nation for good or ill.

The Victorious North

In the years immediately following the Civil War, the North entered a period of unprecedented prosperity. Profits reached record levels, wages were higher than at any previous time in the nation's history, and farmers had little difficulty in disposing of their products at favorable prices. Turning their backs on the reforms that they had espoused before the war, northerners plunged wholeheartedly into the more prosaic—but equally serious—business of making money. Few doubted that the end justified the means, and most agreed that the end was the accumulation of wealth.

Proposed Arcade Railway, New York City, 1876

[NEW YORK PUBLIC LIBRARY]

The postwar boom was sustained by the rapid development of northern industry. A friendly government, an expanding domestic market, and a seemingly limitless supply of natural resources combined to produce a spectacular growth in all forms of business activity. Men who had accumulated wartime profits invested their surplus funds in new and old enterprises, and Europeans poured money into the American economy. The government, which before the war had devoted its energies to promoting the interests of the farmers, now aided industrialists by raising tariffs, encouraging the immigration of cheap labor, depriving southern agrarians of a voice in national affairs, and turning over to private corporations extensive tracts of the public domain. Entrepreneurs were quick to take advantage of these opportunities, and for almost a decade after Appomattox the North steadily enlarged its manufacturing facilities, extended and improved its transportation system, and exploited its mineral resources.

Almost every branch of American industry grew with amazing rapidity during the war and postwar years. From 1860 to 1870, the number of factories in the United States increased by 80 per cent, railroad lines increased by 22,000 miles, oil refining developed into a major industry, and the United States became one of the world's leading producers of iron and steel. Comparable advances were made in the consumer goods industries. The output of shoes, for example, rose from 5,000,000 pairs in 1864 to 25,000,000 in 1870; the number of woolen mills increased from 1,559 in 1850 to 2,891 in 1870, the number of workers employed in the mills from 39,352 to 80,053, and the number of pounds of wool turned into cloth from 70,900,000 to 172,100,000. In many fields of manufacturing, moreover, there was a marked increase in the tempo of mechanization, in the subdivision of labor, in mass production, in industrial consolidation, and in the use of high pressure salesmanship to reach a national rather than local market.

The postwar boom gave speculators and freebooters unexampled opportunities for quick profits. The inexperience of a large part of the investing public and the absence of restrictive regulations made it comparatively easy for economic adventurers to water stock, turn security exchanges into gambling casinos, and sell stock in any one of a variety of bogus enterprises. In an age that was perhaps the most corrupt in the nation's history, Daniel Drew, Jay Gould, and Jim Fisk earned well-merited reputations as practitioners of the art of fraudulent manipulation. One of their most notorious exploits was the "Erie War" waged against Cornelius Vanderbilt in 1867.

When Vanderbilt, who was head of the New York Central, attempted to obtain control of the Erie from Drew, Gould, and Fisk, they prevented him from securing a majority of the stock and crippled him financially at the same time by issuing $10,000,000 of worthless Erie securities which they dumped on the market at just the moment when Vanderbilt's heavy purchases had pushed the price to record levels. In the legal quarrels that followed, Gould and Fisk more than matched the bribes that Vanderbilt had paid to both judges and legislators. In the summer of 1868, they issued still more Erie stock, sold it to a gullible public, and put their profits in New York City's leading national banks. Because the National Banking Act of 1863 required every national bank in New York to maintain a reserve in greenbacks or other legal tender equal to 25 per cent of its indebtedness, Drew, Gould, and Fisk were able to disrupt the money market by demanding that the banks repay them in greenbacks. To meet this demand the banks had to call in their loans, and the resulting money stringency produced a decline in both trade and security prices. The Erie triumvirate immediately capitalized on this situation by buying up large blocks of securities at a fraction of their former value. As gold had also fallen in price, they purchased it at bargain rates and pushed up its

"The Commodore" Cornelius Vanderbilt

price to record figures by withdrawing it from the market. In the fall of 1869, after inducing President Grant to refrain from any move that might lower the price of gold, Gould and Fisk again cornered the country's gold supply. On September 24, 1869—or "Black Friday"—gold, which had been quoted at 132* on September 2, had reached 160; and the country was saved from financial ruin only after Grant had belatedly authorized the government to place $4,000,000 in gold on the market.

Drew, Gould, and Fisk were the most notorious—but not the only —examples of business corruption in the postwar decade. In an age in which misrepresentation was often synonymous with "good business," a premium was placed on results regardless of how they were achieved.

* This figure represents the price of gold in relation to greenbacks.

"Gentleman Jim" James Fisk, Jr.

Convinced that there was no greater crime than to die poor, many businessmen felt that they were forced by circumstances to be ruthless, predatory, and dishonest. Ethically it is difficult to distinguish between a railroad-wrecker like Daniel Drew and a professional desperado like Jesse James, and perhaps all that is left for the social historian to record is that the first died in his bed and that the second was killed by a bullet in the back of his head.

The correct practices of some of the nation's businessmen were matched by the fraudulent activities of numerous officials in the local, state, and federal governments. The success of many of the business ventures undertaken during the Civil War depended in part on some form of governmental assistance, and after the war the politicians soon made it clear that they expected to be reimbursed for any aid that they provided. Judicial decisions more than once went to the highest bidder, and legislators at every level of government were paid for subsidies, utility franchises, contracts for public works, monopolistic grants, and the assurance that the authorities would neither investigate nor regulate certain business practices. Because the politician had favors to sell and the entrepreneur had the money to purchase them, bribery became an accepted way of doing business. In Mark Twain and Charles Dudley Warner's *The Gilded Age* (1873), one of the characters tells how to obtain a congressional appropriation for a "public improvement" company—a description that provides some indication (even after adequate allowance has been made for the satirist's right to exaggerate) of the techniques of political corruption:

> Why the matter is simple enough. A Congressional appropriation costs money. Just reflect, for instance. A majority of the House committee, say $10,000 apiece—$40,000; a majority of the Senate committee, the same each—say $40,000; a little extra to one or two chairmen of one or two such committees, say $10,000 each—$20,000; and there's $100,000 of the money gone, to begin with. Then, seven male lobbyists, at $3,000 each—$21,000; one female lobbyist, $10,000; a high moral Congressman or Senator here and there—the high moral ones cost more . . . ten of these at $3,000 each, is $30,000; then a lot of small-fry country members, who won't vote for anything whatever without pay—say twenty at $500 apiece is $10,000; a lot of dinners to members—say $10,000 altogether; lot of jim-cracks for Congressmen's wives and children—those go a long way—you can't spend too much . . . in that line—those . . . cost in a lump, say $10,000—along there somewhere;—and then comes your printed documents—your maps, your tinted engravings, your pamphlets, your illuminated show-cards, your advertisements in a hundred and fifty papers at ever so much a line—because you've got to keep the papers all right or you are gone up, you know. Oh, my dear sir, printing bills are destruction itself. Ours so far amount to—let me see—10; 52; 22; 13;—and then there's 11; 14; 33—well, never mind the details, the total in clean numbers foots up $118,254.42 thus far!

Although every major American city was looted by designing politicians during the postwar years, New York City enjoyed the dubious distinction of being the most corruptly governed municipality in the nation. A Tammany "ring," headed by William Marcy Tweed, a former chair-maker and volunteer fireman, robbed the city of millions of dollars annually. Under the direction of Boss Tweed, Mayor A. Oakey Hall, Peter B. Sweeny, and "Slippery Dick" Connolly, New York increased its debt tenfold within a decade. A county courthouse, worth approximately $25,000, cost the taxpayers $8,000,000, and the building's furnishings added another $3,000,000 to the total. Paving con-

"Boss" William Tweed

tracts, public printing, sewers, parks, and hospitals all provided profits for members of the ring, which had stolen more than $20,000,000 by 1871. Tweed, who boasted that he would soon be as rich as Vanderbilt, moved to a large mansion on Fifth Avenue, kept his blooded horses in mahogany stables, and replied to his critics by asking: "What are you going to do about it?" And for a time it seemed as though nothing could be done. With the support of his henchmen in the state legislature and a subservient governor, he secured a revision of the city charter that placed New York completely at his mercy. At the same time, a committee of prominent citizens, after investigating the city's finances, announced that they could discover no irregularities. Although Thomas Nast had waged a merciless campaign against Tweed in his cartoons in *Harper's*, it was not until an attempt was made to bribe both the *Times* and *Harper's* that public opinion turned against the boss. The chance installation of one of Tweed's enemies in the city comptroller's office led to a split in Tammany, a series of revelations, and the eventual prosecution of the machine leaders. Tweed, who was convicted of stealing $6,000,000, escaped to Spain; but he was subsequently extradited and returned to jail, where he died in 1878.

State governments were as corrupt as those of the nation's cities. Most New York state legislators—whether they were merchants, lawyers, up-state farmers, or members of Tammany Hall—had their price; and at the height of the Erie War, one New York senator accepted $75,000 from Vanderbilt and $100,000 from Gould, and then voted for Gould. At Harrisburg, the capital of Pennsylvania, Simon Cameron and Matthew S. Quay saw to it that almost no bill of importance could be put through unpurchased. For years the Illinois legislature was run by the state's corporations, contractors, and land speculators. In Wisconsin a powerful railway lobby crushed unfriendly measures, while in Kansas, Missouri, and a number of other western states the giving and taking of bribes was an accepted part of the legislative process.

Because the federal government could offer businessmen particularly favorable prizes, its members were able to make enormous sums of money from graft and bribery. Politics was converted into a business, and, like any good businessman, the politician sold his wares and services to the highest bidder. Vernon L. Parrington, in describing what he called "the great barbecue," has written:

Congress had rich gifts to bestow—in lands, tariffs, subsidies, favors of all sorts; and when influential citizens made their wishes known to the reigning statesmen, the sympathetic politicians were quick to turn the government into the fairy godmother the voters wanted it to be. A huge barbecue was spread to which all presumably were invited. Not quite all, to be sure; inconspicuous persons, those who were at home on the farm or at work in the mills and offices, were overlooked; a good many indeed out of the total number of the American people. But all the important persons, leading bankers and promoters and business men, received invitations. There wasn't room for everybody and these were presumed to represent the whole. It was a splendid feast. If the waiters saw to it that the choicest portions were served to favored guests, they were not unmindful of their numerous homespun constituency and they loudly proclaimed the fine democratic principle that what belongs to the people should be enjoyed by the people—not with petty bureaucratic restrictions, not as a social body, but as individuals, each free citizen using what came to hand for his own private ends, with no questions asked.*

In aiding the businessman, the government also accelerated the postwar cycle of boom and bust. By the end of the 1860's, there was ample evidence of overexpansion in many areas of northern business enterprise. The number of business firms in the United States jumped from 431,000 in 1870 to 609,904 in 1871. The annual increase in railroad mileage, which averaged about 1,300 miles in 1860–67, rose to about 5,000 in 1869, and to about 5,700 in 1870; and during the next two years 13,000 miles were built. But of 364 railroads in 1872, only 104 paid dividends, and 69 of these paid less than 10 per cent. At the same time, American exports lagged behind imports, and in the early 1870's the United States had to export $130,000,000 annually to cover its trade deficit and interest payments on the capital it had borrowed abroad. The nation's credit structure also was top-heavy, for in the period from 1868 to 1873 the volume of bank loans increased seven times as fast as bank deposits. Perhaps most dangerous were the movements of capital from productive to speculative enterprises and the rise in the number of business failures from 2,915 in 1871 to 4,069 in 1872.

The crash came in 1873. On September 8, the New York Warehouse and Securities Company failed, followed within two weeks by Kenyon, Cox and Company and Jay Cooke and Company. On September 20, the New York Stock Exchange closed for ten days "to save the entire Street from utter ruin"; but nothing could prevent the cumulative effect of the collapse. By the end of 1873, there had been more than 5,000 commercial failures with liabilities totaling $228,500,000, and 89 railroads had defaulted on their bonds. For the next five years, there was little prospect of returning prosperity. In 1876–7, more than 18,000 business firms failed, at least half the nation's mills and factories closed, and unemployment steadily increased. It was not until 1878 that any signs of a business revival appeared, and it was not until 1880 that full recovery had been achieved.

The Defeated South

At the end of the Civil War, the South was bitter and exhausted. In five years the section's white population had declined from almost 5,500,000 to fewer than 5,000,000, and more than 250,000 Confederate

* Vernon L. Parrington: *Main Currents in American Thought*, Vol. III, *The Beginnings of Critical Realism, 1860–1920* (New York: Harcourt, Brace & Company, Inc., 1930), p. 23. Copyright 1930 by, and reprinted with permission of, Harcourt, Brace & Company, Inc.

soldiers had been killed during the war. To those who survived, the present seemed intolerable and the future hopeless, for the war had destroyed not only a large part of the South's physical assets, but also its way of life. With the northern victory, the southerners were left with little to cherish but their memories.

Few parts of the South had escaped the effects of the war. From Harper's Ferry to Newmarket, Virginia—a distance of about eighty miles—barns, mills, haystacks, and houses had been burned to the ground. Livestock, fences, and bridges had been destroyed. The region between Washington and Richmond was a wasteland of gutted villages and farm buildings. In Georgia and the Carolinas, Sherman's army had left a path of destruction that was "heart-sickening," while large parts of Arkansas and northern Alabama presented scenes of appalling ruin. The valley of the Tennessee was so devastated that six years after the war Robert Somers, an English traveler, reported that

> . . . it consists for the most part of plantations in a state of semi-ruin, and plantations of which the ruin is for the present total and complete. . . . The trial of war is visible throughout the valley in burnt-up gin-houses, ruined bridges, mills and factories . . . and in large tracts of once cultivated land stripped of every vestige of fencing.

The towns and cities of the South were almost as desolate as the countryside. Richmond, largely destroyed by fire when it was evacuated by the Confederate troops, was a mass of charred ruins. In Columbia, South Carolina, an area of eighty blocks containing 1,386 buildings had been converted into a dreary stretch of blackened chimneys and crumbling walls. Charleston, which had suffered from repeated bombardments and two disastrous fires, was described by a northern visitor as a city "of ruins, of desolation, of vacant houses, of widowed women, of rotting wharves, of deserted warehouses, of weed-wild gardens, of miles of grass-grown streets, of acres of pitiful and voiceless barrenness." Masses of fire-smoked brick and mortar, burned timber, twisted scraps of tin roofing, and thousands of tons of débris were evidence that Sherman had passed through Atlanta. "Hell has laid her egg," said a Georgian viewing Atlanta, "and right here it hatched." In Mobile, nine blocks had been destroyed by an explosion; a large part of the wharves had been torn up and used for firewood; half the warehouses and shops were closed; and an atmosphere of decay enveloped the narrow, dirty streets in which wretched men loafed dispiritedly. Galveston, according to a reporter, was "a city of dogs and desolation . . . utterly insignificant and Godforsaken." Even in New Orleans, where there was little physical damage, the spirit of the people seemed broken, and business was virtually at a standstill.

The South was devastated, but its people were not completely poverty-stricken. But much of their capital had disappeared in a sea of worthless Confederate stocks, bonds, and currency. Many banks and insurance companies were bankrupt. The property in slaves, estimated at almost two billion dollars, had been wiped out by the Thirteenth Amendment to the Constitution. Farmers and planters lacked tools, stock, seeds, and money. Land values were incredibly low, and many plantations were heavily mortgaged. Mills, factories, and mines that had not been destroyed were closed. All coin had disappeared long before 1865, and stocks of merchandise were practically exhausted. Whitelaw Reid, a New York journalist who visited the South just after the war, wrote:

> Everything has been mended, and generally in the rudest style. Window-glass has given way to thin boards in railway coaches and in the cities. Furniture is marred and broken, and none has been replaced for four years. Dishes are cemented in various styles and half the pitchers have tin handles. A complete set of crockery is never seen, and in very few families is there enough to set a table. . . . A set of forks with whole tines is a curiosity. Clocks and watches have nearly all stopped. . . . Hair brushes and tooth brushes have all worn out; combs are broken. . . . Pins, needles and thread, and a thousand such articles, which seem indispensable to housekeeping, are very scarce.

Despite the widespread destruction and the contemporary sense that the South had been ruined, the former Confederate states had not been fully impoverished. Much of the crudity, rudeness, and even some of the ruins seen by northern and foreign observers at the time had carried over from before 1860, when whole areas of the South had lived in crude conditions. Most of the war devastation and bankruptcy had taken place within the planter class who, whatever the economic facts, were convinced that the war had ruined them and their society. Nevertheless, after 1865, the rebuilding of southern cities, the early postwar expansion of cotton factories and the rebuilding of some railroads were southern financed. Even within the planter group, many men were still wealthy enough to apply for the special presidential pardon for rebellion necessary for ex-Confederates with wealth in excess of $20,000. Mounting evidence seems to indicate that, although there was probably a large shift in ownership, the plantation system did not break up but soon reverted to the prewar pattern of growing at the expense of the middle size and smaller farmers.

In the first year or two after the war, the available southern energy for reconstruction was hindered in several ways. The South's economic problems were aggravated by the almost complete lack of transportation facilities. Horses, mules, wagons, and carriages were scarce; country roads had become practically impassable through neglect; and bridges that had not been burned or washed away were in need of repair. Most of the river steamboats had been captured or destroyed, while the few that were intact were worn out. With the exception of the railroads that had been used by the federal government, southern rail facilities were either destroyed or useless. Two thirds of the railroad companies in the section were bankrupt. Virtually all the Virginia lines were out of commission. Every mile of railway in Georgia and South Carolina that could be used by the Confederacy had been destroyed by Sherman. Alabama's 800 miles of railway were practically worthless, and the New Orleans, Jackson, and Great Northern—Mississippi's leading railroad before the war—was a scrapheap.

With the defeat of the Confederate armies, the region's central, state, and local governments collapsed, and for some time there was little or no check placed on the more unruly elements in the population. Guerrilla and outlaw bands terrorized many parts of the South. In Texas alone, more than 5,000 men secured their livelihood by organized robbery and murder. Almost every neighborhood north of the Arkansas was pillaged by guerrillas, and in Alabama and Mississippi highwaymen made it practically impossible to carry on trade between towns.

Southern economic recovery was also impeded at first by the activities of federal treasury agents, who were paid a commission of approximately 25 per cent to discover and confiscate Confederate army stores. Left largely to their own devices, many of these agents seized and sold private property to which they had no legal claim. Horses, mules, wagons, tobacco, rice, sugar, and cotton were frequently taken in spite of the protests of their rightful owners. "I am sure I sent some honest cotton agents South," Secretary of the Treasury McCulloch wrote, "but it seems doubtful whether any of them remained honest very long." In his special report of 1866, McCulloch stated:

. . . Residents and others in the districts where these peculations were going on took advantage of the unsettled conditions of the country, and representing themselves as agents of this department, went about robbing under such pretended au-

"The Capture of Jefferson Davis, Disguised as a Woman" (*A Myth*)

thority, and thus added to the difficulties of the situation by causing unjust opprobrium and suspicion to rest upon officers engaged in the faithful discharge of their duties. Agents . . . frequently received or collected property . . . which the law did not authorize them to take . . Lawless men, singly and in organized bands, engaged in general plunder; every species of intrigue and speculation and theft were resorted to.

While these agents turned over about $34,000,000 to the United States, it is impossible even to guess how much money they kept for themselves. In subsequent years, 40,000 southern claimants were indemnified for property that had been taken from them illegally. Many thousands of others, unable to prove that they had been defrauded, received nothing.

At the same time that the South was seeking to solve its economic problems, it was also forced to work out a new set of relationships between the region's white groups and the 3,500,000 newly liberated Negroes. The majority of the Negroes were at first too bewildered to appreciate the meaning of their new status. To some, freedom meant a change of name, a new job, and the right to go wherever they pleased. Many freedmen became migrants; some supported themselves by thievery; and still others died from hunger. Many, too, thought that freedom meant education, an opportunity to become the equals of the whites, and a gift from the government of "forty acres and a mule." A relatively large number of Negroes remained with their former masters until their role as freedmen had been clarified. Although freedom meant many different things to the Negroes, the white southerners, like most northerners, were almost unanimous in their agreement that it should not mean equality of the races.

The South started upon this critical period of readjustment without the political services of its former leaders, for the federal government at first barred most members of the planter class from politics in the years immediately following Appomattox. This policy, regardless of its merits, further antagonized a people who were already embittered by war and defeat. At the same time, a large part of the control over southern political affairs passed initially into the hands of northern military and civilian officials. For the white southerners, the hatred engendered by the war was compounded by its aftermath, and in 1866 a Virginia patrician, who had been robbed and pillaged by northern troops, in drawing up his will wrote:

> . . . I give and bequeath to my children and grandchildren, and their descendants throughout all generations, that bitter hatred and everlasting malignity of my heart and soul against the Yankees, including all the people north of Mason and Dixon's line, and I do hereby exhort and entreat my children and grandchildren, if they have any love or veneration for me, to instill in the hearts of their children and grandchildren, and all their future descendants, from their childhood, this bitter hatred and these malignant feelings, against the aforesaid people and their descendants throughout all future time and generations.

To some wealthy and influential southerners, defeat and the prospect of northern domination were so distasteful that they preferred emigration to remaining in America, while others moved to northern cities. But most southern leaders—including Robert E. Lee, Wade Hampton, and Jefferson Davis—believed that the South's difficulties were the very reason why its people should not abandon their homeland. Hampton urged his fellow citizens to "devote their whole energies to the restoration of law and order, the reestablishment of agriculture and commerce, the promotion of education and the rebuilding of our cities and dwellings which have been laid in ashes." And Lee, in arguing against emigration, maintained that all should "share in the fate of their respective states." "The thought of abandoning the country and all that must be left in it [he said] is abhorrent to my feelings . . . The South requires the aid of her sons now more than at any other period of her history."

For the mass of southerners who remained in their section, the most pressing problem was economic rehabilitation. Half a million farms and plantations, many of them bankrupt or on the verge of insolvency, had to be restored; gutted homes and a ruined transportation system had to be rebuilt; credit had to be re-established; and, perhaps most important of all, some substitute had to be found for slave labor. Neither the whites nor the Negroes had had much experience with the wage system, and after the war a number of conditions militated against its use. Because most farmers were penniless, they were unable to pay their hired help until they had marketed their crops. Many southern whites, moreover, were opposed on both social and economic grounds to employing free Negroes. Throughout these years, plans for transporting the freedmen to Africa or the West Indies and importing foreign white labor were seriously discussed in many parts of the South. But an impoverished South could offer few inducements to immigrants from the Old World, and few newcomers settled below Mason and Dixon's line. On the other hand, the Negro, who was reluctant to give up any part of his new freedom and was suspicious of white employers, showed no enthusiasm for hiring-out.

The wage system was tried in some parts of the rural South after the war, but in most instances it proved unworkable. The limitations of southern banking and the scarcity of money so reminiscent of prewar years, prevented all but a small number of planters and farmers from hiring help. The Negroes also generally objected to the terms on which they were employed. Frequently, they complained of low wages, and on numerous occasions—and often with much justification—they insisted that they were being cheated. As most freedmen soon refused to work for wages under these circumstances, and as most southerners had little money to pay out for wages anyway, southern landowners increasingly turned to the share, or cropping, system. Under this arrangement, the planter provided the croppers with land, seed, draft animals, and implements and arranged credit facilities for them at the local store. The croppers, in turn, agreed to plant, cultivate, and harvest the crop in return for a portion of it that usually ranged from one third to one half. The store, which was owned sometimes by a planter but usually by a local merchant, provided the tenant with credit in return for a mortgage on his share in the season's crop. Although the so-called crop-lien system provided the agrarian South with much needed credit facilities, it was also largely responsible for the section's concentration on cotton—a cash crop—to the exclusion of most other products, for the perpetuation of backward methods of farming in the region, and for the creation of a class of virtual peons—both Negro and white—in the rural areas of the South.

The hard times following the war were responsible not only for the growth of share cropping and the crop-lien system, but also for many changes on the section's large plantations. Many old planters were forced to dispose of their lands at a fraction of their prewar value, and the newspapers were filled with advertisements of plantations for sale at a "sacrifice." In 1865, it was possible to buy good land anywhere in the South at from three to five dollars an acre—or at a price that represented one fifth to one sixth of its value in 1860. With cotton prices high, men from all parts of the South took advantage of the unprecedented opportunity to acquire land in the first two years or so after the war. A Georgia editor wrote:

> Never perhaps was there a rural movement accomplished without revolution or exodus, that equalled in extent and swiftness the partition of the plantations of the ex-slaveholders into small farms. As remarkable as was the eagerness of the Negroes—who bought in Georgia alone 6,850 farms in three years—the earth-hunger of the poorer class of the whites, who had been under the slaveholding oligarchy to own land, was even more striking.

Northerners also invested heavily in southern land. A group of Ohioans, believing that they could revolutionize cotton production by introducing scientific methods of cultivation, settled in Noxubee and Lowndes counties, Mississippi; Whitelaw Reid moved to Louisiana; Colonel Henry Lee Higginson and others bought up large tracts of plantation land in Georgia; and John Hay put a considerable sum of money in Florida orange groves.

Census returns seemed to indicate that the plantation system had broken up. Tennessee, which in 1860 had only 82,368 farms, had 118,-141 in 1870. In South Carolina the number increased from 33,000 to 52,000; in Mississippi from 43,000 to 68,000; and in Louisiana from 17,000 to 28,000. At the same time, there was a corresponding decrease in the size of most southern farms. The area of the average Louisiana farm decreased from 536 acres in 1860 to 247 acres ten years later; and even in North Carolina, which before the Civil War had had more small farms than most southern states, the average farm fell from 316 acres to 212. These figures, however, are deceptive. A great number of men listed as landowners in the census returns after the war were actually tenants or even sharecroppers. Although many plantations in most states were divided into a smaller number of units, actual ownership remained with the old planter or the new rural business class that was drawn from wartime profiteers and merchants. New farms, furthermore, which were small at first, very soon were encompassed by neighboring farms or plantations or themselves became the nucleus of larger units. Very swiftly the South resumed the national tendencies to ever larger farms and more commercial farming.

By 1875, southern agriculture, although still relatively backward, had almost regained its prewar footing. Thousands of small growers acquired holdings either as tenants, croppers, or owners. Across the Mississippi, pioneer farmers opened up extensive new cotton lands in Arkansas and Texas. From 1865 to 1875, the area under cotton cultivation averaged 8,810,000 acres annually. With the exception of 1866 and 1867, when the South suffered from severe droughts, yields rose steadily and good prices prevailed. By 1878, the crop equaled that of the off year of 1860, and in 1880 the South surpassed the best prewar cotton year. Many farmers were making money for the first time since the war, and the South was gradually lightening its heavy burden of debt.

The reorganization of southern agriculture was accompanied by fundamental changes in the section's mercantile system. Before the war, the large planters had bought their supplies at wholesale rates in Mobile, Charleston, Richmond, New York, and other urban centers. In the postwar years, the southern farmer—both Negro and white—made his purchases at the village or crossroads store, which in turn obtained its goods from northern merchants. In similar fashion, the individual farmer, instead of consigning his crop directly to commission jobbers, as was the common practice before the war, sold it to a local dealer. As the character of the southern economy altered, both towns and townspeople assumed a position of unprecedented importance in the South's economy. Many planters, who during the antebellum period had devoted their major efforts to the management of their plantations, turned to business enterprise. "The higher planting class," P. A. Bruce has written, "so far as it has survived at all, has been concentrated in the cities. . . . The talent, the energy, the ambition, that formerly sought expression in the management of great estates and the control of hosts of slaves, now seeks a field of action in trade, manufacturing enterprises; or in the general enterprises of development." While the South remained overwhelmingly agrarian, both the mores and economy of the section were increasingly shaped by an ambitious growing middle class—an influence that indicated that the North had won more than a military victory at Appomattox.

Lincoln and Reconstruction

During the postwar years, almost every aspect of southern life was either directly or indirectly affected by the reconstruction policies of the federal government. The course of reconstruction, in turn, was in large part determined by the outcome of the struggle between the Republican factions for the control of the nation's government. Conservatives, who were led by Lincoln and probably composed the bulk of the party during the war, urged that the bitterness of the past be forgotten, that the southern states be restored to their antebellum status as rapidly as possible, and that following the abolition of slavery no further moves be made to alter the social and economic structure of the South.

Radicals were drawn from a number of diverse groups within the Republican party. Abolitionists, who had opposed slavery long before the war, demanded that the freedmen be granted political, social, and economic equality. The abolitionists, who distrusted both the southern whites and the northern conservatives, had a powerful ally in the growing industrial class. The Civil War had stimulated the growth of industry and had driven planter-spokesmen from Congress. If the former Confederates were now kept politically impotent, the way would be clear for the industrialists to push their schemes for transcontinental railroads, large-scale manufactures, high tariffs, and the exploitation of the nation's natural resources. Under the circumstances, they had every reason to desire that the Republican party—champion of free homesteads, unrestricted immigration, internal improvements, protective tariffs, shipping subsidies, and a national banking system—retain its control over the national government. Republican politicians, grown fat on wartime patronage and favors, realized that by giving the Negro the vote and by withholding it from large numbers of white southerners they could ensure the success of their party in the states of the former Confederacy. In these various groups within the Republican party the radicals found a basis for cooperation to break the power of the old white ruling class in the South.

During the postwar years, the leading men favoring a radical policy toward the South were Charles Sumner of Massachusetts, Thaddeus Stevens of Pennsylvania, Benjamin Butler of Massachusetts, Benjamin F. Wade of Ohio, Zachariah Chandler of Michigan, G. W. Julian of Indiana, Henry Wilson of Massachusetts, Richard Yates of Illinois, and James M. Ashley of Ohio. Stevens was pre-eminent in the House, while Sumner was perhaps the outstanding radical in the Senate. Stevens, born in New England, spent most of his life practicing law in Pennsylvania. He had been a member of the Anti-Masonic party, a champion of free public schools, an abolitionist, and a member of the House of Representatives. From the end of the Civil War until his death in 1868, Stevens repeatedly demanded that the southerners be deprived of their political rights, that they be compelled to pay the cost of the war, that their property be confiscated, and that the head of each Negro family in the South be given forty acres of land. Sumner was a Boston aristocrat and intellectual who had opposed slavery all his life. A lawyer, scholar, politician, and reformer, he was one of the ablest opponents of Lincoln's nonvindictive attitude and Johnson's lenient reconstruction program. In Sumner's view, the seceded states occupied the same status as territories, and the prerequisite for any reconstruction plan had to be Negro suffrage. To their enemies, Stevens and Sumner were fanatics; to their supporters, they were selfless crusaders. Both groups were right.

Both the conservatives and the radicals sought to reinforce their respective positions with constitutional arguments. During the war, northern officials had maintained that, since secession was illegal, the South in constitutional law had not withdrawn from the Union. It followed inevitably that there could be no question about readmitting the southern states to a Union that they had never left. The problem then was to restore to the citizens of the South the rights which they had temporarily renounced but to which they were still entitled. While adopting this line of reasoning, the conservatives did not think that constitutional questions should be emphasized at the expense of what they felt were practical considerations. On April 11, 1865, Lincoln spoke for many other conservatives when he said:

We all agree that the seceded states, so-called, are out of their proper practical relation with the Union; and that the sole

Thaddeus Stevens

object of the government, civil and military, in regard to those States is to again get them into that proper practical relation. I believe it is not only possible, but in fact, easier to do this, without deciding, or even considering, whether these States have ever been out of the Union, than with it. Finding themselves safely at home, it would be utterly immaterial whether they had ever been abroad.

In opposing the conservative position, the radicals, some of whom had argued in 1860-1 that the Union was indissoluble, in effect now took over the original southern view of secession and maintained that the states of the Confederacy had actually withdrawn from the Union. By insisting that secession was a fact rather than an untenable constitutional theory, the radicals could conclude that the inhabitants of the seceded states had forfeited the rights and privileges guaranteed by the Constitution. This interpretation of secession left the defeated South completely at the mercy of the victorious North. The inconsistency of the radicals was matched by that of the southerners. Having maintained during the war that their states were irrevocably out of the Union, they proceeded to ask at the end of the war that they be treated as though they had never left the Union.

In their conflicts with the conservatives, the radicals were at first at a marked disadvantage, for Lincoln, as a wartime president, was able to put some generous reconstruction policies into effect even before the final defeat of the Confederacy. Lincoln's best known program, which was called the Ten Per Cent Plan, was first presented to the American people in December, 1863. According to its provisions, participation in the reconstructed state governments in the South was to be denied leading Confederate military, naval, diplomatic, and civil officials. Full pardon as well as restoration of property would be granted to any other Confederates who would take an oath to uphold the Constitution in the future and comply with all executive proclamations and acts of Congress concerning slavery. In any state, as soon as ten per cent of the population that had voted in 1860 had taken the oath, they could proceed to organize a new government loyal to the United States.

Even before the announcement of his Ten Per Cent Plan, Lincoln had taken steps to facilitate the re-establishment of Union governments in those southern states that were controlled at least in part by northern troops. In 1862, he had placed Tennessee, North Carolina, and Louisiana under the supervision of provisional military governors, and by 1864 Tennessee, Louisiana, and Arkansas had organized governments in accordance with the terms of the Ten Per Cent Plan. Lincoln had also recognized the loyal government that had been formed by the Unionists of western Virginia.

Although Lincoln had the authority to set up new governments in the southern states, no state could be restored to the Union without congressional approval. Congress could not only refuse to recognize the validity of the Lincoln governments, but it also had the right to prevent the senators or representatives of any state from being seated. It was through Congress, therefore, that the radicals sought to block the President's reconstruction program. In opposing Lincoln's plan, the radicals in Congress accurately reflected the widespread feeling that grew in the North as the war became more bitter that the southerners should be punished for both secession and the war. The radicals also obtained considerable support from several moderate congressmen who felt that the President, in assuming the initiative in restoring the states of the South to the Union, had encroached on the province of the legislative branch of the government.

The radicals made no attempt to conceal their hostility to the President's program. Largely because of radical opposition, Congress refused to recognize the Lincoln governments; the representatives from the reorganized states were not seated; the Union—or Republican—platform of 1864 contained a plank calling for congressional control of Reconstruction; and the electoral votes of the states with Lincoln governments were not counted in the election of 1864. The radicals spelled out their own reconstruction plan in the Wade-Davis Bill, which was adopted by Congress in July, 1864. This measure, which was based explicitly upon the premise that the seceded states had actually left the Union, put readmission entirely in the hands of Congress and made complete subjugation the first prerequisite to reinstatement. As soon as the military conquest of a state had been completed, a census was to be taken of all adult white males. When a majority of these—not a mere ten per cent as under Lincoln's plan—had taken an oath that they had been loyal to the Union and would be in the future, they would be permitted to elect delegates to a state constitutional convention. The new constitution would need the approval of half the eligible voters. To secure a state's readmission into the Union, its convention had to abolish slavery, repudiate the debts of the Confederate state government, and disfranchise practically all citizens who had held high civilian and military offices under the Confederacy. When Lincoln prevented the adoption of this bill by a pocket veto, the radicals replied with the Wade-Davis Manifesto warning the President to confine himself to his executive duties and to leave the problem of political reconstruction to Congress. In discussing reconstruction with Charles Sumner, however, Lincoln tried for a compromise between his plan and that of the radicals, thereby showing that, while his attitude was humane, he had no one policy to which he was unreservedly committed.

The Wade-Davis Bill and the Manifesto that followed it revealed that there was a strong faction in each house of Congress that opposed both presidential control over reconstruction and a lenient policy toward the defeated South. Although the exigencies of the military conflict prevented the radicals from pressing their views during the war, they did secure the passage of a bill creating a Bureau of Refugees, Freedmen, and Abandoned Lands in March, 1865. The Freedmen's Bureau, as the new agency was generally called, was set up to aid the Negroes in the South and to prevent any move to re-enslave them. Under the direction of General Oliver O. Howard, the bureau assigned "abandoned" and confiscated lands to the freedmen, distributed food and clothing, furnished medical aid, organized Negro schools, supervised Negro employment, and exercised certain judicial powers in cases involving freedmen. The Freedmen's Bureau saved thousands of destitute freedmen from starvation; in three years it distributed

Charles Sumner

[U. S. ARMY SIGNAL CORPS]

nearly 21,000,000 rations, more than 15,000,000 of these to freedmen. In this and other work the agency also helped poorer whites.

The Freedmen's Bureau both antagonized the southern whites and helped to make actual the radical plans for the South. Within a short time, the bureau had also become a branch of the Republican party, and much of its relief work had political as well as humanitarian objectives. In aiding the freedmen, the bureau in effect purchased their votes. Many of the bureau's officials, moreover, were corrupt and on several occasions they misappropriated the agency's funds. To most southern whites, despite its achievements, the bureau was a symbol of all that they hated in reconstruction; to the radicals, on the other hand, it was a highly effective device for creating a social and political revolution in the South.

Johnson and the Radicals

Abraham Lincoln had shown himself remarkably adept at handling the political phases of reconstruction policy during the war. He alien-

Andrew Johnson
[LIBRARY OF CONGRESS]

ated no group entirely and waited for a chance to make the best choice open to him. Although Lincoln had the most generous feelings toward the South, summed up in his famous words, "With malice toward none; with charity for all," he had not wedded himself irrevocably to any one program. Many radicals greeted Lincoln's assassination in April 1865 with unconcealed rejoicing, for they believed that his successor, Andrew Johnson, favored a harsh policy for the South. Andrew Johnson, born in 1808 in North Carolina, was a self-made man and a southern Democrat. Settling at an early age in Greeneville, Tennessee, he earned his living as a tailor and became a forthright spokesman for the more radical elements of the Democratic party in his state. For a decade after 1843, he was a member of the House of Representatives, and during the 1850's he served two terms as governor of Tennessee. Elected to the Senate, he did not secede with his state, in spite of the fact that he had voted for Breckinridge in 1860. During the war, he was named military governor of Tennessee by Lincoln, and repeatedly demonstrated his courage and devotion to the Union cause. His nomination as the Republican vice-presidential candidate in 1864 was largely the result of the desire of the party's leaders to win the support of the War Democrats and to create the impression that the party stood for the Union regardless of partisan considerations. Unfortunately, as a politician, Johnson the Democrat had no chance to acquire claims on Republican loyalties before he became President, only a month after the inauguration.

Despite Johnson's record as an antisecessionist Democrat and a Union military governor of Tennessee, the new President soon revealed that he had none of Lincoln's shrewdness and little sympathy for the radical program. Acting largely under the advice of General Grant and other military men, after a few months Johnson dropped his initial hostility to the defeated Southern elite and made a positive program of Lincoln's mere proposals, but he used much less tact than Lincoln. Consequently, Johnson's reconstruction policy was both mild and militant in character and brought the radicals together against him. Under the Johnson plan, which went into effect soon after he took office, the President granted a general amnesty to all participants in the rebellion who took an oath of allegiance to the United States. Southern states were to be readmitted to the Union as soon as their newly formed governments had repealed the ordinances of secession, abolished slavery by constitutional conventions and by legislative ratification of the Thirteenth Amendment, and had repudiated the debts incurred in the prosecution of the war. Although the radicals denounced the Johnson program, they were powerless to prevent its immediate adoption; for when Johnson became President, Congress was not in session, and it did not reconvene until December, 1865. Johnson gambled that he could present Congress with irreversible facts. By the end of the year, the seven Confederate states that had not been reconstructed under the Lincoln plan had established new governments in accordance with Johnson's proposals, and sent leading Confederates to Washington.

Following their reorganization under either the Lincoln or Johnson plans, the southern states, confronted with their economic and race problems, enacted the "Black Codes"—a series of laws that affected the status of the Negro in the South. This legislation granted the freedmen certain civil rights—to make contracts, to sue and be sued in regular state courts, to acquire and hold property (in most instances), and to be secure in person and estate. But at the same time the Black Codes imposed a number of restrictions on the freedom of the southern Negro. They forbade intermarriage of the races; in some states they forbade Negroes to carry weapons without a license; in several states they did not permit Negroes to be witnesses in court against white persons; and

Lincoln's Remains in New York, 1865 (The garish funeral was used to embitter the North against the South.)

[THE NEW YORK HISTORICAL SOCIETY]

in practically every state they severely circumscribed the freedman's right to work. The laws concerning vagrancy were discriminatory, and in many cases magistrates were given wide discretionary powers in ordering Negroes to be held as vagrants and in assigning them to the highest bidder to work out fines. The most drastic codes were enacted by Mississippi, Louisiana, and South Carolina, the states in which the Negroes outnumbered the whites. In Mississippi, for example, a freedman could not own or rent land except in incorporated towns and cities, while South Carolina forbade them to engage in any trade or business other than husbandry or domestic service except under a license requiring a substantial annual fee.

Although in part the Black Codes had been based on former northern laws to maintain white supremacy, many northerners now condemned them. Horace Greeley thought that they indicated that the South would not "stop short of the extermination of the black race," and the *Chicago Tribune* wrote "that the men of the North will convert the state of Mississippi into a frogpond before they will allow any such laws to disgrace one foot of soil in which the bones of our soldiers sleep and over which the flag of freedom waves." Although the majority of southern whites approved of the Black Codes, there were some who believed that they were both oppressive and politically inexpedient. The *Clarion*, one of the most influential papers in Mississippi, conceded that certain aspects of the Black Codes were "unfortunate," and the *Columbus Sentinel* stated that those responsible for the laws were a "shallow-headed majority more anxious to make capital at home than to propitiate the powers at Washington."

The Black Codes and the election of ex-Confederates aroused radicals against the South and the mild Johnson program. Convinced, as between former rebel leaders among the planters and rebel soldier "poor whites," that there was no other reliable group to deal with in the South, and that both Negro freedom and Republican supremacy depended on Negro political power, when Congress convened in December, 1865, the radicals were prepared to launch an all-out offensive against the President and his reconstruction policies. Their first move was to have the House and Senate establish the Joint Committee of Fifteen on Reconstruction—which the radicals dominated from the outset—to review Johnson's reconstruction program and to pass on questions concerning the admission to Congress of members from the seceded states. A tug of war between Congress and President now followed. Congress approved a measure that extended the life and enlarged the powers of the Freedmen's Bureau, but Johnson vetoed this measure in February, 1866. In the following month, the radicals returned to the attack with a concurrent resolution stating that no senator or representative could be seated until Congress had granted representation to the state in question. At the same time, Congress adopted over Johnson's veto the Civil Rights Bill, which forbade the states to discriminate against citizens because of their color or race and served as a warning to the southern legislatures that their plan to set the Negro apart under the Black Codes would not be tolerated by the federal government. If any doubt remained concerning either congressional or radical supremacy, it was dispelled in July, 1866, when Radical majorities in the House and Senate passed—and then repassed over Johnson's veto—the Second Freedmen's Bureau Bill.

Because the Civil Rights Bill was subject to repeal by any succeeding Congress and because there was always the possibility that the Supreme Court might declare it unconstitutional, the radicals decided to write it into the Constitution. Accordingly, in April, 1866, the Joint Committee on Reconstruction submitted to Congress a proposal that eventually became the Fourteenth Amendment. As finally submitted to the states, Section 1 of the Amendment made the Negro a citizen of the United States and of the state in which he resided, and said that no state could deprive "any person of life, liberty or property, without due process of law" or deny any person the equal protection of the laws.

Section 2 provided that representation among the several states should be now apportioned on the basis of total population instead of by counting only three fifths of the Negroes, but when the right to vote for national or state officials was denied by a state to any male inhabitants "being twenty one years of age, and citizens . . . except for participation in rebellion or other crime," the state's basis of representation should be proportionately reduced. The third section disqualified for either state or federal office all persons, "who, having previously taken an oath . . . to support the Constitution of the United States, shall have engaged in insurrection or rebellion against the same," until Congress by a two-thirds vote of each removed such a disability. Section 4 confirmed the validity of the debt of the United States, outlawed the Confederate debt in all its forms, and denied the legality of all claims arising from the emancipation of the slaves.

The Fourteenth Amendment proved of inestimable aid to the radicals. It enabled them to impose their program on the South and it also provided them with another opportunity to discredit both Johnson and his reconstruction policies. In submitting the amendment to the states for ratification, the President stated that he thought it unconstitutional and urged the eleven southern states to reject it. All but Tennessee, which was readmitted to the Union in July, 1866, followed his advice. In adopting this course, both the President and the southerners played into the hands of the radicals, who now had little difficulty in convincing the voters that Johnson was allied with the former enemies of the North and that the people of the South had shown that they were not fit to govern themselves. In discussing the refusal of the southern states to ratify the Fourteenth Amendment, James A. Garfield of Ohio said: "The last one of the sinful ten has at last with contempt and scorn flung back into our teeth the magnanimous offer of a generous nation. It is now our turn to act."

The conflict over the Fourteenth Amendment set the stage for the midterm elections of 1866. Instead of the traditional type of contest between the two major parties, the campaign quickly developed into a struggle between the President and the radicals. At the "National Union Convention," held by Johnson's followers at Philadelphia in August, in an attempt to rally moderate support behind the President, the Democrats overshadowed the Republicans. During the entire campaign, the President was handicapped by the fact that his program was more appealing to his one-time opponents than to the members of the party that had elected him. Johnson, moreover, was opposed not only by critics of his reconstruction policies but also by many businessmen who feared that he would attempt to deprive northern industry of the many favors that it had been granted by the Republicans. While the business class was still relatively small it provided radical campaigners with invaluable financial assistance.

Throughout the campaign of 1866, radical newspapers and stump speakers attacked Johnson's character as well as his views on reconstruction. On various occasions he was accused of being a drunkard, of maintaining a harem in the White House, and of having had a part in Lincoln's assassination. Although administration spokesmen sought to refute these preposterous charges,* the accusations invariably received more publicity than the denials. At the same time, the radicals gave extensive publicity to reports of floggings and murders in the South, and the race riots in Memphis (May, 1866) and New Orleans (July, 1866) were pictured as the inevitable results of the President's reconstruction program. In an effort to strike back at his detractors, Johnson made his famous—and, as it turned out, disastrous—"swing around the circle." A two-and-a-half week (August 28 to September 15) speaking tour that took Johnson as far west as Chicago, the swing around the circle undoubtedly cost him more votes than he gained. At every stop, heckling by radical groups either drowned out his words or goaded him into making foolhardy and intemperate rejoinders. The effectiveness of such tactics was revealed by the outcome of the election, for the radicals won overwhelming majorities in both houses of Congress.

Congress Takes the Reins

Strengthened by their victory in the congressional elections of 1866, the radicals forced through Congress the first Reconstruction Act of March 2, 1867. Under this act, the South was placed under comprehensive and rigorous military rule. The state governments set up under executive authority were abolished as illegal, and the entire region was divided into five districts, each under the jurisdiction of "an officer of the army not below the rank of brigadier-general and . . . a sufficient military force to enable him to perform his duties and enforce his authority . . ." To gain relief from military rule and to obtain representation in Congress, each state was required to call a convention consisting of delegates "elected by the male citizens . . . of whatever race, color or previous condition." This convention in turn was required to frame a new constitution giving Negroes the right to vote. When such

---

* Johnson was drunk at his inauguration. Being sick and weak at the time, he thought that a drink or two might sustain him during the ceremonies; but he took too much and became intoxicated. He was not, however, a drunkard.

a constitution had been ratified by the same electorate and approved by Congress and when the Fourteenth Amendment had been ratified, the state's congressional delegation could resume its seats in the capitol. Supplementary Reconstruction Acts of March 23 and July 19, 1867, further perfected the administrative machinery for carrying out the objectives of the radicals.

Frustrated in his appeal to the electorate, Johnson now tried to use his patronage and removal powers to undercut radical strength. In response, the radicals sponsored two measures, both of which were enacted on March 2, 1867. The first of these, the Tenure of Office Act, prohibited the President from removing officeholders except with the consent of the Senate. Congress overrode Johnson's veto of this act. The second—a rider to the Army Appropriation Act—forbade the executive to issue orders to the army except through General Grant, to relieve Grant of command, or to assign him to any command away from Washington except at the General's own request or with the previous approval of the Senate. Violation of either of these acts was a misdemeanor punishable by imprisonment. The first measure was designed to prevent Johnson from removing radical officeholders, and the second to prevent the President from exercising his constitutional command of the army.

Johnson soon played into the hands of the radicals again by removing Secretary of War Edwin Stanton from office. A member of Lincoln's cabinet, Stanton had remained in office in spite of his opposition to the President's reconstruction program and his close association with most of the leading radicals in Congress. After Stanton had refused to resign at the President's request in August, 1867, Johnson suspended him and named Grant as his temporary successor. When Congress convened in December, 1867, the Senate failed to approve the suspension of Stanton, and Grant—despite his earlier promise to stand by the President—withdrew and permitted Stanton to resume his duties as Secretary of War. Johnson countered by dismissing Stanton, but the Secretary of War refused to give up his office. In removing Stanton without the consent of the Senate, Johnson violated the Tenure of Office Act.

Stanton's dismissal provided the radicals with a golden opportunity, and, under the leadership of Stevens, the House on February 25, 1868, approved a resolution "That Andrew Johnson, President of the United States, be impeached of high crimes and misdemeanors in office." On March 2–3, the House adopted eleven charges against the President. The first nine charges were concerned with Johnson's violation of the Tenure of Office Act; the tenth charge accused him of attacking Congress with "inflammatory and scandalous harangues"; and the eleventh

Ulysses S. Grant, U. S. A.

charge, or "omnibus article," summed up the earlier accusations and added a few more for good measure.

The trial before the Senate was presided over by Chief Justice Salmon P. Chase and lasted from March 5 to May 26, 1868. The prosecution, under the direction of Stevens and Benjamin F. Butler of Massachusetts, sought by the use of innuendo and unsubstantiated accusations to create the impression that Johnson was no longer "fit to retain the office of President." Johnson's lawyers emphasized that he had committed neither crimes nor misdemeanors, and that he had violated the Tenure of Office Act so that the courts would have an opportunity to decide on the constitutionality of a measure that he had considered unconstitutional from the outset.*

When the vote was taken in the Senate, Johnson was saved by seven Republican senators who put principle above party and voted with twelve Democrats to acquit the President. The final vote was 35 to 19, or one vote short of the two-thirds majority required by the Constitution.

With the failure of the impeachment proceedings, the radicals turned their attention to the presidential campaign of 1868. At the Republican convention in Chicago every delegate voted for Grant on the first ballot, while Schuyler Colfax of Indiana, a radical and Speaker of the House, was nominated for the vice-presidency. From the Republican standpoint Grant, who as far as can be ascertained had no previous party affiliations, was an ideal candidate. He had cooperated with the radicals in the move to impeach Johnson, and his military career was a priceless asset in the North. The party's platform endorsed the radical record in the South, advocated measures to encourage immigration, and reflected the Republican alliance with the business-creditor class by demanding a "hard" rather than "soft" currency.† The leading candidates for the Democratic nomination were Johnson and Chief Justice Salmon Chase, who after his failure to be selected by the Republicans indicated his willingness to lead their opponents. Although Johnson received sixty-five votes on the first ballot and Chase also had considerable support in the convention, the nomination eventually went to Horatio Seymour, a Union Democrat and former governor of New York. As his running mate, the Democrats chose Francis P. Blair, Jr., of Missouri, a former Republican who had become an outspoken opponent of radical reconstruction. The platform, while attacking Congressional reconstruction for subjecting the South to "military despotism and Negro supremacy," had a "soft-money" plank calling for the payment of United States' bonds with greenbacks rather than with gold.

Throughout the campaign, the Republicans enjoyed certain obvious advantages. Because of their monetary plank and the assistance which they had given industry in the past, they could count on liberal financial support from the nation's business groups. In addition, their control over the South assured them of a large colored vote in that

* In 1926, the Supreme Court in *Myers vs. U. S.* ruled that the Tenure of Office Act was unconstitutional.

† Debtors were inflationists because they wished to pay their debts with a cheaper currency than they had borrowed. Creditors were deflationists because they wished to be paid in a dearer currency than that which they had loaned.

area, while Grant's candidacy took advantage of his status as the military savior of the Union. The Democrats' strategy lay in constantly exposing and attacking Republican corruption in both Washington and the South, and they were able to make an unexpectedly strong showing. Although Grant received 214 electoral votes to 80 for Seymour, his popular majority was only 305,458 in a total vote of 5,724,684.

The South Under the Radicals

Having gained control of Congress and with a more passive President at the head of the federal government in Washington, the radicals proceeded to carry out their reconstruction program in the South. With the establishment of a military administration in the South in accordance with the terms of the Reconstruction Act of 1867, control of the section's political affairs passed initially from the hands of the upper-class whites to groups that in the past had had little or no voice in the management of their states' governments. When the new registration of voters was completed under the direction of the district commanders in the South, there were 703,000 Negroes on the rolls and only 627,000 whites. In six of the ten unreconstructed states—Alabama, Louisiana—South Carolina, Florida, Mississippi, and Georgia—there were Negro majorities. In every part of the South, the white electorate was largely composed of "scalawags" and "carpetbaggers." The "scalawags" were native southern whites, sometimes former prewar wealthy Whigs, who in most instances had opposed secession and were now prepared to cooperate with the radicals. The "carpetbaggers" were drawn from every section and class of the North. At best they were humanitarians, and at worst they were adventurers. When the elected representatives of these groups met to draw up new state constitutions, they took as models the constitutions of the more progressive states of the North. Provision was accordingly made—on paper at least—for free public education, democratic local government, and complete civil and political equality regardless of race.

White southerners, who at the close of the war had hoped that the freedmen would look to their former masters for leadership, were at first disillusioned. The Negroes, who quite naturally attributed their changed status to the Republican party, saw no reason why they should now spurn their principal benefactors for an alliance with those who had fought to perpetuate slavery in the South. This view was reinforced by northern spokesmen—including Yankee soldiers, missionaries, school teachers and politicians—who traveled about the South denouncing the Democrats and praising the Republicans. At the same time, the Freedmen's Bureau and the Union, or Loyal, Leagues, which had been organized during the war to promote the northern cause, proved effective agencies for lining up the new Republican voters in the states of the ex-Confederacy.

Because of the undeviating loyalty of the Negroes to the radical Republicans, the leading whites of the South were unable to prevent the ratification of the new state constitutions. By the end of 1868, seven states—the two Carolinas, Georgia, Florida, Alabama, Louisiana, and Arkansas—had ratified the new instruments and had elected new governors and legislators. In 1870, Mississippi, Texas, and Virginia took similar action. In every state but Georgia, Republicans and their allies dominated every branch of the government. Ten of the fourteen United States senators and four of the seven governors were northerners who had moved to the South after the war. Although Negroes and scalawags filled most of the minor offices and every one of the new legislatures contained a substantial number of freedmen, only in South Carolina did the Negro members outnumber the whites, 88 to 67. Most of the new officials were men of little property. The members of the South Carolina legislature in 1868, for example, paid collectively less than $650 in taxes, and 91 of the 155 paid no taxes. In Alabama, the total taxes paid by members of the legislature were estimated at less than $100. In the same period, New York and the five New England states were the only northern states that even permitted the Negro to vote, and four other northern states—Minnesota, Michigan, Kansas, and Ohio—voted down proposals to extend the franchise to the Negroes.

Corruption, incompetence, and extravagance frequently characterized the Carpetbagger-Scalawag-Negro administration of the state governments. The worst experiences of South Carolina, which were not typical, still color the southern memory of "Black Reconstruction." More than $200,000 was spent for State House furniture that was actually worth less than $18,000; bills were submitted for $750 mirrors, $60 chairs, $650 chandeliers, $600 timepieces, and $60 imported china spittoons. Under the heading "Legislative Supplies" appeared such items as Westphalia hams, imported mushrooms, a side of bacon, feather beds, extra-long stockings, garters, chemises, gold watches, corsets, perfumes, three gallons of whisky, and a metal coffin. A barroom with forty different kinds of beverages was maintained in the State House at government expense. On one occasion, the legislature voted the speaker of the house $1,000 to reimburse him for a lost bet on a horse race. Public printing, which from 1790 to 1863 had totaled $609,000 amounted in the years 1868–76 to $1,326,589. In Louisiana the legislative session of 1871 averaged $113.50 a day for "travelling and other expenses for each

senator, representative, clerk, sergeant-at-arms, doorkeeper and page."
In Arkansas the auditor's clerk hire, which was $4,000 in 1866, cost
$92,000, or twenty-three times as much, in 1873.

Under radical control, public indebtedness in the South mounted
rapidly. In two years the public debt of North Carolina increased from
$16,000,000 to $32,000,000; South Carolina's rose from $7,000,000 in
1865 to $29,000,000 in 1873. The debt of New Orleans multiplied
twenty-five times and that of Vicksburg a thousandfold. As state debts
mounted, taxes also increased. In 1870, Louisiana levied $21.85 on every
$1000 worth of property compared with a rate of $7.47 in New York.
Similarly, Mississippi's rate was $17.86 contrasted with $6.44 for Pennsylvania. At the same time, property values declined sharply. The decrease in Alabama amounted to 65 per cent; in Florida 45 per cent; and
in Louisiana from 50 to 75 per cent.

While it is true that such extravagance and graft existed, it is also
true that there was a pressing need to spend large sums of money in the
postwar South. Not only did areas devastated during the war have to
be rebuilt, but for years previous to the war the southern states had
neglected to provide their citizens with many essential services. To
supply these deficiencies cost money, and, even though some legislatures
spent funds on trifles and luxuries, they all provided the South with
several much-needed improvements. The spending programs of the
radical governments were not opposed by all the members of the South's
former ruling class, who later helped distort the achievements of the
so-called black regions. State subsidies to railroads greatly contributed
to the South's debt, and the recipients of these grants found it easy
to place their desire for profits ahead of their loyalty to their section. There is abundant evidence that southern businessmen (regardless of what class they were drawn from) were as willing as those of
the North to accept whatever assistance any government would give
them.

Although the newly constituted southern governments were often
corrupt, no particular locality or party had a monopoly on thieving
politicians in the postwar period. While the carpetbaggers, scalawags,
and freedmen were holding forth in the South, Boss Tweed, a Democrat, was robbing millions in New York City; the state legislatures at
Harrisburg, Pennsylvania, and Albany, New York, were demonstrating
that they could be as corrupt as any south of Mason and Dixon's line;
and the federal government in Washington was being shaken by the
revelation of unprecedented scandals. Corruption was a national rather
than a sectional or racial phenomenon and cannot be attributed exclusively to radical or black misrule. Indeed, some radical governments

were remarkably honest and efficient and the Bourbon regimes that assumed power at the end of Reconstruction were often as corrupt as their predecessors had been. In Mississippi, for example, there were only three instances of official stealing under the Reconstruction government of the state. A Republican treasurer of a hospital stole $7,251; a Negro librarian took some books; and a native white Democratic treasurer stole $61,962. After the southern Democrats had regained control of the state government, they elected an official who stole $315,612.

Care should also be exercised in judging the personnel of the radical state governments. Although all the freedmen were inexperienced and most were illiterate, naive, and susceptible to the influence of designing men, the fact remains that some of them compiled excellent records in public office. Nor were all carpetbaggers rascals. Some went South to put into effect reforms that they had long advocated, others were undoubtedly motivated by a desire to make money—a desire that in other instances Americans have often been prone to commend rather than condemn. Most scalawags, whom their fellow white southerners branded turncoats and traitors to their section, in reality never shifted their allegiance. With a long record of opposition to slavery, planter rule, and secession, they revealed an understandable wish to participate in governments from which they had always been excluded. Moreover, despite the many Negroes elected to the state legislatures, the vast majority of chief state officers and of Representatives and Senators from the South at Washington were white men. Increasingly, as time passed these officials came from the old white elite whose political disabilities were gradually removed by the very "black regimes" against whom they later turned as the white Bourbons gained power and confidence and their resentment rose against high or progressive state taxes, debts, and the remaining limits on their political activity.

Any fair appraisal of the radical state governments of the South should include some mention of their positive accomplishments. Although there was considerable variation from state to state, the radical governments made a sustained—and sometimes successful—effort to provide educational facilities, revise tax laws on the basis of the ability to pay, reorganize voting districts so as to give adequate representation to the more populous but less wealthy regions, reform the judicial system, provide relief for the indigent, and build railroads, roads, schools, hospitals, orphan asylums, and insane asylums.

Of the various reforms advocated by the radicals, those affecting education perhaps provide the best guide to the character of the radical reconstruction program within the southern states. Before 1860, the South had only a semblance of a public-school system, and the war wiped out most of the hard-won gains of the antebellum years. Public and private schools were forced to close; students and teachers were dispersed; many school buildings were burned or converted into hospitals; and public libraries practically disappeared. When the radicals assumed control of the southern state governments, they were faced with the task of restoring the shattered school-system and of furnishing the Negroes with adequate educational facilities. Although their actual accomplishments always fell short of their aspirations, the radicals undoubtedly did more for southern primary education than previous southerners had done in two centuries. By 1876, the constitution of nearly every southern state contained provisions making tax-supported, free public schools for both whites and Negroes mandatory. While lack of funds, racial animosity, and public indifference made it impossible to enforce these constitutional provisions rigidly, considerable progress was made in a relatively short time. In South Carolina, which has been repeatedly cited by opponents of Reconstruction as an outstanding example of radical inefficiency and corruption, there were more than 50,000 white and 70,000 Negro children attending public schools in 1876. In 1860, the total figure had been 20,000.

In the eyes of most white southerners, any accomplishments of the radical state governments were largely, if not entirely, nullified by the means employed and by the grant to the freedmen of equal civil and political rights. Since they were unable to dislodge their opponents by the use of the ballot, many southerners resorted to such extralegal agencies as the Ku-Klux Klan, Knights of the White Camellia, Society of the White Rose, '76 Association, and similar secret societies. Of these the K.K.K. was the most powerful. Organized in 1865 before the Radical take-over, the Klan later spread over the South. Limited in membership to southern whites, the Klan refused admission to Union veterans, Republicans, and Union Leaguers. Its members were pledged to oppose equality of the races, to work for the restoration of the "rights" of the southern whites, and to "defend constitutional government." In 1876, just as the Reconstruction Acts were being put into operation, a grand convention in Nashville transformed the Klan into a sectional organization in which the former slave states, with the exception of Delaware, were erected into the "Invisible Empire." The administration of this empire was entrusted to a hierarchy of officials whose titles were calculated to frighten the ignorant and superstitious: Grand Wizard, Grand Dragons, Grand Titans, Grand Giants, and Grand Cyclops.

By nocturnal visits, warnings inscribed in blood, ghostly parades in white robes and weird-looking masks and other methods, the Klansmen terrified the freedmen. If "peaceful" intimidation failed, violence was used. The results achieved by the Klan and other similar orders were highly successful from the standpoint of the conservative whites. In addition to regulating the conduct of many Negroes, the vigilantes sharply scrutinized the activities and teachings of northern preachers and teachers, dispersed gatherings of freedmen, and forced some Reconstruction officials to leave the South. Above all, by frightening large numbers of Negro voters away from the polls, they substantially reduced the electoral support of the carpetbaggers.

The radicals, who were determined to save the Negro vote, struck back at the southern whites with the Fifteenth Amendment, which prohibited a state from denying any citizen the right to vote on account of race, color, or previous conditions of servitude. Its ratification was required of those southern states which had not at that time been readmitted to the Union, and the new amendment was proclaimed on March 30, 1870. It was immediately followed by the passage of an enforcement act imposing heavy penalties for infringement of either the Fourteenth or the Fifteenth Amendment. To circumvent the probability of loose interpretation in the South, the framers of this bill placed jurisdiction over all cases arising under it in the hands of the federal rather than the state courts. Democratic gains in the elections of 1870, as well as fraud and violence in elections in New York and other northern cities, stimulated the Republicans in Congress to push through another enforcement act (February, 1871) that extended rigorous federal control over congressional elections in the South. Less than two months later, Congress passed the Ku-Klux Act, which gave the federal courts jurisdiction over conspiracies against the freedmen and authorized the President to suspend the writ of *habeas corpus* and to declare martial law in any terrorized community. This measure was so effectively applied that by the fall of 1872 the military, when it chose to, had effective control over the South.

Grantism

While the radicals were attempting to impose their program on the South, Grant was demonstrating in Washington how inadequately his triumphs on the battle field had prepared him for the highest civilian office in the land. The Grant administration was distinctive for the incompetence of most of its officials and the uninhibited fashion in which it, in effect, turned over both the North and South to the country's special interests. Aside from Secretary of State Hamilton Fish, who held his position for the eight years that Grant served as President and for the short tenure of Attorney General E. R. Howe and Secretary of the Interior J. D. Cox, the cabinet was a way station for incompetents and mediocrities. During his two terms, Grant made twenty-four appointments to his seven-man cabinet. Without any experience in politics, Grant turned over the management of most of the government's affairs to hacks or old army cronies. Instead of attempting to check corruption, he stood by dishonest officials on the ground that it was not right to abandon a friend or subordinate in trouble. He had no interest in the reform of the tariff, currency, or civil service; he lacked either the knowledge or inclination to espouse a program for the regulation of business; and he thought that reconstruction could best be left in the hands of those who had controlled the South since 1866. The result was chaos; but it was a kind of chaos that permitted the politicians to get their graft, the businessmen to run the nation's economy with government aid rather than interference, and the radicals to continue their domination of the South.

During Grant's administration, the radical Republicans were able to continue their program of government assistance to the nation's businessmen. The railroads were granted huge tracts of the public domain; the federal land laws were administered in such a way as to aid the speculator rather than the settler; and Congress conducted what amounted to a bargain basement for the sale of subsidies. Although Congress lowered the tariff in 1872 to aid the Republicans in the presidential campaign of that year, in 1875 the old rates were restored. Perhaps most important was the fact that the government gave those northeastern businessmen who were creditors the type of currency that they desired.

The first postwar conflict over the currency issue centered on the question of whether the government's war bonds should be redeemed in gold or in the unsecured greenbacks that had been issued in accordance with the Currency Acts of 1862 and 1864. The inflationists and deflationists advanced the traditional arguments on both sides of the question, and the issue was further complicated by the fact that many of the bonds did not state specifically how they were to be redeemed. To the soft-money advocates, this omission seemed to indicate that greenbacks should be used. The hard-money groups, on the other hand, argued that, since federal bonds had always been redeemed in gold in the past, the government had a moral obligation to abide by this precedent. The question was finally decided in favor of the deflationists. The Republican platform of 1868 included a gold-payment plank, and following the party's victory, Grant announced that the Republicans would observe their pledge. Accordingly, on March 18, 1870, Congress passed a law stating that the government would pay all its debts in "coin or its equivalent"—a phrase that Grant and his successors interpreted to mean gold. While it can be argued that the government was morally committed to this step, the fact remains that this policy resulted in a substantial—and unearned—profit for all those who had purchased bonds with depreciated paper money during the war.

The same groups that argued over the redemption of the war bonds were unable to agree on what policy should be adopted toward the greenbacks. Issued during the war as part of the emergency financing program, the greenbacks were legal-tender notes whose value depended on government fiat rather than on their convertibility into specie. As soon as the war ended, creditors demanded that the government either destroy the greenbacks or make them convertible into specie. Debtors were equally insistent in their opposition to the resumption of specie payments. The first victory, however, went to the hard-money interests, for in 1866, Congress adopted a bill that provided for the gradual retirement of the greenbacks. But in 1868, after $44,000,000 in greenbacks had been withdrawn, Congress halted any further contraction of the currency, and thus helped create a Greenback party.

While Congress was attempting to discover a satisfactory solution to the greenback problem, the Supreme Court was seeking to determine whether or not the legal-tender notes were constitutional. In 1869, in *Hepburn v. Griswold* the Court ruled that the greenbacks were not legal tender. This case, however, concerned a debt that had been contracted before the Legal Tender Act of February 25, 1862, and therefore did not provide an adequate precedent; and in 1871, the Court in *Knox v. Lee* reversed its earlier decision. The majority opinion stated that "Congress has power to enact that the government's promises to pay money shall be, for the time being, equivalent in value to the representation of value determined by the coinage acts or to multiples thereof."

Although the Supreme Court's decision settled the legal status of the greenbacks, it neither precluded nor insured the resumption of specie payments. The soft-money groups were as determined as ever in their opposition to any plans for the contraction of the currency; and when the Panic of 1873 created a money shortage, they seized on this development to urge the government to increase rather than reduce the supply of paper money. Responding to these demands, Congress in April, 1873, adopted a bill authorizing an expansion of the greenbacks from $382,000,000 to $400,000,000. But Grant, to the chagrin of the nation's debtors, vetoed the bill. In his veto message, the President said: "I am not a believer in any artificial method of making paper

money equal to coin, when the coin is not owned or held ready to redeem the promises to pay, for paper money is nothing more than the
promise to pay, and is valuable exactly in proportion to the amount of
coin that it can be converted into."

The inflationists suffered their final defeat in the conflict over the
greenbacks in January, 1875, when Republican majorities in Congress
passed the Resumption Act, which provided that specie payments were
to be resumed on January 1, 1879. John Sherman, Secretary of the
Treasury in President Hayes' cabinet, was the individual most responsible for the successful fulfillment of the Resumption Act. By selling
bonds for gold, he was able to build up an adequate specie reserve; and
when the provisions of the Resumption Act went into effect, paper was
quoted at par. Many students of this subject have commended the government for its adoption of a "sound" monetary policy; but it must be
remembered that the Resumption Act took money from one group and
gave it to another. Resumption was a deflationary measure that increased the value of a debtor's obligations while awarding a bonus to
creditors.

Grant not only acceded to the demands of the businessmen and
politicians, but he also refused to interfere with radical plans for the
control of the South. Although each of the ten unadmitted states had
by 1870 established new governments in accordance with the terms of
the Reconstruction Act, federal interference in the South continued.
Congressional committees repeatedly investigated the new state governments; Southern anti-Republicans were forced to relinquish offices
to which they had been elected; and when the radicals felt that the
occasion warranted it, federal troops were employed. Moreover, the
radicalism of the 1870's had lost most of the idealism that had been a
distinguishing feature of the movement during the Civil War and in
the years immediately after the conflict. The radicals in Grant's administration paid less and less attention to the lot of the Negro, and they
increasingly used Reconstruction as a device to conceal their attempts
to promote the interests of northern businessmen and the Republican
party. Realizing that once the southerners had regained their political
rights, they might team up with other groups to repeal the government's favors to business and to vote the Republicans out of office, the
radicals used every conceivable means to prevent the participation of
the South in national affairs. Many of the radicals of the 1860's had
been reformers who wished to create a social revolution in the South;
their successors, on the other hand, more often than not were spoils
politicians who viewed Reconstruction simply as an instrument to aid
themselves and their allies among the business classes. And this change

in the attitude of the radicals, in turn, accurately reflected the change in the character of the Republican party, which within less than two decades had been transformed from a militant crusading movement to a staunch defender of the nation's leading business groups.

By 1872, a considerable number of northern Republicans were openly opposed to the administration's program in the South. Calling themselves Liberal Republicans, they maintained that the issues of the past were dead and that the government should concentrate on the many pressing problems of the present. As early as 1870, the Liberal Republicans in Missouri had split with the regular party and with the aid of the Democrats had elected B. Gratz Brown as governor. The movement soon spread to other states, and in 1872 the Liberal cause was being supported by such dismayed patricians as Charles Francis Adams, who had been minister to England during the Civil War; Carl Schurz, a German immigrant who represented Missouri in the Senate; Horace Greeley, editor of the New York *Tribune;* Chief Justice Salmon Chase and Justice David Davis of the Supreme Court; and Senator Lyman Trumbull of Illinois. While the Liberals placed their principal emphasis on their demand for the end of the radical reconstruction program, most of them also favored civil service reform. On the tariff and currency questions the group was without unity. As time passed, the movement attracted a number of maverick politicians who weakened whatever call to gentlemanly principle and old virtues the reformers intended making.

When it became clear that the regular Republicans intended to renominate Grant despite opposition within the party, the Liberals, now a rag-bag group, held their own convention at Cincinnati in May, 1872. Their platform called for civil service reform and reconciliation with the South, but the delegates were unable to agree on a tariff plank, and the convention sidestepped the issue by referring "the discussion of the subject to the people in their Congressional Districts, and to the decision of Congress . . . wholly free of Executive interference or dictation." The rift in the convention over the tariff question was further widened by the nomination of Greeley, who for years had advocated a high tariff in the columns of the *Tribune.* Despite Greeley's tariff views and his long association with the Republican party, the Democrats—more in desperation than from conviction— agreed at their convention to support both the platform and candidate of the Liberal Republicans. The combined parties, however, proved no match for the Republicans, and Grant, with 286 votes to 66 for Greeley, carried every state but Georgia, Kentucky, Maryland, Missouri, Tennessee, and Texas. The Republican victory can be attributed to the party's ability to control a large part of the southern electorate, Greeley's ineptitude as a candidate, the prosperous times that prevailed throughout the campaign, and the difficulties encountered by the Liberal Republicans in seeking low-tariff votes with a high-tariff candidate.

The Scandals Break

With the exception of the Resumption Act and the continued efforts of the radicals to retain their control over the South, the most significant developments of Grant's second term were a series of revelations of widespread corruption in practically every branch of the government. As exposure followed exposure, the alliance between business and politics became increasingly clear. It soon became apparent that politicians of every rank had participated in the "great barbecue." Robert Schenck used his post as Ambassador at the Court of St. James to foist bogus mining stock on English investors; Senator James G. Blaine of Maine accepted a thinly disguised bribe in return for his efforts to secure a land grant for a western railroad; General Daniel Butterfield, head of the New York subtreasury, helped Gould and Fisk corner the country's gold supply in 1869; and Secretary of the Treasury William A. Richardson had to resign when it was revealed that he had permitted one John A. Sanborn of Massachusetts to keep half of the $427,000 in back taxes that he had collected as a Federal agent. The internal revenue system was a center of corruption; taxes on tobacco, cigars, and, above all, on distilled liquors, were openly evaded. A "Whisky Ring," composed in part of high government officials, defrauded the treasury of enormous sums. Even General O. E. Babcock, President Grant's private secretary, was involved, and Grant himself was the recipient of many presents from members of the ring. The government practice of rewarding those who gave information about tax evaders encouraged blackmailing, and "hush-money" running into millions of dollars went into the pockets of government agents as the price of silence. The administration of the customs was equally lax and corrupt. When Secretary of War William W. Belknap was accused of selling an appointment to a position in the trading post at Fort Sill, Oklahoma, he hurriedly sent his resignation to the President, who accepted it with "great regret." Nevertheless, the House of Representatives drew up and passed articles of impeachment on which Belknap was duly tried by the Senate. No question existed as to Belknap's guilt, and only the lack of technical jurisdiction saved him from conviction.

Most sensational of all the national scandals of this period was the Crédit Mobilier affair. Following the authorization of the Union Pacific

Railway by Congress, a group of the controlling stockholders formed a construction company called the Crédit Mobilier, headed by Oakes Ames, Congressman from Massachusetts. In 1867, this concern obtained an award from the Union Pacific for building and equipping the railway. In payment, the construction company received nearly all the stock of the Union Pacific at about one third its face value plus the proceeds from its bonds. To keep Congress in a friendly mood, Ames induced the Crédit Mobilier directors to transfer to him as trustee Crédit Mobilier stock that he sold to various members of the House and Senate at par value. Inasmuch as the stock was worth twice its par value, Ames found ready purchasers among his colleagues. Soon after the shares had been distributed where they would "do the most good," the Crédit Mobilier "cut a melon" of nearly $3,500 for every thousand dollars invested. All went well until 1872, when a Crédit Mobilier stockholder, Colonel H. S. McComb of Delaware, after a quarrel with Ames, turned over to the New York *Sun* a series of letters that at once led to a congressional investigation. Ames was found "guilty of selling to members of Congress shares of stock in the Crédit Mobilier . . . with intent . . . to influence the votes and decisions of such members . . ." and his expulsion from the House was recommended. Vice-President Schuyler Colfax, Senator Patterson of New Hampshire, Representatives James Brooks, James A. Garfield, and others were implicated with Ames in varying degree, although they stoutly maintained that they were not "guilty of any impropriety or even indelicacy."

Although Grant did not "cause" the corruption that flourished during his administration, he made no apparent move to prevent or expose it, and his naive trust in a number of unscrupulous individuals undoubtedly helped to create an atmosphere in which official dishonesty seemed to be at least tacitly encouraged. To Grant the presidency was an honor that a grateful people had bestowed upon him for his outstanding record during the war. Under the circumstances, he usually preferred to stand by his friends—regardless of the crimes they committed—rather than to protect the honor of his administration or the interests of the taxpayers.

The Compromise of 1877

Throughout Grant's two terms as President the radicals steadily lost ground in the South. Neither constitutional amendments nor congressional "force acts" could hold the South for the Republicans, and the conservative southern whites gradually reestablished their power by making temporary common cause with the so-called black regimes.

The Republicans were ousted from control of Tennessee as early as 1869, and in Georgia, North Carolina, and Virginia in 1870. Four years later, the conservatives carried Alabama and Arkansas. The following year, Texas and Mississippi swung into the Democratic column. By 1875, only Florida, Louisiana, and South Carolina remained under radical control, and in these states the ruling groups were torn by internal dissension. Attracted by new issues and new interests, the northern electorate showed steadily smaller interest in the welfare of the freedmen. In the short session of the Forty-third Congress (1875) only one measure on the radical program was adopted—the "Supplementary Civil Rights Bill," long urged by Sumner, which prohibited discrimination against Negroes in hotels, theaters, and public conveyances. When President Hayes withdrew the federal armed forces from Louisiana and South Carolina in 1877, the radical governments in those states promptly collapsed. Political reconstruction was practically at an end.

The final collapse of radical rule in the South was the direct result of the disputed presidential election of 1876. The Republicans entered the campaign of 1876 with a number of serious handicaps. The Democrats had gained control of the House in 1874, and for two years a series of House committees had exposed Republican graft and corruption in the federal government; the radicals had been driven from all but three of the southern states; and the country was still suffering from the depression precipitated by the Panic of 1873. Largely because of these considerations, the delegates to the Republican convention passed over a number of prominent men in the party who had been affiliated with the Grant administration and gave the nomination to Rutherford B. Hayes, an advocate of civil service reform and the Governor of Ohio for three terms. To oppose Hayes, the Democrats selected Samuel J. Tilden, a New York corporation lawyer who had taken a prominent part in the destruction of the Tweed Ring and had been elected governor of his state in 1874.

Hayes and Tilden had much in common, for both advocated hard money, the restoration of conservative rule in the South, and civil service reform. But the similarity of the two candidates' views did not detract from the bitterness with which both parties waged their campaigns. While Democratic stump speakers sought to make political capital out of the depression, corruption in high places, and the abuses of radical Reconstruction, Republican orators warned the voters against entrusting the national government to a party that was still "the same in character and spirit as when it sympathized with treason." That Tilden received 4,300,590 popular votes to 4,036,298 for Hayes was due not only to the widespread disgust with the excesses of the Grant ad-

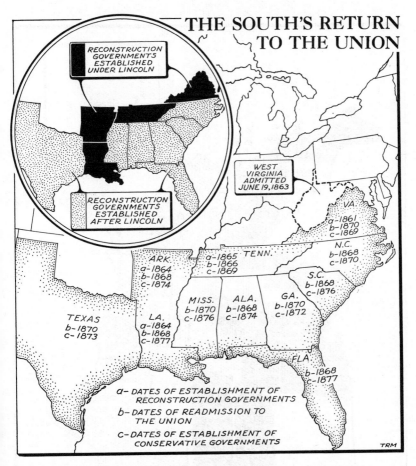

THE SOUTH'S RETURN TO THE UNION

RECONSTRUCTION GOVERNMENTS ESTABLISHED UNDER LINCOLN

RECONSTRUCTION GOVERNMENTS ESTABLISHED AFTER LINCOLN

WEST VIRGINIA ADMITTED JUNE 19,1863

VA.
a-1861
b-1870
c-1869

N.C.
b-1868
c-1870

ARK
a-1864
b-1868
c-1874

TENN.
a-1865
b-1866
c-1869

S.C.
b-1868
c-1876

TEXAS
b-1870
c-1873

LA.
a-1864
b-1868
c-1877

MISS.
b-1870
c-1876

ALA.
b-1868
c-1874

GA.
b-1870
c-1872

FLA.
b-1868
c-1877

a— DATES OF ESTABLISHMENT OF RECONSTRUCTION GOVERNMENTS

b— DATES OF READMISSION TO THE UNION

c— DATES OF ESTABLISHMENT OF CONSERVATIVE GOVERNMENTS

TRM

ministration, but also to the fact that the collapse of radical rule in the South permitted a majority of the states in the region to return to the Democratic column.

Despite Tilden's popular majority, the Republicans were able to prevent his election as President. On the day after the election, when the returns were still incomplete, it was clear that Tilden had 184 electoral votes—or one less than the necessary majority—and that the outcome of the contest would depend on the electoral votes of the three "unreconstructed states of South Carolina, Florida, and Louisiana. Although the Republicans probably had a majority in South Carolina, the Democrats led in Florida and Louisiana. But in all three states the returning boards were controlled by the Republicans, and in each instance they certified the Hayes rather than the Tilden electors. The Democrats, however, refused to accept this decision. The confusion

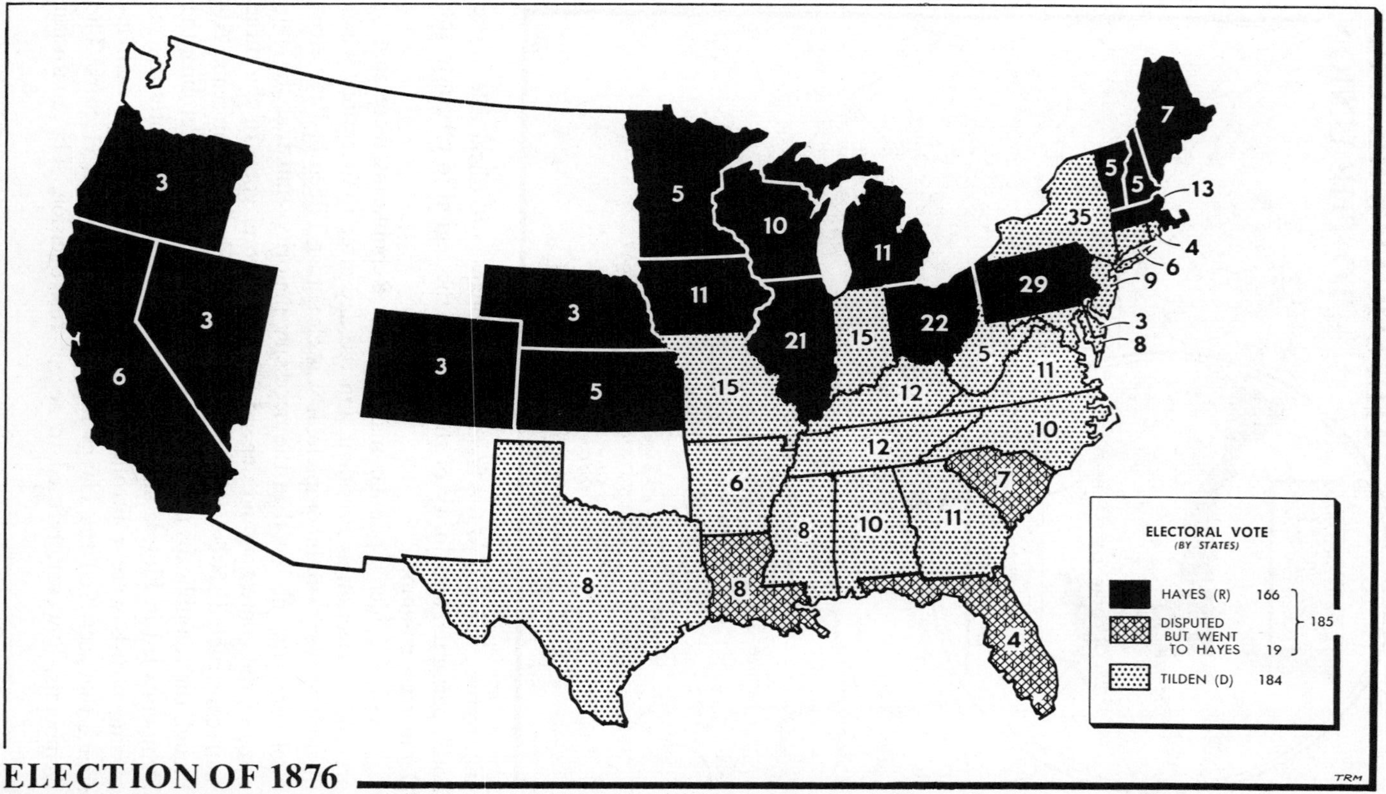

3
3
6
3
5
3
5
10
11
11
21
15
22
29
35
5
5
7
13
4
6
9
3
8
15
5
11
12
12
10
6
8
10
11
7
8
8
4
ELECTORAL VOTE
(BY STATES)
HAYES (R) 166
DISPUTED BUT WENT TO HAYES 19
185
TILDEN (D) 184
TRM

ELECTION OF 1876

was further confounded by the fact that one of the three Oregon electors (all of whom were Republicans) was declared ineligible. The Democrats insisted that the vacancy be filled by the elector with the next highest number of votes (that is, a Democrat), while the Republicans maintained that the two Republican electors had the right to name the third man on the slate.

Although both sides claimed the victory, it was apparent to all that the federal government would have to settle the contest by ruling on the outcome of the election in the disputed states. No one, however, was quite sure which branch of the government should assume this responsibility. The Constitution stated that "The President of the Senate shall, in the presence of the Senate and House of Representatives, open all the certificates and the votes shall then be counted." But it did not state whether the votes should be counted by the President of the Senate, by the House and Senate voting separately, or by the House and Senate voting jointly. And this was the central question, for the President of the Senate was a Republican, the House was Democratic, the Senate was Republican, and the Democrats had a majority of the combined Senate and House membership. Under the circumstances, a decision on who was to count the vote (and thus rule on the disputed returns) was tantamount to a decision on who was to win the election.

After months of haggling and maneuvering, the spokesmen for both parties in Congress decided to resolve the problem by the appointment of an electoral commission of five Senators, five Representatives, and five Supreme Court justices. The original plan for the commission called for the selection of seven Republicans and seven Democrats while the eighth member was to be Justice David Davis, an independent. Davis, however, became ineligible when he resigned from the Court to become a Senator from Illinois. A Republican Justice was appointed to fill his place on the commission which by a vote of 8 to 7 proceeded to uphold all the Republican claims. On March 2, 1877, the final count giving Hayes 185 electoral votes and Tilden 184 was approved by the Senate.

The Republican victory, which was achieved by depriving Tilden of electoral votes that were legitimately his, was made possible by southern Democrats. In return for Republican promises of the withdrawal of the federal troops from the South, of the appointment of at least one southerner to the cabinet, and of generous appropriations for internal improvements in the South, the southern Democrats agreed to join the Republicans in supporting the Electoral Commission's decision. Hayes, in turn, lived up to at least part of the bargain by making

"Another Such Victory and I Am Undone" (Harper's Weekly)

The Republicans' Trick Victory in 1876

David M. Key of Tennessee Postmaster General and by withdrawing the last federal soldiers from the South in April, 1877.

The compromise of 1877, which made possible Hayes' accession to the presidency, was in part the result of the activities of a lobby headed by Thomas A. Scott, president of the Pennsylvania Railroad, and by Grenville Dodge, who had served as chief engineer of the Union Pacific from 1866 to 1870. Both men were backers of the proposed Texas Pacific railroad to the coast and they were able to convince many southern congressmen, first, that such a line would aid the South and, second, that its completion was dependent in turn on a Republican victory.

In a larger sense, the southern support of Hayes in the disputed election of 1876–7 reflected the power of the business interests in the new South. Realizing that the expansion of the southern economy de-

"The Freed Slave": Philadelphia Centennial Exposition, 1876

pended in large measure on federal grants, they backed the Republican party in the hope that it would be as generous to their section as it had been to the North since the end of the war. While these southerners were Democratic in name, many were also ex-Whigs who did not find it difficult to support a party that espoused a program of internal improvements. In short, the only significant difference between the businessmen of the North and those of the South in 1877 was their party labels.

While the radicals had failed to achieve their major objectives in the South, they had been able to carry out their diverse programs in the rest of the nation. By 1877, industry was entrenched in the Northeast, growing in the South and, in both Democratic and Republican parties North and South, the allies of business interests froze out farmers and workingmen. There seemed little or no likelihood that the nation's farmers would ever again be powerful enough to thwart the country's businessmen. The new southern ruling class had quickly revealed that it had little interest in challenging the reign of business. Known collectively as Bourbons, the radicals' successors in the South consisted of remnants of the old planter-class and native whites who had been able to better their fortunes during the Reconstruction period. On the one hand, the Bourbons proclaimed the uniqueness of their section, while, on the other, they sought to make it over in the image of the North. Under the Bourbons and their friends in both parties, coal and iron mines were opened up in Alabama and Tennessee; textile factories were established in the Carolinas, Georgia, and Alabama; New Orleans became the center of a growing gambling empire and the sugar and molasses industry; and by the late 1870's more than 100 tobacco manufacturing establishments were operating in North Carolina alone.

While seeking to create what they referred to as the New South, the Bourbons systematically lessened the power of the Negro in their section's politics, largely by franchise provisions in the new constitutions that ingeniously sidestepped the Fifteenth Amendment. Although Negroes continued to vote in the South for a generation after 1877, it became increasingly difficult for them to do so. The most common new barriers were literacy and educational tests, poll taxes, or property qualifications for voting. Most useful of all was the "grandfather clause" by which any man who could not meet the educational and property qualifications could nevertheless be admitted to the suffrage if he had voted before 1867 or was the son or grandson of a person who had. Obviously, this device strengthened the conservatives, since it acted to disfranchise the Negroes. As for those Negroes who did vote, they were completely controlled by Bourbon leaders.

By 1890, the last physical—if not emotional—traces of Reconstruction rule in the South had been removed, and southern politics were dominated by native politicians who effectively prevented the solution of the grievous social and economic problems of the South. Despite the assumption that in 1877 the South had been "redeemed," political corruption continued, many social gains were cancelled, and the South's economy was controlled by northern capital; many of its Negro and white farmers lived in abject poverty; and its social life was torn by interracial tensions and conflicts. Reconstruction now became a memory that, along with the Civil War, served as a psychological safety valve for those southerners who preferred to think that their present difficulties could be attributed exclusively to their troubled past rather than to their own choices.

FOR SUPPLEMENTARY READING

Much recent scholarship lies behind J. H. Franklin, *Reconstruction After the Civil War* (1961); K. M. Stampp, *The Era of Reconstruction* (1965); and D. Donald, *The Politics of Reconstruction, 1863–1867* (1965).

Highlights in the older views of reconstruction history are W. A. Dunning, *Reconstruction, Political and Economic* (1907); E. M. Coulter, *The South During Reconstruction* (1947); and H. K. Beale, *The Critical Year* (1930). Three state studies pointed out the newer paths: V. L. Wharton, *The Negro in Mississippi Politics, 1865–1890* (1947) (Pb); F. B. Simkins and R. H. Woody, *South Carolina During Reconstruction* (1932); and G. B. Tindall, *South Carolina Negroes 1877–1900* (1952). An excellent retrospect of the years 1865–77 is covered in C. V. Woodward, *The Origins of the New South 1877–1913* (1951). R. W. Shugg, *Origins of Class Struggle in Louisiana* (1939), has important information on the postwar plantation system, and W. L. Rose, *Rehearsal for Reconstruction: The Port Royal Experiment* (1964), is important on an attempt at social reconstruction before 1865.

E. L. McKitrick, *Andrew Johnson and Reconstruction* (1960), and W. R. Brock, *An American Crisis . . . 1865–1867* (1963), deal fully with the Johnson-Congress wars. Allan Nevins's *Hamilton Fish* (1936) is the leading study of the years under Grant. C. V. Woodward, *Reunion and Reaction* (1951) (Pb), analyzes the end of northern rule in the South and the settlement of the election of 1876. R. Current, *Old Thad Stevens* (1942), deals with the symbolic figure of Republican "radicalism."

On the special problems of the freed Negroes, go first to R. W. Logan, *The Negro in American Life and Thought* (1954), and to J. H. Franklin, *From Slavery to Freedom* (1947).

On the liberal Republicans, use E. D. Ross, *The Liberal Republican Movement* (1919). On northern corruption, their target, use S. J. Mandelbaum, *Boss Tweed's New York* (1965).

INDEX

Aberdeen, Lord, 454, 563
abolition societies, 225
abolitionists, 502, 530–5, 562, 595, 596, 601, 604, 626, 640; policies after the Civil War, 719
Abominations, Tariff of, 417–18, 427, 431
Académie Française, 105
Ackerman, Amos T., 793
Adams, Charles Francis, 682, 743
Adams, Henry, *quoted*, 348
Adams, John, 170, 197, 207, 208, 214, 217, 330, 340: on Land Bank, 142; religion in the colonies, 149; Second Continental Congress, 187, 190; Declaration of Independence, 190; refusal to accept British peace proposals, 205; and education, 226; minister to Britain, 243; Vice President, 276; re-elected Vice-President, 287; Presidential candidate, 298–9; elected President, 299; as President, 299–307; Cabinet, 299, 302, 391, 786; son of, becomes President, 411
Adams, Mrs. John (Abigail), *quoted*, 217
Adams, John Quincy: as U. S. representative to Russia, 355; Indians and, 364; as Secretary of State, 386–7, 388, 390, 391, 396, 411; Presidential candidate, 410; background, 411; Cabinet, 411, 788; as President, 411–17; election of 1828, 417; protective tariff, 431; tariff policy, 433; independent treasury opposed by, 447; Baltimore and Ohio Canal, 467; gag rule, 534, 596; slavery issue, 598
Adams, Samuel, 167, 169, 170, 175, 176, 178, 181, 184, 187, 188, 231, 251
Adet, Pierre A., 298, 300
Administration of Justice Act, 179
admission of states to the Union (1789–1877), 182–3
Adventists, 506–7
Africa, medieval Europe and, 5, 6–7

Agassiz, Louis, 517
agriculture: colonial, 28, 61–9; in the South, 63, 64–8, 476–82, 485–6, 582; commercial, expansion of, 476; in the West, 482–5; problems, 483–7; in the South, after the Civil War, 717–19; *see also* farming
Aix-la-Chapelle, Treaty of, 74
Alabama: admission to the Union, 359, 782; secession, 634; area, 782
Alabama (Confederate raider), 682, 686
Alamance, battle of the, 57
Alamo, siege of the, 560
Albany, 69, 110; shipbuilding at, 77
Albany Congress, 152, 229
Albany Regency, 413, 444, 448
alcohol, campaign against, 520
Alcott, Bronson, 537
Algiers, 318
Alien Acts (1798), 303–7, 317
alienation, practice of, 55
Allen, Chief Justice, 58
Allen, Ethan, 205, 236
Allen, Ira, 236
Allen, Levi, 236
Ambrister, Robert, 386
Amendments, Constitutional, 257, 258; Bill of Rights, 264, 267, 278, 393; Thirteenth, 697–8, 712, 726; Fourteenth, 728–9, 739; Fifteenth, 739
American Academy of Arts and Sciences, 226
American Association for the Advancement of Education, 516
American Colonization Society, 531
American Fur Company, 370–2, 378
American Indians, *see* Indians
American party, 513, 613
American Philosophical Society, 106, 226
American Revolution, 194–226: causes, 145; Americans divided over, 194–6; Patriots and, 196, 197–202; inflation during, 200–1; financing of, 200–2; campaigns, 202–14; foreign aid to